# Medieval Europe
# 350 to 1350 C.E.

## HIS 118

Jackson J. Spielvogel
The Pennsylvania State University

Candace Gregory
California State University, Sacramento

Cynthia Kosso
Northern Arizona University

THOMSON

★ ™

WADSWORTH

Australia · Canada · Mexico · Singapore · Spain · United Kingdom · United States

# Medieval Europe 350 to 1350 C.E.
## Spielvogel/Gregory/Kosso

**Custom Editor:**
Lisa Capozzolo

**Project Development Editor:**
Laura Hoevenaar

**Marketing Coordinator:**
Sara Mercurio

**Production/Manufacturing Supervisor:**
Donna M. Brown

**Project Coordinator:**
Terri Daley

**Pre-Media Services Supervisor:**
Dan Plofchan

**Rights and Permissions Specialist:**
Bahman Naraghi

**Senior Prepress Specialist:**
Joel Brennecke

**Cover Design:**
Krista Pierson

**Cover Image:**
© Getty Images

**Printer:**
BR Corporation

Printed in the United States of America
1 2 3 4 5 6 7 8 9 10 11 12 13 14 08 07 06 05

For information about our products, contact us at:
**Thomson Learning Academic Resource Center**
**(800) 423-0563**

For permission to use material from this text or product, submit a request online at **http://www.thomsonrights.com**. Any additional questions about permissions can be submitted by email to
**thomsonrights@thomson.com**.

The Adaptable Courseware Program consists of products and additions to existing Wadsworth products that are produced from camera-ready copy. Peer review, class testing, and accuracy are primarily the responsibility of the author(s).

Student Edition: ISBN 0-495-15862-3

**Thomson Custom Solutions**
**5191 Natorp Boulevard**
**Mason, OH 45040**
www.thomsoncustom.com

**Thomson Higher Education**
**10 Davis Drive**
**Belmont, CA 94002-3098**
**USA**

**Asia (Including India):**
Thomson Learning
60 Albert Street, #15-01
Albert Complex
Singapore 189969
Tel 65 336-6411
Fax 65 336-7411

**Australia/New Zealand:**
Thomson Learning Australia
102 Dodds Street
Southbank, Victoria 3006
Australia

**Latin America:**
Thomson Learning
Seneca 53
Colonia Polano
11560 Mexico, D.F., Mexico
Tel (525) 281-2906
Fax (525) 281-2656

**Canada:**
Thomson Nelson
1120 Birchmount Road
Toronto, Ontario
Canada M1K 5G4
Tel (416) 752-9100
Fax (416) 752-8102

**UK/Europe/Middle East/Africa:**
Thomson Learning
High Holborn House
50-51 Bedford Row
London, WC1R 4L$
United Kingdom
Tel 44 (020) 7067-2500
Fax 44 (020) 7067-2600

**Spain (Includes Portugal):**
Thomson Paraninfo
Calle Magallanes 25
28015 Madrid
España
Tel 34 (0)91 446-3350
Fax 34 (0)91 445-6218

# Brief Contents

CHAPTER

# THE ROMAN EMPIRE

## CHAPTER OUTLINE AND FOCUS QUESTIONS

### The Age of Augustus (31 B.C.–A.D. 14)

● In his efforts to solve the problems Rome had faced during the late Republic, what changes did Augustus make in Rome's political, military, and social institutions?

### The Early Empire (14–180)

● What were the chief features of the Roman Empire at its height during the second century?

### Roman Culture and Society in the Early Empire

● What were the chief intellectual, artistic, and social developments in the Early Empire?

### Transformation of the Roman World: Crises in the Third Century

● What problems did the Roman Empire face during the third century?

### Transformation of the Roman World: The Rise of Christianity

● What characteristics of Christianity enabled it to grow and ultimately to triumph?

### CRITICAL THINKING

● What did one historian mean when he said that the Romans became Christians and the Christians became Romans?

*Entry of Hadrian (with outstretched arms) into Rome*

© Nimatallah/Art Resource, NY

WITH THE VICTORIES OF OCTAVIAN, peace finally settled on the Roman world. Although civil conflict still erupted occasionally, the new imperial state constructed by Octavian experienced a period of remarkable stability for the next two hundred years. The Romans imposed their peace on the largest empire established in antiquity. Indeed, Rome's writers proclaimed that "by heaven's will my Rome shall be capital of the world."[1] Rome's writers were not quite accurate, but few Romans were aware of the Han Empire, which flourished at the same time (202 B.C.–A.D. 221) and extended from Central Asia to the Pacific. Although there was little contact between them, the Han and Roman empires had remarkable similarities: they lasted for centuries, they had remarkable success in establishing centralized control, and they maintained their law and political institutions, their technical skills, and their languages throughout the empire.

To the Romans, their divine mission was clearly to rule nations and peoples. Hadrian, one of the emperors of the second century A.D., was but one of many Roman rulers who believed in Rome's mission. He was a strong

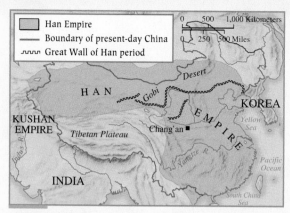

The Han Chinese Empire

and intelligent ruler who took his responsibilities quite seriously. Between 121 and 132, he visited all of the provinces in the empire. According to his Roman biographer, Aelius Spartianus, "Hardly any emperor ever traveled with such speed over so much territory." When he arrived in a province, Hadrian dealt firsthand with any problems and bestowed many favors on the local population. He also worked to establish the boundaries of the provinces and provide for their defense. New fortifications, such as the 80-mile-long Hadrian's Wall across northern Britain, were built to defend the borders. Hadrian insisted on rigid discipline for frontier armies and demanded that the soldiers be kept in training "just as if war were imminent." He also tried to lead by personal example; according to his biographer, he spent time with the troops and "cheerfully ate out of doors such camp food as bacon, cheese, and vinegar." Moreover, he "would walk as much as twenty miles fully armed."

By the third century A.D., however, Rome's ability to rule nations and people began to weaken as the Roman Empire began to experience renewed civil war, economic chaos, and invasions. In the meantime, the growth of Christianity, one of the remarkable success stories of Western civilization, led to the emergence of a new and vibrant institution.

**Augustus.** Octavian, Caesar's adopted son, emerged victorious from the civil conflict that rocked the Republic after Caesar's assassination. The senate awarded him the title Augustus. This marble statue from Prima Porta, an idealized portrait, is based on Greek rather than Roman models. The statue was meant to be a propaganda piece, depicting a youthful general addressing his troops. At the bottom stands Cupid, the son of Venus, goddess of love, meant to be a reminder that the Julians, Caesar's family, claimed descent from Venus, thus emphasizing the ruler's divine background.

# The Age of Augustus (31 B.C.–A.D. 14)

In 27 B.C., Octavian proclaimed the "restoration of the Republic." He understood that only traditional republican forms would satisfy the senatorial aristocracy. At the same time, Octavian was aware that the Republic could not be fully restored and managed to arrive at a compromise that worked, at least during his lifetime. In 27 B.C., the senate awarded him the title of Augustus—"the revered one." He preferred the title *princeps*, meaning chief citizen or first among equals. The system of rule that Augustus established is sometimes called the **principate,** conveying the idea of a constitutional monarch as coruler with the senate. But while Augustus worked to maintain this appearance, in reality, power was heavily weighted in favor of the *princeps*.

## The New Order

In the new constitutional order that Augustus created, the basic governmental structure consisted of the *princeps* (Augustus) and an aristocratic senate. Augustus retained the senate as the chief deliberative body of the Roman state. Its decrees, screened in advance by the *princeps*, now had the effect of law. The title of *princeps*—first citizen of the state—carried no power in itself, but each year until 23 B.C., Augustus held the office of consul, which gave him *imperium*, or the right to command (see Chapter 5). When Augustus gave up the consulship in 23 B.C., he was granted

# THE ACHIEVEMENTS OF AUGUSTUS

HIS EXCERPT IS TAKEN from a text written by Augustus and inscribed on a bronze tablet at Rome. Copies of the text in stone were displayed in many provincial capitals. Called "the most famous ancient inscription," the *Res Gestae* of Augustus summarizes his accomplishments in three major areas: his offices, his private expenditures on behalf of the state, and his exploits in war and peace. Though factual in approach, it is a highly subjective account.

### Augustus, *Res Gestae*

Below is a copy of the accomplishments of the deified Augustus by which he brought the whole world under the empire of the Roman people, and of the moneys expended by him on the state and the Roman people, as inscribed on two bronze pillars set up in Rome.

1. At the age of nineteen, on my own initiative and at my own expense, I raised an army by means of which I liberated the Republic, which was oppressed by the tyranny of a faction [Mark Antony and his supporters]. . . .
2. Those who assassinated my father [Julius Caesar, his adoptive father] I drove into exile, avenging their crime by due process of law; and afterwards when they waged war against the state, I conquered them twice on the battlefield.
3. I waged many wars throughout the whole world by land and by sea, both civil and foreign, and when victorious I spared all citizens who sought pardon. . . .
5. The dictatorship offered to me . . . by the people and the senate, both in my absence and in my presence, I refused to accept. . . .
17. Four times I came to the assistance of the treasury with my own money, transferring to those in charge of the treasury 150,000,000 sesterces. And in the consulship of Marcus Lepidus and Lucius Arruntius I transferred out of my own patrimony 170,000,000 sesterces to the soldiers' bonus fund, which was established on my advice for the purpose of providing bonuses for soldiers who had completed twenty or more years of service. . . .
20. . . . I repaired the conduits of the aqueducts which were falling into ruin in many places because of age. . . .
22. I gave a gladiatorial show three times in my own name, and five times in the names of my sons or grandsons; at these shows about 10,000 fought. . . .
25. I brought peace to the sea by suppressing the pirates. In that war I turned over to their masters for punishment nearly 30,000 slaves who had run away from their owners and taken up arms against the state. . . .
26. I extended the frontiers of all the provinces of the Roman people on whose boundaries were peoples not subject to our empire. . . .
27. I added Egypt to the empire of the Roman people. . . .
28. I established colonies of soldiers in Africa, Sicily, Macedonia, in both Spanish provinces, in Achaea, Asia, Syria, Narbonese Gaul, and Pisidia. Italy, moreover, has twenty-eight colonies established by me, which in my lifetime have grown to be famous and populous. . . .
35. When I held my thirteenth consulship, the senate, the equestrian order, and the entire Roman people gave me the title of "father of the country" and decreed that this title should be inscribed in the vestibule of my house, in the Julian senate house, and in the Augustan Forum on the pedestal of the chariot which was set up in my honor by decree of the senate. At the time I wrote this document I was in my seventy-sixth year.

*maius imperium*—greater *imperium* than all others. The consulship was now unnecessary. Moreover, very probably in 23 B.C., Augustus was given the power of a tribune without actually holding the office itself; this power enabled him to propose laws and veto any item of public business. Although officials continued to be elected, Augustus' authority ensured that his candidates for office usually won. This situation caused participation in elections to decline. Consequently, the popular assemblies, shorn of any real role in elections and increasingly overshadowed by the senate's decrees, gradually declined in importance.

Augustus proved highly popular. As the Roman historian Tacitus commented, "Indeed, he attracted everybody's goodwill by the enjoyable gift of peace. . . . Opposition did not exist."[2] The ending of the civil wars had greatly bolstered Augustus' popularity (see the box above). At the same time, his continuing control of the army, while making possible the Roman peace, was a crucial source of his power.

### The Army

The peace of the Roman Empire depended on the army, and so did the security of the *princeps*. Though primarily responsible for guarding the frontiers of the empire, the army was also used to maintain domestic order within the provinces. Moreover, the army played an important social role. It was an agent of upward mobility for both officers and recruits and provided impetus for Romanization wherever the legions were stationed. The colonies of veterans established by Augustus throughout the empire proved especially valuable in Romanizing the provinces.

Augustus maintained a standing army of twenty-eight legions. Since each legion at full strength numbered 5,400 soldiers, the Roman Empire had an army of about 150,000 men, certainly not large either by modern standards or in terms of the size of the empire itself (the population of the empire was probably close to fifty million). Roman legionaries served twenty years and were recruited only from the citizenry and, under Augustus, largely from Italy. Augustus also maintained a large contingent of auxiliary forces enlisted from the subject peoples. They served as both light-armed troops and cavalry and were commanded by Roman officers as well as tribal leaders. During the principate of Augustus, the **auxiliaries** numbered around 130,000. They were recruited only from noncitizens, served for twenty-four years, and along with their families received citizenship after their terms of service.

**The Praetorian Guard** Augustus was responsible for establishing the **praetorian guard.** These "nine cohorts of elite troops," roughly nine thousand men, had the important task of guarding the person of the *princeps.* They were recruited from Roman citizens in Italy and served for sixteen years. Eventually, the praetorian guard would play an important role in making and deposing emperors.

The role of the *princeps* as military commander gave rise to a title by which this ruler eventually came to be known. When victorious, a military commander was acclaimed by his troops as *imperator.* Augustus was so acclaimed on a number of occasions. *Imperator* is our word

emperor. Although such a title was applied to Augustus and his successors, Augustus still preferred to use the title *princeps*. Not until the reign of Vespasian (69–79) did *emperor* become the common title for the Roman ruler.

## Roman Provinces and Frontiers

Augustus inaugurated a new system for governing the provinces. Under the Republic, the senate had appointed the provincial governors. Now certain provinces were allotted to the *princeps,* who assigned deputies known as *legates* to govern them. These legates were from the senatorial class and held office as long as the emperor chose. The remaining provinces were designated as senatorial provinces. They continued to be ruled by proconsuls and propraetors as governors who were appointed annually by lot for one year and reported directly to the senate. Although a dual system of provincial administration seemed to have been created, in reality the greater proconsular *imperium* that had been granted to Augustus gave him the power to overrule the senatorial governors and thus to establish a unified imperial policy. Because all provincial governors, whether of imperial or senatorial provinces, now received regular salaries, there was less need for the kind of extortion that had characterized provincial administration in the late Republic. In general, although there were still abuses, especially in the area of tax collection, provincial administration under Augustus was more efficient than under the Republic, and provincials were better protected against abuses of power.

Since a governor had relatively few administrative officials to assist him, effective government of the provinces necessitated considerable cooperation from local authorities. By supporting the power of local elites—the upper classes—in return for their cooperation, Roman policy encouraged a substantial degree of self-government and local autonomy in the cities. By fostering municipal life, Rome essentially made cities and city-states the basic units of imperial administration. City councils of leading citizens made for stable local government, and leading city officials were rewarded for their administrative services with Roman citizenship.

**Frontier Policy** Augustus' frontier policy was not wholly defensive, as it is sometimes portrayed. He was not immune to the glories of military conquest and in fact added more territory to the Roman Empire than any other single Roman. In the east, instead of creating new provinces, Augustus encouraged the establishment of client kingdoms, a policy that enabled him to minimize the Roman military presence in the east so that he could use his forces elsewhere. After the final pacification of Spain in 19 B.C., the *princeps* expended his greatest mil-

**The Praetorian Guard.** Augustus was responsible for setting up the praetorian guard as an imperial bodyguard of elite troops. Pictured in this second-century relief are members of the praetorian guard. Their body armor was like that of the legionaries, although the cohort serving in the palace wore togas.

itary efforts along the northern frontiers of the Roman Empire. He conquered the central and maritime Alps and then expanded Roman control of the Balkan peninsula up to the Danube River.

The extension of Roman power to the Danube now opened the door for Augustus' major military project—expansion into Germany. After 15 B.C., Roman forces advanced across the Rhine and by 9 B.C. had reached the Elbe River in eastern Germany. In A.D. 6, the Romans began another advance between the Elbe and the Danube but encountered a series of difficulties, including the great catastrophe of A.D. 9 when three Roman legions under Varus were massacred in the Teutoburg Forest by a coalition of German tribes led by Arminius, a German tribal leader who had served in the Roman auxiliary forces and had even received Roman citizenship. Roman historians blamed Varus for the disaster: "He [Varus] entertained the notion that the Germans were a people who were men only in voice and limbs. . . . With this purpose in mind, he entered the heart of Germany as though he were going among a people enjoying the blessings of peace."[3] The defeat severely dampened Augustus' enthusiasm for continued expansion in central Europe. Thereafter, the Romans were content to use the Rhine as the frontier between the Roman province of Gaul and the German tribes to the east. In fact, Augustus' difficulties had convinced him that "the empire should not be extended beyond its present frontiers."[4] His defeats in Germany taught Augustus that Rome's power was limited. They also left him devastated; for months he would beat his head against a door and shout, "Varus, give me back my legions!"

## Augustan Society

Society in the Early Roman Empire was characterized by a system of social stratification, inherited from the Republic, in which Roman citizens were divided into three basic classes: the senatorial, equestrian, and lower classes.

**The Social Order**   Augustus had accepted the senatorial order as a ruling class for the empire. Senators filled the chief magistracies of the Roman government, held the most important military posts, and governed the provinces. One needed to possess property worth 1 million sesterces (an unskilled laborer in Rome received 3 sesterces a day; a Roman legionary, 900 sesterces a year in pay) to belong to the senatorial order. When Augustus took charge, the senate had over a thousand members. Augustus revised the senatorial list and reduced its size to six hundred but also added new men from wealthy families throughout Italy. Overall, Augustus was successful in winning the support of the senatorial class for his new order.

The equestrian order was expanded under Augustus and given a share of power in the new imperial state. The order was open to all Roman citizens of good standing who possessed property valued at 400,000 sesterces. They could now hold military and governmental offices, but the positions open to them were less important than those held by the senatorial order. At the end of his career, an equestrian might be rewarded by membership in the senatorial order.

Citizens not of the senatorial or equestrian orders belonged to the lower classes, who obviously constituted the overwhelming majority of the free citizens. The diminution of the power of the Roman assemblies ended whatever political power they may have possessed earlier in the Republic. Many of these people were provided with free grain and public spectacles to keep them from creating disturbances. Nevertheless, by gaining wealth and serving as lower officers in the Roman legions, it was sometimes possible for them to advance to the equestrian order.

**Augustus' Reforms**   Augustus was very concerned about certain aspects of Rome's social health. He believed that the civil strife of the first century B.C. had sapped the strength of public religion, which he considered the cornerstone of a strong state. Therefore, he restored traditional priesthoods that had fallen into disuse in the late Republic, rebuilt many ruined temples and shrines, and constructed new ones to honor the Roman gods.

Augustus also instituted a new religious cult that would serve to strengthen the empire. Since the Roman state was intimately tied to Roman religion, an imperial cult served as a unifying instrument for the Roman world. Augustus did not claim to be a god, but he did permit the construction of temples to his deified adoptive father, Julius Caesar. Augustus also permitted the building of temples to Augustus and Roma, the personification of the Roman state. The worship of Augustus and Roma became the foundation of the imperial cult. Its development was furthered when Augustus was acclaimed as a god upon his death.

Augustus' belief that Roman morals had been corrupted during the late Republic led him to initiate social legislation to arrest the decline. He thought that increased luxury had undermined traditional Roman frugality and simplicity and caused a decline in morals, evidenced by easy divorce, a falling birthrate among the upper classes, and lax behavior manifested in hedonistic parties and the love affairs of prominent Romans with fashionable women and elegant boys.

Through his new social legislation, Augustus hoped to restore respectability to the upper classes and reverse the declining birthrate as well. Expenditures for feasts were limited, and other laws made adultery a criminal offense. In fact, Augustus exiled his own daughter Julia for adultery—a rather hypocritical act in view of Augustus' numerous sexual affairs. Augustus also revised the tax laws to penalize bachelors, widowers, and married persons who had fewer than three children.

## A Golden Age of Latin Literature

The high point of Latin literature was reached in the time of Augustus. The literary accomplishments of the Augustan Age were such that the period has been called the golden age of Latin literature.

**Virgil**   The most distinguished poet of the Augustan Age was Virgil (70–19 B.C.). The son of a small landholder in northern Italy, he welcomed the rule of Augustus and wrote his greatest work in the emperor's honor. Virgil's masterpiece was *The Aeneid,* an epic poem clearly meant to rival the work of Homer. The connection between Troy and Rome is made explicitly. Aeneas, the son of Anchises of Troy, survives the destruction of Troy and eventually settles in Latium; thus Roman civilization is linked to Greek history. The character of Aeneas is portrayed in terms that remind us of the ideal Roman—his virtues are duty, piety, and faithfulness. Virgil's overall purpose was to show that Aeneas had fulfilled his mission to establish the Romans in Italy and thereby start Rome on its divine mission to rule the world:

> Let others fashion from bronze more lifelike, breathing
>     images—
> For so they shall—and evoke living faces from marble;
> Others excel as orators, others track with their
>     instruments
> The planets circling in heaven and predict when stars will
>     appear.
> But, Romans, never forget that government is your
>     medium!
> Be this your art:—to practice men in the habit of peace,
> Generosity to the conquered, and firmness against
>     aggressors.[5]

As Virgil expressed it, ruling was Rome's gift.

**Horace**   Another prominent Augustan poet was Horace (65–8 B.C.), a friend of Virgil. Horace was a very sophisticated writer whose overriding concern seems to have been to point out to his contemporaries the "follies and vices of his age." In the *Satires,* a medley of poems on a variety of subjects, Horace is revealed as a detached observer of human weaknesses. He directed his attacks against movements, not living people, and took on such subjects as sexual immorality, greed, and job dissatisfaction ("How does it happen, Maecenas, that no man alone is content with his lot?"[6]). Horace mostly laughs at the weaknesses of humankind and calls for forbearance: "Supposing my friend has got liquored and wetted my couch. . . . Is he for such a lapse to be deemed less dear as a friend, or because when hungry he snatched up before me a chicken from my side of the dish?"[7] In his final work, the *Epistles,* Horace used another Greek form—the imaginary letter in verse—to provide a portrait of his friends and society and the things he held most dear: a simple life, good friends, and his beloved countryside.

**Ovid**   Ovid (43 B.C.–A.D. 18) was the last of the great poets of the golden age. He belonged to a privileged group of Roman youths who liked to ridicule old Roman values. In keeping with the spirit of this group, Ovid wrote a frivolous series of love poems known as the *Amores.* Intended to entertain and shock, they achieved their goal. Ovid's most popular work was the *Metamorphoses,* a series of fifteen complex mythological tales involving transformations

of shapes, such as the change of chaos into order. A storehouse of mythological information, the *Metamorphoses* inspired many Western painters, sculptors, and writers, including Shakespeare.

Another of Ovid's works was *The Art of Love.* This was essentially a takeoff on didactic poems. Whereas authors of earlier didactic poems had written guides to farming, hunting, or some such subject, Ovid's work was a handbook on the seduction of women (see the box on p. 143). *The Art of Love* appeared to applaud the loose sexual morals of the Roman upper classes at a time when Augustus was trying to clean up the mores of upper-class Rome. The *princeps* was not pleased. Ovid chose to ignore the wishes of Augustus and paid a price for it. In A.D. 8, Ovid was implicated in a sexual scandal, possibly involving the emperor's daughter Julia. He was banished to a small town on the coast of the Black Sea and died in exile.

**Livy**   The most famous Latin prose work of the golden age was written by the historian Livy (59 B.C.–A.D. 17). Livy's masterpiece was a history of Rome from the foundation of the city to 9 B.C., written in 142 books. Only 35 of the books have survived, although we do possess brief summaries of the whole work from other authors. Livy perceived history in terms of moral lessons. He stated in the preface:

> The study of history is the best medicine for a sick mind; for in history you have a record of the infinite variety of human experience plainly set out for all to see; and in that record you can find for yourself and your country both examples and warnings: fine things to take as models, base things, rotten through and through, to avoid.[8]

For Livy, human character was the determining factor in history.

Livy's history celebrated Rome's greatness. He built scene upon scene that not only revealed the character of the chief figures but also demonstrated the virtues that had made Rome great. Of course, he had serious weaknesses as a historian. He was not always concerned about the factual accuracy of his stories and was not overly critical of his sources. But he did tell a good tale, and his work remained the standard history of Rome for centuries.

The Augustan Age was a lengthy one. Augustus died in A.D. 14 after dominating the Roman world for forty-five years. He had created a new order while placating the old by restoring and maintaining traditional values, a fitting combination for a leader whose favorite maxim was "Make haste slowly." By the time of his death, his new order was so well established that few Romans agitated for an alternative. Indeed, as the Roman historian Tacitus pointed out, "Actium had been won before the younger men were born. Even most of the older generation had come into a world of civil wars. Practically no one had ever seen truly Republican government. . . . Political equality was a thing of the past; all eyes watched for imperial commands."[9] The Republic was now only a memory and, given its last century of warfare, an unpleasant one at that. The new order was here to stay.

## OVID AND THE ART OF LOVE

*O*VID HAS BEEN CALLED the last great poet of the Augustan golden age of literature. One of his most famous works was *The Art of Love,* a guidebook for the seduction of women. Unfortunately for Ovid, the work appeared at a time when Augustus was anxious to improve the morals of the Roman upper class. Augustus considered the poem offensive, and Ovid soon found himself in exile.

### Ovid, *The Art of Love*

Now I'll teach you how to captivate and hold the woman of your choice. This is the most important part of all my lessons. Lovers of every land, lend an attentive ear to my discourse; let goodwill warm your hearts, for I am going to fulfill the promises I made you.

First of all, be quite sure that there isn't a woman who cannot be won, and make up your mind that you will win her. Only you must prepare the ground. Sooner would the birds cease their song in the springtime, or the grasshopper be silent in the summer, . . . than a woman resist the tender wooing of a youthful lover. . . .

Now the first thing you have to do is to get on good terms with the fair one's maid. She can make things easy for you. Find out whether she is fully in her mistress's confidence, and if she knows all about her secret dissipations. Leave no stone unturned to win her over. Once you have her on your side, the rest is easy. . . .

In the first place, it's best to send her a letter, just to pave the way. In it you should tell her how you dote on her; pay her pretty compliments and say all the nice things lovers always say. . . . And promise, promise, promise. Promises will cost you nothing. Everyone's a millionaire where promises are concerned. . . .

If she refuses your letter and sends it back unread, don't give up; hope for the best and try again. . . .

Don't let your hair stick up in tufts on your head; see that your hair and your beard are decently trimmed. See also that your nails are clean and nicely filed; don't have any hair growing out of your nostrils; take care that your breath is sweet, and don't go about reeking like a billy-goat. . . .

When you find yourself at a feast where the wine is flowing freely, and where a woman shares the same couch with you, pray to that god whose mysteries are celebrated during the night, that the wine may not overcloud your brain. 'Tis then you may easily hold converse with your mistress in hidden words whereof she will easily divine the meaning. . . .

By subtle flatteries you may be able to steal into her heart, even as the river insensibly overflows the banks which fringe it. Never cease to sing the praises of her face, her hair, her taper fingers and her dainty foot. . . .

Tears, too, are a mighty useful resource in the matter of love. They would melt a diamond. Make a point, therefore, of letting your mistress see your face all wet with tears. Howbeit, if you can't manage to squeeze out any tears— and they won't always flow just when you want them to— put your finger in your eyes.

# The Early Empire (14–180)

There was no serious opposition to Augustus' choice of successor, his stepson Tiberius. By designating a family member as *princeps*, Augustus established the Julio-Claudian dynasty; the next four rulers were related either to his own family or to that of his wife, Livia.

### The Julio-Claudians (14–68)

The Julio-Claudian rulers varied greatly in ability. Tiberius (14–37) was a competent general and an able administrator who tried initially to involve the senate in government. Caligula (37–41) was a grandnephew of Tiberius and great-grandson of Augustus. He exhibited tyrannical behavior and was excessively erratic. Claudius (41–54) had been mistreated by his family because of a physical disability due to partial paralysis, but he was intelligent, well educated, and competent. He was followed by Nero (54–68), who was only sixteen when he came to power. Nero's interest in the arts caused him to neglect affairs of state, especially the military, and that proved to be his undoing.

Several major tendencies emerged during the reigns of the four Julio-Claudians. In general, more and more of the responsibilities that Augustus had given to the senate tended to be taken over by the emperors. Moreover, an imperial bureaucracy was instituted under Claudius. He rationalized the central government by developing bureaucratic departments with talented freedmen as their chiefs. This practice further undermined the authority of the senators, who had previously shared in these responsibilities.

As the Julio-Claudian successors of Augustus began to behave openly like real rulers rather than "first citizens of the state," the opportunity for arbitrary and corrupt acts increased. Caligula, who became mentally unbalanced, wanted to be hailed as a god and neglected affairs of state while indulging his passions. Nero freely eliminated people he wanted out of the way, including his own mother, whom he had murdered. Without troops, the senators proved unable to oppose these excesses. Only the praetorian guard established by Augustus seemed capable of interfering with these rulers but did so in a manner that did not bode well for future stability. Caligula proved so capricious that the officers of the praetorian guard hatched a plot and assassinated him before he had ruled for four complete years. Afterward, they chose Claudius, uncle of Caligula, as the next emperor and forced the senate to confirm their act, thereby demonstrating the power of the military units stationed around Rome.

## THE FATE OF CREMONA IN THE YEAR OF THE FOUR EMPERORS

**A**FTER THE DEATH of Nero in A.D. 68, a power struggle ensued that resulted in a year of confusion with four different emperors, each the leader of a field army. Galba replaced Nero and was succeeded by Otho, who was then defeated by Vitellius. Finally, Vespasian established a new dynasty. Some of the Italian cities suffered greatly in these struggles between Roman legions loyal to their commanders. This excerpt is from Tacitus' account of the destruction of Cremona by the forces that had declared for Vespasian.

### Tacitus, *The Histories*

Forty thousand armed men forced their way into the city.... Neither rank nor years saved the victims from an indiscriminate orgy in which rape alternated with murder and murder with rape. Graybeards and frail old women, who had no value as loot, were dragged off to raise a laugh. But any full-grown girl or good-looking lad who crossed their path was pulled this way and that in a violent tug-of-war between the would-be captors, and finally drove them to destroy each other. A single looter trailing a hoard of money or temple-offerings of massive gold was often cut to pieces by others who were stronger. Some few turned up their noses at the obvious finds and inflicted flogging and torture on the owners in order to rummage after hidden valuables and dig for buried treasure. In their hands they held firebrands, which, once they had got their spoil away, they wantonly flung into the empty houses and rifled temples. It is not surprising that, in an army of varied tongues and conventions, including Romans, allies and foreigners [auxiliaries], there was a diversity of wild desires, differing conceptions of what was lawful, and nothing barred. Cremona lasted them four days. While all its buildings, sacred and secular, collapsed in flames, only the temple of Melitis [goddess of pestilential vapors] outside the walls remained standing, defended by its position or the power of the divinity.

---

The downfall of the Julio-Claudian dynasty came during the reign of Nero. His early reign had been quite successful. The young emperor worked hard and with the assistance of his childhood tutor, the philosopher Seneca, gave the empire a sound government. But Nero soon tired of his duties and began to pursue other interests, including singing, acting, horse racing, and sexual activities. After Seneca resigned his position in disgust in 62, Nero's rule deteriorated. His obsession with singing and acting in public was greeted with contempt by the senatorial class. At the same time, he aroused animosity by executing a number of prominent figures, including a popular general, on a charge of treason. His actions finally led to a conspiracy, not by the praetorian guard, but by the Roman legions themselves. In 68, Galba, governor of one of the Spanish provinces, rose in revolt and secured the principate for himself. Nero, abandoned by his guards, chose to commit suicide by stabbing himself in the throat after uttering his final words, "What an artist the world is losing in me."

### The Flavians (69–96)

Galba, however, was not readily accepted by the other provincial armies, which led to civil wars in 69, known as the year of the four emperors (see the box above). Finally, Vespasian, commander of the legions in the east, established himself as sole ruler and his family as a new dynasty known as the Flavians. The significance of the year 69 was summed up precisely by Tacitus when he stated that "a well-hidden secret of the principate had been revealed: it was possible, it seemed, for an emperor to be chosen outside Rome"[10]—chosen, of course, by members of the Roman army.

The accession of Vespasian to the imperial power demonstrated that it was no longer necessary to be descended from an ancient aristocratic family to be emperor. In fact, the family of Vespasian (69–79) was from the equestrian order. Once in control, he managed to reestablish the economy on a sound basis after the extravagances of Nero and the destruction wrought by the civil wars of 69. More important, Vespasian had no compunctions whatever about establishing the principle of dynastic succession for the principate. He was followed by his sons Titus (79–81) and Domitian (81–96). The Flavians, especially Domitian, dropped the pretense of the word *princeps* and began to use the title of *imperator*, emperor, freely. The emperor was rapidly becoming an absolute monarch.

### The Five "Good Emperors" (96–180)

Many historians see the **Pax Romana** (the Roman peace) and the prosperity it engendered as the chief benefits of Roman rule during the first and second centuries A.D. These benefits were especially noticeable during the reigns of the five so-called **good emperors**. These rulers treated the ruling classes with respect, cooperated with the senate, ended arbitrary executions, maintained peace in the empire, and supported domestic policies generally beneficial to the empire. Though absolute monarchs, they were known for their tolerance and diplomacy.

The first of the five good emperors was Nerva (96–98), chosen by the senate after the assassination of Domitian. By chance, Nerva and his next three successors had no sons and had to resort to adoption to obtain heirs. According to one Roman historian, "Nerva, therefore, finding himself held in such contempt by reason of his old age, ascended the Capital and said in a loud voice: 'May good success

| | |
|---|---|
| *Julio-Claudian Dynasty* | |
| Augustus | 31 B.C.–A.D. 14 |
| Tiberius | 14–37 |
| Caligula | 37–41 |
| Claudius | 41–54 |
| Nero | 54–68 |
| *Flavian Dynasty* | |
| Vespasian | 69–79 |
| Titus | 79–81 |
| Domitian | 81–96 |
| *Five Good Emperors* | |
| Nerva | 96–98 |
| Trajan | 98–117 |
| Hadrian | 117–138 |
| Antoninus Pius | 138–161 |
| Marcus Aurelius | 161–180 |

attend the Roman senate and people and myself: I hereby adopt Marcus Ulpius Nerva Trajan."[11] Trajan (98–117) was a capable man who was also acceptable to the army, an increasingly important requirement. He had been born in Spain to an old Roman family and was the first emperor born outside Italy.

Trajan was succeeded by his second cousin Hadrian (117–138), who spent years inspecting the provinces and restoring the military forces to good order. Hadrian adopted as his successor Antoninus Pius (138–161), who achieved a reputation as the most beneficent of the five good emperors. It was said of him that "one should behave in all things like a pupil of Antoninus: his energy on behalf of what was done in accord with reason, his equability everywhere, his serene expression, his sweetness, his disdain of glory, his ambition to grasp affairs."[12] Unlike Hadrian, who traveled extensively in the provinces, Antonius Pius stayed in Rome and made even greater use of the senate. He in turn adopted Marcus Aurelius (161–180), who has been viewed as a philosopher-king of the sort Plato envisioned (see Chapter 3). Highly influenced by Stoicism, Marcus Aurelius wrote his *Meditations,* reflecting the ideal of Stoic duty as a religious concept.

Under the five good emperors, the powers of the emperor continued to expand at the expense of the senate. Increasingly, imperial officials appointed and directed by the emperor took over the running of the government. The five good emperors also extended the scope of imperial administration to areas previously untouched by the imperial government. Trajan established a program that provided state funds to assist poor parents in raising and educating their children. He was not motivated simply by benevolence, since he believed that such assistance would materially aid in creating a larger pool of young men in Italy eligible for military service.

The five good emperors were widely praised by their subjects for their extensive building programs. Trajan and Hadrian were especially active in constructing public works—aqueducts, bridges, roads, and harbor facilities—throughout the provinces and in Rome. Trajan built a new forum in Rome to provide a setting for his celebrated victory column. Hadrian's Pantheon, a temple of "all the gods," is one of the grandest ancient buildings surviving in Rome.

## The Roman Empire at Its Height: Frontiers and Provinces

At its height in the second century, the Roman Empire (see Map 6.1) covered about 3.5 million square miles and had a population, like that of Han China, estimated at more than fifty million. While the emperors and the imperial administration provided a degree of unity, considerable leeway was given to local customs, and the privileges of Roman citizenship were extended to many people throughout the empire. In A.D. 212, the emperor Caracalla completed the process by giving Roman citizenship to every free inhabitant of the empire. Latin was the language of the western part of the empire, while Greek was used in the east. Although Roman culture spread to all parts of the empire, there were limits to Romanization since local languages persisted and many of the empire's residents spoke neither Latin nor Greek.

**Roman Frontiers**   With the exception of Claudius' annexation of Britain, the first-century successors of Augustus had largely followed his advice to curb expansion and remain within the natural frontiers of the empire—the ocean to the west, the rivers in the north, and the desert in the east and south. Two areas prompted special concern. The Rhine-Danube frontier in the north became the most heavily fortified border area because of the threat from restless barbarian tribes. In the east, the Romans used a system of client states to serve as a buffer against the troublesome Parthians.

Although Trajan broke with Augustus' policy of defensive imperialism by extending Roman rule into Dacia (modern Romania), Mesopotamia, and the Sinai peninsula, his conquests represent the high-water mark of Roman expansion. His successors recognized that the empire was overextended and pursued a policy of retrenchment. Hadrian withdrew Roman forces from much of Mesopotamia. Although he retained Dacia and Arabia, he went on the defensive in his frontier policy, reinforcing the fortifications along a line connecting the Rhine and Danube Rivers and building a defensive wall 80 miles long across northern Britain. By the end of the second century, the vulnerability of the empire had become apparent. Frontiers were stabilized, and the Roman forces were established in permanent bases behind the frontiers. But when one frontier was attacked, troops had to be drawn from other

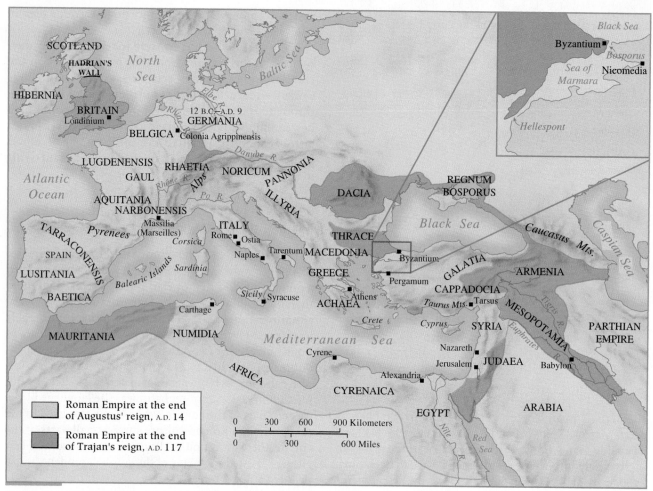

**MAP 6.1** **The Roman Empire from Augustus to Trajan (14–117).** Augustus and later emperors continued the expansion of the Roman Empire, adding more resources but also increasing the tasks of administration and keeping the peace. Compare this map with Map 5.3. ❓ Which territories were conquered by Augustus, and which were added by the end of Trajan's reign? 🖱 **View an animated version of this map or related maps at** http://history.wadsworth.com/spielvogel06/

frontiers, leaving them vulnerable. The empire lacked a real strategic reserve, and its weakness would become ever more apparent.

**Role of the Army** The Roman army was the primary instrument for the defense of the Roman frontiers. In A.D. 14, it numbered twenty-five legions but had increased to thirty by the time of Trajan. The auxiliaries were increased correspondingly, making a Roman army of about 400,000 by the end of the second century. Since legionaries had to be Roman citizens, most recruits in Augustus' time were from Italy. But in the course of the first century, the Italians' reluctance to serve in the military led to the recruitment of citizens from the provinces. By A.D. 100, only one in five of the legionaries was Italian.

In addition to defense and protection, the Roman army also served as an important instrument for Romanizing the provinces. Roman military camps became centers for the spread of the Latin language and Roman institutions and ways of thought and conduct. The presence of large num-

bers of troops and their dependent women and slaves encouraged the development of trade and local production to meet the army's need for supplies. Urban centers developed around army bases or nearby colonies. Many cities along the Rhine had their roots in legionary bases or auxiliary forts. The city of Cologne, for example, grew out of the military colony the Romans called Colonia Agrippinensis.

**Importance of Cities** The administration and cultural life of the Roman Empire depended greatly on cities and towns. A provincial governor's staff was not large, so it was left to local city officials to act as Roman agents in carrying out many government functions, especially those related to taxes. Most towns and cities were not large by modern standards. The largest was Rome, but there were also some large cities in the east: Alexandria in Egypt numbered over 300,000 inhabitants, Ephesus in Asia Minor had 200,000, and Antioch in Syria had around 150,000. In the west, cities were usually small, with only a few thousand inhabitants. Cities were important in the spread of things Roman. They

**Rome in Germany.** The Roman army helped bring Roman culture and institutions to the provinces. Local production and trade grew up around the military camps to meet the soldiers' needs, and cities often developed from the bases themselves or from colonies located nearby. Pictured are the remains of the Porta Nigra, or gateway to the Roman city of Augusta Treverorum (modern Trier). In the Early Empire, Trier became the headquarters of the imperial procurator of Belgica and the two Germanies. Its close location to Roman military camps along the Rhine enabled it to flourish as one of the most significant cities in the western Roman Empire.

were also uniform in physical appearance, with similar temples, markets, amphitheaters, and other public buildings.

Magistrates and town councillors chosen from the ranks of the wealthy upper classes directed municipal administration. These municipal offices were unsalaried but were nevertheless desired by wealthy citizens because the offices conferred prestige and power at the local level as well as Roman citizenship. Roman municipal policy effectively tied the upper classes to Roman rule and ensured that these classes would retain control over the rest of the population.

The process of Romanization in the provinces was reflected in significant changes in the governing classes of the empire. In the course of the first century, there was a noticeable decline in the number of senators from Italian families. By the end of the second century, Italian senators made up less than half the total. Increasingly, the Roman senate was being recruited from wealthy provincial equestrian families. The provinces also provided many of the legionaries for the Roman army and, beginning with Trajan, supplied many of the emperors.

## Prosperity in the Early Empire

The Early Empire was a period of considerable prosperity. Internal peace resulted in unprecedented levels of trade (see Map 6.2). Merchants from all over the empire came to the chief Italian ports of Puteoli on the Bay of Naples and Ostia at the mouth of the Tiber. Trade extended beyond the Roman boundaries and included even goods from China. Chinese merchants traveled across Central Asia, forming part of the Silk Road, which became a regular overland route between west and east. By the first century A.D., Chinese goods, including silk and lacquerware, were being sent into the eastern part of the Roman Empire, in southwestern Asia, where they were traded for woolen textiles, glass, and precious stones. Moreover, the importation of large quantities of grain to feed the populace of Rome and an incredible quantity of luxury items for the wealthy upper classes in the west led to a steady drain of gold and silver coins from Italy and the west to the eastern part of the empire.

**The Shipping of Grain.** Trade was an important ingredient in the prosperity of the Early Empire. This tomb painting from Ostia, the port of Rome at the mouth of the Tiber River, shows workers loading grain onto the *Isis Giminiana,* a small merchant vessel, for shipment upriver to Rome. The captain of the ship stands by the rudder. Next to him is Abascantus, the ship's owner.

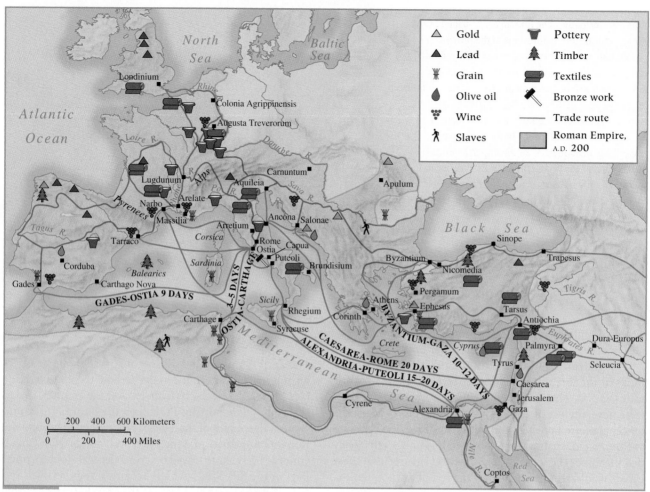

**MAP 6.2 Trade Routes and Products in the Roman Empire, c. 200.** Although still primarily an agrarian economy, the Roman Empire provided the single currency and stable conditions necessary for an expansion of trade in various commodities and products. An extensive system of roads and shipping routes also facilitated trade. [?] What truth is there to the statement "All roads lead to Rome"?

View an animated version of this map or related maps at http://history.wadsworth.com/spielvogel06/

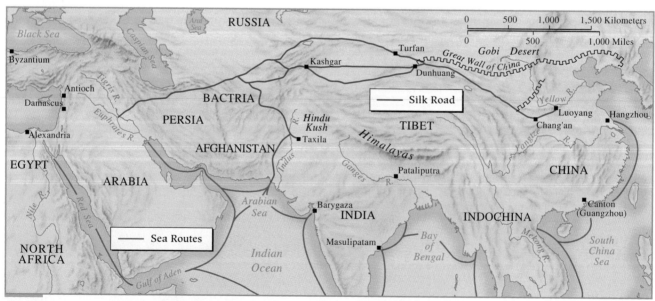

**The Silk Road**

Increased trade helped stimulate manufacturing. The cities of the east still produced the items made in Hellenistic times (see Chapter 4). The first two centuries of the empire also witnessed the high point of industrial development in Italy. Some industries became concentrated in certain areas, such as bronze work in Capua and pottery in Arretium in Etruria. Other industries, such as brickmaking, were pursued in rural areas on large landed estates. Much industrial production remained small-scale and was done by individual artisans, usually freedmen or slaves. In the course of the first century, Italian centers of industry experienced increasing competition from the provinces. Pottery produced in Gaul, for example, began to outsell Italian pottery from Arretium.

Despite the prosperity from trade and commerce, agriculture remained the chief occupation of most people and the underlying basis of Roman prosperity. While the large landed estates, the *latifundia*, still dominated agriculture, especially in southern and central Italy, small peasant farms persisted, particularly in Etruria and the Po valley. Although large estates concentrating on sheep and cattle raising used slave labor, the lands of some *latifundia* were worked by free tenant farmers called *coloni.* The *colonus* was essentially a sharecropper who paid rent in labor, produce, or sometimes cash.

In considering the prosperity of the Roman world, it is important to remember the enormous gulf between rich and poor underlying it (see the box above). The development of towns and cities, so important to the creation of any civilization, is based to a large degree on the agricultural surpluses of the countryside. In ancient times, the margin of surplus produced by each farmer was relatively small. Therefore, the upper classes and urban populations had to be supported by the labor of a large number of agricultural producers who never found it easy to produce much more than enough for themselves. In lean years, when there were no surpluses, the townspeople often took what they wanted, leaving little for the peasants.

# Roman Culture and Society in the Early Empire

Although the cultural and social developments of the Early Empire were similar to those of the last century of the Republic, there were also significant changes as a result of the new imperial order.

## The Silver Age of Latin Literature

In the history of Latin literature, the century and a half after Augustus is often labeled the "silver age" to indicate that the literary efforts of the period, while good, were not equal to the high standards of the Augustan "golden age." The popularity of rhetorical training encouraged the use of clever literary expressions, often at the expense of original and meaningful content. A good example of this trend can be found in the works of Seneca.

**Seneca** Educated in Rome, Seneca (c. 4 B.C.–A.D. 65) became strongly attached to the philosophy of Stoicism (see Chapter 4). After serving as tutor to Nero, he helped run the government during the first five years of Nero's reign. Seneca began to withdraw from politics after Nero took a more active role in government. In 65, he was charged with involvement in a conspiracy against Nero and committed suicide at Nero's command.

In letters written to a young friend, Seneca expressed the basic tenets of Stoicism: living according to nature, accepting events dispassionately as part of the divine plan, and a universal love for all humanity. Thus "the first thing philosophy promises us is the feeling of fellowship, of belonging to mankind and being members of a community. . . . Philosophy calls for simple living, not for doing penance, and the simple way of life need not be a crude one."[13] Viewed in retrospect, Seneca displays some glaring inconsistencies. While preaching the virtues of simplicity, he amassed a fortune and was ruthless at times in protecting it. His letters show humanity, benevolence, and fortitude, but his sentiments are often undermined by an attempt to be clever with words.

The silver age also produced a work called the *Satyricon,* described by some literary historians as the first picaresque novel in Western literature. It was written by Petronius (d. 66), probably a former governor of Bithynia who had joined Nero's inner circle. The *Satyricon* is a humorous satire on the excesses of the Roman social scene. Basically, it is the story of a young man and his two male companions who engage in a series of madcap escapades and homosexual antics. The longest surviving episode contains a description of an elaborate and vulgar dinner party given by Trimalchio, a freedman who had become a millionaire through an inheritance from his former master. In Trimalchio, Petronius gave a hilarious, satirical portrait of Rome's new rich.

**Tacitus** The greatest historian of the silver age was Tacitus (c. 56–120). His main works included the *Annals* and the *Histories,* which presented a narrative account of Roman history from the reign of Tiberius through the assassination of Domitian in 96. Tacitus believed that history had a moral purpose: "It seems to me a historian's foremost duty to ensure that merit is recorded, and to confront evil deeds and words with the fear of posterity's denunciations."[14] As a member of the senatorial class, Tacitus was disgusted with the abuses of power perpetrated by the emperors and was determined that the "evil deeds" of wicked men would not be forgotten. Many historians believe he went too far in projecting the evils of his own day back into his account of the past. Tacitus' work *Germania* is especially important as a source of information about the early Germans. But it too is colored by his attempt to show the Germans as noble savages in contrast to the decadent Roman upper classes.

**Juvenal** By the second century A.D., though still influenced by the familiar Greek models, Latin authors were increasingly imitating the great Latin writers of earlier ages. This was evident in the work of Juvenal, the best poet of the silver age. Juvenal (c. 55–c. 128) wrote five books of satires in which he pilloried the manners and vices of his generation. He attacked the affectations of Roman women, the abuse of slaves, the excesses of emperors, the eastern and Greek immigrants, his own poverty, and the inequities of Roman society. For example: "They demand that the teacher shall mold these tender minds. . . . 'See to it,' you're told, and when the school year's ended, you'll get as much as a jockey makes from a single race."[15] But Juvenal was not a reformer. Though he attacked many vices, he offered no basic critique of his society.

## Art in the Early Empire

The Romans contributed little that was original to painting and scupture. Much work was done by Greek artists and craftspeople who adhered to the Roman desire for realism and attention to details. Wall paintings and frescoes in the houses of the rich realistically depicted landscapes, portraits, and scenes from mythological stories.

In architecture, the Romans continued to imitate Greek styles and made use of colonnades, rectangular structures, and post-and-lintel construction. But the Romans were innovative in their own way. They made considerable use of curvilinear forms: the arch, vault, and dome. The Romans were the first people in antiquity to use concrete on a massive scale. By combining concrete and curvilinear forms, they were able to construct massive buildings—public baths, such as those of Caracalla, and amphitheaters, the most famous of which was the Colosseum in Rome. These large buildings were made possible by Roman engineering skills. These same skills were put to use in constructing roads (the Romans built a network of 50,000 miles of roads throughout their empire), aqueducts (in Rome, almost a dozen aqueducts kept the population supplied with water), and bridges.

## Imperial Rome

At the center of the colossal Roman Empire was the ancient city of Rome (see Map 6.3). Truly a capital city, Rome had the largest population of any city in the empire. It is estimated that its population was close to one million by the time of Augustus. For anyone with ambitions, Rome was the place to be. A magnet to many people, Rome was extremely

**The Pantheon.** Shown here is the Pantheon, one of Rome's greatest buildings. Constructed of brick, six kinds of concrete, and marble, it was a stunning example of the Romans' engineering skills. The outside porch of the Pantheon contained eighteen Corinthian granite columns, but it was the inside of the temple that amazed onlookers. The interior is a large circular space topped by a huge dome. A hole in the center of the roof was the only source of light. The dome, built up layer by layer, was made of concrete, weighing 5,000 tons. The walls holding the dome are almost 20 feet thick.

cosmopolitan. Nationalities from all over the empire resided there, with entire neighborhoods inhabited by specific groups, such as Greeks and Syrians.

Rome was no doubt an overcrowded and noisy city. Because of the congestion, cart and wagon traffic was banned from the streets during the day. The noise from the resulting vehicular movement at night often made sleep difficult. Evening pedestrian travel was dangerous. Although Augustus had organized a police force, lone travelers might be assaulted, robbed, or soaked by filth thrown out of the upper-story windows of Rome's massive apartment buildings.

An enormous gulf existed between rich and poor in the city of Rome. While the rich had comfortable villas, the poor lived in apartment blocks called *insulae*, which might be six stories high. Constructed of concrete, they were often poorly built and prone to collapse. The use of wooden beams in the floors and movable stoves, torches, candles, and lamps for heat and light made the danger of fire constant. Once started, fires were extremely difficult to put out. The famous conflagration of 64, which Nero was unjustly accused of starting, devastated a good part of the city.

**Roman Aqueduct.** The engineering skills of the Romans enabled them to build massive constructions, including aqueducts such as this one in southern France, known as the Pont du Gard. The Pont du Gard is a three-story bridge built of blocks of stone without cement, at the top of which was a channel that carried water. Nîmes received its water from a source 30 miles away. Since gravity kept the water flowing, channels holding the water had to have a gradual decline from the source of water to its final destination. The Pont du Gard, which crosses the Gardon River outside Nîmes, was built to the exact height needed to maintain the flow of water into the city.

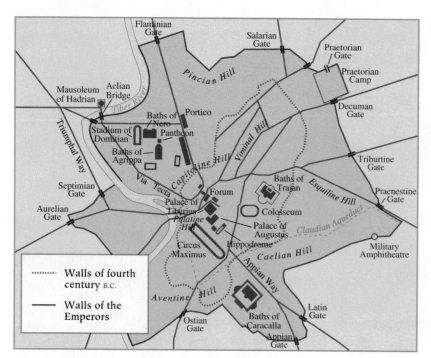

MAP 6.3 **Imperial Rome.** A large, overcrowded, and dirty city, Rome was the political, economic, social, and cultural hub of the Roman Empire. Squalid and desperate living conditions for the poor contrasted dramatically with the city's magnificent architectural works. ❓ How did roads from outside enter Rome, and what could possibly explain this? 🔊 **View an animated version of this map or related maps at** http://history .wadsworth .com/spielvogel06/

Besides the hazards of collapse and fire, living conditions were miserable. High rents forced entire families into one room. In the absence of plumbing and central heating, conditions were so uncomfortable that poorer Romans spent most of their time outdoors in the streets.

Fortunately for these people, Rome boasted public buildings unequaled anywhere in the empire. Its temples, forums, markets, baths, theaters, triumphal arches, governmental buildings, and amphitheaters gave parts of the city an appearance of grandeur and magnificence (see the box on p. 153).

Though the center of a great empire, Rome was also a great parasite. Beginning with Augustus, the emperors accepted responsibility for providing food for the urban populace, with about 200,000 people receiving free grain. Rome needed about six million sacks of grain a year and imported large quantities from its African and Egyptian provinces to meet these requirements. But even the free grain did not change the grim condition of the poor. Early in the second century A.D., a Roman doctor claimed that rickets was common among the city's children.

In addition to food, entertainment was also provided on a grand scale for the inhabitants of Rome. The poet Juvenal said of the Roman masses: "Nowadays, with no vote to sell, their motto is 'Couldn't care less.' Time was when their vote elected generals, heads of state, commanders of legions: but now they've pulled in their horns, there's only two things that concern them: Bread and Circuses."[16] The emperor and other state officials provided public spectacles as part of the great festivals—most of them religious in origin—celebrated by the state. More than one hundred days a year were given over to these public holidays. The festivals included three major types of entertainment. At the Circus Maximus, horse and chariot races attracted hundreds of thousands, while dramatic and other performances were held in theaters. But the most famous of all the public spectacles were the gladiatorial shows.

## The Gladiatorial Shows

The gladiatorial shows were an integral part of Roman society. They took place in amphitheaters; the first permanent one was constructed at Rome in 29 B.C. Perhaps the most famous was the Flavian amphitheater, called the Colosseum, constructed at Rome under Vespasian and his son Titus to seat fifty thousand spectators. Amphitheaters were constructed throughout the empire. They varied in size, with capacities ranging from a few thousand to tens of thousands. Considerable resources and ingenuity went into building them, especially in the arrangements for moving wild beasts efficiently into the arena. In most cities and towns, amphitheaters came to be the biggest buildings, rivaled only by the circuses for races and the public baths. As we shall see repeatedly in the course of Western civilization, where a society invests its money gives an idea of its priorities. Since the amphitheater was the primary location for the gladiatorial games, it is fair to say that public slaughter was an important part of Roman culture.

Programs of gladiatorial games lasted from dawn to dusk. Their main features were contests to the death between trained fighters. Most gladiators were slaves or condemned criminals, although some free men, lured by the hope of popularity and patronage by wealthy fans, participated voluntarily. They were trained for combat in special gladiatorial schools.

Gladiatorial games included other forms of entertainment as well. Criminals of all ages and both sexes were sent into the arena without weapons to face certain death from

# THE PUBLIC BATHS OF THE ROMAN EMPIRE

THE PUBLIC BATHS in Rome and other cities played an important role in urban life. Introduced to Rome in the second century B.C. as a result of Greek influence, the number of public baths grew at a rapid pace in the Early Empire as the emperors contributed funds for their construction. The public baths were especially noisy near the end of the afternoon when Romans stopped in after work to use the baths before dinner. The following description is by Lucian, a traveling lecturer who lived in the second century. This selection is taken from *Hippias, or the Bath.*

### Lucian, *Hippias, or the Bath*

The building suits the magnitude of the site, accords well with the accepted idea of such an establishment, and shows regard for the principles of lighting. The entrance is high, with a flight of broad steps of which the tread is greater than the pitch, to make them easy to ascend. On entering, one is received into a public hall of good size, with ample accommodations for servants and attendants. On the left are the lounging rooms, also of just the right sort for a bath, attractive, brightly lighted retreats. Then, besides them, a hall larger than need be for the purposes of a bath, but necessary for the reception of richer persons. Next, capacious locker rooms to undress in, on each side, with a very high and brilliantly lighted hall between them, in which are three swimming pools of cold water. . . .

On leaving this hall, you come into another which is slightly warmed instead of meeting you at once with fierce heat; it is oblong, and has an apse on each side. Next to it, on the right, is a very bright hall, nicely fitted up for massage. . . . Then near this is another hall, the most beautiful in the world, in which one can stand or sit with comfort, linger without danger, and stroll about with profit. It also is radiant with Phrygian marble clear to the roof. Next comes the hot corridor, faced with Numidian marble. The hall beyond it is very beautiful, full of abundant light and aglow with color like that of purple hangings. It contains three hot tubs.

When you have bathed you need not go back through the same rooms, but can go directly to the cold room through a slightly warmed chamber. Everywhere there is copious illumination and full indoor daylight. . . . Why should I go on to tell you of the exercising floor and the cloak rooms? . . . Moreover, it is beautiful with all other marks of thoughtfulness—with two toilets, many exits, and two devices for telling time, a water clock that makes a bellowing sound and a sundial.

**Interior of the Colosseum of Rome.**
The Colosseum was a large amphitheater constructed under the emperor Vespasian and his son Titus. Such amphitheaters, in which gladiatorial contests were held, were built throughout the empire. They varied in size, but the one at Rome was the largest. The Colosseum was named after the Colossus of Nero, a large statue of the first-century A.D. emperor that stood nearby. Although scene to many bloody gladiatorial spectacles, the arena of the Colosseum was also flooded for a spectacular naval battle when the emperor Titus held the first games there.

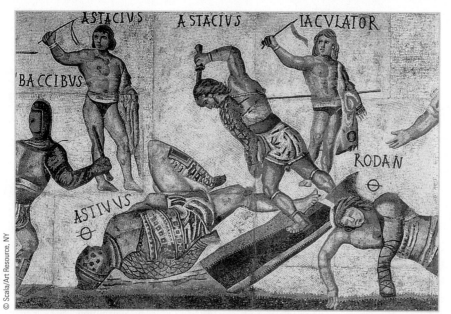

ASTACIVS   A STACIVS   IACVLATOR

BACCIBVS

RODAN

ASTIVS

**The Gladiatorial Games.** Although some gladiators were free men enticed by the possibility of rewards, most were condemned criminals, slaves, or prisoners of war who were trained in special schools. A great gladiator could win his freedom through the games. This mosaic from the fourth century A.D. depicts different aspects of gladiatorial fighting and clearly shows the bloody nature of the contests.

wild animals who would tear them to pieces. Numerous kinds of animal contests were also held: wild beasts against each other, such as bears against buffalo; staged hunts with men shooting safely from behind iron bars; and gladiators in the arena with bulls, tigers, and lions. Reportedly, five thousand beasts were killed in one day of games when the emperor Titus inaugurated the Colosseum in A.D. 80. Enormous resources were invested in capturing and shipping wild animals for slaughter, and whole species were hunted to extinction in parts of the empire.

These bloodthirsty spectacles were extremely popular with the Roman people. Tacitus reported, "Few indeed are to be found who talk of any other subjects in their homes, and whenever we enter a classroom, what else is the conversation of the youths."[17] But the gladiatorial games served a purpose beyond mere entertainment. Like the other forms of public entertainment, the games fulfilled both a political and a social function. Certainly, the games served to divert the idle masses from political unrest. It was said of the emperor Trajan that he understood that although the distribution of grain and money satisfied the individual, spectacles were necessary for the "contentment of the masses."

### Disaster in Southern Italy

Gladiatorial spectacles were contrived by humans, but the Roman Empire also experienced some horrific natural spectacles. One of the greatest was the eruption of Mount Vesuvius on August 24, 79. Although known to be a volcano, Vesuvius was thought to be extinct, its hillsides green with flourishing vineyards. Its eruption threw up thousands of tons of lava and ash. Toxic fumes killed many people, and the nearby city of Pompeii was quickly buried under volcanic ash. To the west, Herculaneum and other communities around the Bay of Naples were submerged beneath a mud flow (see the box on p. 155). Not for another 1,700 years were systematic excavations begun on the buried towns. The examination of their preserved remains have enabled archaeologists to reconstruct the everyday life and art of these Roman towns. Their discovery in the eighteenth century was an important force in stimulating both scholarly and public interest in classical antiquity and helped give rise to the Neoclassical style of that century.

### The Art of Medicine

Although early Romans had no professional physicians, they did possess an art of medicine. Early Roman medicine was essentially herbal. The *paterfamilias* would prepare various remedies to heal wounds and cure illnesses. Knowledge of the healing properties of plants was passed down from generation to generation. This traditional approach to medicine continued in the Early Empire. Of course, numerous recipes for nonillnesses, such as remedies to prevent baldness, were also passed on. One such formula consisted of wine, saffron, pepper, vinegar, *laserpicium* (the queen of Roman medicinal plants, now extinct), and rat dung.

As in other areas of Roman life, Greek influence was also felt in medicine. At the end of the third century B.C., scientific medicine entered the Roman world through professional practitioners from the Hellenistic world. Doctors became fashionable in Rome, although prejudice against them was never completely abandoned. Many were Greek slaves who belonged to the households of large aristocratic families. The first public doctors in Rome were attached to the Roman army. Military practices were then extended to imperial officials and their families in the provinces and included the establishment of public hospitals. Gladiatorial schools had their own resident doctors as well. In fact, one of the most famous physicians, the Greek Galen (129–199), emerged from the ranks of gladiatorial doctors

# THE ERUPTION OF MOUNT VESUVIUS

PLINY THE YOUNGER, whose description of his villa we read in the box on p. 149, also wrote a letter to the Roman historian Tacitus describing the death of his uncle, Pliny the Elder, as a result of the eruption of Mount Vesuvius. Pliny the Elder was the commander of a fleet at Misenum. When the eruption occurred, his curiosity led him to take a detachment of his fleet to the scene. He landed at Stabiae, where he died from the toxic fumes.

### Pliny, Letter to Cornelius Tacitus

Thank you for asking me to send you a description of my uncle's death so that you can leave an accurate account of it for posterity. . . . It is true that he perished in a catastrophe which destroyed the loveliest regions of the earth, a fate shared by whole cities and their people, and one so memorable that it is likely to make his name live for ever. . . .

My uncle was stationed at Misenum, in active command of the fleet. On 24 August, in the early afternoon, my mother drew his attention to a cloud of unusual size and appearance. . . . He called for his shoes and climbed up to a place which would give him the best view of the phenomenon. It was not clear at that distance from which mountain the cloud was rising (it was afterwards known to be Vesuvius); its general appearance can best be expressed as being like an umbrella pine, for it rose to a great height on a sort of trunk and then split off into branches, I imagine because it was thrust upwards by the first blast and then left unsupported as the pressure subsided, or else it was borne down by its own weight so that it spread out and gradually dispersed. In places it looked white, elsewhere blotched and dirty, according to the amount of soil and ashes it carried with it. My uncle's scholarly acumen saw at once that it was important enough for a closer inspection, and he ordered a boat to be made ready. . . .

[Unable to go further by sea, he lands at Stabiae.]

Meanwhile on Mount Vesuvius broad sheets of fire and leaping flames blazed at several points, their bright glare emphasized by the darkness of night. My uncle tried to allay the fears of his companions by repeatedly declaring that these were nothing but bonfires left by the peasants in their terror, or else empty houses on fire in the districts they had abandoned. . . .

They debated whether to stay indoors or take their chance in the open, for the buildings were now shaking with violent shocks, and seemed to be swaying to and fro as if they were torn from their foundations. Outside on the other hand, there was the danger of falling pumice-stones, even though these were light and porous; however, after comparing the risks they chose the latter. In my uncle's case one reason outweighed the other, but for the others it was a choice of fears. As a protection against falling objects they put pillows on their heads tied down with cloths.

Elsewhere there was daylight by this time, but they were still in darkness, blacker and denser than any ordinary night, which they relieved by lighting torches and various kinds of lamp. My uncle decided to go down to the shore and investigate on the spot the possibility of any escape by sea, but he found the waves still wild and dangerous. A sheet was spread on the ground for him to lie down, and he repeatedly asked for cold water to drink. Then the flames and smell of sulphur which gave warning of the approaching fire drove the others to take flight and roused him to stand up. He stood leaning on two slaves and then suddenly collapsed, I imagine because the dense fumes choked his breathing by blocking his windpipe which was constitutionally weak and narrow and often inflamed. When daylight returned on the 26th—two days after the last day he had seen—his body was found intact and uninjured, still fully clothed and looking more like sleep than death.

---

to become court physician to the emperor Marcus Aurelius. Roman scientific medicine also witnessed the development of numerous specialists. For example, Alcon, the famous surgeon of the Flavian age, specialized in bone diseases and hernia operations.

### Roman Law in the Early Empire

The Early Empire experienced great progress in the study and codification of law. The second and early third centuries A.D. witnessed the "classical age of Roman law," a period in which a number of great jurists classified and compiled basic legal principles that have proved valuable to the Western world. Most jurists emphasized the emperor as the source of law: "What has pleased the emperor has the force of law."

In the "classical age of Roman law," the identification of the law of nations with natural law led to a concept of natural rights. According to the jurist Ulpian (d. 228), natural rights implied that all men are born equal and should therefore be equal before the law. In practice, however, the principle was not applied.

The Romans did, however, establish standards of justice, applicable to all people, that included principles that we would immediately recognize. A person was considered innocent until proved otherwise. People accused of wrongdoing were allowed to defend themselves before a judge. A judge was expected to weigh evidence carefully before arriving at a decision. These principles lived on in Western civilization long after the fall of the Roman Empire.

# THE ROMAN FEAR OF SLAVES

HE LOWEST STRATUM of the Roman population consisted of slaves. They were used extensively in households and the court, as craftspeople in industrial enterprises, as business managers, and in numerous other ways. Although some historians have argued that slaves were treated more humanely during the Early Empire, these selections by the Roman historian Tacitus and the Roman statesman Pliny indicate that slaves still rebelled against their masters because of mistreatment. Many masters continued to live in fear of their slaves, as witnessed by the saying "as many enemies as you have slaves."

### Tacitus, *The Annals of Imperial Rome*

The City Prefect, Lucius Pedanius Secundus, was murdered by one of his slaves [in A.D. 61]. Either Pedanius had refused to free the murderer after agreeing to a price, or the slave, in a homosexual infatuation, found competition from his master intolerable. After the murder, ancient custom required that every slave residing under the same roof must be executed. But a crowd gathered, eager to save so many innocent lives; and rioting began. The senate-house was besieged. Inside, there was feeling against excessive severity, but the majority opposed any change. Among the latter was Gaius Cassius Longinus, who when his turn came spoke as follows. . . .

"An ex-consul has been deliberately murdered by a slave in his own home. None of his fellow-slaves prevented or betrayed the murderer, though the senatorial decree threatening the whole household with execution still stands. Exempt them from the penalty if you like. But then, if the City Prefect was not important enough to be immune, who will be? Who will have enough slaves to protect him if Pedanius' 400 were too few? Who can rely on his household's help if even fear for their own lives does not make them shield us?" [The sentence of death was carried out.]

### Pliny, Letter to Acilius

This horrible affair demands more publicity than a letter—Larcius Macedo, a senator and ex-praetor, has fallen a victim to his own slaves. Admittedly he was a cruel and overbearing master, too ready to forget that his father had been a slave, or perhaps too keenly conscious of it. He was taking a bath in his house at Formiae when suddenly he found himself surrounded; one slave seized him by the throat while the others struck his face and hit him in the chest and stomach and—shocking to say—in his private parts. When they thought he was dead they threw him on to the hot pavement, to make sure he was not still alive. Whether unconscious or feigning to be so, he lay there motionless, thus making them believe that he was quite dead. Only then was he carried out, as if he had fainted with the heat, and received by his slaves who had remained faithful, while his concubines ran up, screaming fanatically. Roused by their cries and revived by the cooler air he opened his eyes and made some movement to show that he was alive, it being now safe to do so. The guilty slaves fled, but most of them have been arrested and a search is being made for the others. Macedo was brought back to life with difficulty, but only for a few days; at least he died with the satisfaction of having revenged himself, for he lived to see the same punishment meted out as for murder. There you see the dangers, outrages, and insults to which we are exposed. No master can feel safe because he is kind and considerate; for it is their brutality, not their reasoning capacity, which leads slaves to murder masters.

## Slaves and Their Masters

The number of slaves had increased dramatically in the Roman Republic as the empire was expanded through warfare. Consequently, slaves were highly visible in the Early Empire. The residences of the rich were filled with slaves. Possessing a large number of slaves was a status symbol; a single household might include dozens of slaves, serving as hairdressers, footmen, messengers, accountants, secretaries, carpenters, plumbers, librarians, goldsmiths, and doctors as well as ordinary domestic servants. The reliance on slaves, especially as skilled craftspeople, undoubtedly created unemployment among the free population. Some slaves worked at high-status jobs as architects and managers of businesses, while some imperial slaves held positions in the government bureaucracy. Slaves were also used on landed estates.

But the number of slaves probably peaked in the Early Empire. The defensive imperial policies pursued after Augustus led to a decline in the supply of slaves from foreign conquest. Manumission also contributed to the decline in the number of slaves. It had been customary in Rome for "good masters" to free their slaves, especially well-educated ones or good workers. Although freedmen became Roman citizens, they were not given full rights of citizenship. They could vote but not run for office.

Many authors have commented on the supposed advance in humanitarian attitudes toward slaves in the Early Empire, especially in the second century. They argue that the philosophy of Stoicism, with its emphasis on the universality of humanity, had an influence in this direction. Seneca stressed the need for kindness to slaves. Very likely, however, the practical Romans were as much, if not more, concerned about the usefulness of their slaves than about any humanitarian attitudes. New laws in the second century moralized more than they actually improved the condition of slaves. Hadrian, for example, forbade the sale of slaves for immoral or gladiatorial purposes. Such laws had little impact, however, on how masters actually treated their slaves. Despite the changes, there were still instances of slaves murdering their owners, and Romans continued to live in unspoken fear of their slaves (see the box above).

## The Upper-Class Roman Family

By the second century A.D., significant changes were occurring in the Roman family. The foundations of the authority of the *paterfamilias* over his family, which had already begun to weaken in the late Republic, were further undermined. The *paterfamilias* no longer had absolute authority over his children; he could no longer sell his children into slavery or have them put to death. Moreover, the husband's absolute authority over his wife also disappeared, a process that had begun in the late Republic. In the Early Empire, the idea of male guardianship continued to weaken significantly, and by the late second century, it had become a mere formality.

Upper-class Roman women in the Early Empire had considerable freedom and independence. They had acquired the right to own, inherit, and dispose of property. Upper-class women could attend races, the theater, and events in the amphitheater, although in the latter two places they were forced to sit in separate female sections. Moreover, ladies of rank were still accompanied by maids and companions when they went out. Some women operated businesses, such as shipping firms. Women still could not participate in politics, but the Early Empire saw a number of important women who influenced politics through their husbands, including Livia, the wife of Augustus; Agrippina, the mother of Nero; and Plotina, the wife of Trajan.

At the end of the first century and beginning of the second, there was a noticeable decline in the number of children among the upper classes, a trend that had already begun in the late Republic. Especially evident was an increase in childless marriages. Despite imperial laws aimed at increasing the number of children, the low birthrate persisted. Not only did **infanticide** continue to be practiced, but upper-class Romans also used contraception and abortion to limit their families. There were numerous techniques for contraception. Though highly touted, amulets, magical formulas, and potions to induce temporary sterility proved ineffective, as did the rhythm method, since Roman medical writers believed that a woman was most fertile just when menstruation was ending. A more dependable practice involved the use of oils, ointments, and soft wool to obstruct the opening of the uterus. Contraceptive techniques for males were also advocated. An early version of a condom involved using the bladder of a goat, but it was prohibitively expensive. Although the medical sources do not mention it, the Romans may also have used the ubiquitous coitus interruptus. Abortion was practiced, using drugs or surgical instruments. Ovid chastises Corinna: "Ah, women, why will you thrust and pierce with the instrument, and give dire poisons to your children yet unborn?"[18]

Women also faced great dangers in childbirth. The birth of a child occurred at home with the assistance of a midwife and a few female relatives. Fathers-to-be and other males were not present. Although exact numbers are not available, we do know that many upper-class women between the ages of sixteen and thirty-five died in childbirth. Prominent women who died in childbirth or soon after due to complications include Cicero's daughter Tullia and Caesar's daughter Julia.

# Transformation of the Roman World: Crises in the Third Century

During the reign of Marcus Aurelius, the last of the five good emperors, a number of natural catastrophes struck Rome. Floods of the Tiber, famine, and plague brought back from the east by the army led to considerable loss of population and a shortage of military manpower. To many Romans, these natural disasters seemed to portend an ominous future for Rome. New problems arose soon after the death of Marcus Aurelius.

## Political and Military Woes

Unlike the first four good emperors, who chose capable successors by adopting competent men as their sons, Marcus Aurelius allowed his own son, Commodus (180–192), to become emperor. A cruel man, Commodus was a poor choice, and his assassination led to a brief renewal of civil war until Septimius Severus (193–211), who was born in North Africa and spoke Latin with an accent, used his legions to seize power. On his deathbed, Septimius Severus advised his sons, "Live in harmony, make the soldiers rich, and don't give a damn for anything else." His advice set the tone for the new dynasty he established. The Severan rulers (193–235) began to create a military monarchy. The army was expanded, soldiers' pay was increased, and military officers were appointed to important government positions. A new stability seemed at hand, but the increased power of the military led new military leaders to aspire to become emperor, and the military monarchy of the Severan rulers degenerated into military anarchy.

For the next fifty years (235–284), the empire was mired in the chaos of continual civil war. Contenders for the imperial throne found that bribing soldiers was an effective way to become emperor. In these five decades, there were twenty-two emperors, only two of whom did not meet a violent end. At the same time, the empire was beset by a series of invasions, no doubt encouraged by the internal turmoil. In the east, the Sassanid Persians made inroads into Roman territory. A fitting symbol of Rome's crisis was the capture of the Roman emperor, Valerian (253–260), by the Persians and his death in captivity, an event unprecedented in Roman history. Valerian's body was displayed in the chief towns of Persia. Germanic tribes also poured into the empire. The Goths overran the Balkans and moved into Greece and Asia Minor. The Franks advanced into Gaul and Spain. Not until the reign of Aurelian (270–275) were most of the boundaries restored. Although he abandoned the Danubian province of Dacia, Aurelian reconquered Gaul and reestablished order in the east and along the Danube. He also built a new defensive wall

**Septimius Severus and His Family.** This portrait painted on wood about A.D. 200, found in Egypt, is the only existing painted likeness of a Roman emperor. The emperor is portrayed with gray hair and beard in memory of Marcus Aurelius. To legitimize his authority, Septimius Severus had himself adopted into the Antonine dynasty, calling himself the son of Marcus Aurelius. The emperor stands next to his wife with their two sons in front of them. The face of his son Geta has been blotted out, no doubt by order of the other son standing next to him, Caracalla, who had his brother killed when he succeeded to the throne.

around Rome to defend the city against invaders. Grateful citizens hailed him as "restorer of the world."

As civil wars and invasions wore down the central government, provinces began to break away from the empire. A military commander named Postumus seized control of Gaul and then gained the support of Britain and Spain. He defended his "Gallic empire" until he was killed by his own soldiers in 269. In the east, Zenobia, the wife of the ruler of Syria, seized power after his death and then in 270 extended her control over Egypt and much of Asia Minor. In 272, Emperor Aurelian ended this threat to imperial power by defeating Zenobia and her forces in Syria.

### Economic and Social Crises

Invasions, civil wars, and a recurrence of the plague came close to causing an economic collapse of the Roman Empire in the third century. The population declined drastically, possibly by as much as one-third. There was a significant decline in trade and small industry. The manpower shortage created by the plague affected both military recruiting and the economy. Farm production deteriorated as fields were ravaged by barbarians and even more often by the defending Roman armies. Many farmers complained that Roman commanders and their soldiers were confiscating produce and livestock. Provincial governors seemed powerless to stop these depredations, and some even joined in the frenzy.

The monetary system began to show signs of collapse as a result of debased coinage and the onset of serious inflation. Gold coins disappeared from circulation, and silver coins were diluted. The standard coin, the denarius, was now worth less than half of its first-century value. After further decline, it was replaced by new coins of even less value. Goods began to replace money as a medium of exchange.

Armies were needed more than ever, but financial strains made it difficult to enlist and pay the necessary soldiers. Short of cash, the imperial government paid its soldiers with produce, causing bitter resentment. Whereas in the second century the Roman army had been recruited among the inhabitants of frontier provinces, by the mid-third century, the state had to rely on hiring barbarians to fight under Roman commanders. These soldiers had no understanding of Roman traditions and no real attachment to either the empire or the emperors. By the end of the third century, a new form of political structure would emerge (see Chapter 7).

## Transformation of the Roman World: The Rise of Christianity

The advent of Christianity marks a fundamental break with the dominant values of the Greco-Roman world. Christian views of God, human beings, and the world were quite different from those of the Greeks and Romans. Nevertheless, to understand the rise of Christianity, we must first examine both the religious environment of the Roman world and the Jewish background from which Christianity emerged.

## The Religious World of the Roman Empire

Augustus had taken a number of steps to revive the Roman state religion, which had declined during the turmoil of the late Republic. The official state religion focused on the worship of a pantheon of Greco-Roman gods and goddesses, including Jupiter, Juno, Minerva, and Mars. Observance of proper ritual by state priests theoretically brought the Romans into proper relationship with the gods and guaranteed security, peace, and prosperity. The polytheistic Romans were extremely tolerant of other religions. The Romans allowed the worship of native gods and goddesses throughout their provinces and even adopted some of the local gods. In addition, the imperial cult of Roma and Augustus was developed to bolster support for the emperors. After Augustus, dead emperors deified by the Roman senate were included in the official imperial cult.

The desire for a more emotional spiritual experience led many people to the mystery religions of the Hellenistic east, which flooded into the western Roman world during the Early Empire. The mystery religions offered secret teachings that supposedly brought special benefits. They promised their followers advantages unavailable through Roman religion: an entry into a higher world of reality and the promise of a future life superior to the present one. They also featured elaborate rituals with deep emotional appeal. By participating in their ceremonies and performing their rites, an adherent could achieve communion with spiritual beings and undergo purification that opened the door to life after death.

Although many mystery cults vied for attention in the Roman world, perhaps the most important was Mithraism. Mithra was the chief agent of Ahuramazda, the supreme god of light in Persian Zoroastrianism (see Chapter 2). In the Roman world, Mithra came to be identified with the sun god and was known by his Roman title of the Unconquered Sun. Mithraism had spread rapidly in Rome and the western provinces by the second century A.D. and was especially favored by soldiers, who viewed Mithra as their patron deity. It was a religion for men only and featured an initiation ceremony in which devotees were baptized in the blood of a sacrificed bull. Mithraists paid homage to the sun on the first day of the week (Sunday), commemorated the sun's birthday around December 25, and celebrated ceremonial meals.

## The Jewish Background

Christianity emerged out of Judaism, and so it is to the Jewish political-religious world that we must turn to find the beginnings of Christianity. In Hellenistic times, the Jewish people had enjoyed considerable independence under their Seleucid rulers (see Chapter 4). Roman involvement with the Jews began in 63 B.C., and by A.D. 6, Judaea had been made a province and placed under the direction of a Roman procurator. But unrest continued, augmented by divisions among the Jews themselves. The Sadducees favored a rigid adherence to Hebrew law, rejected the possibility of personal immortality, and favored cooperation with the Romans. The Pharisees adhered strictly to Jewish ritual and, although they wanted Judaea to be free from Roman control, did not advocate violent means to achieve this goal. The Essenes were a Jewish sect that lived in a religious community near the Dead Sea. As revealed in the Dead Sea Scrolls, a collection of documents first discovered in 1947, the Essenes, like many other Jews, awaited a Messiah who would save Israel from oppression, usher in the kingdom of God, and establish a paradise on earth. A fourth group, the Zealots, were militant extremists who advocated the violent overthrow of Roman rule. A Jewish revolt in A.D. 66 was crushed by the Romans four years later. The Jewish Temple in Jerusalem was destroyed, and Roman power once more stood supreme in Judaea.

## The Origins of Christianity

Jesus of Nazareth (c. 6 B.C.–A.D. 30) was a Palestinian Jew who grew up in Galilee, an important center of the militant Zealots. He began his itinerant public preaching as a young adult amid the confusion and conflict in Judaea. Jesus' message was basically simple. He reassured his fellow Jews that he did not plan to undermine their traditional religion: "Do not think that I have come to abolish the Law or the Prophets; I have not come to abolish them but to fulfill them."[19] According to Jesus, what was important was not strict adherence to the letter of the law and attention to rules and prohibitions but the transformation of the inner person: "So in everything, do to others what you would have them do to you, for this sums up the Law and the Prophets."[20] God's command was simply to love God and one another: "Love the Lord your God with all your heart and with all your soul and with all your mind and with all your strength. The second is this: Love your neighbor as yourself."[21] In the Sermon on the Mount (see the box on p. 160), Jesus presented the ethical concepts—humility, charity, and brotherly love—that would form the basis for the value system of medieval Western civilization. As we have seen, these were not the values of classical Greco-Roman civilization.

Although some Jews welcomed Jesus as the Messiah who would save Israel from oppression and establish God's kingdom on earth, Jesus spoke of a heavenly kingdom, not an earthly one: "My kingdom is not of this world."[22] Consequently, he disappointed the radicals. At the same time, conservative religious leaders believed Jesus was another false Messiah who was undermining respect for traditional Jewish religion. To the Roman authorities of Palestine and their local allies, the Nazarene was a potential revolutionary who might transform Jewish expectations of a messianic kingdom into a revolt against Rome. Therefore, Jesus found himself denounced on many sides and was given

# CHRISTIAN IDEALS: THE SERMON ON THE MOUNT

CHRISTIANITY WAS SIMPLY one of many religions competing for attention in the Roman Empire during the first and second centuries. The rise of Christianity marked a fundamental break with the value system of the upper-class elites who dominated the world of classical antiquity. As these excerpts from the Sermon on the Mount in the Gospel of Matthew illustrate, Christians emphasized humility, charity, brotherly love, and a belief in the inner being and a spiritual kingdom superior to this material world. These values and principles were not those of classical Greco-Roman civilization as exemplified in the words and deeds of its leaders.

## The Gospel According to Matthew

Now when he saw the crowds, he went up on a mountainside and sat down. His disciples came to him, and he began to teach them saying:

> Blessed are the poor in spirit: for theirs is the kingdom of heaven.
> Blessed are those who mourn: for they will be comforted.
> Blessed are the meek: for they will inherit the earth.
> Blessed are those who hunger and thirst for righteousness: for they will be filled.
> Blessed are the merciful: for they will be shown mercy.
> Blessed are the pure in heart: for they will see God.
> Blessed are the peacemakers: for they will be called sons of God.
> Blessed are those who are persecuted because of righteousness: for theirs is the kingdom of heaven. . . .

You have heard that it was said, "Eye for eye, and tooth for tooth." But I tell you, Do not resist an evil person. If someone strikes you on the right cheek, turn to him the other also. . . .

You have heard that it was said, "Love your neighbor, and hate your enemy." But I tell you, Love your enemies and pray for those who persecute you. . . .

Do not store up for yourselves treasures on earth, where moth and rust destroy, and where thieves break in and steal. But store up for yourselves treasures in heaven, where moth and rust do not destroy, and where thieves do not break in and steal. For where your treasure is, there your heart will be also. . . .

No one can serve two masters. Either he will hate the one and love the other, or he will be devoted to the one and despise the other. You cannot serve both God and Money.

Therefore I tell you, do not worry about your life, what you will eat or drink; or about your body, what you will wear. Is not life more important than food, and the body more important than clothes? Look at the birds of the air; they do not sow or reap to store away in barns, and yet your heavenly Father feeds them. Are you not much more valuable than they? . . . So do not worry, saying, What shall we eat? or What shall we drink? or What shall we wear? For the pagans run after all these things, and your heavenly Father knows that you need them. But seek first his kingdom and his righteousness, and all these things will be given to you as well.

---

over to the Roman authorities. The procurator Pontius Pilate ordered his crucifixion. But that did not solve the problem. A few loyal disciples of Jesus spread the story, common to mystery cults (see Chapter 4), that he had overcome death, been resurrected, and then ascended into heaven. The belief in Jesus' resurrection became an important tenet of Christian doctrine. Jesus was now hailed by his followers as the "anointed one" (*Christ* in Greek), the Messiah who would return and usher in the kingdom of God on earth.

**The Importance of Paul**   Christianity began, then, as a religious movement within Judaism and was viewed that way by Roman authorities for many decades. Although tradition holds that one of Jesus' disciples, Peter, founded the Christian church at Rome, the most important figure in early Christianity after Jesus was Paul of Tarsus (c. 5–c. 67). Paul reached out to non-Jews and transformed Christianity from a Jewish sect into a broader religious movement.

Called the "second founder of Christianity," Paul was a Jewish Roman citizen who had been strongly influenced by Hellenistic Greek culture. He believed that the message of Jesus should be preached not only to Jews but to Gentiles (non-Jews) as well. Paul was responsible for founding Christian communities throughout Asia Minor and along the shores of the Aegean.

It was Paul who provided a universal foundation for the spread of Jesus' ideas. He taught that Jesus was, in effect, a savior-God, the son of God, who had come to earth to save all humans, who were basically sinners as a result of Adam's original sin of disobedience against God. By his death, Jesus had atoned for the sins of all humans and made it possible for all men and women to experience a new beginning with the potential for individual salvation. By accepting Jesus as their savior, they, too, could be saved.

**The Spread of Christianity**   At first, Christianity spread slowly. Although the teachings of early Christianity were mostly disseminated by the preaching of convinced Christians, written materials also appeared. Paul had written a series of letters, or epistles, outlining Christian beliefs for different Christian communities. Some of Jesus' disciples may also have preserved some of the sayings of the master in writing and would have passed on personal memo-

**Jesus and His Apostles.** Pictured is a fourth-century fresco from a Roman catacomb depicting Jesus and his apostles. Catacombs were underground cemeteries where early Christians buried their dead. Christian tradition holds that in times of imperial repression, Christians withdrew to the catacombs to pray and hide.

ries that became the basis of the written *gospels*—the "good news" concerning Jesus—which attempted to give a record of Jesus' life and teachings and formed the core of the New Testament. Although Jerusalem was the first center of Christianity, its destruction by the Romans in A.D. 70 left individual Christian churches with considerable independence. By 100, Christian churches had been established in most of the major cities of the east and in some places in the western part of the empire. Many early Christians came from the ranks of Hellenized Jews and the Greek-speaking populations of the east. But in the second and third centuries, an increasing number of followers were Latin-speaking people. A Latin translation of the Greek New Testament that appeared soon after 200 aided this process.

**Early Christian Communities** Early Christian groups met in private homes in the evening to share a common meal called an *agape* or love feast and to celebrate what became known as the sacrament of the **Eucharist** or Lord's Supper—the communal celebration of Jesus' Last Supper:

> While they were eating, Jesus took bread, gave thanks and broke it, and gave it to the disciples, saying, Take and eat; this is my body. Then he took the cup, gave thanks, and offered it to them, saying, Drink from it, all of you. This is my blood of the covenant, which is poured out for many for the forgiveness of sins.[23]

Early Christian communities were loosely organized, with both men and women playing significant roles. Some women held important positions, often as preachers. Local churches were under the leadership of boards of elders (*presbyters*), but by the beginning of the second century, officials known as *bishops* came to exercise considerable authority over the presbyters. These bishops based their superior position on apostolic succession—as the successors to Jesus' original twelve apostles (disciples), they were living representatives of Jesus' power. As Ignatius of Antioch wrote in 107, "It is clear that we must regard a bishop as the Lord Himself. . . . Your clergy . . . are attuned to their

bishop like the strings of a harp, and the result is a hymn of praise to Jesus Christ from minds that are in unison."[24] Bishops were men, a clear indication that by the second century A.D., most Christian communities were following the views of Paul that Christian women should be subject to Christian men.

Although some of the fundamental values of Christianity differed markedly from those of the Greco-Roman world, the Romans initially did not pay much attention to the Christians, whom they regarded at first as simply another sect of Judaism. The structure of the Roman Empire itself aided the growth of Christianity. Christian missionaries, including some of Jesus' original twelve apostles, used Roman roads to travel throughout the empire spreading their "good news."

**The Changing Roman View of Christianity** As the popular appeal of Christianity grew, the Roman attitude toward it began to change. As we have seen, the Romans were tolerant of other religions except when they threatened public order or public morals. Many Romans came to view Christians as harmful to the order of the Roman state. These views were often based on misperceptions. The celebration of the Lord's Supper, for example, led to rumors that Christians practiced horrible crimes, such as the ritualistic murder of children. Although we know these rumors are untrue, some Romans believed them and used them to incite people against the Christians during times of crisis. Moreover, because Christians held their meetings in secret and seemed to be connected to Christian groups in distant areas, the government could view them as potentially dangerous to the state.

Some Romans felt that Christians were overly exclusive and hence harmful to the community and public order. The Christians did not recognize other gods and therefore abstained from public festivals honoring the popular deities. Finally, Christians refused to participate in the worship of the state gods and the imperial cult. Since the

Romans regarded these as important to the state, the Christians' refusal undermined the security of the state and hence constituted an act of treason, punishable by death. It was also proof of atheism (disbelief in the gods) and subject to punishment on those grounds. But to the Christians, who believed there was only one real God, the worship of state gods and the emperors was idolatry and would endanger their own salvation.

Roman persecution of Christians in the first and second centuries was never systematic but sporadic and local. Persecution began during the reign of Nero. After the fire that destroyed much of Rome, the emperor used the Christians as scapegoats, accusing them of arson and hatred of the human race and subjecting them to cruel deaths in Rome. In the second century, Christians were often ignored as harmless. By the end of the reigns of the five good emperors, Christians still represented a small minority, but one of considerable strength. That strength lay in their conviction of the rightness of their path, a conviction that had been reinforced by the willingness of the first Christians to become martyrs for their faith.

## The Growth of Christianity

The sporadic persecution of Christians by the Romans in the first and second centuries had done nothing to stop the growth of Christianity. It had, in fact, served to strengthen Christianity as an institution in the second and third centuries by causing it to shed the loose structure of the first century and move toward a more centralized organization of its various church communities. Crucial to this change was the emerging role of the bishops. Though still chosen by the community, bishops began to assume more control, with the bishop serving as leader and the presbyters emerging as clergy subject to the bishop's authority. By the third century, bishops were nominated by the clergy, simply approved by the congregation, and then officially ordained into office. The Christian church was creating a well-defined hierarchical structure in which the bishops and clergy were salaried officers separate from the laity or regular church members.

**The Appeal of Christianity** Christianity grew slowly in the first century, took root in the second, and had spread widely by the third. Why was Christianity able to attract so many followers? Historians are not really sure but have offered several answers. Certainly, the Christian message had much to offer the Roman world. The promise of salvation, made possible by Jesus' death and resurrection, had immense appeal in a world full of suffering and injustice. Christianity seemed to imbue life with a meaning and purpose beyond the simple material things of everyday reality. Second, Christianity was not entirely unfamiliar. It could be viewed as simply another eastern mystery religion, offering immortality as the result of the sacrificial death of a savior-god. At the same time, it offered advantages that the other mystery religions lacked. Jesus had been a human figure, not a mythological one, such as Isis or Mithra. Moreover, Christianity had universal appeal. Unlike Mithraism, it was not restricted to men. Furthermore, it did not require a difficult or expensive initiation rite as other mystery religions did. Initiation was accomplished simply by baptism—a purification by water—by which one entered into direct communion with Jesus. In addition, Christianity gave new meaning to life and offered what the Roman state religions could not—a personal relationship with God and a link to higher worlds.

Finally, Christianity fulfilled the human need to belong. Christians formed communities bound to one another in which people could express their love by helping each other and offering assistance to the poor, sick, widows, and orphans. Christianity satisfied the need to belong in a way that the huge, impersonal, and remote Roman Empire could never do.

Christianity proved attractive to all classes. The promise of eternal life was for all—rich, poor, aristocrats, slaves, men, and women. As Paul stated in his Epistle to the Colossians: "And [you] have put on the new self, which is being renewed in knowledge in the image of its Creator. Here there is no Greek nor Jew, circumcised or uncircumcised, barbarian, Scythian, slave or free, but Christ is all, and is in all."[25] Although it did not call for revolution or social upheaval, Christianity emphasized a sense of spiritual equality for all people.

Many women found that Christianity offered them new roles and new forms of companionship with other women. Christian women fostered the new religion in their own homes and preached their convictions to other people in their towns and villages. Many also died for their faith. Perpetua (d. 203) was an aristocratic woman who converted to Christianity. Her pagan family begged her to renounce her new faith, but she refused. Arrested by the Roman authorities, she chose instead to die for her faith and was one of a group of Christians who were slaughtered by wild beasts in the arena at Carthage on March 7, 203.

**Persecution** As the Christian church became more organized, two emperors in the third century responded with more systematic persecutions. The emperor Decius (249–251) blamed the Christians for the disasters befalling the Roman Empire in the terrible third century: it was they who had failed to acknowledge the state gods and consequently brought on the gods' retribution against the Romans. Moreover, as the administrative organization of the church grew, Christianity appeared to Decius even more like a state within a state that was undermining the empire. Accordingly, he initiated the first systematic persecution of Christians. All citizens were required to appear before their local magistrates and offer sacrifices to the Roman gods. Christians of course refused to do so. Decius' scheme, however, failed to work. Local officials did not cooperate, and Decius' reign was also not that long. The last great persecution was by Diocletian at the beginning of the fourth century, but by then it was too late. Christianity had become too strong to be eradicated by force.

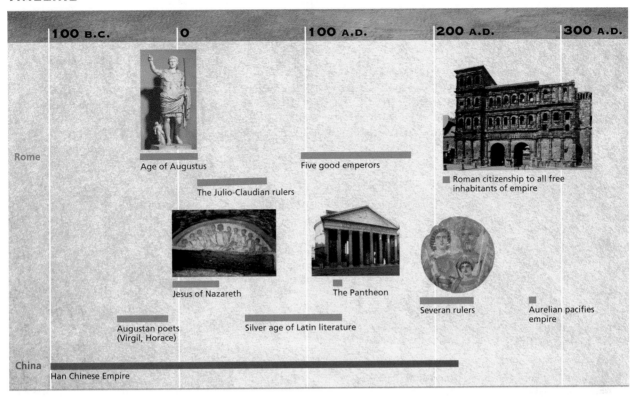

| 100 B.C. | 0 | 100 A.D. | 200 A.D. | 300 A.D. |

Rome

Age of Augustus

Five good emperors

Roman citizenship to all free inhabitants of empire

The Julio-Claudian rulers

Jesus of Nazareth

The Pantheon

Severan rulers

Aurelian pacifies empire

Augustan poets (Virgil, Horace)

Silver age of Latin literature

China

Han Chinese Empire

## CONCLUSION

*T*HE ROMAN REPUBLIC had created one of the largest empires in antiquity, but its republican institutions had proved inadequate for the task of ruling an empire. After a series of bloody civil wars, Augustus created a new order that began the Roman Empire, which experienced a lengthy period of peace and prosperity between 14 and 180. During this Pax Romana, trade flourished and the provinces were governed efficiently. In addition, within their empire, the Romans developed a remarkable series of achievements that were bequeathed to the future.

These achievements were fundamental to the development of Western civilization. The Romance languages of today (French, Italian, Spanish, Portuguese, and Romanian) are based on Latin. Western practices of impartial justice and trial by jury owe much to Roman law. As great builders, the Romans left monuments to their skills throughout Europe, some of which, including aqueducts and roads, are still in use today. Other monuments provided models for public buildings in the West for hundreds of years. Aspects of Roman administrative practices survived in the Western world for centuries. The Romans also preserved the intellectual heritage of the Greco-Roman world of antiquity.

By the third century, the Roman world was being buffeted by civil wars, invasions, and economic problems. At the same time, a new religion—Christianity—was spreading throughout the empire. As we shall see in the next chapter, the response to these developments slowly brought a transformation of the Roman Empire.

## NOTES

1. Livy, *The Early History of Rome*, trans. Aubrey de Sélincourt (Harmondsworth, England, 1960), p. 35.
2. Tacitus, *The Annals of Imperial Rome*, trans. Michael Grant (Harmondsworth, England, 1956), p. 30.
3. Velleius Paterculus, *Compendium of Roman History*, trans. Frederick Shipley (Cambridge, Mass., 1967), 2.117.
4. Tacitus, *Annals of Imperial Rome*, p. 37.
5. Virgil, *The Aeneid*, trans. C. Day Lewis (Garden City, N.Y., 1952), p. 154.
6. Horace, *Satires*, in *The Complete Works of Horace*, trans. Lord Dunsany and Michael Oakley (London, 1961), 1.1.
7. Ibid., 1.3.
8. Livy, *Early History of Rome*, p. 18.
9. Tacitus, *Annals of Imperial Rome*, p. 31.
10. Tacitus, *The Histories*, trans. Kenneth Wallesley (Harmondsworth, England, 1964), p. 23.

11. Quoted in Martin Goodman, *The Roman World, 44 B.C.–A.D. 180* (London, 1997), p. 67.
12. Quoted in ibid., p. 72.
13. Seneca, *Letters from a Stoic,* trans. Robin Campbell (Harmondsworth, England, 1969), let. 5.
14. Tacitus, *Annals of Imperial Rome,* p. 147.
15. Juvenal, *The Sixteen Satires,* trans. Peter Green (Harmondsworth, England, 1967), satire 7, p. 171.
16. Ibid., satire 10, p. 207.
17. Tacitus, *A Dialogue on Oratory,* in *The Complete Works of Tacitus,* trans. Alfred Church and William Brodribb (New York, 1942), 29, p. 758.
18. Ovid, *The Amores,* trans. Grant Showerman (Cambridge, Mass., 1963), 2.14.26–27.
19. Matthew 5:17.
20. Matthew 7:12.
21. Mark 12:30–31.
22. John 18:36.
23. Matthew 26:26–28.
24. *Early Christian Writings* (Harmondsworth, England, 1968), pp. 76–77.
25. Colossians 3:10–11.

---

## SUGGESTIONS FOR FURTHER READING

For a general account of the Roman Empire, see **J. Boardman, J. Griffin, and O. Murray, eds.,** *The Oxford History of the Roman World* (Oxford, 1991), and **G. Wolf, ed.,** *Cambridge Illustrated History of the Roman World* (Cambridge, 2003). Good surveys of the Early Empire include **P. Garnsey and R. P. Saller,** *The Roman Empire: Economy, Society and Culture* (London, 1987); **C. Wells,** *The Roman Empire,* 2d ed. (London, 1992); **M. Goodman,** *The Roman World, 44 B.C.–A.D. 180* (London, 1997); **J. Wacher,** *The Roman Empire* (London, 1987); and **F. Millar,** *The Roman Empire and Its Neighbours,* 2d ed. (London, 1981).

Studies of Roman emperors of the first and second centuries include **W. Eck,** *The Age of Augustus,* trans. **D. L. Schneider** (Oxford, 2003); **R. Seager,** *Tiberius* (London, 1972); **A. Barrett,** *Caligula: The Corruption of Power* (New Haven, Conn., 1998); **A. Momigliano,** *Claudius: The Emperor and His Achievement,* trans. **W. D. Hogarth** (Cambridge, 1961); **E. Champlin,** *Nero* (Cambridge, Mass., 2003); **E. Speller,** *Following Hadrian* (Oxford, 2003); and **M. Hammond,** *The Antonine Monarchy* (Rome, 1959). For brief biographies of all the Roman emperors, see **M. Grant,** *The Roman Emperors* (New York, 1985). On the wife of Augustus, see **A. A. Barrett,** *Livia: First Lady of Imperial Rome* (New Haven, Conn., 2002).

The Roman army is examined in **J. B. Campbell,** *The Emperor and the Roman Army* (Oxford, 1984). On the provinces and Roman foreign policy, see **E. N. Luttwak,** *The Grand Strategy of the Roman Empire from the First Century A.D. to the Third* (Baltimore, 1976); **B. Isaac,** *The Limits of Empire: The Roman Empire in the East* (Oxford, 1990); and **S. L. Dyson,** *The Creation of the Roman Frontier* (Princeton, N.J., 1985). On the battle in the Teutoburg Forest, see **P. S. Wells,** *The Battle That Stopped Rome: Emperor Augustus, Arminius and the Slaughter of the Legions in the Teutoburg Forest* (New York, 2003).

A good survey of Roman literature can be found in **R. M. Ogilvie,** *Roman Literature and Society* (Harmondsworth, England, 1980). More specialized studies include **R. O. Lyne,** *The Latin Love Poets from Catullus to Horace* (Oxford, 1980), and **K. Galinsky,** *Augustan Culture* (Princeton, N.J., 1996).

A survey of Roman art can be found in **D. E. Strong,** *Roman Art* (Harmondsworth, England, 1976). Architecture is covered in the standard work by **J. B. Ward-Perkins,** *Roman Imperial Architecture* (Harmondsworth, England, 1981).

Various aspects of Roman society are covered in **L. Adkins and R. A. Adkins,** *Handbook to Life in Ancient Rome* (New York, 1994). Also useful on urban life is **J. E. Stambaugh,** *The Ancient Roman City* (Baltimore, 1988). On public festivals, see **P. Veyne,** *Bread and Circuses* (London, 1992). On the gladiators, see **T. Wiedemann,** *Emperors and Gladiators* (New York, 1992). Studies on Roman women include **J. P. V. D. Balsdon,** *Roman Women: Their History and Habits* (London, 1969), and **S. B. Pomeroy,** *Goddesses, Whores, Wives, and Slaves: Women in Classical Antiquity* (New York, 1975), pp. 149–226. On slavery, see **K. Bradley,** *Slavery and Society at Rome* (New York, 1994).

For a general introduction to early Christianity, see **J. Court and K. Court,** *The New Testament World* (Cambridge, 1990). Useful works on early Christianity include **W. A. Meeks,** *The First Urban Christians* (New Haven, Conn., 1983); **W. H. C. Frend,** *The Rise of Christianity* (Philadelphia, 1984); and **R. MacMullen,** *Christianizing the Roman Empire* (New Haven, Conn., 1984). For a detailed analysis of Christianity in the 30s and 40s of the first century A.D., see **J. D. Crossan,** *The Birth of Christianity* (New York, 1998). On Christian women, see **D. M. Scholer, ed.,** *Women in Early Christianity* (New York, 1993), and **R. Kraemer,** *Her Share of the Blessings: Women's Religion Among the Pagans, Jews and Christians in the Graeco-Roman World* (Oxford, 1995).

## History  Now™

Enter *HistoryNow* using the access card that is available for *Western Civilization. HistoryNow* will assist you in understanding the content in this chapter with lesson plans generated for your needs. In addition, you can read the following documents, and many more, online:

Virgil, Book 1 of *The Aeneid*

Horace, Satire 1 of Book 1

The Gospel of Mark (New Testament)

Eusebius, Edict of Milan

Ignatius, "Letter to the Ephesians"

### INFOTRAC SEARCH TERMS

 For additional reading, go to InfoTrac College Edition, your online research library at http://infotrac.thomsonlearning.com

| Key Term Search | Subject Guide Search |
| --- | --- |
| Roman Empire | Roman mythology |
|  | Roman law |

### WESTERN CIVILIZATION RESOURCES

Visit the *Western Civilization* Companion Web site for resources specific to this book:

http://history.wadsworth.com/spielvogel06/

For a variety of tools to help you succeed in this course, visit the Western Civilization Resource Center at

http://history.wadsworth.com/western/

Included are quizzes; images; documents; interactive simulations; maps and timelines; movie explorations; and a wealth of other sources.

# LATE ANTIQUITY AND THE EMERGENCE OF THE MEDIEVAL WORLD

## CHAPTER OUTLINE AND FOCUS QUESTIONS

### The Late Roman Empire

● What reforms did Diocletian and Constantine institute, and to what extent were the reforms successful?

### The Germanic Kingdoms

● What changes did the Germanic peoples make to the political, economic, and social conditions of the Western Roman Empire?

### Development of the Christian Church

● What were the chief characteristics of Benedictine monasticism, and what role did monks play in both the conversion of Europe to Christianity and the intellectual life of the Germanic kingdoms?

### The Byzantine Empire

● How did the Byzantine Empire that had emerged by the eighth century differ from the empire of Justinian and from the Germanic kingdoms in the west?

### The Rise of Islam

● What was the basic message of Islam, and why was it able to expand so successfully?

### CRITICAL THINKING

● In what ways were the Byzantine and Islamic civilizations different from the civilization developing in western Europe? In what ways were they similar?

© Giraudon/Bridgeman Art Library

*A fourteenth-century French manuscript illustration of the baptism of Clovis*

BY THE THIRD CENTURY, the Roman Empire was experiencing a number of problems as well as witnessing the growth of a new religion—Christianity. To restore the empire, the emperors Diocletian and Constantine initiated a number of reforms that created the so-called Late Empire. Constantine also converted to Christianity, starting a process that gave the Late Empire a new state religion.

After Constantine, the Late Roman Empire survived, but it was increasingly faced in the west by the incursions of Germanic tribes. By the second half of the fifth century, new political arrangements were taking shape that brought the collapse of the old imperial structure in the west and the emergence of a series of German kingdoms in western Europe that would form the basis of a new civilization. In these kingdoms, the Christian church also played a role as it drew these Germanic tribes to its faith.

The conversion to Christianity of the pagan leaders of German tribes was sometimes dramatic, at least as reported by the sixth-century historian Gregory of Tours. Clovis, leader of the Franks, married Clotilde, daughter of the king of the Burgundians. She was a Christian, but Clovis refused her pleas to become a Christian, telling her, "Your god can do nothing." But during a battle with the Alemanni, when Clovis's army was close to utter destruction, "he saw the danger; his heart was stirred; and he raised his eyes to heaven, saying, 'Jesus Christ, I beseech the glory of your aid. If you shall grant me victory over these enemies, I will believe in you and be baptized in your name.'" When he had uttered these words, the Alemanni began to flee. Clovis kept his vow and became a Christian.

While the Germanic kingdoms were putting down roots in the west, the eastern part of the old Roman Empire, increasingly Greek in culture, continued as the Byzantine Empire. Serving as a buffer between Europe and the peoples to the east, the Byzantine or Eastern Roman Empire also preserved the intellectual and legal accomplishments of Greek and Roman antiquity. At the same time, a new culture centered on Islam emerged in the east; it spread through large parts of the old Roman Empire, preserved much of Greek culture, and created its own flourishing civilization. This chapter, then, concerns the transformation of the Roman world in late antiquity, the heirs of the Roman Empire, and the new world–the medieval world–they began to create.

# The Late Roman Empire

At the end of the third century and the beginning of the fourth, the Roman Empire gained a new lease on life through the efforts of two strong emperors, Diocletian and Constantine, who restored order and stability. The empire was virtually transformed into a new state, the Late Roman Empire, which included a new governmental structure, a rigid economic and social system, and a new state religion—Christianity.

### The Reforms of Diocletian and Constantine

Diocletian had risen through the ranks to become a prominent military leader. After the murder of the emperor Numerian by his praetorian prefect, Diocletian executed the prefect and was then hailed as emperor by his soldiers. Diocletian's own rise to power led him to see the need for a new system for ruling the Roman Empire.

**Political Reforms**   Diocletian (284–305) created a new administrative system for a restructured empire. The number of provinces was increased to almost one hundred by creating smaller districts superintended by more officials. The provinces were in turn grouped into twelve dioceses, each headed by an official called a vicar. The twelve dioceses were grouped into four prefectures (see Map 7.1), and the entire Roman Empire was divided into two parts, east and west. Each part contained two prefectures and was ruled by an "Augustus." Diocletian ruled the east, and Maximian, a strong military commander, the west. Each Augustus was assisted by a chief lieutenant or "vice-emperor"

called a "Caesar," who theoretically would eventually succeed to the position of Augustus. This new system was called the **tetrarchy** (rule by four). Diocletian had obviously come to believe that one man was incapable of ruling such an enormous empire, especially in view of the barbarian invasions of the third century. Each of the four tetrarchs—two Augusti and two Caesars—resided in a different administrative capital. Diocletian, for example, established his base at Nicomedia in Bithynia. Despite the appearance of four-man rule, however, it is important to note that Diocletian's military seniority enabled him to claim a higher status and hold the ultimate authority.

Soon after Diocletian's retirement in 305, a new struggle for power ensued. The victory of Constantine (306–337) in 312 led to his control of the entire west, although he continued to share imperial authority with Licinius, a fellow emperor. Twelve years later, in 324, Constantine's army routed Licinius' forces, and Constantine established himself as the sole ruler.

Constantine continued and even expanded the autocratic policies of Diocletian. Under these two rulers, the Roman Empire was transformed into a system where the emperor had far more personal power than Augustus, Trajan, or any of the other emperors had had during the Pax Romana. The emperor, now clothed in jewel-bedecked robes of gold and blue, was seen as a divinely sanctioned monarch whose will was law. Government officials were humble servants required to kneel before the emperor and kiss his robe. The Roman senate was stripped of any power and became merely the city council for Rome.

Diocletian and Constantine greatly strengthened and enlarged the administrative bureaucracies of the Roman Empire. Henceforth, civil and military bureaucracies were sharply separated. Each contained a hierarchy of officials who exercised control at the various levels. The emperor presided over both hierarchies and served as the only link between them. New titles of nobility—such as *illustres* ("illustrious ones") and *illustrissimi* ("most illustrious ones")—were instituted to dignify the holders of positions in the civil and military bureaucracies.

**Military Reforms**   Additional military reforms were also instituted. The army was enlarged to 400,000 men, including units filled with Germans. By the end of Constantine's reign, a new organization of the army had also been put in place. Military forces were divided into two kinds: garrison troops, which were located on the frontiers and intended as a first line of defense against invaders, and mobile units, which were located behind the frontier but could be quickly moved to support frontier troops when the borders were threatened. This gave the empire greater flexibility in responding to invasion.

**Economic and Social Trends**   The political and military reforms of Diocletian and Constantine greatly enlarged two institutions—the army and the civil service—that drained most of the public funds. Although more revenues were needed to pay for the military and the bureaucracy, the

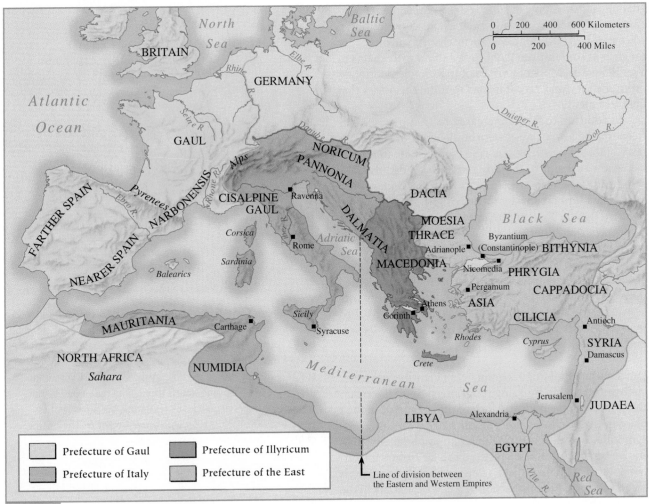

**MAP 7.1** **Divisions of the Late Roman Empire, c. 300.** Diocletian imposed order and a new economic and administrative structure on the Late Empire. He divided the Roman Empire into four regions, each ruled by either an "Augustus" or a "Caesar," although Diocletian retained supreme power.
❓ Compare this map with Map 6.1. How much territory was lost by the time of Diocletian?
🌐 **View an animated version of this map or related maps at** http://history.wadsworth.com/spielvogel06/

population was not growing, so the tax base could not be expanded. Diocletian and Constantine devised new economic and social policies to deal with these financial burdens. Like their political policies, these economic and social policies were all based on coercion and loss of individual freedom.

To fight **inflation,** in 301 Diocletian resorted to issuing an edict that established maximum wages and prices for the entire empire. It was applied mostly in the east, but despite severe penalties, like most wage and price controls, it was largely unenforceable. The decline in circulation of coins led Diocletian to collect taxes and make government payments in produce. Constantine, however, managed to introduce a new gold coin, the solidus, and new silver coins that remained in circulation during his reign.

In the third century, the city councils, which had formed one of the most important administrative units of the empire, had begun to decline. Since the *curiales* (the city councillors) were forced to pay expenses out of their own pocket when the taxes they collected were insufficient, the wealthy no longer wanted to serve in these positions. Diocletian and Constantine responded by issuing edicts that forced the rich to continue in their posts as *curiales,* virtually making the positions hereditary. Some *curiales* realized that their fortunes would be wiped out and fled the cities to escape the clutches of the imperial bureaucracy. If caught, however, they were returned to their cities like runaway slaves and forced to resume their duties.

Coercion also came to form the underlying basis for numerous occupations in the Late Roman Empire. To ensure the tax base and keep the empire going despite the shortage of labor, the emperors issued edicts that forced people to remain in their designated vocations. Hence basic jobs, such as bakers and shippers, became hereditary.

Free tenant farmers—the *coloni*—continued to decline and soon found themselves bound to the land as well. Large landowners took advantage of depressed agricultural conditions to enlarge their landed estates. Free tenant farmers, unable to survive on their own, became dependent on these large estates and soon found that landlords, in order to guarantee their supply of labor, gained government cooperation in attaching them to their estates. One imperial edict stated: "And as for *coloni* themselves, it will be proper for such as contemplate flight to be bound with chains to a servile status, so that by virtue of such condemnation to servitude they may be compelled to fulfill the duties that befit free men."[1]

In addition to facing increased restrictions on their freedom, the lower classes were burdened with enormous taxes, since the wealthiest classes in the Late Roman Empire were either exempt from paying taxes or evaded them by bribing the tax collectors. These tax pressures undermined lower-class support for the regime. A fifth-century writer reported that the Roman peasants welcomed the Visigothic invaders of southern Gaul as liberators because the enemy was more lenient to them than the tax collectors.

In general, the economic and social policies of Diocletian and Constantine were based on an unprecedented degree of control and coercion. Though temporarily successful, in the long run such authoritarian policies stifled the very vitality the Late Empire needed to revive its sagging fortunes.

**Constantine's Building Program**   Constantine was especially interested in building programs despite the strain they placed on the budget. Much of the construction took place in the provinces, since Rome had become merely a symbolic capital. It was no longer an imperial administrative center, as it was considered too far from the frontiers. Between 324 and 330, Constantine engaged in his biggest project, the construction of a new capital city in the east, on the site of the Greek city of Byzantium, on the shores of the Bosporus. Named the "city of Constantine," or Constantinople (modern Istanbul), it was developed for defensive reasons; it had an excellent strategic location. Calling it his "New Rome," Constantine endowed the city with a forum, large palaces, and a vast amphitheater. It was officially dedicated on May 11, 330, "by the commandment of God," and in the following years, many Christian churches were built there.

Constantine did not entirely forget Rome. Earlier he was responsible for building public baths and the triumphal Arch of Constantine, built between 312 and 315. Constantine was also the first emperor to build churches for the Christian faith in Rome, including the first basilica dedicated to Saint Peter, built on the supposed site of Saint Peter's burial. Constantine also gave grants to Christian leaders in Rome, enabling them to assume a more conspicuous role in the city. These acts by Constantine are a reminder of the new role Christianity was beginning to play in the Late Empire.

## The Empire's New Religion

In the fourth century, Christianity prospered as never before, and the emperor Constantine played an important role in its status.

**The Emperor Constantine.**   Constantine played an important role in restoring order and stability to the Roman Empire at the beginning of the fourth century. This marble head of Constantine, which is 8 feet 6 inches high, was part of an enormous 30-foot-tall seated statue of the emperor in the New Basilica in Rome. Constantine used these awe-inspiring statues throughout the empire to build support for imperial policies by reminding his subjects of his position as an absolute ruler with immense power. The casting of his eyes toward heaven also emphasized Constantine's special relationship with God.

**The Conversion of Constantine**   Constantine's support for Christianity supposedly began in 312, when his army was about to fight a crucial battle against the forces of Maxentius at the Milvian Bridge, which crossed the Tiber River just north of the city of Rome. According to the traditional story, before the battle, Constantine saw a vision of a Christian cross with the words, "In this sign you will conquer." Having won the battle, the story goes, Constantine was convinced of the power of the Christian God. Although he was not baptized until the end of his life, in 313 he issued the famous Edict of Milan, which officially tolerated the existence of Christianity.

After Constantine, the emperors were Christian with the exception of Julian (360–363), who tried briefly to restore the traditional Greco-Roman polytheistic religion. But he died in battle, and his reign was too short to make a difference. Under Theodosius "the Great" (378–395), Christianity was made the official religion of the Roman Empire. Once in control, Christian leaders used their influence and power to outlaw pagan religious practices. Christianity had triumphed.

**Organization and Religious Disputes**   By the fourth century, the Christian church had developed a system of government based on a territorial plan borrowed from Roman administration. The Christian community in each city was headed by a bishop, whose area of jurisdiction was known as a bishopric or diocese. The bishoprics of each Roman province were clustered together under the direction of an archbishop. The bishops of four great cities, Rome, Jerusalem, Alexandria, and Antioch, held positions of special power in church affairs because the churches in these cities all asserted that they had been founded by the original apostles sent out by Jesus.

One reason the church needed a more formal organization was the problem of **heresy.** As Christianity developed and spread, contradictory interpretations of important doctrines emerged. Heresy came to be viewed as a teaching different from the official "catholic" or universal beliefs of the church. In a world where people were concerned about salvation, the question of whether Jesus' nature is divine or human took on great significance. These doctrinal differences also became political issues, creating political factions that actually warred with one another. It is highly unlikely, though, that ordinary people understood what these debates meant.

The two major heresies of the fourth century were Donatism and Arianism. Donatus was a priest in North Africa who taught that the sacraments of the church, the channels by which a Christian received God's grace, were not valid if administered by an immoral priest or one who had denied his faith under persecution. Donatus' deviation from traditional teaching on the subject created so much dissension that it came to the attention of the Emperor Constantine, who convened a council of western bishops to denounce it. It was not until a century later, in 411, however, that the church declared authoritatively that the efficacy of the sacraments was not dependent on the moral state of the priest administering them as long as the priest had been properly ordained.

**Arianism** was a product of the followers of Arius, a priest from Alexandria in Egypt. Arius postulated that Jesus had been human and thus not truly God. Arius was opposed by Athanasius, a bishop of Alexandria, who argued that Jesus was human but also truly God. Emperor Constantine, disturbed by the controversy, called the first ecumenical council of the church, a meeting composed of representatives from the entire Christian community. The Council of Nicaea, held in 325, condemned Arianism and stated that Jesus was of "the same substance" as God: "We believe in one God the Father All-sovereign, maker of all things visible and invisible; And in one Lord Jesus Christ, the Son of God, begotten of the Father, only-begotten, that is, of the substance of the Father, God of God, Light of Light, true God of true God, begotten not made, of one substance with the Father."[2] The Council of Nicaea did not end the controversy, however; not only did Arianism persist in some parts of the Roman Empire for many years, but even more important, many of the Germanic Goths who established states in the west converted to Arian Christianity (see "The Germanic Kingdoms" later in this chapter). As a result of these fourth-century religious controversies, the Roman emperor came to play an increasingly important role in church affairs.

## The End of the Western Empire

Constantine had reunited the Roman Empire and restored a semblance of order. After his death, however, the empire continued to divide into western and eastern parts as fighting erupted on a regular basis between elements of the Roman army backing the claims of rival emperors. By 395, the western and eastern parts of the empire became virtually two independent states. In the course of the fifth century, while the empire in the east remained intact under the Roman emperor in Constantinople (see "The Byzantine Empire" later in this chapter), the administrative structure of the empire in the west collapsed and was replaced by an assortment of Germanic kingdoms. The process was a gradual one, involving the movement of Germans into the empire, military failures, the struggles for power on the part of both Roman and German military leaders, and the efforts of wealthy aristocrats to support the side that seemed to offer them the greatest security.

**The Germans**    During the first and second centuries A.D., the Romans had established the Rhine and Danube Rivers as the empire's northern boundary. The Romans called all the peoples to the north of the rivers "Germans" and regarded them as uncivilized barbarians. In fact, the Germans consisted of different groups with their own customs and identities, but these constantly changed as tribes broke up and came together in new configurations. At times they formed larger confederations under strong warrior leaders. The Germans lived by herding and farming and also traded with people living along the northern frontiers of the Roman Empire.

Although the Romans had established a series of political frontiers along the Rhine and Danube Rivers, Romans and Germans often came into contact across these boundaries. For some time, the Romans had hired Germanic tribes to fight other Germanic tribes that threatened Rome or enlisted groups of Germans to fight for Rome. In any case, until the fourth century, the empire had proved capable of absorbing these people without harm to its political structure. In the second half of the fourth century, this situation began to change.

**German Migrations**    In the late fourth century, the Germanic tribes came under new pressure when the Huns, a fierce tribe of nomads from the steppes of Asia (see the box on p. 170), moved into the Black Sea region, possibly attracted by the riches of the empire to its south. One of the groups displaced by the Huns was the Visigoths, who in 376 asked the Roman emperor Valens (364–378) to allow them to cross the Danube and farm in the Balkans in return for providing troops for the Roman military. But the Roman military commanders mistreated them, as one ancient German historian recounted:

> [They] crossed the Danube and settled Dacia Ripensis, Moesia, and Thrace by permission of the Emperor. Soon famine and want came upon them. . . . Their leaders . . . begged the Roman commanders to open a market. But to what will not the "cursed

# THE HUNS

HE FIRST SELECTION is a description of the Huns by Ammianus Marcellinus (c. 330–c. 393), who has been called the "last great Roman historian." Ammianus wrote a history of Rome from A.D. 96 to his own day. Only the chapters that deal with the period from 354 to 378 have survived. Historians believe that his account of the Huns is largely based on stereotypes. The second selection is taken from an account by Priscus, an envoy from the Eastern Roman Empire to the court of Attila, king of the Huns from 434 to 453. His description of the Huns in 448 is quite different from that of Ammianus Marcellinus.

## Ammianus Marcellinus, *The Later Roman Empire*

The Huns . . . are quite abnormally savage. From the moment of their birth they make deep gashes in their children's cheeks, so that when in due course hair appears its growth is checked by the wrinkled scars. . . . They have squat bodies, strong limbs, and thick necks, and are so prodigiously ugly and bent that they might be two-legged animals, or the figures crudely carved from stumps which are seen on the parapets of bridges. Still, their shape, however disagreeable, is human; but their way of life is so rough that they have no use for fire or seasoned food, but live on the roots of wild plants and the half-raw flesh of any sort of animal, which they warm a little by placing it between their thighs and the backs of their horses. They have no buildings to shelter them, but avoid anything of the kind; . . . not so much as a hut thatched with reeds is to be found among them. . . . They wear garments of linen or of the skins of field-mice stitched together, and there is no difference between their clothing whether they are at home or abroad. Once they have put their necks in some dingy shirt they never take it off or change it till it rots and falls to pieces from incessant wear. They have round caps of fur on their heads, and protect their hairy legs with goatskins. Their shapeless shoes . . . make it hard to walk easily. In consequence they are ill-fitted to fight on foot, and remain glued to their horses, hardy but ugly beasts, on which they sometimes sit like women to perform their everyday business. Buying or selling, eating or drinking, are all done by day or night on horseback, and they even bow forward over their beasts' narrow necks to enjoy a deep and dreamy sleep. . . .

They sometimes fight by challenging their foes to single combat, but when they join battle they advance in packs, uttering their various warcries. Being lightly equipped and very sudden in their movements they can deliberately scatter and gallop about at random, inflicting tremendous slaughter; their extreme nimbleness enables them to force a rampart or pillage an enemy's camp before one catches sight of them. . . . None of them plows or ever touches a plow-handle. They have no fixed abode, no home or law or settled manner of life, but wander like refugees with the wagons in which they live. In these their wives weave their filthy clothing, mate with their husbands, and give birth to their children, and rear them to the age of puberty.

## Priscus, *An Account of the Court of Attila the Hun*

[We were invited to a banquet with Attila.] When the hour arrived we went to Attila's palace, along with the embassy from the western Romans, and stood on the threshold of the hall in the presence of Attila. The cup-bearers gave us a cup, according to the national custom, that we might pray before we sat down. Having tasted the cup, we proceeded to take our seats, all the chairs being ranged along the walls of the room on either side. Attila sat in the middle on a couch; a second couch was set behind him, and from it steps led up to his bed, which was covered with linen sheets and coverlets. . . .

[First the king and his guests pledged one another with the wine.] When this ceremony was over the cup-bearers retired and tables, large enough for three or four, or even more, to sit at, were placed next the table of Attila, so that each could take of the food on the dishes without leaving his seat. The attendant of Attila first entered with a dish full of meat, and behind him came the other attendants with bread and other dishes, which they laid on the tables. A luxurious meal, served on silver plate, had been made ready for us and the other guests, but Attila ate nothing but meat on a wooden platter. In everything else, too, he showed himself temperate; his cup was of wood, while to the guests were given goblets of gold and silver. His dress, too, was quite simple, affecting only to be clean.

lust for gold" compel men to assent? The generals, swayed by greed, sold them at a high price not only the flesh of sheep and oxen, but even the carcasses of dogs and unclean animals. . . . When their goods and chattels failed, the greedy traders demanded their sons in return for the necessities of life. And the parents consented even to this.[3]

Outraged at the Romans' behavior, the Visigoths revolted. In 378, Emperor Valens and an army of forty thousand soldiers confronted the Visigoths at Adrianople. The emperor was killed, and two-thirds of the Roman army was left dead on the battlefield.

The loss was not fatal, although the new emperor, Theodosius I (379–395), resettled the Visigoths and incorporated many of their soldiers into the Roman army. Some of the Visigoths even became army leaders. By the second half of the fourth century, Roman policy continued to allow Roman army units to be composed entirely of Germanic tribes, known as **federates,** or allies of Rome.

**The Threat of the Germans**    The existence of such military groups proved dangerous to the Late Empire. This was especially evident after Alaric became the leader of the

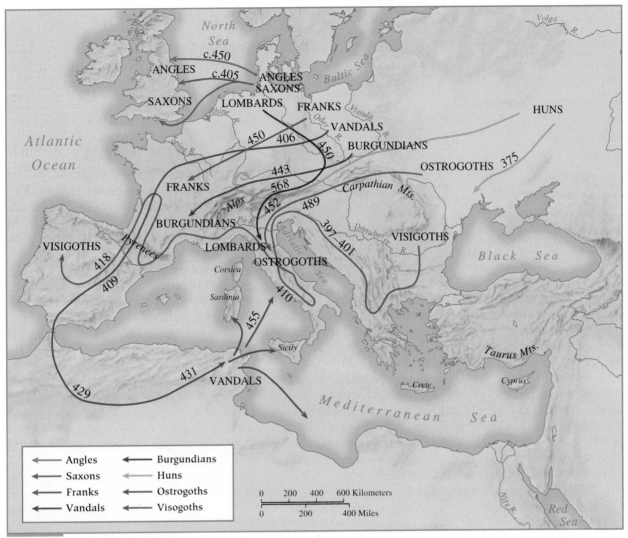

North Sea
Baltic Sea
ANGLES c.450
ANGLES c.405
SAXONS
ANGLES SAXONS
LOMBARDS
FRANKS
Rhine
VANDALS
Vistula R.
Oder R.
HUNS
Atlantic
Ocean
Seine R.
450  406
450
BURGUNDIANS
OSTROGOTHS 375
FRANKS
443
568
Alps
452
489
Po R.
Carpathian Mts.
VISIGOTHS
418
Ebro R.
Pyrenees
409
BURGUNDIANS
397-401
Danube R.
VISIGOTHS
LOMBARDS
OSTROGOTHS
Corsica
Adriatic Sea
410
Black Sea
Sardinia
455
431
VANDALS
Sicily
429
Crete
Taurus Mts.
Cyprus
Mediterranean Sea
Nile R.
Red Sea
Volga R.

← Angles      ← Burgundians
← Saxons      ← Huns
← Franks      ← Ostrogoths
← Vandals     ← Visogoths

0   200   400   600 Kilometers
0        200        400 Miles

**MAP 7.2  German Migration Routes.** In the fifth century, German groups migrated throughout the Western Roman Empire. Pressure from Huns in the east forced some tribes west into the empire, and many tribes already in the empire experienced conflict. Some fought the empire, while others were induced to move to the empire's far regions. ❓ How far did the Vandals travel in what period of time? 🌐 **View an animated version of this map or related maps at** http://history.wadsworth.com/spielvogel06/

Visigoths. Between 395 and 401, Alaric and his soldiers moved through the Balkans and then into Italy, seeking food and cash payments from Roman officials. When the city of Rome refused his demands in 408, Alaric marched to the gates and besieged the city, causing the senate of Rome to agree to pay 5,000 pounds of gold and 30,000 pounds of silver for his withdrawal. Two years later, frustrated in his demand that the Visigoths be given part of northern Italy, Alaric and his forces sacked Rome for three days. Alaric died soon after, and his Visigothic followers left Italy, crossed the Alps, and moved into Spain and southern Gaul as Roman allies (see Map 7.2).

By this time, other Germanic tribes were also passing into the Roman Empire and settling down. At the end of 406, several groups crossed the frozen Rhine River, making their way into Gaul and then Spain. One of these groups, the Vandals, under their leader Gaiseric, crossed the Strait of Gibraltar into North Africa and seized Carthage, the capital city, in 439.

As the Germanic tribes moved into the empire and settled down, Roman forces were often withdrawn from the provinces, effectively reducing the central authority of the emperors. In Britain, for example, the emperor Honorius removed the last Roman legions in 410. As one ancient commentator remarked, "Honorius sent letters to the cities in Britain, urging them to fend for themselves."[4] With the withdrawal, the Saxons, who had arrived earlier as Roman allies, now expanded their control in Britain. Within another decade, both Spain and Gaul had also become free of imperial authority.

**Role of Masters of the Soldiers**   By the middle of the fifth century, the western provinces of the Roman Empire had been taken over by Germanic peoples who were in the process of creating independent kingdoms. At the same time, a semblance of imperial authority remained in Rome, although the real power behind the throne tended to rest in the hands of important military officials known as Masters of the Soldiers. These military commanders controlled the government and dominated the imperial court. The three most prominent in the fifth century were Stilicho, Aetius, and Ricimer. Stilicho and Ricimer were both Germans, and although all three propped up emperors to maintain the fiction of imperial rule, they were also willing to cooperate with the Germans to maintain their power. But even the Masters of the Soldiers were never safe in the bloody world of fifth-century Roman political life. Stilicho was executed by order of Emperor Honorius. Aetius was killed by Emperor Valentinian III, who was in turn assassinated by a group of Aetius' German bodyguards, who sought to avenge their betrayed leader. Ricimer died a natural death, an unusual event in fifth-century Rome. No doubt, the constant infighting at the center of the Western Empire added to the instability of imperial rule.

By the mid-fifth century, imperial authority in the west remained operating only in Italy and small parts of Gaul. But Rome itself was not safe. In 455, after a treaty made between Rome and Gaiseric, leader of the Vandals, was broken by the Romans, Gaiseric sent a Vandal fleet to Italy and sacked the undefended city of Rome. Twenty-one years later, in 476, Odoacer, a new Master of the Soldiers, himself of German origin, deposed the Roman emperor, the boy Romulus Augustulus. To many historians, the deposition of Romulus signaled the end of the Roman Empire. Of course, this is only a symbolic date, since much of direct imperial rule had already been lost in the course of the fifth century. Even then the empire remained, as Odoacer presented himself as a German king obedient in theory to the Roman emperor Zeno in Constantinople.

By the end of the fifth century, Roman imperial authority in the west had ceased. Nevertheless, the intellectual, governmental, and cultural traditions of the Late Roman Empire continued to live in the new Germanic kingdoms.

# The Germanic Kingdoms

By 500, the Western Roman Empire was being replaced politically by a series of kingdoms ruled by German kings (see Map 7.3). The pattern of settlement and the fusion of the Romans and Germans took different forms in the various Germanic kingdoms.

## The Ostrogothic Kingdom of Italy

Zeno, the Roman emperor in Constantinople, was not pleased with Odoacer's actions and plotted to unseat him. In his desire to act against the German leader, Zeno brought another German tribe, the Ostrogoths, into Italy. The Ostrogoths had recovered from a defeat by the Huns in the fourth century and under their king Theodoric (493–526) had attacked Constantinople. To divert them, Emperor Zeno had invited Theodoric to act as his deputy to defeat Odoacer and bring Italy back into the empire. Theodoric accepted the challenge, marched into Italy, killed Odoacer, and then, contrary to Zeno's wishes, established himself as ruler of Italy in 493.

**Theodoric's Rule**   More than any other Germanic state, the Ostrogothic kingdom of Italy managed to maintain the Roman tradition of government. The Ostrogothic king, Theodoric, had received a Roman education while a hostage in Constantinople. After taking control of Italy, he was eager to create a synthesis of Ostrogothic and Roman practices (see the box on p. 173). In addition to maintaining the entire structure of imperial Roman government, he established separate systems of rule for the Ostrogoths and Romans. The Italian population lived under Roman law administered by Roman officials. The Ostrogoths were governed by their own customs and their own officials. However, while the Roman administrative system was kept intact, it was the Ostrogoths alone who controlled the army. Despite the apparent success of this "dual approach," Theodoric's system was unable to keep friction from developing between the Italian population and their Germanic overlords.

Religion proved to be a major source of trouble between Ostrogoths and Romans. The Ostrogoths had been converted earlier to Christianity, but to Arian Christianity, and consequently were viewed by western Christians and the Italians as heretics. Theodoric's rule grew ever harsher as discontent with Ostrogothic rule deepened.

**End of the Ostrogothic Kingdom**   After Theodoric's death in 526, it quickly became apparent that much of his success had been due to the force of his own personality. His successors soon found themselves face to face with opposition from the imperial forces of the Byzantine or Eastern Roman Empire. Under Emperor Justinian (527–565) (see "The Reign of Justinian" later in this chapter), Byzantine armies reconquered Italy between 535 and 552, devastating much of the peninsula and destroying Rome as one of the great urban centers of the Mediterranean world.

# THEODORIC AND OSTROGOTHIC ITALY

THE OSTROGOTHIC KING Theodoric (493–526), who had been educated in Constantinople, was determined to maintain Roman culture rather than destroy it. His attempt to preserve *civilitas,* the traditional Roman civic culture, was well expressed in the official letters written in his name by Cassiodorus, who became master of offices in 525. Theodoric's efforts were largely undone by opposition from the Roman nobility and especially by Justinian's reconquest of the Italian peninsula shortly after Theodoric's death.

## Letters of Cassiodorus

### King Theodoric to Colossaeus

We delight to entrust our mandates to persons of approved character. . . .

Show forth the justice of the Goths, a nation happily situated for praise, since it is theirs to unite the forethought of the Romans and the virtue of the Barbarians. Remove all ill-planted customs, and impress upon all your subordinates that we would rather that our Treasury lost a suit than that it gained one wrongfully, rather that we lost money than the taxpayer was driven to suicide.

### King Theodoric to Unigis, the Sword-Bearer

We delight to live after the law of the Romans, whom we seek to defend with our arms; and we are as much interested in the maintenance of morality as we can possibly be in war. For what profit is there in having removed the turmoil of the Barbarians, unless we live according to law?

. . . Let other kings desire the glory of battles won, of cities taken, of ruins made; our purpose is, God helping us, so to rule that our subjects shall grieve that they did not earlier acquire the blessing of our dominion.

### King Theodoric to All the Jews of Genoa

The true mark of *civilitas* is the observance of law. It is this which makes life in communities possible, and which separates man from the brutes. We therefore gladly accede to your request that all the privileges which the foresight of antiquity conferred upon the Jewish customs shall be renewed to you, for in truth it is our great desire that the laws of the ancients shall be kept in force to secure the reverence due to us. Everything which has been found to conduce to *civilitas* should be held fast with enduring devotion.

### King Theodoric to All the Goths Settled in Picenum and Samnium

The presence of the Sovereign doubles the sweetness of his gifts, and that man is like one dead whose face is not known to his lord. Come therefore by God's assistance, come all into our presence on the eighth day before the Ides of June [June 7], there solemnly to receive our royal largesse. But let there be no excesses by the way, no plundering the harvest of the cultivators nor trampling down their meadows, since for this cause do we gladly defray the expense of our armies that *civilitas* may be kept intact by armed men.

**Amalsuntha, Theodoric's Successor.** After Theodoric's death in 526, his daughter Amalsuntha, acting as regent for her son Athalaric, took control of Italy. But she was murdered by relatives in 535, and Italy soon fell subject to the forces of Justinian. This ivory panel of 530 shows Amalsuntha seated on a throne. The frame probably depicts part of Theodoric's palace at Ravenna.

The Byzantine reconquest proved ephemeral, however. Another German tribe, the Lombards, invaded Italy in 568 and conquered much of northern and central Italy. Unlike the Ostrogoths, the Lombards were harsh rulers and cared little for Roman structures and traditions. The Lombards' fondness for fighting each other enabled the Byzantines to retain control of some parts of Italy, especially the area around Ravenna, which became the capital of imperial government.

## The Visigothic Kingdom of Spain

The Visigothic kingdom in Spain demonstrated a number of parallels to the Ostrogothic kingdom of Italy. Both favored coexistence between the Roman and German populations, both featured a warrior caste dominating a larger

**Political Divisions of Britain**
- Angles
- Saxons
- Jutes
- Britons

PICTS
Lindisfarne
North Sea
JUTES
DANES
Baltic Sea
Whitby
CELTS
NORTHUMBRIA
MERCIA EAST ANGLIA
FRISIANS
SAXONS
ESSEX
London
KENT
WESSEX SUSSEX
Rhine R.
Elbe R.
Oder R.
Vistula
Atlantic Ocean
AUSTRASIA
**KINGDOM OF THE FRANKS**
Paris
NEUSTRIA
Seine R.
ALEMANNI
LOMBARDS
BURGUNDIANS
BAVARIANS
BURGUNDY
Alps
**KINGDOM OF THE OSTROGOTHS**
Danube R.
SUEVES BASQUES
Toulouse
Po R.
Ravenna
Pyrenees
Toledo
Barcelona
Corsica
Rome
**KINGDOM OF THE VISIGOTHS**
Sardinia
Mediterranean Sea
Sicily
VANDALS Carthage
**BYZANTINES**

0  200  400  600 Kilometers
0  200  400 Miles

**MAP 7.3** **The Germanic Kingdoms of the Old Western Empire.** The Germanic tribes filled the power vacuum caused by the demise of the Roman Empire, building states that blended elements of Germanic customs and laws with those of Roman culture, including large-scale conversions to Christianity. The Franks established the most durable of these Germanic states.

❓ How did the movements of Franks during this period correspond to the borders of present-day France?

🌐 View an animated version of this map or related maps at http://history.wadsworth .com/spielvogel06/

native population, and both continued to maintain much of the Roman structure of government while largely excluding Romans from power. There were also noticeable differences, however. Perceiving that their Arianism was a stumbling block to good relations, the Visigothic rulers in the late sixth century converted to Latin or Catholic Christianity and ended the tension caused by this heresy. Laws preventing intermarriage were dropped, and the Visigothic and Hispano-Roman peoples began to fuse together. A new body of law common to both peoples also developed.

The kingdom possessed one fatal weakness, however—the Visigoths fought constantly over the kingship. The Visigoths had no hereditary monarchy and no established procedure for choosing new rulers. Church officials tried to help develop a sense of order, as this canon from the Fourth Council of Toledo in 633 illustrates: "No one of us shall dare to seize the kingdom; no one shall arouse sedition among the citizenry; no one shall think of killing the king...." Church decrees failed to stop the feuds, however,

and assassinations remained a way of life in Visigothic Spain. In 711, Muslim invaders destroyed the Visigothic kingdom itself (see "The Rise of Islam" later in this chapter).

### The Frankish Kingdom

Only one of the German states on the European continent proved long-lasting—the kingdom of the Franks. The establishment of a Frankish kingdom was the work of Clovis (c. 482–511), the leader of one group of Franks who eventually became king of them all.

**The Rule of Clovis** Around 500, Clovis became a Catholic Christian. He was not the first German king to convert to Christianity, but the others had joined the Arian sect of Christianity. The Christian church in Rome, which had become known as the Roman Catholic church, regarded the Arians as heretics, people who believed in teachings that departed from the official church doctrine. Clovis found that his conversion to Catholic Christianity gained him the sup-

**Baptism of Clovis.** The conversion of Clovis to Catholic Christianity around 500 was an important factor in gaining papal support for his Frankish kingdom. In this illustration from a medieval manuscript, bishops and nobles look on while Clovis is baptized. One of the nobles holds a crown while a dove, symbol of the Holy Spirit, descends from heaven bringing sacred oil for the ceremony.

**CHRONOLOGY**   **The Germanic Kingdoms**

| | |
|---|---|
| Theodoric establishes an Ostrogothic kingdom in Italy | 493 |
| Frankish king Clovis converts to Christianity | c. 500 |
| Reconquest of Italy by Byzantines | 535–552 |
| Lombards begin conquest of Italy | 568 |
| Muslims shatter Visigoths in Spain | 711 |
| Charles Martel defeats Muslims | 732 |

port of the Roman Catholic church, which was only too eager to obtain the friendship of a major Germanic ruler who was a Catholic Christian. The conversion of the king also paved the way for the conversion of the Frankish peoples. Finally, Clovis could pose as a defender of the orthodox Catholic faith in order to justify his expansion at the beginning of the sixth century. He defeated the Alemanni in southwest Germany and the Visigoths in southern Gaul. By 510, Clovis had established a powerful new Frankish kingdom stretching from the Pyrenees in the west to German lands in the east (modern-day France and western Germany).

Clovis was responsible, then, for establishing a Frankish kingdom under the Merovingian dynasty, a name derived from Merovech, their semilegendary ancestor. Clovis came to rely on his Frankish followers to rule in the old Roman city-states under the title of count. Often these officials were forced to share power with the Gallo-Roman Catholic bishops, producing a gradual fusion of Latin and German cultures, with the church serving to preserve the Latin culture. Clovis spent the last years of his life ensuring the survival of his dynasty by killing off relatives who were leaders of other groups of Franks.

**The Successors of Clovis**  After the death of Clovis, his sons divided the newly created kingdom, as was the Frankish custom. During the sixth and seventh centuries, the once-united Frankish kingdom came to be partitioned into three major areas: Neustria in northern Gaul; Austrasia, consisting of the ancient Frankish lands on both sides of the Rhine; and the former kingdom of Burgundy. All three were ruled by members of the Merovingian dynasty. Within the three territories, members of the dynasty were assisted

by powerful nobles. Frankish society possessed a ruling class that gradually intermarried with the old Gallo-Roman senatorial class to form a new nobility. These noble families took advantage of their position to strengthen their own lands and wealth at the expense of the monarchy. Within the royal household, the position of *major domus,* or mayor of the palace, the chief officer of the king's household, began to overshadow the king. Essentially, both nobles and mayors of the palace were expanding their power at the expense of the kings.

At the beginning of the eighth century, the most important political development in the Frankish kingdom was the rise of Charles Martel, who served as mayor of the palace of Austrasia beginning in 714. Charles Martel led troops that defeated the Muslims near Poitiers in 732 and by the time of his death in 741 had become virtual ruler of the three Merovingian kingdoms. Though he was not king, Charles Martel's dynamic efforts put his family on the verge of creating a new dynasty that would establish an even more powerful Frankish state (see Chapter 8).

During the sixth and seventh centuries, the Frankish kingdom witnessed a process of fusion between Gallo-Roman and Frankish cultures and peoples, a process accompanied by a significant decline in Roman standards of civilization and commercial activity. The Franks were warriors and did little to encourage either urban life or trade. Commerce declined in the interior, though seacoast towns maintained some activity. By 750, Frankish Gaul was basically an agricultural society in which the old Roman *latifundia* system of the Late Empire continued unimpeded. Institutionally, however, Germanic concepts of kingship and customary law had replaced the Roman governmental structure.

### Anglo-Saxon England

The barbarian pressures on the Western Roman Empire had forced the emperors to withdraw the Roman armies and abandon Britain by the beginning of the fifth century. This opened the door to the Angles and Saxons, Germanic tribes from Denmark and northern Germany. Although these same peoples had made plundering raids for a century, the withdrawal of the Roman armies enabled them to make settlements instead. They met with resistance from the Celtic Britons, however, who still controlled the western regions of Cornwall, Wales, and Cumberland at the beginning of the seventh century (see Map 7.3). The German invaders eventually succeeded in carving out small kingdoms throughout the island, Kent in southeast England being one of them. This wave of German invaders would eventually be converted to Christianity by new groups of Christian missionaries (see "The Conversion of England" later in this chapter).

## The Society of the Germanic Kingdoms

As the Germans infiltrated the Roman Empire, they were influenced by the Roman society they encountered. Consequently, the Germanic peoples of the fifth, sixth, and seventh centuries were probably quite different from the Germans that the forces of Augustus encountered in the first century A.D. Moreover, there was a meaningful fusion of Roman and German upper classes in the new kingdoms. In Merovingian Frankish lands, upper-class Gallo-Romans intermarried with Frankish nobles to produce a new ruling class. Each influenced the other. Franks constructed Roman-style villas; Gallo-Romans adopted Frankish weapons.

The crucial social bond among the Germanic peoples was the family, especially the extended or patriarchal family of husbands, wives, children, brothers, sisters, cousins, and grandparents. In addition to working the land together and passing it down to succeeding generations, the extended family provided protection, which was sorely needed in the violent atmosphere of Merovingian times.

**Germanic Law** The German conception of family and kinship affected the way Germanic law treated the problem of crime and punishment. In the Roman system, as in our own, a crime such as murder was considered an offense against society or the state and was handled by a court that heard evidence and arrived at a decision. Germanic law tended to be personal. An injury by one person against another could mean a blood feud in which the family of the injured party took revenge on the kin of the wrongdoer. Feuds could lead to savage acts of revenge, such as hacking off hands or feet, gouging out eyes, or slicing off ears and noses. Since this system had a tendency to get out of control and allow mayhem to multiply, an alternative system arose that made use of a fine called *wergeld*. This was the amount paid by a wrongdoer to the family of the person who had been injured or killed. *Wergeld,* which means "money for a man," was the value of a person in monetary terms. That value varied considerably according to social status. The law of the Salic Franks, which was first written down under Roman influence at the beginning of the sixth century, stated, "If any one shall have killed a free Frank, or a barbarian living under the Salic law, and it have been proved on him, he shall be sentenced to 8,000 denars. . . . But if any one has slain a man who is in the service of the king, he shall be sentenced to 24,000 denars."[5] An offense against a noble obviously cost considerably more than one against a free person or a slave.

Under German customary law, compurgation and the ordeal were the two most commonly used procedures for determining whether an accused person was guilty and should have to pay *wergeld*. Compurgation was the swearing of an oath by the accused person, backed up by a group of "oathhelpers," numbering twelve or twenty-five, who would also swear that the accused person should be believed. The ordeal functioned in a variety of ways, all of which were based on the principle of divine intervention; divine forces (whether pagan or Christian) would not allow an innocent person to be harmed (see the box on p. 177).

**The Frankish Family and Marriage** For the Franks, like other Germanic peoples of the Early Middle Ages, the extended family was at the center of social organization. The Frankish family structure was quite simple. Males were dominant and made all the important decisions. A woman obeyed her father until she married and then fell under the legal domination of her husband. A widow, however, could hold property without a male guardian. In Frankish law, the *wergeld* of a wife of childbearing age—of value because she could produce children—was considerably higher than that of a man. The Salic law stated: "If any one killed a free woman after she had begun bearing children, he shall be sentenced to 24,000 denars. . . . After she can have no more children, he who kills her shall be sentenced to 8,000 denars."[6]

Since marriage affected the extended family group, fathers or uncles could arrange marriages for the good of the family without considering their children's wishes. Most important was the engagement ceremony in which a prospective son-in-law made a payment symbolizing the purchase of paternal authority over the bride. The essential feature of the marriage itself involved placing the married couple in bed to achieve their physical union. In first marriages, it was considered important that the wife be a virgin so as to ensure that any children would be the husband's. A virgin symbolized the ability of the bloodline to continue. For this reason, adultery was viewed as pollution of the woman and her offspring, poisoning the future. Adulterous wives were severely punished (an adulterous woman could be strangled or even burned alive); adulterous husbands were not. Divorce was relatively simple and was initiated primarily by the husband. Divorced wives simply returned to their families.

For most women in the new Germanic kingdoms, their legal status reflected the material conditions of their lives. Archaeological evidence suggests that most women had life expectancies of only thirty or forty years and that about 10 to 15 percent of women died in their childbearing years, no doubt due to complications associated with childbirth. For most women, life consisted of domestic labor: providing food and clothing for the household, caring for the children, and assisting with numerous farming chores. Of all the duties of women, the most important was childbearing, because it was crucial to the maintenance of the family and its properties.

# GERMANIC CUSTOMARY LAW: THE ORDEAL

IN GERMANIC CUSTOMARY LAW, the ordeal came to be a means by which accused persons might clear themselves. Although the ordeal took different forms, all involved a physical trial of some sort, such as holding a red-hot iron. It was believed God would protect the innocent and allow them to come through the ordeal unharmed. The sixth-century account by Gregory of Tours describes an ordeal by hot water.

### Gregory of Tours, *An Ordeal of Hot Water* (c. 580)

An Arian priest disputing with a deacon of our religion made venomous assertions against the Son of God and the Holy Ghost, as is the habit of that sect [the Arians]. But when the deacon had discoursed a long time concerning the reasonableness of our faith and the heretic, blinded by the fog of unbelief, continued to reject the truth, . . . the former said: "Why weary ourselves with long discussions? Let acts approve the truth; let a kettle be heated over the fire and someone's ring be thrown into the boiling water. Let him who shall take it from the heated liquid be approved as a follower of the truth, and afterward let the other party be converted to the knowledge of the truth. And do you also understand, O heretic, that this our party will fulfill the conditions with the aid of the Holy Ghost; you shall confess that there is no discordance, no dissimilarity in the Holy Trinity [belief that God, Jesus (son of God), and Holy Spirit (Ghost) are three manifestations of the same unique Deity]." The heretic consented to the proposition and they separated after appointing the next morning for the trial. But the fervor of faith in which the deacon had first made this suggestion began to cool through the instigation of the enemy. Rising with the dawn he bathed his arm in oil and smeared it with ointment. But nevertheless he made the round of the sacred places and called in prayer on the Lord. . . . About the third hour they met in the market place. The people came together to see the show. A fire was lighted, the kettle was placed upon it, and when it grew very hot the ring was thrown into the boiling water. The deacon invited the heretic to take it out of the water first. But he promptly refused, saying, "You who did propose this trial are the one to take it out." The deacon all of a tremble bared his arm. And when the heretic saw it besmeared with ointment he cried out: "With magic arts you have thought to protect yourself, that you have made use of these salves, but what you have done will not avail." While they were thus quarreling there came up a deacon from Ravenna named Iacinthus and inquired what the trouble was about. When he learned the truth he drew his arm out from under his robe at once and plunged his right hand into the kettle. Now the ring that had been thrown in was a little thing and very light so that it was thrown about by the water as chaff would be blown about by the wind; and searching for it a long time he found it after about an hour. Meanwhile the flame beneath the kettle blazed up mightily so that the greater heat might make it difficult for the ring to be followed by the hand; but the deacon extracted it at length and suffered no harm, protesting rather that at the bottom the kettle was cold while at the top it was just pleasantly warm. When the heretic beheld this he was greatly confused and audaciously thrust his hand into the kettle saying, "My faith will aid me." As soon as his hand had been thrust in all the flesh was boiled off the bones clear up to the elbow. And so the dispute ended.

# Development of the Christian Church

By the end of the fourth century, Christianity had become the predominant religion of the Roman Empire. As the official Roman state disintegrated, the Christian church played an increasingly important role in the new civilization built on the ruins of the old Roman Empire.

### The Church Fathers

Many early Christians expressed considerable hostility toward the pagan culture of the classical world. Tertullian (c. 160–c. 225), a Christian writer from Carthage, had proclaimed: "What has Jerusalem to do with Athens, the Church with the Academy, the Christian with the heretic? . . . After Jesus Christ we have no need of speculation, after the Gospel no need of research."[7] To many early Christians, the Bible contained all the knowledge anyone needed.

Others, however, thought it was not possible to separate Christian theological thought from classical traditions and education and encouraged Christians to absorb the classical heritage. As it spread in the eastern Roman world, Christianity adopted Greek as its language. The New Testament was written in Greek. Christians also turned to Greek thought for help in expressing complicated theological concepts. An especially important influence was Neoplatonism, a revival of Platonic thought that reached its high point in the third century A.D. Neoplatonists believed that one could use reason to perceive the link between the invisible spiritual world and the visible material world. Christian theologians used Neoplatonic concepts to explain doctrines on Jesus, especially the distinction between his human and divine natures. In many ways, then, Christianity served to preserve Greco-Roman culture.

**The Work of Augustine** The work of Saint Augustine (354–430) provides one of the best examples of how Christian theologians used pagan culture in the service of Christianity.

# THE CONFESSIONS OF AUGUSTINE

AINT AUGUSTINE'S spiritual and intellectual auto-biography is a revealing self-portrait of the inner struggles of one of the intellectual giants of early Christianity. The first excerpt is taken from Book 8, in which Augustine describes how he heard a voice from heaven and was converted from his old habits. In the second excerpt, from Book 9, Augustine expresses joy and gratitude for his conversion.

## Augustine, *Confessions*

 ### From Book 8

So was I speaking and weeping in the most bitter contrition of my heart, when, lo! I heard from a neighboring house a voice as of boy or girl, I know not, chanting, and oft repeating, "Take up and read; Take up and read." Instantly, my countenance altered, I began to think most intently whether children were wont in any kind of play to sing such words: nor could I remember ever to have heard the like. So checking the torrent of my tears, I arose; interpreting it to be no other than a command from God to open the book, and read the first chapter I should find. For I had heard of Antony, that coming in during the reading of the Gospel, he received the admonition, as if what was being read was spoken to him: Go, sell all that you have, and give to the poor, and you shall have treasure in heaven, and come and follow me:

and by such oracle he was forthwith converted unto You. Eagerly then I returned to the place where Alypius was sitting; for there I had laid the volume of the Apostle [Paul] when I arose thence. I seized, opened, and in silence read that section on which my eyes first fell: Not in rioting and drunkenness, not in chambering and wantonness, not in strife and envying; but put you on the Lord Jesus Christ, and make not provision for the flesh. . . . No further would I read; nor need I: for instantly at the end of this sentence, by a light as it were of serenity infused into my heart, all the darkness of doubt vanished away.

### From Book 9

O Lord I am your servant; I am your servant, and the son of your handmaid: You have broken my bonds in sunder. I will offer to You the sacrifice of praise. Let my heart and my tongue praise You; yea, let all my bones say, O Lord, who is like unto You? Let them say, and answer You me, and say unto my soul, I am your salvation. Who am I, and what am I? What evil have not been either my deeds, or if not my deeds, my words, or if not my words, my will? But You, O Lord, are good and merciful, and your right hand had respect unto the depth of my death, and from the bottom of my heart emptied that abyss of corruption.

---

Augustine came to be seen as one of the Latin Fathers of the Catholic church, intellectuals who wrote in Latin and profoundly influenced the development of Christian thought in the west.

Born in North Africa, Augustine was reared by his mother, an ardent Christian. He eventually became a professor of rhetoric at Milan in 384. But two years later, after experiencing a profound and moving religious experience, Augustine gave up his teaching position and went back to North Africa, where he served as bishop of Hippo from 396 until his death in 430.

Augustine's two most famous works are the *Confessions* and *The City of God*. Written in 397, the *Confessions* was a self-portrait not of Augustine's worldly activities but of the "history of a heart," an account of his own personal and spiritual experiences, written to help others with their search. Augustine describes how he struggled throughout his early life to find God until in his thirty-second year he experienced a miraculous conversion (see the box above).

*The City of God*, Augustine's other major work, was a profound expression of a Christian philosophy of government and history. It was written in response to a line of argument that arose soon after the sack of Rome in 410. Some pagan philosophers maintained that Rome's problems stemmed from the Roman state's recognition of Christianity and abandonment of the old, traditional gods. Augustine argued that Rome's troubles began long before

Christianity arose in the empire. In *The City of God*, Augustine theorized on the ideal relations between two kinds of societies existing throughout time—the City of God and the City of the World. Those who loved God would be loyal to the City of God, whose ultimate location was the kingdom of heaven. Earthly society would always be insecure because of human beings' imperfect nature and inclination to violate God's commandments. And yet the City of the World was still necessary, for it was the duty of rulers to curb the depraved instincts of sinful humans and maintain the peace necessary for Christians to live in the world. Hence Augustine posited that secular government and authority were necessary for the pursuit of the true Christian life on earth; in doing so, he provided a justification for secular political authority that would play an important role in medieval thought.

Augustine was also important in establishing the Christian church's views on sexual desire. Many early Christians had seen **celibacy,** or complete abstinence from sexual activity, as the surest way to holiness. Augustine, too, believed Christians should reject sex, but he maintained that many Christians were unable to do so. For them, marriage was a good alternative, but with the understanding that even in marriage, sex between a man and woman had to serve a purpose—the procreation of children. It was left to the clergy of the church to uphold the high ideal of celibacy.

**Jerome and the Bible**    Another Latin Father was Jerome (345–420), who pursued literary studies in Rome and became a master of Latin prose. Jerome had mixed feelings about his love for liberal studies, however, and like Augustine experienced a spiritual conversion, after which he tried to dedicate himself more fully to Jesus. He had a dream in which Jesus appeared as his judge:

> Asked who and what I was, I replied: "I am a Christian." But He who presided said: "You lie, you are a follower of Cicero, not of Christ. For where your treasure is, there will your heart be also." Instantly, I became dumb. . . . Accordingly I made oath and called upon His name, saying: "Lord, if ever again I possess worldly books [the classics], or if ever again I read such, I have denied You."

After this dream, Jerome determined to "read the books of God with a zeal greater than I had previously given to the books of men."[8]

Ultimately, Jerome found a compromise by purifying the literature of the pagan world and then using it to further the Christian faith. Jerome was the greatest scholar among the Latin Fathers, and his extensive knowledge of both Hebrew and Greek enabled him to translate the Old and New Testaments into Latin. In the process, he created the so-called Latin Vulgate, or common text, of the Scriptures that became the standard edition for the Catholic church in the Middle Ages.

## The Power of the Pope

In the early centuries of Christianity, the churches in the larger cities had great influence in the administration of the church. It was only natural, then, that the bishops of those cities would also exercise considerable power. One of the far-reaching developments in the history of the Christian church was the emergence of one bishop—that of Rome—as the recognized leader of the western Christian church.

The doctrine of **Petrine supremacy,** based on the belief that the bishops of Rome occupied a preeminent position in the church, was grounded in Scripture. According to the Gospel of Matthew, when Jesus asked his disciples, "Who do you say I am?" Simon Peter answered:

> You are the Christ, the Son of the living God. Jesus replied, Blessed are you, Simon, son of Jonah, for this was not revealed by man, but by my Father in heaven. And I tell you that you are Peter, and on this rock I will build my church, and the gates of hell will not overcome it. I will give you the keys of the kingdom of heaven; whatever you bind on earth will be bound in heaven; and whatever you loose on earth will be loosed in heaven.[9]

According to church tradition, Jesus had given the keys to the kingdom of heaven to Peter, who was considered the chief apostle and the first bishop of Rome. Subsequent bishops of Rome were considered Peter's successors and later the "vicars of Christ" on earth. Though this exalted view of the bishops of Rome was by no means accepted by all early Christians, Rome's position as the traditional capital of the Roman Empire served to buttress this claim.

By the end of the fourth century, the bishops of Rome were using the title of *papa,* "father" (which became the English *pope*). Pope Leo I (440–461) was especially energetic in systematically expounding the doctrine of Petrine supremacy. He portrayed himself as the heir of Peter, whom Jesus had chosen to be head of the Christian church. But state authorities were also claiming some power over the church.

## Church and State

Once the Roman emperors became Christians, they came to play a significant role in the affairs of the church. Christian emperors viewed themselves as God's representatives on earth. They not only built churches and influenced the structure of the church's organization but also became involved in church government and doctrinal controversies.

While emperors were busying themselves in church affairs, the spiritual and political vacuum left by the disintegration of the Roman state allowed bishops to play a more active role in imperial government. Increasingly, they served as advisers to Christian Roman emperors. Moreover, as imperial authority declined, bishops often played a noticeably independent political role. Ambrose (c. 339–397) of Milan was an early example of a strong and independent bishop. Through his activities and writings, Ambrose created an image of the ideal Christian bishop. Among other things, this ideal bishop would defend the independence of the church against the tendency of imperial officials to oversee church policy: "Exalt not yourself, but if you would reign the longer, be subject to God. It is written, God's to God and Caesar's to Caesar. The palace is the Emperor's, the Churches are the Bishop's."[10] When Emperor Theodosius I ordered the massacre of many citizens in Thessalonika for refusing to obey his commands, Ambrose denounced the massacre and refused to allow the emperor to take part in church ceremonies. Theodosius finally agreed to do public penance in the cathedral of Milan for his dastardly deed. Ambrose proved himself a formidable advocate of the position that spiritual authority should take precedence over temporal power, at least in spiritual matters.

The weakness of the political authorities on the Italian peninsula also contributed to the church's independence in that area. In the Germanic kingdoms, the kings controlled both churches and bishops. But in Italy, a different tradition prevailed, fed by semilegendary accounts of papal deeds. Pope Leo I, for example, supposedly caused Attila the Hun to turn away from Rome in 452. Although plague rather than papal persuasion was probably more to account for Attila's withdrawal, the pope got the credit. Popes, then, played significant political roles in Italy, which only added to their claims of power vis-à-vis the secular authorities. Pope Gelasius I (492–496) could write to the emperor at Constantinople:

> There are two powers, august Emperor, by which this world is ruled from the beginning: the consecrated authority of the bishops, and the royal power. In these matters the priests bear the heavier burden because they will render account, even for

rulers of men, at the divine judgment. Besides, most gracious son, you are aware that, although you in your office are the ruler of the human race, nevertheless you devoutly bow your head before those who are leaders in things divine and look to them for the means of your salvation.[11]

According to Gelasius, though there were two ruling powers, spiritual and temporal, with different functions, the church was ultimately the higher authority because all men, including emperors, must look to the church "for the means of . . . salvation."

## Pope Gregory the Great

Although western Christians came to accept the bishop of Rome as head of the church, there was no unanimity on the extent of the powers the pope possessed as a result of his position. Nevertheless, the emergence in the sixth century of a strong pope, Gregory I, known as Gregory the Great, set the papacy and the Roman Catholic church on an energetic path that enabled the church in the seventh and eighth centuries to play an increasingly prominent role in civilizing the Germans and aiding the emergence of a distinctly new European civilization.

**Pope Gregory I.** Pope Gregory the Great became one of the most important popes of the Early Middle Ages. This ninth-century manuscript illustration shows Gregory dictating a work to two monks. Over Gregory's right shoulder is a dove, symbol of the Holy Spirit, which is providing divine inspiration for what he is dictating.

As pope, Gregory I (590–604) assumed direction of Rome and its surrounding territories, which had suffered enormously from the Ostrogothic-Byzantine struggle and the Lombard invasion of the sixth century. Gregory described the conditions in a sermon to the people of Rome:

> What Rome herself, once deemed the Mistress of the World, has now become, we see—wasted away with afflictions grievous and many, with the loss of citizens, the assaults of enemies, the frequent fall of ruined buildings. . . . Where is the Senate? Where is the people? The bones are all dissolved, the flesh is consumed, all the pomp of the dignities of this world is gone.[12]

Gregory took charge and made Rome and its surrounding area into an administrative unit that eventually came to be known as the Papal States. Although historians disagree about Gregory's motives in establishing papal temporal power, no doubt Gregory was probably only doing what he felt needed to be done: to provide for the defense of Rome against the Lombards, to establish a government for Rome, and to feed the people. Gregory remained loyal to the empire and continued to address the Byzantine emperor as the rightful ruler of Italy.

Gregory also pursued a policy of extending papal authority over the Christian church in the west. He intervened in ecclesiastical conflicts throughout Italy and corresponded with the Frankish rulers, urging them to reform the church in Gaul. He successfully initiated the efforts of missionaries to convert England to Christianity and was especially active in converting the pagan peoples of Germanic Europe. His primary instrument was the monastic movement.

## The Monks and Their Missions

A **monk** (Latin *monachus,* meaning "someone who lives alone") was a man who sought to live a life divorced from the world, cut off from ordinary human society, in order to pursue an ideal of godliness or total dedication to the will of God. Christian **monasticism,** which developed first in Egypt, was initially based on the model of the solitary hermit who forsakes all civilized society to pursue spirituality. Saint Anthony (c. 250–350) was a prosperous Egyptian peasant who decided to follow Jesus' injunction in the Gospel of Mark: "Go your way, sell whatsoever you have, and give to the poor, and you shall have treasure in heaven: and come, take up the cross, and follow me."[13] Anthony gave his 300 acres of land to the poor and went into the desert to pursue his ideal of holiness (see the box on p. 181). Others did likewise, often to extremes. Saint Simeon the Stylite lived for three decades in a basket atop a pillar over 60 feet high. These spiritual gymnastics established a new ideal for Christianity. Whereas the early Christian model had been the martyr who died for the faith and achieved eternal life in the process, the new ideal was the monk who died to the world and achieved spiritual life through denial, asceticism, and mystical experience of God.

# THE LIFE OF SAINT ANTHONY

N THE THIRD and early fourth centuries, the lives of martyrs had provided important models for early Christianity. But in the course of the fourth century, monks who attempted to achieve spiritual perfection through asceticism, the denial of earthly life, and the struggle with demons became the new spiritual ideal for Christians. Consequently, spiritual biographies of early monks became a significant new form of Christian literature. Especially noteworthy was *The Life of Saint Anthony* by Saint Athanasius, the defender of Catholic orthodoxy against the Arians. His work had been translated into Latin before 386. This excerpt describes how Anthony fought off the temptations of Satan.

## Athanasius, *The Life of Saint Anthony*

Now when the Enemy [Satan] saw that his craftiness in this matter was without profit, and that the more he brought temptation into Saint Anthony, the more strenuous the saint was in protecting himself against him with the armor of righteousness, he attacked him by means of the vigor of early manhood which is bound up in the nature of our humanity. With the goadings of passion he sued to trouble him by night, and in the daytime also he would vex him and pain him with the same to such an extent that even those who saw him knew from his appearance that he was waging war against the Adversary. But the more the Evil One brought unto him filthy and maddening thoughts, the more Saint Anthony took refuge in prayer and in abundant supplication, and amid them all he remained wholly chaste. And the Evil One was working upon him every shameful deed according to his wont, and at length he even appeared unto Saint Anthony in the form of a woman; and other things which resembled this he performed with ease, for such things are a subject for boasting to him.

But the blessed Anthony knelt down upon his knees on the ground, and prayed before Him who said, "Before you criest unto Me, I will answer you," and said, "O my Lord, this I entreat you. Let not Your love be blotted out from my mind, and behold, I am, by Your grace, innocent before You." And again the Enemy multiplied in him the thoughts of lust, until Saint Anthony became as one who was being burned up, not through the Evil One, but through his own lusts; but he girded himself about with the threat of the thought of the Judgment, and of the torture of Gehenna [Hell], and of the worm which does not die. And while meditating on the thoughts which could be directed against the Evil One, he prayed for thoughts which would be hostile to him. Thus, to the reproach and shame of the Enemy, these things could not be performed; for he who imagined that he could be God was made a mock of by a young man, and he who boasted over flesh and blood was vanquished by a man who was clothed with flesh.

---

These early monks, however, soon found themselves unable to live in solitude. Their feats of holiness attracted followers on a wide scale, and as the monastic ideal spread throughout the east, a new form of monasticism, based on the practice of communal life, soon became the dominant form. Monastic communities soon came to be seen as the ideal Christian society that could provide a moral example to the wider society around them.

**Benedictine Monasticism** Saint Benedict of Nursia (c. 480–c. 543), who founded a monastic house for which he wrote a set of rules sometime between 520 and 530, established the fundamental form of monastic life in the western Christian church. Benedict's rules largely rejected the ascetic ideals of eastern monasticism, which had tended to emphasize such practices as fasting and self-inflicted torments (such as living atop pillars for thirty years), in favor of an ideal of moderation. In Chapter 40 of the rules, on the amount of drink a monk should imbibe, this sense of moderation becomes apparent:

> "Every man has his proper gift from God, one after this manner, another after that." And therefore it is with some misgiving that we determine the amount of food for someone else. Still, having regard for the weakness of some brothers, we believe that a hemina [a quarter liter] of wine per day will suffice for all. Let those, however, to whom God gives the gift of abstinence, know that they shall have their proper reward. But if either the circumstances of the place, the work, or the heat of summer necessitates more, let it lie in the discretion of the abbot to grant it. But let him take care in all things lest satiety or drunkenness supervene.

At the same time, moderation did not preclude a hard and disciplined existence based on the ideals of poverty, chastity, and obedience.

Benedict's rules divided each day into a series of activities with primary emphasis on prayer and manual labor. Physical work of some kind was required of all monks for several hours a day because "idleness is the enemy of the soul." At the very heart of community practice was prayer, the proper "work of God." While this included private meditation and reading, all monks gathered together seven times during the day for common prayer and chanting of psalms. A Benedictine life was a communal one; monks ate, worked, slept, and worshiped together.

Each Benedictine monastery was strictly ruled by an **abbot,** or "father" of the monastery, who had complete authority over the monks, who bent unquestioningly to the will of the abbot. Each Benedictine monastery owned lands that enabled it to be a self-sustaining community, isolated from and independent of the world surrounding it. Within

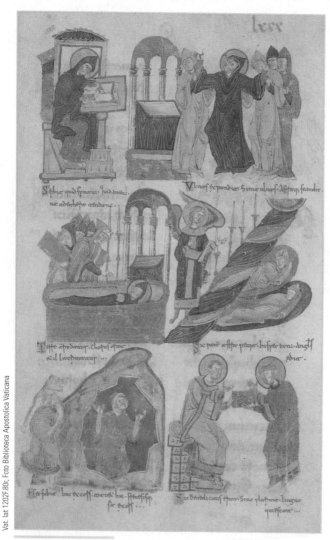

**Life of Saint Benedict.** This illustration with its six scenes is from an eleventh-century manuscript of Pope Gregory the Great's *Life of Saint Benedict,* written in 593 or 594. *Top left,* Benedict writes his rules; *top right,* the death of Benedict; *middle left,* his burial; *middle right* and *bottom left,* scenes of miracles attributed to Saint Benedict's intercession; *bottom right,* Gregory finishes his *Life of Saint Benedict.*

the monastery, however, monks were to fulfill their vow of poverty: "Let all things be common to all, as it is written, lest anyone should say that anything is his own or arrogate it to himself."[14] By the eighth century, Benedictine monasticism had spread throughout the west.

Women, too, sought to withdraw from the world to dedicate themselves to God. Already in the third century, groups of women abandoned the cities to form communities in the deserts of Egypt and Syria. The first monastic rules for western women were produced by Caesarius of Arles for his sister in the fifth century. They strongly emphasized a rigid cloistering of female religious, known as **nuns,** to preserve them from dangers. Later in the west, in the seventh and eighth centuries, the growth of double monasteries allowed monks and nuns to reside close by and follow a common set of rules. Not all women pursued the celibate life in the desert, however. In a number of cities in the fourth century, women organized religious communities in their own homes.

Monasticism played an indispensable role in early medieval civilization. Monks became the new heroes of Christian civilization. Their dedication to God became the highest ideal of Christian life. Moreover, the monks played an increasingly significant role in spreading Christianity to all of Europe.

**Irish Monks as Missionaries**   Ireland had remained a Celtic outpost beyond the reach of the Roman Empire and the Germanic invaders. The most famous of the Christian missionaries to Ireland in the fifth century was Saint Patrick (c. 390–461). Son of a Romano-British Christian, Patrick was kidnapped as a young man by Irish raiders and kept as a slave in Ireland. After his escape to Gaul, he became a monk and chose to return to Ireland to convert the Irish to Christianity. Irish tradition ascribes to Patrick the title of "founder of Irish Christianity," a testament to his apparent success.

Since Ireland had not been part of the Roman world and was fairly isolated from the European continent even after its conversion, Irish Christianity tended to develop along lines somewhat different from Roman Christianity. Whereas Catholic ecclesiastical structure had followed Roman government models, the absence of these models in Ireland engendered a different pattern of church organization. Rather than bishoprics, monasteries became the fundamental units of church organization, and abbots, the heads of the monasteries, exercised far more control over the Irish church than bishops did.

By the sixth century, Irish monasticism was a flourishing institution with its own striking characteristics. It was strongly ascetic. Monks performed strenuous fasts, prayed and meditated frequently under extreme privations, and confessed their sins on a regular basis to their superiors. In fact, Irish monasticism gave rise to the use of penitentials or manuals that provided a guide for examining one's life to see what offenses against the will of God one had committed (see the box on p. 183).

A great love of learning also characterized Irish monasticism. The Irish eagerly absorbed both Latin and Greek culture and fostered education as a major part of their monastic life. Irish monks were preserving classical Latin at the same time spoken Latin was being corrupted on the Continent into new dialects that eventually became the Romance languages, such as Italian, French, and Spanish. Irish monasteries produced extraordinary illuminated manuscripts illustrated with abstract geometric patterns.

The emphasis on asceticism led many Irish monks to go into voluntary exile. This "exile for the love of God" was not into isolation, however, but into missionary activity. Irish monks became fervid missionaries. Saint Columba (521–597) left Ireland in 565 as a "pilgrim for Christ" and founded a highly influential monastic community off the coast of Scotland on the island of Iona. From there Irish missionaries went to northern England to begin the process

# IRISH MONASTICISM AND THE PENITENTIAL

IRISH MONASTICISM became well known for its ascetic practices. Much emphasis was placed on careful examination of conscience to determine if one had committed a sin against God. To facilitate this examination, penitentials were developed that listed possible sins with appropriate penances. Penance usually meant fasting a number of days each week, taking only bread and water. Although these penitentials were eventually used throughout Christendom, they were especially important in Irish Christianity. This excerpt from the penitential of Cummean, an Irish abbot, was written about 650 and demonstrates a distinctive feature of the penitentials, an acute preoccupation with sexual sins.

### The Penitential of Cummean

A bishop who commits fornication shall be degraded and shall do penance for twelve years.

A priest or a deacon who commits natural fornication, having previously taken the vow of a monk, shall do penance for seven years. He shall ask pardon every hour; he shall perform a special fast during every week except in the days between Easter and Pentecost.

He who defiles his mother shall do penance for three years, with perpetual pilgrimage.

So shall those who commit sodomy do penance every seven years.

He who merely desires in his mind to commit fornication, but is not able, shall do penance for one year, especially in the three forty-day periods.

He who is willingly polluted during sleep shall arise and sing nine psalms in order, kneeling. On the following day, he shall live on bread and water.

A cleric who commits fornication once shall do penance for one year on bread and water; if he begets a son he shall do penance for seven years as an exile; so also a virgin.

He who loves any woman, but is unaware of any evil beyond a few conversations, shall do penance for forty days.

He who is in a state of matrimony ought to be continent during the three forty-day periods and on Saturday and on Sunday, night and day, and in the two appointed week days [Wednesday and Friday], and after conception, and during the entire menstrual period.

After a birth he shall abstain, if it is a son, for thirty-three [days]; if a daughter, for sixty-six [days].

Boys talking alone and transgressing the regulations of the elders [in the monastery], shall be corrected by three special fasts.

Children who imitate acts of fornication, twenty days; if frequently, forty.

But boys of twenty years who practice masturbation together and confess [shall do penance] twenty or forty days before they take communion.

---

of converting the Angles and Saxons. Aidan of Iona, for example, founded the island monastery of Lindisfarne in the Anglo-Saxon kingdom of Northumbria. Lindisfarne in turn became a training center for monks who spread out to different parts of Anglo-Saxon England. Meanwhile, other Irish monks traveled to the European mainland. New monasteries founded by the Irish became centers of learning wherever they were located.

**The Conversion of England** At the same time the Irish monks were busy bringing their version of Christianity to the Anglo-Saxons of Britain, Pope Gregory the Great had set in motion his own effort to convert England to Roman Christianity. His most important agent was Augustine, a monk from Saint Andrew's monastery in Rome, who arrived in England in 597. England at that time had a number of Germanic kingdoms. Augustine went first to Kent, where he converted King Ethelbert, whereupon most of the king's subjects followed suit. Pope Gregory's conversion techniques emphasized persuasion rather than force, and as seen in this excerpt from one of his letters, he was willing to assimilate old pagan practices in order to coax the pagans into the new faith:

We wish you [Abbot Mellitus] to inform him [Augustine] that we have been giving careful thought to the affairs of the English, and have come to the conclusion that the temples of the idols among that people should on no account be destroyed. The idols are to be destroyed, but the temples themselves are to be sprinkled with holy water, altars set up in them, and relics deposited there. For if these temples are well-built, they must be purified from the worship of demons and dedicated to the service of the true God. In this way, we hope that the people, seeing that their temples are not destroyed, may abandon their error and, flocking more readily to their accustomed resorts, may come to know and adore the true God.[15]

Freed of their pagan past, temples had become churches, as one Christian commentator noted with joy: "The dwelling place of demons has become a house of God. The saving light has come to shine, where shadows covered all. Where sacrifices once took place and idols stood, angelic choirs now dance. Where God was angered once, now God is made content."[16]

Likewise, old pagan feasts were to be given new names and incorporated into the Christian calendar. No doubt Gregory was aware that early Christians had done the same. The Christian feast of Christmas, for example, was held on December 25, the day of the pagan celebration of the winter solstice.

As Roman Christianity spread northward in Britain, it encountered Irish Christianity moving southward. Soon arguments arose over the differences between Celtic and Roman Christianity, especially over matters of discipline. At the Synod of Whitby, held in the kingdom of Northumbria

**The Book of Kells.** Art historians use the term *Hiberno-Saxon* (Hibernia was the ancient name for Ireland) or *Insular* to refer to works produced primarily in the monasteries of the British Isles, especially Ireland. The best example of Hiberno-Saxon art is *The Book of Kells,* a richly decorated illuminated manuscript of the Christian Gospels. Kells was the name of the monastery that owned it, but the work was produced by the monks of Iona, who combined Celtic and Anglo-Saxon abstract designs with elaborate portrayals of human figures and animals. A twelfth-century priest who viewed it observed: "Look . . . keenly at it and you . . . will make out intricacies, so delicate and subtle, so exact and compact, so full of knots and links, with colors so fresh and vivid, that you might say that all this was the work of an angel, and not of a man." Shown here is a page centered on the figure of Jesus.

in 664, the king of Northumbria accepted the arguments of the representatives of Roman Christianity and decided the issue in favor of Roman practices. A gradual fusion of Celtic and Roman Christianity now ensued. Despite its newfound unity and loyalty to Rome, the English church retained some Irish features. Most important was the concentration on monastic culture with special emphasis on learning and missionary work. By 700, the English clergy had become the best trained and most learned in western Europe.

Following the Irish example, English monks journeyed to the European continent to carry on the work of conversion (see Map 7.4). Most important was Boniface (c. 675–754), who undertook the conversion of pagan Germans in Frisia, Bavaria, and Saxony. By 740, Saint Boniface, the "Apostle of the Germans," had become the most famous churchman in Europe. Fourteen years later, he was killed while trying to convert the pagan Frisians. Boniface was a brilliant example of the numerous Irish and English monks whose tireless efforts made Europe the bastion of the Roman Catholic faith.

**Women and Monasticism**   Women, too, played an important role in the monastic missionary movement and the conversion of the Germanic kingdoms. Double monasteries, where both monks and nuns lived in separate houses but attended church services together, were found in both the English and Frankish kingdoms. The monks and nuns followed common rules under a common head—frequently an **abbess** rather than an abbot. Many of these abbesses belonged to royal houses, especially in Anglo-Saxon England. In the kingdom of Northumbria, for example, Saint Hilda founded the monastery of Whitby in 657. As abbess, she was responsible for giving learning an important role in the life of the monastery; five future bishops were educated under her tutelage (see the box on p. 185). For female intellectuals, monasteries offered opportunities for learning not found elsewhere in the society of their day.

Nuns of the seventh and eighth centuries were not always as heavily cloistered as they once had been and were therefore able to play an important role in the spread of Christianity. The great English missionary Boniface relied on nuns in England for books and money. He also asked the abbess of Wimborne to send groups of nuns to establish convents in newly converted German lands. A nun named Leoba established the first convent in Germany at Bischofsheim.

**The Path of Celibacy**   The monastic movement enabled some women to pursue a new path to holiness. Cloisters for both men and women offered the ideal place to practice the new Christian ideal of celibacy. This newfound emphasis on abstaining from sexual relations, especially evident in the emphasis on virginity, created a new image of the human body in late antiquity. To many Greeks and Roman, the human body had been a source of beauty, joy, and enjoyment, noticeable in numerous works of art.

# An Anglo-Saxon Abbess: Hilda of Whitby

*H*ILDA, ABBESS OF the monastery of Whitby, is a good example of the abbesses from royal families in Anglo-Saxon England who played important roles in English monastic institutions. Hilda was especially known for her exemplary life and high regard for learning. This account of her life is taken from Bede, considered by many the first major historian of the Middle Ages.

### Bede, *The Ecclesiastical History of the English People*

In the following year, that is the year of our Lord 680, Hilda, abbess of the monastery of Whitby, a most religious servant of Christ, passed away to receive the reward of eternal life on the seventeenth of November at the age of sixty-six, after a life full of heavenly deeds. Her life fell into two equal parts, for she spent thirty-three years most nobly in secular occupations, and dedicated the remainder of her life even more nobly to our Lord in the monastic life. She was nobly born, the daughter of Hereric, nephew to King Edwin, with whom she received the Faith and sacraments of Christ through the preaching of Paulinus of blessed memory, first bishop of the Northumbrians, and she preserved this Faith inviolate until she was found worthy to see him in heaven. . . .

When she had ruled this monastery (Heruteu) for some years, constantly occupied in establishing the regular life, she further undertook to found or organize a monastery at a place known as Streaneshalch, and carried out this appointed task with great energy. She established the same regular life as in her former monastery, and taught the observance of justice, devotion, purity, and other virtues, but especially in peace and charity. After the example of the primitive Church, no one there was rich or poor, for everything was held in common, and none possessed any personal property.

So great was her prudence that not only ordinary folk, but kings and princes used to come and ask her advice in their difficulties. Those under her direction were required to make a thorough study of the Scriptures and occupy themselves in good works, in order that many might be found fitted for Holy Orders and the service of God's altar. Subsequently, five bishops were chosen from this monastery—Bosa, Hedda, Oftfor, John, and Wilfrid—all of them men of outstanding merit and holiness. . . .

Christ's servant Abbess Hilda, whom all her acquaintances called Mother because of her wonderful devotion and grace, was not only an example of holy life to members of her own community, for she also brought about the amendment and salvation of many living far distant, who heard the inspiring story of her industry and goodness. . . . When Hilda ruled this monastery for many years, it pleased the Author of our salvation to try her holy soul by a long sickness, in order that, like the Apostle, her strength might be perfected in weakness. She was attacked by a burning fever that racked her continually for six years; but during all this time she never ceased to give thanks to her Maker, or to instruct the flock committed to her both privately and publicly. For her own example taught them all to serve God rightly when in health, and to render thanks to him faithfully when in trouble or bodily weakness. In the seventh year of her illness she suffered interior pains, and her last day came. About dawn she received holy Communion, and when she had summoned all the servants of Christ in the monastery, she urged them to maintain the gospel peace among themselves and with others. And while she was still speaking, she joyfully welcomed death, and in the words of our Lord, passed from death to life.

---

To many Christians, the body was seen as a hindrance to a spiritual connection with God. The refusal to have sex was a victory over the desires of the flesh and thus an avenue to holiness.

In the fourth and fifth centuries, a cult of virginity also moved beyond the walls of monasteries and convents. Throughout the Mediterranean world, groups of women met together to study the importance and benefits of celibacy. In Rome, a woman named Marcella supported a group of aristocratic women who studied the ideas of celibacy and also aided Jerome, the church father, with his work on translating the Bible into Latin.

### Christian Intellectual Life in the Germanic Kingdoms

Although the Christian church came to accept classical culture, it was not easy to do so in the new German kingdoms.

Nevertheless, some Christian scholars managed to keep learning alive.

**Cassiodorus**  Most prominent was Cassiodorus (c. 490–585), who came from an aristocratic Roman family and served as an official of the Ostrogothic king Theodoric. The conflicts that erupted after the death of Theodoric led Cassiodorus to withdraw from public life and retire to his landed estates in southern Italy, where he wrote his final work, *Divine and Human Readings*, a compendium of the literature of both Christian and pagan antiquity. Cassiodorus accepted the advice of earlier Christian intellectuals to make use of classical works while treasuring the Scriptures above all else.

Cassiodorus continued the tradition of late antiquity of classifying knowledge according to certain subjects. In assembling his compendium of authors, he followed the works of late ancient authors in placing all secular knowledge into

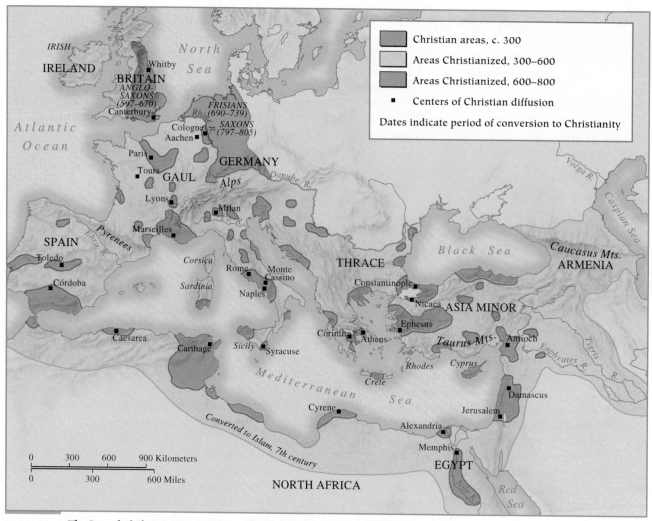

**MAP 7.4** **The Spread of Christianity, 400–800.** The Christian church had penetrated much of the Roman Empire by the end of the fifth century. It emerged as a major base of power after the fall of the empire, and it pushed its influence into new areas through the activities of missionaries. ❓ What aspects of geography help explain the relatively late conversions of the Anglo-Saxons in Britain and the Frisians and Saxons east of the Rhine River? 🔊 **View an animated version of this map or related maps at** http://history.wadsworth.com/spielvogel06/

the categories of the seven **liberal arts,** which were divided into two major groups: the *trivium,* consisting of grammar, **rhetoric,** and dialectic or logic, and the *quadrivium,* consisting of arithmetic, geometry, astronomy, and music. The seven liberal arts would be the cornerstone of Western education for nearly twelve hundred years.

**Bede** The Venerable Bede (c. 672–735) was a scholar and product of Christian Anglo-Saxon England. He entered a monastery at Jarrow as a small boy and remained there most of the rest of his life. His *Ecclesiastical History of the English People,* completed in 731, was a product of the remarkable flowering of English ecclesiastical and monastic culture in the eighth century. His history of England begins with the coming of Christianity to Britain. Although Bede shared the credulity of his age in regard to stories of miracles, he had a remarkable sense of history. He used his

sources so judiciously that they remain our chief source of information about early Anglo-Saxon England (see the box on p. 185). His work was a remarkable accomplishment for a monk from a small corner of England and reflects the high degree of intellectual achievement of England in the eighth century.

# The Byzantine Empire

As noted earlier, in the fourth century, a separation between the western and eastern parts of the Roman Empire began to occur. Even as the Germans moved into the western part of the empire and established various kingdoms over the course of the fifth century, the Roman Empire in the east, centered on Constantinople, solidified and prospered.

**Justinian and His Court.** Ravenna remained the center of the Byzantine presence in Italy for two hundred years. The Church of San Vitale at Ravenna contains some of the finest examples of sixth-century Byzantine mosaics (works of art made by assembling small colored pieces of glass or rock). This mosaic depicts the Byzantine emperor Justinian and his court dressed in their elaborate robes. Justinian is seen with soldiers, his staff, and members of the clergy.

## The Reign of Justinian (527–565)

In the sixth century, the empire in the east came under the control of one of its most remarkable rulers, the emperor Justinian. As the nephew and heir of the previous emperor, Justinian had been well trained in imperial administration. He was determined to reestablish the Roman Empire in the entire Mediterranean world and began his attempt to reconquer the west within a year after the revolt had failed.

Justinian's army under Belisarius, probably the best general of the late Roman world, presented a formidable force. Belisarius sailed to North Africa and quickly destroyed the Vandals in two major battles. From North Africa, he led his forces onto the Italian peninsula after occupying Sicily in 535. But it was not until 552 that the Ostrogoths were finally defeated. The struggle devastated Italy, which suffered more from Justinian's reconquest than from all of the previous barbarian invasions.

Justinian has been criticized for overextending his resources and bankrupting the empire. Historians now think, however, that a devastating plague in 542 and long-term economic factors were far more damaging to the Eastern Roman Empire than Justinian's conquests. Before he died, Justinian appeared to have achieved his goals. He had restored the imperial Mediterranean world; his empire included Italy, part of Spain, North Africa, Asia Minor, Palestine, and Syria (see Map 7.5). But the conquest of the Western Empire proved fleeting. Only three years after Justinian's death, the Lombards entered Italy. Although the Eastern Empire maintained the fiction of Italy as a province, its forces were limited to southern and central Italy, Sicily, and coastal areas, such as the territory around Ravenna.

**The Codification of Roman Law** Though his conquests proved short-lived, Justinian made a lasting contribution to Western civilization through his codification of Roman law. The Eastern Empire was heir to a vast quantity of materials connected to the development of Roman law. These included laws passed by the senate and assemblies, legal commentaries of jurists, decisions of praetors, and the edicts of emperors. Justinian had been well trained in imperial government and was thoroughly acquainted with Roman law. He wished to codify and simplify this mass of materials.

To accomplish his goal, Justinian authorized the jurist Trebonian to make a systematic compilation of imperial edicts. The result was the Code of Law, the first part of the *Corpus Iuris Civilis* (Body of Civil Law), completed in 529. Four years later, two other parts of the *Corpus* appeared: the *Digest,* a compendium of writings of Roman jurists, and the *Institutes,* a brief summary of the chief principles of Roman law that could be used as a textbook on Roman law. The fourth part of the *Corpus* was the *Novels,* a compilation of the most important new edicts issued during Justinian's reign.

Justinian's codification of Roman law became the basis of imperial law in the Byzantine Empire until its end in 1453. More important, however, since it was written in Latin (it was, in fact, the last product of eastern Roman culture to be written in Latin, which was soon replaced by Greek), it was also eventually used in the west and in fact became the basis of the legal system of all of continental Europe.

**Intellectual Life Under Justinian** The intellectual life of the Eastern Roman Empire was highly influenced by the traditions of classical civilization. Scholars actively strived to preserve the works of the ancient Greeks while basing a great deal of their own literature on classical models. Initially, however, the most outstanding literary achievements of the Eastern Empire were historical and religious works.

The best known of the early Byzantine historians was Procopius (c. 500–c. 562), court historian during the reign

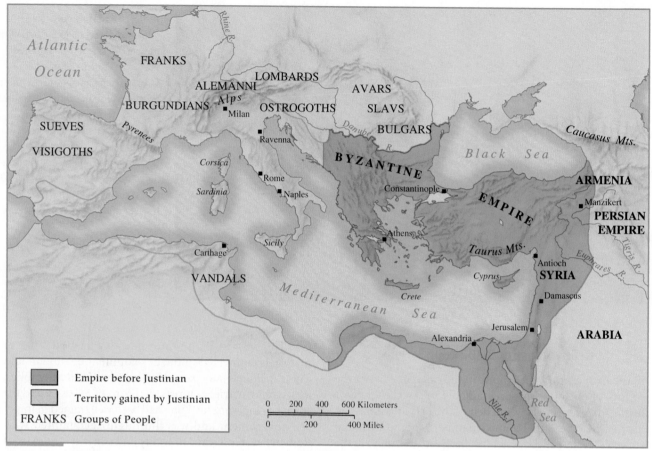

**MAP 7.5** **The Byzantine Empire in the Time of Justinian.** The Byzantine emperor Justinian briefly restored much of the Mediterranean portion of the old Roman Empire. His general Belisarius quickly conquered the Vandals in North Africa but wrested Italy from the Ostrogoths only after a long and devastating struggle. ⚡ Examine Map 6.1. What former Roman territories lay outside Justinian's control?

🌐 **View an animated version of this map or related maps at** http://history.wadsworth.com/spielvogel06/

of Justinian. Procopius served as secretary to the great general Belisarius and accompanied him on his wars on behalf of Justinian. Procopius' best historical work, the *Wars,* is a firsthand account of Justinian's wars of reconquest in the western Mediterranean and his wars against the Persians in the east. Deliberately modeled after the work of his hero, the Greek historian Thucydides (see Chapter 3), Procopius' narrative features vivid descriptions of battle scenes, clear judgment, and noteworthy objectivity.

Procopius also wrote a work that many historians consider mostly scandalous gossip, his infamous *Secret History.* At the beginning of this work, Procopius informed his readers that "what I shall write now follows a different plan, supplementing the previous formal chronicle with a disclosure of what really happened throughout the Roman Empire."[17] What he revealed constituted a scathing attack on Justinian and his wife Theodora for their alleged misdeeds.

**The Empress Theodora** Theodora was the daughter of the "keeper of bears" for the games at Constantinople, who died when she was a child. Theodora followed in her mother's footsteps by becoming an actress, which at that time was considered a lowborn activity. Often actresses also worked as prostitutes, and Theodora was no exception. At the age of twenty-five, she met Justinian, who was forty. His father, the Emperor Justin, had to change the law to allow an aristocratic senator to marry a woman who had been an actress. After his father died in 527, Justinian became emperor and Theodora empress, a remarkable achievement for a woman from the lower classes.

Justinian and Theodora were close and loving companions. She also influenced her husband in both church and state affairs. A strong-willed and intelligent woman, she proved especially valuable in 532, when the two factions of charioteer supporters in Constantinople joined forces and rioted against the emperor. The riots soon became a revolt as the rioters burned and looted the center of the city, shouting "*Nika!*" ("win"), a word normally used to cheer on their favorite charioteer teams. Justinian seemed ready to flee, but Theodora strengthened his resolve by saying, "My opinion then is that the present time, above all others, is inopportune for flight, even though it bring safety. . . . For one who has been emperor it is unendurable to be a fugitive, . . . and may I not live that day on which those who

**Theodora and Attendants.** This mosaic, located on the south wall of the apse of the Church of San Vitale (Justinian is on the north wall), depicts Theodora and her attendants. Her presence on the wall of this church indicates the important role she played in the Byzantine state. At the bottom of her robe is a scene of the three Wise Men, an indication that Theodora was special enough to have belonged in the company of the three kings who visited the newborn Jesus.

meet me shall not address me as mistress."[18] Justinian resolved to fight. Many of the protesters were killed, and the so-called Nika Revolt was ended.

**The Emperor's Building Program** After riots destroyed much of Constantinople, Justinian rebuilt the city and gave it the appearance it would keep for almost a thousand years (see Map 7.6). Earlier, Emperor Theodosius II (408–450) had constructed an enormous defensive wall to protect the city on its land side. The city was dominated by an immense palace complex, a huge arena known as the Hippodrome, and hundreds of churches. No residential district was particularly fashionable; palaces, tenements, and slums ranged alongside one another. Justinian added many new

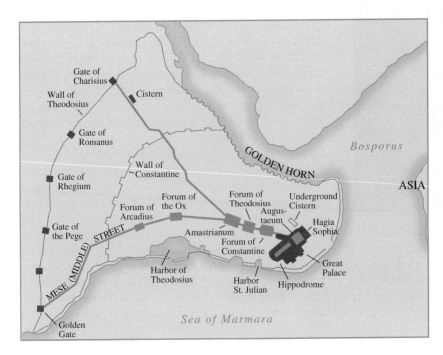

**MAP 7.6 Constantinople.** Constantinople was the largest European city, and until the twelfth century, it was the nexus of trade between east and west. Emperor Justinian oversaw a massive building program that produced important architectural monuments such as Hagia Sophia. ❓ What natural and human-built aspects of the city helped protect it from invasion? 🖰 **View an animated version of this map or related maps at** http://history .wadsworth.com/spielvogel06/

buildings. His public works projects included roads, bridges, walls, public baths, law courts, and colossal underground reservoirs to hold the city's water supply. He also built hospitals, schools, monasteries, and churches. Churches were his special passion, and in Constantinople alone he built or rebuilt thirty-four of them. His greatest achievement was the famous Hagia Sophia, the Church of the Holy Wisdom.

Completed in 537, Hagia Sophia was designed by a Greek architect who departed radically from the simple, flat-roofed basilica of Western architecture. The center of Hagia Sophia consisted of four huge piers crowned by an enormous dome, which seemed to be floating in space. This effect was emphasized by Procopius, the court historian, who, at Justinian's request, wrote a treatise on the emperor's building projects: "From the lightness of the building, it does not appear to rest upon a solid foundation, but to cover the place beneath as though it were suspended from heaven by the fabled golden chain." In part, this impression was created by putting forty-two windows around the base of the dome, which allowed an incredible play of light within the cathedral. Light served to remind the worshipers of God; as Procopius commented:

> Whoever enters there to worship perceives at once that it is not by any human strength or skill, but by the favor of God that this work has been perfected; his mind rises sublime to commune with God, feeling that He cannot be far off, but must especially love to dwell in the place which He has chosen; and this takes place not only when a man sees it for the first time, but it always makes the same impression upon him, as though he had never beheld it before.[19]

As darkness is illumined by invisible light, so too it was believed the world is illumined by invisible spirit.

The royal palace complex, Hagia Sophia, and the Hippodrome were the three greatest buildings in Constantinople. This last was a huge amphitheater, constructed of brick covered by marble, holding as many as sixty thousand spectators. Although gladiator fights were held there, the main events were the chariot races; twenty-four would usually be presented in one day. The citizens of Constantinople were passionate fans of chariot racing. Successful charioteers were acclaimed as heroes and honored with public statues. Crowds in the Hippodrome also took on political significance. Being a member of the two chief factions of charioteers—the Blues or the Greens—was the only real outlet for political expression. Even emperors had to be aware of their demands and attitudes: the loss of a race in the Hippodrome frequently resulted in bloody riots, and rioting could threaten the emperor's power.

**Life in Constantinople**   With a population estimated in the hundreds of thousands, Constantinople was the largest city in Europe during the Middle Ages. It viewed itself as the center of an empire and a special Christian city.

Until the twelfth century, Constantinople was Europe's greatest commercial center. The city was the chief entrepôt for the exchange of products between west and east. Highly desired in Europe were the products of the east: silk from China, spices from Southeast Asia and India, jewelry and ivory from India (the latter used by artisans for church items), wheat and furs from southern Russia, and flax and honey from the Balkans. Many of these eastern goods were then shipped to the Mediterranean area and northern Europe. Despite the Germanic incursions, European trade did not entirely end.

Moreover, imported raw materials were used in Constantinople for local industries. During Justinian's reign, two Christian monks smuggled silkworms from China to begin a silk industry. The state had a monopoly on the production of silk cloth, and the workshops themselves were housed in Constantinople's royal palace complex. European demand for silk cloth made it the city's most lucrative product. It is interesting to note that the upper classes, including emperors and empresses, were not discouraged from making money through trade and manufacturing. Indeed, one empress even manufactured perfumes in her bedroom.

© Digital Vision/Getty Images

**Interior of Hagia Sophia.** This view of the interior of the Church of the Holy Wisdom, constructed under Justinian by Anthemius of Tralles and Isidore of Milan, gives an idea of how the windows around the base of the dome produced a special play of light within the cathedral. The pulpits and plaques bearing inscriptions from the Qur'an were introduced when the Turks converted this church to a mosque in the fifteenth century.

## From Eastern Roman to Byzantine Empire

Justinian's accomplishments had been spectacular, but when he died, he left the Eastern Roman Empire with serious problems: too much distant territory to protect, an empty treasury, a smaller population after the plague, and renewed threats to the frontiers. In the first half of the seventh century, during the reign of Heraclius (610–641), the empire faced attacks from the Persians to the east and the Slavs to the north.

The empire was left exhausted by these struggles. In the midst of them, it had developed a new system of defense by creating a new administrative unit, the *theme,* which combined civilian and military offices in the hands of the same person. Thus the civil governor was also the military leader of the area. Although this innovation helped the empire survive, it also fostered an increased militarization of the empire. By the mid-seventh century, it had become apparent that a restored Mediterranean empire was simply beyond the resources of the Eastern Empire, which now increasingly turned its back on the Latin west. A renewed series of external threats in the second half of the seventh century strengthened this development.

The most serious challenge to the Eastern Empire was the rise of Islam, which unified the Arab tribes and created a powerful new force that swept through the east (see "The Rise of Islam" later in this chapter). The defeat of an eastern Roman army at Yarmuk in 636 meant the loss of the provinces of Syria and Palestine. The Arabs also moved into the old Persian Empire and conquered it. An Arab attempt to besiege Constantinople failed, in large part due to the use of Greek fire against the Arab fleets. Greek fire was a petroleum-based compound containing quicklime and sulfur. Because it would burn under water, the Byzantines created the equivalent of modern flamethrowers by using tubes to blow Greek fire onto wooden ships, with frightening effect. Arabs and eastern Roman forces now faced each other along a frontier in southern Asia Minor.

Problems also arose along the northern frontier, especially in the Balkans, where an Asiatic people known as the Bulgars had arrived earlier in the sixth century. In 679, the Bulgars defeated the eastern Roman forces and took possession of the lower Danube valley, setting up a strong Bulgarian kingdom.

By the beginning of the eighth century, the Eastern Roman Empire was greatly diminished in size, consisting only of the eastern Balkans and Asia Minor. It was now an eastern Mediterranean state. These external challenges had important internal repercussions as well. By the eighth century, the Eastern Roman Empire had been transformed into what historians call the Byzantine Empire, a civilization with its own unique character that would last until 1453

| | |
| --- | --- |
| Protective walls of Theodosius II | 408–450 |
| Justinian codifies Roman law | 529–533 |
| Reconquest of Italy by the Byzantines | 535–552 |
| Completion of Hagia Sophia | 537 |
| Attacks on the empire in reign of Heraclius | 610–641 |
| Arab defeat of Byzantines at Yarmuk | 636 |
| Defeat by the Bulgars; losses in the Balkans | 679 |

(Constantinople was built on the site of an older city named Byzantium—hence the term *Byzantine*).

**The Byzantine Empire in the Eighth Century**  The Byzantine Empire was a Greek state. Justinian's *Corpus Iuris Civilis* had been the last official work published in Latin. Increasingly, Latin fell into disuse as Greek became not only the common language of the Byzantine Empire but its official language as well.

The Byzantine Empire was also a Christian state, built on a faith in Jesus that was shared in a profound way by almost all its citizens. An enormous amount of artistic talent was poured into the construction of churches, church ceremonies, and church decoration. Spiritual principles deeply permeated Byzantine art. The importance of religion to the Byzantines explains why theological disputes took on an exaggerated form. The most famous of these disputes, the so-called iconoclastic controversy, threatened the stability of the empire in the first half of the eighth century.

Beginning in the sixth century, the use of religious images, especially in the form of icons or pictures of sacred figures, became so widespread that charges of idolatry, the worship of images, began to be heard. The use of images or icons had been justified by the argument that icons were not worshiped but were simply used to help illiterate people understand their religion. This argument failed to stop the **iconoclasts,** as the opponents of icons were called. Beginning in 730, the Byzantine emperor Leo III (717–741) outlawed the use of icons. Strong resistance ensued, especially from monks. Leo also used the iconoclastic controversy to add to the prestige of the patriarch of Constantinople, the highest church official in the east and second in dignity only to the bishop of Rome. The Roman popes were opposed to the iconoclastic edicts, and their opposition created considerable dissension between the popes and the Byzantine emperors. Late in the eighth century, the Byzantine rulers reversed their stand on the use of images, but not before considerable damage had been

**The Byzantine Empire, c. 750**

done to the unity of the Christian church. Although the final separation between Roman Catholicism and Greek Orthodoxy (as the Christian church in the Byzantine Empire was called) did not occur until 1054, the iconoclastic controversy was important in moving both sides in that direction.

The emperor occupied a crucial position in the Byzantine state. Portrayed as chosen by God, the Byzantine emperor was crowned in sacred ceremonies, and his subjects were expected to prostrate themselves in his presence. His power was considered absolute and was limited in practice only by deposition or assassination. Because the emperor appointed the patriarch, he also exercised control over both church and state. The Byzantines believed that God had commanded their state to preserve the true faith—Orthodox Christianity. Emperor, clergy, and civic officials were all bound together in service to this ideal. It can be said that spiritual values truly held the Byzantine state together.

By 750, it was apparent that two of Rome's heirs, the Germanic kingdoms and the Byzantine Empire, were moving in different directions. Nevertheless, Byzantine influence on the Western world was significant. The images of a Roman imperial state that continued to haunt the west lived on in Byzantium. The legal system of the west came to owe much to Justinian's codification of Roman law. In addition, the Byzantine Empire served in part as a buffer state, protecting the west for a long time from incursions from the east. Although the Byzantine Empire would continue to influence the west until its demise in 1453, it went its own unique way. One of its bitterest enemies was the new power known as Islam.

# The Rise of Islam

Like the Hebrews and the Assyrians, the Arabs were a Semitic-speaking people of the Near East with a long history. In Roman times, the Arabian peninsula came to be dominated by Bedouin nomads who moved constantly to find water and food for their animals. Although some Arabs prospered from trading activities, especially in the north, the majority of the Arabs consisted of poor Bedouins, whose tribes were known for their independence, their warlike qualities, and their dislike of urban-dwelling Arabs.

Although these early Arabs were polytheistic, there was a supreme God named Allah (Arabic for "God") who ruled over the other gods. There was no priesthood; all members of the tribe were involved in the practice of the faith. Allah was symbolized by a sacred stone, and each tribe had its own stone. All tribes, however, worshiped a massive black meteorite—the Black Stone, which had been placed in a central shrine called the *Ka'ba* in the city of Mecca.

In the fifth and sixth centuries A.D., the Arabian peninsula took on new importance. As a result of political disorder in Mesopotamia and Egypt, the usual trade routes in the region began to change. A new trade route—from the Mediterranean through Mecca to Yemen and then by ship across the Arabian Sea and the Indian Ocean—became more popular, and communities in that part of the Arabian peninsula, such as Mecca, began to prosper from this caravan trade. As a result, tensions arose between the Bedouins in the desert and the increasingly wealthy merchant classes in the towns. Into this intense world came Muhammad.

## Muhammad

Born in Mecca to a merchant family, Muhammad (c. 570–632) was orphaned at the age of five. He grew up to become a caravan manager and eventually married a rich widow who was also his employer. In his middle years, he began to experience visions that he believed were inspired by Allah. Muhammad believed that although Allah had already revealed himself in part through Moses and Jesus—and thus through the Hebrew and Christian traditions—the final revelations were now being given to him. Out of these revelations, which were eventually written down, came the Qur'an or Koran, which contained the guidelines by which followers of Allah were to live. Muhammad's teachings formed the basis for the religion known as Islam, which means "submission to the will of Allah." Allah was the all-powerful being who had created the universe and everything in it. Humans must subject themselves to Allah if they wished to achieve everlasting life. His followers were called Muslims, meaning "practitioners of Islam."

After receiving the revelations, Muhammad set out to convince the people of Mecca that the revelations were true. At first, many thought he was insane, and others feared that his attacks on the corrupt society around him would upset the established social and political order. Discouraged by the failure of the Meccans to accept his message, in 622 Muhammad and some of his closest supporters left the city and moved north to the rival city of Yathrib, later renamed Medina ("city of the Prophet"). The year of the journey to Medina, known in history as the *Hegira* ("departure"), became year 1 in the official calendar of Islam.

Muhammad, who had been invited to the town by a number of prominent residents, soon began to win support from people in Medina as well as from members of Bedouin tribes in the surrounding countryside. From these groups, he formed the first Muslim community. Muslims saw no separation between political and religious authority; submission to the will of Allah meant

**Arabia in the Time of Muhammad**

submission to his Prophet, Muhammad. Muhammad soon became both a religious and a political leader. His political and military skills enabled him to put together a reliable military force, with which he returned to Mecca in 630, conquering the city and converting the townspeople to the new faith. From Mecca, Muhammad's ideas spread quickly across the Arabian peninsula and within a relatively short time had resulted in both the religious and the political unification of Arab society.

## The Teachings of Islam

At the heart of Islam was its sacred book, the Qur'an, with its basic message that there is no God but Allah and Muhammad is his Prophet. Essentially, the Qur'an contains Muhammad's revelations of a heavenly book written down by secretaries. Consisting of 114 chapters, the Qur'an recorded the beliefs of the Muslims and served as their code of ethics and law.

Islam was a direct and simple faith, emphasizing the need to obey the will of Allah. This meant following a basic ethical code consisting of the Five Pillars of Islam: belief in Allah and Muhammad as his Prophet; standard prayer five times a day and public prayer on Friday at midday to worship Allah; observance of the holy month of Ramadan (the ninth month on the Muslim calendar) by fasting from dawn to sunset; making a pilgrimage (known as the *hajj*) to Mecca in one's lifetime, if possible (see the box on p. 194); and giving alms to the poor and unfortunate. The faithful who observed the law were guaranteed a place in an eternal paradise.

Islam was not just a set of religious beliefs but a way of life as well. After the death of Muhammad, Muslim scholars drew up a law code, called the *Shari'a*, to provide believers with a set of prescriptions to regulate their daily lives. Much of the *Shari'a* was drawn from the Qur'an. Believers'

behavior was subject to strict guidelines. In addition to the Five Pillars, Muslims were forbidden to gamble, to eat pork, to drink alcoholic beverages, and to engage in dishonest behavior. Sexual practices were also strict. Marriages were to be arranged by parents, and contacts between unmarried men and women were discouraged. In accordance with Bedouin custom, males were permitted to have more than one wife, but Muhammad attempted to limit the practice by restricting the number of wives to four.

## The Spread of Islam

The death of Muhammad presented his followers with a dilemma. Although Muhammad had not claimed to be divine, Muslims saw no separation between religious and political authority. Submission to the will of Allah was the same thing as submission to his Prophet, Muhammad. According to the Qur'an: "Whoever obeys the messenger obeys Allah." But Muhammad had never named a successor, and although he had several daughters, he left no sons. In a male-oriented society, who would lead the community of the faithful? Shortly after Muhammad's death, a number of his closest followers selected Abu Bakr, a wealthy merchant who was Muhammad's father-in-law, as **caliph,** or temporal leader, of the Islamic community.

Muhammad and the early caliphs who succeeded him took up the Arab tribal custom of the *razzia* or raid in the struggle against their enemies. Some have called this activity a *jihad,* which they misleadingly interpret as a holy war. *Jihad* actually means "striving in the way of the Lord" to achieve personal betterment, although it can also mean fair, defensive fighting to preserve one's life and one's faith. Arab conquests were not carried out to convert others, since conversion to Islam was purely voluntary. Those who did not convert were required only to submit to Muslim rule and pay taxes.

**Muslims Celebrate the End of Ramadan.** Ramadan is the holy month of Islam during which all Muslims must fast from dawn to sunset. Observance of this holy month is regarded as one of the Five Pillars of the faith. Muhammad instituted the fast during his stay at Medina. It was designed to replace the single Jewish Day of Atonement. This Persian miniature depicts Muslims on horseback celebrating the end of Ramadan.

# THE QUR'AN: THE PILGRIMAGE

*T*HE QUR'AN IS the sacred book of the Muslims, comparable to the Bible in Christianity. This selection from Chapter 22, titled "Pilgrimage," discusses the importance of making a pilgrimage to Mecca, one of the Five Pillars of Islam. The pilgrim's final destination was the Ka'ba at Mecca, containing the Black Stone.

### Qur'an, Chapter 22: "Pilgrimage"

Exhort all men to make the pilgrimage. They will come to you on foot and on the backs of swift camels from every distant quarter; they will come to avail themselves of many a benefit, and to pronounce on the appointed days the name of God over the cattle which He has given them for food. Eat of their flesh, and feed the poor and the unfortunate.

Then let the pilgrims tidy themselves, make their vows, and circle the Ancient House. Such is God's commandment. He that reveres the sacred rites of God shall fare better in the sight of his Lord.

The flesh of cattle is lawful for you, except for that which has been specified before. Guard yourselves against the filth of idols; and avoid the utterance of falsehoods.

Dedicate yourselves to God, and serve none besides Him. The man who serves other deities besides God is like him who falls from heaven and is snatched by the birds or carried away by the wind to some far-off region. Even such is he.

He that reveres the offerings made to God shows the piety of his heart. Your cattle are useful to you in many ways until the time of their slaughter. Then they are offered for sacrifice at the Ancient House.

For every community We have ordained a ritual, that they may pronounce the name of God over the cattle which He has given them for food. Your God is one God; to Him surrender yourselves. Give good news to the humble, whose hearts are filled with awe at the mention of God; who endure adversity with fortitude, attend to their prayers, and give in alms from what We gave them.

We have made the camels a part of God's rites. They are of much use to you. Pronounce over them the name of God as you draw them up in line and slaughter them; and when they have fallen to the ground eat of their flesh and feed the uncomplaining beggar and the demanding supplicant. Thus have We subjected them to your service, so that you may give thanks.

Their flesh and blood does not reach God; it is your piety that reaches Him. Thus has He subjected them to your service, so that you may give glory to God for guiding you.

Give good news to the righteous. God will ward off evil from true believers. God does not love the treacherous and the thankless.

---

Once the Arabs had become unified under Abu Bakr, they began to direct the energy they had once expended against each other outward against neighboring peoples. The Byzantines and the Persians were the first to feel the strength of the newly united Arabs. At Yarmuk in 636, the Muslims defeated the Byzantine army, and by 640, they had taken possession of the province of Syria (see Map 7.7). To the east, the Arabs defeated Persian forces in 637 and then went on to conquer the entire Persian Empire by 650. In the meantime, Egypt and other areas of northern Africa had been added to the new Muslim empire. Led by a series of brilliant generals, the Arabs had put together a large and highly motivated army, whose valor was enhanced by the belief that Muslim warriors were guaranteed a place in paradise if they died in battle.

Early caliphs, ruling from Medina, organized their newly conquered territories into taxpaying provinces. By the mid-seventh century, problems arose again over the succession to the Prophet until Ali, Muhammad's son-in-law, was assassinated and the general Muawiya, the governor of Syria and one of Ali's chief rivals, became caliph in 661. Muawiya was known for one outstanding virtue: he used force only when necessary. As he said, "I never use my sword when my whip will do, nor my whip when my tongue will do."[20] Muawiya moved quickly to make the caliphate hereditary in his own family, thus establishing the Umayyad dynasty. As one of their first actions, the Umayyads moved the capital of the Muslim empire from Medina to Damascus in Syria. This internal dissension over the caliphate created a split in Islam between the Shi'ites, or those who accepted only the descendants of Ali, Muhammad's son-in-law, as the true rulers, and the Sunnites, who claimed that the descendants of the Umayyads were the true caliphs. This seventh-century split in Islam has lasted until the present day.

Internal dissension did not stop the expansion of Islam, however. At the beginning of the eighth century, new attacks were made at both the western and eastern ends of the Mediterranean. After sweeping across North Africa, the Muslims crossed the Strait of Gibraltar and moved into Spain around 710. The Visigothic kingdom collapsed, and by 725, most of Spain had become a Muslim state with its center at Córdoba. In 732, a Muslim army, making a foray into southern France, was defeated at the Battle of Tours near Poitiers. Muslim expansion in Europe came to a halt.

Meanwhile, in 717, another Muslim force had launched a naval attack on Constantinople with the hope of destroying the Byzantine Empire. In the spring of 718, the Byzantines destroyed the Muslim fleet and saved the Byzantine Empire and indirectly Christian Europe, since the fall of Constantinople would no doubt have opened the door to Muslim invasion of eastern Europe. The Byzantine Empire and Islam now established an uneasy frontier in southern Asia Minor.

The Arab advance had finally come to an end, but not before the southern and eastern Mediterranean parts of the old Roman Empire had been conquered. Islam had truly become heir to much of the old Roman Empire. The Umayyad dynasty at Damascus now ruled an enormous empire. While expansion had conveyed untold wealth and new ethnic groups into the fold of Islam, it also brought contact with Byzantine and Persian civilization. As a result, the new Arab empire would be influenced by Greek culture as well as the older civilizations of the ancient Near East. The children of the conquerors would be educated in new ways and produce a brilliant culture that would eventually influence western Europe intellectually.

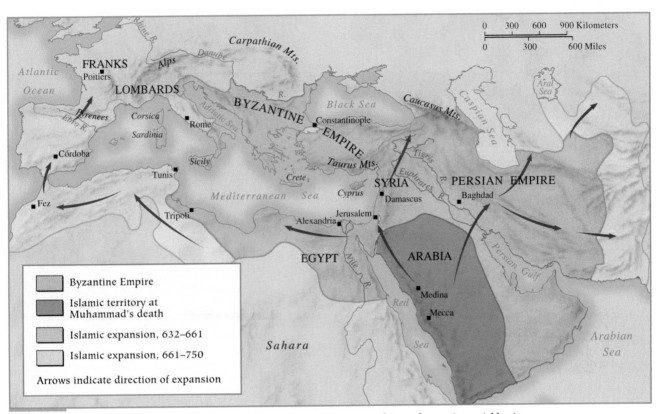

MAP 7.7 **The Expansion of Islam.** Muhammad, the prophet of Islam, engaged in warfare against neighboring tribes. Militaristic expansion continued with great zeal under the Prophet's successors. Islamic rule spread rapidly in the decades after Muhammad's death, stopped finally by the Byzantine Empire and the Franks. ❓ Why was the continuance of the Byzantine Empire a key factor in stopping the spread of Islam into Europe?

🌐 **View an animated version of this map or related maps at** http://history.wadsworth.com/spielvogel06/

## CONCLUSION

𝒯HE PERIOD FROM the mid-third century to the mid-eighth century was both chaotic and creative. During late antiquity, the Roman world of the Mediterranean was gradually transformed. Three new entities fell heir to Roman civilization: the Germanic kingdoms of western Europe, the Byzantine Empire, and the world of Islam.

In the west, Roman elements combined with German and Celtic influences; in the east, Greek and eastern elements of late antiquity were of more consequence. Although the Germanic kingdoms of the west and the Byzantine civilization of the east came to share a common bond in Christianity, it proved incapable of keeping them in harmony politically as the two civilizations continued to move apart. Christianity, however, remained a dominant influence in both civilizations and in the west was especially important as a civilizing agent that brought pagan peoples into the new European civilization that was slowly being born. The rise of Islam, Rome's third heir, resulted in the loss of the southern and eastern Mediterranean portions of the old Roman Empire to a religious power that was neither Roman nor Christian. The new Islamic empire forced Europe proper back on itself, and slowly, a new civilization emerged that became the heart of what we know as Western civilization.

## NOTES

1. Naphtali Lewis and Meyers Reinhold, eds., *Roman Civilization,* vol. 2 (New York, 1955), p. 191.
2. "The Creed of Nicaea," in Henry Bettenson, ed., *Documents of the Christian Church* (London, 1963), p. 35.
3. Charles C. Mierow, trans., *The Gothic History of Jordanes* (Princeton, N.J., 1915), pp. 88–89.
4. Quoted in Averil Cameron, *The Mediterranean World in Late Antiquity* (London, 1993), p. 37.
5. Ernest F. Henderson, *Selected Historical Documents of the Middle Ages* (London, 1892), p. 182.
6. Ibid., p. 181.
7. Tertullian, "The Prescriptions Against the Heretics," in *The Library of Christian Classics,* vol. 5, *Early Latin Theology,* ed. and trans. S. L. Greenslade (Philadelphia, 1956), p. 36.
8. Anne Fremantle, ed., *A Treasury of Early Christianity* (New York, 1953), p. 91.
9. Matthew 16:15–19.
10. R. C. Petry, ed., *A History of Christianity: Readings in the History of Early and Medieval Christianity* (Englewood Cliffs, N.J., 1962), p. 70.
11. Brian Pullan, ed., *Sources for the History of Medieval Europe* (Oxford, 1966), p. 46.

## TIMELINE

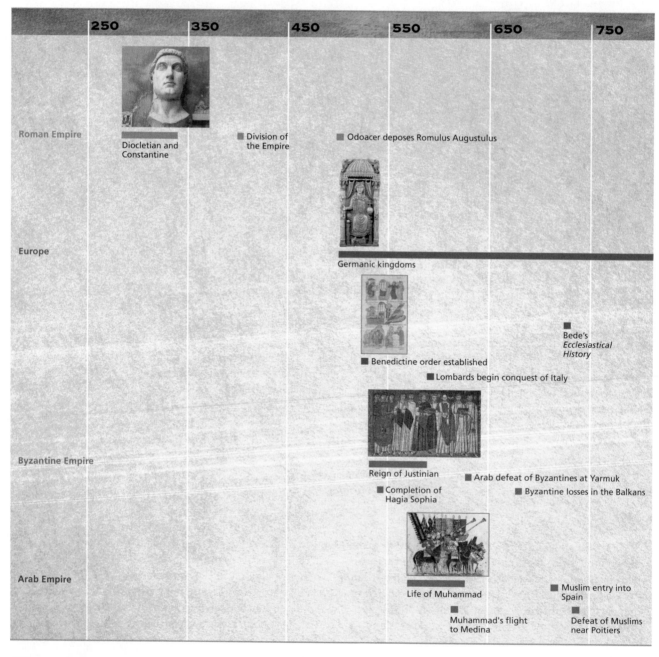

250  350  450  550  650  750

Roman Empire

Diocletian and Constantine

Division of the Empire

Odoacer deposes Romulus Augustulus

Europe

Germanic kingdoms

Bede's *Ecclesiastical History*

Benedictine order established

Lombards begin conquest of Italy

Byzantine Empire

Reign of Justinian

Completion of Hagia Sophia

Arab defeat of Byzantines at Yarmuk

Byzantine losses in the Balkans

Arab Empire

Life of Muhammad

Muhammad's flight to Medina

Muslim entry into Spain

Defeat of Muslims near Poitiers

12. Quoted in Sidney Painter and Brian Tierney, *Western Europe in the Middle Ages, 300–1475* (New York, 1983), p. 106.

13. Mark 10:21.

14. Norman F. Cantor, ed., *The Medieval World, 300–1300* (New York, 1963), pp. 104, 101, 108, 103.

15. Bede, *A History of the English Church and People,* trans. Leo Sherley-Price (Harmondsworth, England, 1968), pp. 86–87.

16. Quoted in Peter Brown, *The Rise of Western Christendom: Triumph and Adversity,* A.D. *200–1000* (Oxford, 1997), p. 98.

17. Procopius, *Secret History,* trans. Richard Atwater (Ann Arbor, Mich., 1963), p. 3.

18. H. B. Dewing, trans., *Procopius,* vol. 1 (Cambridge, Mass., 1914), p. 48.

19. Procopius, *Buildings of Justinian* (London, 1897), pp. 9, 6–7, 11.

20. Quoted in Arthur Goldschmidt Jr., *A Concise History of the Middle East,* 4th ed. (Boulder, Colo., 1991), p. 56.

## SUGGESTIONS FOR FURTHER READING

For good introductions to late antiquity, see **P. Brown, *The World of Late Antiquity,*** A.D. *150–750* (New York, 1989); **J. Moorhead, *The Roman Empire Divided, 400–700*** (London, 2001); **A. Cameron, *The Mediterranean World in Late Antiquity,*** A.D. *395–600* (London, 1993); and **R. Collins, *Early Medieval Europe, 300–1000*** (New York, 1991). There is an excellent collection of essays and encyclopedic entries in **G. W. Bowersock, P. Brown, and O. Grabar, *Late Antiquity: A Guide to the Postclassical World*** (Cambridge, Mass., 1999).

On the Late Roman Empire, see **A. Cameron, *The Later Roman Empire*** (Cambridge, Mass., 1993). On the fourth century, see **M. Grant, *Constantine the Great: The Man and His Times*** (New York, 1993), and **T. D. Barnes, *The New Empire of Diocletian and Constantine*** (Cambridge, Mass., 1982). Studies analyzing the aristocratic circles, the barbarian invasions, and the military problem include **E. A. Thompson, *Romans and Barbarians*** (Madison, Wis., 1982); **A. Ferrill, *The Fall of the Roman Empire: The Military Explanation*** (London, 1986); and **J. M. O'Flynn, *Generalissimos of the Western Roman Empire*** (Edmonton, Canada, 1983).

For surveys of the German tribes and their migrations, see **L. Musset, *The German Invasions*** (University Park, Pa., 1975); **T. S. Burns, *A History of the Ostrogoths*** (Bloomington, Ind., 1984); **F. P. Heather, *Goths and Romans*** (Oxford, 1991); **E. James, *The Franks*** (Oxford, 1988); **H. Wolfram, *The Goths, trans.* T. J. Dunlop** (Berkeley, Calif., 1988); and **I. N. Wood, *Merovingian Kingdoms*** (London, 1994). On the relationship between the Romans and the Germans, see **T. S. Burns, *Rome and the Barbarians, 100*** B.C.–A.D. *400* (Baltimore, 2003).

For a superb introduction to early Christianity, see **P. Brown, *The Rise of Western Christendom: Triumph and Adversity,*** A.D. *200–1000, 2d ed.* (Oxford, 2002). On Saints Augustine and Jerome, see **H. Chadwick, *Augustine*** (Oxford, 1986), and **J. N. D. Kelly, *Saint Jerome*** (London, 1975). For a good account of early monasticism, see **C. H. Lawrence, *Medieval Monasticism,* 2d ed.** (London, 1989). On Saint Benedict, see **O. Chadwick, *The Making of the Benedictine Ideal*** (London, 1981). For women in monastic life, see **S. F. Wemple, *Women in Frankish Society: Marriage and the Cloister, 500–900*** (Philadelphia, 1981). On women in general, see **G. Clark, *Women in Late Antiquity: Pagan and Christian Life-Styles*** (Oxford, 1993).

A brief survey of the development of the papacy can be found in **G. Barraclough, *The Medieval Papacy*** (New York, 1968). **J. Richards, *The Popes and the Papacy in the Early Middle Ages, 476–752*** (Boston, 1979), is a more detailed study of the early papacy. On Pope Gregory the Great, see **C. Straw, *Gregory the Great: Perfection in Imperfection*** (Berkeley, Calif., 1988). On Irish monasticism, see **L. M. Bitel, *Isle of the Saints: Monastic Settlement and Christian Community in Early Ireland*** (Ithaca, N.Y., 1990).

Brief but good introductions to Byzantine history can be found in **J. Haldon, *Byzantium: A History*** (Charleston, S.C., 2000), and **W. Treadgold, *A Concise History of Byzantium*** (London, 2001). The best single political history is **G. Ostrogorsky, *A History of the Byzantine State,* 2d ed.** (New Brunswick, N.J., 1968). For a comprehensive survey of the Byzantine Empire, see **W. Treadgold, *A History of the Byzantine State and Society*** (Stanford, Calif., 1997). See also **C. Mango, ed., *The Oxford History of Byzantium*** (Oxford, 2002). On Justinian, see **J. Moorhead, *Justinian*** (London, 1995), and **J. A. S. Evans, *The Age of Justinian*** (New York, 1996). On Constantinople, see **D. T. Rice, *Constantinople: From Byzantium to Istanbul*** (New York, 1965). The role of the Christian church is discussed in **J. Hussey, *The Orthodox Church in the Byzantine Empire*** (Oxford, 1986).

Good brief surveys of the Islamic Middle East include **A. Goldschmidt Jr. , *A Concise History of the Middle East,* 7th ed.** (Boulder, Colo., 2001), and **S. N. Fisher and W. Ochsenwald, *The Middle East: A History*** (New York, 2003). On the rise of Islam, see **F. E. Peters, *Muhammad and the Origins of Islam*** (Albany, N.Y., 1994); **M. Lings, *Muhammad: His Life Based on the Earliest Sources*** (New York, 1983); **K. Armstrong, *Muhammad: A Biography of the Prophet*** (New York, 1992); and **F. Donner, *The Early Islamic Conquests*** (Princeton, N.J., 1980).

## History  Now™

Enter *HistoryNow* using the access card that is available for *Western Civilization. HistoryNow* will assist you in understanding the content in this chapter with lesson plans generated for your needs. In addition, you can read the following documents, and many more, online:

Saint Paul's First Epistle to the Corinthians

Pliny the Younger, Letter 97

Plotinus, excerpts from the first book of the Six Enneads

## INFOTRAC SEARCH TERMS

 For additional reading, go to InfoTrac College Edition, your online research library at http://infotrac.thomsonlearning.com

| Key Term Search | Subject Guide Search |
| --- | --- |
| early Christianity | Byzantium |
| Augustine | |

## WESTERN CIVILIZATION RESOURCES

Visit the *Western Civilization* Companion Web site for resources specific to this book:

http://history.wadsworth.com/spielvogel06/

For a variety of tools to help you succeed in this course, visit the Western Civilization Resource Center at

http://history.wadsworth.com/western/

Included are quizzes; images; documents; interactive simulations; maps and timelines; movie explorations; and a wealth of other sources.

C H A P T E R

# 8

# EUROPEAN CIVILIZATION
# IN THE EARLY MIDDLE AGES,
# 750–1000

## CHAPTER OUTLINE AND FOCUS QUESTIONS

### Europeans and the Environment

● What were the main features of the physical environment of the Early Middle Ages?

### The World of the Carolingians

● In what ways did the political, intellectual, and daily life in the Carolingian Empire represent a fusion of Gallo-Roman, Germanic, and Christian practices?

### Disintegration of the Carolingian Empire

● What impact did the Vikings have on the history and culture of medieval Europe?

### The Emerging World of Lords and Vassals

● What was fief-holding, and how was it related to manorialism?

### The Zenith of Byzantine Civilization

● What were the chief developments in the Byzantine Empire between 750 and 1000?

### The Slavic Peoples of Central and Eastern Europe

● What patterns of development occurred in central and eastern Europe as a result of the Slavic peoples?

### The Expansion of Islam

● What were the chief developments in the Islamic world between 750 and 1000?

## CRITICAL THINKING

● Why can it be said that the Islamic civilization was superior to the civilization of western Europe in the ninth and tenth centuries?

*A medieval French manuscript illustration of the coronation of Charlemagne by Pope Leo III*

IN 800, CHARLEMAGNE, the king of the Franks, journeyed to Rome to help Pope Leo III, who was barely clinging to power in the face of rebellious Romans. On Christmas Day, Charlemagne and his family, attended by Romans, Franks, and visitors from the Byzantine Empire, crowded into Saint Peter's Basilica to hear Mass. Quite unexpectedly, according to a Frankish writer, "as the king rose from praying before the tomb of the blessed apostle Peter, Pope Leo placed a golden crown on his head." In keeping with ancient tradition, the people in the church shouted, "Long life and victory to Charles Augustus, crowned by God the great and pacific Emperor of the Romans." Seemingly, the Roman Empire in the west had been reborn, and Charles had become the first western emperor since 476. But this "Roman emperor" was actually a German king, and he had been crowned by the head of the western Christian church. In truth, the coronation of Charlemagne was a sign not of the rebirth of the Roman Empire but of the emergence of a new European civilization.

By the year of Charlemagne's coronation, the contours of this new European civilization were beginning to emerge in western Europe. Increasingly,

Europe would become the focus and center of Western civilization. Building on a fusion of Germanic, Greco-Roman, and Christian elements, the medieval European world first became visible in the Carolingian Empire of Charlemagne. The agrarian foundations of the eighth and ninth centuries proved inadequate to maintain a large monarchical system, however, and a new political and military order based on the decentralization of political power subsequently evolved to become an integral part of the political world of the Middle Ages.

European civilization began on a shaky and uncertain foundation, however. In the ninth century, Vikings, Magyars, and Muslims posed threats that could easily have stifled the new society. But the Vikings and Magyars were assimilated, and recovery slowly began to set in. By 1000, European civilization was ready to embark on a period of dazzling vitality and expansion.

# Europeans and the Environment

The number of people in early medieval Europe is a matter of considerable uncertainty. In all probability, the population of the eighth century had still not recovered from the losses caused by the plagues of the sixth and seventh centuries. Historians generally believe that in the Early Middle Ages, Europe was a sparsely populated landscape dotted with villages and clusters of villages of farmers and warriors. Although rivers, such as the Loire, Seine, Rhine, Elbe, and Oder, served as major arteries of communication, villages were still separated from one another by forests, swamps, and mountain ridges. Forests, which provided building and heating materials as well as game, covered the European landscape. In fact, it has been estimated that less than 10 percent of the land was cultivated, a figure so small that some economic historians believe that Europe had difficulty feeding even its modest population. Thus hunting and fishing were necessary to supplement the European diet.

## Farming

The cultivation of new land proved especially difficult in the Early Middle Ages. Given the crude implements of the time, it was not easy to clear forests and prepare the ground for planting. Moreover, German tribes had for centuries considered trees sacred and resisted cutting them down to make room for farms. Even conversion to Christianity did not entirely change these attitudes. In addition, the heavy soils of northern Europe were not easily plowed. Agricultural methods also worked against significant crop yields. Land was allowed to lie fallow (unplanted) every other year to regain its fertility, but even so it produced low yields. Evidence indicates that Frankish estates yielded incredibly low ratios of two measures of grain to one measure of seed.

## The Climate

Climatic patterns show that European weather began to improve around 700 after several centuries of wetter and colder conditions. Nevertheless, natural disasters were always a threat, especially since the low yields meant that little surplus could be saved for bad times. Drought or too much rain could mean meager harvests, famine, and dietary deficiencies that made people susceptible to a wide range of diseases. This was a period of low life expectancy. One study of Hungarian graves found that of every five skeletons, one was a child below the age of one, and two were children between one and fourteen; more than one in five was a woman below the age of twenty. Overall, then, the picture of early medieval Europe is of a relatively small population subsisting on the basis of a limited agricultural economy and leading, in most cases, a precarious existence.

# The World of the Carolingians

By the eighth century, the Merovingian dynasty was losing its control of the Frankish lands. Charles Martel, the Carolingian mayor of the palace of Austrasia, became the virtual ruler of these territories. When Charles Martel died in 741, his son, Pepin, deposed the Merovingians and assumed the kingship of the Frankish state for himself and his family. Pepin's actions, which were approved by the pope, created a new form of Frankish kingship. Pepin (751–768) was crowned king and formally anointed by a representative of the pope with holy oil in imitation of an Old Testament practice. The anointing not only symbolized that the kings had been entrusted with a sacred office but also provides yet another example of how a Germanic institution fused with a Christian practice in the Early Middle Ages.

## Charlemagne and the Carolingian Empire (768–814)

Pepin's death in 768 brought to the throne of the Frankish kingdom his son, a dynamic and powerful ruler known to history as Charles the Great or Charlemagne (*Carolus magnus* in Latin—hence our word *Carolingian*). Charlemagne was a determined and decisive man, intelligent and inquisitive. A fierce warrior, he was also a wise patron of learning and a resolute statesman (see the box on p. 200). He greatly expanded the territory of the Carolingian Empire during his lengthy rule.

**Expansion of the Carolingian Empire**   In the tradition of the Germanic kings, Charlemagne was a determined warrior who undertook fifty-four military campaigns. Even though the Frankish army was relatively small—only eight thousand men gathered each spring for campaigning—supplying it and transporting it to distant areas could still present serious problems. The Frankish army comprised mostly infantry, with some cavalry armed with swords and spears.

# THE ACHIEVEMENTS OF CHARLEMAGNE

*E*INHARD, THE BIOGRAPHER of Charlemagne, was born in the valley of the Main River in Germany about 775. Raised and educated in the monastery of Fulda, an important center of learning, he arrived at the court of Charlemagne in 791 or 792. Although he did not achieve high office under Charlemagne, he served as private secretary to Louis the Pious, Charlemagne's son and successor. Einhard's *Life of Charlemagne,* written between 817 and 830, was modeled on Suetonius' *Lives of the Caesars,* especially his biography of Augustus. In this selection, Einhard discusses some of Charlemagne's acccomplishments.

## Einhard, *Life of Charlemagne*

Such are the wars, most skillfully planned and successfully fought, which this most powerful king waged during the forty-seven years of his reign. He so largely increased the Frank kingdom, which was already great and strong when he received it at his father's hands, that more than double its former territory was added to it. . . . He subdued all the wild and barbarous tribes dwelling in Germany between the Rhine and the Vistula, the Ocean and the Danube, all of which speak very much the same language, but differ widely from one another in customs and dress. . . .

He added to the glory of his reign by gaining the good will of several kings and nations; so close, indeed, was the alliance that he contracted with Alfonso, King of Galicia and Asturias, that the latter, when sending letters or ambassadors to Charles, invariably styled himself his man. . . . The Emperors of Constantinople [the Byzantine emperors] sought friendship and alliance with Charles by several embassies; and even when the Greeks [the Byzantines] suspected him of designing to take the empire from them, because of his assumption of the title Emperor, they made a close alliance with him, that he might have no cause of offense. In fact, the power of the Franks was always viewed with a jealous eye, whence the Greek proverb, "Have the Frank for your friend, but not for your neighbor."

This King, who showed himself so great in extending his empire and subduing foreign nations, and was con-stantly occupied with plans to that end, undertook also very many works calculated to adorn and benefit his kingdom, and brought several of them to completion. Among these, the most deserving of mention are the basilica of the Holy Mother of God at Aix-la-Chapelle, built in the most admirable manner, and a bridge over the Rhine River at Mainz, half a mile long, the breadth of the river at this point. . . . Above all, sacred buildings were the object of his care throughout his whole kingdom; and whenever he found them falling to ruin from age, he commanded the priests and fathers who had charge of them to repair them, and made sure by commissioners that his instructions were obeyed. . . . Thus did Charles defend and increase as well as beautify his kingdom. . . .

He cherished with the greatest fervor and devotion the principles of the Christian religion, which had been instilled into him from infancy. Hence it was that he built the beautiful church at Aix-la-Chapelle, which he adorned with gold and silver and lamps, and with rails and doors of solid brass. He had the columns and marbles for this structure brought from Rome and Ravenna, for he could not find such as were suitable elsewhere. He was a constant worshiper at this church as long as his health permitted, going morning and evening, even after nightfall, besides attending Mass. . . .

He was very forward in caring for the poor, so much so that he not only made a point of giving in his own country and his own kingdom, but when he discovered that there were Christians living in poverty in Syria, Egypt, and Africa, at Jerusalem, Alexandria, and Carthage, he had compassion on their wants, and used to send money over the seas to them. . . . He sent great and countless gifts to the popes, and throughout his whole reign the wish that he had nearest at heart was to reestablish the ancient authority of the city of Rome under his care and by his influence, and to defend and protect the Church of St. Peter, and to beautify and enrich it out of his own store above all other churches.

---

Charlemagne's campaigns took him to many areas of Europe. In 773, he led his army into Italy, crushed the Lombards, and took control of the Lombard state. Although his son was crowned king of Italy, Charlemagne was its real ruler. Four years after his invasion of Italy, Charlemagne and his forces advanced into northern Spain. This campaign proved disappointing; not only did the Basques harass his army as it crossed the Pyrenees on the way home, but they also ambushed and annihilated his rear guard.

Charlemagne was considerably more successful with his eastern campaigns into Germany, especially against the Saxons, who had settled between the Elbe River and the North Sea. As Einhard, Charlemagne's biographer, re-counted it:

No war ever undertaken by the Frank nation was carried on with such persistence and bitterness, or cost so much labor, because the Saxons, like almost all the tribes of Germany, were a fierce people, given to the worship of devils, and hostile to our religion, and did not consider it dishonorable to transgress and violate all law, human and divine.[1]

Charlemagne's insistence that the Saxons convert to Christianity simply fueled their resistance. Not until 804, after eighteen campaigns, was Saxony finally pacified and added to the Carolingian domain.

In southeastern Germany, Charlemagne invaded the land of the Bavarians in 787 and brought them into his empire by the following year, an expansion that brought him into contact with the southern Slavs and the Avars. The

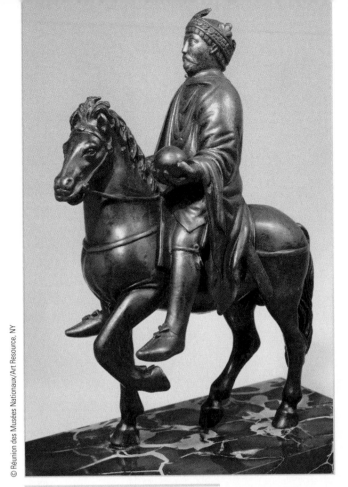

**Bronze Equestrian Statue of Charlemagne.** This small bronze statue is believed to represent the emperor Charles the Great, although some scholars believe it is his grandson, Charles the Bald. The figure dates from the ninth century, but the horse is a sixteenth-century restoration. The attire on the figure accords with Einhard's account of how Charlemagne dressed. The imperial crown rests on his head, and in his left hand he grasps a globe, a symbol of world power and a reminder that the power of the Roman Empire had been renewed.

| CHRONOLOGY | The Carolingian Empire |
| --- | --- |
| Pepin crowned king of the Franks | 751 |
| Reign of Charlemagne | 768–814 |
| Campaign in Italy | 773–774 |
| Campaign in Spain | 778 |
| Conquest of Bavarians | 787–788 |
| Charlemagne crowned emperor | 800 |
| Final conquest of Saxons | 804 |
| Reign of Louis the Pious | 814–840 |
| Treaty of Verdun divides Carolingian Empire | 843 |

representatives in local areas, although in dangerous border districts officials known as margraves (literally, *mark graf,* count of the border district) were used. Counts were members of the nobility who had already existed under the Merovingians. They had come to control public services in their own lands and thus acted as judges, military leaders, and agents of the king. Gradually, as the rule of the Merovingian kings weakened, many counts had simply attached the royal lands and services performed on behalf of the king to their own family possessions.

In an effort to gain greater control over his kingdom, Charlemagne attempted to limit the power of the counts. They were required to serve outside their own family lands and were moved about periodically rather than being permitted to remain in a county for life. By making the offices appointive, Charlemagne tried to prevent the counts' children from automatically inheriting their offices. Moreover, as another check on the counts, Charlemagne instituted the *missi dominici* ("messengers of the lord king"), two men, one lay lord and one church official, who were sent out to local districts to ensure that the counts were executing the king's wishes. The counts also had assistants, but they were members of their households, not part of a bureaucratic office.

The last point is an important reminder that we should not think of Carolingian government in the modern sense of government offices run by officials committed to an impersonal ideal of state service. The Carolingian system was glaringly inefficient. Great distances had to be covered on horseback, making it impossible for Charlemagne and his household staff to exercise much supervision over local affairs. What held the system together was personal loyalty to a single ruler who was strong enough to ensure loyalty by force when necessary.

Charlemagne also realized that the Catholic church could provide valuable assistance in governing his kingdom. By the late seventh century, the system of ecclesiastical government within the Christian church that had been created in the Late Roman Empire had largely disintegrated. Many church offices were not filled or were held by grossly unqualified relatives of the royal family. Both Pepin and his son Charlemagne took up the cause of church

latter disappeared from history after their utter devastation at the hands of Charlemagne's army. Now at its height, Charlemagne's empire covered much of western and central Europe (see Map 8.1); not until the time of Napoleon in the nineteenth century would an empire of this size be seen again in Europe.

**Governing the Empire** Charlemagne continued the efforts of his father in organizing the Carolingian kingdom. Because there was no system of public taxation, Charlemagne was dependent on the royal estates for the resources he needed to govern his empire. Food and goods derived from these lands provided support for the king, his household staff, and officials. To keep the nobles in his service, Charlemagne granted part of the royal lands as lifetime holdings to nobles who assisted him.

Besides the household staff, the administration of the empire depended on counts, who were the king's chief

**MAP 8.1  The Carolingian Empire.** Charlemagne inherited the Carolingian Empire from his father, Pepin. He expanded his territories in several directions, creating an empire that would not be rivaled in size until the conquests of Napoleon in the early nineteenth century. ❓ How might Charlemagne's holdings in northern Italy have influenced his relationship with the pope?

🔊 **View an animated version of this map or related maps at** http://history.wadsworth.com/spielvogel06/

reform by creating new bishoprics and archbishoprics, restoring old ones, and seeing to it that the clergy accepted the orders of their superiors and executed their duties.

**Charlemagne as Emperor**  As Charlemagne's power grew, so did his prestige as the most powerful Christian ruler; one monk even wrote of his empire as the "kingdom of Europe." Charlemagne acquired a new title—emperor of the Romans—in 800, but substantial controversy surrounds this event, and it can only be understood within the context of the relationship between the papacy and the Frankish monarchs.

Already during the reign of Pepin, a growing alliance had emerged between the kingdom of the Franks and the papacy. The popes welcomed this support, and in the course of the second half of the eighth century, they severed more and more of their ties with the Byzantine Empire

and drew closer to the Frankish kingdom. Charlemagne encouraged this development. In 799, after a rebellion against his authority, Pope Leo III (795–816) managed to escape from Rome and flee to safety at Charlemagne's court. Charlemagne offered assistance, and when he went to Rome in November 800 to settle affairs, he was received by the pope like an emperor. On Christmas Day in 800, after Mass, Pope Leo placed a crown on Charlemagne's head and proclaimed him emperor of the Romans.

The significance of this imperial coronation has been much debated by historians. We are not even sure whether the pope or Charlemagne initiated the idea or whether Charlemagne was pleased or displeased. His biographer Einhard claimed that "at first [he] had such an aversion that he declared that he would not have set foot in the Church the day that [it was] conferred, although it was a great feast-day, if he could have foreseen the design of the Pope."[2]

**The Coronation of Charlemagne.** After a rebellion in 799 forced Pope Leo III to seek refuge at Charlemagne's court, Charlemagne went to Rome to settle the affair. There, on Christmas Day in 800, he was crowned emperor of the Romans by the pope. This manuscript illustration shows Leo III placing a crown on Charlemagne's head.

But Charlemagne also perceived the usefulness of the imperial title; after all, he was now on a level of equality with the Byzantine emperor, a status he did not reject. Moreover, the papacy now had a defender of great stature, although later popes in the Middle Ages would become involved in fierce struggles with emperors over who possessed the higher power.

In any case, Charlemagne's coronation as Roman emperor certainly demonstrated the strength, even after three hundred years, of the concept of an enduring Roman Empire. More important, it symbolized the fusion of the Roman, Christian, and Germanic elements that constituted the foundation of European civilization. A Germanic king had been crowned emperor of the Romans by the spiritual leader of western Christendom. A new civilization had emerged.

## The Carolingian Intellectual Renewal

Charlemagne had a strong desire to revive learning in his kingdom, an attitude that stemmed from his own intellectual curiosity as well as the need to provide educated clergy for the church and literate officials for the government. His efforts led to a revival of learning and culture that some historians have labeled a Carolingian Renaissance, or "rebirth" of learning.

For the most part, the revival of classical studies and the efforts to preserve Latin culture took place in the monasteries, many of which had been established by the Irish and English missionaries of the seventh and eighth centuries (see Chapter 7). By the ninth century, the work required of Benedictine monks was the copying of manuscripts. Monasteries established **scriptoria,** or writing rooms, where monks copied not only the works of early Christianity, such as the Bible and the treatises of the church fathers, but also the works of Latin classical authors.

Following the example of the Irish and English monks, their Carolingian counterparts developed new ways of producing books. Their texts were written on pages made of parchment or sheepskin rather than papyrus and then bound in covers decorated with jewels and precious metals. The use of parchment made books very expensive; an entire herd of sheep could be required to make a Bible. (Papyrus was no longer available because Egypt was in Muslim hands, and the west could no longer afford to import it.) Carolingian monastic scribes also developed a new writing style called the Carolingian minuscule (see the illustration on p. 208). This was really hand printing rather than cursive writing and was far easier to read than the Merovingian script.

The production of manuscripts, some of which were illustrated, in Carolingian monastic scriptoria was a crucial factor in the preservation of the ancient legacy. About eight thousand manuscripts survive from Carolingian times. Virtually 90 percent of the ancient Roman works that we have today exist because they were copied by Carolingian monks.

Charlemagne personally promoted learning by establishing a palace school and encouraging scholars from all over Europe to come to the Carolingian court. These included men of letters from Italy, Spain, Germany, and Ireland. Best known was Alcuin, called by Einhard the "greatest scholar of that day." He was from the famous school at York that was a product of the great revival of learning in the Anglo-Saxon kingdom of Northumbria. From 782 to 796, while serving at Charlemagne's court as an adviser on ecclesiastical affairs, Alcuin also provided the leadership for the palace school. He concentrated on teaching classical Latin and adopted Cassiodorus' sevenfold division of knowledge known as the liberal arts (see Chapter 7), which became the basis for all later medieval education. All in all, the Carolingian Renaissance played a crucial role in keeping the classical heritage alive as well as maintaining the intellectual life of the Catholic church.

**Monks as Copyists.** The copying of manuscripts was a major task of monastic establishments in the Middle Ages. This work took place in a scriptorium or writing room. This medieval manuscript illustration from the early eleventh century shows two German monks at work in the scriptorium of a monastery in Echternach. To copy a whole book was considered a work of special spiritual merit. Copying the Bible was especially important because it was considered a sacred object.

© Dr. Ludwig Reichert Verlag, Wiesbaden

## Life in the Carolingian World

In daily life as well as intellectual life, the Europe of the Carolingian era witnessed a fusion of Roman, Germanic, and Christian practices. The last in particular seem to have exercised an ever-increasing influence.

**The Family and Marriage**   By Carolingian times, the Catholic church had begun to make a significant impact on Frankish family life and marital and sexual attitudes. Marriages in Frankish society were arranged by fathers or uncles to meet the needs of the extended family. Although wives were expected to be faithful to their husbands, Frankish aristocrats often kept concubines, either slave girls or free women from their estates. Even the "most Christian king" Charlemagne had a number of concubines.

To limit such sexual license, the church increasingly emphasized its role in marriage and attempted to Christianize it. Although marriage was a civil arrangement, priests tried to add their blessings and strengthen the concept of a special marriage ceremony. Moreover, the church tried to serve as the caretaker of marriage by stipulating that a girl over fifteen must give her consent to her guardian's choice of a husband or her marriage would not be valid in the eyes of the church.

To stabilize marriages, the church also began to emphasize **monogamy** and permanence. A Frankish church council in 789 stipulated that marriage was an "indissoluble sacrament" and condemned the practice of concubinage and easy divorce; during the reign of Emperor Louis the Pious (814–840), the church finally established the right to prohibit divorce. Now a man who married was expected to remain with his wife "even though she were sterile, deformed, old, dirty, drunken, a frequenter of bad company, lascivious, vain, greedy, unfaithful, quarrelsome, abusive . . . for when that man was free, he freely engaged himself."[3] This was not easily accepted, since monogamy and indissoluble marriages were viewed as obstacles to the well-established practice of concubinage. Not until the thirteenth century was divorce largely stamped out among both the common people and the nobility.

The acceptance and spread of the Catholic church's views on the indissolubility of marriage encouraged the development of the **nuclear family** at the expense of the extended family. Although the kin was still an influential social and political force, the conjugal unit came to be seen as the basic unit of society. The new practice of young couples establishing their own households had a significant impact on women (see the box on p. 205). In the extended family, the eldest woman controlled all the other female members; in the nuclear family, the wife was still dominated by her husband, but at least she now had control of her own household and children.

**Christianity and Sexuality**   The early church fathers had stressed that celibacy and complete abstinence from sexual activity constituted an ideal state superior to marriage. Subsequently, the early church gradually developed a case for clerical celibacy, although it proved impossible to enforce in the Early Middle Ages.

The early fathers had also emphasized, however, that not all people had the self-discipline to remain celibate. It was thus permissible to marry, as Paul had indicated in his first epistle to the Corinthians: "It is good for a man not to touch a woman. Nevertheless, to avoid fornication, let every man have his own wife, and let every woman have her own husband. . . . I say therefore to the unmarried and widows, It is good for them if they abide even as I. But if they cannot contain, let them marry: for it is better to marry than to burn [with passion]."[4] The church thus viewed marriage as the lesser of two evils; it was a concession to human weakness and fulfilled the need for companionship, sex, and children. Although marriage was the subject of much debate in the early medieval church, it was generally agreed that marriage gave the right to indulge in sexual intercourse. Sex, then, was permissible

# ADVICE FROM A CAROLINGIAN MOTHER

THE WIFE OF a Carolingian aristocrat bore numerous responsibilities. She was entrusted with the management of the household and even the administration of extensive landed estates while her husband was absent in the royal service or on a military campaign. A wife was also expected to bear larger numbers of children and to supervise their upbringing. This selection by Dhouda, wife of Bernard, marquis of Septimania (in southern France), is taken from a manual she wrote to instruct her son on his duties to his new lord, King Charles the Bald (840–877).

### Dhouda, *Handbook for William*

Direction on your comportment toward your lord.

You have Charles as your lord; you have him as lord because, as I believe, God and your father, Bernard, have chosen him for you to serve at the beginning of your career, in the flower of your youth. Remember that he comes from a great and noble lineage on both sides of his family. Serve him not only so that you please him in obvious ways, but also as one clearheaded in matters of both body and soul. Be steadfastly and completely loyal to him in all things. . . .

This is why, my son, I urge you to keep this loyalty as long as you live, in your body and in your mind. For the advancement that it brings you will be of great value both to you and to those who in turn serve you. May the madness of treachery never, not once, make you offer an angry insult. May it never give rise in your heart to the idea of being disloyal to your lord. There is harsh and shameful talk about men who act in this fashion. I do not think that such will befall you or those who fight alongside you because such an attitude has never shown itself among your ancestors. It has not been seen among them, it is not seen now, and it will not be seen in the future.

Be truthful to your lord, my son William, child of their lineage. Be vigilant, energetic, and offer him ready assistance as I have said here. In every matter of importance to royal power take care to show yourself a man of good judgment—in your own thoughts and in public—to the extent that God gives you strength. Read the sayings and the lives of the holy Fathers who have gone before us. You will there discover how you may serve your lord and be faithful to him in all things. When you understand this, devote yourself to the faithful execution of your lord's commands. Look around as well and observe those who fight for him loyally and constantly. Learn from them how you may serve him. Then, informed by their example, with the help and support of God, you will easily reach the celestial goal I have mentioned above. And may your heavenly Lord God be generous and benevolent toward you. May he keep you safe, be your kind leader and your protector. May he deign to assist you in all your actions and be your constant defender.

within marriage, but only so long as it was used for the purpose of procreation, or the begetting of children, not for pleasure.

Because the church developed the tradition that sexual relations between man and wife were legitimate only if engaged in for procreation, it condemned all forms of contraception. The church also strongly condemned abortion, although its prohibition failed to stop the practice. Various herbal potions, whose formulas appear in writings from Roman and Byzantine doctors, were available to prevent conception or cause abortion. The Catholic church accepted only one way to limit children: abstinence from intercourse, either periodic or total.

The church's condemnation of sexual activity outside marriage also included homosexuality. Neither Roman religion nor Roman law had recognized any real difference between homosexual and heterosexual eroticism, and the Roman Empire had taken no legal measures against the practice of homosexuality between adults. Later, in the Byzantine Empire, Emperor Justinian in 538 condemned homosexuality, emphasizing that such practices brought down the wrath of God ("we have provoked Him to anger") and endangered the welfare of the state:

> For because of such crimes, there are famines, earthquakes, and pestilences; wherefore we admonish men to abstain from the aforesaid unlawful acts, that they may not lose their souls. . . .

> We order the most illustrious prefect of the capital to arrest those who persist in the aforesaid lawless and impious acts after they have been warned by us, and to inflict on them the extreme punishments, so that the city and the state may not come to harm by reason of such wicked deeds.[5]

Justinian recommended that the guilty parties be punished by castration. Although the church in the Early Middle Ages similarly condemned homosexuality, it also pursued a flexible policy in its treatment of homosexuals. In the Early Middle Ages, homosexuals were treated less harshly than married couples who practiced contraception.

**New Attitudes Toward Children**    The Catholic church also had an impact on another aspect of family life—children. The ancient Romans had limited their family size through infanticide, primarily the exposure of unwanted children, which was accepted in classical society. Romans then paid much attention to the children chosen to survive, as is especially evident in the education of upper-class children. In the emerging early medieval world, barbarian practices of child rearing became influential. As we saw in Chapter 7, the Germanic law codes listed *wergelds*, whose size represented a crude evaluation of a person's importance. According to a Visigothic code of the mid-seventh century, for example, male children were valued at 60 solidi. At the age of twenty, when they had become warriors, the *wergeld* increased fivefold to 300 solidi, where it remained until the adult male reached fifty, after which it again declined. The value of females was only half that of males, although it also jumped tremendously (to 250 solidi) for women between the ages of fifteen and forty because of their importance as bearers of children.

Although the Christian church condemned infanticide, it was not able to eliminate the practice, especially among the poor and among victims of seduction who did not want to keep their illegitimate offspring. Nevertheless, priests tried to discourage such practices by urging people to abandon unwanted children in churches. Often such children were taken in by monasteries and convents and raised to be monks and nuns. Following the example of Jesus' love for children, monks and nuns tended to respect and preserve the virtues of childhood. As children grew older, however, it was thought necessary to use strict discipline to control what was considered the natural inclination of children to sin, especially by disobeying their elders.

**Travel and Hospitality**   Monasteries served another important function in the early medieval world as providers of hospitality. Both monasteries and aristocratic households were expected to provide a place to stay for weary travelers, who were ever at risk from thieves or violence of many kinds. Indeed, Burgundian law stipulated that "anyone who refused to offer a visitor shelter and warmth shall pay a fine of three solidi."⁶ Hospitality, then, was a sacred duty, and

**Travelers Arriving at an Inn.** Inns provided refuge for the many pilgrims, merchants, and others who traveled Europe's dangerous roads in the Middle Ages. In this illustration, a group of merchants has stopped at an inn, which like most medieval inns provided basic necessities but not individual beds. Medieval people generally slept in the nude.

monasteries were especially active in providing it. It was customary for monasteries to have two guest houses, one for the rich and another for the poor. The plan for the monastery of Saint Gall, for example, provided pilgrims and paupers with a house containing benches, two dormitories, and outbuildings. For travelers of high rank, there was a separate guest house with two heated rooms, servants' bedrooms, and stables for horses. One could not always be sure of hospitality in the Early Middle Ages, however. The famous English missionary to Germany, Saint Boniface, reported that female pilgrims to Rome had been forced to become prostitutes in every town along their route in order to obtain their sustenance and reach their goal. The church responded by forbidding females to go on such pilgrimages.

**Diet**   For both rich and poor, the main staple of the Carolingian diet was bread. The aristocratic classes, as well as the monks, consumed it in large quantities. Ovens at the monastery of Saint Gall were able to bake a thousand loaves of bread. Sometimes a gruel made of barley and oats was substituted for bread in the peasant diet.

The upper classes in Carolingian society enjoyed a much more varied diet than the peasants. Pork was the major meat. Domestic pigs, allowed to run wild in the forests to find their own food, were collected and slaughtered in the fall, then smoked and salted to be eaten during the winter months. Because Carolingian aristocrats were especially fond of roasted meat, hunting wild game became one of their favorite activities. They ate little beef or mutton, however, because cattle were kept as dairy cows and oxen to draw plows, and sheep were raised for wool.

Dairy products became prevalent in the Carolingian diet. Milk, which spoiled rapidly, was made into cheese and butter. Chickens were raised for their eggs. Vegetables also formed a crucial part of the diet of both rich and poor. These included legumes, such as beans, peas, and lentils, and roots, such as garlic, onions, and carrots.

The Carolingian diet, especially of the upper classes, was also heavily dependent on honey and spices. Honey was used as a sweetener, both for foods and for many drinks, including wine and ale. Spices included domestic varieties that were grown in home gardens, such as thyme, sage, and chives, and more exotic—and outrageously expensive—varieties imported from the East, such as pepper, cumin, cloves, and cinnamon. Aristocrats were especially fond of spicy dishes, not just for their taste but as a sign of prestige and wealth; spices were also believed to aid the digestion.

Both gluttony and drunkenness were vices shared by many people in Carolingian society. Monastic rations were greatly enlarged in the eighth century to include a daily allotment of 3.7 pounds of bread (nuns were permitted 3 pounds), 1½ quarts of wine or ale, 2 or 3 ounces of cheese, and 8 ounces of vegetables (4 ounces for nuns). These rations provided a total of 6,000 calories a day, and since only heavy and fatty foods—bread, milk, and cheese—were considered nourishing, we begin to understand why some

# MEDICAL PRACTICES IN THE EARLY MIDDLE AGES

*A* NUMBER OF medical manuscripts written in Old English have survived from Anglo-Saxon England. Although most of the medical texts date from the tenth to twelfth centuries, scholars believe that they include copies of earlier works and contain older influences as well. As the following selections from three of these treatises illustrate, herbs were the basic materials of the Anglo-Saxon physicians (or *leeches,* as they were called), and treatments consequently focused almost entirely on botanical remedies. The identity of many of the plants used remains unknown.

## *The Anglo-Saxon Herbal*

### Cress (Nasturtium)

1. In case a man's hair falls out, take juice of the plant which one names nasturtium and by another name cress, put it on the nose, the hair shall grow.
2. This plant is not sown but it is produced of itself in springs and in brooks; also it is written that in some lands it will grow against walls.
3. For a sore head, that is for scurf [dandruff] and for itch, take the seed of this same plant and goose grease, pound together, it draws from off the head the whiteness of the scurf.
4. For soreness of the body [indigestion], take this same plant nasturtium and pennyroyal, soak them in water and give to drink; the soreness and the evil departs.

## *The Leechbook of Bald*

Here are wound salves for all wounds and drinks and cleansings of every sort, whether internally or externally.

Waybroad beaten and mixed with old lard, the fresh is of no use. Again, a wound salve: take waybroad seed, crush it small, shed it on the wound and soon it will be better.

For a burn, if a man be burned with fire only, take woodruff and lily and brooklime; boil in butter and smear therewith. If a man be burned with a liquid, let him take elm rind and roots of the lily, boil them in milk, smear thereon three times a day. For sunburn, boil in butter tender ivy twigs and smear thereon.

## *The Peri-Didaxeon*

### For a Broken Head

For a broken or wounded head which is caused by the humors of the head. Take betony and pound it and lay it on the wound and it will relieve all the pain.

### For Sleep

Thus must one do for the man who cannot sleep; take wormwood and rub it into wine or warm water and let the man drink it and soon it will be better with him.

### For Sore Hands

This leechcraft is good for sore hands and for sore fingers which is called chilblains. Take white frankincense and silver cinders and brimstone and mingle together, then take oil and add it into this mixture, then warm the hands and smear them with the mixture thus made. Wrap up the hands in a linen cloth.

---

Carolingians were known for their potbellies. Malnutrition, however, remained a widespread problem for common people in this period.

Everyone in Carolingian society, including abbots and monks, drank heavily and often to excess. Taverns became a regular feature of life and were found everywhere: in marketplaces, at pilgrimage centers, and on royal, episcopal, and monastic estates. Drinking contests were not unusual; one penitential stated: "Does drunken bravado encourage you to attempt to out-drink your friends? If so, thirty days' fast."

The aristocrats and monks favored wine above all other beverages, and much care was lavished on its production, especially by monasteries. Although ale was considered inferior in some quarters, it was especially popular in the northern and eastern parts of the Carolingian world. Water was also drunk as a beverage, but much care had to be taken to obtain pure sources from wells or clear streams. Monasteries were particularly active in going to the sources of water and building conduits to bring it to the cloister or kitchen fountains.

Water was also used for bathing. Although standards of personal hygiene were not high, medieval people did not ignore cleanliness. A royal palace, such as Charlemagne's, possessed both hot and cold baths. Carolingian aristocrats changed clothes and bathed at least once a week, on Saturdays. The Saturday bath was also a regular practice in many Carolingian monasteries. To monks, bathing more than once a week seemed an unnecessary luxury; to aristocrats, it often seemed desirable.

**Health** Medical practice in Carolingian times stressed the use of medicinal herbs (see the box above) and bleeding. Although the latter was practiced regularly, moderation was frequently recommended. Some advised carefulness as well: "Who dares to undertake a bleeding should see to it that his hand does not tremble."

Physicians were also available when people faced serious illnesses. Many were clerics, and monasteries trained their own. Monastic libraries kept medical manuscripts copied from ancient works and grew herbs to provide stocks of medicinal plants. Carolingian medical manuscripts contained scientific descriptions of illnesses, recipes for medical potions, and even gynecological advice, although monks in particular expended little effort on female medical needs. Some manuals even included instructions for operations, especially for soldiers injured in battle. Some sources clearly demonstrate that there were accurate techniques for amputating gangrenous limbs:

> If you must cut off an unhealthy limb from a healthy body, then do not cut to the limit of the healthy flesh, but cut further into the whole and quick flesh, so that a better and quicker cure may be obtained. When you set fire on the man [i.e., cauterize], take leaves of tender leek and grated salt, overlay the places so that the heat of the fire be more quickly drawn away.[7]

Although scholars are not sure whether anesthesia was used for such operations, medieval manuals recommended poppy, mandrake, and henbane for their narcotic properties.

Physicians of the Early Middle Ages supplemented their medicines and natural practices with appeals for otherworldly help. Magical rites and influences were carried over from pagan times; the Germanic tribes had used magical medicine for centuries. Physicians recommended that patients wear amulets and charms around their bodies to ward off diseases:

> Procure a little bit of the dung of a wolf, preferably some which contains small bits of bone, and pack it in a tube which the patient may easily wear as an amulet.

For epilepsy take a nail of a wrecked ship, make it into a bracelet and set therein the bone of a stag's heart taken from its body whilst alive; put it on the left arm; you will be astonished at the result.[8]

But as pagans were converted to Christianity, miraculous healing through the intervention of God, Jesus, or the saints soon replaced pagan practices. Medieval chronicles abound with accounts of people healed by touching a saint's body. The use of Christian prayers, written down and used as amulets, however, reminds us that for centuries Christian and pagan medical practices survived side by side.

# Disintegration of the Carolingian Empire

The Carolingian Empire began to disintegrate soon after Charlemagne's death. Charlemagne was succeeded by his son Louis the Pious (814–840). Though a decent man, Louis was not a strong ruler and was unable to control either the Frankish aristocracy or his own four sons, who fought continually. In 843, after their father's death, the three surviving brothers signed the Treaty of Verdun. This agreement divided the Carolingian Empire among them into three major sections: Charles the Bald (843–877) obtained the western Frankish lands, which formed the

**The First Bible of Charles the Bald.** Charles the Bald, who took control of the western Frankish lands, is pictured here in an illustration from his first Bible, which dates from between 843 and 851. Illustrated Bibles were one of the finest achievements of Carolingian art. Also pictured is a page from the Bible, showing the use of the Carolingian minuscule style of writing.

core of the eventual kingdom of France; Louis the German (843–876) took the eastern lands, which became Germany; and Lothar (840–855) received the title of emperor and a "Middle Kingdom" extending from the North Sea to the Mediterranean, including the Netherlands, the Rhineland, and northern Italy. The territories of the Middle Kingdom became a source of incessant struggle between the other two Frankish rulers and their heirs. Indeed, France and Germany would fight over the territories of this Middle Kingdom for centuries.

Although this division of the Carolingian Empire was made for political and not nationalistic reasons (dividing a kingdom among the male heirs was a traditional Frankish custom), two different cultures began to emerge. By the ninth century, inhabitants of the western Frankish area were speaking a Romance language derived from Latin that became French. Eastern Franks spoke a Germanic dialect. The later kingdoms of France and Germany did not yet exist, however. In the ninth century, the frequent struggles among the numerous heirs of the sons of Louis the Pious led to further disintegration of the Carolingian Empire. In the meantime, while powerful aristocrats acquired even more power in their own local territories at the expense of the squabbling Carolingian rulers, the process of disintegration was abetted by external attacks on different parts of the old Carolingian world.

**Division of the Carolingian Empire by the Treaty of Verdun, 843**

## Invasions of the Ninth and Tenth Centuries

In the ninth and tenth centuries, western Europe was beset by a wave of invasions by several non-Christian peoples— one old enemy, the Muslims, and two new ones, the Magyars and the Vikings (see Map 8.2 on p. 212). Although battered by these onslaughts, Christian Europe hung on and, with the exception of the Muslims, wound up assimilating its assailants into Christian European civilization.

**Muslims and Magyars**   The first great wave of Muslim expansion had ended at the beginning of the eighth century (see Chapter 7). Gradually, the Muslims built up a series of sea bases in their occupied territories in North Africa, Spain, and southern Gaul and began a new series of attacks in the Mediterranean in the ninth century. They raided the southern coasts of Europe, especially Italy, and even threatened Rome in 843. Their invasion of Sicily in 827 eventually led to a successful occupation of the island. Muslim forces also destroyed the Carolingian defenses in northern Spain and conducted forays into southern France.

The Magyars were a people from western Asia. When the Byzantine emperors encouraged them to attack the troublesome Bulgars, the latter in turn encouraged a people known as the Pechenegs to attack the Magyars instead.

Consequently, the Magyars, under severe Pecheneg pressure, had moved west into eastern and central Europe by the end of the ninth century. They established themselves on the plains of Hungary and from there made raids into western Europe. The Magyars were finally crushed at the Battle of Lechfeld in Germany in 955. At the end of the tenth century, they were converted to Christianity and settled down to establish the kingdom of Hungary.

**The Vikings**   By far the most devastating and far-reaching attacks of the time came from the Northmen or Norsemen of Scandinavia, also known to us as the Vikings. The Vikings were a Germanic people based in Scandinavia and constitute, in a sense, the final wave of Germanic migration. Why they moved is not very clear to historians. One common explanation focuses on overpopulation, although recent research indicates that this may have been true only in western Norway. Other reasons have included the Vikings' great love of adventure and their search for wealth and new avenues of trade.

Two features of Viking society help explain what the Vikings accomplished. First of all, they were warriors. Second, they were superb shipbuilders and sailors. Their ships were the best of the period. Long and narrow with beautifully carved arched prows, the Viking dragon ships carried about fifty men. They had banks of oars as well as a single great sail. Their shallow draft enabled them to sail up European rivers and attack places at some distance inland. Although Viking raids in the eighth century tended to be small-scale and sporadic, they became more regular and more devastating in the ninth (see the box on p. 210). Vikings sacked villages and towns, destroyed churches, and easily defeated small local armies. Viking attacks frightened people and led many a clergyman to exhort his parishioners to change their behavior to appease God's anger, as in this sermon by an English archbishop in 1014:

> Things have not gone well now for a long time at home or abroad, but there has been devastation and persecution in every district again and again, and the English have been for a long time now completely defeated and too greatly disheartened through God's anger; and the pirates [Vikings] so strong with God's consent that often in battle one puts to flight ten, and sometimes less, sometimes more, all because of our sins. . . . We pay them continually and they humiliate us daily; they ravage and they burn, plunder, and rob and carry on board; and lo, what else is there in all these events except God's anger clear and visible over this people?[9]

Because there were different groups of Scandinavians, Viking expansion varied a great deal. Norwegian Vikings moved into Ireland and western England; Danes attacked eastern England, Frisia, and the Rhineland and navigated

# THE VIKINGS INVADE ENGLAND

NEAR THE END of the ninth century, a number of monks in England began to compile a series of chronicles, or yearly records of events. Although there are several chronicles, they have come to be known as the *Anglo-Saxon Chronicle*. Although much of the chronicle focuses on politics, there are also numerous accounts of events of immediate concern to the monks, such as the death of a bishop or inclement weather conditions. This selection from the *Anglo-Saxon Chronicle* focuses on the Danish Viking invasions of England. These selections, taken from the accounts for the years 994, 997, 998, 999, and 1003, show how regular and devastating the Viking invasions were.

### Anglo-Saxon Chronicle

**994.** Olaf and Swein came to London, on the Nativity of St. Mary, with ninety-four ships, fighting constantly the city, and they meant, moreover, to set it on fire. But they there suffered more harm and evil than they ever believed any town-dwellers could have done them. In this God's holy mother showed her mercy to the town-dwellers and delivered them from their enemies; then they went from there, and wrought the most evil that any force had ever done, in burning, ravaging and killing, both along the sea-coast, in Essex, and in Kent, Sussex and Hampshire; finally they seized horses for themselves, and rode as widely as they would, working unspeakable evil.

**997.** The Danes went around Devonshire into the mouth of the Severn, and there ravaged in Cornwall, Wales and Devon. Then they put in at Watchet and did much evil by burning and slaughtering. After that, they went around Land's End again on the south side, and went into the mouth of the Tamar, continuing up until they came to Lydford, burning or killing each thing they met—they burnt down Ordulf's monastery at Tavistock, and brought with them to their ships indescribable plunder.

**998.** The force went eastward again into the mouth of the Frome, and went inland as widely as they pleased into Dorset. Troops were often gathered against them, but as soon as they should have come together, always, in some way, flight was ordered, and they always had the victory in the end. Another time they settled themselves on the Isle of Wight, and fed themselves from Hampshire and Sussex.

**999.** The force came again into the Thames, and went up along Medway to Rochester; there the Kentish troops came against them, and they came together resolutely. But alas, they moved too quickly, and fled because they had not the help they should have had—then the Danes had the power of the battlefield, seized horses, and rode as widely as they pleased. They ravaged and destroyed nearly all West Kent.

**1003.** Exeter was ruined, because of the Frankish peasant Hugh, whom the lady had set up as her reeve [local official]; the Danish force destroyed the town completely, and took much booty. A very great army was gathered from Wiltshire and Hampshire, and went very resolutely against the force. The ealdorman [town official] Aelfric should have led the army, but he displayed his old wiles. As soon as they were close enough to look on one another, he feigned sickness, and began retching to vomit, and said that he was taken ill; so he betrayed the people he should have led, as it is said: 'When the war-leader weakens, all the army is greatly hindered.' When Swein saw that they were not resolute, and all scattering, he led his force into Wilton, ravaged and burnt the borough, went to Salisbury, and from there went back to the sea, where he knew his wave-coursers were.

---

rivers to enter western Frankish lands. Swedish Vikings dominated the Baltic Sea and progressed into the Slavic areas to the east. Moving into northwestern Russia, they went down the rivers of Russia to Novgorod and Kiev and established fortified ports throughout these territories. There they made contact with the Byzantine Empire, either as traders or as invaders. They also made contact with Arab traders on the Volga River and the Sea of Azov.

Early Viking raids had been carried out largely in the summer; by the mid-ninth century, however, the Norsemen had begun to establish winter settlements in Europe from which they could make expeditions to conquer and settle new lands. By 850, groups of Norsemen had settled in Ireland, and the Danes occupied an area known as the Danelaw in northeastern England by 878. Agreeing to accept Christianity, the Danes were eventually assimilated into a larger Anglo-Saxon kingdom. Beginning in 911, the ruler of the western Frankish lands gave one band of Vikings land at the mouth of the Seine River, forming a section of France that ultimately came to be known as Normandy. This policy of settling the Vikings and converting them to Christianity was a deliberate one, since the new inhabitants served as protectors against additional Norseman attacks.

The Vikings were also daring explorers. After 860, they sailed westward in their long ships across the North Atlantic Ocean, reaching Iceland in 874. Erik the Red, a Viking exiled from Iceland, traveled even farther west and discovered Greenland in 985. The only known Viking site in North America was found in Newfoundland.

By the tenth century, Viking expansion was drawing to a close. Greater control by the monarchs of Denmark, Norway, and Sweden over their inhabitants and the increasing Christianization of both the Scandinavian kings and peoples tended to inhibit Viking expansion, but not before Viking settlements had been established through-

**The Vikings Attack England.** An illustration from an eleventh-century English manuscript depicts a group of armed Vikings invading England. Two ships have already reached the shore, and a few Vikings are shown walking down a long gangplank onto English soil. Also shown is a replica of a well-preserved Viking ship found at Oseberg, Norway. The Oseberg ship was one of the largest Viking ships in its day.

out many parts of Europe. Like the Magyars, the Vikings were also assimilated into European civilization. Once again, Christianity proved a decisive civilizing force in Europe. Europe and Christianity were becoming virtually synonymous.

The Viking raids and settlements also had important political repercussions. The inability of royal authorities to protect their peoples against these incursions caused local populations to turn instead to the local aristocrats to provide security for them. In the process, the landed aristocrats not only increased their strength and prestige but also assumed even more of the functions of local government that had previously belonged to the kings; over time these developments led to a new political and military order.

# The Emerging World of Lords and Vassals

The renewed invasions and the disintegration of the Carolingian Empire led to the emergence of a new type of relationship between free individuals. When governments ceased to be able to defend their subjects, it became important to find some powerful lord who could offer protection in exchange for service. The contract sworn between a lord and his subordinate is the basis of a form of social organization that later generations of historians called *feudalism*. But feudalism was never a system, and many historians today prefer to avoid using the term.

## Vassalage

The practice of **vassalage** was derived from Germanic society, in which warriors swore an oath of loyalty to their leader. They fought for their chief, and he in turn took care of their needs. By the eighth century, an individual who served a lord in a military capacity was known as a *vassal*.

With the breakdown of governments, powerful nobles took control of large areas of land. They needed men to fight

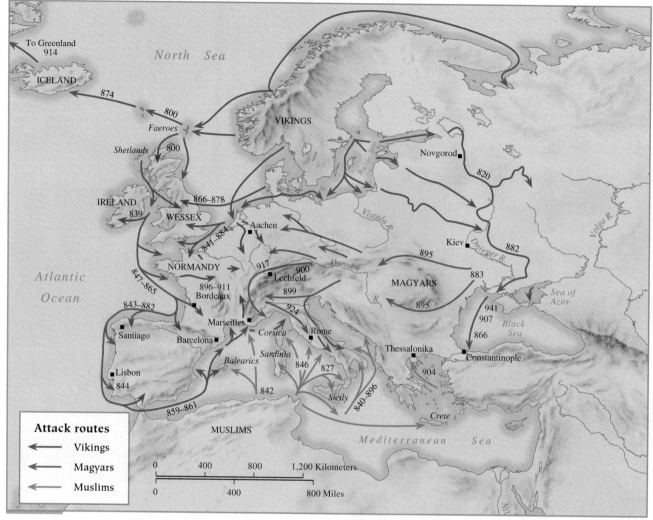

**MAP 8.2  Invasions of the Ninth and Tenth Centuries.**  Attacks by invading Vikings, Magyars, and Muslims terrorized much of Europe in the ninth and tenth centuries, disrupting economic development and spurring the development of fief-holding. The Vikings were the biggest problem, but they eventually formed settlements, converted to Christianity, and were assimilated. ❓ Why was it important for the marauding Vikings to build sound boats and develop good seafaring skills?

🌐 **View an animated version of this map or related maps at** http://history.wadsworth.com/spielvogel06/

for them, so the practice arose of giving grants of land to vassals, who would in return fight for their lord. The Frankish army had originally consisted of foot soldiers, dressed in coats of mail and armed with swords. But in the eighth century, when larger horses and the stirrup were introduced, a military change began to occur. Earlier, horsemen had been throwers of spears. Now they wore armored coats of mail (the larger horse could carry the weight) and wielded long lances that enabled them to act as battering rams (the stirrups kept the riders on their horses). For almost five hundred years, warfare in Europe would be dominated by heavily armored cavalry, or *knights,* as they came to be called.

Of course, a horse, armor, and weapons were expensive to purchase and maintain, and learning to wield these instruments skillfully from horseback took much time and practice. Consequently, lords who wanted men to fight for them had to grant each vassal a piece of land that provided

for the support of the vassal and his family. In return for the land, the vassal provided his lord with one major service, his fighting skills. Each needed the other. In the society of the Early Middle Ages, where there was little trade and wealth was based primarily on land ownership, land became the most important gift a lord could give to a vassal in return for military service.

The relationship between lord and vassal was made official by a public ceremony. To become a vassal, a man performed an act of homage to his lord, as described in this passage from a medieval treatise of law:

> The man should put his hands together as a sign of humility, and place them between the two hands of his lord as a token that he vows everything to him and promises faith to him; and the lord should receive him and promise to keep faith with him. Then the man should say: "Sir, I enter your homage and faith and become your man by mouth and hands [i.e., by taking the oath and

Leiden, University Library, BPL 20, f.60r

**A Knight's Equipment Showing Saddle and Stirrups.** In return for his fighting skills, a knight received a piece of land from his lord that provided for his economic support. Pictured here is a charging knight with his equipment. The introduction of the high saddle, stirrup, and larger horses allowed horsemen to wear heavier armor and to wield long lances, vastly improving the fighting ability of the cavalry.

placing his hands between those of the lord], and I swear and promise to keep faith and loyalty to you against all others, and to guard your rights with all my strength.[10]

As in the earlier Germanic band, loyalty to one's lord was the chief virtue.

## Fief-Holding

The land granted to a vassal in return for military service came to be known as a **fief.** In time, many vassals who held such grants of land came to exercise rights of jurisdiction or political and legal authority within their fiefs. As the Carolingian world disintegrated politically under the impact of dissension within and invasions from without, an increasing number of powerful lords arose. Instead of a single government, many people were now responsible for keeping order. In some areas of France, for example, some lords—called *castellans*—constructed castles and asserted their authority to collect taxes and dispense justice to the local population. Lack of effective central control led to ever larger numbers of castles and castellans.

Fief-holding also became increasingly complicated as **subinfeudation** developed. The vassals of a king, who were themselves great lords, might also have vassals who would owe them military service in return for a grant of land from their estates. Those vassals, in turn, might likewise have vassals, who at such a level would be simple knights with barely enough land to provide their equipment. The lord-vassal relationship, then, bound together both greater and lesser landowners. Historians used to speak of a hierarchy with the king at the top, greater lords on the next level, lesser lords on the next, and simple knights at the bottom; however, this was only a model and rarely reflected reality. Such a hierarchy implies a king at the top. The reality in the tenth-century west Frankish kingdom was that the Capetian kings (see "New Political Configurations in the Tenth Century" later in this chapter) actually controlled no more land than the region around Paris. They possessed little real power over the great lords who held fiefs throughout France.

The lord-vassal relationship at all levels always constituted an honorable relationship between free men and did not imply any sense of servitude. Since kings could no longer provide security in the midst of the breakdown created by the invasions of the ninth century, the system of subinfeudation became ever more widespread. With their rights of jurisdiction, fiefs gave lords virtual possession of the rights of government.

The new practice of lordship was basically a product of the Carolingian world, but it also spread to England, Germany, central Europe, and in modified form to Italy. Fief-holding came to be characterized by a set of practices worked out in the course of the tenth century, although they became more prominent after 1000. These practices included a series of mutual obligations of lord toward vassal and vassal toward lord, but it is crucial to remember that such obligations varied considerably from place to place and even from fief to fief. As usual, practice almost always diverged from theory.

**Mutual Obligations** Because the basic objective of fief-holding was to provide military support, it is no surprise to learn that the major obligation of a vassal to his lord was to perform military service. In addition to his own personal service, a great lord was also responsible for providing a group of knights for the king's army. Moreover, vassals had to furnish suit at court; this meant that a vassal was obliged to appear at his lord's court when summoned, either to give advice to the lord or to sit in judgment in a legal case, since the important vassals of a lord were peers, and only they could judge each other. Many vassals were also obliged to provide hospitality for their lord when he stayed at a vassal's castle. This obligation was especially important to medieval kings because they tended to be itinerant. Finally, vassals were responsible for aids, or financial payments, to the lord on a number of occasions, among them the knighting of the lord's eldest son, the marriage of his eldest daughter, and the ransom of the lord's person if the lord was held captive (see the box on p. 214).

EUROPEAN CIVILIZATION IN THE EARLY MIDDLE AGES, 750–1000    213

# LORDS, VASSALS, AND FIEFS

*T*HE UPHEAVALS of the Early Middle Ages produced a number of new institutions—lordship, vassalage, fiefs. The first selection records the granting of a fief by a lord to a vassal. The second is the classic statement by Bishop Fulbert of Chartres in 1020 on the mutual obligations between lord and vassal.

### Record of a Grant Made by Abbot Faritius to Robert, a Knight

Abbot Faritius also granted to Robert, son of William Mauduit, the land of four hides in Weston which his father had held from the former's predecessor, to be held as a fief. And he should do this service for it, to wit: that whenever the church of Abingdon should perform its knight's service he should do the service of half a knight for the same church; that is to say, in castle ward, in military service beyond and on this side of the sea, in giving money in proportion to the knights on the capture of the king, and in the rest of the services which the other knights of the church perform.

### Bishop Fulbert of Chartres

Asked to write something concerning the form of fealty, I have noted briefly for you, on the authority of the books, the things which follow. He who swears fealty to his lord ought always to have these six things in memory: what is harmless, safe, honorable, useful, easy, practicable. *Harmless,* that is to say, that he should not injure his lord in his body; *safe,* that he should not injure him by betraying his secrets or the defenses upon which he relies for safety; *honorable,* that he should not injure him in his justice or in other matters that pertain to his honor; *useful,* that he should not injure him in his possessions; *easy* and *practicable,* that that good which his lord is able to do easily he make not difficult, nor that which is practicable he make not impossible to him.

That the faithful vassal should avoid these injuries is certainly proper, but not for this alone does he deserve his holding; for it is not sufficient to abstain from evil, unless what is good is done also. It remains, therefore, that in the same six things mentioned above he should faithfully counsel and aid his lord, if he wishes to be looked upon as worthy of his benefice and to be safe concerning the fealty which he has sworn.

The lord also ought to act toward his faithful vassal reciprocally in all these things. And if he does not do this, he will be justly considered guilty of bad faith, just as the former, if he should be detected in avoiding or consenting to the avoidance of his duties, would be perfidious and perjured.

---

In turn, a lord had responsibilities toward his vassals. His major obligation was to protect his vassal, either by defending him militarily or by taking his side in a court of law if necessary. The lord was also responsible for the maintenance of the vassal, usually by granting him a fief.

As this system of mutual obligations between lord and vassal evolved, certain practices became common. If a lord acted improperly toward his vassal, the bond between them could be dissolved. Likewise, if a vassal failed to fulfill his vow of loyalty, he was subject to forfeiture of his fief. Upon a vassal's death, his fief theoretically reverted to the lord, since it had been granted to the vassal for use, not as a possession. In practice, however, fiefs by the tenth century tended to be hereditary. Following the principle of primogeniture, the eldest son inherited the father's fief. If a man died without heirs, the lord could reclaim the fief.

### New Political Configurations in the Tenth Century

In the tenth century, Europe began to recover from the invasions of the century before. The disintegration of the Carolingian Empire and the emergence of great and powerful lords soon produced new political configurations.

**The Eastern Franks**   In the east Frankish kingdom, the last Carolingian king died in 911, whereupon local rulers, especially the powerful dukes (the title of *duke* is derived from the Latin word *dux,* meaning "leader") of the Saxons, Swabians, Bavarians, Thuringians, and Franconians, who exercised much power in their large dukedoms, elected one of their own number, Conrad of Franconia, to serve as king of Germany (as we think of it) or of the eastern Franks (as contemporaries thought of it). But Conrad did not last long, and after his death, the German dukes chose Henry the Fowler, duke of Saxony, as the new king of Germany (919–936). The first of the Saxon dynasty of German kings, Henry was not particularly successful in creating a unified eastern Frankish kingdom, lacking the resources to impose effective rule over the entire area.

The best known of the Saxon kings of Germany was Henry's son, Otto I (936–973). He defeated the Magyars at the Battle of Lechfeld in 955 and encouraged an ongoing program of Christianization of both the Slavic and Scandinavian peoples. Even more than his father, he relied on bishops and abbots in governing his kingdom. This practice was in part a response to the tendency of the lay lords to build up their power at the expense of the king. Since the clergy were theoretically celibate, bishops and abbots could not make their offices hereditary, thus allowing the king to maintain more control over them.

Otto also intervened in Italian politics and for his efforts was crowned emperor of the Romans by the pope in 962, reviving a title that had fallen into disuse with the disintegration of Charlemagne's empire. Once again a pope had conferred the Roman imperial title on a king of the Franks, even though he was a Saxon king of the eastern Franks. Otto's creation of a new "Roman Empire" in the hands of the eastern Franks (or Germans) added a tremendous burden to the kingship of Germany. To the difficulties of governing Germany was appended the onerous task of ruling Italy as well. It proved a formidable and ultimately impossible task.

**The Western Franks**   In the ninth and tenth centuries, the Carolingian kings had little success in controlling the great lords of the western Frankish kingdom. The counts, who were supposed to serve as the chief administrative officials, often paid little attention to the wishes of the Carolingian kings. In 987, when the Carolingian king died, the western Frankish nobles and chief prelates of the church chose Hugh Capet, count of Orléans and Paris, as the new king (987–996).

The nobles who elected Hugh Capet did not intend to establish a new royal dynasty. After all, although Hugh was officially king of the western Franks and overlord of the great nobles of the kingdom, his own family controlled only the Île-de-France, the region around Paris. Other French nobles possessed lands equal to or greater than those of the Capetians and assumed that the king would be content to live off the revenues of his personal lands and not impose any burdensome demands on the nobility. Hugh Capet did succeed in making his position hereditary, however. He asked the nobles, and they agreed, to choose his eldest son, Robert, as his anointed associate in case Hugh died on a campaign to Spain in 987. And although Hugh Capet could not know it then, the Capetian dynasty would rule the western Frankish kingdom, or France, as it eventually came to be known, for centuries. In the late tenth century, however, the territory that would become France was not a unified kingdom but a loose alliance of powerful lords who treated the king as an equal. They assisted him only when it was in their own interests to do so.

**Anglo-Saxon England**   England's development in the ninth and tenth centuries took a course somewhat different from that of the Frankish kingdoms. The long struggle of the Anglo-Saxon kingdoms against the Viking invasions ultimately produced a unified kingdom. Alfred the Great, king of Wessex (871–899), played a crucial role. He defeated a Danish army in 879, according to an account by Asser, his adviser, who wrote a biography of the king:

> [Alfred] gained the victory through God's will. He destroyed the Vikings with great slaughter, and pursued those who fled as far as the stronghold, hacking them down; he seized everything which he found outside the stronghold—men (whom he killed

**CHRONOLOGY**   **New Political Configurations of the Tenth Century**

| *Eastern Franks* | |
|---|---|
| Conrad of Franconia | 911–918 |
| Saxon dynasty: Henry I | 919–936 |
| Otto I | 936–973 |
| Defeat of Magyars | 955 |
| Coronation as emperor | 962 |
| *Western Franks* | |
| Election of Hugh Capet as king | 987 |
| *Anglo-Saxon England* | |
| Alfred the Great, king of Wessex | 871–899 |
| Peace with the Danes | 886 |
| Reign of King Edgar | 959–975 |

immediately), horses and cattle—and boldly made camp in front of the gate of the Viking stronghold with all his army. When he had been there for fourteen days the Vikings, thoroughly terrified by hunger, cold and fear, and in the end by despair, sought peace.[11]

Alfred eventually made peace with the Danes after strengthening his army and creating a navy.

Alfred also believed in the power of education. He invited scholars to his court and encouraged the translation of the works of such church fathers as Augustine and Gregory the Great from Latin into Anglo-Saxon (Old English), the vernacular, or the language spoken by the people. Old English was also soon used for official correspondence as well.

Alfred's successors reconquered the remaining areas occupied by the Danes and established a unified Anglo-Saxon monarchy. By the time of King Edgar (959–975), Anglo-Saxon England had a well-developed and strong monarchical government. Although the kingship was elective, only descendants of Alfred were chosen for the position. In the counties or *shires,* the administrative units into which England was divided, the king was assisted by an agent appointed and controlled by him, the shire-reeve or sheriff. An efficient chancery or writing office was responsible for issuing writs (or royal letters) conveying the king's orders to the sheriffs.

## The Manorial System

The landholding class of nobles and knights comprised a military elite whose ability to function as warriors depended on having the leisure time to pursue the arts of war. Landed estates worked by a dependent peasant class provided the economic sustenance that made this way of life possible. A **manor** (see Map 8.3) was simply an agricultural estate operated by a lord and worked by peasants. Lords

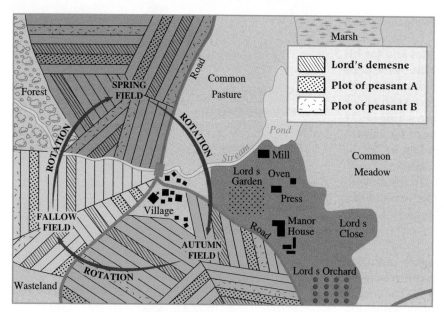

**MAP 8.3** **A Typical Manor.** The manorial system created small, tightly knit communities in which peasants were economically and physically bound to their lord. Crops were rotated, with roughly one-third of the fields lying fallow at any one time, which helped replenish soil nutrients (see Chapter 9). ❓ How does the area of the lord's manor, other buildings, garden, and orchard compare to that of the peasant holdings in the village?

🌐 View an animated version of this map or related maps at http://history.wadsworth.com/spielvogel06/

provided protection; peasants gave up their freedom, became tied to the lord's land, and provided labor services for him.

Manorialism grew out of the unsettled circumstances of the Early Middle Ages, when small farmers often needed protection or food in a time of bad harvests. Free peasants gave up their freedom to the lords of large landed estates in return for protection and use of the lord's land. Although a large class of free peasants continued to exist, increasing numbers of them became bound to the land as serfs. Unlike slaves, **serfs** could not be bought and sold, but they were subservient to their lords in a variety of ways. Serfs were required to provide labor services, pay rents, and be subject to the lord's jurisdiction. By the ninth century, probably 60 percent of the population of western Europe had become serfs.

A serf's labor services consisted of working the lord's **demesne,** the land retained by the lord, which might consist of one-third to one-half of the cultivated lands scat-

tered throughout the manor (the rest would have been allotted to the serfs for their maintenance), as well as building barns and digging ditches. Although labor requirements varied from manor to manor and person to person, a common work obligation was three days a week.

The serfs paid rents by giving the lords a share of every product they raised. Serfs also paid the lord for the use of the manor's common pasturelands, streams, ponds, and surrounding woodlands. For example, if tenants fished in the pond or stream on a manor, they turned over part of the catch to their lord. For grazing a cow in the common pasture, a serf paid a rent in cheese produced from the cow's milk. Serfs were also obliged to pay a **tithe** (a tenth of their produce) to their local village church.

Lords also possessed a variety of legal rights over their serfs. Serfs were legally bound to the lord's land; they could not leave without his permission. Although free to marry, serfs could not marry anyone outside their manor without the lord's approval. Moreover, lords sometimes exercised

**Peasants in the Manorial System.** In the manorial system, peasants were required to provide labor services for their lord. This thirteenth-century illustration shows a group of English peasants harvesting grain. Overseeing their work is a bailiff, or manager, who supervised the work of the peasants.

# THE MANORIAL COURT

THE WAY OF LIFE of the medieval lord was made possible by the labors of the serfs on his manor. In addition to his right to collect rents, labor services, and fees from his serfs, the lord also possessed political authority over them, including the right to hold a manorial court to try tenants for crimes and infractions of the manor's rules. This selection, taken from the records of an English manorial court, lists the cases heard, the decisions of the jurors, and the subsequent penalties.

## Select Pleas in Manorial Courts

John Sperling complains that Richard of Newmere on the Sunday next before S. Bartholomew's day [August 24] last past with his cattle, horses, and pigs wrongfully destroyed the corn on his (John's) land to his damage to the extent of one thrave of wheat, and to his dishonor to the extent of two shillings; and of this he produces suit. And Richard comes and defends all of it. Therefore let him go to the law six handed [with three companions who will swear to his innocence]. His pledges, Simon Combe and Hugh Frith [like bail bondsmen, pledges stood surety for a person ordered to show up in court or pay a fine].

Hugh Free in mercy [fined] for his beast caught in the lord's garden. Pledges, Walter Hill and William Slipper, Fine 6d. [sixpence].

(The) twelve jurors say that Hugh Cross has right in the bank and hedge about which there was a dispute between him and William White. Therefore let him hold in peace and let William be distrained [forced to comply by seizing his property] for his many trespasses. (Afterwards he made fine for 12d.)

From the whole township of Little Ogbourne, except seven, for not coming to wash the lord's sheep, 6s. 8d. [six shillings, eight pence].

Gilbert Richard's son gives 5s. for license to marry a wife. Pledge, Seaman. Term (for payments), the Purification [February 2].

William Jordan in mercy for bad plowing on the lord's land. Pledge, Arthur. Fine, 6d.

The parson of the Church is in mercy for his cow caught in the lord's meadow. Pledges, Thomas Ymer and William Coke.

From Martin Shepherd 6d. for the wound that he gave Pekin.

Ragenhilda of Bec. gives 2s. for having married without license. Pledge, William of Primer.

Walter Hull gives 13s. 4d. for license to dwell on the land of the Prior of Harmondsworth so long as he shall live and as a condition finds pledges, to wit, William Slipper, John Bisuthe, Gilbert Bisuthe, Hugh Tree, William Johnson, John Hulle, who undertake that the said Walter shall do to the lord all the services and customs which he would do if he dwelt on the lord's land. . . .

It was presented that Robert Carter's son by night invaded the house of Peter Burgess and in felony threw stones at his door so that the said Peter raised the hue [alarm]. Therefore let the said Robert be committed to prison. Afterwards he made fine with 2s.

All the plowmen of Great Ogbourne are convicted by the oath of twelve men . . . because by reason of their default (the) land of the lord is damaged to the amount of 9s. . . . And Walter Reaper is in mercy for concealing (i.e., not giving information as to) the said bad plowing. Afterwards he made fine with the lord with 1 mark [thirteen shillings, four pence].

public rights or political authority on their lands. This gave the lord the right to try serfs in his own court, although only for lesser crimes (called "low justice"). In fact, the lord's manorial court provided the only law that most serfs knew (see the box above). Finally, the lord's political authority enabled him to establish monopolies on certain services that provided additional revenues. Serfs could be required to bring their grain to the lord's mill and pay a fee to have it ground into flour. Thus the rights a lord possessed on his manor gave him virtual control over both the lives and property of his serfs.

The administration of manors varied considerably. If the lord of a manor was a simple knight, he would probably live on the estate and supervise it in person. Great lords possessed many manors and relied on a steward or bailiff to run each estate. Note that manors were controlled not only by lay lords but also by monasteries and cathedral churches. Monasteries tended to be far more conscientious about keeping accurate records of their manorial estates than lay lords, and their surveys provide some of the best sources of information on medieval village life. The relationship between manors and villages was highly variable. A single village might constitute a manor, or a large manor might encompass several villages.

In the Early Middle Ages, a vast majority of men and women, free or unfree—possibly as many as 90 percent—worked the land. This period had witnessed a precipitous decline in trade. Coins and jewelry were often hoarded, and at the local level, goods were frequently bartered because so few coins were in circulation. But trade never entirely disappeared. Even in an agrarian society, surplus products could be exchanged at local markets. More significant, however, was that both aristocrats and wealthy clerics desired merchandise not produced locally, such as spices, silk cloth, wine, gold, and silver jewelry, and it took trade to obtain these items.

Much trade in luxury goods, especially beginning in the ninth century, was with the Byzantine Empire, particularly the city of Constantinople, and the Islamic caliphs of Baghdad. Products from the west included iron, timber, furs, and slaves (many from eastern Europe, including captured Slavs, from whom the modern word *slave* is derived). Traders, often Jews, carried goods by boat on European rivers or on caravans with horses or mules. An Arab geographer of the ninth century left this account of Jewish traders from southern France:

> [They] speak Arabic, Persian, Greek, Frankish, Spanish, and Slavonic. They travel from west to east and from east to west, by land and by sea. From the west they bring eunuchs, slave-girls, boys, brocade, marten and other furs, and swords. They take ship from Frankland in the western Mediterranean sea and land at Farama, whence they take their merchandise on camel-back to Qulzum. . . . Then they sail on the eastern [Red] sea from Qulzum, and onward to India and China. From China they bring back musk, aloes, camphor, cinnamon, and other products of those parts, and return to Qulzum. Then they transport them to Farama and sail again on the western sea. Some sail with their goods to Constantinople and sell them to the Greeks, and some take them to the king of the Franks and sell them there.[12]

By 900, Italian merchants, especially the Venetians, were entering the trade picture. Overall, however, compared to the Byzantine Empire or Muslim caliphates, western Europe in the Early Middle Ages was an underdeveloped, predominantly agrarian society and could not begin to match the splendor of either of the other heirs of the Roman Empire.

# The Zenith of Byzantine Civilization

In the seventh and eighth centuries, the Byzantine Empire had lost much of its territory to Slavs, Bulgars, and Muslims. By 750, the empire consisted only of Asia Minor, some lands in the Balkans, and the southern coast of Italy. Although Byzantium was beset with internal dissension and invasions in the ninth century, it was able to deal with them and not only endured but even expanded, reaching its high point in the tenth century, which some historians have called the golden age of Byzantine civilization.

During the reign of Michael III (842–867), the Byzantine Empire began to experience a revival. Iconoclasm was finally abolished in 843, and reforms were made in education, church life, the military, and the peasant economy. There was a noticeable intellectual renewal. But the Byzantine Empire under Michael was still plagued by persistent

**The Byzantine Empire in 1025**

problems. The Bulgars mounted new attacks, and the Arabs continued to harass the empire. Moreover, a new church problem with political repercussions erupted over differences between the pope as leader of the western Christian church and the patriarch of Constantinople as leader of the eastern (or Orthodox) Christian church. Patriarch Photius condemned the pope as a heretic for accepting a revised form of the Nicene Creed stating that the Holy Spirit proceeded from the Father and the Son instead of "the Holy Spirit, who proceeds from the Father." A council of eastern bishops followed Photius' wishes and excommunicated the pope, creating the so-called Photian schism. Although the differences were later papered over, this controversy served to further the division between the eastern and western Christian churches.

## The Macedonian Dynasty

The problems that arose during Michael's reign were effectively dealt with by a new dynasty of Byzantine emperors known as the Macedonians (867–1081), who managed to hold off the external enemies, go over to the offensive, and reestablish domestic order. Supported by the church, the emperors thought of the Byzantine Empire as a continuation of the Christian Roman Empire of late antiquity. Although for diplomatic reasons they occasionally recognized the imperial title of western emperors, such as Charlemagne and Otto I, they still regarded them as little more than barbarian parvenus.

The Macedonian emperors could boast of a remarkable number of achievements in the late ninth and tenth centuries. They worked to strengthen the position of the free farmers, who felt threatened by the attempts of landed aristocrats to expand their estates at the expense of the farmers. The emperors were well aware that the free farmers made up the rank and file of the Byzantine cavalry and provided the military strength of the empire. The Macedonian emperors also fostered a burst of economic prosperity by expanding trade relations with western Europe, especially by selling silks and metalwork. Thanks to this prosperity, the city of Constantinople flourished. Foreign visitors continued to be astounded by its size, wealth, and physical surroundings. To western Europeans, it was the stuff of legends and fables (see the box on p. 219).

In the midst of this prosperity, Byzantine cultural influence expanded due to the active missionary efforts of eastern Byzantine Christians. Eastern Orthodox Christianity was spread to eastern European peoples, such as the Bulgars and Serbs. Perhaps the greatest missionary success occurred when the prince of Kiev in Russia converted to Christianity in 987.

Under the Macedonian rulers, Byzantium enjoyed a strong civil service, talented emperors, and

# A Western View of the Byzantine Empire

BISHOP LIUDPRAND of Cremona undertook diplomatic missions to Constantinople on behalf of two western kings, Berengar of Italy and Otto I of Germany. This selection is taken from the bishop's description of his mission to the Byzantine emperor Constantine VII as an envoy for Berengar, king of Italy from 950 until his overthrow by Otto I of Germany in 964. Liudprand had mixed feelings about Byzantium: admiration, yet also envy and hostility because of its superior wealth.

### Liudprand of Cremona, *Antapodosis*

Next to the imperial residence at Constantinople there is a palace of remarkable size and beauty which the Greeks call Magnavra . . . the name being equivalent to "fresh breeze." In order to receive some Spanish envoys, who had recently arrived, as well as myself . . . , Constantine gave orders that his palace should be got ready. . . .

Before the emperor's seat stood a tree, made of bronze gilded over, whose branches were filled with birds, also made of gilded bronze, which uttered different cries, each according to its varying species. The throne itself was so marvelously fashioned that at one moment it seemed a low structure, and at another it rose high into the air. It was of immense size and was guarded by lions, made either of bronze or of wood covered over with gold, who beat the ground with their tails and gave a dreadful roar with open mouth and quivering tongue. Leaning upon the shoulders of two eunuchs I was brought into the emperor's presence. At my approach the lions began to roar and the birds to cry out, each according to its kind; but I was neither terrified nor surprised, for I had previously made enquiry about all

these things from people who were well acquainted with them. So after I had three times made obeisance to the emperor with my face upon the ground, I lifted my head, and behold! the man whom just before I had seen sitting on a moderately elevated seat had now changed his raiment and was sitting on the level of the ceiling. How it was done I could not imagine, unless perhaps he was lifted up by some such sort of device as we use for raising the timbers of a wine press. On that occasion he did not address me personally . . . but by the intermediary of a secretary he enquired about Berengar's doings and asked after his health. I made a fitting reply and then, at a nod from the interpreter, left his presence and retired to my lodging.

It would give me some pleasure also to record here what I did then for Berengar. . . . The Spanish envoys . . . had brought handsome gifts from their masters to the emperor Constantine. I for my part had brought nothing from Berengar except a letter and that was full of lies. I was very greatly disturbed and shamed at this and I began to consider anxiously what I had better do. In my doubt and perplexity it finally occurred to me that I might offer the gifts, which on my account I had brought for the emperor, as coming from Berengar, and trick out my humble present with fine words. I therefore presented him with nine excellent curaisses, seven excellent shields with gilded bosses, two silver gilt cauldrons, some swords, spears and spits, and what was more precious to the emperor than anything, four carzimasia; that being the Greek name for young eunuchs who have had both their testicles and their penis removed. This operation is performed by traders at Verdun, who take the boys into Spain and make a huge profit.

---

military advances. The Byzantine civil service was staffed by well-educated, competent aristocrats from Constantinople who oversaw the collection of taxes, domestic administration, and foreign policy. At the same time, the Macedonian dynasty produced some truly outstanding emperors skilled in administration and law, including Leo VI (886–912) and Basil II (976–1025). In the tenth century, competent emperors combined with a number of talented generals to mobilize the empire's military resources and take the offensive. The Bulgars were defeated, and both the eastern and western parts of Bulgaria were annexed to the empire. The Byzantines went on to add the islands of Crete and Cyprus to the empire and defeat the Muslim forces in Syria, expanding the empire to the upper Euphrates. By the end of the reign of Basil II in 1025, the Byzantine Empire was the largest it had been since the beginning of the seventh century.

## The Slavic Peoples of Central and Eastern Europe

North of Byzantium and east of the Carolingian Empire lay a spacious plain through which a number of Asiatic nomads, including the Huns, Bulgars, Avars, and Magyars, had pushed their way westward, terrorizing and plundering the settled peasant communities. Eastern Europe was ravaged by these successive waves of invaders, who found it relatively easy to create large empires that were in turn overthrown by the next invaders. Over a period of time, the invaders themselves were largely assimilated with the native Slavic peoples of the area.

The Slavic peoples were originally a single people in central Europe who through mass migrations and nomadic invasions were gradually divided into three major groups: the western, southern, and eastern Slavs (see Map 8.4).

**Emperor Leo VI.** Under the Macedonian dynasty, the Byzantine Empire achieved economic prosperity through expanded trade and gained new territories through military victories. This mosaic over the western door of Hagia Sophia in Constantinople depicts the Macedonian emperor Leo VI prostrating himself before Jesus. This act of humility symbolized the emperor's function as an intermediary between God and the empire.

Byzantine Visual Resources, Dumbarton Oaks, Washington, D.C., © 1996

## 🖋 Western Slavs

In the region east of the Germanic kingdom emerged the Polish and Bohemian kingdoms of the western Slavs. The Germans assumed responsibility for the conversion of these Slavic peoples because German emperors considered it their duty to spread Christianity to the "barbarians." Of course, it also gave them the opportunity to extend their political authority as well. German missionaries had converted the Czechs in Bohemia by the end of the ninth cen-

tury, and a bishopric eventually occupied by a Czech bishop was established at Prague in the tenth century. The Slavs in Poland were not converted until the reign of Prince Mieszko (c. 960–992). In 1000, an independent Polish archbishopric was set up at Gniezno by the pope. The non-Slavic kingdom of Hungary, which emerged after the Magyars settled down after their defeat at Lechfeld in 955, was also converted to Christianity by German missionaries. Saint Stephen, king of Hungary from 997 to 1038, facilitated the acceptance of Christianity by his people. The

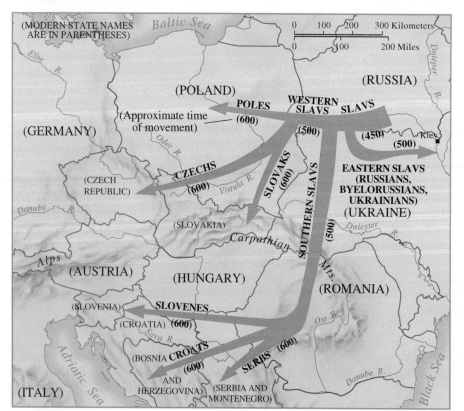

**MAP 8.4** **The Migrations of the Slavs.** Originally from east-central Europe, the Slavic people broke into three groups. The western Slavs converted to Catholic Christianity, while the eastern Slavs and southern Slavs, under the influence of the Byzantine Empire, embraced the Eastern Orthodox faith. ❓ What connections do these Slavic migrations have with what we today characterize as eastern Europe?

🖰 View an animated version of this map or related maps at http://history.wadsworth.com/spielvogel06/

# A Muslim's Description of the Rus

DESPITE THE DIFFICULTIES that travel presented, early medieval civilization did witness some contact among the various cultures. This might occur through trade, diplomacy, or the conquest and migration of peoples. This document is a description of the Swedish Rus who eventually merged with the native Slavic peoples to form the principality of Kiev, commonly regarded as the first Russian state. This account was written by Ibn Fadlan, a Muslim diplomat sent from Baghdad in 921 to a settlement on the Volga River. His comments on the filthiness of the Rus reflect the Muslim preoccupation with cleanliness.

### Ibn Fadlan, *Description of the Rus*

I saw the Rus folk when they arrived on their trading-mission and settled at the river Atul (Volga). Never had I seen people of more perfect physique. They are tall as date-palms, and reddish in color. They wear neither coat nor kaftan, but each man carried a cape which covers one half of his body, leaving one hand free. No one is ever parted from his axe, sword, and knife. Their swords are Frankish in design, broad, flat, and fluted. Each man has a number of trees, figures, and the like from the fingernails to the neck. Each woman carried on her bosom a container made of iron, silver, copper or gold—its size and substance depending on her man's wealth. . . .

They [the Rus] are the filthiest of God's creatures. They do not wash after discharging their natural functions, neither do they wash their hands after meals. They are as lousy as donkeys. They arrive from their distant river, and there they build big houses on its shores. Ten or twenty of them may live together in one house, and each of them has a couch of his own where he sits and diverts himself with the pretty slave girls whom he had brought along for sale. He will make love with one of them while a comrade looks on; sometimes they indulge in a communal orgy, and, if a customer should turn up to buy a girl, the Rus man will not let her go till he has finished with her.

They wash their hands and faces every day in incredibly filthy water. Every morning the girl brings her master a large bowl of water in which he washes his hands and face and hair, then blows his nose into it and spits into it. When he has finished the girl takes the bowl to his neighbor—who repeats the performance. Thus the bowl goes the rounds of the entire household. . . .

If one of the Rus folk falls sick they put him in a tent by himself and leave bread and water for him. They do not visit him, however, or speak to him, especially if he is a serf. Should he recover he rejoins the others; if he dies they burn him. But if he happens to be a serf they leave him for the dogs and vultures to devour. If they catch a robber they hang him to a tree until he is torn to shreds by wind and weather. . . .

Poles, Czechs, and Hungarians all accepted Catholic or western Christianity and became closely tied to the Roman Catholic church and its Latin culture.

## Southern Slavs

The southern and eastern Slavic populations took a different path because of their proximity to the Byzantine Empire. The southern Slavic peoples were converted to the Eastern Orthodox Christianity of the Byzantine Empire by two Byzantine missionary brothers, Cyril and Methodius, who began their activities in 863. They created a Slavonic (Cyrillic) alphabet, translated the Bible into Slavonic, and developed Slavonic church services. Although the southern Slavic peoples accepted Christianity, a split eventually developed between the Croats, who accepted the Roman church, and the Serbs, who remained loyal to eastern Christianity.

Although the Bulgars were originally an Asiatic people who conquered much of the Balkan peninsula, they were eventually absorbed by the larger native southern Slavic population. Together, by the ninth century, they formed a largely Slavic Bulgarian kingdom. Although the conversion to Christianity of this state was complicated by the rivalry between the Roman Catholic and Eastern Orthodox churches, the Bulgarians eventually accepted the latter. By the end of the ninth century, they embraced the Slavonic church services earlier developed by Cyril and Methodius. The acceptance of Eastern Orthodoxy by the southern Slavic peoples, the Serbs and Bulgarians, meant that their cultural life was also linked to the Byzantine state.

## Eastern Slavs

The eastern Slavic peoples, from whom the modern Russians, White Russians (Byelorussians), and Ukrainians are descended, had settled in the territory of present-day Ukraine and European Russia. There, beginning in the late eighth century, they began to contend with Viking invaders. Swedish Vikings, known to the eastern Slavs as Varangians, moved down the extensive network of rivers into the lands of the eastern Slavs in search of booty and new trade routes. After establishing trading links with the Byzantine state, the Varangians built trading settlements, became involved in the civil wars among the Slavic peoples, and eventually came to dominate the native peoples, just as their fellow Vikings were doing in parts of western Europe. According to the traditional version of the story, the semilegendary Rurik secured his ruling dynasty in the Slavic settlement of Novgorod in 862. Rurik and his fellow Vikings were called the Rus, from which the name that eventually became attached to the state they founded, Russia, is derived (see the box above). Although much about Rurik is unclear, it is certain that his follower Oleg (c. 873–913) took up residence in Kiev and created the Rus state, a union of eastern Slavic territories known as the principality of Kiev. Oleg's successors extended their control over the eastern Slavs and expanded the territory of Kiev until it encompassed the lands between the Baltic and Black Seas and the Danube and Volga Rivers. By marrying Slavic wives, the Viking ruling class was gradually assimilated into the Slavic population, a process confirmed by their assumption of Slavic names.

The growth of the principality of Kiev attracted religious missionaries, especially from the Byzantine Empire. One Rus ruler, Vladimir (c. 980–1015), married the Byzantine emperor's sister and officially accepted Christianity for himself and his people in 987. His primary motive was probably not spiritual. By all accounts, Vladimir was a cruel and vicious man who believed an established church would be helpful in developing an organized state. From the end of the tenth century on, Byzantine Christianity became the model for Russian religious life, just as Byzantine imperial ideals came to influence the outward forms of Russian political life.

## The Expansion of Islam

The Umayyad dynasty of caliphs had established Damascus as the center of an Islamic empire created by Arab expansion in the seventh and eighth centuries. But Umayyad rule created resentment, and the Umayyad's corrupt behavior also helped bring about their end. One caliph, for example, supposedly swam in a pool of wine and drank enough of it to lower the wine level considerably. Finally, in 750, Abu al-Abbas, a descendant of the uncle of Muhammad, brought an end to the Umayyad dynasty and established the Abbasid dynasty, which lasted until 1258.

### ≫ The Abbasid Dynasty

The Abbasid rulers brought much change to the world of Islam. They tried to break down the distinctions between Arab and non-Arab Muslims. All Muslims, regardless of their ethnic background, could now hold both civil and military offices. This helped open Islamic life to the influences of the conquered civilizations. Many Arabs now began to intermarry with their conquered peoples.

In 762, the Abbasids built a new capital city, Baghdad, on the Tigris River far to the east of Damascus. The new capital was well placed. It took advantage of river traffic to the Persian Gulf and at the same time was located on the caravan route from the Mediterranean to Central Asia. The move eastward allowed Persian influence to come to the fore, encouraging a new cultural orientation. Under the Abbasids, judges, merchants, and government officials, rather than warriors, were viewed as the ideal citizens.

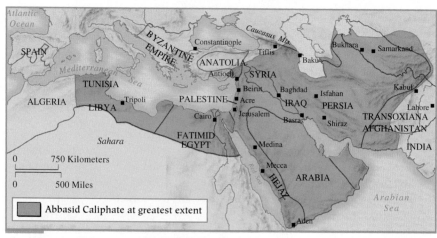

**The Abbasid Caliphate at the Height of Its Power**

The new Abbasid dynasty experienced a period of splendid rule well into the ninth century. Best known of the caliphs of the time was Harun al-Rashid (786–809), whose reign is often described as the golden age of the Abbasid caliphate. His son al-Ma'mun (813–833) was a great patron of learning. He founded an astronomical observatory and created a foundation for translating classical Greek works. This was also a period of growing economic prosperity. The Arabs had conquered many of the richest provinces of the old Roman Empire, and they now controlled the trade routes to the east. Baghdad became the center of an enormous trade empire that extended into Europe, Asia, and Africa, greatly adding to the wealth of the Islamic world.

Despite the prosperity, all was not quite well in the empire of the Abbasids. There was much fighting over the succession to the caliphate. When Harun al-Rashid died, his two sons fought to succeed him in a struggle that almost destroyed the city of Baghdad. As the tenth-century Muslim historian al-Mas'udi wrote: "Mansions were destroyed, most remarkable monuments obliterated; prices soared. . . . Brother turned his sword against brother, son against father, as some fought for Amin, others for Ma'mun. Houses and palaces fueled the flames; property was put to the sack."[13]

Vast wealth also gave rise to financial corruption. By awarding important positions to court favorites, the Abbasid caliphs began to undermine the foundations of their own power and soon became figureheads. Provincial rulers broke away from the control of the caliphs and established their own independent dynasties. Even earlier, in the eighth century, a separate caliphate had already been established in Spain when Abd al-Rahman of the Umayyad dynasty had fled there. In 756, he seized control of southern Spain and then expanded his power into the center of the peninsula. He took the title of *emir,* or commander, and set up the emirate of al-Andalus (the Arabic name for Spain) with its center at Córdoba. In 929, Abd al-Rahman III (912–961) proclaimed himself caliph. The rulers of al-Andalus developed a unique society in which all religions were tolerated. The court also supported writers and artists, creating a brilliant and flourishing culture.

The fragmentation of the Islamic empire accelerated in the tenth century. The Fatimid family established a caliphate in Egypt in 973, and an independent dynasty also operated in North Africa. Despite the political disunity of the Islamic world, however, there was an underlying Islamic civilization based on two common bonds, the Qur'an and the Arabic language.

## Islamic Civilization

From the beginning of their empire, Muslim Arabs had demonstrated a willingness to absorb the culture of their conquered territories. The Arabs were truly heirs to the remaining Greco-Roman culture of the Roman Empire. Just as readily, they assimilated Byzantine and Persian culture. In the eighth and ninth centuries, numerous Greek, Syrian, and Persian scientific and philosophical works were translated into Arabic. As the chief language in the southern Mediterranean and the Near East and the required language of Muslims, Arabic became a truly international tongue.

The Muslims created a brilliant urban culture at a time when western Europe was predominantly a rural world of farming villages. This can be seen in such new cities as Baghdad and Cairo, but also in Córdoba, the capital of the Umayyad caliphate in Spain. With a population of possibly 100,000, Córdoba was Europe's largest city after Constantinople. It had seventy public libraries, and the number of manuscripts in the caliph's private library reached 400,000. One caliph, al-Hakem (961–976), collected books from different parts of the world and then had them translated into Arabic and Latin. These included works on geography that later proved valuable to Western sailors and merchants. Schools were also established, and the Great Mosque of Córdoba became a center for scholars from all over the Islamic world. Large numbers of women served as teachers and librarians in Córdoba.

Islamic cities had a distinctive physical appearance due to their common use of certain architectural features, such as the pointed arch and traceried windows, and specific kinds of buildings. The latter included palaces and public buildings with fountains and secluded courtyards, mosques for worship, public baths, and bazaars or marketplaces. Muslims embellished their buildings with a unique decorative art that avoided representation of living things because of their religion's prohibition of the making of graven images. Islamic cities other than Córdoba were also distinguished by their numerous libraries. Baghdad had more than thirty libraries, and the library in Cairo contained 1.1 million manuscripts.

During the first few centuries of the Arab empire, it was the Islamic world that saved and spread the scientific

**Mosque at Córdoba.** The first Great Mosque of Córdoba was built by Abd al-Rahman, founder of the Umayyad dynasty of Spain, in the eighth century. The mosque was later enlarged in the tenth century. Shown here is the interior of the sanctuary, with its two levels of arches. Although the Umayyad caliphs of Damascus were overthrown and replaced by the Abbasid dynasty in the eighth century, the independent Umayyad dynasty in Spain lasted until the eleventh century.

© Photodisc Green/Getty Images

and philosophical works of ancient civilizations. At a time when the ancient Greek philosophers were largely unknown in Europe, key works by Plato and Aristotle were translated into Arabic. They were put in a library called the House of Wisdom in Baghdad, where they were read and studied by Muslim scholars. The library also contained texts on mathematics brought from India. The preservation of ancient texts was aided by the use of paper. The making of paper was introduced from China in the eighth century, and by the end of that century, paper factories had been established in Baghdad. Booksellers and libraries soon followed. European universities later benefited from this scholarship when these works were translated from Arabic into Latin.

Although Islamic scholars are rightly praised for preserving much of classical knowledge for the West, they also made considerable advances of their own. Nowhere is this more evident than in their contributions to mathematics and the natural sciences. The list of achievements in mathematics and astronomy alone is impressive. The Muslims adopted and passed on the numerical system of India, including the use of the zero. In Europe, it became known as the Arabic system. Al-Khwarizmi, a ninth-century Persian mathematician, created the discipline of algebra. Muslim astronomers studied the positions of the stars from the observatory established by al-Ma'mun at Baghdad. They were aware that the earth was round and named many stars. They also perfected the astrolabe, an instrument used by sailors to determine their location by observing the positions of heavenly bodies. It was the astrolabe that later made it possible for Europeans to sail to the Americas.

Muslim scholars also made many new discoveries in chemistry and developed medicine as a field of scientific study. Especially renowned was Ibn Sina (known as Avicenna in the West, 980–1037), who wrote a medical encyclopedia that, among other things, stressed the contagious nature of certain diseases and showed how they could be spread by contaminated water supplies. After its translation into Latin, Avicenna's work became a basic medical textbook for medieval European university students. Avicenna was but one of many Muslim scholars whose work was translated into Latin and contributed to the development of intellectual life in Europe in the twelfth and thirteenth centuries.

## TIMELINE

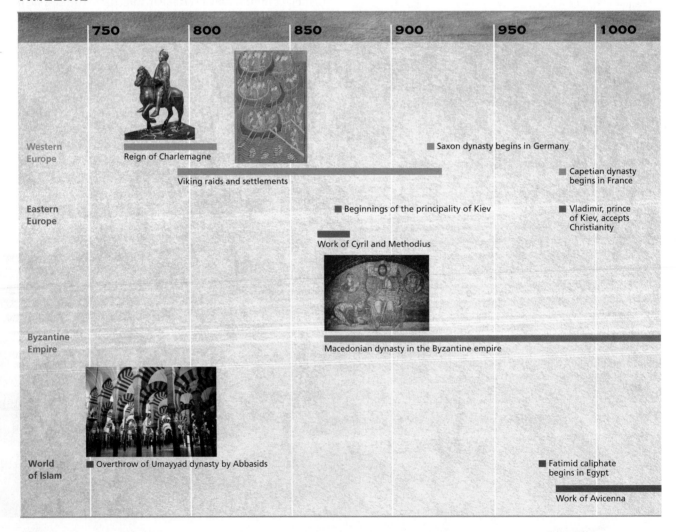

12. Quoted in Bernard Lewis, *The Arabs in History* (London, 1958), p. 90.
13. al-Mas'udi, *The Meadows of Gold: The Abbasids,* ed. Paul Lunde and Caroline Stone (London, 1989), p. 151.

## CONCLUSION

![drop cap A] FTER THE TURMOIL OF the disintegration of the Roman Empire and the establishment of the Germanic states, a new European civilization began to emerge slowly in the Early Middle Ages. The coronation of Charlemagne, descendant of a Germanic tribe converted to Christianity, as Roman emperor in 800 symbolized the fusion of the three chief components of the new European civilization: the German tribes, the classical tradition, and Christianity. In the long run, the creation of a western empire fostered the idea of a distinct European identity and marked a shift of power from the south to the north. Italy and the Mediterranean had been the center of the Roman Empire. The lands north of the Alps now became the political center of Europe.

With the disintegration of the Carolingian Empire, new forms of political institutions in which lords exercised legal, administrative, and military power began to develop in Europe. The practice of fief-holding transferred public power into many private hands and seemed to provide the security sorely lacking in a time of weak central government and new invasions by Muslims, Magyars, and Vikings. While Europe struggled, the Byzantine and Islamic worlds continued to prosper and flourish, the brilliance of their urban cultures standing in marked contrast to the underdeveloped rural world of Europe. By 1000, however, that rural world had not only recovered but was beginning to expand in ways undreamed of by previous generations. Europe stood poised for a giant leap.

## NOTES

1. Einhard, *The Life of Charlemagne,* trans. Samuel Turner (Ann Arbor, Mich., 1960), p. 30.
2. Ibid., p. 57.
3. Quoted in Pierre Riché, *Daily Life in the World of Charlemagne,* trans. Jo Ann McNamara (Philadelphia, 1978), p. 56.
4. 1 Corinthians 7:1–2, 8–9.
5. Quoted in Derrick Bailey, *Homosexuality and the Western Christian Tradition* (London, 1955), p. 73.
6. Quoted in Paul Veyne, ed., *A History of Private Life,* vol. 1, *From Pagan Rome to Byzantium,* trans. Arthur Goldhammer (Cambridge, Mass., 1987), p. 440.
7. Stanley Rubin, *Medieval English Medicine* (New York, 1974), p. 136.
8. Quoted in Brian Inglis, *A History of Medicine* (New York, 1965), p. 51.
9. Quoted in Simon Keynes, "The Vikings in England, c. 790–1016," in Peter Sawyer, ed., *The Oxford Illustrated History of the Vikings* (Oxford, 1997), p. 81.
10. Quoted in Oliver Thatcher and Edgar McNeal, *A Source Book for Medieval History* (New York, 1905), p. 363.
11. Simon Keynes and Michael Lapidge, *Alfred the Great: Asser's "Life of King Alfred" and Other Contemporary Sources* (Harmondsworth, England, 1983), pp. 84–85.

## SUGGESTIONS FOR FURTHER READING

Good general histories of the entire medieval period can be found in **S. Painter and B. Tierney, *Western Europe in the Middle Ages, 300–1475*** (New York, 1983); **E. Peters, *Europe and the Middle Ages,*** 2d ed. (Englewood Cliffs, N.J., 1989); **D. Nicholas, *The Evolution of the Medieval World: Society, Government, and Thought in Europe, 312–1500*** (London, 1993); and **G. Holmes, ed., *The Oxford Illustrated History of Medieval Europe*** (Oxford, 1988). For a good general survey of the social history of the Middle Ages, see **C. B. Bouchard, *Life and Society in the West: Antiquity and the Middle Ages*** (San Diego, Calif., 1988). For excellent reference works on medieval history, see **N. F. Cantor, *The Encyclopedia of the Middle Ages*** (New York, 1999), and **J. R. Strayer, ed., *Dictionary of the Middle Ages,*** 13 vols. (New York, 1982–1989). For a brief history of the period covered in this chapter, see **R. Collins, *Early Medieval Europe, 300–1000*** (New York, 1991). See also the brief works by **B. Rosenwein, *A Short History of the Middle Ages*** (Orchard Park, N.Y., 2002), and **C. W. Hollister and J. Bennett, *Medieval Europe: A Short History,*** 9th ed. (New York, 2001). For a good collection of essays, see **R. McKitterick, ed., *Early Middle Ages: Europe, 400–1000*** (Oxford, 2001).

Surveys of Carolingian Europe include **D. Bullough, *The Age of Charlemagne*** (New York, 1966); **P. Riché, *The Carolingians: A Family Who Forged Europe*** (Philadelphia, 1993); **L. Halphen, *Charlemagne and the Carolingian Empire*** (New York, 1977); and **R. McKitterick, *The Frankish Kingdoms Under the Carolingians, 751–987*** (London, 1983). On Charlemagne, see **H. R. Loyn and J. Percival, *The Reign of Charlemagne*** (New York, 1976), and the popular biography by **R. Winston, *Charlemagne: From the Hammer to the Cross*** (Indianapolis, Ind., 1954). On Carolingian culture, see *The Carolingians and the Written Word* (Cambridge, 1989), *Carolingian Culture: Emulation and Innovation* (New York, 1994), and the collection of essays titled *The Frankish Kings and Culture in the Early Middle Ages* (Brookfield, Vt., 1995), all by **R. McKitterick.**

Various aspects of social life in the Carolingian world are examined in **P. Riché, *Daily Life in the World of Charlemagne,*** trans. **J. A. McNamara** (Philadelphia, 1978); **M. Rouche,** "The Early Middle Ages in the West," in **P. Veyne, ed., *A History of Private Life*** (Cambridge, Mass., 1987), vol. 1, pp. 411–549; **C. B. Bouchard,** *Life and Society in the West: Antiquity and the Middle Ages* (San Diego, Calif., 1988), ch. 5; and **S. F. Wemple, *Women in Frankish Society: Marriage and the Cloister*** (Philadelphia, 1981). On children, see **S. Shamar, *Childhood in the Middle Ages,* trans.** C. Galai (London, 1992), and **J. Boswell, *The Kindness of Strangers*** (New York, 1988). On attitudes toward sexuality in the early Christian church, see the important works by **P. Brown, *The Body and Society*** (New York, 1988), and **E. Pagels, *Adam, Eve, and the Serpent*** (New York, 1988).

The Vikings are examined in **P. Sawyer, *Kings and Vikings*** (London, 1982); **F. D. Logan, *The Vikings in History,*** 2d ed. (London, 1991); **G. Jones, *A History of the Vikings,*** rev. ed. (Oxford, 2001); and **P. Sawyer, ed., *The Oxford Illustrated History of the Vikings*** (New York, 1997).

Two introductory works on fief-holding are **J. R. Strayer, *Feudalism*** (Princeton, N.J., 1985), and the classic work by **M. Bloch, *Feudal Society,* trans.** L. A. Manyon (London, 1961). For an important revisionist view, see **S. Reynolds, *Fiefs and Vassals*** (Oxford, 1994). Works on the new political configurations that emerged in the tenth century are cited in Chapter 9.

For the economic history of the Early Middle Ages, see **G. Duby,** *The Early Growth of the European Economy: Warriors and Peasants from the Seventh to the Twelfth Century* (Ithaca, N.Y., 1974). On the manorial court, see **Z. Razi and R. Smith, eds.,** *Medieval Society and the Manor Court* (New York, 1996).

Byzantine civilization in this period is examined in **R. Jenkins,** *Byzantium: The Imperial Centuries, 610–1071* (New York, 1969), and **W. Treadgold,** *The Byzantine Revival, 780–842* (Stanford, Calif., 1988). On the Slavic peoples of central and eastern Europe, see **F. Dvornik,** *The Slavs in European History and Civilization* (New Brunswick, N.J., 1962); **A. P. Vlasto,** *The Entry of the Slavs into Christendom* (Cambridge, 1970); **Z. Vana,** *The World of the Ancient Slavs* (London, 1983); and **S. Franklin and J. Shepard,** *The Emergence of Rus, 750–1200* (New York, 1996). The world of Islam in this period is discussed in **H. Kennedy,** *The Prophet and the Age of the Caliphates: The Islamic Near East from the Sixth to the Eleventh Century* (London, 1986), and **J. Lassner,** *The Shaping of Abbasid Rule* (Princeton, N.J., 1980). For a broad view on the relations between Islam and the West, see **B. Lewis,** *Islam and the West* (Oxford, 1994).

# History ⧗ Now™

Enter *HistoryNow* using the access card that is available for *Western Civilization*. *HistoryNow* will assist you in understanding the content in this chapter with lesson plans generated for your needs. In addition, you can read the following documents, and many more, online:

Saint Benedict, Rule

Saint Finnian of Clonard, Penitential

Einhard, *Life of Charlemagne*

## INFOTRAC SEARCH TERMS

For additional reading, go to InfoTrac College Edition, your online research library at http://infotrac.thomsonlearning.com

| *Key Term Search* | *Subject Guide Search* |
| --- | --- |
| Carolingian | feudal |
| Charlemagne | feudalism |
| Vikings not Minnesota | |

## WESTERN CIVILIZATION RESOURCES

Visit the *Western Civilization* Companion Web site for resources specific to this book:

http://history.wadsworth.com/spielvogel06/

For a variety of tools to help you succeed in this course, visit the Western Civilization Resource Center at

http://history.wadsworth.com/western/

Included are quizzes; images; documents; interactive simulations; maps and timelines; movie explorations; and a wealth of other sources.

# THE RECOVERY AND GROWTH OF EUROPEAN SOCIETY IN THE HIGH MIDDLE AGES

*Town street scene in thirteenth-century England*

Mary Evans Picture Library

THE NEW EUROPEAN CIVILIZATION that had emerged in the ninth and tenth centuries began to come into its own in the eleventh and twelfth centuries as Europeans established new patterns that reached their zenith in the thirteenth century. The High Middle Ages (1000–1300) was a period of recovery and growth for Western civilization, characterized by a greater sense of security and a burst of energy and enthusiasm. New agricultural practices that increased the food supply helped give rise to a commercial and urban revival that, accompanied by a rising population, created new dynamic elements in a formerly static society.

Townspeople themselves were often great enthusiasts for their new way of life. In the twelfth century, William Fitz-Stephen spoke of London as one of the noble cities of the world: "It is happy in the healthiness of its air, in the Christian religion, in the strength of its defences, the nature of its site, the honor of its citizens, the modesty of its women; pleasant in sports; fruitful of noble men." To Fitz-Stephen, London offered myriad opportunities and pleasures. Fairs and markets were held regularly, and "practically anything that man may need is brought daily not only into special places but even into the open squares." Any man, according to Fitz-Stephen, "if he is healthy and not a good-for-nothing, may earn his living expenses and esteem according to his station." Then, too, there are the happy inhabitants of the city: Where else has one "ever met such a wonderful show of people this side or the other side of the sea?" Sporting events and leisure activities are available in every season of the year: "In Easter holidays they fight battles on water." In summer, "the youths are exercised in leaping, dancing, shooting, wrestling, casting the stone; the maidens dance as long as they can well see." In winter, "when the great fen, or moor, which waters the walls of the city on the north side, is frozen, many young men play upon the ice; some, striding as wide as they may, do slide swiftly." To Fitz-Stephen, "every convenience for human pleasure is known to be at hand" in London. One would hardly know from his cheerful description that medieval cities faced over-crowded conditions, terrible smells from rotting garbage and raw sewage, and the constant challenge of epidemics and fires.

By the twelfth and thirteenth centuries, both the urban centers and the urban population of Europe were experiencing a dramatic expansion. New forms of cultural and intellectual expression also arose in this new urban world. Although European society in the High Middle Ages remained overwhelmingly agricultural, the growth of trade and cities along with the development of a money economy and new commercial practices and institutions constituted a veritable commercial revolution that affected most of Europe.

# Land and People in the High Middle Ages

The period from 1000 to 1300 witnessed an improvement in climate as a small but nevertheless significant rise in temperature made for longer and better growing seasons. At the same time, the European population experienced a dramatic increase, virtually doubling between 1000 and 1300, from 38 million to 74 million people. As Table 9.1 indicates, the rate of growth tended to vary from region to region. This rise in population was physically evident in the growth of agricultural villages, towns, and cities and the increase in arable land.

What accounted for this dramatic increase in population? Obviously, fertility rates increased sufficiently to gradually outstrip the relatively high mortality rates of medieval society, which were especially acute in infancy and the childhood years. Traditionally, historians have cited two factors to explain the population increase: increased security stemming from more settled and peaceful conditions after the invasions of the Early Middle Ages had stopped and a dramatic increase in agricultural production capable of sustaining a larger population.

**TABLE 9.1** **Population Estimates (in millions), 1000 and 1340**

| Area | 1000 | 1340 |
|---|---|---|
| *Mediterranean* | | |
| Greece and Balkans | 5 | 6 |
| Italy | 5 | 10 |
| Iberia | 7 | 9 |
| Total | 17 | 25 |
| *Western and Central Europe* | | |
| France and Low Countries | 6 | 19 |
| British Isles | 2 | 5 |
| Germany and Scandinavia | 4 | 11.5 |
| Total | 12 | 35.5 |
| *Eastern Europe* | | |
| Russia | 6 | 8 |
| Poland | 2 | 3 |
| Hungary | 1.5 | 2 |
| Total | 9.5 | 13 |
| *Grand Total* | 38.5 | 73.5 |

SOURCE: J. C. Russell, *The Control of Late Ancient and Medieval Population* (Philadelphia: American Philosophical Society, 1985), p. 36. Demographic specialists admit that these are merely estimates. Some figures, especially those for eastern Europe, could be radically revised by new research.

## The New Agriculture

During the High Middle Ages, significant changes occurred in the way Europeans farmed. Although the warmer climate played an underlying role by improving growing conditions, another important factor in increasing the production of food was the expansion of cultivated or arable land. This was done primarily by clearing forested areas for cultivation. Millions of acres of forests were also cut down to provide timber for fuel, houses, mills, bridges, fortresses, ships, and charcoal for the iron industry (see the box on p. 229). Eager for land, peasants cut down trees, drained swamps, and in the Netherlands even began to reclaim land from the sea. By the thirteenth century, the total acreage available for farming in Europe was greater than at any time before or since.

**Technological Changes** Technological changes also furthered the expansion of agriculture. Many of them depended on the use of iron, which was mined in various areas of Europe and traded to places where it was not found. Iron was in demand to make swords and armor as well as scythes, axheads, new types of farming implements such as hoes, and saws, hammers, and nails for building purposes. It was crucial to the development of the heavy, wheeled plow, the *carruca*, which made an enormous impact on medieval agriculture north of the Alps.

The plow of the Mediterranean and Near Eastern worlds had been the *aratum*, a nonwheeled, light scratch plow made mostly of wood that was sufficient to break the top layer of the light soils of those areas. It could be pulled by a single donkey, ox, or horse. But such a light plow was

church were Christmas (celebrating the birth of Jesus), Easter (celebrating the resurrection of Jesus), and Pentecost (celebrating the descent of the Holy Spirit on Jesus' disciples fifty days after his resurrection). Numerous other feasts dedicated to saints or the Virgin Mary, the mother of Jesus, were also celebrated, making a total of over fifty holidays.

Religious feast days, Sunday Mass, baptisms, marriages, and funerals all brought peasants into contact with the village church, a crucial part of manorial life. In the village church, the peasant was baptized as an infant, confirmed in the faith, sometimes married, and given the sacrament of Holy Communion as well as the last rites of the church before death. The village priest instructed the peasants in the basic elements of Christianity so that they might attain the Christian's ultimate goal—salvation. But village priests were often barely literate peasants themselves, and it is hard to know how much church doctrine the peasants actually understood. Very likely, they regarded God as an all-powerful force who needed to be appeased by prayer to bring good harvests.

**The Peasant Household**    Peasant dwellings were very simple. In timber-rich areas, peasant cottages had wood frames filled in with wattling (a lattice of laths) and plastered with a "daub" of clay, straw, animal hair, and dung. Roofs were often thatched with reeds or straw. In timber-poor areas, peasants built their houses out of stone. The houses of poorer peasants consisted of a single room, but others had at least two rooms—a main room for cooking, eating, and other activities and another room for sleeping. There was little privacy in a medieval household. A hearth in the main room was used for heating and cooking, but since there were few or no windows and no chimney, the smoke from fires in the hearth went out a hole in the roof or gable.

**Family and the Role of Women**    Surveys of monastic manors reveal that the typical peasant household consisted of a husband and wife with two or three children. Infant mortality rates were high. Peasant women occupied both an important and a difficult position in manorial society. They were expected to carry and bear children, do the spinning and weaving that provided the household's clothes, tend the family's vegetable garden, and provide the meals. A woman's ability to manage the household might determine whether her family would starve or survive in difficult times. At the same time, peasant women often worked with men in the fields, especially at harvest time.

**The Peasant Diet**    Though simple, a peasant's daily diet was potentially nutritious when food was available. The basic staple of the peasant diet, and the medieval diet in general, was bread. While women made the dough for the bread, the loaves were usually baked in community ovens, which were a monopoly of the lord of the manor. Peasant bread was made of the cheaper grains (rye, barley, millet, and oats), rather than expensive wheat. It was dark and had

a very heavy, hard texture. Bread was supplemented by legumes (peas and beans) from the household gardens, bacon from the family pig, cheese from cow's or goat's milk, and where available, wild game and fish from hunting and fishing. Manorial lords tended to regulate fishing, however, and were especially reluctant to allow peasants to hunt for fear that insufficient game would remain for the nobility. Woodlands also provided nuts, berries, and a foraging area for pigs. Fruits, such as apples, pears, and cherries, were also available. Chickens provided eggs and occasionally meat. Peasants usually ate fresh meat only on the great feast days, such as Christmas, Easter, and Pentecost.

Grains were important not only for bread but also for making ale. In many northern European countries, ale was the most common drink of the poor. If records are accurate, enormous quantities of ale were consumed. A monastery in the twelfth century recorded a daily allotment of three gallons a day to each monk, far above the weekend consumption of many present-day college students. Peasants in the field undoubtedly consumed even more. This high consumption of alcohol might explain the large number of fights and accidents recorded in medieval court records.

## The Aristocracy of the High Middle Ages

In the High Middle Ages, European society was dominated by a group of men whose primary preoccupation was warfare. King Alfred of England had said that a "well-peopled land" must have "men of prayer, men of war, and men of work," and medieval ideals held to a tripartite division of society into these three basic groups. The "men of war" were the **aristocracy** who came to form a distinct social group, albeit one with considerable variation in wealth among its members. Nevertheless, they, along with their wives and children, shared a common ethos and a distinctive lifestyle.

**The Significance of the Aristocracy**    King Alfred's "men of war" were the lords and vassals of medieval society. The lords were the kings, dukes, counts, barons, and viscounts (and even bishops and archbishops) who held extensive lands and considerable political power. They formed an aristocracy or nobility that consisted of people who held real political, economic, and social power. Nobles relied for military help on knights, mounted warriors who fought for them in return for weapons and daily sustenance. Knights were by no means the social equals of nobles; many knights in fact possessed little more than peasants. But in the course of the twelfth and thirteenth centuries, knights improved their social status and joined the ranks of the nobility. In the process, *noble* and *knight* came to mean much the same thing, and warfare likewise tended to become a distinguishing characteristic of the nobleman. The great lords and knights came to form a common caste. Although social divisions based on extremes of wealth and landholdings persisted, they were all warriors united by the institution of knighthood.

**The Men of War**    Medieval theory maintained that the warlike qualities of the nobility were justified by their role as defenders of society. Knights, however, were also notorious for fighting each other. The Catholic church intervened, and though it could not stop the incessant bloodletting, it did at least try to limit it by instituting the "Peace of God." Beginning in the eleventh century, the church encouraged knights to take an oath to respect churches and pilgrimage centers and to refrain from attacking noncombatants, such as clergy, poor people, merchants, and women. It was, of course, permissible to continue killing each other. At the same time, the church initiated the "Truce of God," which forbade fighting on Sundays and the primary feast days.

In addition to trying to diminish fighting, the church also worked to redirect the nobility's warlike energy into different channels, such as the Crusades against the Muslims (see Chapter 10), and was quite willing to justify violence when used against peace-breakers and especially against non-Christians. Hence being a warrior on behalf of God easily vindicated the nobles' love of war and in fact justified their high social status as the defenders of Christian society. The church furthered this process by steeping knighthood in Christian symbols. A knight formally received his arms in a religious ceremony, and weapons were blessed by a priest for Christian service. Throughout the Middle Ages, a constant tension existed between the ideals of a religion founded on the ideal of peace and the ethos of a nobility based on the love of war.

**Castles**    The growth of the European nobility in the High Middle Ages was made visible by an increasing number of castles scattered across the landscape. Although castle architecture varied considerably, castles did possess two common features: they were permanent residences for the noble family, its retainers, and servants, and they were defensible fortifications. For defensive purposes, castles were surrounded by open areas and large stone walls. At the heart of the castle was the keep, a large, multistoried building that housed kitchens, stables, storerooms, a great hall for visitors, dining, and administrative business, and numerous rooms for sleeping and living. The growing wealth of the High Middle Ages made it possible for the European nobility to build more secure castles with thicker walls and more elaborately decorated interiors. As castles became more sturdily built, they proved to be more easily defended and harder to seize by force.

**Aristocratic Women**    Although women could legally hold and inherit property, most women remained under the control of men—their fathers until they married and their husbands after they married. Nevertheless, aristocratic women had numerous opportunities to play important roles. Because the lord was often away at war, on a Crusade, or at court, the lady of the castle had to manage the estate, a considerable responsibility in view of the fact that households, even of lesser aristocrats, could include large numbers of officials and servants. Supervising financial accounts, both for the household and for the landed estate,

**Castle and Aristocrats.** This illustration is from the *Très Riches Heures* (Very Sumptuous Hours) of Jean, duke of Berry. The three Limbourg brothers created this Book of Hours, which was a book containing prayers to be recited at different times each day. This scene depicts the château at Dourdan, France, and its surrounding lands. In the foreground, elaborately dressed aristocratic men and women are seen amusing themselves.

alone required considerable financial knowledge. The lady of the castle was also often responsible for overseeing the food supply and maintaining all other supplies for the smooth operation of the household.

Childhood ended early for the daughters of aristocrats. Since aristocratic girls were married in their teens (usually at the age of fifteen or sixteen) and were expected by their husbands to assume their responsibilities immediately, the training of girls in a large body of practical knowledge could never start too early. Sent at a young age to the castles of other nobles to be brought up, girls were trained as ladies-in-waiting. The lady of the castle taught them how to sew and weave and instructed them in all the skills needed for running an estate. They also learned how to read and write, dance, sing, and play musical instruments.

# Women in Medieval Thought

W HETHER A NUN or the wife of an aristocrat, towns- man, or peasant, a woman in the Middle Ages was considered inferior to a man and subject to a man's authority. Although there are a number of examples of strong women who ignored such attitudes, church teachings also reinforced these notions. The first selection from Gratian, the twelfth- century jurist who wrote the first systematic work on canon law, supports this view. The second selection was written in the 1390s by a wealthy fifty-year-old Parisian who wanted to instruct his fifteen-year-old bride on how to be a good wife.

## Gratian, *Decretum*

Women should be subject to their men. The natural order for mankind is that women should serve men and children their parents, for it is just that the lesser serve the greater.

The image of God is in man and it is one. Women were drawn from man, who has God's jurisdiction as if he were God's vicar, because he has the image of one God. Therefore woman is not made in God's image.

Woman's authority is nil; let her in all things be subject to the rule of man. . . . And neither can she teach, nor be a witness, nor give a guarantee, nor sit in judgment.

Adam was beguiled by Eve, not she by him. It is right that he whom woman led into wrongdoing should have her under his direction, so that he may not fail a second time through female levity.

## A Merchant of Paris, *On Marriage*

I entreat you to keep his linen clean, for this is up to you. Because the care of outside affairs is men's work, a husband must look after these things, and go and come, run here and there in rain, wind, snow, and hail—sometimes wet, sometimes dry, sometimes sweating, other times shivering, badly fed, badly housed, badly shod, badly bedded—and nothing harms him because he is cheered by the anticipa- tion of the care his wife will take of him on his return— of the pleasures, joys, and comforts she will provide, or have provided for him in her presence: to have his shoes off before a good fire, to have his feet washed, to have clean shoes and hose, to be well fed, provided with good drink, well served, well honored, well bedded in white sheets and white nightcaps, well covered with good furs, and comforted with other joys and amusements, intimacies, affections, and secrets about which I am silent. And on the next day fresh linen and garments. . . .

Also keep peace with him. Remember the country proverb that says there are three things that drive a good man from his home: a house with a bad roof, a smoking chimney, and a quarrelsome woman. I beg you, in order to preserve your husband's love and good will, be loving, amiable, and sweet with him. . . . Thus protect and shield your husband from all troubles, give him all the comfort you can think of, wait on him, and have him waited on in your home. . . . If you do what is said here, he will always have his affection and his heart turned toward you and your service, and he will forsake all other homes, all other women, all other help, and all other households.

---

Although women were expected to be subservient to their husbands (see the box above), there were many strong women who advised and sometimes even dominated their husbands. Perhaps the most famous was Eleanor of Aquitaine (c. 1122–1204), heiress to the duchy of Aquitaine in southwestern France. Married first to King Louis VII of France (1137–1180), Eleanor even accompanied her husband on a Crusade, but her failure to bear sons led Louis to have their marriage annulled. Eleanor then mar- ried Henry, count of Anjou, who became King Henry II of England (1154–1189) and duke of Normandy. She bore him both sons and daughters and took an active role in pol- itics, even assisting her sons in rebelling against Henry in 1173–1174. Imprisoned by her husband for her activities, after Henry's death she again assumed an active political life, providing both military and political support for her sons.

Blanche of Castile (1188–1252) was another power- ful medieval queen. She became regent while her son Louis IX was a boy and ruled France with a powerful hand dur- ing much of the 1220s and 1230s. She repelled the attempt of some rebellious French nobles to seize her son, the young king, and defeated Henry III of England when he tried to incite an uprising in France in order to reconquer Nor- mandy. Blanche's political sense was so astute that even when Louis IX came of age, he continued to rely on her as his chief adviser. One medieval chronicler gave her the highest compliment he could think of: "she ruled as a man."

**The Way of the Warrior**   At the age of seven or eight, aris- tocratic boys were sent either to a clerical school to pur- sue a religious career or to another nobleman's castle, where they prepared for the life of a noble. Their chief lessons were military; they learned how to joust, hunt, ride, and handle weapons properly. Occasionally, aristocrats' sons might also learn the basic fundamentals of reading and writing. After his apprenticeship in knighthood, at about the age of twenty-one, a young man formally entered the adult world in the ceremony of "knighting." A sponsor girded a sword on the young candidate and struck him on the cheek or neck with an open hand (or later touched him three times on the shoulder with the blade of a sword), possibly signifying the passing of the sponsor's military valor to the new knight.

In the eleventh and twelfth centuries, under the influence of the church, an ideal of civilized behavior called **chivalry** gradually evolved among the nobility. Chivalry represented a code of ethics that knights were supposed to uphold. In addition to their oath to defend the church and the defenseless, knightly honor also demanded that unarmed knights should not be attacked. Chivalry also implied that knights should fight only for glory, but this account of a group of English knights by a medieval writer reveals another motive for battle: "The whole city was plundered to the last farthing, and then they proceeded to rob all the churches throughout the city, . . . and seizing gold and silver, cloth of all colors, women's ornaments, gold rings, goblets, and precious stones. . . . They all returned to their own lords rich men."[1] Apparently, not all chivalric ideals were taken seriously.

After his formal initiation into the world of warriors, a young man returned home to find himself once again subject to his parents' authority. Young men were discouraged from marrying until their fathers died, at which time they could marry and become lords of the castle. Trained to be warriors but with no adult responsibilities, young knights naturally gravitated toward military activities and often furthered the private warfare endemic to the noble class.

**The Role of Tournaments**   In the twelfth century, tournaments began to appear as an alternative to the socially destructive fighting that the church was trying to curb. Initially, tournaments consisted of the "melee," in which warriors on horseback fought with blunted weapons in free-for-all combat. The goal was to take prisoners who would then be ransomed, making success in tournaments a path to considerable gain. Within an eight-month span, the English knight William Marshall made a tour of the tournament circuit, defeated 203 knights, and made so much money that he had to hire two clerks to take care of it.

By the late twelfth century, the melee was preceded by the joust, or individual combat between two knights. Gradually, jousts became the main part of the tournament. No matter how much the church condemned tournaments, knights themselves continued to see them as an excellent way to train for war. As one knight explained: "A knight cannot distinguish himself in that [war] if he has not trained for it in tourneys. He must have seen his blood flow, heard his teeth crack under fist blows, felt his opponent's

**The Tournament.**   The tournament arose as a socially acceptable alternative to the private warfare that plagued the nobility in the Middle Ages. This fifteenth-century Flemish illustration shows a joust between two heavily armored knights. Shown watching are King Richard II in the middle and other onlookers at the right.

weight bear down upon him as he lay on the ground and, after being twenty times unhorsed, have risen twenty times to fight."[2]

## Marriage Patterns of the Aristocracy

Aristocratic marriages were expected to establish alliances with other families, bring new wealth, and provide heirs to carry on the family line. Parents therefore supervised the choice of spouses for their children. One of the most noticeable features of aristocratic marriages was the usually wide discrepancy in the ages of the marital partners.

**Marriage.**   Marriage festivities for members of the aristocracy were usually quite elaborate. As seen in this illustration of the marriage of Renaud de Montauban and Clarisse, daughter of the ruler of Gascogne, after the festivities, the wedding party would accompany the new couple to their bedroom to prepare them for the physical consummation of their marriage. Only after physical union was a medieval marriage considered valid.

# An Italian Banker Discusses Trading Between Europe and China

*W* ORKING ON BEHALF of a banking guild in Florence, Francesco Balducci Pegolotti journeyed to England and Cyprus. As a result of his contacts with many Italian merchants, he acquired considerable information about long-distance trade between Europe and China. In this account, written in 1340, he provides advice for Italian merchants.

### Francesco Balducci Pegolotti, *An Account of Traders Between Europe and China*

In the first place, you must let your beard grow long and not shave. And at Tana [modern Rostov] you should furnish yourself with a guide. And you must not try to save money in the matter of guides by taking a bad one instead of a good one. For the additional wages of the good one will not cost you so much as you will save by having him. And besides the guide it will be well to take at least two good menservants who are acquainted with the Turkish tongue. . . .

The road you travel from Tana to China is perfectly safe, whether by day or night, according to what the merchants say who have used it. Only if the merchant, in going or coming, should die upon the road, everything belonging to him will become the possession of the lord in the country in which he dies. . . . And in like manner if he dies in China. . . .

China is a province which contains a multitude of cities and towns. Among others there is one in particular, that is to say the capital city, to which many merchants are attracted, and in which there is a vast amount of trade; this city is called Khanbaliq [modern Beijing]. And the said city has a circuit of one hundred miles, and is all full of people and houses and of dwellers in the said city. . . .

Whatever silver the merchants may carry with them as far as China, the emperor of China will take from them and put into his treasury. And to merchants who thus bring silver they give that paper money of theirs in exchange . . . and with this money you can readily buy silk and all other merchandise that you have a desire to buy. And all the people of the country are bound to receive it. And yet you shall not pay a higher price for your goods because your money is of paper.

---

Daughters of the nobles married at fifteen or sixteen, but their husbands might be in their thirties or even forties, since men did not marry until they came into their inheritances.

By the twelfth century, the efforts of the church since Carolingian times to end divorce (see Chapter 8) had borne much fruit. As a sacrament, marriage was intended to last for a lifetime and could not be dissolved. In certain cases, however, the church accepted the right of married persons to separate by granting them an annulment or official recognition that their marriage had not been valid in the first place. If it could be established that the couple had not consented to the marriage, that one or the other suffered from a sexual incapacity that prevented the consummation of the marriage, or that the couple were related by blood (more closely than sixth or, after 1215, third cousins), the church would approve an annulment of their marriage, and the partners would be free to marry again.

## The New World of Trade and Cities

Medieval Europe was an overwhelmingly agrarian society with most people living in small villages. In the eleventh and twelfth centuries, however, new elements were introduced that began to transform the economic foundation of Western civilization: a revival of trade, considerable expansion in the circulation of money, a restoration of specialized craftspeople and artisans, and the growth and development of towns. These changes were made possible by the new agricultural practices and subsequent increase in food production, which freed some European families from the need to produce their own food. Merchants and craftspeople could now buy their necessities.

### The Revival of Trade

The revival of commercial activity was a gradual process. During the chaotic conditions of the Early Middle Ages, large-scale trade had declined in western Europe except for Byzantine contacts with Italy and the Jewish traders who moved back and forth between the Muslim and Christian worlds. By the end of the tenth century, however, people with both the skills and the products for commercial activity were emerging in Europe.

Cities in Italy assumed a leading role in the revival of trade (see Map 9.1). By the end of the eighth century, Venice, on the northeastern coast, had emerged as a town with close trading ties to the Byzantine Empire. Venice developed a trading fleet and by the end of the tenth century had become the chief western trading center for Byzantine and Islamic commerce. Venice sent wine, grain, and timber to Constantinople in exchange for silk cloth, which was then peddled to other communities. Other coastal communities in western Italy, such as Genoa and Pisa, also opened new trade routes. By 1100, Italian merchants began to benefit from the Crusades and were able to establish new trading centers in eastern ports. There the merchants obtained silks, sugar, and spices, which they subsequently carried back to Italy and the West.

In the High Middle Ages, Italian merchants became even more daring in their trade activities. They established trading posts in Cairo, Damascus, and a number of Black Sea ports, where they acquired goods brought by Muslim merchants from India, China, and Southeast Asia. A few Italian merchants even journeyed to India and China in search of trade (see the box above).

While the northern Italian cities were busy trading in the Mediterranean, the towns of Flanders were doing

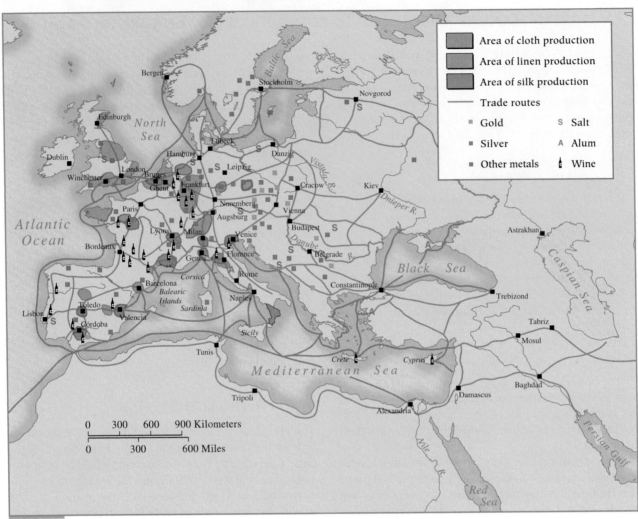

**MAP 9.1 Medieval Trade Routes.** Italian cities and Flanders were the centers of gradually expanding trade in Europe. They fostered the exchange of goods from the Byzantine Empire and the Far East with those of various regions of Europe. The diminishing threats of violence over time greatly helped trade. ❓ Look at Map 6.2. In what areas had trade expanded, and how can you account for this? 🌐 **View an animated version of this map or related maps at** http://history.wadsworth.com/spielvogel06/

likewise in northern Europe. Flanders, the area along the coast of present-day Belgium and northern France, was known for the production of a much desired high-quality woolen cloth. Flanders's location made it a logical entrepôt for the traders of northern Europe. Merchants from England, Scandinavia, France, and Germany converged there to trade their wares for woolen cloth. Flanders prospered in the eleventh and twelfth centuries, and such Flemish towns as Bruges and Ghent became centers for the trade and manufacture of woolen cloth.

By the twelfth century, it was almost inevitable that a regular exchange of goods would develop between Flanders and Italy. To encourage this trade, the counts of Champagne in northern France devised a series of six fairs held

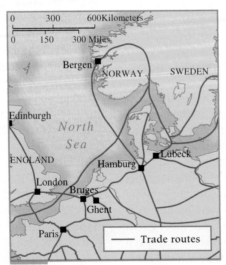

**Flanders as a Trade Center**

annually in the chief towns of their territory. They guaranteed the safety of visiting merchants, supervised the trading activities, and of course collected a sales tax on all goods exchanged at the fairs. The fairs of Champagne became the largest commercial marketplace in western Europe where the goods of northern Europe could be exchanged for the goods of southern Europe and the East. Northern merchants brought the furs, woolen cloth, tin, hemp, and honey of northern Europe and exchanged them for the cloth and swords of northern Italy and the silks, sugar, and spices of the East. The prosperity of the Champagne fairs caused lords everywhere to follow their example and establish trading fairs.

As trade increased, both gold and silver came to be in demand at fairs and trading markets of all kinds. Slowly, a money economy began to emerge. New trading companies as well as banking firms were set up to manage the exchange and sale of goods. All of these new practices were part of the rise of **commercial capitalism,** an economic system in which people invested in trade and goods in order to make profits.

## The Growth of Cities

The revival of trade led to a revival of cities. Merchants needed places where they could live and build warehouses to store their goods. Towns had greatly declined in the Early Middle Ages, especially in Europe north of the Alps. Old Roman cities continued to exist but had dwindled in size and population. With the revival of trade, merchants began to settle in these old cities, followed by craftworkers or artisans, people who had developed skills on manors or elsewhere and now perceived the opportunity to ply their trade producing objects that could be sold by the merchants. In the course of the eleventh and twelfth centuries, the old Roman cities came alive with new residents. By 1100, the old areas of these cities had been repopulated; soon the population outgrew the walls, necessitating the construction of new city walls outside the old.

In the Mediterranean world, cities had survived in a more visible fashion. Spain's Islamic cities had a flourishing urban life, and southern Italy still possessed such thriving cities as Bari, Salerno, Naples, and Amalfi. Although greatly reduced in size, Rome, the old capital of the Roman world, had survived as the center of papal administration. In northern Italy, Venice had already emerged as a town by the end of the eighth century because of its commercial connections to the Byzantine Empire.

**Founding of New Cities and Towns** Beginning in the late tenth century, many new cities or towns were founded, particularly in northern Europe. Usually, a group of artisans and merchants established a settlement near some fortified stronghold, such as a castle or monastery. Castles were particularly favored because they were usually located along major routes of transportation or at the intersection of two trade routes; the lord of the castle also offered protection. If the settlement prospered and expanded, walls were built to protect it. The original meaning of the English *borough* or *burgh* and the German *Burg* as a fortress or walled enclosure is still evident in the names of many cities, such as Edinburgh and Hamburg. The merchants and artisans of these boroughs and burghs came to be called burghers or **bourgeoisie.**

**Fortified Town of Carcassonne.** The expansion of commerce and industry led to an ongoing growth of towns and cities in the High Middle Ages. As seen in this picture of the French town of Carcassonne, medieval towns were surrounded by walls (here, double walls) strengthened by defensive towers and punctuated by gates. As is evident here, medieval urban skylines were dominated by towers of all kinds.

Most towns were closely tied to their surrounding territories because they were dependent on the countryside for their food supplies. In addition, they were often part of the territory belonging to a lord and were subject to his jurisdiction. Although lords wanted to treat towns and townspeople as they would their vassals and serfs, cities had totally different needs and a different perspective. Townspeople needed mobility to trade. Consequently, the merchants and artisans of the towns constituted a revolutionary group who needed their own unique laws to meet their requirements. Since the townspeople were profiting from the growth of trade and sale of their products, they were willing to pay for the right to make their own laws and govern themselves. In many instances, lords and kings saw the potential for vast new sources of revenues and were willing to grant (or more accurately, sell) to the townspeople the liberties they were beginning to demand.

### The Rights of Townspeople

By 1100, townspeople were obtaining charters of liberties from their territorial lords that granted them the privileges they wanted, including the right to bequeath goods and sell property, freedom from military obligation to the lord, written urban law that guaranteed their freedom, and the right for serfs to become free after residing a year and a day in the town. The last provision made it possible for a runaway serf who could avoid capture to become a free person in a city. Almost all new urban communities gained these elementary liberties, but only some towns obtained the right to govern themselves by choosing their own officials and administering their own courts of law. Where townspeople experienced difficulty in obtaining privileges, they often swore an oath, forming an association called a **commune,** and resorted to force against their lay or ecclesiastical lords.

Communes made their first appearance in Italy, where urban communities existed even in the Early Middle Ages. In northern Italy, in the regions called Tuscany and Lombardy, towns were governed by their bishops, but the nobles whose lands surrounded the towns took an active interest in them. Bishops were usually supported by the emperors, who used them as their chief administrators. In the eleventh century, city residents rebelled against the rule of the bishops, swore communal associations with the bishops' noble vassals, and overthrew the authority of the bishops by force. The alliance between town residents and rural nobles was overwhelming, and in the course of the eleventh and twelfth centuries, bishops were shorn of their authority. Communes took over the rights of government and created new offices, such as consuls and city councils, for self-rule. Pisa, Milan, Arezzo, and Genoa all attained self-government by the end of the eleventh century.

Although communes were also sworn in northern Europe, especially in France and Flanders, townspeople did not have the support of rural nobles. Revolts against lay lords were usually brutally suppressed; those against bishops, as in Laon at the beginning of the twelfth century (see the box on p. 239), were more frequently successful. When they succeeded, communes received the right to choose their own officials, hold their own courts, and run their own cities. Unlike the towns in Italy, however, where the decline of the emperor's authority ensured that the northern Italian cities could function as self-governing republics, towns in France and England did not become independent city-states but remained ultimately subject to royal authority.

Medieval cities, then, possessed varying degrees of self-government, depending on the amount of control retained over them by the lord or king in whose territory they were located. Nevertheless, all towns, regardless of the degree of outside control, evolved institutions of government for running the affairs of the community.

**City Governments** Medieval cities defined citizenship narrowly and accorded it only to males who had been born in the city or who had lived there for some time. In many cities, citizens elected members of a city council that bore primary responsibility for running the affairs of the city. City councilors (known as *consuls* in Italy and southern France) not only enacted legislation but also served as judges and city magistrates. The electoral process was carefully engineered to ensure that only members of the wealthiest and most powerful families, who came to be called the *patricians,* were elected. They kept the reins of government in their hands despite periodic protests from lesser merchants and artisans. In the twelfth and thirteenth centuries, cities added some kind of sole executive leader, even if he was only a figurehead. Although the title varied from town to town, this executive officer was frequently called a *mayor.*

City governments kept close watch over the activities of their community. To care for the welfare and safety of the community, a government might regulate air and water pollution; provide water barrels and delegate responsibility to people in every section of the town to fight fires, which were an ever-present danger; construct warehouses to stockpile grain in the event of food emergencies; and establish and supervise the standards of weights and measures used in the various local trades and industries.

Crime was not a major problem in the towns of the High Middle Ages because the relatively small size of communities made it difficult for criminals to operate openly. Nevertheless, medieval urban governments did organize town guards to patrol the streets by night and the city walls by day. People caught committing criminal acts were quickly tried for their offenses. Serious offenses, such as murder, were punished by execution, usually by hanging. Lesser crimes were punished by fines, flogging, branding, public exposure (as in the pillory), or expulsion.

Medieval cities remained relatively small in comparison to either ancient or modern cities. A large trading city would number about five thousand inhabitants. By 1300, London was the largest city in England, with eighty thousand people or more. Otherwise, north of the Alps, only a few great commercial urban centers, such as Bruges and Ghent, had a population close to forty thousand. Italian cities tended to be larger, with Venice, Florence, Genoa, Milan, and Naples numbering almost one hundred thou-

# A COMMUNAL REVOLT

HE GROWTH OF TOWNS and cities was a major aspect of economic life in the High Middle Ages. When townspeople were unable to gain basic liberties for themselves from the lord in whose territory their town was located, they sometimes swore a "commune" to gain these privileges by force. This selection by a contemporary abbot describes the violence that accompanied the formation of a commune at Laon in France in 1116. The bishop of Laon, lord of the town, had granted privileges to the townspeople in return for a large payment. Later he rescinded his grant but kept the money, thereby angering the citizens.

### The Autobiography of Guibert, Abbot of Nogent-sous-Coucy

All the efforts of the prelate and nobles in these days were reserved for fleecing their inferiors. But those inferiors were no longer moved by mere anger, but goaded into a murderous lust for the death of the bishop and his accomplices and bound themselves by oath to effect their purpose. Now they say that 400 took the oath. Such a mob could not be secret and when it came to the ears of Anselm [the bishop's assistant] toward evening of the holy Sabbath, he sent word to the bishop, as he was retiring to rest, not to go out to the early morning service, knowing that if he did he must certainly be killed. But he, infatuated with excessive pride said, "Fie, surely I shall not perish at the hands of such. . . ."

The next day, that is, the fifth in Easter week, after midday, as he [the bishop] was engaged in business with Archdeacon Walter about the getting of money, behold there arose a disorderly noise throughout the city, men shouting "Commune!" and . . . citizens now entered the bishop's court with swords, battle-axes, bows and hatchets, and carrying clubs and spears, a very great company. As soon as this sudden attack was discovered, the nobles rallied from all sides to the bishop, having sworn to give him aid against such an onset, if it should occur. . . . [Despite the assistance of the nobles, the commoners were victorious.]

Next the outrageous mob attacking the bishop and howling before the walls of his palace, he with some who were aiding him fought them off by hurling of stones and shooting of arrows. For he now, as at all times, showed great spirit as a fighter, but because he had wrongly and in vain taken up another sword, by the sword he perished. Therefore, being unable to stand against the reckless assaults of the people, he put on the clothes of one of his servants and flying to the vaults of the church hid himself in a cask, shut up in which with the head fastened on by a faithful follower he thought himself safely hidden. And as they ran hither and thither demanding where, not the bishop, but the hangdog, was, they seized one of his pages, but through his faithfulness could not get what they wanted. Laying hands on another, they learned from the traitor's nod where to look for him. Entering the vaults therefore, and searching everywhere, at last they found [him]. . . .

[The bishop] therefore, sinner though he was, yet the Lord's anointed, was dragged forth from the cask by the hair, beaten with many blows and brought out into the open air in the narrow lane of the clergy's cloister before the house of the chaplain Godfrey. And as he piteously implored them, ready to take oath that he would henceforth cease to be their bishop, that he would leave the country, and as they with hardened hearts jeered at him, one named Bernard . . . lifting his battle-axe brutally dashed out the brains of that sacred, though sinner's, head, and he slipping between the hands of those who held him, was dead before he reached the ground stricken by another thwart blow under the eye-sockets and across the middle of the nose. There brought to his end, his legs were cut off and many another wound inflicted. But Thibaut seeing the ring on the finger of the erstwhile prelate and not being able to draw it off, cut off the dead man's finger and took it. And so stripped to his skin he was thrown into a corner in front of his chaplain's house. My God, who shall recount the mocking words that were thrown at him by passersby, as he lay there, and with what clods and stones and dirt his corpse was covered?

---

sand. Even the largest European city, however, seemed insignificant alongside the Byzantine capital of Constantinople or the Arab cities of Damascus, Baghdad, and Cairo. For a long time to come, Europe remained predominantly rural, but in the long run, the rise of towns and the growth of trade laid the foundation for the eventual transformation of Europe from a rural agricultural society to an urban industrial one.

**Life in the Medieval City**   Medieval towns were surrounded by stone walls that were expensive to build, so the space within was precious and tightly filled. This gave medieval cities their characteristic appearance of narrow, winding streets with houses crowded against each other. Streets were generally left unpaved until the thirteenth century, and buildings fronted directly on them. To gain more space, inhabitants frequently added balconies or built the second and third stories of their dwellings out over the streets. Since dwellings were crowded so closely together and candles and wood fires were used for light and heat, the danger of fire was great.

A medieval urban skyline was dominated by the towers of castles and town halls, but especially of churches, whose number could be staggering. At the beginning of the thirteenth century, London had 120 monastic and parish churches. If a city was the center of a bishop's see, a large cathedral would dominate the other buildings and be visible for miles outside the city.

**The Execution of Criminals.** Violence was a common feature of medieval life. Criminals, if apprehended, were punished quickly and severely, and public executions were considered a deterrent to crime. As one can surmise from this illustration, executions were also a form of entertainment.

Most of the people who lived in the cities were merchants involved in trade and artisans engaged in manufacturing of some kind. Sometimes merchants and artisans had their own sections in a city. The merchant area included warehouses, inns, and taverns. Artisan sections were usually divided along craft lines, and each craft might have its own street where its activity was pursued.

The physical environment of medieval cities was not pleasant. They were often dirty and rife with smells from animal and human waste deposited in backyard privies or on the streets (see the box on p. 241). In some places, city governments required citizens to periodically collect garbage and waste and cart it outside the town. Atmospheric pollution was also a fact of life, not only from the ubiquitous wood fires but also from the use of coal, a cheap fuel that was used industrially by lime-burners, brewers, and dyers. Burning coal emitted ill-smelling, noxious fumes and was sometimes prohibited under pain of fine.

Cities were also unable to stop water pollution, especially from the animal-slaughtering and tanning industries. Butchers dumped blood and other waste products from their butchered animals into the river, while tanners

**Shops in a Medieval Town.** Most urban residents were merchants involved in trade and artisans who manufactured a wide variety of products. Master craftspeople had their workshops in the ground-level rooms of their houses. In this illustration, two well-dressed burghers are touring the shopping districts of a French town. Tailors, furriers, a barber, and a grocer (from left to right) are visible at work in their shops.

# POLLUTION IN A MEDIEVAL CITY

*E*NVIRONMENTAL POLLUTION is not new. Medieval cities and towns had their own problems with filthy living conditions. This excerpt is taken from an order sent by the king of England to the town of Boutham, a suburb of York, which was then being used by the king as headquarters in a war with the Scots. It demands rectification of the town's pitiful physical conditions.

## The King's Command to Boutham

To the bailiffs of the abbot of St. Mary's, York, at Boutham. Whereas it is sufficiently evident that the pavement of the said town of Boutham is so very greatly broke up that all and singular passing and going through that town sustain immoderate damages and grievances, and in addition the air is so corrupted and infected by the pigsties situated in the king's highways and in the lanes of that town and by the swine feeding and frequently wandering about in the streets and lanes and by dung and dunghills and many other foul things placed in the streets and lanes, that great repugnance overtakes the king's ministers staying in that town and also others there dwelling and passing through, the advantage of more wholesome air is impeded; the state of men is grievously injured, and other unbearable inconveniences and many other injuries are known to proceed from such corruption, to the nuisance of the king's ministers aforesaid and of others there dwelling and passing through, and to the peril of their lives.... The king, being unwilling longer to tolerate such great and unbearable defects there, orders the bailiffs to cause the pavement to be suitably repaired within their liberty before All Saints next, and to cause the pigsties, aforesaid streets and lanes to be cleansed from all dung and dunghills, and to cause proclamation to be made throughout their bailiwick forbidding any one, under pain of grievous forfeiture, to cause or permit their swine to feed or wander outside his house in the king's streets or the lanes aforesaid.

---

unloaded tannic acids, dried blood, fat, hair, and the other waste products of their operations. Forcing both industries to locate downstream to avoid polluting the water used by the city upstream was only partly effective. Tanneries and slaughterhouses existed in every medieval town, so the river could rapidly become polluted from other towns' wastes.

Because of the pollution, cities were not inclined to use the rivers for drinking water but relied instead on wells. Occasionally, communities repaired the system of aqueducts or conduits left over from Roman times and sometimes even constructed new ones. Private and public baths also existed in medieval towns. Paris, for example, had thirty-two public baths for men and women. City laws did not allow lepers and people with "bad reputations" to use them, but such measures did not prevent the public baths from being known for permissiveness due to public nudity. One contemporary commented on what occurred in public bathhouses: "Shameful things. Men make a point of staying all night in the public baths and women at the break of day come in and through 'ignorance' find themselves in the men's rooms."[3] Authorities came under increasing pressure to close the baths down, and the great plague of the fourteenth century sealed their fate. The standards of medieval hygiene broke down, and late medieval and early modern European society would prove to be remarkably dirty.

Because of the limited space in medieval towns, houses were narrow, built next to one another, and usually multistoried. In many houses, the shops or workrooms of merchants and craftspeople occupied the ground floor. Inhabitants, who might include husband and wife, children, servants, and apprentices, would live upstairs.

For most ordinary merchants and artisans, home life and work life were thus closely intertwined. Merchants and artisans taught their trades to their children and their wives and apprentices, or their children might be apprenticed to another merchant or artisan. Women, in addition to supervising the household, purchasing food and preparing meals, washing clothes, and managing the family finances, were also often expected to help their husbands in their trades. While men produced goods at home, their wives often peddled them at markets or fairs.

Some women also developed their own trades, such as brewing ale or making glass, to earn extra money. Other women worked at making hats and cloth. Widows often carried on their husband's trade. Some women in medieval towns were thus able to lead lives of considerable independence.

## Industry in Medieval Cities

The revival of trade enabled cities and towns to become important centers for manufacturing a wide range of goods, such as cloth, metalwork, shoes, and leather goods. A host of crafts were carried on in houses along the narrow streets of the medieval cities. From the twelfth century on, merchants and artisans began to organize themselves into **guilds,** which came to play a leading role in the economic life of the cities.

By the thirteenth century, virtually every group of craftspeople, such as tanners, carpenters, and bakers, had their own guild, and specialized groups of merchants, such as dealers in silk, spices, wool, or banking, had their separate guilds as well. Florence alone, for example, had fifty different guilds. Some communities were so comprehensive in covering all trades that they even had guilds for prostitutes.

Craft guilds directed almost every aspect of the production process. They set standards for the articles produced, specified the actual methods of production to be used, and even fixed the price at which the finished goods could be sold. Guilds also determined the number of individuals who could enter a specific trade and the procedure they must follow to do so.

A person who wanted to learn a trade first became an apprentice to a master craftsman, usually at around the age of ten. Apprentices were not paid but did receive room and board from their masters. After five to seven years of service, during which they learned their craft, apprentices became journeymen (or journeywomen, although most were male) who then worked for wages for other masters. Journeymen aspired to become masters as well. To do so, a journeyman had to produce a "masterpiece," a finished piece in his craft that allowed the master craftsmen of the guild to judge whether the journeyman was qualified to become a master and join the guild.

Craft guilds continued to dominate manufacturing in industries where raw materials could be acquired locally and the products sold locally. But in industries that required raw materials from outside the local area to produce high-quality products for growing markets abroad, a new form of industry dependent on large concentrations of capital and unskilled labor began to emerge. It was particularly evident in the "putting-out" or domestic system used in the production of woolen cloth in both Flanders and northern Italy. An entrepreneur, whose initial capital outlay probably came from commercial activities, bought raw wool and distributed it to workers who carried out the various stages of carding, spinning, weaving, dyeing, and fulling to produce a finished piece of woolen cloth. These laborers worked in their own homes and were paid wages. As wage earners, they were dependent on their employers and the fluctuations in prices that occurred periodically in the international market for the finished goods. The entrepreneur collected the final products and sold the finished cloth, earning a profit that could then be invested in more production. Woolen industries operated by capitalist entrepreneurs in seventeen principal centers in northern Europe, mostly in Flanders, produced most of the woolen cloth used in northern Europe. An Italian chronicler at the beginning of the fourteenth century estimated that the woolen industry in Florence produced eighty thousand pieces of cloth a year and employed thirty thousand men, women, and children, usually at pitiful wages.

# The Intellectual and Artistic World of the High Middle Ages

The High Middle Ages was a time of tremendous intellectual and artistic vitality. The period witnessed the growth of educational institutions, a rebirth of interest in ancient culture, a quickening of theological thought, the revival of law, the development of a vernacular literature, and a burst of activity in art and architecture. Although monks continued to play an important role in intellectual activity, increasingly the secular clergy, cities, and courts, whether of kings, princes, or high church officials, began to exert a newfound influence. Especially significant were the new cultural expressions that emerged in towns and cities.

## The Rise of Universities

The university as we know it with faculty, students, and degrees was a product of the High Middle Ages. The word *university* is derived from the Latin word *universitas*, meaning a corporation or guild, and referred to either a guild of teachers or a guild of students. Medieval universities were educational guilds or corporations that produced educated and trained individuals.

**The Origins of Universities** Education in the Early Middle Ages rested primarily with the clergy, especially the monks. Although monastic schools were the centers of learning from the ninth century, they were surpassed in the course of the eleventh century by the cathedral schools organized by the secular (nonmonastic) clergy. Cathedral schools, like the cities in which they were located, expanded rapidly in the eleventh century. There were twenty of them in 900, but by 1100 the number had grown to at least two hundred since every cathedral city felt compelled to establish one. The most famous were Chartres, Reims, Paris, Laon, and Soissons, all in France, which was the intellectual center of Europe by the twelfth century (see Map 9.2). Although the primary purpose of cathedral schools was to educate priests to be more literate men of God, they also attracted other individuals who desired some education but did not want to become priests. Many university administrators today carry titles, such as chancellor, provost, and dean, that were originally used for the officials of cathedral chapters.

The first European university appeared in Bologna, Italy (unless one accords this distinction to the first medical school, established earlier at Salerno, Italy). The emergence of the University of Bologna coincided with the revival of interest in Roman law, especially the rediscovery of Justinian's *Corpus Iuris Civilis* (see "The Revival of Roman Law" later in this chapter). In the twelfth century, a great teacher, such as Irnerius (1088–1125), attracted students from all over Europe. Most of them were laymen, usually older individuals who served as administrators to kings and princes and were eager to learn more about law so they could apply it in their jobs. To protect themselves, students at Bologna formed a guild or *universitas*, which was recognized by Emperor Frederick Barbarossa and given a charter in 1158. Although the faculty also organized itself as a group, the *universitas* of students at Bologna was far more influential. It obtained a promise of freedom for students from local authorities, regulated the price of lodging, and determined the curriculum, fees, and standards for their masters. Teachers were fined if they missed a class or began their lectures late. The University of Bologna remained the greatest law school in Europe throughout the Middle Ages.

In northern Europe, the University of Paris became the first recognized university. A number of teachers or mas-

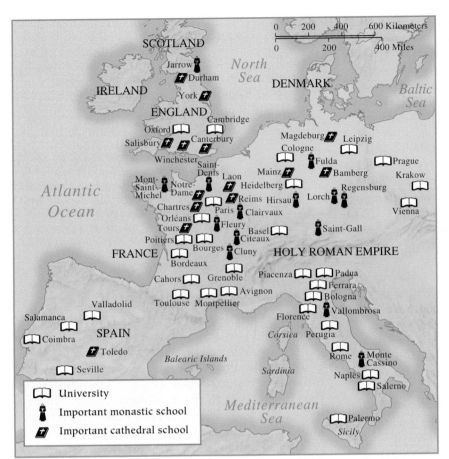

MAP 9.2 **Intellectual Centers of Medieval Europe.** Products of the High Middle Ages, universities provided students with a basic liberal arts education and the opportunity to pursue further studies in law, medicine, or theology. Courses were taught in Latin, primarily by professors reading from books. There were no exams in individual courses, but students had to pass a comprehensive oral exam to gain a degree. **?** In what ways did France qualify as the intellectual capital of Europe? ◈ **View an animated version of this map or related maps at** http://history.wadsworth.com/spielvogel06/

ters who had received licenses to teach from the cathedral school of Notre-Dame in Paris began to take on extra students for a fee. By the end of the twelfth century, these masters teaching at Paris had formed a *universitas* or guild of masters. By 1200, the king of France, Philip Augustus, officially acknowledged the existence of the University of Paris. The University of Oxford in England, organized on the Paris model, first appeared in 1208. A migration of scholars from Oxford in 1209 led to the establishment of Cambridge University. In the Late Middle Ages, kings, popes, and princes vied to found new universities. By the end of the Middle Ages, there were eighty universities in Europe, most of them located in France, Italy, Germany, and England.

**Teaching in the Medieval University** A student's initial studies at a medieval university centered around the traditional liberal arts curriculum.

The *trivium* consisted of grammar, rhetoric, and logic, and the *quadrivium* was comprised of arithmetic, geometry, astronomy, and music. All classes were conducted in Latin, which provided a common means of communication for students, regardless of their country of origin. Basically, medieval university instruction used the lecture method.

**University Classroom.** This illustration shows a university classroom in fourteenth-century Germany. As was customary in medieval classrooms, the master is reading from a text. The students vary considerably in age and in the amount of attention they are willing to give the lecturer.

The word *lecture* is derived from Latin and means "to read." Before the development of the printing press in the fifteenth century, books were expensive, and few students could afford them, so masters read from a text (such as a collection of laws if the subject were law) and then added commentaries, which came to be known as *glosses*. No exams were given after a series of lectures, but when a student applied for a degree, he (women did not attend universities in the Middle Ages) was given a comprehensive oral examination by a committee of teachers. These exams were taken after a four- or six-year period of study. The first degree a student could earn was an A.B., the *artium baccalaureus*, or bachelor of arts; later he might receive an A.M., *artium magister*, master of arts. All degrees were technically licenses to teach, although most students receiving them did not become teachers.

After completing the liberal arts curriculum, a student could go on to study law, medicine, or theology, which was the most highly regarded subject of the medieval curriculum. The study of law, medicine, or theology was a long process that could take a decade or more. A student who passed his final oral examinations was granted a doctor's degree, which officially enabled him to teach his subject. Most students who pursued advanced degrees received their master's degrees first and taught the arts curriculum while continuing to pursue their advanced degrees. Students who received degrees from medieval universities could pursue other careers besides teaching that proved to be much more lucrative. A law degree was deemed essential for those who wished to serve as advisers to kings and princes. The growing administrative bureaucracies of popes and kings also demanded a supply of clerks with a university education who could keep records and draw up official documents.

**Students in the Medieval University**   Students at medieval universities stemmed predominantly from the middle groups of medieval society, the families of lesser knights, merchants, and artisans. All were male; many were poor but ambitious and upwardly mobile. Many medieval students started when they were fourteen to eighteen years old and received their bachelor's or master's degrees by their early twenties. Study for a doctorate in one of the specialized schools of law, medicine, or theology entailed at least another ten years. It was not unusual for men to receive their doctorates in their late thirties or early forties.

There are obvious similarities between medieval and modern students. Then as now, many students took their studies seriously and worked hard. Then as now, alcohol, sex, and appeals for spending money were all too common. In medieval universities, handbooks provided form letters that students could use in requesting money from their fathers, guardians, or patrons. This is an example from Oxford:

> B. to his venerable master A., greeting. This is to inform you that I am studying at Oxford with the greatest of diligence, but the matter of money stands greatly in the way of my promotion, as it is now two months since I have spent the last of what

you sent me. The city is expensive and makes many demands; I have to rent lodgings, buy necessaries, and provide for many other things which I cannot now specify. Wherefore I respectfully beg your paternity that by the promptings of divine pity you may assist me, so that I may be able to complete what I have well begun.[4]

Lack of studiousness is not just a modern phenomenon, as this letter from a medieval father to his son illustrates:

> To his son G. residing at Orléans, P. of Besançon sends greetings with paternal zeal. It is written, "He also that is slothful in his work is brother to him that is a great waster." I have recently discovered that you live dissolutely and slothfully, preferring license to restraint and play to work and strumming a guitar while the others are at their studies, whence it happens that you have read but one volume of law while your more industrious companions have read several. Wherefore I have decided to exhort you herewith to repent utterly of your dissolute and careless ways, that you may no longer be called a waster and your shame may be turned to good repute.[5]

We have no idea whether the letter convinced the student to change his ways.

Medieval universities shared in the violent atmosphere of the age. Records from courts of law reveal numerous instances of disturbances at European universities. One German professor was finally dismissed for stabbing one too many of his colleagues in faculty meetings. A student in Bologna was attacked in the classroom by another student armed with a sword. Oxford regulations attempted to dampen the violence by forbidding students to bring weapons to class. Not uncommonly, town and gown struggles (gown refers to the academic robe worn by teachers and students) escalated into bloody riots between townspeople and students (see the box on p. 245).

Despite the violence, universities proved important to medieval civilization, not only for the growth of learning, which, after all, is the main task of the university, but also by providing a mechanism for training the personnel who served as teachers, administrators, lawyers, and doctors in an increasingly specialized society.

## A Revival of Classical Antiquity

Another aspect of the intellectual revival of the High Middle Ages was a resurgence of interest in the works of classical antiquity—the works of the Greeks and Romans. In the twelfth century, western Europe was introduced to a large number of Greek scientific and philosophical works, including those of Galen and Hippocrates on medicine, Ptolemy on geography and astronomy, and Euclid on mathematics. Above all, the West now had available the complete works of Aristotle. During the second half of the twelfth century, all of Aristotle's scientific works were translated into Latin, which served as an international language for both speaking and writing in the West. This great influx of Aristotle's works had an overwhelming impact on the West. He came to be viewed as the "master of those who know," the man who seemed to have understood every field of knowledge.

# UNIVERSITY STUDENTS AND VIOLENCE AT OXFORD

*M*EDIEVAL UNIVERSITIES shared in the violent atmosphere of their age. Town and gown quarrels often resulted in bloody conflicts, especially during the universities' formative period. This selection is taken from an anonymous description of a student riot at Oxford at the end of the thirteenth century.

### A Student Riot at Oxford

They [the townsmen] seized and imprisoned all scholars on whom they could lay hands, invaded their inns [halls of residence], made havoc of their goods and trampled their books under foot. In the face of such provocation the proctors [university officials] sent their assistants about the town, forbidding the students to leave their inns. But all commands and exhortations were in vain. By nine o'clock next morning, bands of scholars were parading the streets in martial array. If the proctors failed to restrain them, the mayor was equally powerless to restrain his townsmen. The great bell of St. Martin's rang out an alarm; oxhorns were sounded in the streets; messengers were sent into the country to collect rustic allies. The clerks [students and teachers], who numbered 3,000 in all, began their attack simultaneously in various quarters. They broke open warehouses in the Spicery, the Cutlery and elsewhere. Armed with bow and arrows, swords and bucklers, slings and stones, they fell upon their opponents. Three they slew, and wounded fifty or more. One band . . . took up a position in High Street between the Churches of St. Mary and All Saints', and attacked the house of a certain Edward Hales. This Hales was a longstanding enemy of the clerks. There were no half measures with him. He seized his crossbow, and from an upper chamber sent an unerring shaft into the eye of the pugnacious rector. The death of their valiant leader caused the clerks to lose heart. They fled, closely pursued by the townsmen and country-folk. Some were struck down in the streets, and others who had taken refuge in the churches were dragged out and driven mercilessly to prison, lashed with thongs and goaded with iron spikes.

Complaints of murder, violence and robbery were lodged straightway with the king by both parties. The townsmen claimed 3,000 pounds' damage. The commissioners, however, appointed to decide the matter, condemned them to pay 200 marks, removed the bailiffs, and banished twelve of the most turbulent citizens from Oxford.

---

The recovery of Greek scientific and philosophical works was not a simple process, however. Little knowledge of Greek had survived in Europe. Thus it was through the Muslim world that the West recovered Aristotle and other Greek works. The translation of Greek works into Arabic had formed but one aspect of a brilliant Muslim civilization. In the twelfth century, these writings were now translated from Arabic into Latin, making them available to the West. Wherever Muslim and Christian cultures met—in the Norman kingdom of Sicily, southern Italy, and above all Spain—the work of translation was carried on by both Arabic and Jewish scholars.

The Islamic world had more to contribute intellectually to the West than translations, however. Scientific work in the ninth and tenth centuries had enabled it to forge far ahead of the Western world, and in the twelfth and thirteenth centuries, Arabic works on physics, mathematics, medicine, and optics became available to the West in Latin translations. Adelard of Bath (1090–1150) was one source of these works. Having traveled throughout the Mediterranean region, he later translated an Arabic version of Euclid's *Elements* (see Chapter 4) into Latin, as well as the mathematical works of al-Khwarizmi (see Chapter 8). Adelard also introduced to Europeans the astrolabe, an Arabic astronomical instrument that proved valuable to sailors.

When Aristotle's works arrived in the West in the second half of the twelfth century, they were accompanied by commentaries written by outstanding Arabic and Jewish philosophers. One example was Ibn-Rushd, or Averroës (1126–1198), who lived in Córdoba and composed a systematic commentary on virtually all of Aristotle's surviving works. The works of Arabic philosophers proved highly influential to Western intellectuals.

The West was also receptive to the works of Jewish scholars living in the Islamic world. Perhaps the best known is Moses ben Maimon, or Maimonides (1135–1204), who also lived in Córdoba. He was conversant with Greek and Arabic traditions and interested in the problem of reconciling faith and reason. In his *Guide for the Perplexed*, written in Arabic, Maimonides attempted to harmonize the rational and natural philosophy of Aristotle with the basic truths of Judaism. Although it was attacked by some Orthodox Jews, Western scholars in the thirteenth century paid close attention to it after its translation into Latin.

### The Development of Scholasticism

Christianity's importance in medieval society probably made inevitable theology's central role in the European intellectual world. Whether in monastic or cathedral schools or the new universities, theology, the formal study of religion, reigned as "queen of the sciences."

Beginning in the eleventh century, the effort to apply reason or logical analysis to the church's basic theological doctrines had a significant impact on the study of theology. The word *scholasticism* is used to refer to the philosophical and theological system of the medieval schools. A primary preoccupation of scholasticism was the attempt to reconcile faith and reason, to demonstrate that what was accepted on faith was in harmony with what could be learned by reason. The scholastic method came to be the basic instructional mode of the universities. In essence, this method consisted of posing a question, presenting contradictory authorities on that question, and then arriving at conclusions. It was a system that demanded rigorous analytical thought. Although scholasticism reached its high point in the thirteenth century, it had its beginnings in the theological world of the eleventh and twelfth centuries, especially in the work of Abelard.

**Abelard**   Peter Abelard (1079–1142) studied in northern France but scorned his teachers as insignificant and took up the teaching of theology in Paris. Possessed of a colorful personality, Abelard was a very popular teacher who attracted many students. A man with a strong ego, he became known for the zest with which he entered into arguments with fellow students as well as for his affair with his student Heloise. Heloise bore a child by Abelard and secretly married him. But her uncle, who had hired Abelard as a tutor for his niece, sought revenge, as Abelard related in an account of his life titled *History of My Misfortunes:* "One night they took from me a most cruel and shameful vengeance, as I was resting and sleeping in the inner room of my lodging. . . . For they cut off those parts of my body, by which I had committed the deed which sorrowed them."[6]

Above all others, Abelard was responsible for furthering the new scholastic approach to theology. In his most famous work, *Sic et Non* (*Yes and No*), he listed passages from Scripture and the church fathers that stood in direct contradiction to one another and stressed the need to use logic or dialectical reasoning to reconcile the apparent differences systematically. He summed up his method thus: "By doubting we come to inquiry, through inquiry to the truth."

**The Problem of Universals**   Beginning in the twelfth century, a major controversy—the problem of universals—began to occupy many theologians. The basic issue involved the nature of reality itself: What constitutes what is real? Theologians were divided into two major schools of thought reflecting the earlier traditions of Greek thought, especially the divergent schools of Plato and Aristotle.

Following Plato, the scholastic **realists** took the position that the individual objects that we perceive with our senses, such as trees, are not real but merely manifestations of universal ideas ("treeness") that exist in the mind of God. All knowledge, then, is based on the ideas implanted in human reason by the creator. To the realists, truth can be discovered only by contemplating universals. The **nominalists** were adherents of Aristotle's ideas and believed that only individual objects are real. In their view, universal ideas and concepts were simply names (Latin *nomina*, hence *nominalism*). Truth could be discovered only by examining individual objects.

By the thirteenth century, the scholastics were confronting a new challenge—how to harmonize Christian revelation with the work of Aristotle. The great influx of Aristotle's works into the West in the High Middle Ages

threw many theologians into consternation. Aristotle was so highly regarded that he was called "the philosopher," yet he had arrived at his conclusions by rational thought, not revelation, and some of his doctrines, such as the mortality of the individual soul, contradicted the teachings of the church. The most famous attempt to reconcile Aristotle and the doctrines of Christianity was that of Saint Thomas Aquinas.

**Aquinas**   Thomas Aquinas (1225–1274) studied theology at Cologne and Paris and taught at both Naples and Paris, and it was at the latter that he worked on his famous *Summa Theologica* (*A Summa of Theology*—a summa was a compendium of knowledge that attempted to bring together all the received learning of the preceding centuries on a given subject into a single whole). Aquinas' masterpiece was organized according to the dialectical method of the scholastics. Aquinas first posed a question, cited sources that offered opposing opinions on the question, and then resolved them by arriving at his own conclusions. In this fashion, Aquinas raised and discussed some six hundred articles or issues (see the box on p. 247).

Aquinas' reputation derives from his masterful attempt to reconcile faith and reason. He took it for granted that there were truths derived by reason and truths derived by faith. He was certain, however, that the two truths could not be in conflict with each other:

> The light of faith that is freely infused into us does not destroy the light of natural knowledge [reason] implanted in us naturally. For although the natural light of the human mind is insufficient to show us these things made manifest by faith, it is nevertheless impossible that these things which the divine principle gives us by faith are contrary to these implanted in us by nature [reason]. Indeed, were that the case, one or the other would have to be false, and since both are given to us by God, God would have to be the author of untruth, which is impossible. . . . It is impossible that those things which are of philosophy can be contrary to those things which are of faith.[7]

The natural mind, unaided by faith, could arrive at truths concerning the physical universe. Without God's help, however, unaided reason alone could not grasp spiritual truths, such as the Trinity (the belief that God, Jesus, and the Holy Spirit are three manifestations of the same unique deity) or the Incarnation (the belief that Jesus in his lifetime was God in human form).

## The Revival of Roman Law

A systematic approach to knowledge was also expressed in the area of law. Of special importance was the rediscovery of the great legal work of Justinian, the *Corpus Iuris Civilis*, known to the medieval West before 1100 only at second hand. Initially, teachers of law, such as Irnerius of Bologna, were content merely to explain the meaning of Roman legal terms to their students. Gradually, they became more sophisticated so that by the mid-twelfth century, "doctors of law" had developed commentaries and

# The Dialectical Method of Thomas Aquinas

*N HIS MASTERPIECE* of scholastic theology, the *Summa Theologica*, Thomas Aquinas attempted to resolve some six hundred theological issues by the dialectical method. This method consisted of posing a question, stating the objections to it, and then replying to the objections. This selection from the *Summa Theologica* focuses on Article 4 of Question 92, "The Production of the Woman."

## Thomas Aquinas, *Summa Theologica*

### Question 92: The Production of the Woman (in Four Articles)

We must next consider the production of the woman. Under this head there are four points of inquiry: (1) Whether the woman should have been made in that first production of things? (2) Whether the woman should have been made from man? (3) Whether of man's rib? (4) Whether the woman was made immediately by God? . . .

### Fourth Article: Whether the Woman Was Formed Immediately by God?

We proceed thus to the Fourth Article:—

*Objection 1.* It would seem that the woman was not formed immediately by God. For no individual is produced immediately by God from another individual alike in species. But the woman was made from a man who is of the same species. Therefore she was not made immediately by God.

*Objection 2.* Further, Augustine says that corporeal things are governed by God through the angels. But the woman's body was formed from corporeal matter. Therefore it was made through the ministry of the angels, and not immediately by God.

*Objection 3.* Further, those things which preexist in creatures as to their causal virtues are produced by the power of some creature, and not immediately by God. But the woman's body was produced in its causal virtues among the first created works, as Augustine says. Therefore it was not produced immediately by God.

*On the contrary,* Augustine says, in the same work: *God alone, to Whom all nature owes its existence, could form or build up the woman from the man's rib.*

I answer that, as was said above, the natural generation of every species is from some determinate matter. Now the matter whence man is naturally begotten is the human semen of man or woman. Wherefore from any other matter an individual of the human species cannot naturally be generated. Now God alone, the Author of nature, can produce an effect into existence outside the ordinary course of nature. Therefore God alone could produce either a man from the slime of the earth, or a woman from the rib of a man.

*Reply Objection 1.* This argument is verified when an individual is begotten, by natural generation, from that which is like it in the same species.

*Reply Objection 2.* As Augustine says, we do not know whether the angels were employed by God in the formation of the woman; but it is certain that, as the body of man was not formed by the angels from the slime of the earth, so neither was the body of the woman formed by them from the man's rib.

*Reply Objection 3.* As Augustine says, The first creation of things did not demand that woman should be made thus; it made it possible for her to be thus made. Therefore the body of the woman did indeed preexist in these causal virtues, in the things first created; not as regards active potentiality, but as regards a potentiality passive in relation to the active potentiality of the Creator.

---

systematic treatises on the legal texts. Italian cities, above all Pavia and Bologna, became prominent centers for the study of Roman law. By the thirteenth century, Italian jurists were systematizing the various professional commentaries on Roman law into a single commentary known as the ordinary gloss. Study of Roman law at the universities came to consist of learning the text of the law along with this gloss.

This revival of Roman law occurred in a world dominated by a body of law quite different from that of the Romans. European law comprised a hodgepodge of Germanic law codes, feudal customs, and urban regulations. The desire to know a more orderly world, already evident in the study of theology, perhaps made it inevitable that Europeans would enthusiastically welcome the more systematic approach of Roman law.

The training of students in Roman law at medieval universities led to further application of its principles as these students became judges, lawyers, scribes, and councilors for the towns and monarchies of western Europe. By the beginning of the thirteenth century, the old system of the ordeal was being replaced by a rational, decision-making process based on the systematic collection and analysis of evidence, a clear indication of the impact of Roman law on the European legal system.

### Literature in the High Middle Ages

Latin was the universal language of medieval civilization. Used in the church and schools, it enabled learned people to communicate anywhere in Europe. The intellectual revival of the High Middle Ages included an outpouring of

Latin literature. While Latin continued to be used for literary purposes, by the twelfth century much of the creative literature was being written in the **vernacular** (the local language, such as Spanish, French, English, or German). Throughout the Middle Ages, there had been a popular vernacular literature, especially manifest in the Germanic, Celtic, Old Icelandic, and Slavonic sagas. But a new market for vernacular literature appeared in the twelfth century when educated laypeople at courts and in the new urban society sought fresh avenues of entertainment.

**Troubadour Poetry**    Perhaps the most popular vernacular literature of the twelfth century was *troubadour poetry,* chiefly the product of nobles and knights. This poetry focused on themes of courtly love, the love of a knight for a lady, generally a married noble lady, who inspires him to become a braver knight and a better poet. A good example is found in the laments of a crusading noble Jaufré Rudel, who cherished a dream lady from afar whom he said he would always love but feared he would never meet:

> *Most sad, most joyous shall I go away,*
> *Let me have seen her for a single day,*
> *    My love afar,*
> *I shall not see her, for her land and mine*
> *Are sundered, and the ways are hard to find,*
> *So many ways, and I shall lose my way,*
> *    So wills it God.*
>
> *Yet shall I know no other love but hers,*
> *And if not hers, no other love at all.*
> *    She has surpassed all.*
> *So fair she is, so noble, I would be*
> *    A captive with the hosts of paynimrie [the Muslims]*
> *In a far land, if so be upon me*
> *    Her eyes might fall.*[8]

Although it originated in southern France, troubadour poetry also spread to northern France, Italy, and Germany.

**The Heroic Epic**    Another type of vernacular literature was the *chanson de geste,* or heroic epic. The earliest and finest example is the *Chanson de Roland* (*The Song of Roland*), which appeared around 1100 and was written in a dialect of French, a Romance language derived from Latin (see the box on p. 249). The *chansons de geste* were written for a male-dominated society. The chief events described in these poems, as in *The Song of Roland,* are battles and political contests. Their world is one of combat in which knights fight courageously for their kings and lords. Women play little or no role in this literary genre.

**The Courtly Romance**    Although *chansons de geste* were still written in the twelfth century, a different kind of long poem, the *courtly romance,* also became popular. It was composed in rhymed couplets and dwelt on romantic subjects: brave knights, virtuous ladies, evil magicians, bewitched palaces, fairies, talking animals, and strange forests. The story of King Arthur, the legendary king of the fifth-century Britons, became a popular subject for the courtly romance. The best versions of the Arthurian legends survive in the works of Chrétien de Troyes, a French writer in the second half of the twelfth century, whose courtly romances were viewed by contemporaries as the works of a master storyteller.

## Romanesque Architecture: "A White Mantle of Churches"

The eleventh and twelfth centuries witnessed an explosion of building, both private and public. The construction of castles and churches absorbed most of the surplus resources of medieval society and at the same time reflected its basic preoccupations, warfare and God. The churches were by far the most conspicuous of the public buildings. As a chronicler of the eleventh century commented:

> [After the] year of the millennium, which is now about three years past, people all over the world, but especially in Italy and France, began to rebuild their churches. Although most of them were well built and in little need of alterations, Christian

**Barrel Vaulting.**   The eleventh and twelfth centuries witnessed an enormous amount of church construction. Utilizing the basilica shape, master builders replaced flat wooden roofs with long, round stone vaults known as barrel vaults. As this illustration of a Romanesque church in Vienne, France, indicates, the barrel vault limited the size of a church and left little room for windows.

# THE SONG OF ROLAND

*THE SONG OF ROLAND* is one of the best examples of the medieval *chanson de geste*, or heroic epic. Inspired by a historical event, it recounts the ambush of the rear guard of Charlemagne's Frankish army in the Pyrenees. It was written three hundred years after the event it supposedly describes, however, and reveals more about the eleventh century than about the age of Charlemagne. Christian Basques who ambushed Charlemagne's army have been transformed into Muslims, the Frankish soldiers into French knights. This selection describes the death of Roland, Charlemagne's nephew, who was the commander of the ill-fated rear guard.

### The Song of Roland

Now Roland feels that he is at death's door;
Out of his ears the brain is running forth.
Now for his peers he prays God call them all,
And for himself St. Gabriel's aid implores;
Then in each hand he takes, lest shame befall,
His Olifant [horn] and Durendal his sword.
Far as a quarrel flies from a cross-bow drawn,
Toward land of Spain he goes, to a wide lawn,
And climbs a mound where grows a fair tree tall,
And marble stones beneath it stand by four.

Face downward there on the green grass he falls,
And swoons away, for he is at death's door. . . .
Now Roland feels death press upon him hard;
It's creeping down from his head to his heart.
Under a pine-tree he hastens him apart,
There stretches him face down on the green grass,
And lays beneath him his sword and Olifant.
He's turned his head to where the Paynims [Muslims] are,
And this he does for the French and for Charles,
Since fain is he that they should say, brave heart,
That he has died a conqueror at last.
He beats his breast full many a time and fast,
Gives, with his glove, his sins into God's charge.

Now Roland feels his time is at an end;
On the steep hill-side, toward Spain he's turned his head,
And with one hand he beats upon his breast;
Saying: "Mea culpa; Thy mercy, Lord, I beg
For all the sins, both the great and the less,
That e'er I did since first I drew my breath
Unto this day when I'm struck down by death."
His right-hand glove he unto God extends;
Angels from Heaven now to his side descend.

---

nations were rivaling each other to have the most beautiful edifices. One might say the world was shaking herself, throwing off her old garments, and robing herself with a white mantle of churches. Then nearly all the cathedrals, the monasteries dedicated to different saints, and even the small village chapels were reconstructed more beautifully by the faithful.[9]

Hundreds of new cathedrals and abbey and pilgrimage churches, as well as thousands of parish churches in rural villages, were built in the eleventh and twelfth centuries. This building spree reflected both the revived religious culture and the increased wealth of the period produced by agriculture, trade, and the growth of cities.

The cathedrals of the eleventh and twelfth centuries were built in a truly international style, the **Romanesque.** The construction of churches required the services of professional master builders, whose employment throughout Europe guaranteed an international unity in basic features. Prominent examples of Romanesque churches can be found in Germany, France, and Spain.

Romanesque churches were normally built in the rectangular basilica shape used in the construction of churches in the Late Roman Empire. Romanesque builders made a significant innovation by replacing the earlier flat wooden ceiling with a long, round stone vault called a barrel vault or a cross vault where two barrel vaults intersected (a vault is simply a curved roof made of masonry). The latter was used when a transept was added to create a church plan in the shape of a cross. Although barrel and cross vaults were technically difficult to construct, they were considered aesthetically pleasing and technically proficient and had fine acoustics.

Because stone vaults were extremely heavy, Romanesque churches required massive pillars and walls to hold them up. This left little space for windows, making Romanesque churches notoriously dark on the inside. Their massive walls and pillars gave the churches a sense of solidity and almost the impression of a fortress. Indeed, massive walls and slit windows were also characteristic of the castle architecture of the period.

### The Gothic Cathedral

Begun in the twelfth century and brought to perfection in the thirteenth, the **Gothic** cathedral remains one of the greatest artistic triumphs of the High Middle Ages. Soaring skyward, almost as if to reach heaven, it was a fitting symbol for medieval people's preoccupation with God.

Two fundamental innovations of the twelfth century made Gothic cathedrals possible. The combination of ribbed vaults and pointed arches replaced the barrel vault of Romanesque churches and enabled builders to make Gothic churches higher than their Romanesque counterparts.

**The Gothic Cathedral.** The Gothic cathedral was one of the great artistic triumphs of the High Middle Ages. Shown here is the cathedral of Notre-Dame in Paris. Begun in 1163, it was not completed until the beginning of the fourteenth century.

© Russell Thompson/OmniPhoto Communications

© The Art Archive/Dagli Orti

**Interior of a Gothic Cathedral.** The use of ribbed vaults and pointed arches gave the Gothic cathedral a feeling of upward movement. Moreover, due to the flying buttress, the cathedral could have thin walls with stained-glass windows that filled the interior with light. The flying buttress was a heavy pier of stone built onto the outside of the walls to bear the brunt of the weight of the church's vaulted ceiling. The flying buttresses are visible at the left in the illustration of the cathedral of Notre-Dame.

The use of pointed arches and ribbed vaults created an impression of upward movement, a sense of weightless upward thrust that implied the energy of God. Another technical innovation, the flying buttress, a heavy arched pier of stone built onto the outside of the walls, made it possible to distribute the weight of the church's vaulted ceilings outward and downward and thereby eliminate the heavy walls used in Romanesque churches to hold the weight of the massive barrel vaults. Thus Gothic cathedrals could be built with thin walls that were filled with magnificent stained-glass windows, which created a play of light inside that varied with the sun at different times of the day.

Medieval craftspeople of the twelfth and thirteenth centuries perfected the art of stained glass. Small pieces of glass were stained in glowing colors like jewels. The preoccupation with colored light in Gothic cathedrals was not accidental but was executed by people inspired by the belief that natural light was a symbol of the divine light of God. Light is invisible but enables people to see; so too is God invisible, but the existence of God allows the world of matter to be. Those impressed by the mystical significance of light were also impressed by the mystical significance of number. The proportions of Gothic cathedrals were based on mathematical ratios that their builders believed were derived from the ancient Greek school of Pythagoras and expressed the intrinsic harmony of the world as established by its creator.

The first fully Gothic church was the abbey church of Saint-Denis near Paris, inspired by Suger, the famous abbot of the monastery from 1122 to 1151, and built between 1140 and 1150. Although the Gothic style was the prod-uct of northern France, by the mid-thirteenth century French Gothic architecture had spread to England, Spain, Germany—indeed, to virtually all of Europe. This French Gothic style was seen most brilliantly in cathedrals in Paris (Notre-Dame), Reims, Amiens, and Chartres.

A Gothic cathedral was the work of an entire community. All classes contributed to its construction. Money was raised from wealthy townspeople who had profited from the new trade and industries as well as from kings and nobles. Master masons who were both architects and engineers designed the cathedrals. They drew up the plans and supervised the work of construction. Stonemasons and other craftspeople were paid a daily wage and provided the skilled labor to build the cathedrals. Indeed, these buildings were the first monumental structures of consequence built by free, salaried labor.

The building of cathedrals often became highly competitive as communities vied with one another to build the

**Chartres Cathedral: Stained-Glass Window.** The stained glass of Gothic cathedrals is remarkable for the beauty and variety of its colors. Stained-glass windows depicted a remarkable variety of scenes. The windows of Chartres cathedral, for example, present the saints, views of the everyday activities of ordinary men and women, and, as in this panel, scenes from the life of Jesus.

© Sonia Halliday Photographs

highest tower, a rivalry that sometimes ended in disaster. The cathedral of Beauvais in northern France collapsed in 1284 after reaching the height of 157 feet. Gothic cathedrals also depended on a community's faith. After all, it often took two or more generations to complete a cathedral, and the first generation of builders must have begun with the knowledge that they would not live to see the completed project. Most important, a Gothic cathedral symbolized the chief preoccupation of a medieval Christian community, its dedication to a spiritual ideal. As we have observed before, the largest buildings of an era reflect the values of its society. The Gothic cathedral, with its towers soaring toward heaven, gave witness to an age when a spiritual impulse still underlay most of existence.

## CONCLUSION

𝒯HE NEW EUROPEAN CIVILIZATION that had emerged in the Early Middle Ages began to flourish in the High Middle Ages. Better growing conditions, an expansion of cultivated land, and technological and agricultural changes combined to enable Europe's food supply to increase significantly after 1000. This increase helped sustain a dramatic rise in population that was physically apparent in the expansion of towns and cities.

The High Middle Ages witnessed economic and social changes that some historians believe set European civilization on a path that lasted until the eighteenth century. The revival of trade, the expansion of towns and cities, and the development of a money economy did not mean the end of a predominantly rural European society, but they did open the door to new ways to make a living and new opportunities for people to expand and enrich their lives. Eventually, they created the foundations for the development of a mostly urban industrial society.

The High Middle Ages also gave birth to a cultural revival. This cultural revival led to a rediscovery of important aspects of the classical heritage, to new centers of learning in the universities, to the use of reason to systematize the study of theology and law, to the development of a vernacular literature that appealed both to knights and to townspeople, and to a dramatic increase in the number and size of churches.

### NOTES

1. Quoted in Joseph Gies and Frances Gies, *Life in a Medieval Castle* (New York, 1974), p. 175.
2. Quoted in Robert Delort, *Life in the Middle Ages,* trans. Robert Allen (New York, 1972), p. 218.
3. Quoted in Jean Gimpel, *The Medieval Machine* (Harmondsworth, England, 1976), p. 92.
4. Quoted in Charles H. Haskins, *The Rise of Universities* (Ithaca, N.Y., 1957), pp. 77–78.
5. Ibid., pp. 79–80.
6. Quoted in David Herlihy, *Medieval Culture and Society* (New York, 1968), p. 204.
7. Quoted in John H. Mundy, *Europe in the High Middle Ages, 1150–1309* (New York, 1973), pp. 474–475.
8. Helen Waddell, *The Wandering Scholars* (New York, 1961), p. 222.
9. Quoted in John W. Baldwin, *The Scholastic Culture of the Middle Ages, 1000–1300* (Lexington, Mass., 1971), p. 15.

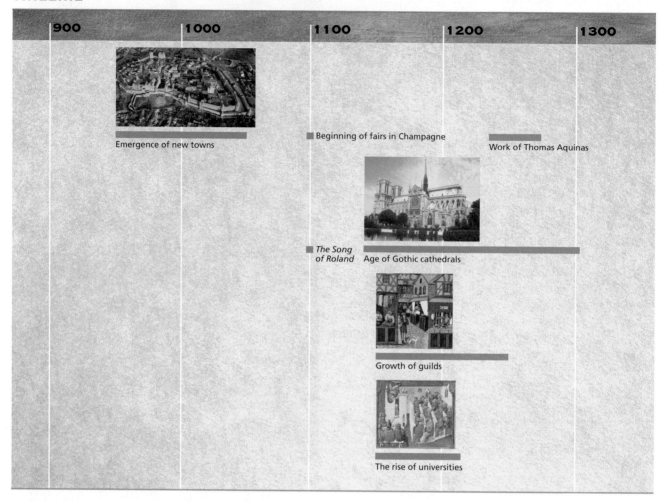

900     1000     1100     1200     1300

Emergence of new towns

Beginning of fairs in Champagne

Work of Thomas Aquinas

*The Song of Roland*   Age of Gothic cathedrals

Growth of guilds

The rise of universities

## SUGGESTIONS FOR FURTHER READING

For a good introduction to this period, see **W. C. Jordan,** *Europe in the High Middle Ages* (New York, 2003); **J. H. Mundy,** *Europe in the High Middle Ages, 1150–1309,* 3d ed. (New York, 1999); **C. N. L. Brooke,** *Europe in the Central Middle Ages, 962–1154,* rev. ed. (New York, 1988); **M. Barber,** *The Two Cities: Medieval Europe, 1050–1320* (London, 1992); and **R. Bartlett,** *The Making of Europe: Conquest, Colonization, and Cultural Change, 950–1350* (Princeton, N.J., 1993). There is a good collection of essays on various facets of medieval history in **P. Linehan and J. L. Nelson, eds.,** *The Medieval World* (London, 2001). On peasant life, see **R. Fossier,** *Peasant Life in the Medieval West* (New York, 1988). Technological changes are discussed in **J. Gimpel,** *The Medieval Machine* (Harmondsworth, England, 1976), and **J. Langdon,** *Horses, Oxen, and Technological Innovation* (New York, 1986).

Works on the function and activities of the nobility in the High Middle Ages include **S. Reynolds,** *Kingdoms and Communities in Western Europe, 900–1300* (Oxford, 1984); **R. W. Barber,** *The Knight and Chivalry* (Rochester, N.Y., 1995); and the classic work by **M. Bloch,** *Feudal Society* (London, 1961). Various aspects of the social history of the nobility can be found in **G. Duby,** *The Knight, the Lady, and the Priest* (London, 1984), on noble marriages; **R. Barber and J. Barker,** *Tournaments: Jousts, Chivalry, and Pageants in the Middle Ages* (New York, 1989), on tournaments; **N. J. G. Pounds,** *The Medieval Castle in*

*England and Wales: A Social and Political History* (New York, 1990); and **C. B. Bouchard,** *Life and Society in the West: Antiquity and the Middle Ages* (San Diego, Calif., 1988), ch. 6. On women, see **R. T. Morewedge, ed.,** *The Role of Women in the Middle Ages* (Albany, N.Y., 1975), and **S. M. Stuard, ed.,** *Women in Medieval Society* (Philadelphia, 1976).

On the revival of trade, see **R. S. Lopez,** *The Commercial Revolution of the Middle Ages, 950–1350* (Englewood Cliffs, N.J., 1971). Urban history is covered in **D. Nicholas,** *The Growth of the Medieval City: From Late Antiquity to the Early Fourteenth Century* (New York, 1997), and the classic work of **H. Pirenne,** *Medieval Cities* (Princeton, N.J., 1969). For a good collection of essays on urban culture, see **B. Hanawalt and K. I. Reyerson, eds.,** *City and Spectacle in Medieval Europe* (Minneapolis, Minn., 1994). On women in the cities, see **B. Hanawalt, ed.,** *Women and Work in Preindustrial Europe* (Bloomington, Ind., 1986).

A general work on medieval intellectual life is **M. L. Colish,** *Medieval Foundations of the Western Intellectual Tradition, 400–1400* (New Haven, Conn., 1997). See also the classic study by **F. Artz,** *The Mind of the Middle Ages,* 3d ed. (Chicago, 1980). The development of universities is covered in **S. Ferruolo,** *The Origin of the University* (Stanford, Calif., 1985); **A. B. Cobban,** *The Medieval Universities* (London, 1975); and the brief older work by **C. H. Haskins,** *The Rise of Universities* (Ithaca, N.Y., 1957). Various aspects of the intellectual and literary developments of the High Middle Ages are examined in **J. W. Baldwin**, *The Scholastic Culture of the Middle Ages, 1000–1300* (Lexington, Mass., 1971); **J. Marenbon**, *The Philosophy of Peter Abelard* (New York, 1997); and **H. Waddell**, *The Wandering Scholars* (New York, 1961). A good biography of Thomas Aquinas is **J. Weisheipl**, *Friar Thomas d'Aquino: His Life, His Thought and Work* (New York, 1974).

For a good introduction to the art and architecture of the Middle Ages, see **A. Shaver-Crandell**, *The Middle Ages,* in the Cambridge Introduction to Art Series (Cambridge, 1982). A good introduction to Romanesque style is **A. Petzold**, *Romanesque Art* (New York, 1995). On the Gothic movement, see **M. Camille**, *Gothic Art: Glorious Visions* (New York, 1996). Good books on the construction of Gothic cathedrals are **J. Gimpel**, *The Cathedral Builders* (New York, 1961), and **A. Erlande-Brandenburg**, *Cathedrals and Castles: Building in the Middle Ages* (New York, 1995).

## History  Now™

Enter *HistoryNow* using the access card that is available for *Western Civilization*. *HistoryNow* will assist you in understanding the content in this chapter with lesson plans generated for your needs. In addition, you can read the following documents, and many more, online:

Dante, first five cantos of the *Inferno* and Canto 33 of *Paradiso*

Giovanni Boccaccio, Introduction to the *Decameron*

Peter Abelard, *Story of My Misfortunes*

Thomas Aquinas, Part 1, Question 2, Article 3 of
    *Summa Theologica*

# *10*

# THE RISE OF KINGDOMS AND THE GROWTH OF CHURCH POWER

## CHAPTER OUTLINE AND FOCUS QUESTIONS

### The Emergence and Growth of European Kingdoms, 1000–1300

● What steps did the rulers of England and France take during the High Middle Ages to reverse the decentralizing tendencies of fief-holding?

● What were the major developments in Spain, the Holy Roman Empire, and northern and eastern Europe during the High Middle Ages?

### The Recovery and Reform of the Catholic Church

● What was at issue in the Investiture Controversy, and what effect did the controversy have on the church and on Germany?

### Christianity and Medieval Civilization

● What were the characteristics of the papal monarchy and the new religious orders of the High Middle Ages, and what role did women play in the religious life of the period?

### The Crusades

● What were the reasons for the Crusades, and who or what benefited the most from the experience of the Crusades?

### CRITICAL THINKING

● Why did centralized kingdoms develop in some parts of Europe and not in others?

*A medieval monk and his abbot*

akg-images/British Library

THE RECOVERY AND GROWTH of European civilization in the High Middle Ages also affected the state and the church. Both lords and vassals and the Catholic church recovered from the invasions and internal dissension of the Early Middle Ages. Although lords and vassals seemed forever mired in endless petty conflicts, some medieval kings began to exert a centralizing authority and inaugurated the process of developing new kinds of monarchical states. By the thirteenth century, European monarchs were solidifying their governmental institutions in pursuit of greater power.

The recovery of the Catholic church produced a reform movement that led to exalted claims of papal authority and subsequent conflict with state authorities. At the same time, vigorous papal leadership combined with new dimensions of religious life to make the Catholic church a forceful presence in every area of life. The role of the church in the new European civilization was quite evident in the career of a man named Samson, who became abbot, or head, of the great English abbey of Bury St. Edmonds in 1182. According to Jocelyn of Brakeland, a monk who assisted him, Abbot Samson was a devout man who wore "undergarments of horsehair and a horsehair shirt."

He loved virtue and "abhorred liars, drunkards and talkative folk." His primary concern was the spiritual well-being of his monastery, but he spent much of his time working on problems in the world beyond the abbey walls. Since the monastery had fallen into debt under his predecessors, Abbot Samson toiled tirelessly to recoup the abbey's fortunes by carefully supervising its manors. He also rounded up murderers to stand trial in St. Edmunds and provided knights for the king's army. But his actions were not always tolerant or beneficial. He was instrumental in driving the Jews from the town and was not above improving the abbey's possessions at the expense of his neighbors: "He built up the bank of the fish-pond at Babwell so high, for the service of a new mill, that by keeping back the water there is not a man, rich or poor, but has lost his garden and his orchards." The abbot's worldly cares weighed heavily on him, but he had little choice if his abbey were to flourish and fulfill its spiritual and secular functions. But he did have regrets, as he confided to Jocelyn: "If he could have returned to the circumstances he had enjoyed before he became a monk, he would never have become a monk or an abbot."

# The Emergence and Growth of European Kingdoms, 1000–1300

The domination of society by the nobility reached its apex in the High Middle Ages. During this time, however, kings began the process of extending their power in more effective ways. Out of this growth in the monarchies would eventually come the European states that dominated much of later European history.

In theory, kings were regarded as the heads of their kingdoms and were expected to lead their vassals and subjects into battle. The king's power, however, was strictly limited. He had to honor the rights and privileges of his vassals, and if he failed to observe his vassals' rights, they could and did rebel. Weak kings were overthrown or, like the later Carolingians, replaced by another ruling dynasty.

However, kings did possess some sources of power that other lords did not. Kings were anointed by holy oil in ceremonies reminiscent of Old Testament precedents; thus their positions seemed sanctioned by divine favor. War and marriage alliances enabled them to increase their power, and their conquests enabled them to reward their followers with grants of land and bind powerful nobles to them. In the High Middle Ages, kings found ways to strengthen governmental institutions and consequently to extend their powers. The revival of commerce, the growth of cities, and the emergence of a money economy eventually enabled monarchs to hire soldiers and officials and to rely less on their vassals.

## England in the High Middle Ages

At the beginning of the eleventh century, Anglo-Saxon England had fallen subject to Scandinavian control after a successful invasion by the Danes in 1016. King Canute (1016–1035), however, continued English institutions and laws and even supported the Catholic church. His dynastic line proved unable to maintain itself, and in 1042, the Anglo-Saxon line of kings was restored in the person of Edward the Confessor (1042–1066). After his death, the kingship was taken by Harold Godwinson, who belonged to one of England's greatest noble families.

A cousin of Edward the Confessor, William of Normandy, laid claim to the throne of England, however, and invaded England in the fall of 1066. The forces of Harold Godwinson and Duke William met at Hastings on October 14, 1066. The Saxon infantry was soundly defeated by the heavily armed Norman knights, and William was crowned king of England at Christmas in London.

**William of Normandy**  After his conquest, William (1066–1087) treated all of England as a royal possession. Based on the Domesday Book, which William commissioned in 1086 by sending out royal officials to ascertain who owned or held land in tenancy, modern historians have estimated that the Norman royal family took possession of about one-fifth

**Norman Conquest of England.** The Bayeux tapestry, which consists of woolen embroidery on a linen backing, was made by English needlewomen before 1082 for Bayeux Cathedral. It depicts scenes from the Norman invasion of England. This segment shows the Norman cavalry charging the shield wall of the Saxon infantry during the Battle of Hastings.

© Michael Holford

of the land in England as the royal demesne (domain). The remaining English land was held by nobles or the church as fiefs of the king; each of these vassals was in turn responsible for supplying a quota of knights for the royal army. The great landed nobles were allowed to divide their lands among their subvassals as they wished. In 1086, however, by the Oath of Salisbury Plain, William required all subvassals to swear loyalty to him as their king and liege lord. Henceforth, all subvassals owed their primary loyalty to the king rather than to their immediate lords.

Thus the Norman conquest of England had brought a dramatic change. In Anglo-Saxon England, the king had held limited lands while great families controlled large stretches of land and acted rather independently of the king. In contrast, the Normans established a hierarchy of nobles holding land as fiefs from the king. William of Normandy had created a strong, centralized monarchy. Gradually, a process of fusion between the victorious Normans and the defeated Anglo-Saxons created a new England. Although the Norman ruling class spoke French, the intermarriage of the Norman-French with the Anglo-Saxon nobility gradually merged Anglo-Saxon and French into a new English language.

William maintained the Anglo-Saxon administrative system in which counties (shires) were divided into hundreds (groups of villages). Within each shire, the sheriff was the chief royal officer responsible for leading the military forces of the county, collecting royal tolls, and presiding over the county court. William retained the office but replaced the Anglo-Saxon sheriffs with Normans. William also more fully developed the system of taxation and royal courts begun by the Anglo-Saxon and Danish kings of the tenth and eleventh centuries.

The Norman conquest of England had repercussions in France as well. Because the new king of England was still the duke of Normandy, he was both a king (of England) and at the same time a vassal to a king (of France), but a vassal who was now far more powerful than his lord. This connection with France kept England heavily involved in Continental affairs throughout the High Middle Ages.

**Henry II** In the twelfth century, the power of the English monarchy was greatly enlarged during the reign of Henry II (1154–1189), the founder of the Plantagenet dynasty. The new king was particularly successful in developing administrative and legal institutions that strengthened the royal government. First of all, Henry continued the development of the **exchequer,** or permanent royal treasury. Royal officials, known as "barons of the exchequer," received taxes collected by the sheriffs while seated around a table covered by a checkered cloth that served as a counting device. (*Exchequer* is derived from the French word for chessboard.) The barons gave receipts to the sheriffs, while clerks recorded the accounts on sheets of parchment that were then rolled up. These so-called pipe rolls have served as an important source of economic and social information for historians.

Perhaps even more significant than Henry's financial reforms were his efforts to strengthen the royal courts. Henry expanded the number of criminal cases tried in the king's court and also devised ways of taking property cases from local courts to the royal courts. Henry's goals were clear: expanding the jurisdiction of royal courts extended the king's power and, of course, brought revenues into his coffers. Moreover, because the royal courts were now found throughout England, a body of **common law** (law that was common to the whole kingdom) began to replace the local law codes, which varied from place to place.

Henry was less successful at imposing royal control over the church. The king claimed the right to punish clergymen in the royal courts, but Thomas à Becket, archbishop of Canterbury and therefore the highest-ranking English cleric, claimed that only church courts could try clerics. Attempts at compromise failed, and the angry king publicly expressed the desire to be rid of Becket: "Who will free me of this priest?" he screamed. Four knights took the challenge, went to Canterbury, and murdered the archbishop in the cathedral (see the box on p. 257). Faced with public outrage, Henry was forced to allow the right of appeal from English church courts to the papal court.

**King John and Magna Carta** Many English nobles came to resent the ongoing growth of the king's power and rose in rebellion during the reign of Henry's son, King John (1199–1216). At Runnymede in 1215, John was forced to assent to Magna Carta, the "great charter" of feudal liberties. Much of Magna Carta was aimed at limiting government practices that affected the relations between the king and his vassals on the one hand and between the king and the church on the other (see the box on p. 258).

Magna Carta remains, above all, a feudal document. Feudal custom had always recognized that the relationship between king and vassals was based on mutual rights and obligations. Magna Carta gave written recognition to that fact and was used in subsequent years to underscore the concept that the monarch should be limited rather than absolute.

**Edward I and the Emergence of Parliament** In the late thirteenth century, a very talented and powerful monarch ascended the throne in the person of Edward I (1272–1307). He began the process of uniting all of the British Isles into a single kingdom. Although Wales was eventually conquered and pacified, his attempt to subdue Scotland failed. Edward managed merely to begin a lengthy conflict between England and Scotland that lasted for centuries.

Edward was successful in reestablishing monarchical rights after a period of baronial control. During his reign, the role of the English Parliament, an institution of great importance in the development of representative government, began to be defined.

Originally, the word *parliament* was applied to meetings of the king's Great Council in which the greater barons and chief prelates of the church met with the king's judges and principal advisers to deal with judicial affairs. But in need of money in 1295, Edward I invited two knights from every county and two residents (known as burgesses) from

# MURDER IN THE CATHEDRAL

HE CONFLICT BETWEEN King Henry II and Thomas à Becket, archbishop of Canterbury, was the most dramatic confrontation between church and state in English medieval history. Although Henry did not order the archbishop's murder, he certainly caused it by his reckless public words expressing his desire to be free of Becket. This excerpt is from a letter by John of Salisbury, who served as secretary to Theobald, archbishop of Canterbury, and his successor, Thomas à Becket. John was present at the murder of the archbishop in 1170.

## John of Salisbury to John of Canterbury, Bishop of Poitiers

The martyr [Becket] stood in the cathedral, before Christ's altar, as we have said, ready to suffer; the hour of slaughter was at hand. When he heard that he was sought—heard the knights who had come for him shouting in the throng of clerks and monks "Where is the archbishop?"—he turned to meet them on the steps which he had almost climbed, and said with steady countenance: "Here am I! What do you want?" One of the knight-assassins flung at him in fury: "That you die now! That you should live longer is impossible." No martyr seems ever to have been more steadfast in his agony than he, . . . and thus, steadfast in speech as in spirit, he replied: "And I am prepared to die for my God, to preserve justice and my church's liberty. If you seek my head, I forbid you on behalf of God almighty and on pain of anathema to do any hurt to any other man, monk, clerk or layman, of high or low degree. Do not involve them in the punishment, for they have not been involved in the cause: on my head not on theirs be it if any of them have supported the church in its troubles. I embrace death readily, so long as peace and liberty for the Church follow from the shedding of my blood. . . ." He spoke, and saw that the assassins had drawn their swords; and bowed his head like one in prayer. His last words were "To God and St. Mary and the saints who protect and defend this church, and to the blessed Denis, I commend myself and the church's cause." No one could dwell on what followed without deep sorrow and choking tears. A son's affection forbids me to describe each blow the savage assassins struck, spurning all fear of God, forgetful of all fealty and any human feeling. They defiled the cathedral and the holy season [Christmas] with a bishop's blood and with slaughter; but that was not enough. They sliced off the crown of his head, which had been specially dedicated to God by anointing with holy oil—a fearful thing even to describe; then they used their evil swords, when he was dead, to spill his brain and cruelly scattered it, mixed with blood and bones, over the pavement. . . . Through all the agony the martyr's spirit was unconquered, his steadfastness marvelous to observe; he spoke not a word, uttered no cry, let slip no groan, raised no arm nor garment to protect himself from an assailant, but bent his head, which he had laid bare to their swords with wonderful courage, till all might be fulfilled. Motionless he held it, and when at last he fell his body lay straight; and he moved neither hand nor foot.

---

each city and town to meet with the Great Council to consent to new taxes. This was the first Parliament.

The English Parliament, then, came to be composed of two knights from every county and two burgesses from every town or city, as well as the barons and ecclesiastical lords. Eventually, the barons and church lords formed the House of Lords; the knights and burgesses, the House of Commons. The Parliaments of Edward I granted taxes, discussed politics, passed laws, and handled judicial business. Although not yet the important body it would eventually become, the English Parliament had clearly emerged as an institution by the end of the thirteenth century. The law of the realm was beginning to be determined not by the king alone but by the king in consultation with representatives of various groups that constituted the community. By the beginning of the fourteenth century, England had begun to develop a unique system of national monarchy.

## The Growth of the French Kingdom

The Capetian dynasty of French kings had emerged at the end of the tenth century. Although they bore the title of king, the Capetians had little real power. They controlled as the royal domain (the lands of the king) only the lands around Paris known as the Île-de-France. As kings of France, the Capetians were formally the overlords of the great lords of France, such as the dukes of Normandy, Brittany, Burgundy, and Aquitaine. In reality, however, many of the dukes were considerably more powerful than the Capetian kings. It would take the Capetian dynasty hundreds of years to create a truly centralized monarchical authority in France.

**The Conquests of Philip II** The reign of King Philip II Augustus (1180–1223) was an important turning point. He perceived that the power of the French monarch would never be extended until the Plantagenets' power was defeated. After all, Henry II and his sons were not only kings of England but also rulers of the French territories of Normandy, Maine, Anjou, and Aquitaine. Accordingly, Philip II waged war against the Plantagenet rulers of England and was successful in wresting control of Normandy, Maine, Anjou, and Touraine from the English kings (see Map 10.1). Through these conquests, Philip II quadrupled the income of the French monarchy and greatly enlarged its power. To administer justice and collect royal revenues in his new territories, Philip appointed new royal officials, thus inaugurating a French royal bureaucracy.

# MAGNA CARTA

*A*FTER THE DISMAL FAILURE of King John to reconquer Normandy from the French king, some of the English barons rebelled against their king. At Runnymede in 1215, King John agreed to seal Magna Carta, the "great charter" of liberties regulating the relationship between the king and his vassals. What made Magna Carta an important historical document was its more general clauses defining rights and liberties. These were later interpreted in broader terms to make them applicable to all the English people.

## Magna Carta

John, by the Grace of God, king of England, lord of Ireland, duke of Normandy and Aquitaine, count of Anjou, to the archbishops, bishops, abbots, earls, barons, justiciars, foresters, sheriffs, reeves, servants, and all bailiffs and his faithful people greeting.

1. In the first place we have granted to God, and by this our present charter confirmed, for us and our heirs forever, that the English church shall be free, and shall hold its rights entire and its liberties uninjured. . . . We have granted moreover to all free men of our kingdom for us and our heirs forever all the liberties written below, to be had and holden by themselves and their heirs from us and our heirs.

2. If any of our earls or barons, or others holding from us in chief by military service shall have died, and when he had died his heir shall be of full age and owe relief, he shall have his inheritance by the ancient relief; that is to say, the heir or heirs of an earl for the whole barony of an earl a hundred pounds; the heir or heirs of a baron for a whole barony a hundred pounds; the heir or heirs of a knight, for a whole knight's fee, a hundred shillings at most; and who owes less let him give less according to the ancient custom of fiefs.

3. If moreover the heir of any one of such shall be under age, and shall be in wardship, when he comes of age he shall have his inheritance without relief and without a fine. . . .

12. No scutage or aid shall be imposed in our kingdom except by the common council of our kingdom, except for the ransoming of our body, for the making of our oldest son a knight, and for once marrying our oldest daughter, and for these purposes it shall be only a reasonable aid. . . .

13. And the city of London shall have all its ancient liberties and free customs, as well by land as by water. Moreover, we will and grant that all other cities and boroughs and villages and ports shall have all their liberties and free customs.

14. And for holding a common council of the kingdom concerning the assessment of an aid otherwise than in the three cases mentioned above, or concerning the assessment of a scutage we shall cause to be summoned the archbishops, bishops, abbots, earls, and greater barons by our letters under seal; and besides we shall cause to be summoned generally, by our sheriffs and bailiffs, all those who hold from us in chief, for a certain day, that is at the end of forty days at least, and for a certain place; and in all the letters of that summons, we will express the cause of the summons, and when the summons has thus been given, the business shall proceed on the appointed day, on the advice of those who shall be present, even if not all of those who were summoned have come. . . .

39. No free man shall be taken or imprisoned or dispossessed, or outlawed, or banished, or in any way destroyed, nor will we go upon him, nor send upon him, except by the legal judgment of his peers or by the law of the land. . . .

60. Moreover, all those customs and franchises mentioned above in which we have conceded in our kingdom, and which are to be fulfilled, as far as pertains to us, in respect to our men; all men of our kingdom, as well as clergy as laymen, shall observe as far as pertains to them, in respect to their men.

---

**The Saintly Louis IX**   Capetian rulers after Philip II continued to add lands to the royal domain. Although Philip had used military force, other kings used both purchase and marriage to achieve the same end. Much of the thirteenth century was dominated by Louis IX (1226–1270), one of the most celebrated of the medieval French kings. A deeply religious man, he was later canonized as a saint by the church, an unusual action regardless of the century. Louis was known for his attempts to bring justice to his people and ensure their rights. He sent out royal agents to check on the activities of royal officials after hearing complaints that they were abusing their power. Sharing in the religious sentiments of his age, Louis played a major role in two of the later Crusades (see "The Crusades" later in this chapter). Both were failures, and he met his death during an invasion of North Africa.

**Philip IV and the Estates-General**   One of Louis's successors, Philip IV the Fair (1285–1314), was particularly effective in strengthening the French monarchy. The machinery of government became even more specialized. French kings going back to the early Capetians had possessed a household staff for running their affairs. In effect, the division and enlargement of this household staff produced the three major branches of royal administration: a council for advice; a chamber of accounts, for finances; and the *Parlement*, or royal court. By the beginning of the fourteenth century, the Capetians had established an efficient royal bureaucracy.

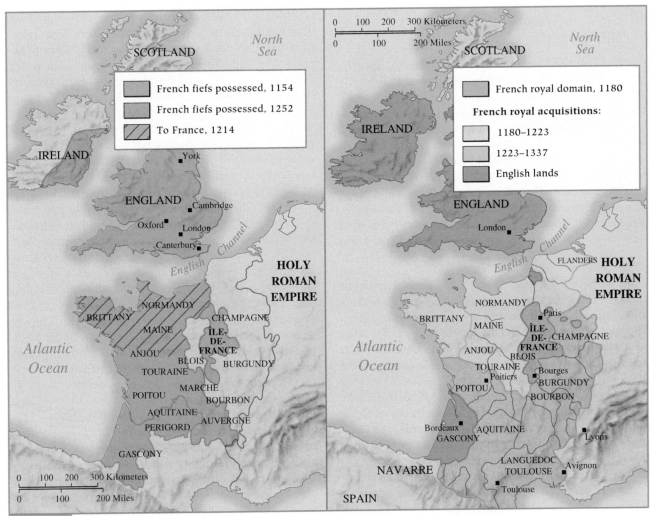

**MAP 10.1** **England and France in the High Middle Ages:** (*left*) **England and Its French Holdings;** (*right*) **Growth of the French State.** King Philip II Augustus of France greatly expanded the power of the Capetian royal family through his victories over the Plantagenet monarchy of England, which enabled Philip to gain control over much of north-central France. ❓ How could the presence of the English Channel have made it more difficult for England to rule its French possessions?  View an animated version of this map or related maps at http://history.wadsworth.com/spielvogel06/

**Louis IX Departs for Tunis.** The pious French king Louis IX organized the last two major Crusades of the thirteenth century. Both failed miserably. This illustration shows a robust Louis IX setting out for Tunis in 1270. In truth, the king was so weak that he had to be carried to the ship.

Philip IV also brought a French parliament into being. After he became involved in a struggle with the pope, Philip summoned representatives of the church, nobility, and towns to meet with him in 1302, thereby inaugurating the Estates-General, the first French parliament. The Estates-General came to function as an instrument to bolster the king's power because he could ask representatives of the major French social classes to change the laws or grant new taxes. By the end of the thirteenth century, France was the largest, wealthiest, and best-governed monarchical state in Europe.

## Christian Reconquest: The Spanish Kingdoms

Much of Spain had been part of the Islamic world since the eighth century. Muslim Spain had flourished in the Early Middle Ages. Córdoba became a major urban center with a population exceeding 300,000 people. Agriculture prospered, and Spain became known for excellent leather, wool, silk, and paper. Beginning in the tenth century, however, the most noticeable feature of Spanish history was the weakening of Muslim power and the beginning of a Christian reconquest that lasted until the final expulsion of the Muslims at the end of the fifteenth century. The *Reconquista,* as the Spaniards called it, became over a period of time a sacred mission to many of the Christian rulers and inhabitants of the peninsula.

**The Reconquest**  By the eleventh century, a number of small Christian kingdoms—Leon, Castile, Navarre, Aragon, and Barcelona—had become established in northern Spain. Muslim disunity and the support of French nobles, who were eager to battle the Muslim infidel, enabled these Spanish Christian states to take the offensive against the Muslims. Rodrigo Díaz de Vivar, known as El Cid, was the most famous military adventurer of the time. Unlike the Christian warriors of France, El Cid fought under either Christian or Muslim rulers. He carved out his own kingdom of Valencia in 1094 but failed to create a dynasty when it was reconquered by the Muslims after his death.

By the end of the twelfth century, the Christian reconquest of Spain had slowed considerably. The northern half had been consolidated into the Christian kingdoms of Castile, Navarre, Aragon, and Portugal, which had emerged by 1179 as a separate kingdom (see Map 10.2). The southern half of Spain remained under the control of the Muslims.

In the thirteenth century, Christian rulers took the offensive again in the reconquest of Muslim territory. Aragon and Castile had become the two strongest Spanish kingdoms, and Portugal had reached its modern boundaries. All three states made significant conquests of Muslim territory. Castile subdued most of Andalusia in the south, down to the Atlantic and the Mediterranean; at the same time, Aragon conquered Valencia. The crucial battle occurred in 1212 at Las Navas de Tolosa. Alfonso VIII of Castile (1155–1214) had amassed an army of sixty thousand men and crushed the Muslim forces, leading to Christian victories over the next forty years. By the mid-thirteenth century, the Muslims remained only in the kingdom of Granada, along the southeastern edge of the Iberian peninsula.

As the Christian armies moved down the peninsula, rulers followed a policy known as *repartimiento.* Rulers distributed houses, land, and property in the countryside to individuals who had made the conquests and new Christian colonists. The former—consisting of nobles, important churchmen, high-ranking soldiers, and royal officials—often received the best lands. The colonists, some of them ordinary foot soldiers, also received land. Muslims who were not expelled or killed and chose to stay under Christian rule were known as *mudejares,* most of whom continued to work in small industrial enterprises or as farmers.

To encourage other settlers to move into the newly conquered regions, Spanish kings issued written privileges that guaranteed rule in accordance with the law for most of the communities in their kingdoms. These privileges, or *fueros,* stipulated the punishments for crimes committed within community boundaries and the means for resolving civil disputes. They also established regulations for acquiring citizenship in the community, rules for service in the local militia, and laws protecting the rights of women and children living in the towns. Kings of the different regions of Spain freely borrowed from the *fueros* of other regions in an effort to develop attractive customs for their towns so that immigrants would be lured into establishing residency there. By the thirteenth century, kings were increasingly required to swear that they would respect

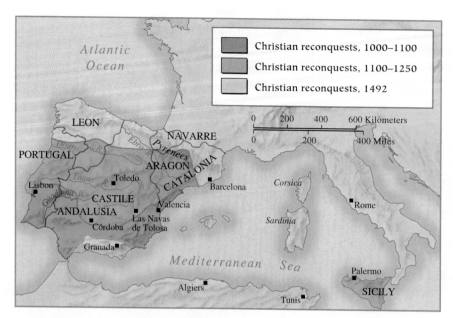

**MAP 10.2** **Christian Reconquests in the Western Mediterranean.** Muslims seized most of Spain in the eighth century, near the end of the period of rapid Islamic expansion. In the eleventh century, small Christian kingdoms in the north began the *Reconquista,* finally conquering the last Moors near the end of the fifteenth century. **?** How can you explain the roughly north-to-south conquest of the Muslim lands in Spain? **View an animated version of this map or related maps at** http://history.wadsworth.com/spielvogel06/

these community customs before they were confirmed in office by assemblies of their leading citizens.

The Spanish kingdoms followed no consistent policy in the treatment of the conquered Muslim population. Muslim farmers continued to work the land but were forced to pay very high rents in Aragon. In Castile, King Alfonso X (1252–1284), who called himself the "King of Three Religions," encouraged the continued development of a cosmopolitan culture shared by Christians, Jews, and Muslims.

## The Lands of the Holy Roman Empire: Germany and Italy

The Saxon kings of the tenth century had strengthened their hold over the German kingdom and revived the empire of Charlemagne. A new dynasty, known as the Salian kings, began in 1024 with the election of Conrad II (1024–1039) of Franconia (see Map 10.3). Both Conrad and his successors, Henry III (1039–1056) and Henry IV (1056–1106), managed to create a strong German monarchy and a powerful empire by leading armies into Italy.

The great lords of Germany took advantage of the early death of Henry III and the minority of Henry IV to extend their own power at the expense of the latter. The elective nature of the German monarchy posed a problem for the German kings. Although some dynasties were strong enough for their members to be elected regularly, the great lords who were the electors did at times deliberately choose otherwise. It was to their advantage to select a weak king.

To compensate for their weaknesses, German kings had come to rely on their ability to control the church and select bishops and abbots whom they could then use as royal administrators. But the struggle between church and state during the reign of Henry IV weakened the king's ability to use church officials in this way.

**Involvement in Italy**  The German kings also tried to bolster their power by using their position as emperors to exploit the resources of Italy. Italy seemed a likely area for intervention because it had no central political authority. While important nobles struggled to dominate northern Italy, central Italy remained under the control of the Papal States. In southern Italy, the Lombard dukes, Muslims, and Byzantines seemed to be in constant conflict.

In the latter half of the eleventh century, a group of Norman adventurers led by Robert Guiscard ("the cunning") conquered much of southern Italy. Robert's brother Roger subdued Muslim Sicily in 1091 after a thirty-year struggle. In 1130, Roger II, the son of Roger of Sicily, was crowned king of Sicily. By the end of the twelfth century, the Norman kingdom was one of the most powerful in Europe as well as one of the most fascinating. A melting pot of Christian, Jewish, and Muslim culture, the state issued its official documents in Latin, Greek, and Arabic.

The Norman kingdom in southern Italy was beyond any claims of the German kings, but the wealthy cities of northern Italy, which by the twelfth century had become virtually independent after overthrowing the rule of their bishops, were a tempting prize to the German kings, who never entirely gave up their dreams of a restored empire. No German dynasty proved more susceptible to the allure of this dream than the Hohenstaufens.

**Frederick I**  Both Frederick I (1152–1190) and Frederick II (1212–1250) tried to create a foundation for a new kind of empire. Frederick I, known as Barbarossa (Redbeard) to the Italians, was a powerful lord from the Swabian house of Hohenstaufen when he was

MAP 10.3 **The Lands of the Holy Roman Empire in the Twelfth Century.** The Hohenstaufen rulers Frederick I and Frederick II sought to expand the Holy Roman Empire to include all of Italy. Frederick II had only fleeting success: after his death, several independent city-states arose in northern Italy, while at home, German nobles had virtually free reign within their domains. ❓ Why did the territorial conquests of the Holy Roman Empire cause alarm in the papacy? 🌐 **View an animated version of this map or related maps at** http://history.wadsworth.com/spielvogel06/

# THE DEEDS OF EMPEROR FREDERICK II

REDERICK II, king of Germany and Sicily and would-be ruler of all Italy, was viewed even by contemporaries as one of the most unusual rulers of his time. This account of his "idiosyncrasies" is by Salimbene de Adam, a Franciscan friar whose *Chronicle* is one of the richest sources of information about medieval life in thirteenth-century Italy. He was, however, also known to be notoriously biased against Frederick II.

## Salimbene de Adam, *Chronicle*

Note that Frederick almost always enjoyed having discord with the Church and fighting her on all sides, although she had nourished him, defended him, and raised him up. He held the true faith to be worthless. He was a cunning, crafty man, avaricious, lecherous, and malicious, easily given to wrath.

At times, however, Frederick was a worthy man, and when he wished to show his good, courtly side, he could be witty, charming, urbane, and industrious. He was adept at writing and singing, and was well-versed in the art of writing lyrics and songs. He was a handsome, well-formed man of medium height. I myself saw him and, at one time, loved him. For he once wrote Brother Elias, Minister General of the Friars Minor, on my behalf asking him to return me to my father. He also could speak many and various languages. In short, if he had been a good Catholic and had loved God, the Church, and his own soul, he would scarcely have had an equal as an emperor in the world. . . .

Now, it is necessary to speak of Frederick's idiosyncrasies. His first idiosyncrasy is that he had the thumb of a certain notary cut off because he had written his name in a way different from the way the Emperor desired. . . .

His second idiosyncrasy was that he wanted to discover what language a child would use when he grew up if he had never heard anyone speak. Therefore, he placed some infants in the care of wet-nurses, commanding them to bathe and suckle the children, but by no means ever to speak to or fondle them. For he wanted to discover whether they would speak Hebrew, the first language, or Greek, Latin, Arabic, or the language of their parents. But he labored in vain, because all of the infants died. . . .

Furthermore, Frederick had many other idiosyncrasies: idle curiosity, lack of faith, perversity, tyranny, and accursedness, some of which I have written about in another chronicle. Once, for example, he sealed up a live man in a cask and kept him there until he died in order to prove that the soul totally perished with the body. . . . For Frederick was an Epicurean, and so he and the learned men of his court searched out whatever Biblical passage they could find to prove that there is no life after death. . . .

This sixth example of Frederick's idiosyncrasy and idle curiosity . . . was that he fed two men a fine meal, and he sent one to bed to sleep, the other out hunting. And that evening he had both men disemboweled in his presence, in order to determine which one had digested his food the best. The decisions by his doctors went to the man who had slept after the meal. . . .

I have heard and known many other idiosyncrasies of Frederick, but I keep quiet for the sake of brevity, and because reporting so many of the Emperor's foolish notions is tedious to me.

---

elected king. Previous German kings had focused on building a strong German kingdom, to which Italy might be added as an appendage. Frederick I, however, planned to get his chief revenues from Italy as the center of a "holy empire," as he called it—the Holy Roman Empire. But his attempt to conquer northern Italy ran into severe difficulties. The pope opposed him, fearful that the emperor wanted to incorporate Rome and the Papal States into his empire. The cities of northern Italy, which had become used to their freedom, were also not willing to be Frederick's subjects. An alliance of these northern Italian cities, with the support of the papacy, defeated the forces of the Emperor Frederick at Legnano in 1176.

Later Frederick returned to Italy and arranged a settlement with the northern Italian cities by which they retained their independence in return for an annual payment to the emperor. Frederick now had the financial base he had sought. Moreover, by marrying his son (who became Henry VI, 1190–1197) to the heiress of the Norman kingdom of southern Italy, Frederick seemed to be creating the foundation for making the Holy Roman Empire a reality and for realizing the pope's nightmare: the encirclement of Rome and the Papal States. After Frederick's death, Henry VI's control of Germany and both northern and southern Italy made him the strongest European ruler since Charlemagne. Henry's empire soon collapsed, however, for he died prematurely, leaving as his heir a son only two years old.

**Frederick II** The son, Frederick II, grew up to become the most brilliant of the Hohenstaufen rulers. King of Sicily in 1198, king of Germany in 1212, and crowned emperor in 1220, Frederick II was a truly remarkable man who awed his contemporaries (see the box above). Frederick was raised in Sicily, with its diverse peoples, languages, and religions. His court there brought together a brilliant array of lawyers, poets, artists, and scientists, and he himself took a deep interest in their work.

Until he was crowned emperor, Frederick spent much time in Germany; once he left in 1220, he rarely returned. He gave the German princes full control of their territories, voluntarily surrendering any real power over Germany in exchange for revenues while he pursued his main goal, the establishment of a strong centralized state in Italy dom-

**The Coronation of Frederick II.** Shown here is the coronation of Frederick II of Germany as Holy Roman Emperor by Pope Honorius II in Rome on November 22, 1220. The pope agreed to do so after Frederick promised to lead a Crusade to the Holy Land, a promise that he took years to fulfill. This scene is taken from a fifteenth-century French manuscript on the monarchs of Europe.

inated by his kingdom in Sicily. Frederick's major task was to gain control of northern Italy. In reaching to extend his power in Italy, he became involved in a deadly struggle with the popes, who realized that a single ruler of northern and southern Italy meant the end of papal secular power in central Italy. The northern Italian cities were also unwilling to give up their freedom. Frederick waged a bitter struggle in northern Italy, winning many battles but ultimately losing the war.

Frederick's preoccupation with the creation of an empire in Italy left Germany in confusion and chaos until 1273, when the major German princes, serving as electors, chose an insignificant German noble, Rudolf of Habsburg, as the new German king. In choosing a weak king, the princes were ensuring that the German monarchy would remain impotent and incapable of reestablishing a centralized monarchical state. The failure of the Hohenstaufens had led to a situation where his exalted majesty, the German king and Holy Roman Emperor, had no real power over either Germany or Italy. Unlike France and England, neither Germany

**Settlements of the Teutonic Knights**

nor Italy created a unified national monarchy in the Middle Ages. Both became geographical designations for loose confederations of hundreds of petty independent states under the vague direction of king or emperor. In fact, neither Germany nor Italy would become united until the nineteenth century.

Following the death of Frederick II, Italy fell into political confusion. While the papacy remained in control of much of central Italy, the defeat of imperial power left the cities and towns of northern Italy independent of any other authority. Gradually, the larger ones began to emerge as strong city-states. Florence assumed the leadership of Tuscany, while Milan, under the guidance of the Visconti family, took control of the Lombard region. With its great commercial wealth, the republic of Venice dominated the northeastern part of the peninsula.

## New Kingdoms in Northern and Eastern Europe

The Scandinavian countries of northern Europe had little political organization before 1000, and it was not until the second half of the tenth century and the first half of the eleventh that the three Scandinavian kingdoms—Denmark, Norway, and Sweden (see Map 10.4)—emerged with a noticeable political structure. At the same time, the three kingdoms were converted to Christianity by kings who believed that an organized church was a necessary accompaniment to an organized state. The adoption of Christianity, however, did not eliminate the warlike tendencies of the Scandinavians. Not only did the three kingdoms fight each other in the eleventh and twelfth centuries, but rival families were in regular conflict over the throne in each state. This period also witnessed the growth of a powerful noble landowning class.

To the south, in eastern Europe, Hungary, which had been a Christian state since 1000, remained relatively stable throughout the High Middle Ages, but the history of Poland and Russia was more turbulent. In the thirteenth century, eastern Europe was beset by two groups of invaders, the Teutonic Knights from the west and the Mongols from the east.

In the eleventh century, a Polish kingdom existed as a separate state but with no natural frontiers. Consequently, German settlers encroached on its territory on a regular basis, leading to considerable intermarriage between Slavs and Germans. During the thirteenth century, relations between the Germans and the Slavs of eastern Europe worsened due to the aggression of the Teutonic Knights. The Teutonic Knights had been founded near the end of the twelfth century to protect the Christian Holy Land. In the early thirteenth century, however, these Christian knights found greater opportunity to the east of Germany, where they

NORWAY
SWEDEN
DENMARK
Baltic Sea
ESTONIANS
Novgorod
LITHUANIANS
POMERANIA
PRUSSIANS
*Elbe*
R.
*Rhine R.*
POLAND
Lublin
*Oder R.*
*Vistula R.*
KINGDOM OF RUS
HOLY ROMAN EMPIRE
Prague
Krakow
*Danube*
Carpathian Mts.
*Dnieper R.*
R.
Vienna
*Alps*
HUNGARY
MOLDAVIA
*Po R.*
CROATS
Belgrade
WALLACHIA
SERBS
BULGARIANS
BYZANTINE EMPIRE
KINGDOM OF SICILY

0     200     400     600 Kilometers
0        200        400 Miles

**MAP 10.4** **Northern and Eastern Europe.** Acceptance of Christianity gave many northern and eastern European kingdoms greater control over their subjects. Warfare was common in the region: dynastic struggles occurred in Scandinavia, and the Teutonic Knights, based in East Prussia, attacked pagan Slavs. **?** Which areas of northern and eastern Europe had large Slavic populations? (Look back at Map 8.4.)

📹 View an animated version of this map or related maps at http://history.wadsworth.com/spielvogel06/

Temuchin, unified the Mongol tribes and gained the title of Genghis Khan (c. 1162–1227), which means "universal ruler." From that time on, Genghis Khan created a powerful military force and devoted himself to fighting. "Man's highest joy," Genghis Khan remarked, "is in victory: to conquer one's enemies, to pursue them, to deprive them of their possessions, to make their beloved weep, to ride on their horses, and to embrace their wives and daughters."[1] Genghis Khan was succeeded by equally competent sons and grandsons.

The Mongols burst onto the scene in the thirteenth century. They advanced eastward, eventually conquering China and Korea. One of Genghis Khan's grandsons, Khubilai Khan, completed the conquest of China and established a new Chinese dynasty of rulers known as the Yuan. In 1279, Khubilai Khan moved the capital of China northward to Khanbaliq ("city of the khan"), which would later be known by the Chinese name Beijing.

The Mongols also moved westward against the Islamic empire. Persia fell by 1233, and by 1258, they had conquered Baghdad and destroyed the Abbasid caliphate. Beginning in the 1230s, the Mongols had moved into Europe. They conquered Russia, advanced into Poland and Hungary, and destroyed a force of Poles and Teutonic Knights in Silesia in 1241 (see Map 10.5). Europe then seemingly got lucky when the Mongol hordes turned back because of internal fighting; western and southern Europe escaped the wrath of the Mongols. Overall, the Mongols had little impact in Europe, although their occupation of Russia had some residual effects.

attacked the pagan Slavs. East Prussia was given to the military order in 1226, and five years later, the knights moved beyond the Vistula River, where they waged war against the Slavs for another thirty years. By the end of the thirteenth century, Prussia had become German and Christian as the pagan Slavs were forced to convert.

Central and eastern Europe had periodically been subject to invasions from fierce Asiatic nomads, such as the Huns, Avars, Bulgars, and Magyars. In the thirteenth century, the Mongols exploded onto the scene, causing far more disruption than earlier invaders.

## 🖋 The Mongol Empire

The Mongols rose to power in Asia with stunning speed. They were a pastoral people in the region of modern-day Mongolia organized loosely into clans and tribes, often warring with each other. This changed when one leader,

## 🖋 The Development of Russia

The Kievan Rus state, which had become formally Christian in 987, prospered considerably afterward, reaching its high point in the first half of the eleventh century. Kievan society was dominated by a noble class of landowners

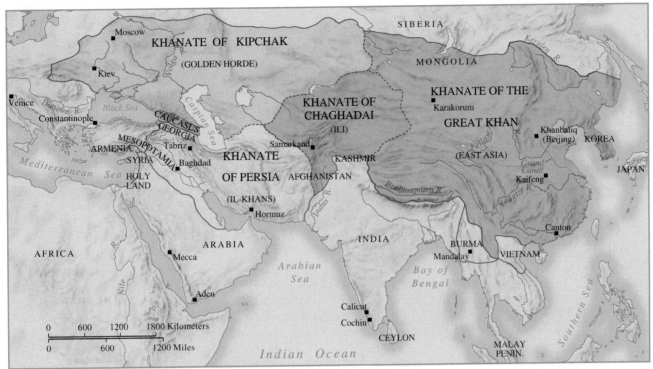

**MAP 10.5  The Mongol Empire.** Beginning with the exploits of Genghis Khan, the Mongols used unorthodox but effective military tactics to establish an empire that stretched from Russia to China and included India and South Asia. The empire was divided into khanates. The Golden Horde, the khanate in Russia, was eventually overwhelmed by Moscow princes who went on to establish the Russian state. ❓ Why would it be difficult for one khan to effectively rule the entire Mongol Empire?

View an animated version of this map or related maps at http://history.wadsworth.com/spielvogel06/

known as the **boyars.** Kievan merchants maintained regular trade with Scandinavia to the northwest and the Islamic and Byzantine worlds to the south. But destructive civil wars and new invasions by Asiatic nomads caused the principality of Kiev to disintegrate into a number of constituent parts. The sack of Kiev by North Russian princes in 1169 brought an inglorious end to the first Russian state.

The fundamental civilizing and unifying force of early Russia was the Christian church. The Russian church imitated the liturgy and organization of the Byzantine Empire, whose Eastern Orthodox priests had converted the Kievan Rus to Christianity at the end of the tenth century. The Russian church became known for its rigid religious orthodoxy. Although Christianity provided a common bond between Russian and European civilization, Russia's religious development guaranteed an even closer affinity between Russian and Byzantine civilization.

In the thirteenth century, the Mongols conquered Russia and cut it off even more from western Europe. The Mongols were not numerous enough to settle the vast Russian lands but were content to rule directly an area along the lower Volga and north of the Caspian and Black Seas to Kiev and rule indirectly elsewhere. In the latter territories, Russian princes were required to pay tribute to the Mongol overlords.

One Russian prince soon emerged as more visible and powerful than the others. Alexander Nevsky (c. 1220–1263), prince of Novgorod, defeated a German invading army at Lake Peipus in northwestern Russia in 1242. His cooperation with the Mongols, which included denouncing his own brother and crushing native tax revolts, won him their favor. The khan, the acknowledged leader of the western part of the Mongol Empire, rewarded Alexander Nevsky with the title of grand-prince, enabling his descendants to become the princes of Moscow and eventually leaders of all Russia.

# The Recovery and Reform of the Catholic Church

In the Early Middle Ages, the Catholic church had played a leading role in converting and civilizing first the Germanic invaders and later the Vikings and Magyars. Although highly successful, this had not been accomplished without challenges that undermined the spiritual life of the church itself.

### The Problems of Decline

Since the eighth century, the popes of the Catholic church had reigned supreme over the affairs of the church. They had also come to exercise control over the territories in central Italy known as the Papal States; this kept popes involved

| England | |
|---|---|
| King Canute | 1016–1035 |
| Battle of Hastings | 1066 |
| William the Conqueror | 1066–1087 |
| Henry II, first of the Plantagenet dynasty | 1154–1189 |
| Murder of Thomas à Becket | 1170 |
| John | 1199–1216 |
| Magna Carta | 1215 |
| Edward I | 1272–1307 |
| The "greater Parliaments" | 1295, 1297 |
| France | |
| Philip II Augustus | 1180–1223 |
| Louis IX | 1226–1270 |
| Philip IV | 1285–1314 |
| First Estates-General | 1302 |
| Spain | |
| El Cid in Valencia | 1094–1099 |
| Establishment of Portugal | 1179 |
| Alfonso VIII of Castile | 1155–1214 |
| Battle of Las Navas de Tolosa | 1212 |
| Alfonso X of Castile | 1252–1284 |
| Germany, the Holy Roman Empire, and Italy | |
| Conrad II, first of the Salian dynasty | 1024–1039 |
| Henry III | 1039–1056 |
| Henry IV | 1056–1106 |
| Frederick I Barbarossa | 1152–1190 |
| Lombard League defeats Frederick at Legnano | 1176 |
| Henry VI | 1190–1197 |
| Frederick II | 1212–1250 |
| Election of Rudolf of Habsburg as king of Germany | 1273 |
| Eastern Europe | |
| East Prussia given to the Teutonic Knights | 1226 |
| Genghis Khan and the rise of the Mongols | c. 1162–1227 |
| Mongol conquest of Russia | 1230s |
| Alexander Nevsky, prince of Novgorod | c. 1220–1263 |
| Defeat of the Germans | 1242 |

in political matters, often at the expense of their spiritual obligations. At the same time, the church became increasingly entangled in the evolving lord-vassal relationships. High officials of the church, such as bishops and abbots, came to hold their offices as fiefs from nobles. As vassals, they were obliged to carry out the usual duties, including military service. Of course, lords assumed the right to choose their vassals, even when those vassals included bishops and abbots. Because lords often selected their vassals

from other noble families for political reasons, these bishops and abbots were often worldly figures who cared little about their spiritual responsibilities.

The monastic ideal had also suffered during the Early Middle Ages. Benedictine monasteries had sometimes been exemplary centers of Christian living and learning, but the invasions of Vikings, Magyars, and Muslims wreaked havoc with many monastic establishments. Discipline declined, and with it the monastic reputation for learning and holiness. At the same time, a growing number of monasteries fell under the control of local lords, as did much of the church. A number of people believed that the time for reform had come.

## The Cluniac Reform Movement

Reform of the Catholic church began in Burgundy in eastern France in 910 when Duke William of Aquitaine founded the abbey of Cluny. The monastery began with a renewed dedication to the highest spiritual ideals of the Benedictine rules and was fortunate in having a series of abbots in the tenth century who maintained these ideals. Cluny was deliberately kept independent from any local control. As Duke William stipulated in his original charter, "It has pleased us also to insert in this document that, from this day, those same monks there congregated shall be subject neither to our yoke, nor to that of our relatives, nor to the sway of the royal might, nor to that of any earthly power."[2] The new monastery at Cluny tried to eliminate some of the abuses that had crept into religious communities by stressing the need for work, replacing manual labor with the copying of manuscripts, and demanding more community worship and less private prayer.

The Cluniac reform movement sparked an enthusiastic response, first in France and eventually in all of western and central Europe. Hundreds of new monasteries were founded based on Cluniac ideals, and previously existing monasteries rededicated themselves by adopting the Cluniac program. The movement also began to reach beyond monasticism and into the papacy itself, which was in dire need of help.

## Reform of the Papacy

By the eleventh century, a movement for change, led by a series of reforming popes, was sweeping through the Catholic church. One of the reformers' primary goals was to free the church from the interference of lords in the election of church officials. This issue was dramatically taken up by the greatest of the reform popes of the eleventh century, Gregory VII (1073–1085).

**Pope Gregory VII and Reform**    Elected pope in 1073, Gregory was absolutely certain that he had been chosen by God to reform the church. In pursuit of those aims, Gregory claimed that he—the pope—was God's "vicar on Earth" and that the pope's authority extended over all of Chris-

# The "Gregorian Revolution": Papal Claims

N THE ELEVENTH CENTURY, a dynamic group of reformers pushed for the "freedom of the church." This came to mean not only papal control over the affairs of the church but also the elimination of lay investiture. The reformers saw the latter as the chief issue at the heart of lay control of the church. In trying to eliminate it, the reforming popes, especially Gregory VII, extended papal claims to include the right to oversee the secular authorities and, in particular, to depose rulers under certain circumstances. The following selection is from a document that was entered in the papal register in 1075. It consisted of twenty-seven assertions that probably served as headings, or a table of contents, for a collection of ecclesiastical writings that supported the pope's claims.

## The Dictates of the Pope

1. That the Roman church was founded by God alone.
2. That the Roman pontiff alone can with right be called universal.
3. That he alone can depose or reinstate bishops.
4. That, in a council, his legate, even if a lower grade, is above all bishops, and can pass sentence of deposition against them.
5. That the pope may depose the absent.
6. That, among other things, we ought not to remain in the same house with those excommunicated by him. . . .
8. That he alone may use the imperial insignia.
9. That of the pope alone all princes shall kiss the feet.
10. That his name alone shall be spoken in the churches.
11. That this is the only name in the world.
12. That it may be permitted to him to depose emperors.
13. That he may be permitted to transfer bishops if need be. . . .
17. That no chapter and no book shall be considered canonical without his authority.
18. That a sentence passed by him may be retracted by no one; and that he himself, alone of all, may retract it.
19. That he himself may be judged by no one.
20. That no one shall dare to condemn one who appeals to the apostolic chair.
21. That to the latter should be referred the more important cases of every church.
22. That the Roman church has never erred; nor will it err to all eternity, the Scripture bearing witness.
23. That the Roman pontiff, if he have been canonically ordained, is undoubtedly made a saint by the merits of St. Peter. . . .
25. That he may depose and reinstate bishops without assembling a synod.
26. That he who is not at peace with the Roman church shall not be considered catholic.
27. That he may absolve subjects from their fealty to wicked men.

---

tendom and included the right to depose emperors if they disobeyed his wishes. Gregory sought nothing less than the elimination of **lay investiture** (both interference by nonmembers of the clergy in elections and their participation in the installation of prelates). Only in this way could the church regain its freedom, by which Gregory meant the right of the church to elect prelates and to run its own affairs. If rulers did not accept these "divine" commands, they could be deposed by the pope acting in his capacity as the vicar of Christ (see the box above). Gregory VII soon found himself in conflict with the king of Germany over these claims. (The king of Germany was also the emperor-designate since it had been accepted by this time that only kings of Germany could be emperors, but they did not officially use the title "emperor" until they were crowned by the pope.)

King Henry IV (1056–1106) of Germany was just as determined as the pope. For many years, German kings had appointed high-ranking clerics, especially bishops, as their vassals in order to use them as administrators. Without them, the king could not hope to maintain his own power vis-à-vis the powerful German nobles. In 1075, Pope Gregory issued a decree forbidding important clerics from receiving investiture from lay leaders: "We decree that no one of the clergy shall receive the investiture with a bishopric or abbey or church from the hand of an emperor or king or of any lay person."[3] Henry had no intention of obeying a decree that challenged the very heart of his administration.

**The Investiture Controversy**    The immediate cause of the so-called Investiture Controversy was a disputed election to the bishopric of Milan in northern Italy, an important position because the bishop was also the ruler of the city. Control of the bishopric was crucial if the king wished to reestablish German power in northern Italy. Since Milan was considered second only to Rome in importance as a bishopric, papal interest in the office was also keen. Pope Gregory VII and King Henry IV backed competing candidates for the position.

To gain acceptance of his candidate, the pope threatened the king with **excommunication.** Excommunication is a censure by which a person is deprived of receiving the sacraments of the church. To counter this threat, the king called a synod or assembly of German bishops, all of whom he had appointed, and had them depose the pope.

Pope Gregory VII responded by excommunicating the king and freeing his subjects from their allegiance to him. The latter was a clever move. The German nobles were only too eager to diminish the power of a centralized monarchy because of the threat it posed to their own power, and they welcomed this opportunity to rebel against the king.

Both the nobles and the bishops of Germany agreed to hold a meeting in Germany with the pope to solve the problem, possibly by choosing a new king. Gregory set out for Germany. Henry, realizing the threat to his power, forestalled the pope by traveling to northern Italy, where he met the pope at Canossa, a castle belonging to Countess Matilda of Tuscany, an avid supporter of the papal reform program. There, in January 1077, the king admitted his transgressions and begged for forgiveness and absolution. Although he made the king wait three days, the pope was constrained by his priestly responsibility to grant absolution to a penitent sinner and lifted the ban of excommunication. This did not end the problem, however. Within three years, pope and king were again locked in combat.

The struggle continued until 1122, when a new German king and a new pope achieved a compromise called the Concordat of Worms. Under this agreement, a bishop in Germany was first elected by church officials. After election, the nominee paid homage to the king as his secular lord, who in turn invested him with the symbols of temporal office. A representative of the pope then invested the new bishop with the symbols of his spiritual office.

This struggle between church and state was an important element in the history of Europe in the High Middle Ages. In the Early Middle Ages, popes had been dependent on emperors and had allowed them to exercise considerable authority over church affairs. But a set of new ideals championed by activist reformers in the eleventh century now supported the "freedom of the church," which meant not only the freedom of the church to control its own affairs but also extreme claims of papal authority. Not only was the pope superior to all other bishops, but popes now claimed the right to depose kings under certain circumstances. Such papal claims ensured further church-state confrontations.

# Christianity and Medieval Civilization

Christianity was an integral part of the fabric of medieval European society and the consciousness of Europe. Papal directives affected the actions of kings and princes alike, while Christian teaching and practices touched the economic, social, intellectual, cultural, and daily lives of all Europeans.

## Growth of the Papal Monarchy

The popes of the twelfth century did not abandon the reform ideals of Gregory VII, but they were less dogmatic and more inclined to consolidate their power and build a strong administrative system. By the twelfth century, the Catholic church possessed a clearly organized, hierarchical structure. The pope and **papal curia** were at the apex of the administrative structure. The curia was staffed by high church officials known as cardinals, who served as major advisers and administrators to the popes; at the pope's death, the college of cardinals, as they were collectively called, elected the new pope. Below the pope and cardinals were the archbishops, each of whom controlled a large region called an archdiocese. Each archdiocese was divided into smaller units called dioceses, each headed by a bishop. Each diocese was divided into parishes, each headed by a priest. Theoretically, the bishop chose all priests in his diocese, administered his diocese, and was responsible only to the pope.

**The Pontificate of Innocent III** In the thirteenth century, the Catholic church reached the height of its political, intellectual, and secular power. The papal monarchy extended its sway over both ecclesiastical and temporal affairs, as was especially evident during the papacy of Pope Innocent III (1198–1216). At the beginning of his pontificate, in a letter to a priest, Innocent made a clear statement of his views on papal supremacy:

> As God, the creator of the universe, set two great lights in the firmament of heaven, the greater light to rule the day, and the lesser light to rule the night, so He set two great dignities in the firmament of the universal church, . . . the greater to rule the day, that is, souls, and the lesser to rule the night, that is, bodies. These dignities are the papal authority and the royal power. And just as the moon gets her light from the sun, and is inferior to the sun . . . so the royal power gets the splendor of its dignity from the papal authority.[4]

Innocent's actions were those of a man who believed that he, the pope, was the supreme judge of European affairs. He forced King Philip II Augustus of France to take back his wife and queen after Philip had coerced a group of French prelates into annulling his marriage. The pope intervened in German affairs and installed his candidate as emperor. He compelled King John of England to accept the papal choice for the position of archbishop of Canterbury. To achieve his political ends, Innocent did not hesitate to use the spiritual weapons at his command, especially the interdict. An **interdict** was imposed on a region or country rather than a person; it forbade priests there to dispense the sacraments of the church in the hope that the people, deprived of the comforts of religion, would exert pressure against their ruler. Pope Innocent's interdict was so effective that it caused King Philip Augustus to restore his wife to her rightful place as queen of France.

## New Religious Orders and Spiritual Ideals

In the second half of the eleventh century and the first half of the twelfth, a wave of religious enthusiasm seized Europe, leading to a spectacular growth in the number of monasteries and the emergence of new monastic orders. Most important was the Cistercian order, founded in 1098 by a group of monks dissatisfied with the lack of strict discipline at their Benedictine monastery. Cistercian monasticism spread rapidly from southern France into the rest of Europe.

The Cistercians were strict. They ate a simple diet and possessed only a single robe apiece. All decorations were

**Pope Innocent III.** Innocent III was an active and powerful pope during the High Middle Ages. He approved the creation of the Franciscan and Dominican religious orders and inaugurated the Fourth Crusade. He is shown here with the papal bull he issued to establish the monastery of Sacro Speco in Subiaco, Italy.

© Scala/Art Resource, NY

eliminated from their churches and monastic buildings. More time for prayer and manual labor was provided by shortening the number of hours spent at religious services. The Cistercians played a major role in developing a new activist spiritual model for twelfth-century Europe. A Benedictine monk often spent hours in prayer to honor God. The Cistercian ideal had a different emphasis: "Arise, soldier of Christ, arise! Get up off the ground and return to the battle from which you have fled! Fight more boldly after your flight, and triumph in glory!"[5] These were the words of Saint Bernard of Clairvaux (1090–1153), who more than any other person embodied the new spiritual ideal of Cistercian monasticism (see the box on p. 270).

**Women in Religious Orders**  Women were also active participants in the spiritual movements of the age. The number of women joining religious houses increased perceptibly with the spread of the new orders of the twelfth century. In the High Middle Ages, most nuns were from the ranks of the landed aristocracy. Convents were convenient for families unable or unwilling to find husbands for their daughters and for aristocratic women who did not wish to marry. Female intellectuals found them a haven for their activities. Most of the learned women of the Middle Ages, especially in Germany, were nuns. One of the most distinguished

was Hildegard of Bingen (1098–1179), who became abbess of a convent at Disibodenberg in western Germany.

Hildegard shared in the religious enthusiasm of the twelfth century. Soon after becoming abbess, she began to write an account of the mystical visions she had experienced for years. "A great flash of light from heaven pierced my brain and . . . in that instant my mind was imbued with the meaning of the sacred books," she wrote in a description typical of the world's mystical literature. Eventually she produced three books based on her visions. Hildegard gained considerable renown as a mystic and prophet, and popes, emperors, kings, dukes, and bishops eagerly sought her advice.

Hildegard of Bingen was also one of the first important female composers and a major contributor to the body of music known as Gregorian chant or plainsong. Gregorian chant was basically monophonic—a single line of unaccompanied vocal music—set to Latin texts and chanted by a group of monks or nuns during church services. Hildegard's work is especially remarkable because she succeeded at a time when music in general, and sacred music in particular, was almost exclusively the domain of men.

**Living the Gospel Life**  In the early thirteenth century, two religious leaders, Saint Francis and Saint Dominic, founded

# A MIRACLE OF SAINT BERNARD

*S*AINT BERNARD OF CLAIRVAUX has been called the most widely respected holy man of the twelfth century. He was an outstanding preacher, wholly dedicated to the service of God. His reputation reportedly influenced many young men to join the Cistercian order. He also inspired a myriad of stories dealing with his miracles.

## 🔖 A Miracle of Saint Bernard

A certain monk, departing from his monastery . . ., threw off his habit, and returned to the world at the persuasion of the Devil. And he took a certain parish living; for he was a priest. Because sin is punished with sin, the deserter from his Order lapsed into the vice of lechery. He took a concubine to live with him, as in fact is done by many, and by her he had children.

But as God is merciful and does not wish anyone to perish, it happened that many years after, the blessed abbot [Saint Bernard] was passing through the village in which the same monk was living, and went to stay at his house. The renegade monk recognized him, and received him very reverently, and waited on him devoutly . . . but as yet the abbot did not recognize him.

On the morrow, the holy man said Matins and prepared to be off. But as he could not speak to the priest, since he had got up and gone to the church for Matins, he said to the priest's son "Go, give this message to your master." Now the boy had been born dumb. He obeyed the command and feeling in himself the power of him who had given it, he ran to his father and uttered the words of the Holy Father clearly and exactly. His father, on hearing his son's voice for the first time, wept for joy, and made him repeat the same words . . . and he asked what the abbot had done to him. "He did nothing to me," said the boy, "except to say, 'Go and say this to your father.'"

At so evident a miracle the priest repented, and hastened after the holy man and fell at his feet saying "My Lord and Father, I was your monk so-and-so, and at such-and-such a time I ran away from your monastery. I ask your Paternity to allow me to return with you to the monastery, for in your coming God has visited my heart." The saint replied unto him, "Wait for me here, and I will come back quickly when I have done my business, and I will take you with me." But the priest, fearing death (which he had not done before), answered, "Lord, I am afraid of dying before then." But the saint replied, "Know this for certain, that if you die in this condition, and in this resolve, you will find yourself a monk before God."

The saint [eventually] returned and heard that the priest had recently died and been buried. He ordered the tomb to be opened. And when they asked him what he wanted to do, he said, "I want to see if he is lying as a monk or a clerk in his tomb." "As a clerk," they said; "we buried him in his secular habit." But when they had dug up the earth, they found that he was not in the clothes in which they had buried him; but he appeared in all points, tonsure and habit, as a monk. And they all praised God.

---

two new religious orders whose members did not remain in the cloister like the monks of the contemplative orders, such as the Benedictines and Cistercians, but rather went out into the secular arena of the towns to preach the word of God. By their example, the new orders, known as mendicant ("begging") orders for their deliberate poverty, strove to provide a more personal religious experience for ordinary people.

Saint Francis of Assisi (1182–1226) was born to a wealthy Italian merchant family, but as a young man he abandoned all worldly goods and began to live and preach in poverty after a series of dramatic spiritual experiences. His simplicity, joyful nature, and love for others soon attracted a band of followers, all of whom took vows of absolute poverty, agreeing to reject all property and live by working and begging for their food. Francis drew up a simple rule for his followers that consisted merely of biblical precepts focusing on the need to preach and the importance of poverty. He sought approval for his new rule from Pope Innocent III, who confirmed the new order as the Order of Friars Minor, more commonly known as the

© Giraudon/Art Resource, NY

---

**Saint Bernard.** One of the most important religious figures of the twelfth century was Saint Bernard of Clairvaux, who advocated a militant expression of Christian ideas while favoring a more personalized understanding of the relationship between humans and God. Here Saint Bernard is shown preaching a sermon to his fellow Cistercians.

Franciscans. The Franciscans struck a responsive chord among many Europeans and became very popular. The Franciscans lived among the people, preaching repentance and aiding the poor. Their calls for a return to the simplicity and poverty of the early church, reinforced by their own example, were especially effective. The Franciscans had a female branch as well, known as the Poor Clares, which was founded by Saint Clare, an aristocratic lady of Assisi who was a great admirer of Francis.

The second new religious order of the early thirteenth century arose out of the desire to defend orthodox church teachings from heresy (see "Voices of Protest and Intolerance" later in this chapter). The Order of Preachers, popularly known as the Dominicans, was created through the efforts of a Spanish priest, Dominic de Guzmán (1170–1221). Unlike Francis, Dominic was an intellectual who was particularly appalled by the recent growth of heretical movements. He came to believe that a new religious order of men who lived lives of poverty but were learned and capable of preaching effectively would best be able to attack heresy. With the approval of Pope Innocent III, the Dominicans became an order of mendicant friars in 1215.

In addition to the friars, the thirteenth century witnessed the development of yet another kind of religious order. Known as Beguines, these were communities of women dwelling together in poverty. Devout and dedicated to prayer, they begged for their daily support or worked as laundresses in hospitals or at other menial tasks. They did not take religious vows and were free to leave the community at will. Although the Beguines originated in the Low Countries, they eventually became quite strong in the Rhineland area of Germany as well.

## Popular Religion in the High Middle Ages

We have witnessed the actions of popes, bishops, and monks. But what of ordinary clergy and laypeople? What were their religious hopes and fears? What were their spiritual aspirations?

The **sacraments** of the Catholic church ensured that the church was an integral part of people's lives, from birth to death. There were (and still are) seven sacraments—the Eucharist (the Lord's Supper), baptism, marriage, penance, extreme unction, holy orders, and confirmation—administered only by the clergy. The sacraments were viewed as outward symbols of an inward grace (grace was God's freely given gift that enabled humans to be saved) and were considered imperative for a Christian's salvation. Therefore, the clergy were seen to have a key role in the attainment of salvation.

**The Importance of Saints** Other church practices were also important to ordinary people. Saints, it was believed, were men and women who, through their holiness, had achieved a special position in heaven, enabling them to act as intercessors before God. The saints' ability to protect poor souls enabled them to take on great importance at the popular level. Jesus' apostles were, of course, recognized throughout Europe as saints, but there were also numerous local saints that were of special significance to the area. New cults rapidly developed, particularly in the intense religious atmosphere of the eleventh and twelfth centuries. The English introduced Saint Nicholas, the patron saint of children, who remains instantly recognizable today through his identification with Santa Claus.

Of all the saints, the Virgin Mary, the mother of Jesus, occupied the foremost position in the High Middle Ages. Mary was viewed as the most important mediator with her son Jesus, the judge of all sinners. Moreover, from the eleventh century on, a fascination with Mary as Jesus' human mother became more evident. A sign of Mary's importance was the growing number of churches all over Europe that were dedicated to her in the twelfth and thirteenth centuries, including the cathedral of Notre-Dame in Paris.

**The Use of Relics** Emphasis on the role of the saints was closely tied to the use of **relics,** which also increased noticeably in the High Middle Ages. Relics were usually the bones of saints or objects intimately connected to saints that were considered worthy of veneration by the faithful. A twelfth-century English monk began his description of the abbey's relics by saying, "There is kept there a thing more precious than gold, . . . the right arm of St. Oswald. . . . This we have seen with our own eyes and have kissed, and have handled with our own hands. . . . There are kept here also part of his ribs and of the soil on which he fell."[6] The monk went on

© Bibliothèque royale Albert Ier (Ms IV 119, fol.72 verso)

**A Group of Nuns.** Although still viewed by the medieval church as inferior to men, women were as susceptible to the spiritual fervor of the twelfth century as men, and female monasticism grew accordingly. This miniature shows a group of Flemish nuns listening to the preaching of an abbot, Gilles li Muisis. The nun at the far left wearing a white robe is a novice.

to list additional purported relics possessed by the abbey, which included two pieces of Jesus' swaddling clothes, pieces of Jesus' manger, and parts of the five loaves of bread with which Jesus miraculously fed five thousand people. Because the holiness of the saint was considered to be inherent in his relics, these objects were believed to be capable of healing people or producing other miracles.

In the High Middle Ages, it became a regular practice of the church to attach **indulgences** to these relics. Indulgences brought a remission of time spent in **purgatory.** Purgatory was believed to be a place of punishment in which the soul of the departed could be purified before ascending to heaven. The living could ease that suffering through Masses and prayers offered on behalf of the deceased or through indulgences. Indulgences were granted for good works such as charitable contributions and viewing the relics of saints. The church specified the number of years and days of each indulgence, enabling the soul to spend less time in purgatory.

**The Pilgrimage**   Medieval Christians believed that a pilgrimage to a holy shrine was of particular spiritual benefit. The greatest shrine but the most difficult to reach was the Holy City of Jerusalem (see Map 10.6). On the European continent, two pilgrim centers were especially pop-ular in the High Middle Ages: Rome, which contained the relics of Saints Peter and Paul, and the town of Santiago de Compostela, supposedly the site of the tomb of the Apostle James. Local attractions, such as shrines dedicated to the Virgin Mary, also became pilgrimage centers.

## Voices of Protest and Intolerance

The desire for more personal and deeper religious experience, which characterized the spiritual revival of the High Middle Ages, also led people into directions hostile to the institutional church. From the twelfth century on, **heresy,** the holding of religious doctrines different from the orthodox teachings of the church as determined by church authorities, became a serious problem for the Catholic church.

The best-known heresy of the twelfth and thirteenth centuries was Catharism. The Cathars (the word *Cathar* means "pure") were often called Albigensians after the city of Albi, one of their strongholds in southern France. They believed in a dualist system in which good and evil were separate and distinct. The things of the spirit were good because they were created by the God of light; the things of the world were evil because they were created by Satan, the prince of darkness. Humans, too, were enmeshed in **dualism.** Their souls, which were good, were trapped in material bodies, which were evil. According to the Cathars, the Catholic church, itself a materialistic institution, had nothing to do with God and was essentially evil. There was no need to follow its teachings or recognize its authority. The Cathar movement gained valuable support from important nobles in southern France and northern Italy.

The spread of heresy in southern France alarmed the church authorities. Pope Innocent III appealed to the nobles of northern France for a **Crusade** (a military campaign in defense of Christendom) against the heretics. The Crusade against the Albigensians, which began in the summer of 1209 and lasted for almost two decades, was a bloody one. Thousands of heretics (and the innocent) were slaughtered, including entire populations of some towns. In Béziers, for example, seven thousand men, women, and children were massacred when they took refuge in the local church.

Southern France was devastated, but Catharism remained, which caused the Catholic church to devise a regular method for discovering and dealing with heretics. This led to the emergence of the Holy Office, as the papal Inquisition was called, a formal court whose job it was to ferret out and try heretics.

**Mass of the Holy Relics.**  It was customary for churches that possessed relics to hold a special Mass honoring those saints. At that time, the reliquaries would be brought out for the faithful to venerate. The large picture shows the celebration of this special Mass of the holy relics. The reliquary is shown on a table to the left. The small pictures illustrate various stages of the Mass.

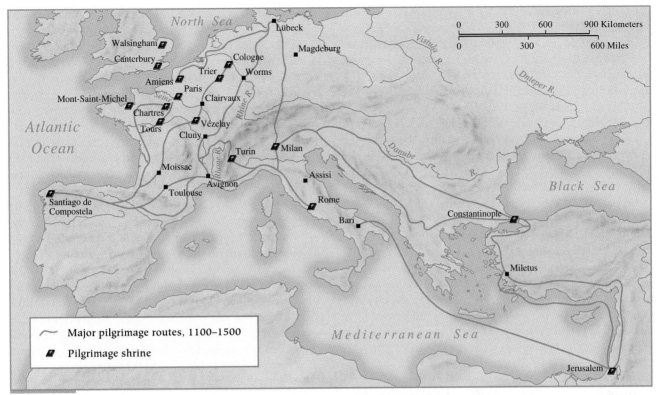

**MAP 10.6** **Pilgrimage Routes in the Middle Ages.** Some Christians sought spiritual solace by traveling to pilgrimage sites. Many went to local shrines honoring the Virgin Mary, but Jerusalem, Rome, and Santiago de Compostela were the most desired locations. **?** Roughly how far would a pilgrim from Lübeck have to travel to reach Jerusalem, and how long would the journey take if he walked 20 miles per day? View an animated version of this map or related maps at
http://history.wadsworth.com/spielvogel06/

Gradually, the Holy Office developed its inquisitorial procedure. Anyone could be accused of heresy, since the identity of the accuser was not revealed to the indicted heretic. If the accused heretic confessed, he or she was forced to perform public penance and was subjected to punishment, such as flogging; the heretic's property was then confiscated and divided between the secular authorities and the church. Beginning in 1252, those not confessing voluntarily were subjected to torture. Relapsed heretics—who confessed, did penance, and then reverted to heresy—were turned over to the secular authorities for execution.

To the Christians of the thirteenth century, who believed that there was only one path to salvation, heresy was a crime against God and against humanity, and force was justified to save souls from damnation. The fanaticism and fear unleashed in the struggle against heretics were also used against others, especially the best-known outgroup of Western society, the Jews.

**Persecution of the Jews** The Jews constituted the only religious minority in Christian Europe that was allowed to practice a non-Christian religion. In the Early Middle Ages, Jews were actively involved in trade and crafts. Later, after being excluded from practicing most trades by the guild system, some Jews turned to moneylending as a way to survive.

**Expulsion of Albigensian Heretics.** In 1209, Pope Innocent III authorized a Crusade against the heretical Albigensians. In this medieval illustration, French knights are shown expelling Albigensian heretics from the town of Caracassonne near Albi, an Albigensian stronghold in southern France.

There is little certainty about the number of Jews in Europe. England had relatively few Jews, probably 2,500 to 3,000, or one of every thousand inhabitants. Larger numbers lived in southern Italy, Spain, France, and Germany. In southern Europe, Jews served an important function as cultural and intellectual intermediaries between the Muslim and Christian worlds.

The religious enthusiasm of the High Middle Ages produced an outburst of intolerance against the supposed enemies of Christianity. Although this was evident in the Crusades against the Muslims (see "The Crusades" in the next section), Christians also took up the search for enemies at home, persecuting Jews in France and the Rhineland at the time of the first Crusades. Jews in Speyer, Worms, Mainz, and Cologne were all set upon by bands of Christian crusaders. A contemporary chronicler described how a band of English crusaders who stopped at Lisbon, Portugal, en route to the Holy Land "drove away the pagans and Jews, servants of the king, who dwelt in the city and plundered their property and possessions, and burned their houses; and they then stripped their vineyards, not leaving them so much as a grape or a cluster."[7] Even people who tried to protect the Jews were in danger. When the archbishop of Mainz provided shelter for the Jews, a mob stormed his palace and forced him to flee. Popes also came to the Jews' defense by issuing decrees ordering that Jews were not to be persecuted.

Nevertheless, in the thirteenth century, in the supercharged religious atmosphere created by the struggle with heretics, Jews were persecuted more and more (see the box on p. 275). Friars urged action against these "murderers of Christ," referring to the traditional Christian view of the Jews as being responsible for the death of Jesus, and organized public burnings of Jewish books. The Fourth Lateran Council in 1215 decreed that Jews must wear distinguishing clothing to separate themselves from Christians. The same council encouraged the development of Jewish ghettos, or walled enclosures, not to protect the Jews but to isolate them from Christians. The persecutions and the new image of the hated Jew stimulated a tradition of anti-Semitism that proved to be one of Christian Europe's most insidious contributions to the Western heritage.

By the end of the thirteenth century, European kings, who had earlier portrayed themselves as protectors of the Jews, had fleeced the Jewish communities of their money and then renounced their protection. Edward I expelled all Jews from England in 1290. The French king followed suit in 1306 but readmitted the Jews in 1315. They then left on their own accord in 1322. As the policy of expulsion spread into central Europe, most northern European Jews were forced to move into Poland as a last refuge.

**Intolerance of Homosexuality** The climate of intolerance that characterized thirteenth-century attitudes toward Muslims, heretics, and Jews was also evident toward homosexuals. Although the church had condemned homosexuality in the Early Middle Ages, it had not been overly concerned with homosexual behavior, an attitude also prevalent in the secular world. By the thirteenth century, however, these tolerant attitudes had altered drastically. Some historians see this change as part of the century's climate of fear and intolerance toward any group that deviated from the standards of the majority. A favorite approach of the critics was to identify homosexuals with other detested groups. Homosexuality was portrayed as a regular practice of Muslims and such notorious heretics as the Albigensians. Between 1250 and 1300, what had been tolerated in most of Europe became a criminal act deserving of death.

The legislation against homosexuality commonly referred to it as a "sin against nature." This is precisely the argument developed by Thomas Aquinas, who formed Catholic opinion on the subject for centuries to come. In his *Summa Theologica,* Aquinas argued that because the purpose of sex was procreation, it could legitimately take place only in ways that did not exclude this possibility. Hence homosexuality was "contrary to nature" and a deviation from the natural order established by God. This argument and laws prohibiting homosexual activity on pain of severe punishment remained the norm in Europe and elsewhere in the Christian world until the twentieth century.

# The Crusades

Another manifestation of the wave of religious enthusiasm that seized Europe in the High Middle Ages was the series of Crusades mounted against the Muslims. The Crusades gave the revived papacy of the High Middle Ages yet another opportunity to demonstrate its influence over European society. The Crusades were a curious mix of God and warfare, two of the chief concerns of the Middle Ages.

## Background to the Crusades

Although European civilization developed in relative isolation, it had never entirely lost contact with the lands and empires of the East. At the end of the eleventh century, that contact increased, in part because developments in the Islamic and Byzantine worlds prompted the first major attempt of the new European civilization to expand beyond Europe proper.

**Islam and the Seljuk Turks** By the mid-tenth century, the Islamic empire led by the Abbasid caliphate in Baghdad was disintegrating. An attempt was made in the tenth century to unify the Islamic world under the direction of a Shi'ite dynasty known as the Fatimids. Their origins lay in North Africa, but they managed to conquer Egypt and establish the new city of Cairo as their capital. In establishing a Shi'ite caliphate, they became rivals to the Sunni caliphate of Baghdad and divided the Islamic world.

Nevertheless, the Fatimid dynasty prospered and surpassed the Abbasid caliphate as the dynamic center of Islam. Benefiting from their position in the heart of the Nile

# TREATMENT OF THE JEWS

*T*HE NEW RELIGIOUS SENSIBILITIES that emerged in the High Middle Ages also had a negative side, the turning of Christians against their supposed enemies. Although the Crusades provide the most obvious example, Christians also turned on the "murderers of Christ," the Jews. As a result, Jews suffered increased persecution. These three documents show different sides of the picture. The first is Canon 68 of the decrees of the Fourth Lateran Council called by Pope Innocent III in 1215. The decree specifies the need for special dress, one of the ways Christians tried to separate Jews from their community. The second excerpt is a chronicler's account of the most deadly charge levied against the Jews—that they were guilty of the ritual murder of Christian children to obtain Christian blood for the Passover service. This charge led to the murder of many Jews. The third document, taken from a list of regulations issued by the city of Avignon, France, illustrates the contempt Christian society held for the Jews.

## Canon 68

In some provinces a difference in dress distinguishes the Jews or Saracens [Muslims] from the Christians, but in certain others such a confusion has grown up that they cannot be distinguished by any difference. Thus it happens at times that through error Christians have relations with the women of Jews or Saracens, and Jews or Saracens with Christian women. Therefore, that they may not, under pretext of error of this sort, excuse themselves in the future for the excesses of such prohibited intercourse, we decree that such Jews and Saracens of both sexes in every Christian province and at all times shall be marked off in the eyes of the public from other peoples through the character of their dress. . . .

Moreover, during the last three days before Easter and especially on Good Friday, they shall not go forth in public at all, for the reason that some of them on these very days, as we hear, do not blush to go forth better dressed and are not afraid to mock the Christians who maintain the memory of the most holy Passion by wearing signs of mourning.

## An Accusation of the Ritual Murder of a Christian Child by Jews

. . . [The eight-year-old boy] Harold, who is buried in the Church of St. Peter the Apostle, at Gloucester . . . is said to have been carried away secretly by Jews, in the opinion of many, on Feb. 21, and by them hidden till March 16. On that night, on the sixth of the preceding feast, the Jews of all England coming together as if to circumcise a certain boy, pretend deceitfully that they are about to celebrate the feast [Passover] appointed by law in such case, and deceiving the citizens of Gloucester with the fraud, they tortured the lad placed before them with immense tortures. It is true no Christian was present, or saw or heard the deed, nor have we found that anything was betrayed by any Jew. But a little while after when the whole convent of monks of Gloucester and almost all the citizens of that city, and innumerable persons coming to the spectacle, saw the wounds of the dead body, scars of fire, the thorns fixed on his head, and liquid wax poured into the eyes and face, and touched it with the diligent examination of their hands, those tortures were believed or guessed to have been inflicted on him in that manner. It was clear that they had made him a glorious martyr to Christ, being slain without sin, and having bound his feet with his own girdle, threw him into the river Severn.

## The Regulations of Avignon, 1243

Likewise, we declare that Jews or whores shall not dare to touch with their hands either bread or fruit put out for sale, and that if they should do this they must buy what they have touched.

---

delta, the Fatimids played a major role in the regional trade passing from the Mediterranean to the Red Sea and beyond. They were tolerant in matters of religion and created a strong army by using nonnative peoples as mercenaries. One of these peoples, the Seljuk Turks, soon posed a threat to the Fatimids themselves

The Seljuk Turks were a nomadic people from Central Asia who had been converted to Islam and flourished as military mercenaries for the Abbasid caliphate. Moving gradually into Persia and Armenia, their numbers grew until by the eleventh century they were able to take over the eastern provinces of the Abbasid empire. In 1055, a Turkish leader captured Baghdad and assumed command of the Abbasid empire with the title of **sultan** ("holder of power"). By the latter part of the eleventh century, the Seljuk Turks were exerting military pressure on Egypt and the Byzantine Empire. When the Byzantine emperor foolishly challenged the Turks, the latter routed the Byzantine army at Manzikert in 1071. In dire straits, the Byzantines looked west for help, setting in motion the papal pleas that led to the Crusades. To understand the complexities of the situation, however, we need to look first at the Byzantine Empire.

**The Byzantine Empire**    The Macedonian dynasty of the tenth and eleventh centuries had restored much of the power of the Byzantine Empire; its incompetent successors, however, reversed most of the gains. After the Macedonian dynasty was extinguished in 1056, the empire was beset by internal struggles for power between ambitious military leaders and aristocratic families who attempted to buy the support of the great landowners of Anatolia by allowing them greater control over their peasants. This policy was self-destructive, however, because the peasant-warrior was the traditional backbone of the Byzantine state.

The growing division between the Catholic church of the West and the Eastern Orthodox church of the Byzantine Empire also weakened the Byzantine state. The Eastern Orthodox church was unwilling to accept the pope's claim that he was the sole head of the church. This dispute reached a climax in 1054 when Pope Leo IX and Patriarch Michael Cerularius, head of the Byzantine church, formally excommunicated each other, initiating a schism between the two great branches of Christianity that has not been healed to this day.

The Byzantine Empire faced external threats to its security as well. The greatest challenge came from the Seljuk Turks who had moved into Asia Minor—the heartland of the empire and its main source of food and manpower. After defeating the Byzantine forces at Manzikert in 1071, the Turks advanced into Anatolia, where many peasants, already disgusted by their exploitation at the hands of Byzantine landowners, readily accepted Turkish control.

A new dynasty, however, soon breathed new life into the Byzantine Empire. The Comneni, under Alexius I Comnenus (1081–1118), were victorious on the Greek Adriatic coast against the Normans, defeated the Pechenegs in the Balkans, and stopped the Turks in Anatolia. Lacking the resources to undertake additional campaigns against the Turks, Emperor Alexius I turned to the West for military assistance. The positive response to the emperor's request led to the Crusades. The Byzantine Empire lived to regret it.

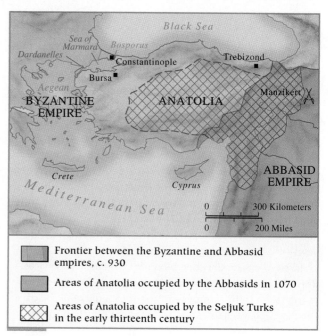

Frontier between the Byzantine and Abbasid empires, c. 930

Areas of Anatolia occupied by the Abbasids in 1070

Areas of Anatolia occupied by the Seljuk Turks in the early thirteenth century

**The Seljuk Turks and the Byzantines**

## 🖋 The Early Crusades

The Crusades were based on the idea of a holy war against the infidel or unbeliever. The wrath of Christians was directed against the Muslims, and at the end of the eleventh century, Christian Europe found itself with a glorious opportunity to attack them. The immediate impetus for the Crusades came when the Byzantine emperor, Alexius I, asked Pope Urban II (1088–1099) for help against the Seljuk Turks. The pope saw a golden opportunity to provide papal leadership for a great cause: to rally the warriors of Europe for the liberation of Jerusalem and the Holy Land from the infidel. At the Council of Clermont in southern France near the end of 1095, Urban challenged Christians to take up their weapons against the infidel and join in a holy war to recover the Holy Land (see the box on p. 277). The pope promised remission of sins: "All who die by the way, whether by land or by sea, or in battle against the pagans, shall have immediate remission of sins. This I grant them through the power of God with which I am invested."[8]

The warriors of western Europe, particularly France, formed the first crusading armies. The knights who made up this first serious crusading host were motivated by religious fervor, but there were other attractions as well. Some sought adventure and welcomed a legitimate opportunity to pursue their favorite pastime—fighting. Others saw an opportunity to gain territory, riches, status, possibly a title, and even salvation—had the pope not offered a full remission of sins for those who participated in these "armed pilgrimages"? From the perspective of the pope and European monarchs, the Crusades offered a way to rid Europe of contentious young nobles who disturbed the peace and wasted lives and energy fighting each other. And merchants in many Italian cities relished the prospect of new trading opportunities in Muslim lands.

**The First Crusade** In the First Crusade, begun in 1096, three organized bands of noble warriors, most of them French, made their way to the east (see Map 10.7 on p. 279). The crusading army probably numbered several thousand cavalry and as many as ten thousand foot soldiers. After the capture of Antioch in 1098, much of the crusading host proceeded down the coast of Palestine, evading the garrisoned coastal cities, and reached Jerusalem in June 1099. After a five-week siege, the Holy City was taken amid a horrible massacre of the inhabitants, men, women, and children (see the box on p. 278).

After further conquest of Palestinian lands, the crusaders ignored the wishes of the Byzantine emperor (who foolishly believed the crusaders were working on his behalf) and organized four crusader states (Edessa, Antioch, Tripoli, and Jerusalem). Because the crusader states were surrounded by Muslim enemies, they grew increasingly dependent on the Italian commercial cities for supplies from Europe. Some Italian cities, such as Genoa, Pisa, and especially Venice, became rich and powerful in the process.

**The Second Crusade** The crusader states soon foundered, and by the 1120s, the Muslims were striking back. In 1144, Edessa became the first of the four Latin states to be recaptured. Its fall led to renewed calls for another Crusade, especially from the monastic firebrand Saint Bernard of Clairvaux, who exclaimed, "Now, on account of our sins, the sacrilegious enemies of the cross have begun to show their

# POPE URBAN II PROCLAIMS A CRUSADE

OWARD THE END OF the eleventh century, the Byzantine emperor Alexius I sent Pope Urban II a request for aid against the Seljuk Turks. At the Council of Clermont, Urban II appealed to a large crowd to take up weapons and recover Palestine from the Muslims. This description of Urban's appeal is taken from an account by Fulcher of Chartres.

### Pope Urban II

Pope Urban II . . . addressed them [the French] in a very persuasive speech, as follows: "O race of the Franks, O people who live beyond the mountain [that is, north of the Alps], O people loved and chosen of God, as is clear from your many deeds, distinguished over all nations by the situation of your land, your catholic faith, and your regard for the holy church, we have a special message and exhortation for you. For we wish you to know what a grave matter has brought us to your country. The sad news has come from Jerusalem and Constantinople that the people of Persia, an accursed and foreign race [the Seljuk Turks], enemies of God, . . . have invaded the lands of those Christians and devastated them with the sword, rapine, and fire. Some of the Christians they have carried away as slaves, others they have put to death. The churches they have either destroyed or turned into mosques. They desecrate and overthrow the altars. They circumcise the Christians and pour the blood from the circumcision on the altars or in the baptismal fonts. Some they kill in a horrible way by cutting open the abdomen, taking out a part of the entrails and tying them to a stake; they then beat them and compel them to walk until all their entrails are drawn out and they fall to the ground. Some they use as targets for their arrows. They compel some to stretch out their necks and then they try to see whether they can cut off their heads with one strike of the sword. It is better to say nothing of their horrible treatment of the women. They have taken from the Greek empire a tract of land so large that it takes more than two months to walk through it. Whose duty is to avenge this and recover that land, if not yours? For to you more than to any other nations the Lord has given the military spirit, courage, agile bodies, and the bravery to strike down those who resist you. Let your minds be stirred to bravery by the deeds of your forefathers, and by the efficiency and greatness of Karl the Great [Charlemagne], . . . and of the other kings who have destroyed Turkish kingdoms, and established Christianity in their lands. You should be moved especially by the holy grave of our Lord and Savior which is now held by unclean peoples, and by the holy places which are treated with dishonor and irreverently befouled with their uncleanness. . . .

"O bravest of knights, descendants of unconquered ancestors, do not be weaker than they, but remember their courage. . . . Set out on the road to the holy sepulchre, take the land from that wicked people, and make it your own. . . . Jerusalem is the best of all lands, more fruitful than all others. . . . This land our Savior made illustrious by his birth, beautiful with his life, and sacred with his suffering. . . . This royal city is now held captive by her enemies, and made pagan by those who know not God. She asks and longs to be liberated and does not cease to beg you to come to her aid. . . . Set out on this journey and you will obtain the remission of your sins and be sure of the incorruptible glory of the kingdom of heaven."

When Pope Urban had said this and much more of the same sort, all who were present were moved to cry out with one accord, "It is the will of God, it is the will of God." When the pope heard this he raised his eyes to heaven and gave thanks to God, and commanding silence with a gesture of his hand, he said: "My dear brethren, today there is fulfilled in you that which the Lord says in the Gospel, 'Where two or three are gathered together in my name, there am I in the midst.' For unless the Lord God had been in your minds you would not all have said the same thing. . . . So I say unto you, God, who put those words into your hearts, has caused you to utter them. Therefore let these words be your battle cry, because God caused you to speak them. Whenever you meet the enemy in battle, you shall all cry out, 'It is the will of God, it is the will of God. . . .' Whoever therefore shall determine to make this journey and shall make a vow to God and shall offer himself as a living sacrifice, holy, acceptable to God, shall wear a cross on his brow or on his breast. And when he returns after having fulfilled his vow he shall wear the cross on his back."

---

faces. . . . What are you doing, you servants of the cross? Will you throw to the dogs that which is most holy? Will you cast pearls before swine?"[9] Bernard aimed his message at knights and even managed to enlist two powerful rulers, King Louis VII of France and Emperor Conrad III of Germany. Their Second Crusade, however, proved to be a total failure.

**The Third Crusade**   The Third Crusade was a reaction to the fall of the Holy City of Jerusalem in 1187 to the Muslim forces under Saladin. Now all of Christendom was ablaze with calls for a new Crusade in the Middle East.

Three major monarchs agreed to lead new crusading forces in person: Emperor Frederick Barbarossa of Germany (1152–1190), King Richard I the Lionhearted of England (1189–1199), and Philip II Augustus, king of France (1180–1223). Some of the crusaders finally arrived in the Middle East by 1189 only to encounter problems. Frederick Barbarossa drowned while swimming in a local river, and his army quickly fell apart. The English and French arrived by sea and met with success against the coastal cities, where they had the support of their fleets, but when they moved inland, they failed miserably. Eventually, after Philip went home, Richard negotiated a settlement whereby

# THE SIEGE OF JERUSALEM: CHRISTIAN AND MUSLIM PERSPECTIVES

*D*URING THE FIRST CRUSADE, Christian knights laid siege to Jerusalem in June 1099. The first excerpt is taken from an account by Fulcher of Chartres, who accompanied the crusaders to the Holy Land. The second selection is by a Muslim writer, Ibn al-Athir, whose account of the First Crusade can be found in his history of the Muslim world.

### Fulcher of Chartres, *Chronicle of the First Crusade*

Then the Franks entered the city magnificently at the noonday hour on Friday, the day of the week when Christ redeemed the whole world on the cross. With trumpets sounding and with everything in an uproar, exclaiming: "Help, God!" they vigorously pushed into the city, and straightway raised the banner on the top of the wall. All the heathen, completely terrified, changed their boldness to swift flight through the narrow streets of the quarters. The more quickly they fled, the more quickly they put to flight.

Count Raymond and his men, who were bravely assailing the city in another section, did not perceive this until they saw the Saracens [Muslims] jumping from the top of the wall. Seeing this, they joyfully ran to the city as quickly as they could, and helped the others pursue and kill the wicked enemy.

Then some, both Arabs and Ethiopians, fled into the Tower of David; others shut themselves in the Temple of the Lord and of Solomon, where in the halls a very great attack was made on them. Nowhere was there a place where the Saracens could escape swordsmen.

On the top of Solomon's Temple, to which they had climbed in fleeing, many were shot to death with arrows and cast down headlong from the roof. Within this Temple, about ten thousand were beheaded. If you had been there,

your feet would have been stained up to the ankles with the blood of the slain. What more shall I tell? Not one of them was allowed to live. They did not spare the women and children.

### Account of Ibn al-Athir

In fact Jerusalem was taken from the north on the morning of Friday 22 Sha'ban 492 / 15 July 1099. The population was put to the sword by the Franks, who pillaged the area for a week. A band of Muslims barricaded themselves into the Oratory of David and fought on for several days. They were granted their lives in return for surrendering. The Franks honored their word, and the group left by night for Ascalon. In the Masjid al-Aqsa the Franks slaughtered more than 70,000 people, among them a large number of Imams and Muslim scholars, devout and ascetic men who had left their homelands to live lives of pious seclusion in the Holy Place. The Franks stripped the Dome of the Rock of more than forty silver candelabra, each of them weighing 3,600 drams, and a great silver lamp weighing forty-four Syrian pounds, as well as a hundred and fifty smaller candelabra and more than twenty gold ones, and a great deal more booty. Refugees from Syria reached Baghdad in Ramadan, among them the qadi Abu sa'd al-Harawi. They told the Caliph's ministers a story that wrung their hearts and brought tears to their eyes. On Friday they went to the Cathedral Mosque and begged for help, weeping so that their hearers wept with them as they described the sufferings of the Muslims in that Holy City: the men killed, the women and children taken prisoner, the homes pillaged. Because of the terrible hardships they had suffered, they were allowed to break the fast.

Saladin agreed to allow Christian pilgrims free access to Jerusalem.

### The Crusades of the Thirteenth Century

After the death of Saladin in 1193, Pope Innocent III initiated the Fourth Crusade. On its way to the Holy Land, the crusading army became involved in a dispute over the succession to the Byzantine throne. The Venetian leaders of the Fourth Crusade saw an opportunity to neutralize their greatest commercial competitor, the Byzantine Empire. Diverted to Constantinople, the crusaders sacked the great capital city in 1204 and created a new Latin Empire of Constantinople. Not until 1261 did a Byzantine army recapture Constantinople. The Byzantine Empire had been saved, but it was no longer a great Mediterranean power. The restored empire now comprised only the city of Constantinople and its surrounding territory as well as some lands in Asia Minor. Though reduced in size, the empire limped along for another 190 years until its weakened condition finally enabled the Ottoman Turks to conquer it in 1453.

Despite the failures, the crusading ideal was not yet completely lost. In Germany in 1212, a youth known as Nicholas of Cologne announced that God had inspired him to lead a Children's Crusade to the Holy Land. Thousands of young people joined Nicholas and made their way down the Rhine and across the Alps to Italy, where the pope told them to go home. Most tried to do so. The next Crusade of adult warriors was hardly more successful. The Fifth Crusade (1219–1221) attempted to recover the Holy Land by way of the powerful Muslim state of Egypt. The Crusade achieved some early successes, but its ultimate failure marked an end to papal leadership of the western crusaders.

The Sixth Crusade, which was led by the German emperor Frederick II, took place without papal support because the emperor had been excommunicated by the pope for starting late. In 1228, Frederick marched into Jerusalem and accepted the crown as king of Jerusalem after he had made an agreement with the sultan of Egypt. The Holy City had been taken without a fight and without papal support. Once Frederick left, however, the city fell once

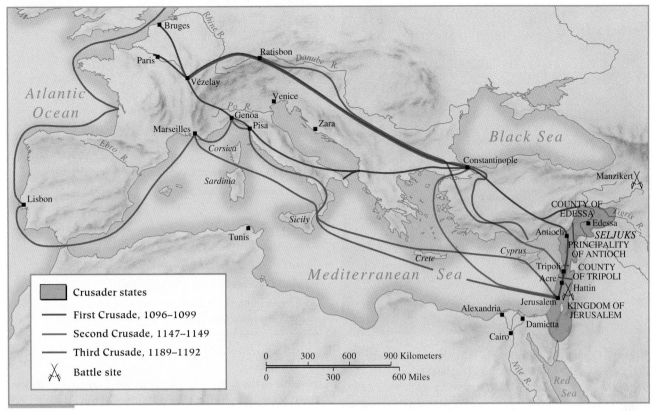

**MAP 10.7 The Early Crusades.** Pope Urban II launched the Crusades to recapture the Holy Land from the "enemies of God," a call met with great enthusiasm in Europe. The fighters of the First Crusade massacred the inhabitants of Jerusalem and established the Crusader States. ❓ In the Third Crusade, which countries sent crusaders by land and which by sea, and why would they choose these methods of travel? 🌐 **View an animated version of this map or related maps at** http://history.wadsworth.com/spielvogel06/

again, this time to a group of Turks allied with the sultan of Egypt. The last two major Crusades, poorly organized by the pious king of France, Louis IX, were complete failures. Soon the remaining Christian possessions in the Middle East were retaken. Acre, the last foothold of the crusaders, surrendered in 1291. All in all, the Crusades had failed to accomplish their primary goal of holding the Holy Land for the Christian West.

### ⚜ Effects of the Crusades

Whether the Crusades had much effect on European civilization is debatable. The crusaders made little long-term impact on the Middle East, where the only visible remnants of their conquests were their castles. There may have been some broadening of perspective that comes from the exchange between two cultures, but the interaction of Christian Europe with the Muslim world was actually both more intense and more meaningful in Spain and Sicily than in the Holy Land.

Did the Crusades help stabilize European society by removing large numbers of young warriors who would have fought each other in Europe? Some historians think so and believe that Western monarchs established their control more easily as a result. There is no doubt that the

**Richard the Lionhearted Executing Muslims at Acre.** The Third Crusade was organized in response to the capture of the kingdom of Jerusalem by the Sunni Muslims under the leadership of Saladin. Though Saladin forbade the massacre of Christians, his Christian foes were more harsh. Here Richard the Lionhearted (at right with crown) watches the execution of 2,700 Muslims at Acre.

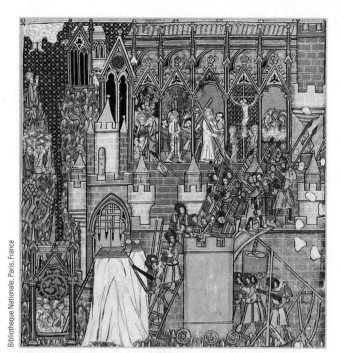

Bibliotheque Nationale, Paris, France

**Siege and Capture of Constantinople.** This thirteenth-century miniature is a depiction of the siege and capture of Constantinople during the Fourth Crusade in 1204. At the right, soldiers use a catapult to shower the city with stones while knights use a tower to attack the walls. In the stained-glass windows above the battle are scenes from the Passion of Christ, a deliberate and ironic reminder that the purpose of the Crusades was to capture the Holy City of Jerusalem.

Crusades did contribute to the economic growth of the Italian port cities, especially Genoa, Pisa, and Venice. But it is important to remember that the growing wealth and population of twelfth-century Europe had made the Crusades possible in the first place. The Crusades may have enhanced the revival of trade, but they certainly did not cause it. Even without the Crusades, Italian merchants would have pursued new trade contacts with the Eastern world.

The Crusades prompted evil side effects that would haunt European society for generations. The first widespread attacks on the Jews began with the Crusades. As some Christians argued, to undertake holy wars against infidel Muslims while the "murderers of Christ" ran free at home was unthinkable. The massacre of Jews became a regular feature of medieval European life.

## CONCLUSION

𝕿HE PERIOD FROM 1000 to 1300 was a dynamic one in the development of Western civilization. The nobles, whose warlike attitudes were rationalized by labeling themselves as the defenders of Christian society, continued to dominate the medieval world politically, economically, and socially. But kings gradually began to expand their powers. Although the popes sometimes treated rulers as if they were the popes' servants, by the thirteenth century, monarchs themselves were developing the machinery of government that would enable them to challenge exalted claims of papal power and become the centers of political authority in Europe. Although they could not know it then, the actions of these medieval monarchs laid the foundation for the European kingdoms that in one form or another have dominated the European political scene ever since.

The Catholic church shared in the challenge of new growth by reforming itself and striking out on a path toward greater papal power, both within the church and over European society. The High Middle Ages witnessed a spiritual renewal that led to numerous and even divergent paths: revived papal leadership, the development of centralized administrative machinery that buttressed papal authority, and new dimensions to the religious life of the clergy and laity. At the same time, this spiritual renewal also gave rise to the crusading "holy warrior" who killed for God.\

The religious enthusiasm of the twelfth century continued well into the thirteenth as new orders of friars gave witness to spiritual growth and passion, but underneath the calm exterior lay seeds of discontent and change. Dissent from church teaching and practices grew, leading to a climate of fear and intolerance as the church responded with inquisitorial procedures to

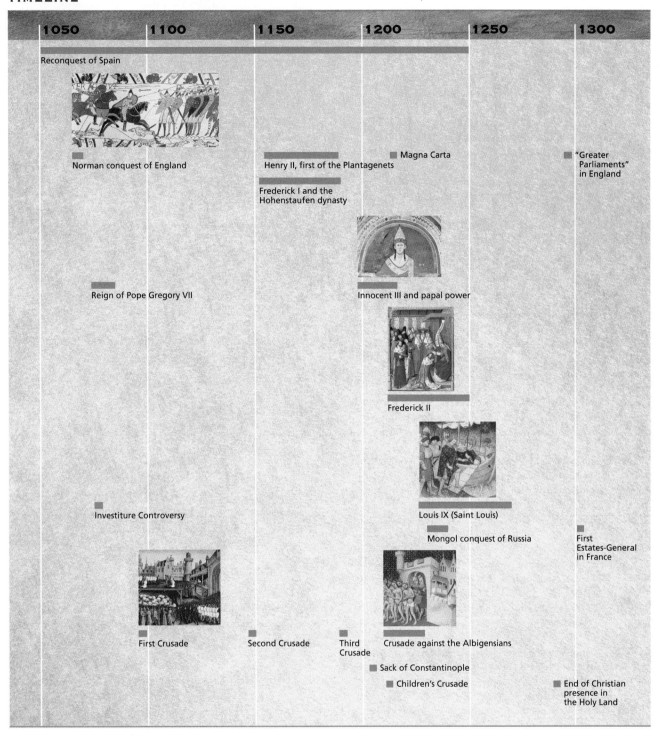

| 1050 | 1100 | 1150 | 1200 | 1250 | 1300 |
|------|------|------|------|------|------|

Reconquest of Spain

Norman conquest of England

Henry II, first of the Plantagenets

Magna Carta

"Greater Parliaments" in England

Frederick I and the Hohenstaufen dynasty

Reign of Pope Gregory VII

Innocent III and papal power

Frederick II

Investiture Controversy

Louis IX (Saint Louis)

Mongol conquest of Russia

First Estates-General in France

First Crusade

Second Crusade

Third Crusade

Crusade against the Albigensians

Sack of Constantinople

Children's Crusade

End of Christian presence in the Holy Land

enforce conformity to its teachings. At the same time, papal claims of supremacy over secular authorities were increasingly challenged by the rising power of monarchical authorities, who, thanks to the growth of cities, the revival of trade, and the emergence of a money economy, were now able to hire soldiers and officials to carry out their wishes.

The High Middle Ages of the eleventh, twelfth, and thirteenth centuries had been a period of great innovation, evident in significant economic, social, political, religious, intellectual, and cultural changes. And yet by the end of the thirteenth century, certain tensions had begun to creep into European society. As we shall see in the next chapter, these tensions soon became a torrent of troubles.

## NOTES

1. Quoted in John K. Fairbank, Edwin O. Reischauer, and Albert M. Craig, *East Asia: Tradition and Transformation* (Boston, 1973), p. 164.

2. Ernest F. Henderson, ed., *Selected Historical Documents of the Middle Ages* (London, 1892), p. 332.

3. Ibid., p. 365.

4. Oliver J. Thatcher and Edgar H. McNeal, eds., *A Source Book for Medieval History* (New York, 1905), p. 208.

5. Quoted in R. H. C. Davis, *A History of Medieval Europe from Constantine to Saint Louis,* 2d ed. (New York, 1988), p. 252.

6. Quoted in Rosalind Brooke and Christopher N. L. Brooke, *Popular Religion in the Middle Ages* (London, 1984), p. 19.

7. Henry T. Riley, ed., *Memorials of London and London Life in the Thirteenth, Fourteenth, and Fifteenth Centuries* (London, 1868), vol. 2, pp. 148–149.

8. Thatcher and McNeal, *Source Book for Medieval History,* p. 517.

9. Quoted in Hans E. Mayer, *The Crusades,* trans. John Gillingham (New York, 1972), pp. 99–100.

## SUGGESTIONS FOR FURTHER READING

There are numerous works on the different medieval states. On England, see **R. Frame, *The Political Development of the British Isles, 1100–1400*** (Oxford, 1990), and **M. T. Clanchy, *England and Its Rulers, 1066–1272*** (New York, 1983). On France, see **J. Dunbabin, *France in the Making, 843–1180*** (Oxford, 1985), and **E. M. Hallam, *Capetian France, 987–1328*** (London, 1980), a well-done general account. On Spain, see **B. F. Reilly, *The Medieval Spains*** (Cambridge, 1993), and **M. R. Menocal, *The Ornament of the World*** (Boston, 2002). On Germany, see **A. Haverkamp, *Medieval Germany*** (Oxford, 1988); **H. Fuhrmann, *Germany in the High Middle Ages, c. 1050–1250*** (Cambridge, 1986), an excellent account; and **B. Arnold, *Princes and Territories in Medieval Germany*** (Cambridge, 1991). On Italy, see **P. Jones, *The Italian City-State: From Commune to Signoria*** (Oxford, 1997). On eastern Europe and Scandinavia, see **N. Davies, *God's Playground: A History of Poland*** (Oxford, 1981); **T. K. Derry, *A History of Scandinavia*** (London, 1979); **J. Fennell, *The Crisis of Medieval Russia, 1200–1304*** (New York, 1983); and the books listed for Chapter 8.

For specialized studies in the political history of the thirteenth century, see **D. Abulafia, *Frederick II: A Medieval Emperor*** (London, 1987); **M. W. Labarge, *St. Louis: The Life of Louis IX of France*** (London, 1968); and **C. J. Halperin, *Russia and the Golden Horde: The Mongol Impact on Medieval Russian History*** (Bloomington, Ind., 1987).

For a good survey of religion in medieval Europe, see **B. Hamilton, *Religion in the Medieval West*** (London, 1986). On Europe during the time of the Investiture Controversy, see **U.-R. Blumenthal, *The Investiture Controversy*** (Philadelphia, 1988). For a general survey of church life, see **R. W. Southern, *Western Society and the Church in the Middle Ages,*** rev. ed. (New York, 1990).

On the papacy in the High Middle Ages, see the general surveys by **C. Morris, *The Papal Monarchy*** (Oxford, 1989), and **I. S. Robinson, *The Papacy*** (Cambridge, 1990). The papacy of Innocent III is covered in **J. E. Sayers, *Innocent III, Leader of Europe, 1198–1216*** (New York, 1994).

Good works on monasticism include **B. Bolton, *The Medieval Reformation*** (London, 1983), and **C. H. Lawrence, *Medieval Monasticism*** (London, 1984), a good general account. On the Cistercians, see **L. J. Lekai, *The Cistercians*** (Kent, Ohio, 1977). On the impact of the Franciscans and Dominicans, see **C. H. Lawrence, *The Friars: The Impact of the Early Mendicant Movement on Western Society*** (New York, 1994). On Saint Francis, see **A. House, *Francis of Assisi:*** *A Revolutionary Life* (London, 2001). **S. Flanagan, *Hildegard of Bingen,*** 2d ed. (London, 1998), is a good account of the twelfth-century mystic. For a good introduction to popular religion in the eleventh and twelfth centuries, see **R. Brooke and C. N. L. Brooke, *Popular Religion in the Middle Ages*** (London, 1984). The image of women in the secular and religious realms is discussed in **P. S. Gold, *The Lady and the Virgin: Image, Attitude, and Experience in Twelfth-Century France*** (Chicago, 1985).

On dissent and heresy, see **M. Lambert, *Medieval Heresy,*** 2d ed. (New York, 1992), and **J. Strayer, *The Albigensian Crusades,*** 2d ed. (New York, 1992). On the Inquisition, see **B. Hamilton, *The Medieval Inquisition*** (New York, 1981). The persecution of Jews in the thirteenth century can be examined in **J. Cohen, *The Friars and the Jews*** (Oxford, 1985). The basic study on intolerance and homosexuality is **J. Boswell, *Christianity, Social Tolerance, and Homosexuality*** (Chicago, 1980).

Two good general surveys of the Crusades are **H. E. Mayer, *The Crusades,*** 2d ed. (New York, 1988), and **J. Riley-Smith, *The Crusades: A Short History*** (New Haven, Conn., 1987). Also see **J. Riley-Smith, ed., *The Oxford Illustrated History of the Crusades*** (New York, 1995), and **A. Konstam, *Historical Atlas of the Crusades*** (New York, 2002). For works on the Byzantine and Islamic empires, see the reading suggestions at the end of Chapter 8 and **M. Angold, *The Byzantine Empire, 1025–1204*** (London, 1984). The disastrous Fourth Crusade is examined in **J. Godfrey, *1204: The Unholy Crusade*** (Oxford, 1980). On the later Crusades, see **N. Housley, *The Later Crusades, 1274–1580*** (New York, 1992).

## History  Now™

Enter *HistoryNow* using the access card that is available for *Western Civilization. HistoryNow* will assist you in understanding the content in this chapter with lesson plans generated for your needs. In addition, you can read the following documents, and many more, online:

*Song of Roland*

John of Salisbury, Book 5 of *Policraticus*

## INFOTRAC SEARCH TERMS

 For additional reading, go to InfoTrac College Edition, your online research library at http://infotrac.thomsonlearning.com

| Key Term Search | Subject Guide Search |
|---|---|
| medieval Germany | Crusades |
| medieval England | |
| Saint Francis | |

## WESTERN CIVILIZATION RESOURCES

Visit the *Western Civilization* Companion Web site for resources specific to this book:

http://history.wadsworth.com/spielvogel06/

For a variety of tools to help you succeed in this course, visit the Western Civilization Resource Center at

http://history.wadsworth.com/western/

Included are quizzes; images; documents; interactive simulations; maps and timelines; movie explorations; and a wealth of other sources.

# *11*

# THE LATER MIDDLE AGES: CRISIS AND DISINTEGRATION IN THE FOURTEENTH CENTURY

*Mass burial of plague victims*

© The Granger Collection, New York

$\mathcal{A}$ S A RESULT OF THEIR CONQUESTS in the thirteenth and four-teenth centuries, the Mongols created a vast empire stretching from Russia in the west to China in the east. Mongol rule brought stability to the Eurasian trade routes; increased trade brought prosperity but also avenues for the spread of flea-infested rats that carried bubonic plague to both East Asia and Europe. The mid-fourteenth century witnessed one of the most destructive natural disasters in history—the Black Death. One contemporary observer named Henry Knighton, a canon of Saint Mary of the Meadow Abbey in Leicester, England, was simply overwhelmed by the magnitude of the catas-trophe. Knighton began his account of the great plague with these words: "In this year [1348] and in the following one there was a general mortality of people throughout the whole world." Few were left untouched; the plague struck even isolated monasteries: "At Montpellier, there remained out of a hundred and forty friars only seven." Animals, too, were devastated: "During this same year, there was a great mortality of sheep everywhere in the king-dom; in one place and in one pasture, more than five thousand sheep died and became so putrefied that neither beast nor bird wanted to touch them."

Knighton was also stunned by the economic and social consequences of the Black Death. Prices dropped: "And the price of everything was cheap, because of the fear of death; there were very few who took any care for their wealth, or for anything else." Meanwhile laborers were scarce, so their wages increased: "In the following autumn, one could not hire a reaper at a lower wage than eight pence with food, or a mower at less than twelve pence with food. Because of this, much grain rotted in the fields for lack of harvesting." So many people died that some towns were deserted and some villages disappeared altogether: "Many small villages and hamlets were completely deserted; there was not one house left in them, but all those who had lived in them were dead." Some people thought the end of the world was at hand.

Plague was not the only disaster in the fourteenth century. Signs of disintegration were everywhere: famine, economic depression, war, social upheaval, a rise in crime and violence, and a decline in the power of the universal Catholic church. Periods of disintegration, however, are often fertile ground for change and new developments. Out of the dissolution of medieval civilization came a rebirth of culture that many historians have labeled the Renaissance.

# A Time of Troubles: Black Death and Social Crisis

Well into the thirteenth century, Europe had experienced good harvests and an expanding population. By the end of the century, however, a period of disastrous changes had begun.

## Famine and Population

Toward the end of the thirteenth century, noticeable changes in weather patterns were occurring as Europe entered a period that has been called a "little ice age." A small drop in overall temperatures resulted in shortened growing seasons and disastrous weather conditions, including heavy storms and constant rain. Between 1315 and 1317, heavy rains in northern Europe destroyed harvests and caused serious food shortages, resulting in extreme hunger and starvation. The great famine expanded to other parts of Europe in an all-too-familiar pattern, as is evident in this scene described by a contemporary chronicler:

> We saw a large number of both sexes, not only from nearby places but from as much as five leagues away, barefooted and maybe even, except for women, in a completely nude state, together with their priests coming in procession at the Church of the Holy Martyrs, their bones bulging out, devoutly carrying bodies of saints and other relics to be adorned hoping to get relief.[1]

Some historians estimate that famine killed 10 percent of the European population in the first half of the fourteenth century.

Europe had experienced a great increase in population in the High Middle Ages. By 1300, however, indications are that Europe had reached the upper limit of its population, not in an absolute sense, but in the number of people who could be supported by existing agricultural production and technology. Virtually all productive land was being farmed, including many marginal lands that needed intensive cultivation and proved easily susceptible to changing weather patterns.

We know that there was also a movement from overpopulated rural areas to urban locations. Eighteen percent of the people in the village of Broughton in England, for example, migrated between 1288 and 1340. There is no certainty that these migrants found better economic opportunities in urban areas. We might in fact conclude the opposite, based on the reports of increasing numbers of poor people in the cities. In 1330, for example, one chronicler estimated that of the 100,000 inhabitants of Florence, 17,000 were paupers. Moreover, evidence suggests that because of the increase in population, individual peasant holdings by 1300 were shrinking in size to an acreage that could no longer support a peasant family. Europe seemed to have reached an upper limit to population growth, and the number of poor appeared to have increased noticeably.

Some historians have pointed out that famine may have led to chronic malnutrition, which in turn contributed to increased infant mortality, lower birthrates, and higher susceptibility to disease because malnourished people are less able to resist infection. This, they argue, helps explain the high mortality of the great plague known as the Black Death.

## The Black Death

The **Black Death** of the mid-fourteenth century was the most devastating natural disaster in European history, ravaging Europe and causing economic, social, political, and cultural upheaval. Contemporary chroniclers lamented that parents abandoned their children; one related the words: "Oh father, why have you abandoned me? . . . Mother, where have you gone?"[2] People were horrified by an evil force they could not understand and by the subsequent breakdown of all normal human relations.

Bubonic plague, the most common and most important form of plague in the time of the Black Death, was spread by black rats infested with fleas who were host to the deadly bacterium *Yersinia pestis*. Symptoms of bubonic plague included high fever, aching joints, swelling of the lymph nodes, and dark blotches caused by bleeding beneath the skin. Bubonic plague was actually the least toxic form of plague but nevertheless killed 50 to 60 percent of its victims. In pneumonic plague, the bacterial infection spread to the lungs, resulting in severe coughing, bloody sputum, and the relatively easy spread of the bacillus from human to human by coughing.

**Spread of the Plague**    The Black Death was the first major epidemic disease to strike Europe since the seventh century, an absence that helps explain medieval Europe's remarkable population growth. This great plague originated in Asia. After disappearing from Europe and the Middle East in the Middle Ages, bubonic plague continued to haunt areas of southwestern China, especially isolated rural territories. The arrival of Mongol troops in this area in the mid-thirteenth century became the means for the spread of the plague as flea-infested rats carrying the bacteria accompanied the Mongols into central and northwestern China and Central Asia. From there, trading caravans brought the plague to Caffa on the Black Sea in 1346.

The plague reached Europe in October 1347, when Genoese merchants brought it from Caffa to the island of Sicily off the coast of southern Italy. It spread quickly, reaching southern Italy and southern France and Spain by the end of 1347 (see Map 11.1). Usually, the diffusion of the Black Death followed commercial trade routes. In 1348, the plague spread through France and the Low Countries and into Germany. By the end of that year, it had moved to

England, ravaging it in 1349. By the end of 1349, it had expanded to northern Europe and Scandinavia. Eastern Europe and Russia were affected by 1351, although mortality rates were never as high in eastern Europe as they were in western and central Europe.

Mortality figures for the Black Death were incredibly high. Italy was hit especially hard. As the commercial center of the Mediterranean, Italy possessed scores of ports where the plague could be introduced. Italy's crowded cities, whether large, such as Florence, Genoa, and Venice, with populations near 100,000, or small, such as Orvieto and Pistoia, suffered losses of 50 to 60 percent (see the box on p. 287). France and England were also particularly devastated. In northern France, farming villages suffered mortality rates of 30 percent, while cities such as Rouen were more severely affected and experienced losses as high as 40 percent. In England and Germany, entire villages simply disappeared. In Germany, of approximately 170,000

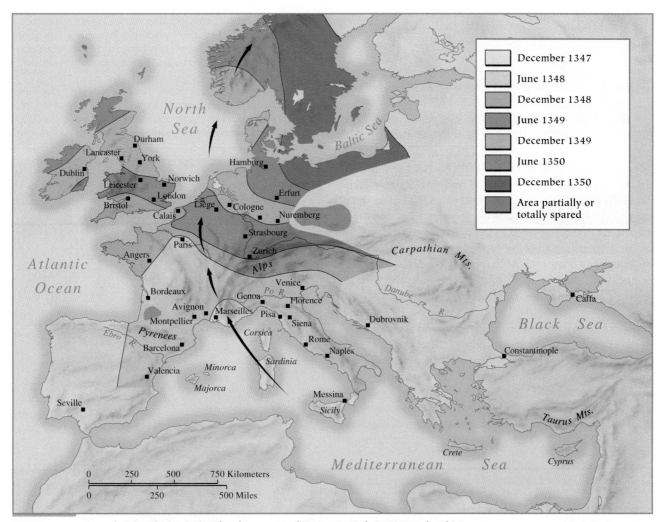

**MAP 11.1** **Spread of the Black Death.** The plague entered Europe in Sicily in 1347 and within three years had killed between one-quarter and one-half of the population. Outbreaks continued into the early eighteenth century, and it took Europe two hundred years to return to the population level it had before the Black Death. [?] Is there a general pattern between distance from Sicily and the elapsed time before a region was infected with the plague? 🌐 **View an animated version of this map or related maps at** http://history.wadsworth.com/spielvogel06/

**Mass Burial of Plague Victims.** The Black Death had spread to northern Europe by the end of 1348. Shown here is a mass burial of victims of the plague in Tournai, located in modern Belgium. As is evident in the illustration, at this stage of the plague, there was still time to make coffins for the victims' burial. Later, as the plague intensified, the dead were thrown into open pits.

inhabited locations, only 130,000 were left by the end of the fourteenth century.

It has been estimated that the European population declined by 25 to 50 percent between 1347 and 1351. If we accept the recent scholarly assessment of a European population of 75 million in the early fourteenth century, this means a death toll of 19 to 38 million people in four years. And the plague did not end in 1351. There were major outbreaks again in 1361–1362 and 1369 and then recurrences every five or six to ten or twelve years, depending on climatic and ecological conditions, until the end of the fifteenth century. The European population thus did not begin to recover until around 1500 and took several generations after that to reattain thirteenth-century levels.

**Life and Death: Reactions to the Plague**   Natural disasters of the magnitude of the great plague produce extreme psychological reactions. Knowing they could be dead in a matter of days, people began living for the moment; some threw themselves with abandon into sexual and alcoholic orgies. The fourteenth-century Italian writer Giovanni Boccaccio gave a classic description of this kind of reaction to the plague in Florence in the preface to his famous *Decameron*:

> [Some people] held that plenty of drinking and enjoyment, singing and free living and the gratification of the appetite in every possible way, letting the devil take the hindmost, was the best preventative . . . ; and as far as they could, they suited the action to the word. Day and night they went from one tavern to another drinking and carousing unrestrainedly. At the least inkling of something that suited them, they ran wild in other people's houses, and there was no one to prevent them, for everyone had abandoned all responsibility for his belongings as well as for himself, considering his days numbered.[3]

Wealthy and powerful people fled to their country estates, as Boccaccio recounted: "Still others . . . maintained that no remedy against plagues was better than to leave them miles behind. Men and women without number . . . , caring for nobody but themselves, abandoned the city, their houses and estates, their own flesh and blood even, and their effects, in search of a country place."[4]

The attempt to explain the Black Death and mitigate its harshness led to extreme sorts of behavior. To many people, the plague had either been sent by God as a punishment for humans' sins or been caused by the devil. Some resorted to extreme asceticism to cleanse themselves of sin and gain God's forgiveness. Such were the flagellants, whose movement became popular in 1348, especially in Germany. Groups of flagellants, both men and women, wandered from town to town, flogging themselves with whips to win the forgiveness of God, whom they believed had sent the plague to punish humans for their sinful ways. One contemporary chronicler described a flagellant procession:

> The penitents went about, coming first out of Germany. They were men who did public penance and scourged themselves with whips of hard knotted leather with little iron spikes. Some made themselves bleed very badly between the shoulder blades and some foolish women had cloths ready to catch the blood and smear it on their eyes, saying it was miraculous blood. While they were doing penance, they sang very mournful songs about the nativity and the passion of Our Lord. The object of this penance was to put a stop to the mortality, for in that time . . . at least a third of all the people in the world died.[5]

**The Flagellants.** Reactions to the plague were extreme at times. Believing that asceticism could atone for humanity's sins and win God's forgiveness, flagellants wandered from town to town flogging themselves and each other with whips, as in this illustration.

# THE BLACK DEATH

HE BLACK DEATH was the most terrifying natural calamity of the Middle Ages. This contemporary description of the great plague in Florence is taken from the preface to the *Decameron* by the fourteenth-century Italian writer Giovanni Boccaccio.

### Giovanni Boccaccio, *Decameron*

In the year of Our Lord 1348 the deadly plague broke out in the great city of Florence, most beautiful of Italian cities. Whether through the operation of the heavenly bodies or because of our own iniquities which the just wrath of God sought to correct, the plague had arisen in the East some years before, causing the death of countless human beings. It spread without stop from one place to another, until, unfortunately, it swept over the West. Neither knowledge nor human foresight availed against it, though the city was cleansed of much filth by chosen officers in charge and sick persons were forbidden to enter it, while advice was broadcast for the preservation of health. Nor did humble supplications serve. Not once but many times they were ordained in the form of processions and other ways for the propitiation of God by the faithful, but, in spite of everything, toward the spring of the year the plague began to show its ravages. . . .

It did not manifest itself as in the East, where if a man bled at the nose he had certain warning of inevitable death. At the onset of the disease both men and women were afflicted by a sort of swelling in the groin or under the armpits which sometimes attained the size of a common apple or egg. Some of these swellings were larger and some smaller, and were commonly called boils. From these two starting points the boils began in a little while to spread and appear generally all over the body. Afterwards, the manifestation of the disease changed into black or livid spots on the arms, thighs, and the whole person. In many these blotches were large and far apart, in others small and closely clus-tered. Like the boils, which had been and continued to be a certain indication of coming death, these blotches had the same meaning for everyone on whom they appeared.

Neither the advice of physicians nor the virtue of any medicine seemed to help or avail in the cure of these diseases. Indeed, . . . not only did few recover, but on the contrary almost everyone died within three days of the appearance of the signs—some sooner, some later. . . . The virulence of the plague was all the greater in that it was communicated by the sick to the well by contact, not unlike fire when dry or fatty things are brought near it. But the evil was still worse. Not only did conversation and familiarity with the diseased spread the malady and even cause death, but the mere touch of the clothes or any other object the sick had touched or used, seemed to spread the pestilence. . . .

More wretched still were the circumstances of the common people and, for a great part, of the middle class, for, confined to their homes either by hope of safety or by poverty, and restricted to their own sections, they fell sick daily by thousands. There, devoid of help or care, they died almost without redemption. A great many breathed their last in the public streets, day and night; a large number perished in their homes, and it was only by the stench of their decaying bodies that they proclaimed their death to their neighbors. Everywhere the city was teeming with corpses. . . .

So many bodies were brought to the churches every day that the consecrated ground did not suffice to hold them, particularly according to the ancient custom of giving each corpse its individual place. Huge trenches were dug in the crowded churchyards and the new dead were piled in them, layer upon layer, like merchandise in the hold of a ship. A little earth covered the corpses of each row, and the procedure continued until the trench was filled to the top.

The flagellants attracted attention and created mass hysteria wherever they went. The Catholic church, however, became alarmed when flagellant groups began to kill Jews and attack clergy who opposed them. Some groups also developed a millenarian aspect, placing their emphasis on the coming end of the world, the return of Jesus, and the establishment of a thousand-year kingdom under his governance. Pope Clement VI condemned the flagellants in October 1349 and urged the public authorities to crush them. By the end of 1350, most of the flagellant movement had been destroyed.

An outbreak of virulent anti-Semitism also accompanied the Black Death. Jews were accused of causing the plague by poisoning town wells. Although Jews were persecuted in Spain, the worst organized massacres, or **pogroms,** against this helpless minority were carried out in Germany; more than sixty major Jewish communities in Germany had been exterminated by 1351 (see the box on p. 288). Many Jews fled eastward to Russia and especially to Poland, where the king offered them protection. Eastern Europe became home to large Jewish communities.

The prevalence of death because of the plague and its recurrences affected people in profound ways. Some survivors apparently came to treat life as something cheap and passing. Violence and violent death appeared to be more common after the plague than before. Postplague Europe also demonstrated a morbid preoccupation with death. In their sermons, priests reminded parishioners that each night's sleep might be their last. Tombstones were decorated with macabre scenes of naked corpses in various stages of decomposition with snakes entwined in their bones and their innards filled with worms.

# A Medieval Holocaust: The Cremation of the Strasbourg Jews

*I*N THEIR ATTEMPT to explain the widespread horrors of the Black Death, medieval Christian communities looked for scapegoats. As at the time of the Crusades, the Jews were blamed for poisoning wells and thereby spreading the plague. This selection by a contemporary chronicler, written in 1349, gives an account of how Christians in the town of Strasbourg in the Holy Roman Empire dealt with their Jewish community. It is apparent that financial gain was also an important motive in killing the Jews.

### Jacob von Königshofen, "The Cremation of the Strasbourg Jews"

In the year 1349 there occurred the greatest epidemic that ever happened. Death went from one end of the earth to the other. . . . And from what this epidemic came, all wise teachers and physicians could only say that it was God's will. . . . This epidemic also came to Strasbourg in the summer of the above-mentioned year, and it is estimated that about sixteen thousand people died.

In the matter of this plague the Jews throughout the world were reviled and accused in all lands of having caused it through the poison which they are said to have put into the water and the wells—that is what they were accused of—and for this reason the Jews were burnt all the way from the Mediterranean into Germany. . . .

[The account then goes on to discuss the situation of the Jews in the city of Strasbourg.]

On Saturday . . . they burnt the Jews on a wooden platform in their cemetery. There were about two thousand people of them. Those who wanted to baptise themselves were spared. [About one thousand accepted baptism.] Many small children were taken out of the fire and baptized against the will of their fathers and mothers. And everything that was owed to the Jews was canceled, and the Jews had to surrender all pledges and notes that they had taken for debts. The council, however, took the cash that the Jews possessed and divided it among the working-men proportionately. The money was indeed the thing that killed the Jews. If they had been poor and if the lords had not been in debt to them, they would not have been burnt. . . .

Thus were the Jews burnt at Strasbourg, and in the same year in all the cities of the Rhine, whether Free Cities or Imperial Cities or cities belonging to the lords. In some towns they burnt the Jews after a trial, in others, without a trial. In some cities the Jews themselves set fire to their houses and cremated themselves.

It was decided in Strasbourg that no Jew should enter the city for 100 years, but before 20 years had passed, the council and magistrates agreed that they ought to admit the Jews again into the city for 20 years. And so the Jews came back again to Strasbourg in the year 1368 after the birth of our Lord.

### Economic Dislocation and Social Upheaval

The population collapse of the fourteenth century had dire economic and social consequences. Economic dislocation was accompanied by social upheaval. Between 1000 and 1300, Europe had been relatively stable. The division of society into the three estates of clergy (those who pray), nobility (those who fight), and laborers (those who work) had already begun to disintegrate in the thirteenth century, however. In the fourteenth century, a series of urban and rural revolts rocked European society.

**Noble Landlords and Peasants**   Both peasants and noble landlords were affected by the demographic crisis of the fourteenth century. Most noticeably, Europe experienced a serious labor shortage that caused a dramatic rise in the price of labor. At Cuxham manor in England, for example, a farm laborer who had received two shillings a week in 1347 was paid seven in 1349 and almost eleven by 1350. At the same time, the decline in population depressed or held stable the demand for agricultural produce, resulting in stable or falling prices for output (although in England prices remained high until the 1380s). The chronicler Henry Knighton observed: "And the price of everything was

cheap. . . . A man could buy a horse for half a mark [six shillings], which before was worth forty shillings."[6] Because landlords were having to pay more for labor at the same time that their rents or incomes were declining, they began to experience considerable adversity and lower standards of living. In England, aristocratic incomes dropped more than 20 percent between 1347 and 1353.

Aristocrats responded to adversity by seeking to lower the wage rate. The English Parliament passed the Statute of Laborers (1351), which attempted to limit wages to pre-plague levels and forbid the mobility of peasants as well. Although such laws proved largely unworkable, they did keep wages from rising as high as they might have in a free market. Overall, the position of landlords continued to deteriorate during the late fourteenth and early fifteenth centuries. At the same time, the position of peasants improved, though not uniformly throughout Europe.

The decline in the number of peasants after the Black Death accelerated the process of converting labor services to rents, freeing peasants from the obligations of servile tenure and weakening the system of manorialism. But there were limits to how much the peasants could advance. They faced the same economic hurdles as the lords, while the latter attempted to impose wage restrictions, reinstate old forms of labor service, and create new obligations. New governmental taxes also hurt. Peasant complaints became widespread and soon gave rise to rural revolts.

**Peasant Revolt in France**   In 1358, a peasant revolt, known as the *Jacquerie*, broke out in northern France. The destruction of normal order by the Black Death and the subsequent economic dislocation were important factors in causing the revolt, but the ravages created by the Hundred Years' War also affected the French peasantry (see "War and Political Instability" later in this chapter). Both the French and English forces followed a deliberate policy of laying waste to peasants' lands while bands of mercenaries lived off the land by taking peasants' produce as well.

Peasant anger was also exacerbated by growing class tensions. Landed nobles were eager to hold on to their politically privileged position and felt increasingly threatened in the new postplague world of higher wages and lower prices. Many aristocrats looked on peasants with utter contempt. A French tale told to upper-class audiences contained this remarkable passage:

> Tell me, Lord, if you please, by what right or title does a villein [peasant] eat beef? . . . Should they eat fish? Rather let them eat thistles and briars, thorns and straw and hay on Sunday and peapods on weekdays. They should keep watch without sleep and have trouble always; that is how villeins should live. Yet each day they are full and drunk on the best wines, and in fine clothes. The great expenditures of villeins come as a high cost, for it is this that destroys and ruins the world. It is they who spoil the common welfare. From the villein comes all unhappiness. Should they eat meat? Rather should they chew grass on the heath with the horned cattle and go naked on all fours.[7]

The peasants reciprocated this contempt for their so-called social superiors.

The outburst of peasant anger led to savage confrontations. Castles were burned and nobles murdered (see the box on p. 290). Such atrocities did not go unanswered, however. The *Jacquerie* soon failed as the privileged classes closed ranks, savagely massacred the rebels, and ended the revolt.

**An English Peasant Revolt**   The English Peasants' Revolt of 1381 was the most prominent of all. It was a product not of desperation but of rising expectations. After the Black Death, the condition of the English peasants had improved as they enjoyed greater freedom and higher wages or lower rents. Aristocratic landlords had fought back with legislation to depress wages and attempted to reimpose old feudal dues. The most immediate cause of the revolt, however, was the monarchy's attempt to raise revenues by imposing a poll tax or a flat charge on each adult member of the population. Peasants in eastern England, the wealthiest part of the country, refused to pay the tax and expelled the collectors forcibly from their villages.

This action sparked a widespread rebellion of both peasants and townspeople led by a well-to-do peasant called Wat Tyler and a preacher named John Ball. The latter preached an effective message against the noble class, as recounted by the French chronicler Jean Froissart:

> Good people, things cannot go right in England and never will, until goods are held in common and there are no more villeins and gentlefolk, but we are all one and the same. In what way are those whom we call lords greater masters than ourselves?

**Peasant Rebellion.** The fourteenth century witnessed a number of revolts of the peasantry against noble landowners. Although the revolts often met with initial success, they were soon crushed. This fifteenth-century illustration shows nobles during the French *Jacquerie* of 1358 massacring the rebels in the town of Meaux, in northern France.

# A Revolt of French Peasants

*I*N 1358, FRENCH PEASANTS rose up in a revolt known as the *Jacquerie*. The relationship between aristocrats and peasants had degenerated as a result of the social upheavals and privations caused by the Black Death and the Hundred Years' War. This excerpt from the chronicle of an aristocrat paints a horrifying picture of the barbarities that occurred during the revolt.

### Jean Froissart, *Chronicles*

There were very strange and terrible happenings in several parts of the kingdom of France. . . . They began when some of the men from the country towns came together in the Beauvais region. They had no leaders and at first they numbered scarcely 100. One of them got up and said that the nobility of France, knights and squires, were disgracing and betraying the realm, and that it would be a good thing if they were all destroyed. At this they all shouted: "He's right! He's right! Shame on any man who saves the nobility from being wiped out!"

They banded together and went off, without further deliberation and unarmed except for pikes and knives, to the house of a knight who lived nearby. They broke in and killed the knight, with his lady and his children, big and small, and set fire to the house. Next they went to another castle and did much worse; for, having seized the knight and bound him securely to a post, several of them violated his wife and daughter before his eyes. Then they killed the wife, who was pregnant, and the daughter and all the other children, and finally put the knight to death with great cruelty and burned and razed the castle.

They did similar things in a number of castles and big houses, and their ranks swelled until there were a good 6,000 of them. Wherever they went their numbers grew, for all the men of the same sort joined them. The knights and squires fled before them with their families. They took their wives and daughters many miles away to put them in safety, leaving their houses open with their possessions inside. And those evil men, who had come together without leaders or arms, pillaged and burned everything and violated and killed all the ladies and girls without mercy, like mad dogs. Their barbarous acts were worse than anything that ever took place between Christians and Saracens [Muslims]. Never did men commit such vile deeds. They were such that no living creature ought to see, or even imagine or think of, and the men who committed the most were admired and had the highest places among them. I could never bring myself to write down the horrible and shameful things which they did to the ladies. But, among other brutal excesses, they killed a knight, put him on a spit, and turned him at the fire and roasted him before the lady and her children. After about a dozen of them had violated the lady, they tried to force her and the children to eat the knight's flesh before putting them cruelly to death.

How have they deserved it? Why do they hold us in bondage? If we all spring from a single father and mother, Adam and Eve, how can they claim or prove that they are lords more than us, except by making us produce and grow the wealth which they spend?[8]

The revolt was initially successful as the rebels burned down the manor houses of aristocrats, lawyers, and government officials and murdered several important officials, including the archbishop of Canterbury. After the peasants marched on London, the young King Richard II, age fifteen, promised to accept the rebels' demands if they returned to their homes. They accepted the king's word and dispersed, but the king reneged and with the assistance of the aristocrats arrested hundreds of the rebels. The poll tax was eliminated, however, and in the end most of the rebels were pardoned.

**Revolts in the Cities**   Revolts also erupted in the cities. Commercial and industrial activity suffered almost immediately from the Black Death. An oversupply of goods and an immediate drop in demand led to a decline in trade after 1350. Some industries suffered greatly. Florence's woolen industry, one of the giants, produced 70,000 to 80,000 pieces of cloth in 1338; in 1378, it was yielding only 24,000 pieces. Bourgeois merchants and manufacturers responded to the decline in trade and production by attempting to restrict competition and resist the demands of the lower classes.

In urban areas, where capitalist industrialists paid low wages and managed to prevent workers from forming organizations to help themselves, industrial revolts broke out throughout Europe. Ghent experienced one in 1381, Rouen in 1382. Most famous, however, was the revolt of the *ciompi* in Florence in 1378. The *ciompi* were wool workers in Florence's most prominent industry. In the 1370s, not only was the woolen industry depressed, but the wool workers saw their real wages decline when the coinage in which they were paid was debased. Their revolt won them some concessions from the municipal government, including the right to form guilds and be represented in the government. But their newly won rights were short-lived; authorities ended *ciompi* participation in the government by 1382.

Although the peasant and urban revolts sometimes resulted in short-term gains for the participants, it is also true that the uprisings were quickly crushed and their gains lost. Accustomed to ruling, the established classes easily combined and quashed dissent. Nevertheless, the rural and urban revolts of the fourteenth century ushered in an age of social conflict that characterized much of later European history.

# War and Political Instability

Famine, plague, economic turmoil, social upheaval, and violence were not the only problems of the fourteenth century. War and political instability must also be added to the list. Of all the struggles that ensued in the fourteenth century, the Hundred Years' War was the most famous and the most violent.

## Causes of the Hundred Years' War

In 1259, the English king, Henry III, had relinquished his claims to all the French territories previously held by the English monarchy except for one relatively small possession known as the duchy of Gascony. As duke of Gascony, the English king pledged loyalty as a vassal to the French king. But this territory gave rise to numerous disputes between the kings of England and France. By the thirteenth century, the Capetian monarchs had greatly increased their power over their more important vassals, the great lords of France. Royal officials interfered regularly in the affairs of the vassals' fiefs, especially in matters of justice. Although this policy irritated all the vassals, it especially annoyed the king of England, who considered himself the peer of the French king.

A dispute over the right of succession to the French throne also complicated the struggle between the French and the English. In the fourteenth century, the Capetian dynasty failed to produce a male heir for the first time in almost four hundred years. In 1328, the last son of King Philip IV died without a male heir. The closest male relative in line to the throne was King Edward III of England (1327–1377), whose mother was Isabella, the daughter of Philip IV. Known for her strong personality (she was nicknamed the "she-wolf of France"), Isabella, with the assistance of her lover, led a revolt against her husband, King Edward II, overthrew him, and ruled England until her teenage son, Edward III, took sole control of the throne in 1330. As the son of the daughter of King Philip IV, King Edward III of England had a claim to the French throne, but the French nobles argued that the inheritance of the monarchy could not pass through the female line and chose a cousin of the Capetians, Philip, duke of Valois, as King Philip VI (1328–1350).

The immediate cause of the war between France and England was yet another quarrel over Gascony. In 1337, when Edward III, the king of England and duke of Gascony, refused to do homage to Philip VI for Gascony, the French king seized the duchy. Edward responded by declaring war on Philip, the "so-called king of France." There is no doubt that the personalities of the two monarchs also had much

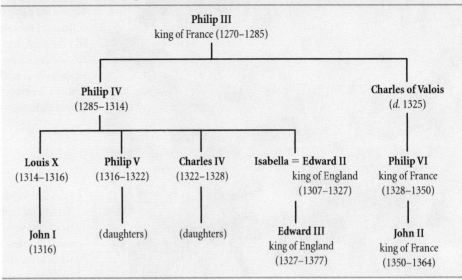

**CHART 11.1  Background to the Hundred Years' War: Kings of France and England**

Philip III
king of France (1270–1285)

Philip IV
(1285–1314)

Charles of Valois
(d. 1325)

Louis X
(1314–1316)

Philip V
(1316–1322)

Charles IV
(1322–1328)

Isabella = Edward II
king of England
(1307–1327)

Philip VI
king of France
(1328–1350)

John I
(1316)

(daughters)

(daughters)

Edward III
king of England
(1327–1377)

John II
king of France
(1350–1364)

to do with the outbreak of the Hundred Years' War. Both Edward and Philip loved luxury and shared a desire for the glory and prestige that came from military engagements. Both were only too willing to use their respective nation's resources to satisfy their own desires. Moreover, for many nobles, the promise of plunder and territorial gain was an incentive to follow the disruptive path of their rulers.

## Conduct and Course of the War

The Hundred Years' War began in a burst of knightly enthusiasm. Trained to be warriors, knights viewed the clash of battle as the ultimate opportunity to demonstrate their fighting abilities. But this struggle would change the nature of warfare, for as it dragged on, the outcomes of battles were increasingly determined not by knights but by peasant foot soldiers. The French army of 1337, with its heavily armed noble cavalry, resembled its twelfth- and thirteenth-century forebears. The noble cavalrymen considered themselves the fighting elite and looked with contempt on the foot soldiers and crossbowmen, their social inferiors.

The English army, however, had evolved differently and had included peasants as paid foot soldiers since at least Anglo-Saxon times. Armed with pikes, many of these foot soldiers had also adopted the longbow, invented by the Welsh. The longbow had a more rapid speed of fire than the more powerful crossbow. Although the English made use of heavily armed cavalry, they relied even more on large numbers of foot soldiers.

**Early Phases of the War**   Edward III's early campaigns in France achieved little. When Edward renewed his efforts in 1346 with an invasion of Normandy, Philip responded by raising a large force to crush the English army and met Edward's forces at Crécy, just south of Flanders. The larger French army followed no battle plan but simply attacked the English lines in a disorderly fashion. The arrows of the English archers devastated the French cavalry. As Jean

**Battle of Crécy.** This fifteenth-century manuscript illustration depicts the Battle of Crécy, the first of several military disasters suffered by the French in the Hundred Years' War, and shows why the English preferred the longbow to the crossbow. At the left, the French crossbowmen stop shooting and prime their weapons by cranking the handle, while English archers continue to shoot their longbows (a skilled archer could launch ten arrows a minute).

Froissart described it, "The English continued to shoot [their longbows] into the thickest part of the crowd, wasting none of their arrows. They impaled or wounded horses and riders, who fell to the ground in great distress, unable to get up again [because of their heavy armor] without the help of several men."[9] It was a stunning victory for the English. Edward followed up by capturing the French port of Calais to serve as a staging ground for future invasions.

The Battle of Crécy was not decisive, however. The English simply did not possess the resources to subjugate all of France. Truces, small-scale hostilities, and some major operations were combined in an orgy of seemingly incessant struggle. The English campaigns were waged by Edward III and his son Edward, the prince of Wales, known as the Black Prince. The Black Prince's campaigns in France were devastating (see the box on p. 293). Avoiding pitched battles, his forces deliberately ravaged the land, burning crops and entire unfortified villages and towns and stealing anything of value. For the English, such campaigns were profitable; for the French people, they meant hunger, deprivation, and death. When the army of the Black Prince was finally forced to do battle, the French, under their king, John II (1350–1364), were once again defeated. This time even the king was captured. This Battle of Poitiers (1356) ended the first phase of the Hundred Years' War. Under the Peace of Brétigny (1359), the French agreed to pay a large ransom for King John, the English territories in Gascony were enlarged, and Edward renounced his claims to the throne of France in return for John's promise to give up control over English lands in France. This first phase of the war made it clear that despite their victories, the English were not really strong enough to subdue all of France and make Edward III's claim to the French monarchy a reality.

Monarchs, however, could be slow learners. The Treaty of Brétigny was never really enforced. In the next phase of the war, in the capable hands of John's son Charles V (1364–1380), the French recovered what they had previously lost. The English returned to plundering the French countryside and avoiding pitched battles. That pleased Charles, who did not want to engage in set battles, preferring to use armed bands to reduce the English fortresses systematically. By 1374, the French had recovered their lost lands, although France itself continued to be plagued by "free companies" of mercenaries who, no longer paid by the English, simply lived off the land by plunder and ransom. Nevertheless, for the time being, the war seemed over, especially when a twenty-year truce was negotiated in 1396.

**Renewal of the War** In 1415, however, the English king, Henry V (1413–1422), renewed the war at a time when the French were enduring civil war as the dukes of Burgundy and Orléans competed to control the weak French king, Charles VI. In the summer of 1413, Paris exploded with bloody encounters. Taking advantage of the chaos, Henry V invaded France in 1415. At the Battle of Agincourt (1415), the French suffered a disastrous defeat, and fifteen hundred French nobles died when the heavy, armor-plated French knights attempted to attack across a field turned to mud by heavy rain. Altogether, French losses were six thousand dead; the English lost only three hundred men.

Henry went on to reconquer Normandy and forge an alliance with the duke of Burgundy, which led Charles VI to agree to the Treaty of Troyes in 1420. By this treaty, Henry V was married to Catherine, daughter of Charles VI, and recognized as the heir to the French throne. By 1420, the English were masters of northern France (see Map 11.2).

The seemingly hopeless French cause fell into the hands of Charles the dauphin (heir to the throne), the son of Charles VI, who, despite being disinherited by the Treaty of Troyes, still considered himself the real heir to the French throne. The dauphin governed the southern two-thirds of French lands from Bourges. Charles was weak and timid and was unable to rally the French against the English, who in 1428 had turned south and were besieging the city of Orléans to gain access to the valley of the Loire. The French monarch was saved, quite unexpectedly, by a French peasant woman.

# THE HUNDRED YEARS' WAR

*N HIS ACCOUNT OF the Hundred Years' War, the fourteenth-century French chronicler Jean Froissart described the sack of the fortified French town of Limoges by the Black Prince, Edward, the prince of Wales. It provides a vivid example of how noncombatants fared during the war.*

### Jean Froissart, *Chronicles*

For about a month, certainly not longer, the Prince of Wales remained before Limoges. During that time he allowed no assaults or skirmishes, but pushed on steadily with the mining. The knights inside and the townspeople, who knew what was going on, started a countermine in the hope of killing the English miners, but it was a failure. When the Prince's miners who, as they dug, were continually shoring up their tunnel, had completed their work, they said to the Prince: "My lord, whenever you like now we can bring a big piece of wall down into the moat, so that you can get into the city quite easily and safely."

The Prince was very pleased to hear this. "Excellent," he said. "At six o'clock tomorrow morning, show me what you can do."

When they knew it was the right time for it, the miners started a fire in their mine. In the morning, just as the Prince had specified, a great section of the wall collapsed, filling the moat at the place where it fell. For the English, who were armed and ready waiting, it was a welcome sight.

Those on foot could enter as they liked, and did so. They rushed to the gate, cut through the bars holding it and knocked it down. They did the same with the barriers outside, meeting with no resistance. It was all done so quickly that the people in the town were taken unawares. Then the Prince, the Duke of Lancaster, the Earl of Cambridge, Sir Guichard d'Angle, with all the others and their men burst into the city, followed by pillagers on foot, all in a mood to wreak havoc and do murder, killing indiscriminately, for those were their orders. There were pitiful scenes. Men, women, and children flung themselves on their knees before the Prince, crying: "Have mercy on us, gentle sir!" But he was so inflamed with anger that he would not listen. Neither man nor woman was heeded, but all who could be found were put to the sword, including many who were in no way to blame. I do not understand how they could have failed to take pity on people who were too unimportant to have committed treason. Yet they paid for it, and paid more dearly than the leaders who had committed it.

There is no man so hard-hearted that, if he had been in Limoges on that day, and had remembered God, he would not have wept bitterly at the fearful slaughter which took place. More than 3,000 persons, men, women, and children, were dragged out to have their throats cut. May God receive their souls, for they were true martyrs.

**Joan of Arc** Joan of Arc was born in 1412 to well-to-do peasants from the village of Domrémy in Champagne. Deeply religious, Joan experienced visions and came to believe that her favorite saints had commanded her to free France and have the dauphin crowned as king. In February 1429, Joan made her way to the dauphin's court, where her sincerity and simplicity persuaded Charles to allow her to accompany a French army to Orléans. Apparently inspired by the faith of the peasant girl, the French armies found new confidence in themselves and liberated Orléans, changing the course of the war. Within a few weeks, the entire Loire valley had been freed of the English. In July 1429, fulfilling Joan's other task, the dauphin was crowned king of France and became Charles VII (1422–1461). In accomplishing the two commands of her angelic voices, Joan had brought the war to a decisive turning point.

Joan, however, did not live to see the war concluded. She was captured by the Burgundian allies of the English in 1430. Wishing to eliminate the "Maid of Orléans" for obvious political reasons, the English turned Joan over to the Inquisition

**Joan of Arc.** Pictured here in a suit of armor, Joan of Arc is holding aloft a banner that shows Jesus and two angels. This portrait dates from the late fifteenth century; there are no known portraits of Joan made from life.

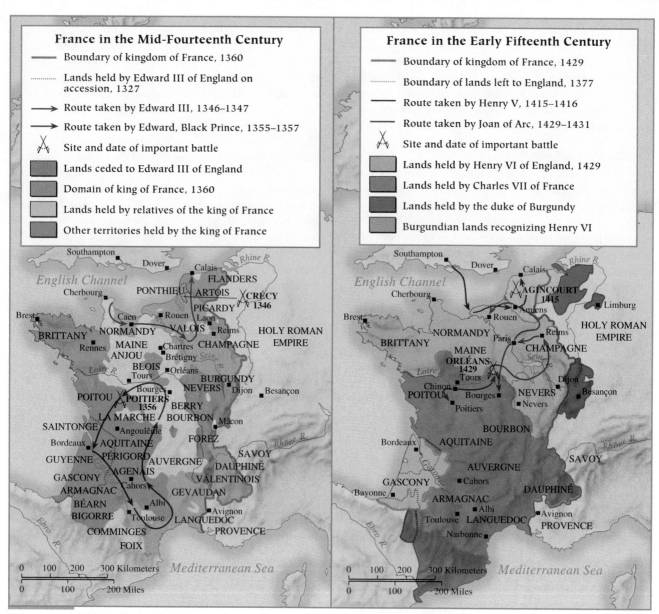

**France in the Mid-Fourteenth Century**

—— Boundary of kingdom of France, 1360

·········· Lands held by Edward III of England on accession, 1327

——→ Route taken by Edward III, 1346–1347

——→ Route taken by Edward, Black Prince, 1355–1357

⚔ Site and date of important battle

▮ Lands ceded to Edward III of England

▮ Domain of king of France, 1360

▮ Lands held by relatives of the king of France

▮ Other territories held by the king of France

**France in the Early Fifteenth Century**

—— Boundary of kingdom of France, 1429

·········· Boundary of lands left to England, 1377

—— Route taken by Henry V, 1415–1416

—— Route taken by Joan of Arc, 1429–1431

⚔ Site and date of important battle

▮ Lands held by Henry VI of England, 1429

▮ Lands held by Charles VII of France

▮ Lands held by the duke of Burgundy

▮ Burgundian lands recognizing Henry VI

**MAP 11.2  The Hundred Years' War.**  This long, exhausting struggle began in 1337 and dragged on until 1453. The English initially gained substantial French territory, but in the later phases of the war, France turned the tide, eventually expelling the English from all Continental lands except the port of Calais.  ❓ What gains had the English made by 1429, and how do they correlate to proximity to England and the ocean?  🌐 **View an animated version of this map or related maps at**

http://history.wadsworth.com/spielvogel06/

on charges of witchcraft. In the fifteenth century, spiritual visions were thought to be inspired by either God or the devil. Because Joan dressed in men's clothing, it was easy for her enemies to believe that she was in league with the "prince of darkness." She was condemned to death as a heretic and burned at the stake in 1431, at the age of nineteen. To the end, as the flames rose up around her, she declared that her voices came from God and had not deceived her. Twenty-five years later, a church court exonerated her of these charges. To a contemporary French writer, Christine de Pizan, she became a feminist heroine (see the box on p. 295). In 1920, she was made a saint of the Roman Catholic church.

**End of the War**  Joan of Arc's accomplishments proved decisive. Although the war dragged on for another two decades, defeats of English armies in Normandy and Aquitaine led to French victory. Important to the French success was the use of the cannon, a new weapon made possible by the invention of gunpowder. The Chinese had invented gunpowder in the eleventh century and devised a simple cannon by the thirteenth century. The Mongols greatly improved this technology, developing more accurate cannons and cannonballs; both spread to the Middle East by the thirteenth century and to Europe by the fourteenth.

# A Feminist Heroine: Christine de Pizan on Joan of Arc

CHRISTINE DE PIZAN, France's "first woman of letters," was witness to the rescue of France from the hands of the English by the efforts of Joan of Arc and was also present at the coronation of Charles VII as king of France. Christine believed that a turning point had arrived in French history and that Joan—a woman—had been responsible for France's salvation. She wrote a poem to honor this great occasion. The following stanzas are taken from her poem.

### Christine de Pizan, *The Poem of Joan of Arc,* July 31, 1429

The year of fourteen twenty-nine
The sun came out to shine again.
It brings the season new and good,
Which we had not directly seen
Too long a time, while many passed
Their lives in sorrow; I am one.
But now, no longer do I grieve
Because I see what pleases me. . . .

And you, the King of France, King Charles,
The seventh of that noble name,
Who fought a mighty war before
Good fortune came at all to you:
Do, now, observe your dignity
Exalted by the Maid, who bent
Your enemies beneath your flag
In record time (that's something new!)

And people thought that it would be
Impossible indeed for you
To ever have your country back,
For it was nearly lost; but now,
It's clearly yours; no matter who
Has done you wrong, it's yours once more,
And through the clever Maid who did
Her part therein—thanks be to God! . . .

When I reflect upon your state,
The youthful maiden that you are,
To whom God gives the force and strength
To be the champion and the one
To suckle France upon her milk
Of peace, the sweetest nourishment,
To overthrow the rebel host:
The wonder passes Nature's work!

That is, if God, through Joshua
Performed so many miracles
In conquering those places where

So many met defeat—a man
Of strength was Joshua. But she's
A woman—simple shepherdess—
More brave than ever man at Rome!
An easy thing for God to do!

But as for us, we've never heard
About a marvel quite so great
For all the heroes who have lived
In history can't measure up
In bravery against the Maid,
Who strives to rout our enemies.

It's God does that, who's guiding her
Whose courage passes that of men . . .
By miracle has she appeared,
Divine commandment sent her here.
God's angel led her in before
The king, to bring her help to him.
There's no illusion in her case
Because it's been indeed borne out
In council (in conclusion, then,
A thing is proved by its effect). . . .

What honor for the female sex!
God's love for it appears quite clear,
Because the kingdom laid to waste
By all those wretched people now
Stands safe, a woman rescued it
(A hundred thousand men could not
Do that) and killed the hostile foe!
A thing beyond belief before! . . .

While ridding France of enemies,
Retaking town and castle both.
No force was ever quite so great,
If hundreds or if thousands strong!
Among our men so brave and apt
She's captain over all; such strength
No Hector or Achilles had.
All this God does, who's guiding her. . . .

The English will be crushed through her,
And never will they rise again
For God who wills it hears the voice
Of guiltless folk they tried to harm!
The blood of those they've killed, who'll walk
No more, cries out. God wants an end
To this; instead He has resolved
To chastise them as evil men.

| | |
|---|---|
| Outbreak of hostilities | 1337 |
| Battle of Crécy | 1346 |
| Battle of Poitiers | 1356 |
| Peace of Brétigny | 1359 |
| Death of Edward III | 1377 |
| Twenty-year truce declared | 1396 |
| Henry V (1413–1422) renews the war | 1415 |
| Battle of Agincourt | 1415 |
| Treaty of Troyes | 1420 |
| French recovery under Joan of Arc | 1429–1431 |
| End of the war | 1453 |

The death of England's best commanders and the instability of the English government under King Henry VI (1421–1471) also contributed to England's defeat. By 1453, the only part of France that was left in England's hands was the coastal town of Calais, which remained English for another century.

## Political Instability

The fourteenth century was a period of adversity for the internal political stability of European governments. Although government bureaucracies grew ever larger, at the same time the question of who should control the bureaucracies led to internal conflict and instability. Like the lord-serf relationship, the lord-vassal relationship based on land and military service was being replaced by a contract based on money. Especially after the Black Death, money payments called **scutage** were increasingly substituted for military service. Monarchs welcomed this development because they could now hire professional soldiers, who tended to be more reliable anyway. As lord-vassal relationships became less personal and less important, new relationships based on political advantage began to be formed, creating new avenues for political influence—and for corruption as well. Especially noticeable as the landed aristocrats suffered declining rents and social uncertainties with the new relationships was the formation of factions of nobles who looked for opportunities to advance their power and wealth at the expense of other noble factions and of their monarchs. Other nobles went to the royal courts, offering to serve the kings.

The kings had their own problems, however. By the mid-fifteenth century, reigning monarchs in many European countries were not the direct descendents of the rulers of 1300. The founders of these new dynasties had to struggle for position as factions of nobles vied to gain material advantages for themselves. As the fifteenth century began, there were two claimants to the throne of France, two aristocratic factions fighting for control of England, and three German princes struggling to be recognized as Holy Roman Emperor.

Fourteenth-century monarchs of old dynasties and new faced financial problems as well. The shift to using mercenary soldiers left monarchs perennially short of cash. Traditional revenues, especially rents from property, increasingly proved insufficient to meet their needs. Monarchs attempted to generate new sources of revenues, especially through taxes, which often meant going through parliaments. This opened the door for parliamentary bodies to gain more power by asking for favors first. Although unsuccessful in most cases, the parliaments simply added another element of uncertainty and confusion to fourteenth-century politics. Turning now to a survey of western and central European states (eastern Europe will be examined in Chapter 12), we can see how these disruptive factors worked.

## The Growth of England's Political Institutions

The fifty-year reign of Edward III (1327–1377) was important for the evolution of English political institutions in the fourteenth century. Parliament increased in prominence and developed its basic structure and functions during Edward's reign. Due to his constant need for money to fight the Hundred Years' War, Edward came to rely on Parliament to levy new taxes. In return for regular grants, Edward made several concessions, including a commitment to levy no direct tax without Parliament's consent and to allow Parliament to examine the government accounts to ensure that the money was being spent properly. By the end of Edward's reign, Parliament had become an important component of the English governmental system.

During this same period, Parliament began to assume the organizational structure it has retained to this day. The Great Council of barons became the House of Lords and evolved into a body composed of the chief bishops and abbots of the realm and aristocratic peers whose position in Parliament was hereditary. The representatives of the shires and boroughs, who were considered less important than the lay and ecclesiastical lords, held collective meetings and soon came to be regarded as the House of Commons. Together, the House of Lords and House of Commons constituted Parliament. Although the House of Commons did little beyond approving measures proposed by the Lords, during Edward's reign the Commons did begin the practice of drawing up petitions, which, if accepted by the king, became law.

After Edward III's death, England began to experience the internal instability of aristocratic factionalism that was racking other European countries. The early years of the reign of Edward's grandson, Richard II (1377–1399), began inauspiciously with the peasant revolt that ended only when the king made concessions. Richard's reign was troubled by competing groups of nobles who sought to pursue their own interests. One faction, led by Henry of Lancaster, defeated the king's forces and then deposed and killed him. Henry of Lancaster became King Henry IV (1399–1413). In the fifteenth century, factional conflict would lead to a devastating series of civil wars known as the War of the Roses.

## The Problems of the French Kings

At the beginning of the fourteenth century, France was the most prosperous monarchy in Europe. By the end of the century, much of its wealth had been dissipated, and rival factions of aristocrats had made effective monarchical rule virtually impossible.

The French monarchical state had always had an underlying inherent weakness that proved its undoing in difficult times. Although Capetian monarchs had found ways to enlarge their royal domain and extend their control by developing a large and effective bureaucracy, the various territories that made up France still maintained their own princes, customs, and laws. The parliamentary institutions of France provide a good example of France's basic lack of unity. The French parliament, known as the Estates-General and composed of representatives of the clergy, the nobility, and the **Third Estate** (everyone else), usually represented only the north of France, not the entire kingdom. The southern provinces had their own estates, and local estates existed in other parts of France. Unlike the English Parliament, which was evolving into a crucial part of the English government, the French Estates-General was simply one of many such institutions.

When Philip VI (1328–1350) became involved in the Hundred Years' War with England, he found it necessary to devise new sources of revenue, including a tax on salt known as the *gabelle* and a hearth tax eventually called the *taille*. These taxes weighed heavily on the French peasantry and middle class. Consequently, when additional taxes were needed to pay for the ransom of King John II after his capture at the Battle of Poitiers, the middle-class inhabitants of the towns tried to use the Estates-General to reform the French government and tax structure.

At the meeting of the Estates-General in 1357, under the leadership of the Parisian provost Étienne Marcel, representatives of the Third Estate granted taxes in exchange for a promise from King John's son, the dauphin Charles, not to tax without the Estates-General's permission and to allow the Estates-General to meet on a regular basis and participate in important political decisions. After Marcel's movement was crushed in 1358, this attempt to make the Estates-General a functioning part of the French government collapsed. The dauphin became King Charles V (1364–1380) and went on to recover much of the land lost to the English. His military successes underscored his efforts to reestablish strong monarchical powers. He undermined the role of the Estates-General by getting it to grant him taxes with no fixed time limit. Charles's death in 1380 soon led to a new time of troubles for the French monarchy, however.

The insanity of Charles VI (1380–1422), which first became apparent in 1392, opened the door to rival factions of French nobles aspiring to power and wealth. The dukes of Burgundy and Orléans competed to control Charles and the French monarchy. Their struggles created chaos for the French government and the French people. Many nobles supported the Orléanist faction, while Paris and other towns favored the Burgundians. By the beginning of the fifteenth century, France seemed hopelessly mired in a civil war. When the English renewed the Hundred Years' War in 1415, the Burgundians supported the English cause and the English monarch's claim to the throne of France.

## The German Monarchy

England and France had developed strong national monarchies in the High Middle Ages. By the end of the fourteenth century, they seemed in danger of disintegrating due to dynastic problems and the pressures generated by the Hundred Years' War. In contrast, the Holy Roman Empire, whose core consisted of the lands of Germany, had already begun to fall apart in the High Middle Ages. Northern Italy, which the German emperors had tried to include in their medieval empire, had been free from any real imperial control since the end of the Hohenstaufen dynasty in the thirteenth century. In Germany itself, the failure of the Hohenstaufens ended any chance of centralized monarchical authority, and Germany became a land of hundreds of virtually independent states. These varied in size and power and included princely states, such as the duchies of Bavaria and Saxony; free imperial city-states (self-governing cities directly under the control of the Holy Roman Emperor rather than a German territorial prince), such as Nuremberg; modest territories of petty imperial knights; and ecclesiastical states, such as the archbishopric of Cologne, in which an ecclesiastical official, such as a bishop, archbishop, or abbot, served in a dual capacity as an administrative official of the Catholic church and as secular lord over the territories of the state. Although all of the rulers of these different states had some obligations to the German king and Holy Roman Emperor, more and more they acted independently.

**Electoral Nature of the German Monarchy** Because of its unique pattern of development in the High Middle Ages, the German monarchy had become established on an elective rather than a hereditary basis. This principle of election was standardized in 1356 by the Golden Bull issued by Emperor Charles IV (1346–1378). This document stated that four lay princes (the count palatine of the Rhine, the duke of Saxony, the margrave of Brandenburg, and the king of Bohemia) and three ecclesiastical rulers (the archbishops of Mainz, Trier, and Cologne) would serve as electors with the legal power to elect the "king of the Romans and future emperor, to be ruler of the world and of the

**The Holy Roman Empire in the Fourteenth Century**

Christian people."[10] "King of the Romans" was the official title of the German king; after his imperial coronation, he would also have the title of emperor.

In the fourteenth century, the electoral principle further ensured that kings of Germany were generally weak. Their ability to exercise effective power depended on the extent of their own family possessions. At the beginning of the fifteenth century, three emperors claimed the throne. Although the dispute was quickly settled, Germany entered the fifteenth century in a condition that verged on anarchy. Princes fought princes and leagues of cities. The emperors were virtually powerless to control any of them.

## The States of Italy

By the fourteenth century, Italy, too, had failed to develop a centralized monarchical state. Papal opposition to the rule of the Hohenstaufen emperors in northern Italy had virtually guaranteed that. Moreover, southern Italy was divided into the kingdom of Naples, ruled by the French house of Anjou, and Sicily, whose kings came from the Spanish house of Aragon. The center of the peninsula remained under the rather shaky control of the papacy. Lack of centralized authority had enabled numerous city-states in northern Italy to remain independent of any political authority.

In fourteenth-century Italy, two general tendencies can be discerned: the replacement of republican governments by tyrants and the expansion of the larger city-states at the expense of the less powerful ones. Nearly all the cities of northern Italy began their existence as free communes with republican governments. But in the fourteenth century, intense internal strife led city-states to resort to temporary expedients, allowing rule by one man with dictatorial powers. Limited rule, however, soon became long-term despotism as tyrants proved willing to use force to maintain themselves in power. Eventually, such tyrants tried to legitimize their power by purchasing titles from the emperor (still nominally ruler of northern Italy as Holy Roman Emperor). In this fashion, the Visconti became the dukes of Milan and the d'Este, the dukes of Ferrara.

The other change of great significance was the development of larger, regional states as the larger states expanded at the expense of the smaller ones. To fight their battles, city-states came to rely on mercenary soldiers, whose leaders, called *condottieri,* sold the services of their bands to the highest bidder. These mercenaries wreaked havoc on the countryside, living by blackmail and looting when they were not actively engaged in battles. Many were foreigners who flocked to Italy during the periods of truce of the Hundred Years' War. By the end of the fourteenth century, three major states came to dominate northern Italy: the despotic state of Milan and the republican states of Florence and Venice.

**Duchy of Milan** In the fertile Po valley, where the chief trade routes from Italian coastal cities to the Alpine passes crossed, Milan was one of the richest city-states in Italy.

**Mercenaries as Looters.** Mercenary soldiers, like medieval armies in general, were notorious for causing havoc by looting when they were not engaged in battle. This mid-fourteenth-century manuscript illustration shows soldiers ransacking a house in Paris.

Politically, it was also one of the most agitated until the Visconti family established itself as the hereditary despots of Milan in 1322. Giangaleazzo Visconti, who ruled from 1385 to 1402, transformed this despotism into a hereditary duchy by purchasing the title of duke from the emperor in 1395. Under Giangaleazzo's direction, the duchy of Milan extended its power over all of Lombardy and even threatened to conquer much of northern Italy until the duke's untimely death before the gates of Florence in 1402.

**Republic of Florence** Florence, like the other Italian towns, was initially a free commune dominated by a patrician class of nobles known as the *grandi*. But the rapid expansion of Florence's economy made possible the development of a wealthy merchant-industrialist class known as the *popolo grasso*—literally the "fat people." In 1293, the *popolo grasso* assumed a dominant role in government by establishing a new constitution known as the Ordinances of Justice. It provided for a republican government controlled by the seven major guilds of the city, which represented the interests of the wealthier classes. Executive power was vested in the hands of a council of elected priors (the *signoria*) and a standard-bearer of justice called the *gonfaloniere,* assisted by a number of councils with advisory and overlapping powers. Near the mid-fourteenth century, revolutionary activity by the *popolo minuto,* the small shopkeepers and artisans, won them a share in the government. Even greater expansion occurred briefly when the *ciompi,* or industrial wool workers, were allowed to be represented in the government after their revolt in 1378. Only four years later, however, a counterrevolution brought the "fat people" back into virtual control of the government. After 1382, the Florentine government was controlled by a small merchant oligarchy that manipulated the supposedly republican government. By that time, Florence had also been successful in a series of wars against its neighbors. It had conquered most of Tuscany and established itself as a major territorial state in northern Italy.

**Republic of Venice** The other major northern Italian state was the republic of Venice, which had grown rich from commercial activity throughout the eastern Mediterranean and into northern Europe. A large number of merchant families became extremely wealthy. In the constitution of 1297, these patricians took control of the republic. In this year, the Great Council, the source of all political power, was closed to all but the members of about two hundred families. Since all other magistrates of the city were chosen either from or by this council, these families now formed a hereditary patriciate that completely dominated the city. Although the doge (or duke) had been the executive head of the

republic since the Early Middle Ages, by 1300 he had become largely a figurehead. Actual power was vested in the hands of the Great Council and the legislative body known as the Senate, while an extraordinary body known as the Council of Ten, first formed in 1310, came to be the real executive power of the state. Venetian government was respected by contemporaries for its stability. A sixteenth- century Italian historian noted that Venice had "the best government of any city not only in our own times but also in the classical world."[11]

In the fourteenth century, Venice also embarked on a policy of expansion. By the end of the century, it had created a commercial empire by establishing colonies and trading posts in the eastern Mediterranean and Black Sea as well as continuing its commercial monopolies in the Byzantine Empire. At the same time, Venice began to conquer the territory adjoining it in northern Italy.

The States of Italy in the Fourteenth Century

# The Decline of the Church

The papacy of the Roman Catholic church reached the height of its power in the thirteenth century. Theories of papal supremacy included a doctrine of "fullness of power" as the spiritual head of Christendom and claims to universal temporal authority over all secular rulers. But papal claims of temporal supremacy were increasingly out of step with the growing secular monarchies of Europe and ultimately brought the papacy into a conflict with the territorial states that it was unable to win.

## Boniface VIII and the Conflict with the State

The struggle between the papacy and the secular monarchies began during the pontificate of Pope Boniface VIII (1294–1303). One major issue appeared to be at stake between the pope and King Philip IV (1285–1314) of France. In his desire to acquire new revenues, Philip claimed the right to tax the French clergy. Boniface VIII responded that the clergy of any state could not pay taxes to their secular ruler without the pope's consent. Underlying this issue, however, was a basic conflict between the claims of the papacy to universal authority over both church and state, which necessitated complete control over the clergy, and the claims of the king that all subjects, including the clergy, were under the jurisdiction of the crown and subject to the king's authority on matters of taxation and justice. In short, the fundamental issue was the universal sovereignty of the papacy versus the royal sovereignty of the monarch.

Boniface VIII asserted his position in a series of papal bulls or letters, the most important of which was *Unam Sanctam*, issued in 1302. It was the strongest statement ever made by a pope on the supremacy of the spiritual authority over the temporal authority (see the box on p. 301).

When it became apparent that the pope had decided to act on his principles by excommunicating Philip IV, the latter sent a small contingent of French forces to capture Boniface and bring him back to France for trial. The pope was captured in Anagni, although Italian nobles from the surrounding countryside soon rescued him. The shock of this experience, however, soon led to the pope's death. Philip's strong-arm tactics had produced a clear victory for the national monarchy over the papacy, and no later pope has dared renew the extravagant claims of Boniface VIII.

To ensure his position and avoid any future papal threat, Philip IV brought enough pressure to bear on the college of cardinals to achieve the election of a Frenchman as pope in 1305, Clement V (1305–1314). Using the excuse of turbulence in the city of Rome, the new pope took up residence in Avignon on the east bank of the Rhône River. Although Avignon was located in the Holy Roman Empire and was not a French possession, it lay just across the river from the territory of King Philip IV. Clement may have intended to return to Rome, but he and his successors remained in Avignon for the next seventy-two years, thereby creating yet another crisis for the church.

## The Papacy at Avignon (1305–1377)

The residency of the popes in Avignon for most of the fourteenth century led to a decline in papal prestige and growing antipapal sentiment. The city of Rome was the traditional capital of the universal church. The pope was the bishop of Rome, and his position was based on being the successor to the Apostle Peter, traditionally considered the first bishop of Rome. It was unseemly that the head of the Catholic church should reside elsewhere. In the 1330s, the popes began to construct a stately palace in Avignon, a clear indication that they intended to stay for some time.

Other factors also led to a decline in papal prestige during the Avignonese residency. It was widely believed that the popes at Avignon were captives of the French monarchy. Although questionable, since Avignon did not belong to the French monarchy, it was easy to believe in view of Avignon's proximity to French lands. Moreover, during the seventy-two years of the Avignonese papacy, of the 134 new cardinals created by the popes, 113 were French.

The papal residency at Avignon was also an important turning point in the church's attempt to adapt itself to the changing economic and political conditions of Europe.

**Pope Boniface VIII.** The conflict between church and state in the Middle Ages reached its height in the struggle between Pope Boniface VIII and Philip IV of France. This fourteenth-century miniature depicts Boniface VIII presiding over a gathering of cardinals.

# BONIFACE VIII'S DEFENSE OF PAPAL SUPREMACY

*O*NE OF THE MOST REMARKABLE documents of the fourteenth century was the exaggerated statement of papal supremacy issued by Pope Boniface VIII in 1302 in the heat of his conflict with the French king Philip IV. Ironically, this strongest statement ever made of papal supremacy was issued at a time when the rising power of the secular monarchies made it increasingly difficult for the premises to be accepted.

### Pope Boniface VIII, *Unam Sanctam*

We are compelled, our faith urging us, to believe and to hold—and we do firmly believe and simply confess—that there is one holy catholic and apostolic church, outside of which there is neither salvation nor remission of sins. . . . In this church there is one Lord, one faith and one baptism. . . . Therefore, of this one and only church there is one body and one head . . . Christ, namely, and the vicar of Christ, St. Peter, and the successor of Peter. For the Lord himself said to Peter, feed my sheep. . . .

We are told by the word of the gospel that in this His fold there are two swords—a spiritual, namely, and a temporal. . . . Both swords, the spiritual and the material, therefore, are in the power of the church; the one, indeed, to be wielded for the church, the other by the church; the one by the hand of the priest, the other by the hand of kings and knights, but at the will and sufferance of the priest. One sword, moreover, ought to be under the other, and the temporal authority to be subjected to the spiritual. . . .

Therefore if the earthly power err it shall be judged by the spiritual power; but if the lesser spiritual power err, by the greater. But if the greatest, it can be judged by God alone, not by man, the apostle bearing witness. A spiritual man judges all things, but he himself is judged by no one. This authority, moreover, even though it is given to man and exercised through man, is not human but rather divine, being given by divine lips to Peter and founded on a rock for him and his successors through Christ himself whom he has confessed; the Lord himself saying to Peter: "Whatsoever you shall bind, etc." Whoever, therefore, resists this power thus ordained by God, resists the ordination of God. . . .

Indeed, we declare, announce and define, that it is altogether necessary to salvation for every human creature to be subject to the Roman pontiff.

---

Like the growing monarchical states, the popes centralized their administration by developing a specialized bureaucracy. In fact, the papal bureaucracy in the fourteenth century under the leadership of the pope and college of cardinals became the most sophisticated administrative system in the medieval world.

At the same time, the popes attempted to find new sources of revenue to compensate for their loss of income from the Papal States and began to impose new taxes on the clergy. Furthermore, the splendor in which the pope and cardinals were living in Avignon led to a highly vocal criticism of both clergy and papacy in the fourteenth century. Avignon had become a powerful symbol of abuses within the church, and many people began to call for the pope's return to Rome.

One of the most prominent calls came from Catherine of Siena (c. 1347–1380), whose saintly demeanor and claims of visions from God led the city of Florence to send her on a mission to Pope Gregory XI (1370–1378) in Avignon. She told the pope, "Because God has given you authority and because you have accepted it, you ought to use your virtue and power; if you do not wish to use it, it might be better for you to resign what you have accepted; it would give more honor to God and health to your soul."[12]

### The Great Schism

Catherine of Siena's admonition seemed to be heeded in 1377, when at long last Pope Gregory XI, perceiving the disastrous decline in papal prestige, returned to Rome. He died soon afterward, however, in the spring of 1378. When the college of cardinals met in conclave to elect a new pope, the citizens of Rome, fearful that the French majority would choose another Frenchman who would return the papacy to Avignon, threatened that the cardinals would not leave Rome alive unless a Roman or at least an Italian were elected pope. Indeed, the guards of the conclave warned the cardinals that they "ran the risk of being torn in pieces" if they did not choose an Italian. Wisely, the terrified cardinals duly elected the Italian archbishop of Bari, who was subsequently crowned as Pope Urban VI (1378–1389) on Easter Sunday. Following his election, Urban VI made clear his plans to reform the papal curia and even to swamp the college of cardinals with enough new Italian cardinals to eliminate the French majority. After many of the cardinals (the French ones) withdrew from Rome in late summer and were finally free of the Roman mob, they issued a manifesto, saying that they had been coerced by the mob and that Urban's election was therefore null and void. The dissenting cardinals thereupon chose one of their number,

**Avignon**

a Frenchman, who took the title of Clement VII and promptly returned to Avignon. Since Urban remained in Rome, there were now two popes, initiating what has been called the **Great Schism** of the church.

Europe's loyalties soon became divided: France, Spain, Scotland, and southern Italy supported Clement, while England, Germany, Scandinavia, and most of Italy supported Urban. These divisions generally followed political lines and reflected the bitter division between the English and the French in the Hundred Years' War. Because the French supported the Avignonese pope, so did their allies; their enemies, particularly England and its allies, supported the Roman pope. The need for political support caused both popes to subordinate their policies to the policies of these states.

The Great Schism lasted for nearly forty years and had a baleful effect on the Catholic church and Christendom in general. The schism greatly aggravated the financial abuses that had developed within the church during the Avignonese papacy. Two papal administrative systems (with only one-half the accustomed revenues) worked to increase taxation. At the same time, the schism badly damaged the faith of Christian believers. The pope was widely believed to be the leader of Christendom and, as Boniface VIII had pointed out, held the keys to the kingdom of heaven. Since each line of popes denounced the other as the Antichrist, such a spectacle could not help but undermine the institution that had become the very foundation of the church.

## New Thoughts on Church and State and the Rise of Conciliarism

As dissatisfaction with the papacy grew, so did the calls for a revolutionary approach to solving the church's institutional problems. One of the most systematic was provided by Marsiglio of Padua (c. 1270–1342), rector of the University of Paris and author of a remarkable book, *Defender of the Peace*.

Marsiglio denied that the temporal authority was subject to the spiritual authority, as popes from Innocent III to Boniface VIII had maintained. Instead, he argued that the church was only one element of society and must confine itself solely to spiritual functions. Furthermore, Marsiglio argued, the church was a community of the faithful in which all authority is ultimately derived from the entire community. The clergy hold no special authority from God but serve only to administer the affairs of the church on behalf of all Christians. Final authority in spiritual matters must reside not with the pope but with a general church council representing all members.

**The Conciliar Movement**   The Great Schism led large numbers of churchmen to take up this theory, known as **conciliarism,** in the belief that only a general council of the church could end the schism and bring reform to the church in its "head and members." The only serious issue left to be decided was who should call the council. Church law held that only a pope could convene a council. Profes-

sors of theology argued, however, that since the competing popes would not do so, either members of the church hierarchy or even secular princes, especially the Holy Roman Emperor, could convene a council to settle all relevant issues.

In desperation, a group of cardinals from both camps finally convened a general council on their own. This Council of Pisa, which met in 1409, deposed the two popes and elected a new one, Alexander V. The council's action proved disastrous when the two deposed popes refused to step down. There were now three popes, and the church seemed more hopelessly divided than ever.

Leadership in convening a new council now passed to the Holy Roman Emperor, Sigismund. As a result of his efforts, a new ecumenical church council met at Constance from 1414 to 1418. Ending the schism proved a surprisingly easy task: after the three competing popes either resigned or were deposed, a new conclave elected Cardinal Oddone Colonna, a member of a prominent Roman family, as Pope Martin V (1417–1431). The Great Schism had finally been ended.

## Popular Religion in an Age of Adversity

The concern of popes and leading clerics with finances and power during the struggles of Boniface VIII, the Avignonese papacy, and the Great Schism could not help but lead to a decline in prestige and respect for the institutional church, especially the papacy. At the same time, in the fourteenth century, the Black Death and its recurrences made an important impact on the religious life of ordinary Christians by heightening their preoccupation with death and salvation. The church often failed to provide sufficient spiritual comfort as many parish priests fled from the plague.

Christians responded in different ways to the adversities of the fourteenth century. First of all, there was a tendency to stress the performance of good works, including acts of charity, as a means of ensuring salvation. Bequests to hospitals and other charitable foundations increased. Family chapels were established, served by priests whose primary responsibility was to say Mass for the good of the souls of deceased family members. These chapels became even more significant as the importance of purgatory rose.

Purgatory was defined by the church as the place where souls went after death to be purged of punishment for sins committed in life. In effect, the soul was purified in purgatory before it ascended into heaven. It was believed that like indulgences, prayers and private Masses for the dead could shorten the amount of time souls spent in purgatory.

All of these developments were part of a larger trend—a new emphasis in late medieval Christianity on a mechanical path to salvation. Chalking up good deeds to ensure salvation was done in numerous ways but was nowhere more evident than in the growing emphasis on indulgences. We should also note that pilgrimages, which became increasingly popular, and charitable contributions were good works that could be accomplished without the involvement of clerics, a reflection of the loss of faith in the institutional church and its clergy and another noticeable feature of popular religious life. At the same time, interest in Christianity itself did not decline. Indeed, people sought to play a more active role in their own salvation. This is particularly evident in the popularity of mysticism and lay piety in the fourteenth century.

**Mysticism and Lay Piety**   The mysticism of the fourteenth century was certainly not new, for Christians throughout the Middle Ages had claimed to have had mystical experiences. Simply defined, **mysticism** is the immediate experience of oneness with God. It is this experience that characterized the teaching of Meister Eckhart (1260–1327), who sparked a mystical movement in western Germany. Eckhart was a well-educated Dominican theologian who wrote learned Latin works on theology, but he was also a popular preacher whose message on the union of the soul with God was typical of mysticism. According to Eckhart, such a union was attainable by all who pursued it wholeheartedly.

Eckhart's movement spread from Germany into the Low Countries, where it took on a new form, called the **Modern Devotion,** founded by Gerard Groote (1340–1384). After a religious conversion, Groote entered a monastery for several years of contemplation before reentering the world. His messages were typical of a practical mysticism. To achieve true spiritual communion with God, people must imitate Jesus and lead lives dedicated to serving the needs of their fellow human beings. Groote emphasized a simple inner piety and morality based on Scripture and an avoidance of the complexities of theology.

Eventually, Groote attracted a group of followers who came to be known as the Brothers of the Common Life. From this small beginning, a movement developed that spread through the Netherlands and back into Germany. Houses of the Brothers, as well as separate houses for women (Sisters of the Common Life), were founded in one city after another. The Sisters and Brothers of the Common Life did not constitute regular religious orders. They were laypeople who took no formal monastic vows but were nevertheless regulated by quasi-monastic rules that they imposed on their own communities. They also established schools throughout Germany and the Netherlands in which they stressed their message of imitating the life of Jesus by serving others. The Brothers and Sisters of the Common Life attest to the vitality of spiritual life among lay Christians in the fourteenth century.

**Unique Female Mystical Experiences**   A number of female mystics had their own unique spiritual experiences. For them, fasting and receiving the Eucharist (the communion wafer that supposedly contains the body of Jesus) became the mainstay of their religious practices. Catherine of Siena, for example, gave up eating any solid food at the age of twenty-three and thereafter lived only on cold water and herbs that she sucked and then spat out. Her primary nourishment, however, came from the Eucharist. She wrote: "The immaculate lamb [Christ] is food, table, and servant. . . . And we who eat at that table become like the food [that is, Christ], acting not for our own utility but for the honor of God and the salvation of neighbor."[13] For Catherine and a number of other female mystics, reception of the Eucharist was their primary instrument in achieving a mystical union with God.

## Changes in Theology

The fourteenth century presented challenges not only to the institutional church but also to its theological framework, especially evidenced in the questioning of the grand synthesis attempted by Thomas Aquinas. In the thirteenth century, Aquinas's grand synthesis of faith and reason was not widely accepted outside his own Dominican order. At the same time, differences with Aquinas were kept within a framework of commonly accepted scholastic thought. In the fourteenth century, however, the philosopher William of Occam (1285–1329) posed a severe challenge to the scholastic achievements of the High Middle Ages.

Occam posited a radical interpretation of nominalism. He asserted that all universals or general concepts were simply names and that only individual objects perceived by the senses were real. Although the mind was capable of analyzing individual objects, it could not establish any truths about the nature of external, higher reality. Reason could not be used to substantiate spiritual truths. It could not, for example, prove the statement "God exists." For William of Occam as a Christian believer, this did not mean that God did not exist, however. It simply indicated that the truths of religion were not demonstrable by reason but could only be known by an act of faith. The acceptance of Occam's nominalist philosophy at the University of Paris brought an element of uncertainty to late medieval theology by seriously weakening the synthesis of faith and reason that had characterized the theological thought of the High Middle Ages. Nevertheless, Occam's emphasis on using reason to analyze the observable phenomena of the world had an important impact on the development of physical science by creating support for rational and scientific analysis. Some late medieval theologians came to accept the compatibility of rational analysis of the material world with mystical acceptance of spiritual truths.

# The Cultural World of the Fourteenth Century

The cultural life of the fourteenth century was also characterized by ferment. In literature, several writers used their vernacular languages to produce notable works. In art, the Black Death and other problems of the century left their mark as many artists turned to morbid themes, but the period also produced Giotto, whose paintings expressed a new realism that would be developed further by the artists of the next century.

## The Development of Vernacular Literature

Although Latin remained the language of the church liturgy and the official documents of both church and state throughout Europe, the fourteenth century witnessed the rapid growth of vernacular literature, especially in Italy. The development of an Italian vernacular literature was mostly the result of the efforts of three writers in the fourteenth century: Dante, Petrarch, and Boccaccio. Their use of the Tuscan dialect common in Florence and its surrounding countryside ensured that it would prevail as the basis of the modern Italian language.

**Dante**    Dante Alighieri (1265–1321) came from an old Florentine noble family that had fallen on hard times. Although he had held high political office in republican Florence, factional conflict led to his exile from the city in 1302. Until the end of his life, Dante hoped to return to his beloved Florence, but his wish remained unfulfilled.

Dante's masterpiece in the Italian vernacular was the *Divine Comedy,* written between 1313 and 1321. Cast in a typical medieval framework, the *Divine Comedy* is basically the story of the soul's progression to salvation, a fundamental medieval preoccupation. The lengthy poem was divided into three major sections corresponding to the realms of the afterworld: hell, purgatory, and heaven or paradise. In the "Inferno" (see the box on p. 305), Dante is led by his guide, the classical author Virgil, who is a symbol of human reason. But Virgil (or reason) can lead the poet only so far on his journey. At the end of "Purgatory," Beatrice (the true love of Dante's life), who represents revelation—which alone can explain the mysteries of heaven—becomes his guide into "Paradise." Here Beatrice presents Dante to Saint Bernard, a symbol of mystical contemplation. The saint turns Dante over to the Virgin Mary, since grace is necessary to achieve the final step of entering the presence of God, where one beholds "the love that moves the sun and the other stars."[14]

**Petrarch**    Like Dante, Francesco Petrarca, known as Petrarch (1304–1374), was a Florentine who spent much of his life outside his native city. Petrarch's role in the revival of the classics made him a seminal figure in the literary Italian Renaissance (see Chapter 12). His primary contribution to the development of the Italian vernacular was made in his sonnets. He is considered one of the greatest European lyric poets. His sonnets were inspired by his love for a married lady named Laura, whom he had met in 1327. While honoring an idealized female figure was a long-standing medieval tradition, Laura was very human and not just an ideal. She was a real woman with whom Petrarch was involved for a long time. He poured forth his lamentations in sonnet after sonnet:

> I am as tired of thinking as my thought
> Is never tired to find itself in you,
> And of not yet leaving this life that brought
> Me the too heavy weight of signs and rue;
>
> And because to describe your hair and face
> And the fair eyes of which I always speak,
> Language and sound have not become too weak
> And day and night your name they still embrace.
>
> And tired because my feet do not yet fail
> After following you in every part,
> Wasting so many steps without avail,
>
> From whence derive the paper and the ink
> That I have filled with you; if I should sink,
> It is the fault of Love, not of my art.[15]

In analyzing every aspect of the unrequited lover's feelings, Petrarch appeared less concerned to sing his lady's praise than to immortalize his own thoughts. This interest in his own personality reveals a sense of individuality stronger than in any previous medieval literature.

**Boccaccio**    Although he too wrote poetry, Giovanni Boccaccio (1313–1375) is known primarily for his prose. Another Florentine, he also used the Tuscan dialect. While working for the Bardi banking house in Naples, he fell in love with a noble lady whom he called his Fiammetta, his Little Flame. Under her inspiration, Boccaccio began to write prose romances. His best-known work, the *Decameron,* however, was not written until after he had returned to Florence. The *Decameron* is set at the time of the Black Death. Ten young people flee to a villa outside Florence to escape the plague and decide to while away the time by telling stories. Although the stories are not new and still reflect the acceptance of basic Christian values, Boccaccio does present the society of his time from a secular point of view. It is the seducer of women, not the knight or philosopher or pious monk, who is the real hero. Perhaps, as some historians have argued, the *Decameron* reflects the immediate easygoing, cynical postplague values. Boccaccio's later work certainly became gloomier and more pessimistic; as he grew older, he even rejected his earlier work as irrelevant. He commented in a 1373 letter, "I am certainly not pleased that you have allowed the illustrious women in your house to read my trifles. . . . You know how much in them is less than decent and opposed to modesty, how much stimulation to wanton lust, how many things that drive to lust even those most fortified against it."[16]

**Chaucer**    Another leading vernacular author was Geoffrey Chaucer (c. 1340–1400), who brought a new level of sophistication to the English vernacular language in his

# DANTE'S VISION OF HELL

THE *DIVINE COMEDY* of Dante Alighieri is regarded as one of the greatest literary works of all time. Many consider it the supreme summary of medieval thought. It combines allegory with a remarkable amount of contemporary history. Indeed, forty-three of the seventy-nine people consigned to hell in the "Inferno" were Florentines. This excerpt is taken from canto 18 of the "Inferno," in which Dante and Virgil visit the eighth circle of hell, which is divided into ten trenches containing the souls of people who had committed malicious frauds on their fellow human beings.

### Dante, "Inferno," *Divine Comedy*

We had already come to where the walk
crosses the second bank, from which it lifts
another arch, spanning from rock to rock.

Here we heard people whine in the next chasm,
and knock and thump themselves with open palms,
and blubber through their snouts as if in a spasm.

Steaming from that pit, a vapor rose
over the banks, crusting them with a slime
that sickened my eyes and hammered at my nose.

That chasm sinks so deep we could not sight
its bottom anywhere until we climbed
along the rock arch to its greatest height.

Once there, I peered down; and I saw long lines
of people in a river of excrement
that seemed the overflow of the world's latrines.

I saw among the felons of that pit
one wraith who might or might not have been tonsured—
one could not tell, he was so smeared with shit.

He bellowed: "You there, why do you stare at me
more than at all the others in this stew?"
And I to him: "Because if memory

serves me, I knew you when your hair was dry.
You are Alessio Interminelli da Lucca.
That's why I pick you from this filthy fry."

And he then, beating himself on his clown's head:
"Down to this have the flatteries I sold
the living sunk me here among the dead."

And my Guide prompted then: "Lean forward a bit
and look beyond him, there—do you see that one
scratching herself with dungy nails, the strumpet

who fidgets to her feet, then to a crouch?
It is the whore Thäis who told her lover
when he sent to ask her, 'Do you thank me much?'

'Much? Nay, past all believing!' And with this
Let us turn from the sight of this abyss."

---

famous *Canterbury Tales*. His beauty of expression and clear, forceful language were important in transforming his East Midland dialect into the chief ancestor of the modern English language. *The Canterbury Tales* is a collection of stories told by a group of twenty-nine pilgrims journeying from the London suburb of Southwark to the tomb of Saint Thomas à Becket at Canterbury. This format gave Chaucer the chance to portray an entire range of English society, both high- and low-born. Among others, he presented the Knight, the Yeoman, the Prioress, the Monk, the Merchant, the Student, the Lawyer, the Carpenter, the Cook, the Doctor, the Plowman, and, of course, "A Good Wife was there from beside the city of Bath—a little deaf, which was a pity." The stories these pilgrims told to while away the time on the journey were just as varied as the storytellers themselves: knightly romances, fairy tales, saints' lives, sophisticated satires, and crude anecdotes.

Chaucer also used some of his characters to criticize the corruption of the church in the late medieval period. His portrayal of the Friar leaves no doubt of Chaucer's disdain for the corrupt practices of clerics. Of the Friar, he says:

He knew the taverns well in every town.
The barmaids and innkeepers pleased his mind
Better than beggars and lepers and their kind.[17]

And yet Chaucer was still a pious Christian, never doubting basic Christian doctrines and remaining optimistic that the church could be reformed.

**Christine de Pizan**   One of the extraordinary vernacular writers of the age was Christine de Pizan (c. 1364–1430). Because of her father's position at the court of Charles V of France, she received a good education. Her husband died when she was only twenty-five (they had been married for ten years), leaving her with little income and three small children and her mother to support. Christine took the unusual step of becoming a writer in order to earn her living. Her poems were soon in demand, and by 1400 she had achieved financial security.

Christine de Pizan is best known, however, for her French prose works written in defense of women. In *The Book of the City of Ladies*, written in 1404, she denounced the many male writers who had argued that women needed to be controlled by men because women by their very nature were prone to evil, unable to learn, and easily swayed. With the help of Reason, Righteousness, and Justice, who appear to her in a vision, Christine refutes these antifeminist attacks. Women, she argues, are not evil by nature, and they could learn as well as men if they were permitted to attend the same schools: "Should I also tell you whether a woman's nature is clever and quick enough to

**The Vision of Christine de Pizan.** Christine de Pizan is one of the extraordinary vernacular writers of the late fourteenth and early fifteenth centuries. She is pictured here in a cover illustration from her *Book of the City of Ladies,* which depicts Reason, Righteousness, and Justice appearing to Christine in a dream.

learn speculative sciences as well as to discover them, and likewise the manual arts. I assure you that women are equally well-suited and skilled to carry them out and to put them to sophisticated use once they have learned them."[18] Much of the book includes a detailed discussion of women from the past and present who have distinguished themselves as leaders, warriors, wives, mothers, and martyrs for their religious faith. She ends by encouraging women to defend themselves against the attacks of men, who are incapable of understanding them.

## Art and the Black Death

The fourteenth century produced an artistic outburst in new directions as well as a large body of morbid work influenced by the Black Death and the recurrences of the plague. The city of Florence witnessed the first dramatic break with medieval tradition in the work of Giotto (1266–1337), often considered a forerunner of Italian Renaissance painting. Born into a peasant family, Giotto acquired his painting skills in a workshop in Florence. Although he worked throughout Italy, his most famous works were done in Padua and Florence. Coming out of the formal Byzantine school, Giotto transcended it with a new kind of realism, a desire to imitate nature that Renaissance artists later identified as the basic component of classical art. Giotto's figures were solid and rounded; placed realistically in relationship to each other and their background, they conveyed three-dimensional depth. The expressive faces and physically realistic bodies gave his sacred figures human qualities with which spectators could identify. Although Giotto had no direct successors, Florentine painting in the early fifteenth century pursued even more dramatically the new direction his work represents.

**Giotto, *Lamentation*.** The work of Giotto marked the first clear innovation in fourteenth-century painting, making him a forerunner of the early Renaissance. This fresco was part of a series done on the walls of the Arena chapel in Padua begun in 1305. Giotto painted thirty-eight scenes on three levels: the lives of Mary, the mother of Jesus, and her parents (top panel); the life and work of Jesus (middle panel); and his passion, crucifixion, and resurrection (bottom panel). Shown here from the bottom panel is the *Lamentation.* A group of Jesus' followers, including his mother and Mary Magdalene, mourn over the body of Jesus before it is placed in its tomb. The solidity of Giotto's human figures gives them a three-dimensional sense. He also captured the grief and despair felt by the mourners.

The Black Death made a visible impact on art. For one thing, it wiped out entire guilds of artists. At the same time, survivors, including the newly rich who patronized artists, were no longer so optimistic. Some were more guilty about enjoying life and more concerned about gaining salvation. Postplague art began to concentrate on pain and death. A fairly large number of artistic works came to exhibit a morbid concern with death, depicting coffins, decomposing bodies, and grim figures of Death, sometimes in the form of a witch flying through the air swinging a large scythe.

# Society in an Age of Adversity

In the midst of disaster, the fourteenth century proved creative in its own way. New inventions made an impact on daily life at the same time that the effects of plague were felt in many areas of medieval urban life.

## Changes in Urban Life

One immediate by-product of the Black Death was greater regulation of urban activities. Authorities tried to keep cities cleaner by enacting new ordinances against waste products in the streets. Viewed as unhealthy places, bathhouses were closed down, leading to a noticeable decline in personal cleanliness. Efforts at regulation also affected the practice of female prostitution.

Medieval society had tolerated prostitution as a lesser evil: it was better for males to frequent prostitutes than to seduce virgins or married women. Since many males in medieval towns married late, the demand for prostitutes was high and was met by a regular supply, derived no doubt from the need of many poor girls and women to survive. The recession of the fourteenth century probably increased the supply of prostitutes, while the new hedonism prevalent after the Black Death also increased demand. As a result, cities intensified their regulation of prostitution.

By organizing brothels, city authorities could supervise as well as tax prostitutes. Officials granted charters to citizens who were allowed to set up brothels, provided they were located only in certain areas of town. Prostitutes were also expected to wear special items of clothing—such as red hats—to distinguish them from other women.

**Family Life and Sex Roles in Late Medieval Cities** The basic unit of the late medieval town was the nuclear family of husband, wife, and children. Especially in wealthier families, there might also be servants, apprentices, and other relatives, including widowed mothers and the husband's illegitimate children.

Before the Black Death, late marriages were common for urban couples. It was not unusual for husbands to be in their late thirties or forties and wives in their early twenties. The expense of setting up a household probably necessitated the delay in marriage. But the situation changed dramatically after the plague, reflecting new economic

opportunities for the survivors and a new reluctance to postpone living in the presence of so much death.

The economic difficulties of the fourteenth century also had a tendency to strengthen the development of sex roles and to set new limits on employment opportunities for women. Based on the authority of Aristotle, Thomas Aquinas and other scholastic theologians had advanced the belief that according to the natural order, men were active and domineering while women were passive and submissive. As more and more lawyers, doctors, and priests, who had been trained in universities where these notions were taught, entered society, these ideas about the different natures of men and women became widely accepted. This was evident in legal systems, many of which limited the legal capacity of women (see the box on p. 308). Increasingly, women were expected to give up any active functions in society and remain subject to direction from males. A fourteenth-century Parisian provost commented that among glass cutters, "no master's widow who keeps working at his craft after her husband's death may take on apprentices, for the men of the craft do not believe that a woman can master it well enough to teach a child to master it, for the craft is a very delicate one."[19] Although this statement suggests that some women were, in fact, running businesses, it also reveals that they were viewed as incapable of undertaking all of men's activities. Europeans in the fourteenth century imposed a division of labor roles between men and women that persisted until the Industrial Revolution.

**Medieval Children** Parents in the High and Later Middle Ages invested considerable resources and affection in rearing their children. The dramatic increase in specialized roles that accompanied the spread of commerce and the growth of cities demanded a commitment to educating children in the marketable skills needed for the new occupations. Philip of Navarre noted in the twelfth century that boys ought to be taught a trade "as soon as possible. Those who early become and long remain apprentices ought to be the best masters."[20] Some cities provided schools to educate the young. A chronicler in Florence related that between eight and ten thousand boys and girls between the ages of six and twelve attended the city's grammar schools, a figure that probably represented half of all school-aged children. Although grammar school completed education for girls, around eleven hundred boys went on to six secondary schools that prepared them for business careers, while another six hundred studied Latin and logic in four other schools that readied them for university training and a career in medicine, law, or the church. In the High Middle Ages, then, urban communities demonstrated a commitment to the training of the young.

As a result of the devastating effects of the plague and its recurrences, these same communities became concerned about investing in the survival and health of children. Although a number of hospitals existed in both Florence and Rome in the fourteenth century, it was not until the 1420s and 1430s that hospitals were established that catered

# THE LEGAL RIGHTS OF WOMEN

URING THE HIGH AND Later Middle Ages, as women were increasingly viewed as weak beings who were unable to play independent roles, legal systems also began to limit the rights of women. These excerpts are taken from a variety of legal opinions in France, England, and a number of Italian cities.

### Excerpts from Legal Opinions

FRANCE, 1270: No married woman can go to court . . . unless someone has abused or beaten her, in which case she may go to court without her husband. If she is a tradeswoman, she can sue and defend herself in matters connected with her business, but not otherwise.

ENGLAND [probably fifteenth century]: Every Feme Covert [married woman] is a sort of infant. . . . It is seldom, almost never that a married woman can have any action to use her wit only in her own name: her husband is her stern, her prime mover, without whom she cannot do much at home, and less abroad. . . . It is a miracle that a wife should commit any suit without her husband.

ENGLAND [probably fifteenth century]: The very goods which a man gives to his wife, are still his own, her chain, her bracelets, her apparel, are all the goodman's goods. . . . A wife however gallant she be, glitters but in the riches of her husband, as the moon has no light but it is the sun's. . . . For thus it is, if before marriage the woman was possessed of horses . . . , sheep, corn, wool, money, plate and jewels, all manner of movable substance is presently . . . the husband's to sell, keep or bequeath if she die.

PESARO, ITALY [exact date unknown]: No wife can make a contract without the consent of her husband.

FLORENCE, ITALY, 1415: A married woman with children cannot draw up a last will in her own right, nor dispose of her dowry among the living to the detriment of husband and children.

LUCCA, ITALY [exact date unknown]: No married woman . . . can seal or give away [anything] unless she has the agreement of her husband and nearest [male] relative.

---

only to the needs of foundlings, supporting them until boys could be taught a trade and girls could marry.

### New Directions in Medicine

The medical community comprised a number of functionaries. At the top of the medical hierarchy were the physicians, usually clergymen, who received their education in the universities, where they studied ancient authorities, such as Hippocrates and Galen. As a result, physicians were highly trained in theory but had little or no clinical practice. By the fourteenth century, they were educated in six chief medical schools—Salerno, Montpellier, Bologna, Oxford, Padua, and Paris. Paris was regarded as the most prestigious.

The preplague medicine of university-trained physicians was theoretically grounded in the classical Greek theory of the "four humors," each connected to a particular organ: blood (from the heart), phlegm (from the brain), yellow bile (from the liver), and black bile (from the spleen). The four humors corresponded in turn to the four elemental qualities of the universe, earth (black bile), air (blood), fire (yellow bile), and water (phlegm), making a human being a microcosm of the cosmos. Good health resulted from a perfect balance of the four humors; sickness meant that the humors were out of balance. The task of the medieval physician was to restore proper order by a number of cures, such as rest, diet, herbal medicines, or bloodletting.

Beneath the physicians in the hierarchy of the medical profession stood the surgeons, whose activities included performing operations, setting broken bones, and bleeding patients. Their knowledge was based largely on practical experience. Below surgeons were midwives, who delivered babies, and barber-surgeons, who were less trained than surgeons and performed menial tasks such as bloodletting and setting simple bone fractures. Barber-surgeons supplemented their income by shaving and cutting hair and pulling teeth. Apothecaries also constituted part of the medical establishment. They filled herbal prescriptions recommended by physicians and also prescribed drugs on their own authority.

All of these medical practitioners proved unable to deal with the plague. When King Philip VI of France requested the opinion of the medical faculty of the University of Paris on the plague, their advice proved worthless. This failure to understand the Black Death, however, produced a crisis in medieval medicine that resulted in some new approaches to health care.

One result was the rise of surgeons to greater prominence because of their practical knowledge. Surgeons were now recruited by universities, which placed them on an equal level with physicians and introduced a greater emphasis on practical anatomy into the university curriculum. Connected to this was a burgeoning of medical textbooks, often written in the vernacular and stressing practical, how-to approaches to medical and surgical problems.

**Medieval Children at Play.** Like children in all ages, medieval children joined with other children in playing a variety of games. Play, as we know, is important to the development of children as it helps them cultivate their physical and mental abilities. In the Middle Ages, a number of writers on children saw play as a basic symbol of childhood itself. In this series of illustrations from a medieval manuscript in the Bodleian Library in Oxford, we see children riding hobbyhorses (undoubtedly popular in a society dependent on horses), shooting arrows at a target, and engaged in throwing snowballs.

**A Medical Textbook.** This illustration is taken from a fourteenth-century surgical textbook that stressed a how-to approach to surgical problems. *Top left,* a surgeon shows how to remove an arrow from a patient; *top right,* how to open a patient's chest; *bottom left,* how to deal with an injury to the intestines; *bottom right,* how to diagnose an abscess.

Finally, as a result of the plague, cities, especially in Italy, gave increased attention to public health and sanitation. Public health laws were instituted, and municipal boards of health came into being. The primary concern of the latter was to prevent plague, but gradually they came to control almost every aspect of health and sanitation. Boards of public health, consisting of medical practitioners and public officials, were empowered to enforce sanitary conditions, report on and attempt to isolate epidemics by quarantine (rarely successful), and regulate the activities of doctors.

## Inventions and New Patterns

Despite its problems, the fourteenth century witnessed a continuation of the technological innovations that had characterized the High Middle Ages.

**The Clock**    The most extraordinary of these inventions, and one that made a visible impact on European cities, was the clock. The mechanical clock was invented at the end of the thirteenth century but not perfected until the fourteenth. The time-telling clock was actually a by-product of a larger astronomical clock. The best-designed one was constructed by Giovanni di Dondi in the mid-fourteenth century. Dondi's clock contained the signs of the zodiac but also struck on the hour. Since clocks were expensive, they were usually installed only in the towers of churches or municipal buildings. The first clock striking equal hours was in a church in Milan; in 1335, a chronicler described it as "a wonderful clock, with a very large clapper which strikes a bell twenty-four times according to the twenty-four hours of the day and night and thus at the first hour of the night gives one sound, at the second two strikes . . . and so distinguishes one hour from another, which is of greatest use to men of every degree."[21]

Clocks introduced a wholly new conception of time into the lives of Europeans; they revolutionized how people thought about and used time. Throughout most of the Middle Ages, time was determined by natural rhythms (daybreak and nightfall) or church bells that were rung at more or less regular three-hour intervals, corresponding to the ecclesiastical offices of the church. Clocks made it possible to plan one's day and organize one's activities around the regular striking of bells. This brought a new regularity into the life of workers and merchants, defining urban existence and enabling merchants and bankers to see the value of time in a new way.

**Eyeglasses and Paper**    Like clocks, eyeglasses were introduced in the thirteenth century but not refined until the fourteenth. Even then they were not particularly effective by modern standards and were still extremely expensive. The high cost of parchment forced people to write in extremely small script; eyeglasses made it more readable. At the same time, a significant change in writing materials occurred in the fourteenth century when parchment was supplemented by much cheaper paper made from cotton rags. Although it was more subject to insect and water damage than parchment, medieval paper was actually superior to modern papers made of high-acid wood pulp.

**Gunpowder and Cannons**    Invented earlier by the Chinese, gunpowder also made its appearance in the West in the fourteenth century. The use of gunpowder eventually brought drastic changes to European warfare. Its primary use was in cannons, although early cannons were prone to blow up, making them as dangerous to the people firing them as to the enemy. Even as late as 1460, an attack on a castle using the "Lion," an enormous Flemish cannon, proved disastrous for the Scottish king James II when the "Lion" blew up, killing the king and a number of his retainers. Continued improvement in the construction of cannons, however, soon made them extremely valuable in reducing both castles and city walls. Gunpowder made castles, city walls, and armored knights obsolete.

## CONCLUSION

*I*N THE ELEVENTH, twelfth, and thirteenth centuries, European civilization developed many of its fundamental features. Territorial states, parliaments, capitalist trade and industry, banks, cities, and vernacular literatures were all products of that fertile period. During the same time, the Catholic church under the direction of the papacy reached its apogee. Fourteenth-century European society, however, was challenged by an overwhelming number of crises. Devastating plague, declining trade and industry, bank failures, peasant revolts pitting lower classes against the upper classes, seemingly constant warfare, aristocratic factional conflict that undermined political stability, the absence of the popes from Rome, and even the spectacle of two popes condemning each other as the Antichrist all seemed to overpower Europeans in this "calamitous century." Not surprisingly, much of the art of the period depicted the Four Horsemen of the Apocalypse described in the New Testament book of Revelation: Death, Famine, Pestilence, and War. No doubt, to some people, the last days of the world appeared to be at hand.

The new European society, however, proved remarkably resilient. Periods of crisis are usually paralleled by the emergence of new ideas and new practices. Intellectuals of the period saw themselves as standing on the threshold of a new age or a rebirth of the best features of classical civilization. It is their perspective that led historians to speak of a Renaissance in the fifteenth century.

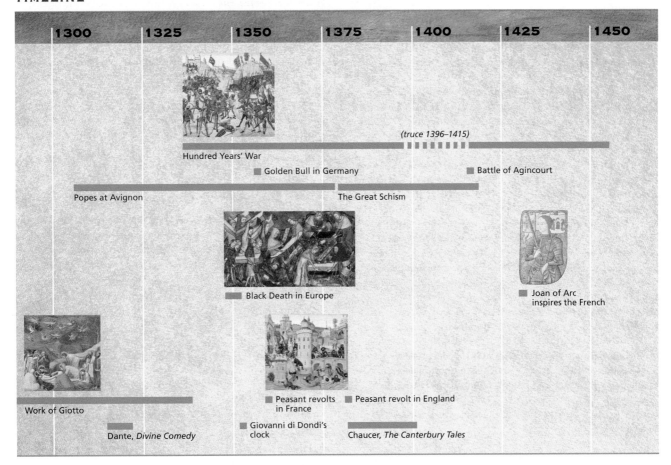

| 1300 | 1325 | 1350 | 1375 | 1400 | 1425 | 1450 |

*(truce 1396–1415)*

Hundred Years' War

■ Golden Bull in Germany

■ Battle of Agincourt

Popes at Avignon

The Great Schism

Black Death in Europe

Joan of Arc
inspires the French

Work of Giotto

■ Peasant revolts
in France

■ Peasant revolt in England

Dante, *Divine Comedy*

■ Giovanni di Dondi's
clock

Chaucer, *The Canterbury Tales*

## NOTES

1. Quoted in H. S. Lucas, "The Great European Famine of 1315, 1316, and 1317," *Speculum* 5 (1930): 359.

2. Quoted in David Herlihy, *The Black Death and the Transformation of the West,* ed. Samuel K. Cohn Jr. (Cambridge, Mass., 1997), p. 9.

3. Giovanni Boccaccio, *Decameron,* trans. Frances Winwar (New York, 1955), p. xxv.

4. Ibid., p. xxvi.

5. Jean Froissart, *Chronicles,* ed. and trans. Geoffrey Brereton (Harmondsworth, England, 1968), p. 111.

6. Quoted in James B. Ross and Mary M. McLaughlin, *The Portable Medieval Reader* (New York, 1949), pp. 218–219.

7. Quoted in Barbara W. Tuchman, *A Distant Mirror* (New York, 1978), p. 175.

8. Froissart, *Chronicles,* p. 212.

9. Ibid., p. 89.

10. Oliver J. Thatcher and Edgar H. McNeal, eds., *A Source Book for Medieval History* (New York, 1905), p. 288.

11. Quoted in D. S. Chambers, *The Imperial Age of Venice, 1380–1580* (London, 1970), p. 30.

12. Quoted in Robert Coogan, *Babylon on the Rhône: A Translation of Letters by Dante, Petrarch, and Catherine of Siena* (Washington, D.C., 1983), p. 115.

13. Quoted in Caroline Walker Bynum, *Holy Feast and Holy Fast: The Religious Significance of Food to Medieval Women* (Berkeley, Calif., 1987), p. 180.

14. Dante Alighieri, *Divine Comedy,* trans. Dorothy Sayers (New York, 1962), "Paradise," canto 33, line 145.

15. Petrarch, *Sonnets and Songs,* trans. Anna Maria Armi (New York, 1968), no. 74, p. 127.

16. Quoted in Millard Meiss, *Painting in Florence and Siena After the Black Death* (Princeton, N.J., 1951), p. 161.

17. Geoffrey Chaucer, *The Canterbury Tales,* in *The Portable Chaucer,* ed. Theodore Morrison (New York, 1949), p. 67.

18. Christine de Pizan, *The Book of the City of Ladies,* trans. E. Jeffrey Richards (New York, 1982), pp. 83–84.

19. Quoted in Susan Mosher Stuard, "The Dominion of Gender, or How Women Fared in the High Middle Ages," in Renate Bridenthal, Claudia Koonz, and Susan Stuard, eds., *Becoming Visible: Women in European History,* 3d ed. (Boston, 1998), p. 147.

20. Quoted in David Herlihy, "Medieval Children," in Bede K. Lackner and Kenneth R. Philp, eds., *Essays on Medieval Civilization* (Austin, Texas, 1978), p. 121.

21. Quoted in Jean Gimpel, The Medieval Machine (New York, 1976), p. 168.

## SUGGESTIONS FOR FURTHER READING

For a general introduction to the fourteenth century, see **D. P. Waley, *Later Medieval Europe,*** 2d ed. (London, 1985); **G. Holmes, *Europe: Hierarchy and Revolt, 1320–1450*** (New York, 1975); and the well-written popular history by **B. Tuchman, *A Distant Mirror*** (New York, 1978).

On famine in the early fourteenth century, see **W. C. Jordan, *The Great Famine: Northern Europe in the Early Fourteenth Century*** (Princeton, N.J., 1996). On the Black Death, see **P. Ziegler, *The Black Death*** (New York, 1969), and **D. Herlihy, *The Black Death and the Transformation of the West,*** ed. **S. K. Cohn Jr.** (Cambridge, Mass., 1997).

Good accounts of the Hundred Years' War include **A. Curry, *The Hundred Years' War*** (New York, 1993), and **R. H. Neillands, *The Hundred Years' War*** (New York, 1990). For a detailed history, see **J. Sumption, *The Hundred Years' War,*** 2 vols. (Philadelphia, 1992–1999). On Joan of Arc, see **M. Warner, *Joan of Arc: The Image of Female Heroism*** (New York, 1981). On the political history of the period, see **B. Guenée, *States and Rulers in Later Medieval Europe,*** trans. **J. Vale** (Oxford, 1985). Works on individual countries include **P. S. Lewis, *Later Medieval France: The Polity*** (London, 1968); **A. R. Myers, *England in the Late Middle Ages*** (Harmondsworth, England, 1952); and **F. R. H. Du Boulay, *Germany in the Later Middle Ages*** (London, 1983). On the Italian political scene, see **J. Larner, *Italy in the Age of Dante and Petrarch, 1216–1380*** (London, 1980).

A good general study of the church in the fourteenth century can be found in **F. P. Oakley, *The Western Church in the Later Middle Ages*** (Ithaca, N.Y., 1980). See also **J. H. Lynch, *The Medieval Church: A Brief History*** (New York, 1992). On the Avignonese papacy, see **Y. Renouard, *The Avignon Papacy, 1305–1403*** (London, 1970). On the role of food in the spiritual practices of medieval women, see **C. W. Bynum, *Holy Feast and Holy Fast: The Religious Significance of Food to Medieval Women*** (Berkeley, Calif., 1987). On late medieval religious practices, see **R. N. Swanson, *Religion and Devotion in Europe, c. 1215–1515*** (Cambridge, 1995).

A classic work on the life and thought of the Later Middle Ages is **J. Huizinga, *The Autumn of the Middle Ages,*** trans. **R. J. Payton** and **U. Mammitzsch** (Chicago, 1996). On the impact of the plague on culture, see the brilliant study by **M. Meiss, *Painting in Florence and Siena After the Black Death*** (New York, 1964). On Dante, see **J. Freccero, *Dante and the Poetics of Conversion*** (Cambridge, Mass., 1986). On Chaucer, see **G. Kane, *Chaucer*** (New York, 1984). The best work on Christine de Pizan is by **C. C. Willard, *Christine de Pizan: Her Life and Works*** (New York, 1984).

A wealth of material on everyday life is provided in the second volume of *A History of Private Life,* edited by **G. Duby, *Revelations of the Medieval World*** (Cambridge, Mass., 1988). On women in the Later Middle Ages, see **S. Shahar, *The Fourth Estate: A History of Women in the Middle Ages,*** trans. **C. Galai** (London, 1983), and **D. Herlihy, *Women, Family, and Society: Historical Essays, 1978–1991*** (Providence, R.I., 1995). On childhood, see **N. Orme, *Medieval Children*** (New Haven, Conn., 2001). The subject of medieval prostitution is examined in **L. L. Otis, *Prostitution in Medieval Society*** (Chicago, 1984). Poor people are discussed in **M. Mollat, *The Poor in the Middle Ages*** (New Haven, Conn., 1986). For a general introduction to the changes in medicine, see **T. McKeown, *The Role of Medicine*** (Princeton, N.J., 1979). The importance of inventions is discussed in **J. Gimpel, *The Medieval Machine*** (New York, 1976). Another valuable discussion of medieval technology can be found in **J. Le Goff, *Time, Work, and Culture in the Middle Ages*** (Chicago, 1980).

## History  Now™

Enter *HistoryNow* using the access card that is available for *Western Civilization.* *HistoryNow* will assist you in understanding the content in this chapter with lesson plans generated for your needs. In addition, you can read the following documents, and many more, online:

> Jean Froissart, The Battle of Crécy, The Burghers of Calais, and The Battle of Poitiers

### INFOTRAC SEARCH TERMS

 For additional reading, go to InfoTrac College Edition, your online research library at http://infotrac.thomsonlearning.com

| Key Term Search | Subject Guide Search |
| --- | --- |
| Black Death | Middle Ages |
| Edward III | |
| Hundred Years' War | |

### WESTERN CIVILIZATION RESOURCES

Visit the *Western Civilization* Companion Web site for resources specific to this book:

> http://history.wadsworth.com/spielvogel06/

For a variety of tools to help you succeed in this course, visit the **Western Civilization Resource Center** at

> http://history.wadsworth.com/western/

**Included are quizzes; images; documents; interactive simulations; maps and timelines; movie explorations; and a wealth of other sources.**

# 12

# RECOVERY AND REBIRTH: THE AGE OF THE RENAISSANCE

*Michelangelo's* Creation of Adam *on the Sistine Chapel ceiling*

© Vatican Museums and Galleries, Vatican City, Italy/Bridgeman Art Library

𝒲 ERE THE FOURTEENTH and fifteenth centuries a continuation of the Middle Ages or the beginning of a new era? Both positions can be defended. Although the disintegrative patterns of the fourteenth century continued into the fifteenth, at the same time there were elements of recovery that made the fifteenth century a period of significant political, economic, artistic, and intellectual change. The humanists or intellectuals of the age called their period (from the mid-fourteenth to the mid-sixteenth century) an age of rebirth, believing that they had restored arts and letters to new glory after they had been "neglected" or "dead" for centuries. The humanists also saw their age as one of accomplished individuals who dominated the landscape of their time. Michelangelo, the great Italian artist of the early sixteenth century, and Pope Julius II, the "warrior pope," were two such titans. The artist's temperament and the pope's temper led to many lengthy and often loud quarrels between the two. The pope had hired Michelangelo to paint the ceiling of the Sistine Chapel in Rome, a difficult task for a man long accustomed to being a sculptor. Michelangelo undertook the project but refused for a long time to allow anyone, including the pope, to see his work. Julius grew anxious, pestering Michelangelo on a regular basis about when the ceiling would be finished. Exasperated by the pope's requests, Michelangelo once replied, according to Giorgio Vasari, his contemporary biographer, that the ceiling would be completed "when it satisfies me as an artist." The pope responded, "And we want you to satisfy us and finish it soon," and then threatened that if Michelangelo did not "finish the ceiling quickly," the pope would "have him thrown down from the scaffolding." Fearing the pope's anger, Michelangelo "lost no time in doing all that was wanted" and quickly completed the ceiling, one of the great masterpieces in the history of Western art.

The humanists' view of their age as a rebirth of the classical civilization of the Greeks and Romans ultimately led historians to use the French word *Renaissance* to identify this age. Although recent historians have emphasized the many elements of continuity between the Middle Ages and the Renaissance, the latter age was also distinguished by its own unique characteristics.

# Meaning and Characteristics of the Italian Renaissance

*Renaissance* means "rebirth." Many people who lived in Italy between 1350 and 1550 believed that they had witnessed a rebirth of antiquity or Greco-Roman civilization, marking a new age. To them, the thousand or so years between the end of the Roman Empire and their own era was a middle period (the "Middle Ages"), characterized by darkness because of its lack of classical culture. Historians of the nineteenth century later used similar terminology to describe this period in Italy. The Swiss historian and art critic Jacob Burckhardt created the modern concept of the **Renaissance** in his celebrated book *The Civilization of the Renaissance in Italy*, published in 1860. He portrayed Italy in the fourteenth and fifteenth centuries as the birthplace of the modern world (the Italians were "the firstborn among the sons of modern Europe") and saw the revival of antiquity, the "perfecting of the individual," and secularism ("worldliness of the Italians") as its distinguishing features. Burckhardt exaggerated the individuality and secularism of the Renaissance and failed to recognize the depths of its religious sentiment; nevertheless, he established the framework for all modern interpretations of the period. Although contemporary scholars do not believe that the Renaissance represents a sudden or dramatic cultural break with the Middle Ages, as Burckhardt argued—there was, after all, much continuity in economic, political, and social life—the Renaissance can still be viewed as a distinct period of European history that manifested itself first in Italy and then spread to the rest of Europe.

Renaissance Italy was largely an urban society. As a result of its commercial preeminence and political evolution, northern Italy by the mid-fourteenth century was mostly a land of independent cities that dominated the country districts around them. These city-states became the centers of Italian political, economic, and social life. Within this new urban society, a secular spirit emerged as increasing wealth created new possibilities for the enjoyment of worldly things (see the box on p. 315).

Above all, the Renaissance was an age of recovery from the calamitous fourteenth century, the slow process of recuperating from the effects of the Black Death, political disorder, and economic recession. This recovery was accompanied by a rediscovery of the culture of classical antiquity. Increasingly aware of their own historical past, Italian intellectuals became intensely interested in the Greco-Roman culture of the ancient Mediterranean world. This revival of classical antiquity (the Middle Ages had in fact preserved much of ancient Latin culture) affected activities as diverse as politics and art and led to new attempts to reconcile the pagan philosophy of the Greco-Roman world with Christian thought, as well as new ways of viewing human beings.

A revived emphasis on individual ability became characteristic of the Italian Renaissance. As the fifteenth-century Florentine architect Leon Battista Alberti expressed it, "Men can do all things if they will."[1] A high regard for human dignity and worth and a realization of individual potentiality created a new social ideal of the well-rounded personality or universal person (*l'uomo universale*) who was capable of achievements in many areas of life.

These general features of the Italian Renaissance were not characteristic of all Italians but were primarily the preserve of the wealthy upper classes, who constituted a small percentage of the total population. The achievements of the Italian Renaissance were the product of an elite, rather than a mass, movement. Nevertheless, indirectly it did have some impact on ordinary people, especially in the cities, where so many of the intellectual and artistic accomplishments of the period were most visible.

# The Making of Renaissance Society

After the severe economic reversals and social upheavals of the fourteenth century, the European economy gradually recovered as the volume of manufacturing and trade increased.

## Economic Recovery

By the fourteenth century, Italian merchants were carrying on a flourishing commerce throughout the Mediterranean and had also expanded their lines of trade north along the Atlantic seaboard. The great galleys of the Venetian Flanders Fleet maintained a direct sea route from Venice to England and the Netherlands, where Italian merchants came into contact with the increasingly powerful Hanseatic League of merchants. Hard hit by the plague, the Italians lost their commercial preeminence while the Hanseatic League continued to prosper.

# A RENAISSANCE BANQUET

*A*S IN GREEK AND ROMAN SOCIETY, the Renaissance banquet was an occasion for good food, interesting conversation, music, and dancing. In Renaissance society, it was also a symbol of status and an opportunity to impress people with the power and wealth of one's family. Banquets were held to celebrate public and religious festivals, official visits, anniversaries, and weddings. The following menu lists the foods served at a grand banquet given by Pope Pius V in the sixteenth century.

## A Sixteenth-Century Banquet

**First Course**
**Cold Delicacies from the Sideboard**
Pieces of marzipan and marzipan balls
Neapolitan spice cakes
Malaga wine and Pisan biscuits
Fresh grapes
Prosciutto cooked in wine, served with capers
and grape pulp
Salted pork tongues cooked in wine, sliced
Spit-roasted songbirds, cold, with their
tongues sliced over them
Sweet mustard

**Second Course**
**Hot Foods from the Kitchen, Roasts**
Fried veal sweetbreads and liver
Spit-roasted skylarks with lemon sauce
Spit-roasted quails with sliced eggplants
Stuffed spit-roasted pigeons with capers
sprinkled over them
Spit-roasted rabbits, with sauce and crushed pine nuts
Partridges larded and spit-roasted, served with lemon
Heavily seasoned poultry with lemon slices
Slices of veal, spit-roasted, with a sauce made
from the juices
Leg of goat, spit-roasted, with a sauce made
from the juices
Soup of almond paste, with the flesh of three
pigeons to each serving

**Third Course**
**Hot Foods from the Kitchen, Boiled Meats and Stews**
Stuffed fat geese, boiled Lombard style and covered
with sliced almonds
Stuffed breast of veal, boiled, garnished with flowers
Very young calf, boiled, garnished with parsley
Almonds in garlic sauce
Turkish-style rice with milk, sprinkled with cinnamon
Stewed pigeons with mortadella sausage and
whole onions
Cabbage soup with sausages
Poultry pie, two chickens to each pie
Fricasseed breast of goat dressed with fried onions
Pies filled with custard cream
Boiled calves' feet with cheese and egg

**Fourth Course**
**Delicacies from the Sideboard**
Bean tarts
Quince pastries
Pear tarts, the pears wrapped in marzipan
Parmesan cheese and Riviera cheese
Fresh almonds on vine leaves
Chestnuts roasted over the coals and served
with salt and pepper
Milk curds
Ring-shaped cakes
Wafers made from ground grain

**Expansion of Trade** As early as the thirteenth century, a number of North German coastal towns had formed a commercial and military association known as the Hansa, or Hanseatic League. By 1500, more than eighty cities belonged to the League, which had established settlements and commercial bases in many cities in England and northern Europe, including the chief towns of Denmark, Norway, and Sweden. For almost two hundred years, the Hansa had a monopoly on northern European trade in timber, fish, grain, metals, honey, and wines. Its southern outlet in Flanders, the port city of Bruges, became the economic crossroads of Europe in the fourteenth century, serving as the meeting place between Hanseatic merchants and the Flanders Fleet of Venice. In the fifteenth century, however, silting of the port caused Bruges to enter a slow decline. So did the Hanseatic League, increasingly unable to compete with the developing larger territorial states.

Overall, trade recovered dramatically from the economic contraction of the fourteenth century. The Italians and especially the Venetians, despite new restrictive pressures on their eastern Mediterranean trade from the Ottoman Turks (see "The Ottoman Turks and the End of the Byzantine Empire" later in this chapter), continued to maintain a wealthy commercial empire. Not until the sixteenth century, when transatlantic discoveries gave new importance to the states along the ocean, did the petty Italian city-states begin to suffer from the competitive advantages of the ever-growing and more powerful national territorial states.

**Industries Old and New** The economic depression of the fourteenth century also affected patterns of manufacturing. The woolen industries of Flanders and the northern Italian cities had been particularly devastated. By the beginning of the fifteenth century, however, the Florentine

Staatliche Landesbildstelle Hamburg

**Harbor Scene at Hamburg.** Hamburg was a founding member of the Hanseatic League. This illustration from a fifteenth-century treatise on the laws of Hamburg shows a busy port with ships of all sizes. At the left, a crane is used to unload barrels. In the building at the right, customs officials collect their dues. Merchants and townspeople are shown talking at dockside.

branches in Venice, Milan, Rome, Avignon, Bruges, London, and Lyons. Moreover, the family had controlling interests in industrial enterprises for wool, silk, and the mining of alum, used in the dyeing of textiles. Except for a brief interruption, the Medici were also the principal bankers for the papacy, a position that produced big profits and influence at the papal court. Despite its great success in the early and middle part of the fifteenth century, the Medici bank suffered a rather sudden decline at the end of the century due to poor leadership and a series of bad loans, especially uncollectible loans to rulers. In 1494, when the French expelled the Medici from Florence and confiscated their property, the Medici financial edifice collapsed.

woolen industry had begun to recover. At the same time, the Italian cities began to develop and expand luxury industries, especially silk, glassware, and handworked items in metal and precious stones.

Other new industries, especially printing, mining, and metallurgy, began to rival the textile industry in importance in the fifteenth century. New machinery and techniques for digging deeper mines and for separating metals from ore and purifying them were developed. When rulers began to transfer their titles to underground minerals to financiers as collateral for loans, these **entrepreneurs** quickly developed large mining operations to produce copper, iron, and silver. Especially valuable were the rich mineral deposits in central Europe, Hungary, the Tyrol, Bohemia, and Saxony. Expanding iron production and new skills in metalworking in turn contributed to the development of firearms that were more effective than the crude weapons of the fourteenth century.

**Banking and the Medici** The city of Florence regained its preeminence in banking in the fifteenth century, due primarily to the Medici family. The Medici had expanded from cloth production into commerce, real estate, and banking. In its best days (in the fifteenth century), the House of Medici was the greatest bank in Europe, with

## Social Changes in the Renaissance

The Renaissance inherited its social structure from the Middle Ages. Society remained fundamentally divided into three **estates:** the First Estate, the clergy, whose preeminence was grounded in the belief that people should be guided to spiritual ends; the Second Estate, the nobility, whose privileges were based on the principle that the nobles provided security and justice for society; and the Third Estate, which consisted of the peasants and inhabitants of the towns and cities. This social order experienced certain adaptations in the Renaissance, which we can see by examining the Second and Third Estates (the clergy will be examined in Chapter 13).

**The Nobility** Throughout much of Europe, the landholding nobles faced declining real incomes during the greater part of the fourteenth and fifteenth centuries, while the expense of maintaining noble status was rising. Nevertheless, members of the old nobility survived, and new blood infused its ranks. A reconstruction of the aristocracy was well under way by 1500.

As a result, the nobles, old and new, who constituted between 2 and 3 percent of the population in most countries, managed to dominate society as they had done in the

Middle Ages, serving as military officers and holding important political posts as well as advising the king. Increasingly in the sixteenth century, members of the aristocracy pursued education as the means to maintain their role in government.

By 1500, certain ideals came to be expected of the aristocrat. These were best expressed in *The Book of the Courtier* by the Italian Baldassare Castiglione (1478–1529). First published in 1528, Castiglione's work soon became popular throughout Europe and remained a fundamental handbook for European aristocrats for centuries. In it, Castiglione described the three basic attributes of the perfect courtier. First, nobles should possess fundamental native endowments, such as impeccable character, grace, talents, and noble birth. The perfect courtier must also cultivate certain achievements. Primarily, he should participate in military and bodily exercises, because the principal profession of a courtier was bearing arms. But unlike the medieval knight, who had been required only to have military skill, the Renaissance courtier was also expected to have a classical education and to adorn his life with the arts by playing a musical instrument, drawing, and painting. In Castiglione's hands, the Renaissance ideal of the well-developed personality became a social ideal of the aristocracy. Finally, the aristocrat was expected to follow a certain standard of conduct. Nobles were to make a good impression; while being modest, they should not hide their accomplishments but show them with grace.

What was the purpose of these courtly standards? Castiglione wrote:

> I think that the aim of the perfect Courtier, which we have not spoken of up to now, is so to win for himself, by means of the accomplishments ascribed to him by these gentlemen, the favor and mind of the prince whom he serves that he may be able to tell him, and always will tell him, the truth about everything he needs to know, without fear or risk of displeasing him; and that when he sees the mind of his prince inclined to a wrong action, he may dare to oppose him . . . so as to dissuade him of every evil intent and bring him to the path of virtue.[2]

The aim of the perfect noble, then, was to serve his prince in an effective and honest way. Nobles would adhere to these principles for hundreds of years while they continued to dominate European life socially and politically.

**Peasants and Townspeople**  Peasants made up the overwhelming mass of the Third Estate and continued to constitute 85 to 90 percent of the European population, except in the highly urbanized areas of northern Italy and Flanders. The most noticeable trend produced by the economic crisis of the fourteenth century was the decline of the manorial system and the continuing elimination of serfdom. This process had already begun in the twelfth century when the introduction of a money economy made possible the conversion of servile labor dues into rents paid in money, although they also continued to be paid in kind or labor. The contraction of the peasantry after the Black

Death simply accelerated this process, since lords found it convenient to deal with the peasants by granting freedom and accepting rents. The lords' lands were then tilled by hired workers or rented out. By the end of the fifteenth century, serfdom was declining in western Europe, and more and more peasants were becoming legally free.

The remainder of the Third Estate centered around the inhabitants of towns and cities, originally the merchants and artisans who formed the bourgeoisie. The Renaissance town or city of the fifteenth century actually possessed a multitude of townspeople widely separated socially and economically.

At the top of urban society were the patricians, whose wealth from capitalistic enterprises in trade, industry, and banking enabled them to dominate their urban communities economically, socially, and politically. Below them were the petty burghers—the shopkeepers, artisans, guildmasters, and guild members, who were largely concerned with providing goods and services for local consumption. Below these two groups were the propertyless workers earning pitiful wages and the unemployed, living squalid and miserable lives; these people constituted 30 to 40 percent of the population living in cities. In many places in Europe in the late fourteenth and fifteenth centuries, urban poverty increased dramatically. One rich merchant of Florence wrote:

> Those that are lazy and indolent in a way that does harm to the city, and who can offer no just reason for their condition, should either be forced to work or expelled from the Commune. The city would thus rid itself of that most harmful part of the poorest class. . . . If the lowest order of society earn enough food to keep them going from day to day, then they have enough.[3]

But even this large group was not at the bottom of the social scale; beneath them were the slaves, especially in the Italian cities.

**Slavery in the Renaissance**  Agricultural slavery existed in the Early Middle Ages but had declined for economic reasons and been replaced by serfdom by the ninth century. Although some domestic slaves remained, slavery in European society had largely disappeared by the eleventh century. It reappeared first in Spain, where both Christians and Muslims used captured prisoners as slaves during the lengthy *Reconquista*. In the second half of the fourteenth century, the shortage of workers after the Black Death led Italians to introduce slavery on a fairly large scale. In 1363, for example, the government of Florence authorized the unlimited importation of foreign slaves.

In the Italian cities, slaves were used as skilled workers, making handcrafted goods for their masters, or as household workers. Girls served as nursemaids and boys as playmates. Fiammetta Adimari wrote to her husband in 1469: "I must remind you that when Alfonso is weaned we ought to get a little slave-girl to look after him, or else one of the black boys to keep him company."[4] In Florence, wealthy merchants might possess two or three slaves. Often men of the household took slaves as concubines, which sometimes led to the birth of illegitimate children. In 1392, the wealthy merchant Francesco Datini fathered an illegitimate daughter by Lucia, his twenty-year-old slave. His wife, Margherita, who was unable to bear any children, reluctantly agreed to raise the girl as their own daughter. Many illegitimate children were not as fortunate.

Slaves for the Italian market were obtained primarily from the eastern Mediterranean and the Black Sea region and included Tartars, Russians, Albanians, and Dalmatians. There were also slaves from Africa, either Moors or Ethiopians, and Muslims from Spain. Because of the lucrative nature of the slave trade, Italian merchants became involved in the transportation of slaves. Between 1414 and 1423, ten thousand slaves were sold on the Venetian market. Most slaves were females, many of them young girls.

By the end of the fifteenth century, slavery had declined dramatically in the Italian cities. Many slaves had been freed by their owners for humanitarian reasons, and the major source of slaves dried up as the Black Sea slave markets were closed to Italian traders after the Turks conquered the Byzantine Empire. Although some other sources remained, prices rose dramatically, further cutting demand. Moreover, a general feeling had arisen that slaves—the "domestic enemy," as they were called—were dangerous and not worth the effort. By the sixteenth century, slaves were in evidence only at princely courts, where they were kept as curiosities; this was especially true of black slaves.

In the fifteenth century, the Portuguese had imported increasing numbers of African slaves for southern European markets. It has been estimated that between 1444 and 1505, some 140,000 slaves were shipped from Africa. The presence of blacks in European society was not entirely new. Saint Maurice, a Christian martyr of the fourth century, was portrayed by medieval artists as a black knight and became the center of a popular cult in the twelfth and thirteenth centuries. The number of blacks in Europe was small, however, until their importation as slaves.

## The Family in Renaissance Italy

The family played an important role in Renaissance Italy. Family meant, first of all, the extended household of parents, children, and servants (if the family was wealthy) and could also include grandparents, widowed mothers, and even unmarried sisters. Families that were related and bore the same surname often lived near each other and might dominate an entire urban district. Old family names—Strozzi, Rucellai, Medici—conferred great status and prestige. The family bond was a source of great security in a dangerous and violent world, and its importance helps explain the vendetta in the Italian Renaissance. A crime committed by one family member fell on the entire family, ensuring that retaliation by the offended family would be a bloody affair involving large numbers of people.

**Marriage**   To maintain the family, careful attention was given to marriages arranged by parents, often to strengthen business or family ties. Details were worked out well in advance, sometimes when children were only two or three, and reinforced by a legally binding marriage contract (see the box on p. 319). The important aspect of the contract was the size of the dowry, money presented by the wife's family to the husband upon marriage. The dowry could involve large sums and was expected of all families. The size of the dowry was an indication of whether the bride was moving upward or downward in society. With a large dowry, a daughter could marry a man of higher social status, thereby enabling her family to move up in society; if the daughter married a man of lower social status, however, her dowry would be smaller because the reputation of her family would raise the status of the husband's family.

**Wedding Banquet.** Parents arranged marriages in Renaissance Italy to strengthen business or family ties. A legally binding marriage contract was considered a necessary part of the marital arrangements. So was a wedding feast. This painting by Botticelli shows the wedding banquet in Florence that celebrated the marriage of Nastagio degli Onesti and the daughter of Paulo Traversaro.

# MARRIAGE NEGOTIATIONS

ARRIAGES WERE so important in maintaining families in Renaissance Italy that much energy was put into arranging them. Parents made the choices for their children, most often for considerations that had little to do with the modern notion of love. This selection is taken from the letters of a Florentine matron of the illustrious Strozzi family to her son Filippo in Naples. The family's considerations were complicated by the fact that the son was in exile.

### Alessandra Strozzi to Her Son Filippo in Naples

[April 20, 1464] . . . Concerning the matter of a wife [for you], it appears to me that if Francesco di Messer Tanagli wishes to give his daughter, that it would be a fine marriage. . . . Now I will speak with Marco [Parenti, Alessandra's son-in-law], to see if there are other prospects that would be better, and if there are none, then we will learn if he wishes to give her [in marriage]. . . . Francesco Tanagli has a good reputation, and he has held office, not the highest, but still he has been in office. You may ask: "Why should he give her to someone in exile?" There are three reasons. First, there aren't many young men of good family who have both virtue and property. Second, she has only a small dowry, 1,000 florins, which is the dowry of an artisan [although not a small sum, either—senior officials in the government bureaucracy earned 300 florins a year]. . . . Third, I believe that he will give her away, because he has a large family and he will need help to settle them. . . .

[July 26, 1465] . . . Francesco is a good friend of Marco and he trusts him. On S. Jacopo's day, he spoke to him discreetly and persuasively, saying that for several months he had heard that we were interested in the girl and . . . that when we had made up our minds, she will come to us willingly. [He said that] you were a worthy man, and that his family had always made good marriages, but that he had only a small dowry to give her, and so he would prefer to send her out of Florence to someone of worth, rather than to give her to someone here, from among those who were available, with little money. . . . We have information that she is affable and competent. She is responsible for a large family (there are twelve children, six boys and six girls), and the mother is always pregnant and isn't very competent. . . .

[August 31, 1465] . . . I have recently received some very favorable information [about the Tanagli girl] from two individuals. . . . They are in agreement that whoever gets her will be content. . . . Concerning her beauty, they told me what I had already seen, that she is attractive and well-proportioned. Her face is long, but I couldn't look directly into her face, since she appeared to be aware that I was examining her . . . and so she turned away from me like the wind. . . . She reads quite well . . . and she can dance and sing. . . .

So yesterday I sent for Marco and told him what I had learned. And we talked about the matter for a while, and decided that he should say something to the father and give him a little hope, but not so much that we couldn't withdraw, and find out from him the amount of the dowry. . . . May God help us to choose what will contribute to our tranquility and to the consolation of us all.

[September 13, 1465] . . . Marco came to me and said that he had met with Francesco Tanagli, who had spoken very coldly, so that I understand that he had changed his mind. . . .

[Filippo Strozzi eventually married Fiametta di Donato Adimari in 1466.]

---

The father-husband was the center of the Italian family. He gave it his name, was responsible for it in all legal matters, managed all finances (his wife had no share in his wealth), and made the crucial decisions that determined his children's lives. A father's authority over his children was absolute until he died or formally freed his children. In Renaissance Italy, children did not become adults on reaching a certain age; adulthood came only when the father went before a judge and formally emancipated them. The age of emancipation varied from early teens to late twenties.

**Children** The wife managed the household, a position that gave women a certain degree of autonomy in their daily lives. Most wives, however, also knew that their primary function was to bear children. Upper-class wives were frequently pregnant; Alessandra Strozzi of Florence, for example, who had been married at the age of sixteen, bore eight children in ten years. Poor women did not conceive at the same rate because they nursed their own babies. Wealthy women gave their infants out to wet nurses, which enabled them to become pregnant more quickly after the birth of a child.

For women in the Renaissance, childbirth was a fearful occasion. Not only was it painful, but it could be deadly; as many as 10 percent of mothers died in childbirth. In his memoirs, the Florentine merchant Gregorio Dati recalled that three of his four wives had died in childbirth. His third wife, after bearing eleven children in fifteen years, "died in childbirth after lengthy suffering, which she bore with remarkable strength and patience."[5] Nor did the tragedies end with childbirth. Surviving mothers often faced the death of their children. In Florence in the fifteenth century, for example, almost 50 percent of the children born to merchant families died before the age of twenty. Given these mortality rates, many upper-class families sought to have as many children as possible to ensure that there would be a surviving male heir to the family fortune.

This concern is evident in the Florentine humanist Leon Battista Alberti's treatise *On the Family,* where one of the characters remarks, "How many families do we see today in decadence and ruin! . . . Of all these families not only the magnificence and greatness but the very men, not only the men but the very names are shrunk away and gone. Their memory . . . is wiped out and obliterated."[6]

**Sexual Norms**   Considering that marriages were arranged, marital relationships ran the gamut from deep emotional attachments to purely formal ties. The lack of emotional attachment from arranged marriages did encourage extramarital relationships, especially among groups whose lifestyle offered special temptations. Although sexual license for males was the norm for princes and their courts, women were supposed to follow different guidelines. The first wife of Duke Filippo Maria Visconti of Milan had an affair with the court musician and was executed for it.

The great age difference between husbands and wives in Italian Renaissance marriage patterns also heightened the need for sexual outlets outside marriage. In Florence in 1427–1428, the average difference was thirteen years. Though females married between the ages of sixteen and eighteen, factors of environment, wealth, and demographic trends favored relatively late ages for the first marriages of males, who were usually in their thirties or even early forties. The existence of large numbers of young, unmarried males encouraged extramarital sex as well as prosti-

tution. Prostitution was viewed as a necessary vice; since it could not be eliminated, it should be regulated. In Florence in 1415, the city fathers established communal brothels:

> Desiring to eliminate a worse evil by means of a lesser one, the lord priors . . . have decreed that the priors . . . may authorize the establishment of two public brothels in the city of Florence, in addition to the one which already exists. . . . [They are to be located] in suitable places or in places where the exercise of such scandalous activity can best be concealed, for the honor of the city and of those who live in the neighborhood in which these prostitutes must stay to hire their bodies for lucre.[7]

A prostitute in Florence was required to wear a traditional garb of "gloves on her hands and a bell on her head."

# The Italian States in the Renaissance

By the fifteenth century, five major powers dominated the Italian peninsula: Milan, Venice, Florence, the Papal States, and Naples (see Map 12.1).

## The Five Major States

Northern Italy was divided between the duchy of Milan and the republic of Venice. After the death of the last Visconti ruler of Milan in 1447, Francesco Sforza, one of the leading *condottieri* of the time (see Chapter 11), turned on his

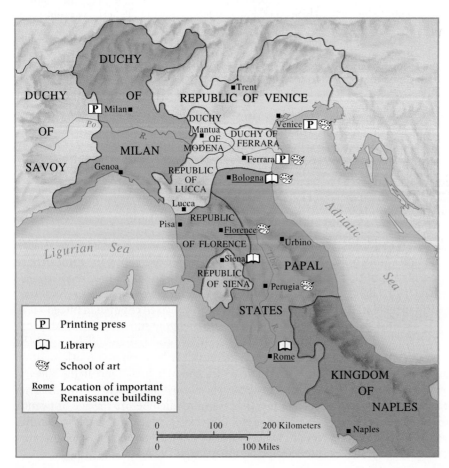

**MAP 12.1  Renaissance Italy.** Italy in the late fourteenth century was a land of five major states and numerous independent city-states. Increased prosperity and a supportive intellectual climate helped create the atmosphere for the middle and upper classes to "rediscover" Greco-Roman culture. Modern diplomacy was also a product of Renaissance Italy **?** Could the presence of several other powers within easy marching distance make a ruler recognize the importance of diplomacy?

**View an animated version of this map or related maps at** http://history .wadsworth.com/spielvogel06/

Milanese employers, conquered the city, and became its new duke. Both the Visconti and the Sforza rulers worked to create a highly centralized territorial state. They were especially successful in devising systems of taxation that generated enormous revenues for the government. The maritime republic of Venice remained an extremely stable political entity governed by a small oligarchy of merchant-aristocrats. Its commercial empire brought in enormous revenues and gave it the status of an international power. At the end of the fourteenth century, Venice embarked on the conquest of a territorial state in northern Italy to protect its food supply and its overland trade routes. Although expansion on the mainland made sense to the Venetians, it frightened Milan and Florence, which worked to curb what they perceived as the expansionary designs of the Venetians.

**Republic of Florence** The republic of Florence dominated the region of Tuscany. By the beginning of the fifteenth century, Florence was governed by a small merchant oligarchy that manipulated the apparently republican government. In 1434, Cosimo de' Medici took control of this oligarchy. Although the wealthy Medici family maintained republican forms of government for appearance's sake, it ran the government from behind the scenes. Through lavish patronage and careful courting of political allies, Cosimo (1434–1464), and later his grandson Lorenzo the Magnificent (1469–1492), were successful in dominating the city at a time when Florence was the center of the cultural Renaissance.

**Papal States** The Papal States lay in central Italy. Nominally under the political control of the popes, papal residence in Avignon and the Great Schism had enabled indi-vidual cities and territories, such as Urbino, Bologna, and Ferrara, to become independent of papal authority. The Renaissance popes of the fifteenth century directed much of their energy toward reestablishing their control over the Papal States (see "The Renaissance Papacy" later in this chapter).

**Kingdom of Naples** The kingdom of Naples, which encompassed most of southern Italy and usually the island of Sicily, was fought over by the French and the Aragonese until the latter established their domination in the mid-fifteenth century. Throughout the Renaissance, the kingdom of Naples remained a backward monarchy with a population consisting largely of poverty-stricken peasants dominated by unruly nobles. It shared little in the cultural glories of the Renaissance.

## Independent City-States

Besides the five major states, there were a number of independent city-states under the control of powerful ruling families that became brilliant centers of Renaissance culture in the fifteenth century. These included Mantua, under the enlightened rule of the Gonzaga lords; Ferrara, governed by the flamboyant d'Este family; and perhaps the most famous, Urbino, ruled by the Montefeltro dynasty.

**Urbino** Federigo da Montefeltro, who ruled Urbino from 1444 to 1482, received a classical education typical of the famous humanist school in Mantua run by Vittorino da Feltre. He had also learned the skills of fighting, since the Montefeltro family compensated for the poverty of Urbino by hiring themselves out as *condottiere*. Federigo was not only a good ruler but also a rather unusual *condottiere* by

**Piero della Francesca, *Duke and Duchess of Urbino*.** Federigo da Montefeltro and his wife, Battista Sforza, ruled the small central Italian principality of Urbino. These profile portraits by Piero della Francesca gave a realistic rendering of the two figures. Visible in the background are the hills and valleys of Urbino.

# THE LETTERS OF ISABELLA D'ESTE

 ANY ITALIAN AND EUROPEAN rulers at the beginning of the sixteenth century regarded Isabella d'Este as an important political figure. These excerpts from her letters reveal Isabella's political skills and her fierce determination. After her husband was taken prisoner by the Venetians in 1509, she refused to accept the condition for his release—namely, that her son Federico be kept as a hostage by the Venetians or the Holy Roman Emperor. She wrote to both the emperor and her husband, refusing to do as they asked.

### Letter of Isabella d'Este to the Imperial Envoy

As to the demand for our dearest first-born son Federico, besides being a cruel and almost inhuman thing for any one who knows the meaning of a mother's love, there are many reasons which render it difficult and impossible. Although we are quite sure that his person would be well cared for and protected by His Majesty [the Holy Roman Emperor], how could we wish him to run the risk of this long and difficult journey, considering the child's tender and delicate age? And you must know what comfort and solace, in his father's present unhappy condition, we find in the presence of this dear son, the hope and joy of all our people and subjects. To deprive us of him, would be to deprive us of life itself, and of all we count good and precious. If you take Federico away you might as well take away our life and state. . . . Once for all, we will suffer any loss rather than part from our son, and this you may take to be our deliberate and unchanging resolution.

### Letter of Isabella d'Este to Her Husband, Who Had Ordered Her to Send the Boy to Venice

If in this matter Your Excellency were to despise me and deprive me of your love and grace, I would rather endure such harsh treatment, I would rather lose our State, than deprive us of our children. I am hoping that in time your own prudence and kindness will make you understand that I have acted more lovingly toward you than you have to yourself.

Have patience! You can be sure that I think continuously of your liberation and when the time comes I will not fail you, as I have not relaxed my efforts. As witness I cite the Pope, the Emperor, the King of France, and all the other reigning heads and potentates of Christendom. Yes, and the infidels as well [she had written to the Turkish sultan for help]. If it were *really* the only means of setting you free, I would not only send Federico but all the other children as well. I will do everything imaginable. Some day I hope I can make you understand. . . .

Pardon me if this letter is badly written and worse composed, but I do not know if I am dead or alive.

*Isabella, who desires the*
*best for Your Excellency,*
*written with her own hand*

[Isabella's husband was not pleased with her response and exclaimed angrily: "That whore of my wife is the cause of it all. Send me into battle alone, do what you like with me. I have lost in one blow my state, my honor and my freedom. If she does not obey, I'll cut her vocal cords."]

---

fifteenth-century standards. Although not a brilliant general, he was reliable and honest. He did not break his promises, even when urged to do so by a papal legate. At the same time, Duke Federigo was one of the greatest patrons of Renaissance culture. Under his direction, Urbino became a well-known cultural and intellectual center. Though a despot, Federigo was also benevolent. It was said of him that he could walk safely through the streets of Urbino unaccompanied by a bodyguard, a feat few Renaissance rulers dared to emulate.

**The Role of Women** A noticeable feature of these smaller Renaissance courts was the important role played by women. Battista Sforza, niece of the ruler of Milan, was the wife of Federigo da Montefeltro. The duke called his wife "the delight of both my public and my private hours." An intelligent woman, she was well versed in both Greek and Latin and did much to foster art and letters in Urbino. As a prominent *condottiere*, Federigo was frequently absent, and like the wives of medieval lords, Battista Sforza was respected for governing the state "with firmness and good sense."

Perhaps the most famous of the Renaissance ruling women was Isabella d'Este (1474–1539), daughter of the duke of Ferrara, who married Francesco Gonzaga, marquis of Mantua. Their court was another important center of art and learning in the Renaissance. Educated at the brilliant court of Ferrara, Isabella was known for her intelligence and political wisdom. Called the "first lady of the world," she attracted artists and intellectuals to the Mantuan court and was responsible for amassing one of the finest libraries in all of Italy. Her numerous letters to friends, family, princes, and artists all over Europe disclose her political acumen as well as a good sense of humor (see the box above). Both before and after the death of her husband, she effectively ruled Mantua and won a reputation as a clever negotiator.

### Warfare in Italy

The fragmented world of the Italian territorial states gave rise to a political practice that was later used on a larger scale by competing European states. This was the concept of a balance of power, designed to prevent the aggrandizement of any one state at the expense of the others. This system was especially evident after 1454 when the Italian states signed the Peace of Lodi, which ended almost a half-century of war and inaugurated a relatively peaceful forty-year era in Italy. An alliance system (Milan, Florence, and Naples versus Venice and the papacy) was then created that led to a workable balance of power within Italy. It failed, however, to establish lasting cooperation among the major powers or a common foreign policy.

The growth of powerful monarchical states (see "The European State in the Renaissance" later in this chapter) led to trouble for the Italians. Italy soon became a battlefield for the great power struggle between the French and Spanish monarchies. Italian wealth and splendor would probably have been inviting to its northern neighbors under any circumstances, but it was actually the breakdown of the Italian balance of power that encouraged the invasions and began the Italian wars. Feeling isolated, Ludovico Sforza, the duke of Milan, foolishly invited the French to intervene in Italian politics. The French king Charles VIII (1483–1498) was eager to do so, and in 1494, with an army of thirty thousand men, he advanced through Italy and occupied the kingdom of Naples. Other Italian states turned to the Spanish for help, and Ferdinand of Aragon indicated his willingness to intervene. For the next fifteen years, the French and Spanish competed to dominate Italy. After 1510, the war was continued by a new generation of rulers, Francis I of France and Charles I of Spain (see Chapter 13). This war was part of a long struggle for power throughout Europe between the Valois and Habsburg dynasties. Italy was only a pawn for the two great powers, a convenient arena for fighting battles. The terrible sack of Rome in 1527 by the armies of the Spanish king Charles I brought a temporary end to the Italian wars. Thereafter, the Spaniards dominated Italy.

Although some Italians had developed a sense of national consciousness and differentiated between Italians and "barbarians" (all foreigners), few Italians conceived of creating an alliance or confederation of states that could repel foreign invaders. Italians remained fiercely loyal to their own petty states, making invasion a fact of life in Italian history for all too long. Italy would not achieve unification and nationhood until 1870.

## The Birth of Modern Diplomacy

The modern diplomatic system was a product of the Italian Renaissance. There were ambassadors in the Middle Ages, but they were used only on a temporary basis. Moreover, an ambassador, regardless of whose subject he was, regarded himself as the servant of all Christendom, not just of his particular employer. As a treatise on diplomacy stated, "An ambassador is sacred because he acts for the general welfare." Since he was the servant of all Christendom, "the business of an ambassador is peace."[8]

This concept of an ambassador changed during the Italian Renaissance because of the political situation in Italy. A large number of states existed, many so small that their security was easily threatened by their neighbors. To survive, the Italian states began to send resident diplomatic agents to each other to ferret out useful information. During the Italian wars, the practice of resident diplomats spread to the rest of Europe, and in the course of the sixteenth and seventeenth centuries, Europeans developed the diplomatic machinery still in use today, such as the rights of ambassadors in host countries and the proper procedures for conducting diplomatic business.

With the use of permanent resident agents or ambassadors, the conception of the purpose of the ambassador also changed. A Venetian diplomat attempted to define the function of an ambassador in a treatise written at the end of the fifteenth century. He wrote, "The first duty of an ambassador is exactly the same as that of any other servant of a government, that is, to do, say, advise, and think whatever may best serve the preservation and aggrandizement of his own state."[9] An ambassador was now simply an agent of the territorial state that sent him, not the larger body of Christendom. He could use any methods that were beneficial to the political interests of his own state. We are at the beginning of modern politics when the interests of the state supersede all other considerations.

## Machiavelli and the New Statecraft

No one gave better expression to the Renaissance preoccupation with political power than Niccolò Machiavelli (1469–1527). He entered the service of the Florentine republic in 1498, four years after the Medici family had been expelled from the city. As a secretary to the Florentine Council of Ten, he made numerous diplomatic missions, including trips to France and Germany, and saw the workings of statecraft at first hand. Since Italy had been invaded in 1494, Machiavelli was active during a period of Italian tribulation and devastation. In 1512, French defeat and Spanish victory led to the reestablishment of Medici power in Florence. Staunch republicans, including Machiavelli, were sent into exile. Forced to give up politics, the great love of his life, Machiavelli now reflected on political power and

**Niccolò Machiavelli.** In *The Prince,* Machiavelli gave concrete expression to the Renaissance preoccupation with political power. This slender volume remains one of the most famous and most widely read Western treatises on politics. Machiavelli is seen here in a portrait by Santi di Tito.

wrote books, including *The Prince* (1513), one of the most famous treatises on political power in the Western world.

***The Prince***   Machiavelli's ideas on politics stemmed from two major sources, his preoccupation with Italy's political problems and his knowledge of ancient Rome. His major concerns in *The Prince* were the acquisition and expansion of political power as the means to restore and maintain order in his time. Late medieval political theorists believed that a ruler was justified in exercising political power only if it contributed to the common good of the people he served. The ethical side of a prince's activity—how a ruler ought to behave based on Christian moral principles—was the focus of many late medieval treatises on politics. Machiavelli bluntly contradicted this approach:

> My hope is to write a book that will be useful, at least to those who read it intelligently, and so I thought it sensible to go straight to a discussion of how things are in real life and not waste time with a discussion of an imaginary world. . . . For the gap between how people actually behave and how they ought to behave is so great that anyone who ignores everyday reality in order to live up to an ideal will soon discover he has been taught how to destroy himself, not how to preserve himself.[10]

Machiavelli considered his approach far more realistic than that of his medieval forebears.

From Machiavelli's point of view, a prince's attitude toward power must be based on an understanding of human nature, which he perceived as basically self-centered: "For of men one can, in general, say this: They are ungrateful, fickle, deceptive and deceiving, avoiders of danger, eager to gain." Political activity, therefore, could not be restricted by moral considerations. The prince acts on behalf of the state and for the sake of the state must be willing to let his conscience sleep. As Machiavelli put it:

> You need to understand this: A ruler, and particularly a ruler who is new to power, cannot conform to all those rules that men who are thought good are expected to respect, for he is often obliged, in order to hold on to power, to break his word, to be uncharitable, inhumane, and irreligious. So he must be mentally prepared to act as circumstances and changes in fortune require. As I have said, he should do what is right if he can; but he must be prepared to do wrong if necessary.[11]

Machiavelli found a good example of the new Italian ruler in Cesare Borgia, the son of Pope Alexander VI, who used ruthless measures to achieve his goal of carving out a new state in central Italy. As Machiavelli said: "So anyone who decides that the policy to follow when one has newly acquired power is to destroy one's enemies, to secure some allies, to win wars, whether by force or by fraud, to make oneself both loved and feared by one's subjects, . . . cannot hope to find, in the recent past, a better model to imitate than Cesare Borgia."[12] Machiavelli was among the first to abandon morality as the basis for the analysis of political activity (see the box on p. 325).

# The Intellectual Renaissance in Italy

**Individualism** and **secularism**—two characteristics of the Italian Renaissance—were most noticeable in the intellectual and artistic realms. Italian culture had matured by the fourteenth century. For the next two centuries, Italy was the cultural leader of Europe. This new Italian culture was primarily the product of a relatively wealthy, urban lay society. The most important literary movement associated with the Renaissance is **humanism.**

### Italian Renaissance Humanism

Renaissance humanism was an intellectual movement based on the study of the classical literary works of Greece and Rome. Humanists studied the liberal arts—grammar, rhetoric, poetry, moral philosophy or ethics, and history—all based on the writings of ancient Greek and Roman authors. These are the subjects we call the humanities.

The central importance of literary preoccupations in Renaissance humanism is evident in the professional status or occupations of the humanists. Some of them were teachers of the humanities in secondary schools and universities, where they either gave occasional lectures or held permanent positions, often as professors of rhetoric.

# MACHIAVELLI: "IS IT BETTER TO BE LOVED THAN FEARED?"

*I*N 1513, NICCOLÒ MACHIAVELLI wrote a short treatise on political power that, justly or unjustly, has given him a reputation as a political opportunist. In this passage from Chapter 17 of *The Prince*, Machiavelli analyzes whether it is better for a ruler to be loved than to be feared.

## Machiavelli, *The Prince*

This leads us to a question that is in dispute: Is it better to be loved than feared, or vice versa? My reply is one ought to be both loved and feared; but, since it is difficult to accomplish both at the same time, I maintain it is much safer to be feared than loved, if you have to do without one of the two. For of men one can, in general, say this: They are ungrateful, fickle, deceptive and deceiving, avoiders of danger, eager to gain. As long as you serve their interests, they are devoted to you. They promise you their blood, their possessions, their lives, and their children, as I said before, so long as you seem to have no need of them. But as soon as you need help, they turn against you. Any ruler who relies simply on their promises and makes no other preparations, will be destroyed. For you will find that those whose support you buy, who do not rally to you because they admire your strength of character and nobility of soul, these are people you pay for, but they are never yours, and in the end you cannot get the benefit of your investment. Men are less nervous of offending someone who makes himself lovable, than someone who makes himself frightening. For love attaches men by ties of obligation, which, since men are wicked, they break whenever their interests are at stake. But fear restrains men because they are afraid of punishment, and this fear never leaves them. Still, a ruler should make himself feared in such a way that, if he does not inspire love, at least he does not provoke hatred. For it is perfectly possible to be feared and not hated. You will only be hated if you seize the property or the women of your subjects and citizens. Whenever you have to kill someone, make sure that you have a suitable excuse and an obvious reason; but, above all else, keep your hands off other people's property; for men are quicker to forget the death of their father than the loss of their inheritance. Moreover, there are always reasons why you might want to seize people's property; and he who begins to live by plundering others will always find an excuse for seizing other people's possessions; but there are fewer reasons for killing people, and one killing need not lead to another.

When a ruler is at the head of his army and has a vast number of soldiers under his command, then it is absolutely essential to be prepared to be thought cruel; for it is impossible to keep an army united and ready for action without acquiring a reputation for cruelty.

---

Others served as secretaries in the chancelleries of Italian city-states or at the courts of princes or popes. All of these occupations were largely secular, and most humanists were laymen rather than members of the clergy.

**The Emergence of Humanism**   Petrarch (1304–1374) has often been called the father of Italian Renaissance humanism (see Chapter 11 on his use of the Italian vernacular). Petrarch had rejected his father's desire that he become a lawyer and took up a literary career instead. Although he lived in Avignon for a time, most of his last decades were spent in Italy as the guest of various princes and city governments. With his usual lack of modesty, Petrarch once exclaimed, "Some of the greatest kings of our time have loved me and cultivated my friendship. . . . When I was their guest it was more as if they were mine."[13]

Petrarch did more than any other individual in the fourteenth century to foster the development of Renaissance humanism. He was the first intellectual to characterize the Middle Ages as a period of darkness, promoting the mistaken belief that medieval culture was ignorant of classical antiquity. Petrarch's interest in the classics led him on a quest for forgotten Latin manuscripts and set in motion a ransacking of monastic libraries throughout Europe. In his preoccupation with the classics and their secular content, Petrarch worried at times whether he was sufficiently attentive to spiritual ideals (see the box on p. 326).

His qualms, however, did not prevent him from inaugurating the humanist emphasis on the use of pure classical Latin, making it fashionable for humanists to use Cicero as a model for prose and Virgil for poetry. As Petrarch said, "Christ is my God; Cicero is the prince of the language."

**Humanism in Fifteenth-Century Italy**   In Florence, the humanist movement took a new direction at the beginning of the fifteenth century when it became closely tied to Florentine civic spirit and pride, giving rise to what one modern scholar has labeled **civic humanism.** Fourteenth-century humanists such as Petrarch had described the intellectual life as one of solitude. They rejected family and a life of action in the community. In the busy civic world of Florence, however, intellectuals began to take a new view of their role as intellectuals. The classical Roman Cicero, who was both a statesman and an intellectual, became their model. Leonardo Bruni (1370–1444), a humanist, Florentine patriot, and chancellor of the city, wrote a biography of Cicero titled *The New Cicero*, in which he waxed enthusiastic about the fusion of political action and literary creation in Cicero's life. From Bruni's time on, Cicero served as the inspiration for the Renaissance ideal that it was the duty of an intellectual to live an active life for one's state. An individual only "grows to maturity—both intellectually and morally—through participation" in the life of the state.

# PETRARCH: MOUNTAIN CLIMBING AND THE SEARCH FOR SPIRITUAL CONTENTMENT

*P*ETRARCH HAS LONG BEEN regarded as the father of Italian Renaissance humanism. One of his literary masterpieces was *The Ascent of Mount Ventoux,* a colorful description of an attempt to climb a mountain in Provence in southern France and survey the world from its top. Petrarch's primary interest is in presenting an allegory of his own soul's struggle to achieve a higher spiritual state. The work is addressed to a professor of theology in Paris who had initially led Petrarch to read Augustine. The latter had experienced a vivid conversion to Christianity almost a thousand years earlier.

## Petrarch, *The Ascent of Mount Ventoux*

Today I ascended the highest mountain in this region, which, not without cause, they call the Windy Peak. Nothing but the desire to see its conspicuous height was the reason for this undertaking. For many years I have been intending to make this expedition. You know that since my early childhood, as fate tossed around human affairs, I have been tossed around in these parts, and this mountain, visible far and wide from everywhere, is always in your view. So I was at last seized by the impulse to accomplish what I had always wanted to do. . . .

[After some false starts, Petrarch finally achieves his goal and arrives at the top of Mount Ventoux.]

I was glad of the progress I had made, but I wept over my imperfection and was grieved by the fickleness of all that men do. In this manner I seemed to have somehow forgotten the place I had come to and why, until I was warned to throw off such sorrows, for which another place would be more appropriate. I had better look around and see what I had intended to see in coming here. The time to leave was approaching, they said. . . . Like a man aroused from sleep, I turned back and looked toward the west. . . . One could see most distinctly the mountains of the province of Lyons to the right and, to the left, the sea near Marseilles as well as the waves that break against Aigues-Mortes. . . . The Rhône River was directly under our eyes.

I admired every detail, now relishing earthly enjoyment, now lifting up my mind to higher spheres after the example of my body, and I thought it fit to look in the volume of Augustine's *Confessions* which I owe to your loving kindness and preserve carefully, keeping it always in my hands, in remembrance of the author as well as the donor. . . . I opened it with the intention of reading whatever might occur to me first: . . . I happened to hit upon the tenth book of the work. . . . Where I fixed my eyes first, it was written: "And men go to admire the high mountains, the vast floods of the sea, the huge streams of the rivers, the circumference of the ocean, and the revolutions of the stars—and desert themselves." I was stunned, I confess. I bade my brother [who had accompanied him], who wanted to hear more, not to molest me, and closed the book, angry with myself that I still admired earthly things. Long since I ought to have learned, even from pagan philosophers, that "nothing is admirable besides the soul; compared to its greatness nothing is great."

I was completely satisfied with what I had seen of the mountain and turned my inner eye toward myself. From this hour nobody heard me say a word until we arrived at the bottom. These words occupied me sufficiently. I could not imagine that this had happened to me by chance: I was convinced that whatever I had read there was said to me and to nobody else. I remembered that Augustine once suspected the same regarding himself, when, while he was reading the Apostolic Epistles, the first passage that occurred to him was, as he himself relates: "Not in banqueting and drunkenness, not in chambering and wantonness, not in strife and envying; but put you on the Lord Jesus Christ, and make no provision for the flesh to fulfill your lusts."

---

Civic humanism reflected the values of the urban society of the Italian Renaissance. Humanists came to believe that their study of the humanities should be put to the service of the state. It is no accident that humanists served the state as chancellors, councillors, and advisers.

Also evident in the humanism of the first half of the fifteenth century was a growing interest in classical Greek civilization. One of the first Italian humanists to gain a thorough knowledge of Greek was Leonardo Bruni, who became an enthusiastic pupil of the Byzantine scholar Manuel Chrysoloras, who taught in Florence from 1396 to 1400. Humanists eagerly perused the works of Plato as well as Greek poets, dramatists, historians, and orators, such as Thucydides, Euripides, and Sophocles, all of whom had been ignored by the scholastics of the High Middle Ages as irrelevant to the theological questions they were examining.

By the fifteenth century, a consciousness of being humanists had emerged. This was especially evident in the career of Lorenzo Valla (1407–1457). Valla was brought up in Rome and educated in both Latin and Greek. Eventually, he achieved his chief ambition of becoming a papal secretary. Valla's major work, *The Elegances of the Latin Language,* was an effort to purify medieval Latin and restore Latin to its proper position over the vernacular. The treatise examined the proper use of classical Latin and created a new literary standard. Early humanists had tended to take as classical models any author (including Christians) who had written before the seventh century A.D. Valla identified different stages in the growth of the Latin language and accepted only the Latin of the last century of the Roman Republic and the first century of the empire.

**Humanism and Philosophy** In the second half of the fifteenth century, a dramatic upsurge of interest in the works of Plato occurred, especially evident among the members of an informal discussion group known as the Florentine Platonic Academy. Cosimo de' Medici, the de facto ruler of Florence, became its patron and commissioned a translation of Plato's dialogues by Marsilio Ficino (1433–1499), one of the academy's leaders. Ficino dedicated his life to the translation of Plato and the exposition of the Platonic philosophy known as **Neoplatonism.**

In two major works, Ficino undertook the synthesis of Christianity and Platonism into a single system. His Neoplatonism was based on two primary ideas, the Neoplatonic hierarchy of substances and a theory of spiritual love. The former postulated the idea of a hierarchy of substances, or great chain of being, from the lowest form of physical matter (plants) to the purest spirit (God), in which humans occupied a central or middle position. They were the link between the material world (through the body) and the spiritual world (through the soul), and their highest duty was to ascend toward that union with God that was the true end of human existence. Ficino's theory of spiritual or Platonic love maintained that just as all people are bound together in their common humanity by love, so too are all parts of the universe held together by bonds of sympathetic love.

**Renaissance Hermeticism** **Hermeticism** was another product of the Florentine intellectual environment of the late fifteenth century. At the request of Cosimo de' Medici, Ficino translated into Latin a Greek work titled *Corpus Hermeticum.* The Hermetic manuscripts contained two kinds of writings. One type stressed the occult sciences, with an emphasis on astrology, alchemy, and magic. The other focused on theological and philosophical beliefs and speculations. Some Hermetic writings espoused **pantheism,** seeing divinity embodied in all aspects of nature and in the heavenly bodies as well as in earthly objects. As Giordano Bruno, one of the most prominent of the sixteenth-century Hermeticists stated, "God as a whole is in all things."[14]

For Renaissance intellectuals, the Hermetic revival offered a new view of humankind. They believed that human beings had been created as divine beings endowed with divine creative power but had freely chosen to enter the material world (nature). Humans could recover their divinity, however, through a regenerative experience or purification of the soul. Thus regenerated, they became true sages or magi, as the Renaissance called them, who had knowledge of God and of truth. In regaining their original divinity, they reacquired an intimate knowledge of nature and the ability to employ the powers of nature for beneficial purposes.

In Italy, the most prominent magi in the late fifteenth century were Ficino and his friend and pupil, Giovanni Pico della Mirandola (1463–1494). Pico produced one of the most famous pieces of writing of the Renaissance, the *Oration on the Dignity of Man.* Pico combed diligently through the works of many philosophers of different backgrounds for the common "nuggets of universal truth" that he believed were all part of God's revelation to humanity. In the *Oration* (see the box on p. 328), Pico offered a ringing statement of unlimited human potential: "To him it is granted to have whatever he chooses, to be whatever he wills."[15] Like Ficino, Pico took an avid interest in Hermetic philosophy, accepting it as the "science of the Divine," which "embraces the deepest contemplation of the most secret things, and at last the knowledge of all nature."[16]

## Education in the Renaissance

The humanist movement had a profound effect on education. Renaissance humanists believed that human beings could be dramatically changed by education. They wrote books on education and developed secondary schools based on their ideas. Most famous was the school founded in 1423 by Vittorino da Feltre (1378–1446) at Mantua, where the ruler of that small Italian state, Gian Francesco I Gonzaga, wished to provide a humanist education for his children. Vittorino based much of his educational system on the ideas of classical authors, particularly Cicero and Quintilian.

At the core of the academic training Vittorino offered were the "liberal studies." The Renaissance view of the value of the liberal arts was most strongly influenced by a treatise on education called *Concerning Character* by Pietro Paolo Vergerio (1370–1444). This work stressed the importance of the liberal arts as the key to true freedom, enabling individuals to reach their full potential. According to Vergerio, "We call those studies liberal which are worthy of a free man; those studies by which we attain and practice virtue and wisdom; that education which calls forth, trains, and develops those highest gifts of body and mind which ennoble men."[17] The liberal studies included history, moral philosophy, eloquence (rhetoric), letters (grammar and logic), poetry, mathematics, astronomy, and music. The purpose of a liberal education was thus to produce individuals who followed a path of virtue and wisdom and possessed the rhetorical skills with which to persuade others to do the same. Following the Greek precept of a sound mind in a sound body, Vittorino's school at Mantua also stressed physical education. Pupils were taught the skills of javelin throwing, archery, and dancing and encouraged frequently to run, wrestle, hunt, and swim.

Although a small number of children from the lower classes were provided free educations, humanist schools such as Vittorino's were primarily geared for the education of an elite, the ruling classes of their communities. Also largely absent from such schools were females. Vittorino's only female pupils were the two daughters of the Gonzaga ruler of Mantua. Though these few female students studied the classics and were encouraged to know some history and to ride, dance, sing, play the lute, and appreciate poetry, they were discouraged from learning mathematics and rhetoric. In the educational treatises of the time, religion and morals were thought to "hold the first place in the education of a Christian lady."

## PICO DELLA MIRANDOLA AND THE DIGNITY OF MAN

*G*IOVANNI PICO DELLA MIRANDOLA was one of the foremost intellects of the Italian Renaissance. Pico boasted that he had studied all schools of philosophy, which he tried to demonstrate by drawing up nine hundred theses for public disputation at the age of twenty-four. As a preface to his theses, he wrote his famous *Oration on the Dignity of Man,* in which he proclaimed the unlimited potentiality of human beings.

### Pico della Mirandola, *Oration on the Dignity of Man*

At last the best of artisans [God] ordained that that creature to whom He had been able to give nothing proper to himself should have joint possession of whatever had been peculiar to each of the different kinds of being. He therefore took man as a creature of indeterminate nature, and assigning him a place in the middle of the world, addressed him thus: "Neither a fixed abode nor a form that is yours alone nor any function peculiar to yourself have we given you, Adam, to the end that according to your longing and according to your judgment you may have and possess what abode, what form, and what functions you yourself desire. The nature of all other beings is limited and constrained within the bounds of laws prescribed by Us. You, constrained by no limits, in accordance with your own free will, in whose hand We have placed you, shall ordain for yourself the limits of your nature. We have set you at the world's center that you may from there more easily observe whatever is in the world. We have made you neither of heaven nor of earth, neither mortal nor immortal, so that with freedom of choice and with honor, as though the maker and molder of yourself, you may fashion yourself in whatever shape you shall prefer. You shall have the power to degenerate into the lower forms of life, which are brutish. You shall have the power, out of your soul's judgment, to be reborn into the higher forms, which are divine."

O supreme generosity of God the Father, O highest and most marvelous felicity of man! To him it is granted to have whatever he chooses, to be whatever he wills. Beasts as soon as they are born bring with them from their mother's womb all they will ever possess. Spiritual beings, either from the beginning or soon thereafter, become what they are to be for ever and ever. On man when he came into life the Father conferred the seeds of all kinds and the germs of every way of life. Whatever seeds each man cultivates will grow to maturity and bear in him their own fruit. If they be vegetative, he will be like a plant. If sensitive, he will become brutish. If rational, he will grow into a heavenly being. If intellectual, he will be an angel and the son of God.

---

Nevertheless, some women in Italy who were educated in the humanist fashion went on to establish their own literary careers. Isotta Nogarola, born to a noble family in Verona, mastered Latin and wrote numerous letters and treatises that brought her praise from male Italian intellectuals. Cassandra Fedele of Venice, who learned both Latin and Greek from humanist tutors hired by her family, became prominent in Venice for her public recitations of orations. Laura Cereta was educated in Latin by her father, a physician from Brescia. Laura defended the ability of women to pursue scholarly pursuits (see the box on p. 329).

Humanist education was thought to be a practical preparation for life. Its aim was not to create great scholars but rather to produce complete citizens who could participate in the civic life of their communities. As Vittorino said, "Not everyone is obliged to excel in philosophy, medicine, or the law, nor are all equally favored by nature; but all are destined to live in society and to practice virtue."[18] Humanist schools, combining the classics and Christianity, provided the model for the basic education of the European ruling classes until the twentieth century.

### Humanism and History

Humanism had a strong impact on the writing of history. Influenced by Roman and Greek historians, the humanists approached the writing of history differently from the chroniclers of the Middle Ages. The humanists' belief that classical civilization had been followed by an age of barbarism (the Middle Ages), which had in turn been succeeded by their own age, with its rebirth of the study of the classics, enabled them to think in terms of the passage of time, of the past as past. Their division of the past into ancient world, dark ages, and their own age provided a new sense of chronology or periodization in history.

The humanists were also responsible for secularizing the writing of history. Humanist historians reduced or eliminated the role of miracles in historical interpretation, not because they were anti-Christian but because they took a new approach to sources. They wanted to use documents and exercised their newly developed critical skills in examining them. Greater attention was paid to the political events and forces that affected their city-states or larger territorial units. Thus Leonardo Bruni wrote the *History of the Florentine People.* The new emphasis on secularization was also evident in the humanists' conception of causation in history. In much medieval historical literature, historical events were often portrayed as being caused by God's active involvement in human affairs. Humanists deemphasized divine intervention in favor of human motives, stressing political forces or the role of individuals in history.

**Guicciardini**   The high point of Renaissance historiography was achieved at the beginning of the sixteenth century in the works of Francesco Guicciardini (1483–1540).

# A WOMAN'S DEFENSE OF LEARNING

*S A YOUNG WOMAN, Laura Cereta was proud of her learning but condemned by a male world that found it unseemly for women to be scholars. One monk said to her father, "She gives herself to things unworthy of her—namely, the classics." Before being silenced, Laura Cereta wrote a series of letters, including one to a male critic who had argued that her work was so good it could not have been written by a woman.*

### ∅ Laura Cereta, *Defense of the Liberal Instruction of Women*

My ears are wearied by your carping. You brashly and publicly not merely wonder but indeed lament that I am said to possess as fine a mind as nature ever bestowed upon the most learned man. You seem to think that so learned a woman has scarcely before been seen in the world. You are wrong on both counts. . . .

I would have been silent. . . . But I cannot tolerate your having attacked my entire sex. For this reason my thirsty soul seeks revenge, my sleeping pen is aroused to literary struggle, raging anger stirs mental passions long chained by silence. With just cause I am moved to demonstrate how great a reputation for learning and virtue women have won by their inborn excellence, manifested in every age as knowledge. . . .

Only the question of the rarity of outstanding women remains to be addressed. The explanation is clear: women have been able by nature to be exceptional, but have chosen lesser goals. For some women are concerned with parting their hair correctly, adorning themselves with lovely dresses, or decorating their fingers with pearls and other gems. Others delight in mouthing carefully composed phrases, indulging in dancing, or managing spoiled puppies. Still others wish to gaze at lavish banquet tables, to rest in sleep, or, standing at mirrors, to smear their lovely faces. But those in whom a deeper integrity yearns for virtue, restrain from the start their youthful souls, reflect on higher things, harden the body with sobriety and trials, and curb their tongues, open their ears, compose their thoughts in wakeful hours, their minds in contemplation, to letters bonded to righteousness. For knowledge is not given as a gift, but [is gained] with diligence. The free mind, not shirking effort, always soars zealously toward the good, and the desire to know grows ever more wide and deep. It is because of no special holiness, therefore, that we [women] are rewarded by God the Giver with the gift of exceptional talent. Nature has generously lavished its gifts upon all people, opening to all the doors of choice through which reason sends envoys to the will, from which they learn and convey its desires. The will must choose to exercise the gift of reason. . . .

I have been praised too much; showing your contempt for women, you pretend that I alone am admirable because of the good fortune of my intellect. . . . Do you suppose, O most contemptible man on earth, that I think myself sprung [like Athena] from the head of Jove? I am a school girl, possessed of the sleeping embers of an ordinary mind. Indeed I am too hurt, and my mind, offended, too swayed by passions, sighs, tormenting itself, conscious of the obligation to defend my sex. For absolutely everything—that which is within us and that which is without—is made weak by association with my sex.

---

He has been called by some Renaissance scholars the greatest historian between Tacitus in the first century (see Chapter 6) and Voltaire and Gibbon in the eighteenth century (see Chapter 17). His *History of Italy* and *History of Florence* represent the beginning of "modern analytical historiography." To Guicciardini, the purpose of writing history was to teach lessons, but he was so impressed by the complexity of historical events that he felt those lessons were not always obvious. From his extensive background in government and diplomatic affairs, he developed the skills that enabled him to analyze political situations precisely and critically. Emphasizing political and military history, his works relied heavily on personal examples and documentary sources.

### ∅ The Impact of Printing

The Renaissance witnessed the invention of printing, one of the most important technological innovations of Western civilization. The art of printing made an immediate impact on European intellectual life and thought.

Printing from hand-carved wooden blocks had been done in the West since the twelfth century and in China even before that. What was new to Europe in the fifteenth century was multiple printing with movable metal type. The development of printing from movable type was a gradual process that culminated between 1445 and 1450; Johannes Gutenberg of Mainz played an important role in bringing the process to completion. Gutenberg's Bible, completed in 1455 or 1456, was the first true book in the West produced from movable type.

The new printing spread rapidly throughout Europe in the second half of the fifteenth century. Printing presses were established throughout the Holy Roman Empire in the 1460s and within ten years had spread to Italy, England, France, the Low Countries, Spain, and eastern Europe. Especially well known as a printing center was Venice, home by 1500 to almost one hundred printers who had produced almost two million volumes.

By 1500, there were more than one thousand printers in Europe who had published almost forty thousand titles (between eight and ten million copies). Probably 50 percent of these books were religious—Bibles and biblical commentaries, books of devotion, and sermons. Next in importance were the Latin and Greek classics, medieval grammars, legal handbooks, works on philosophy, and an ever-growing number of popular romances.

Printing became one of the largest industries in Europe, and its effects were soon felt in many areas of European life. The printing of books encouraged the development of scholarly research and the desire to attain knowledge. Moreover, printing facilitated cooperation among scholars and helped produce standardized and definitive texts. Printing also stimulated the development of an ever-expanding lay reading public, a development that had an enormous impact on European society. Indeed, without the printing press, the new religious ideas of the Reformation would never have spread as rapidly as they did in the sixteenth century.

## The Artistic Renaissance

Leonardo da Vinci, one of the great Italian Renaissance artists, once explained, "Hence the painter will produce pictures of small merit if he takes for his standard the pictures of others, but if he will study from natural objects he will bear good fruit. . . . Those who take for their standard any one but nature . . . weary themselves in vain."[19] Renaissance artists considered the imitation of nature their primary goal. Their search for naturalism became an end in itself:

to persuade onlookers of the reality of the object or event they were portraying. At the same time, the new artistic standards reflected a new attitude of mind as well, one in which human beings became the focus of attention, the "center and measure of all things," as one artist proclaimed.

### Art in the Early Renaissance

Leonardo and other Italians maintained that it was Giotto in the fourteenth century (see Chapter 11) who began the imitation of nature. But what Giotto had begun was not taken up again until the work of Masaccio (1401–1428) in Florence. Masaccio's cycle of frescoes in the Brancacci Chapel has long been regarded as the first masterpiece of Early Renaissance art. With his use of monumental figures, demonstration of a more realistic relationship between figures and landscape, and visual representation of the laws of perspective, a new realistic style of painting was born. Onlookers become aware of a world of reality that appears to be a continuation of their own world. Masaccio's massive, three-dimensional human figures provided a model for later generations of Florentine artists.

This new Renaissance style was absorbed and modified by other Florentine painters in the fifteenth century. Especially important was the development of an experimental trend that took two directions. One emphasized the mathematical side of painting, the working out of the laws of perspective and the organization of outdoor space and light by geometry and perspective. In the work of Paolo

© Scala/Art Resource, NY

**Masaccio, *Tribute Money*.** With the frescoes of Masaccio, regarded by many as the first great works of Early Renaissance art, a new realistic style of painting was born. *Tribute Money* was one of a series of frescoes that Masaccio painted in the Brancacci Chapel of the Church of Santa Maria del Carmine in Florence. In *Tribute Money*, Masaccio illustrated the biblical story of Jesus' confrontation by a tax collector at the entrance to the town of Capernaum (seen at center). Jesus sent Peter to collect a coin from the mouth of a fish from Lake Galilee (seen at left); Peter then paid the tax collector (seen at right). In illustrating this story from the Bible, Masaccio used a rational system of perspective to create a realistic relationship between the figures and their background; the figures themselves are realistic. As one Renaissance observer said, "The works made before Masaccio's day can be said to be painted, while his are living, real, and natural."

**Botticelli, *Primavera*.** This work reflects Botticelli's strong interest in classical antiquity. At the center of the painting is Venus, the goddess of love. At the right stands Flora, a Roman goddess of flowers and fertility, while the Three Graces dance playfully at the left. Cupid, the son of Venus, aims his arrow at the Three Graces. At the far left of the picture is Mercury, the messenger of the gods. Later in his life, Botticelli experienced a profound religious crisis, leading him to reject his earlier preoccupation with pagan gods and goddesses. He burned many of his early paintings and thereafter produced only religious works.

© Erich Lessing/Art Resource, NY

Uccello (1397–1475), figures became mere stage props to show off his mastery of the laws of perspective. The other aspect of the experimental trend involved the investigation of movement and anatomical structure. *The Martyrdom of Saint Sebastian* by Antonio Pollaiuolo (c. 1432–1498) revels in classical motifs and attempts to portray the human body under stress. Indeed, the realistic portrayal of the human nude became one of the foremost preoccupations of Italian Renaissance art. The fifteenth century, then, was a period of experimentation and technical mastery.

During the last decades of the fifteenth century, a new sense of invention emerged in Florence, especially in the circle of artists and scholars who formed part of the court of the city's leading citizen, Lorenzo the Magnificent. One of this group's prominent members was Sandro Botticelli (1445–1510), whose interest in Greek and Roman mythology was well reflected in one of his most famous works, *Primavera* (Spring). The painting is set in the garden of Venus, a garden of eternal spring. Though Botticelli's figures are well defined, they also possess an otherworldly quality that is far removed from the realism that characterized the painting of the Early Renaissance.

**Donatello, *David*.** Donatello's *David* first stood in the courtyard of the Medici Palace. On its base was an inscription praising Florentine heroism and virtue, leading art historians to assume that the statue was meant to commemorate the victory of Florence over Milan in 1428. David's pose and appearance are reminiscent of the nude statues of antiquity.

The revolutionary achievements of Florentine painters in the fifteenth century were matched by equally stunning advances in sculpture and architecture. Donato di Donatello (1386–1466) spent time in Rome studying and copying the statues of antiquity. His subsequent work in Florence reveals how well he had mastered the essence of what he saw. Among his numerous works was a statue of David, which is the first known life-size freestanding bronze nude in European art since antiquity. With the severed head of the giant Goliath beneath David's feet, Donatello's statue celebrated Florentine heroism in the triumph of the Florentines over the Milanese in 1428. Like Donatello's other statues, *David* also radiated a simplicity and strength that reflected the dignity of humanity.

Filippo Brunelleschi (1377–1446) was a friend who accompanied Donatello to Rome. Brunelleschi drew much inspiration from the architectural monuments of Roman antiquity, and when he returned to Florence, he poured his new insights into the creation of a new architecture. His first project involved the challenge of building a dome for the unfinished Cathedral of Florence (the Duomo). The cathedral had been started in 1296, but it was Brunelleschi who devised new building techniques and machinery to create a dome, built between 1420 and 1436, that spanned a 140-foot opening.

An even better example of Brunelleschi's new Renaissance architectural style is evident in the Church of San Lorenzo. When the Medici commissioned him to design the church, Brunelleschi, inspired by Roman models, created a church interior very different from that of the great medieval

© Scala/Art Resource, NY

**Filippo Brunelleschi, Dome of the Duomo.** Brunelleschi was first commissioned in 1417 to design the dome for the unfinished Cathedral of Florence. Work did not begin until 1420. Although Brunelleschi would have preferred the Roman hemispheric dome, for practical reasons he was forced to elevate the center of the dome and then lessen the weight of the structure by building a thin double shell around a structure of twenty-four ribs. The most important ribs were placed on the outside of the dome (four of them are visible in this illustration).

fifteenth century, artists were giving an accurate rendering of their subjects' facial features while revealing the inner qualities of their personalities. The portraits of the duke and duchess of Urbino by Piero della Francesca (c. 1410–1492) provide accurate representations as well as a sense of both the power and the wealth of the rulers of Urbino (see p. 321).

### The Artistic High Renaissance

By the end of the fifteenth century, Italian painters, sculptors, and architects had created a new artistic environment. Many artists had mastered the new techniques for a scientific observation of the world around them and were now ready to move into individualistic forms of creative expression. This final stage of Renaissance art, which flourished between 1480 and 1520, is called the High Renaissance. The shift to the High Renaissance was marked by the increasing importance of Rome as a new cultural center of the Italian Renaissance.

The High Renaissance was dominated by the work of three artistic giants: Leonardo da Vinci (1452–1519), Raphael (1483–1520), and Michelangelo (1475–1564). Leonardo represents a transitional figure in the shift to

cathedrals. San Lorenzo's classical columns, rounded arches, and coffered ceiling created an environment that did not overwhelm the worshiper materially and psychologically, as Gothic cathedrals did, but comforted as a space created to fit human, not divine, measurements. Like painters and sculptors, Renaissance architects sought to reflect a human-centered world.

The new assertion of human individuality, evident in Early Renaissance art, was also reflected in the new emphasis on portraiture. Patrons appeared in the corners of sacred pictures, and monumental tombs and portrait statues honored many of Florence's prominent citizens. By the mid-

**Brunelleschi, Interior of San Lorenzo.** Cosimo de' Medici contributed massive amounts of money to the rebuilding of the Church of San Lorenzo. As seen in this view of the nave and choir of the church, Brunelleschi's architectural designs were based on the basilica plan borrowed by early Christians from pagan Rome. San Lorenzo's simplicity, evident in its rows of slender Corinthian columns, created a human-centered space.

**Leonardo da Vinci, *The Last Supper*.** Leonardo da Vinci was the impetus behind the High Renaissance concern for the idealization of nature, moving from a realistic portrayal of the human figure to an idealized form. Evident in Leonardo's *Last Supper* is his effort to depict a person's character and inner nature by the use of gesture and movement. Unfortunately, Leonardo used an experimental technique in this fresco, which soon led to its physical deterioration.

High Renaissance principles. He carried on the fifteenth-century experimental tradition by studying everything and even dissecting human bodies to more clearly see how nature worked. But Leonardo stressed the need to advance beyond such realism and initiated the High Renaissance's preoccupation with the idealization of nature, or the attempt to generalize from realistic portrayal to an ideal form. Leonardo's *Last Supper,* painted in Milan, is a brilliant summary of fifteenth-century trends in its organization of space and use of perspective to depict subjects three-dimensionally in a two-dimensional medium. But it is also more. The figure of Philip is idealized, and there are profound psychological dimensions to the work. The words of Jesus that "one of you shall betray me" are experienced directly as each of the apostles reveals his personality and his relationship to Jesus. Through gestures and movement, Leonardo hoped to reveal a person's inner life.

Raphael blossomed as a painter at an early age; at twenty-five, he was already regarded as one of Italy's best painters. Raphael was acclaimed for his numerous madonnas, in which he attempted to achieve an ideal of beauty far surpassing human standards. He is well-known for his frescoes in the Vatican Palace; his *School of Athens* reveals a world of balance, harmony, and order—the underlying principles of the art of the classical world of Greece and Rome.

Michelangelo, an accomplished painter, sculptor, and architect, was another giant of the High Renaissance. Fiercely driven by his desire to create, he worked with great passion and energy on a remarkable number of projects. Michelangelo was influenced by Neoplatonism, especially evident in his figures on the ceiling of the Sistine Chapel in Rome. In 1508, Pope Julius II had called Michelangelo to Rome and commissioned him to decorate the chapel ceiling. This colossal project was not completed until 1512. Michelangelo attempted to tell the story of the Fall of Man by depicting nine scenes from the biblical book of Genesis. In his *Creation of Adam* (reproduced at the start of this chapter), the well-proportioned figure of Adam awaits the divine spark. Adam, like the other muscular figures on the ceiling, reveals an ideal type of human being with perfect proportions. In good Neoplatonic fashion, the beauty of these figures is meant to be a reflection of divine beauty; the more beautiful the body, the more God-like the figure.

Another manifestation of Michelangelo's search for ideal beauty was his *David,* a colossal marble statue commissioned by the Florentine government in 1501 and completed in 1504. Michelangelo maintained that the form of a statue already resided in the uncarved piece of stone: "I only take away the surplus, the statue is already there."[20] Out of a piece of marble that had remained unused for fifty years, Michelangelo created a 14-foot-high figure, the largest sculpture in Italy since the time of Rome. An awe-inspiring hero, Michelangelo's *David* proudly proclaims the beauty of the human body and the glory of human beings.

The High Renaissance was also evident in architecture, especially in the work of Donato Bramante (1444–1514).

**Raphael, *School of Athens*.** Raphael arrived in Rome in 1508 and began to paint a series of frescoes commissioned by Pope Julius II for the papal apartments at the Vatican. In *School of Athens,* painted in 1510 or 1511, Raphael created an imaginary gathering of ancient philosophers. In the center stand Plato and Aristotle. At the left is Pythagoras, showing his system of proportions on a slate. At the right is Ptolemy, holding a celestial globe.

He came from Urbino but took up residence in Rome, where he designed a small temple on the supposed site of Saint Peter's martyrdom. The Tempietto, or little temple, with its Doric columns surrounding a sanctuary enclosed by a dome, summarized the architectural ideals of the High Renaissance. Columns, dome, and sanctuary form a monumental and harmonious whole. Inspired by antiquity, Bramante had recaptured the grandeur of ancient Rome. His achievement led Pope Julius II to commission him to design a new basilica for Rome, which eventually became the magnificent Saint Peter's.

**Michelangelo, *David*.** This statue of David, cut from an 18-foot-high piece of marble, exalts the beauty of the human body and is a fitting symbol of the Italian Renaissance's affirmation of human power. Completed in 1504, *David* was moved by Florentine authorities to a special location in front of the Palazzo Vecchio, the seat of the Florentine government.

# THE GENIUS OF LEONARDO DA VINCI

DURING THE RENAISSANCE, artists came to be viewed as creative geniuses with almost divine qualities. One individual who helped create this image was himself a painter. Giorgio Vasari was an avid admirer of Italy's great artists and wrote a series of brief biographies of them. This excerpt is taken from his account of Leonardo da Vinci.

### Giorgio Vasari, *Lives of the Artists*

In the normal course of events many men and women are born with various remarkable qualities and talents; but occasionally, in a way that transcends nature, a single person is marvelously endowed by heaven with beauty, grace, and talent in such abundance that he leaves other men far behind, all his actions seem inspired, and indeed everything he does clearly comes from God rather than from human art.

Everyone acknowledged that this was true of Leonardo da Vinci, an artist of outstanding physical beauty who displayed infinite grace in everything he did and who cultivated his genius so brilliantly that all problems he studied he solved with ease. He possessed great strength and dexterity; he was a man of regal spirit and tremendous breadth of mind; and his name became so famous that not only was he esteemed during his lifetime but his reputation endured and became even greater after his death. . . .

He was marvelously gifted, and he proved himself to be a first-class geometrician in his work as a sculptor and architect. In his youth Leonardo made in clay several heads of women, with smiling faces, of which plaster casts are still being made, as well as some children's heads executed as if by a mature artist. He also did many architectural drawings both of ground plans and of other elevations, and, while still young, he was the first to propose reducing the Arno River to a navigable canal between Pisa and Florence. He made designs for mills, fulling machines, and engines that could be driven by waterpower; and as he intended to be a painter by profession he carefully studied drawing from life. . . . Altogether, his genius was so wonderfully inspired by the grace of God, his powers of expression were so powerfully fed by a willing memory and intellect, and his writing conveyed his ideas so precisely, that his arguments and reasonings confounded the most formidable critics. In addition, he used to make models and plans showing how to excavate and tunnel through mountains without difficulty, so as to pass from one level to another; and he demonstrated how to lift and draw great weights by means of levers and hoists and ways of cleaning harbors and using pumps to suck up water from great depths.

### The Artist and Social Status

Early Renaissance artists began their careers as apprentices to masters in craft guilds. Apprentices with unusual talent might eventually become masters and run their own workshops. As in the Middle Ages, artists were still largely viewed as artisans. Since guilds depended on commissions for their projects, patrons played an important role in the art of the Early Renaissance. The wealthy upper classes determined both the content and purpose of the paintings and pieces of sculpture they commissioned.

By the end of the fifteenth century, a transformation in the position of the artist had occurred. Especially talented individuals, such as Leonardo, Raphael, and Michelangelo, were no longer regarded as artisans but as artistic geniuses with creative energies akin to the divine (see the box above). Artists were heroes, individuals who were praised more for their creativity than for their competence as craftspeople. Michelangelo, for example, was frequently addressed as "Il Divino"—the Divine One. As society excused their

**Bramante, Tempietto.** Ferdinand and Isabella of Spain commissioned Donato Bramante to design a small building in Rome that would commemorate the place where Saint Peter was purportedly crucified. Completed in 1502, the temple reflected Bramante's increasing understanding of ancient Roman remains.

© Art Resource, NY

eccentricities and valued their creative genius, the artists of the High Renaissance became the first to embody the modern concept of the artist.

As respect for artists grew, so did their ability to profit economically from their work and to rise on the social scale. Now welcomed as equals into the circles of the upper classes, they mingled with the political and intellectual elite of their society and became more aware of new intellectual theories, which they then embodied in their art. The Platonic Academy and Renaissance Neoplatonism had an especially important impact on Florentine painters.

## The Northern Artistic Renaissance

In trying to provide an exact portrayal of their world, the artists of the north (especially the Low Countries) and Italy took different approaches. In Italy, the human form became the primary vehicle of expression as Italian artists sought to master the technical skills that allowed them to portray humans in realistic settings. The large wall spaces of Italian churches had given rise to the art of fresco painting, but in the north, the prevalence of Gothic cathedrals with their stained-glass windows resulted in more emphasis on illuminated manuscripts and wooden panel painting for altarpieces. The space available in these works was limited, and great care was required to depict each object, leading northern painters to become masters at rendering details.

The most influential northern school of art in the fifteenth century was centered in Flanders. Jan van Eyck (c. 1390–1441) was among the first to use oil paint, a medium that enabled the artist to use a varied range of colors and make changes to create fine details. In the famous *Giovanni Arnolfini and His Bride,* van Eyck's attention to detail is staggering: precise portraits, a glittering chandelier, and a mirror reflecting the objects in the room. Although each detail was rendered as observed, it is evident that van Eyck's comprehension of perspective was still uncertain. His work is truly indicative of northern Renaissance painters, who, in their effort to imitate nature, did so not by mastery of the laws of perspective and proportion but by empirical observation of visual reality and the accurate portrayal of details. Moreover, northern painters placed great emphasis on the emotional intensity of religious feeling and created great works of devotional art, especially in their altarpieces. Michelangelo summarized the difference between northern and Italian Renaissance painting in these words:

> In Flanders, they paint, before all things, to render exactly and deceptively the outward appearance of things. The painters choose, by preference, subjects provoking transports of piety, like the figures of saints or of prophets. But most of the time they paint what are called landscapes with plenty of figures. Though the eye is agreeably impressed, these pictures have neither choice of values nor grandeur. In short, this art is without power and without distinction; it aims at rendering minutely many things at the same time, of which a single one would have sufficed to call forth a man's whole application.[21]

**Van Eyck,** *Giovanni Arnolfini and His Bride.* Northern painters took great care in depicting each object and became masters at rendering details. This emphasis on a realistic portrayal is clearly evident in this oil painting, supposedly a portrait of Giovanni Arnolfini, an Italian merchant who had settled in Bruges, and his wife, Giovanna Cenami.

By the end of the fifteenth century, however, artists from the north began to study in Italy and were visually influenced by what artists were doing there.

One northern artist of this later period who was greatly affected by the Italians was Albrecht Dürer (1471–1528) from Nuremberg. Dürer made two trips to Italy and absorbed most of what the Italians could teach, as is evident in his mastery of the laws of perspective and Renaissance theories of proportion. He wrote detailed treatises on both subjects. At the same time, as in his famous *Adoration of the Magi,* Dürer did not reject the use of minute details characteristic of northern artists. He did try, however, to integrate those details more harmoniously into his works and, like the Italian artists of the High Renaissance, to achieve a standard of ideal beauty by a careful examination of the human form.

## Music in the Renaissance

For much of the fifteenth century, an extraordinary cultural environment was fostered in the domains of the dukes of

**Dürer, *Adoration of the Magi*.** By the end of the fifteenth century, northern artists had begun to study in Italy and to adopt many of the techniques used by Italian painters. As is evident in this painting, which was the central panel for an altarpiece done for Frederick the Wise in 1504, Albrecht Dürer masterfully incorporated the laws of perspective and the ideals of proportion into his works. At the same time, he did not abandon the preoccupation with detail typical of northern artists. Dürer portrayed himself in the center as the wise man with long hair.

Burgundy in northern Europe. The court of the dukes attracted some of the best artists and musicians of the time. Among them was Guillaume Dufay (c. 1400–1474), perhaps the most important composer of his time. Born in northern France, Dufay lived for a few years in Italy and was thus well suited to combine the late medieval style of France with the early Renaissance style of Italy. One of Dufay's greatest contributions was a change in the composition of the Mass. He was the first to use secular tunes to replace Gregorian chants as the fixed melody that served as the basis for the Mass. Dufay also composed a number of secular songs, an important reminder that during the Renaissance, music ceased to be used chiefly in the service of God and moved into the secular world of courts and cities. In Italy and France, the chief form of secular music was the madrigal.

The Renaissance madrigal was a poem set to music, and its origins were in the fourteenth-century Italian courts. The texts were usually twelve-line poems written in the vernacular, and their theme was emotional or erotic love. By the mid-sixteenth century, most madrigals were written for five or six voices and employed a technique called text painting, in which the music tried to portray the literal meaning of the text. Thus the melody would rise for the word *heaven* or use a wavelike motion to represent the word *water*. By the mid-sixteenth century, the madrigal had also spread to England, where the most popular form was characterized by the *fa-la-la* refrain like that found in the English carol "Deck the Halls."

# The European State in the Renaissance

In the first half of the fifteenth century, European states continued the disintegrative patterns of the previous century. In the second half of the century, however, recovery set in,

and attempts were made to reestablish the centralized power of monarchical governments. To characterize the results, some historians have used the label "Renaissance states"; others have spoken of the "**new monarchies**," especially those of France, England, and Spain at the end of the fifteenth century (see Map 12.2). Although monarchs in western Europe succeeded to varying degrees at extending their political authority, rulers in central and eastern Europe were often weak and unable to impose their authority.

## The Growth of the French Monarchy

The Hundred Years' War had left France prostrate. Depopulation, desolate farmlands, ruined commerce, and independent and unruly nobles had made it difficult for the kings to assert their authority. But the war had also developed a strong degree of French national feeling toward a common enemy that the kings could use to reestablish monarchical power. The need to prosecute the war provided an excuse to strengthen the authority of the king, already evident in the policies of Charles VII (1422–1461) after he was crowned king at Reims. With the consent of the Estates-General, Charles established a royal army composed of cavalry and archers. He received from the Estates-General the right to levy the *taille*, an annual direct tax usually on land or property, without any need for further approval from the Estates-General. Losing control of the purse meant less power for this parliamentary body.

The process of developing a French territorial state was greatly advanced by King Louis XI (1461–1483), known as the Spider because of his wily and devious ways. By retaining the *taille* as a permanent tax imposed by royal authority, Louis secured a sound, regular source of income. Louis was not, however, completely successful in repressing the French nobility, whose independence posed a threat to his own state building. A major problem was his supposed vassal, Charles the Bold, duke of Burgundy (1467–1477).

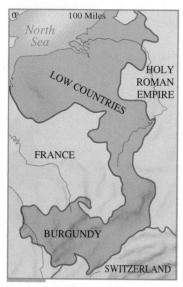

**Lands of Charles the Bold**

Charles attempted to create a middle kingdom between France and Germany, stretching from the Low Countries to Switzerland. Louis opposed his action, and when Charles was killed in 1477 fighting the Swiss, Louis added part of Charles's possessions, the duchy of Burgundy, to his own lands. Three years later, the provinces of Anjou, Maine, Bar, and Provence were brought under royal control. Many historians believe that Louis created a base for the later development of a strong French monarchy.

## England: Civil War and a New Monarchy

The Hundred Years' War had also strongly affected the other protagonist in that conflict. The cost of the war in its final years and the losses in manpower strained the English economy. Moreover, even greater domestic turmoil came to England when the War of the Roses broke out in the 1450s. This civil war pitted the ducal house of Lancaster, whose symbol was a red rose, against the ducal house of York, whose symbol was a white rose. Many aristocratic families of England were drawn into the conflict. Finally, in 1485, Henry Tudor, duke of Richmond, defeated the last Yorkist king, Richard III (1483–1485), at Bosworth Field and established the new Tudor dynasty.

As the first Tudor king, Henry VII (1485–1509) worked to reduce internal dissension and establish a strong monarchical government. Henry ended the private wars of the nobility by abolishing "livery and maintenance," the practice by which wealthy aristocrats maintained private armies

**MAP 12.2 Europe in the Second Half of the Fifteenth Century.** By the second half of the fifteenth century, states in western Europe, particularly France, Spain, and England, had begun the process of modern state building. With varying success, they reined in the power of the church and nobles, increased the ability to levy taxes, and established effective government bureaucracies. ❓ What aspects of Europe's political boundaries help explain why France and the Holy Roman Empire were often at war with each other? 🌐 **View an animated version of this map or related maps at** http://history.wadsworth.com/spielvogel06/

of followers dedicated to the service of their lord. Since England, unlike France and Spain, did not possess a standing army, the king relied on special commissions to trusted nobles to raise troops for a specific campaign, after which the troops were disbanded. Henry also controlled the irresponsible activity of the nobles by establishing the Court of Star Chamber, which did not use juries and allowed torture to be used to extract confessions.

Henry VII was particularly successful in extracting income from the traditional financial resources of the English monarch, such as the crown lands, judicial fees and fines, and customs duties. By using diplomacy to avoid wars, which are always expensive, the king avoided having to call Parliament on any regular basis to grant him funds. By not overburdening the landed gentry and middle class with taxes, Henry won their favor, and they provided much support for his monarchy. Henry's policies enabled him to leave England with a stable and prosperous government and an enhanced status for the monarchy itself.

## The Unification of Spain

During the Middle Ages, several independent Christian kingdoms had emerged in the course of the long reconquest of the Iberian peninsula from the Muslims. Aragon and Castile were the strongest Spanish kingdoms; in the west was the independent monarchy of Portugal; in the north, the small kingdom of Navarre, oriented toward France; and in the south, the Muslim kingdom of Granada (see Map 12.3). Few people at the beginning of the fifteenth century could have predicted the unification of the Iberian kingdoms.

A major step in that direction was taken with the marriage of Isabella of Castile (1474–1504) and Ferdinand of Aragon (1479–1516) in 1469. This was a dynastic union of two rulers, not a political union. Both kingdoms maintained their own parliaments (Cortes), courts, laws, coinage, speech, customs, and political organs. Nevertheless, the two rulers worked to strengthen royal control of government, especially in Castile. The royal council, which was supposed to supervise local administration and oversee the implementation of government policies, was stripped of aristocrats and filled primarily with middle-class lawyers. Trained in the principles of Roman law, these officials operated on the belief that the monarchy embodied the power of the state.

Seeking to replace the undisciplined feudal levies they had inherited with a more professional royal army, Ferdinand and Isabella reorganized the military forces of Spain. The development of a strong infantry force as the heart of the new Spanish army made it the best in Europe by the sixteenth century.

Ferdinand and Isabella recognized the importance of controlling the Catholic church, with its vast power and wealth. They secured from the pope the right to select the most important church officials in Spain, making the clergy virtually an instrument of royal power. Ferdinand and Isabella also pursued a policy of strict religious uniformity. Spain possessed two large religious minorities, Jews and Muslims, both of whom had been largely tolerated in medieval Spain. Increased persecution in the fourteenth century, however, led the majority of Spanish Jews to convert to Christianity. But complaints about the sincerity of these Jewish converts prompted Ferdinand and Isabella to ask the pope to introduce the Inquisition into Spain in 1478. Under royal control, the Inquisition worked with cruel efficiency to guarantee the orthodoxy of the converts but had no authority over practicing Jews. Consequently, in 1492, flush with the success of their conquest of Muslim Granada, Ferdinand and Isabella took the drastic step of expelling all professed Jews from Spain. It is estimated that 150,000 out of possibly 200,000 Jews fled.

Muslims, too, were "encouraged" to convert to Christianity after the conquest of Granada. In 1502, Isabella issued a decree expelling all professed Muslims from her kingdom. To a very large degree, the "Most Catholic" monarchs had achieved their goal of absolute religious orthodoxy as a basic ingredient of the Spanish state. To be Spanish was to be Catholic, a policy of uniformity enforced by the Inquisition.

## The Holy Roman Empire: The Success of the Habsburgs

Unlike France, England, and Spain, the Holy Roman Empire failed to develop a strong monarchical authority. After 1438, the position of Holy Roman Emperor remained

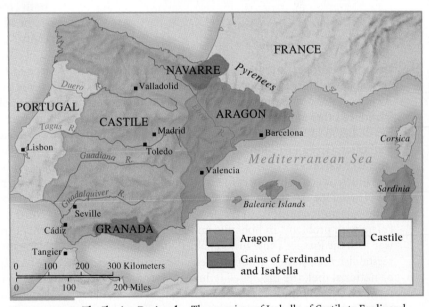

**MAP 12.3** **The Iberian Peninsula.** The marriage of Isabella of Castile to Ferdinand of Aragon laid the foundation for the unification of Spain and its rise as a major European power. The two monarchs instituted military and bureaucratic reforms and forced Jews and Muslims to flee the country. ❓ What aspects of Portugal's geography help explain why it became a major seafaring nation, with little overland trade with Europe? 🐾 **View an animated version of this map or related maps at** http://history.wadsworth.com/spielvogel06/

in the hands of the Habsburg dynasty. Having gradually acquired a number of possessions along the Danube, known collectively as Austria, the house of Habsburg had become one of the wealthiest landholders in the empire and by the mid-fifteenth century began to play an important role in European affairs.

Much of the Habsburg success in the fifteenth century was due not to military success but to a well-executed policy of dynastic marriages. As the old Habsburg motto said, "Leave the waging of wars to others! But you, happy Austria, marry; for the realms which Mars [god of war] awards to others, Venus [goddess of love] transfers to you." By marrying his son Maximilian to Mary, the daughter of Duke Charles the Bold of Burgundy, Emperor Frederick III (1440–1493) gained Franche-Comté in east-central France, Luxembourg, and a large part of the Low Countries. The addition of these territories made the Habsburg dynasty an international power and brought it the undying opposition of the French monarchy because the rulers of France feared they would be surrounded by the Habsburgs.

Much was expected of the flamboyant Maximilian I (1493–1519) when he became emperor. Through the Reichstag, the imperial diet or parliament, Maximilian attempted to centralize the administration by creating new institutions common to the entire empire. Opposition from the German princes doomed these efforts, however. Maximilian's only real success lay in his marriage alliances. Philip of Burgundy, the son of Maximilian's marriage to Mary, was married to Joanna, the daughter of Ferdinand and Isabella. Philip and Joanna produced a son, Charles, who, through a series of unexpected deaths, became heir to all three lines, the Habsburg, Burgundian, and Spanish, making him the leading monarch of his age (see Chapter 13).

### The Struggle for Strong Monarchy in Eastern Europe

In eastern Europe, rulers struggled to achieve the centralization of their territorial states but faced serious obstacles. Although the population was mostly Slavic, there were islands of other ethnic groups that caused untold difficulties. Religious differences also troubled the area, as Roman Catholics, Greek Orthodox Christians, and pagans confronted each other.

Much of Polish history revolved around a bitter struggle between the crown and the landed nobility until the end of the fifteenth century, when the preoccupation of Poland's rulers with problems in Bohemia and Hungary as well as war with the Russians and Turks enabled the aristocrats to reestablish their power. Through their control of the Sejm or national diet, the magnates reduced the peasantry to serfdom by 1511 and established the right to elect their kings. The Polish kings proved unable to establish a strong royal authority.

Bohemia, Poland's neighbor, was part of the Holy Roman Empire, but distrust of the Germans and close ethnic ties to the Poles and Slovaks encouraged the Czechs of Bohemia to associate with their northeastern Slavic

| CHRONOLOGY | Europe in the Renaissance |
|---|---|
| **France** | |
| Charles VII | 1422–1461 |
| Louis XI the Spider | 1461–1483 |
| **England** | |
| War of the Roses | 1450s–1485 |
| Richard III | 1483–1485 |
| Henry VII | 1485–1509 |
| **Spain** | |
| Isabella of Castile | 1474–1504 |
| Ferdinand of Aragon | 1479–1516 |
| Marriage of Ferdinand and Isabella | 1469 |
| Introduction of Inquisition | 1478 |
| Expulsion of the Jews | 1492 |
| Expulsion of the Muslims | 1502 |
| **Holy Roman Empire** | |
| Frederick III | 1440–1493 |
| Maximilian I | 1493–1519 |
| **Eastern Europe** | |
| Battle of Kosovo | 1389 |
| Hungary: Matthias Corvinus | 1458–1490 |
| Russia: Ivan III | 1462–1505 |
| Fall of Constantinople and Byzantine Empire | 1453 |

neighbors. The Hussite wars (see "The Problems of Heresy and Reform" later in this chapter) led to further dissension and civil war. Because of a weak monarchy, the Bohemian nobles increased their authority and wealth at the expense of both crown and church.

The history of Hungary had been closely tied to that of central and western Europe by its conversion to Roman Catholicism by German missionaries. The church became a large and prosperous institution. Wealthy bishops, along with the great territorial lords, became powerful, independent political figures. For a brief while, Hungary developed into an important European state, the dominant power in eastern Europe. King Matthias Corvinus (1458–1490) broke the power of the wealthy lords and created a well-organized bureaucracy. Like a typical Renaissance prince, he patronized the new humanist culture, brought Italian scholars and artists to his capital at Buda, and made his court one of the most brilliant outside Italy. After his death, Hungary returned to weak rule, and the work of Corvinus was largely undone.

Since the thirteenth century, Russia had been under the domination of the Mongols. Gradually, the princes of Moscow rose to prominence by using their close relationship to the Mongol khans to increase their wealth and expand their possessions. In the reign of the great prince Ivan III (1462–1505), a new Russian state—the principality of Moscow—was born. Ivan III annexed other Russian principalities and took advantage of dissension among the Mongols to throw off their yoke by 1480.

## The Ottoman Turks and the End of the Byzantine Empire

Eastern Europe was increasingly threatened by the steadily advancing Ottoman Turks (see Map 12.4). The Byzantine Empire had, of course, served as a buffer between the Muslim Middle East and the Latin West for centuries. It was severely weakened by the sack of Constantinople in 1204 and its occupation by the West. Although the Palaeologus dynasty (1260–1453) had tried to reestablish Byzantine power in the Balkans after the overthrow of the Latin empire, the threat from the Turks finally doomed the long-lasting empire.

Beginning in northeastern Asia Minor in the thirteenth century, the Ottoman Turks spread rapidly, seizing the lands of the Seljuk Turks and the Byzantine Empire. In 1345, they bypassed Constantinople and moved into the Balkans. Under Sultan Murad, Ottoman forces moved through Bulgaria and into the lands of the Serbians, who provided a strong center of opposition under King Lazar.

But in 1389, at the Battle of Kosovo, Ottoman forces defeated the Serbs; both King Lazar and Sultan Murad perished in the battle. Kosovo became a battlefield long revered and remembered by the Serbs. Not until 1480 were Bosnia, Albania, and the rest of Serbia added to the Ottoman Empire in the Balkans.

In the meantime, in 1453, the Ottomans also completed the demise of the Byzantine Empire. With eighty thousand troops ranged against only seven thousand defenders, Sultan Mehmet II laid siege to Constantinople. In their attack on the city, the Turks made use of massive cannons with 26-foot barrels that could launch stone balls weighing up to 1,200 pounds each. Finally, the walls were breached; the Byzantine emperor died in the final battle. Mehmet II, standing before the palace of the emperor, paused to reflect on the passing nature of human glory.

After consolidating their power, the Turks prepared to exert renewed pressure on the West, both in the Mediterranean and up the Danube valley toward Vienna. By the

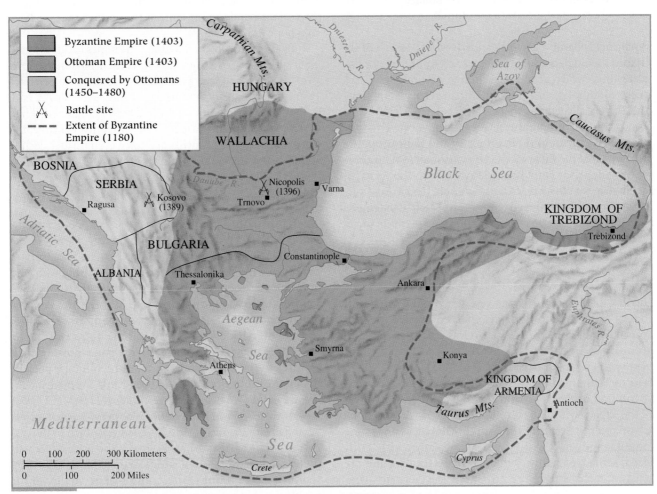

**MAP 12.4** **The Ottoman Empire and Southeastern Europe.** Long a buffer between Christian Europe and the Muslim Middle East, the Byzantine Empire quickly waned in power and territory after Constantinople was sacked by crusaders in 1204. The Ottoman Turks slowly gained Byzantine territory and ended the thousand-year reign with the fall of Constantinople in 1453. ❓ Why would the Byzantine Empire have found it difficult to make alliances by 1403? 👁 **View an animated version** of this map or related maps at http://history.wadsworth.com/spielvogel06/

end of the fifteenth century, they were threatening Hungary, Austria, Bohemia, and Poland. The Holy Roman Emperor, Charles V, became their bitter enemy in the sixteenth century.

# The Church in the Renaissance

As a result of the efforts of the Council of Constance, the Great Schism had finally been brought to an end in 1417 (see Chapter 11). The ending of the schism proved to be the council's easiest task; it was much less successful in dealing with the problems of heresy and reform.

## ⚜ The Problems of Heresy and Reform

Heresy was not a new problem, and in the thirteenth century, the church had developed inquisitorial machinery to deal with it. But two widespread movements in the fourteenth and early fifteenth centuries—Lollardy and Hussitism—posed new threats to the church.

**Wyclif and Lollardy**    English Lollardy was a product of the Oxford theologian John Wyclif (c. 1328–1384), whose disgust with clerical corruption led him to a far-ranging attack on papal authority and medieval Christian beliefs and practices. Wyclif alleged that there was no basis in Scripture for papal claims of temporal authority and advocated that the popes be stripped of their authority and their property. Believing that the Bible should be a Christian's sole authority, Wyclif urged that it be made available in the vernacular languages so that every Christian could read it. Rejecting all practices not mentioned in Scripture, Wyclif condemned pilgrimages, the veneration of saints, and a whole series of rituals and rites that had developed in the medieval church. Wyclif attracted a number of followers who came to be known as Lollards.

**Hus and the Hussites**    A marriage between the royal families of England and Bohemia enabled Lollard ideas to spread to Bohemia, where they reinforced the ideas of a group of Czech reformers led by the chancellor of the university at Prague, John Hus (1374–1415). In his call for reform, Hus urged the elimination of the worldliness and corruption of the clergy and attacked the excessive power of the papacy within the Catholic church. Hus's objections fell on receptive ears, for the Catholic church, as one of the largest landowners in Bohemia, was already widely criticized. Moreover, many clergymen were German, and the native Czechs' strong resentment of the Germans who dominated Bohemia also contributed to Hus's movement.

The Council of Constance attempted to deal with the growing problem of heresy by summoning John Hus to the council. Granted safe conduct by Emperor Sigismund, Hus went in the hope of a free hearing of his ideas. Instead he was arrested, condemned as a heretic (by a narrow vote), and burned at the stake in 1415. This action turned the unrest in Bohemia into revolutionary upheaval, and the resulting Hussite wars racked the Holy Roman Empire until a truce was arranged in 1436.

**Reform of the Church**    The reform of the church was even less successful than the attempt to eradicate heresy. Two reform decrees were passed by the Council of Constance. *Sacrosancta* stated that a general council of the church received its authority from God; hence every Christian, including the pope, was subject to its authority. The decree *Frequens* provided for the regular holding of general councils to ensure that church reform would continue. Taken together, *Sacrosancta* and *Frequens* provided for a legislative system within the church superior to the popes.

Decrees alone, however, proved insufficient to reform the church. Councils could issue decrees, but popes had to execute them, and popes would not cooperate with councils that diminished their authority. Beginning as early as Martin V in 1417, successive popes worked steadfastly for thirty years to defeat the conciliar movement. The final blow came in 1460, when Pope Pius II issued the papal bull *Execrabilis,* condemning appeals to a council over the head of a pope as heretical.

By the mid-fifteenth century, the popes had reasserted their supremacy over the Catholic church. No longer, however, did they have any possibility of asserting supremacy over temporal governments as the medieval papacy had. Although the papal monarchy had been maintained, it had lost much moral prestige. In the fifteenth century, the Renaissance papacy contributed to an even further decline in the moral leadership of the popes.

## ⚜ The Renaissance Papacy

The Renaissance papacy refers to the line of popes from the end of the Great Schism (1417) to the beginnings of the Reformation in the early sixteenth century. The primary concern of the papacy is governing the Catholic church as its spiritual leader. But as heads of the church, popes had temporal preoccupations as well, and the story of the Renaissance papacy is really an account of how the latter came to overshadow the popes' spiritual functions.

The manner in which Renaissance popes pursued their interests in the Papal States and Italian politics, especially their use of intrigue and even bloodshed, seemed shocking. Of all the Renaissance popes, Julius II (1503–1513) was most involved in war and politics. The fiery "warrior-pope" personally led armies against his enemies, much to the disgust of pious Christians, who viewed the pope as a spiritual leader. As one intellectual wrote, "How, O bishop standing in the room of the Apostles, dare you teach the people the things that pertain to war?"

To further their territorial aims in the Papal States, the popes needed loyal servants. Because they were not hereditary monarchs, popes could not build dynasties over several generations and came to rely on the practice of **nepotism** to promote their families' interests. Pope Sixtus IV (1471–1484), for example, made five of his nephews cardinals and gave them an abundance of church offices to

| Council of Constance | 1414–1418 |
|---|---|
| Burning of John Hus | 1415 |
| End of the Great Schism | 1417 |
| Pius II issues the papal bull *Execrabilis* | 1460 |
| The Renaissance papacy | |
| Sixtus IV | 1471–1484 |
| Alexander VI | 1492–1503 |
| Julius II | 1503–1513 |
| Leo X | 1513–1521 |

**A Renaissance Pope: Leo X.**  The Renaissance popes allowed secular concerns to overshadow their spiritual duties. Shown here is the Medici pope Leo X. Raphael portrays the pope as a collector of books, looking up after examining an illuminated manuscript with a magnifying glass. At the left is the pope's cousin Guilio, a cardinal. Standing behind the pope is Luigi de' Rossi, another relative who had also been made a cardinal.

build up their finances (the word *nepotism* is in fact derived from the Greek *nepos,* meaning "nephew"). Alexander VI (1492–1503), a member of the Borgia family who was known for his debauchery and sensuality, raised one son, one nephew, and the brother of one mistress to the cardinalate. A Venetian envoy stated that Alexander, "joyous by nature, thought of nothing but the aggrandizement of his children." Alexander scandalized the church by encouraging his son Cesare to carve a state for himself in central Italy out of the territories of the Papal States.

The Renaissance popes were great patrons of Renaissance culture, and their efforts made Rome a cultural leader at the beginning of the sixteenth century. For the warrior-pope Julius II, the patronage of Renaissance culture was mostly a matter of policy as he endeavored to add to the splendor of his pontificate by tearing down the Basilica of Saint Peter, which had been built by the emperor Constantine, and beginning construction of the greatest building in Christendom, the present Saint Peter's Basilica.

Julius's successor, Leo X (1513–1521), was also a patron of Renaissance culture, not as a matter of policy but as a deeply involved participant. Such might be expected of the son of Lorenzo de' Medici. Made an archbishop at the age of eight and a cardinal at thirteen, he acquired a refined taste in art, manners, and social life among the Florentine Renaissance elite. He became pope at the age of thirty-seven, supposedly remarking to the Venetian ambassador, "Let us enjoy the papacy, since God has given it to us." Raphael was commissioned to do paintings, and the construction of Saint Peter's was accelerated as Rome became the literary and artistic center of the Renaissance.

## CONCLUSION

$\mathcal{T}$HE RENAISSANCE WAS a period of transition that witnessed a continuation of the economic, political, and social trends that had begun in the High Middle Ages. It was also a movement in which intellectuals and artists proclaimed a new vision of humankind and raised fundamental questions about the value and importance of the individual. Of course, intellectuals and artists wrote and painted for the upper classes, and the brilliant intellectual, cultural, and artistic accomplishments of the Renaissance were products of and for the elite. The ideas of the Renaissance did not have a broad base among the masses of the people. As Lorenzo the Magnificent, ruler of Florence, once commented: "Only men of noble birth can obtain perfection. The poor, who work with their hands and have no time to cultivate their minds, are incapable of it."

The Renaissance did, however, raise new questions about medieval traditions. In advocating a return to the early sources of Christianity and criticizing current religious practices, the humanists raised fundamental issues about the Catholic church, which was still an important institution. In the sixteenth century, the intellectual revolution of the fifteenth century gave way to a religious renaissance that touched the lives of people, including the masses, in new and profound ways. After the Reformation, Europe would never again be the unified Christian commonwealth it once believed it was.

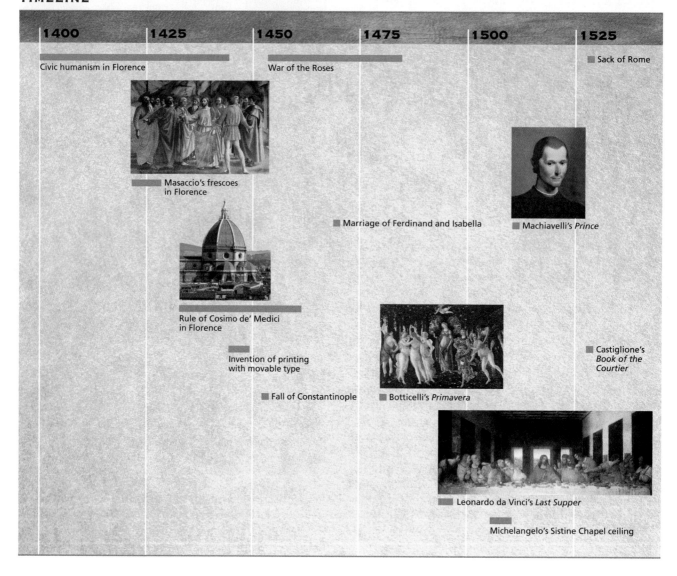

| 1400 | 1425 | 1450 | 1475 | 1500 | 1525 |

Civic humanism in Florence

War of the Roses

Sack of Rome

Masaccio's frescoes in Florence

Marriage of Ferdinand and Isabella

Machiavelli's *Prince*

Rule of Cosimo de' Medici in Florence

Invention of printing with movable type

Castiglione's *Book of the Courtier*

Fall of Constantinople

Botticelli's *Primavera*

Leonardo da Vinci's *Last Supper*

Michelangelo's Sistine Chapel ceiling

**NOTES**

1. Quoted in Jacob Burckhardt, *The Civilization of the Renaissance in Italy,* trans. S. G. C. Middlemore (London, 1960), p. 81.
2. Baldassare Castiglione, *The Book of the Courtier,* trans. Charles S. Singleton (Garden City, N.Y., 1959), pp. 288–289.
3. Quoted in De Lamar Jensen, *Renaissance Europe* (Lexington, Mass., 1981), p. 94.
4. Quoted in Iris Origo, "The Domestic Enemy: The Eastern Slaves in Tuscany in the Fourteenth and Fifteenth Centuries," *Speculum* 30 (1955): 333.
5. Quoted in Gene Brucker, ed., *Two Memoirs of Renaissance Florence* (New York, 1967), p. 132.
6. Quoted in Margaret L. King, *Women of the Renaissance* (Chicago, 1991), p. 3.
7. Quoted in Gene Brucker, ed., *The Society of Renaissance Florence* (New York, 1971), p. 190.
8. Quoted in Garrett Mattingly, *Renaissance Diplomacy* (Baltimore, 1964), p. 42.
9. Ibid., p. 95.
10. Niccolò Machiavelli, *The Prince,* trans. David Wootton (Indianapolis, 1995), p. 48.
11. Ibid., p. 55.
12. Ibid., p. 27.
13. Petrarch, "Epistle to Posterity," *Letters from Petrarch,* trans. Morris Bishop (Bloomington, Ind., 1966), pp. 6–7.
14. Quoted in Frances Yates, *Giordano Bruno and the Hermetic Tradition* (Chicago, 1964), p. 211.
15. Giovanni Pico della Mirandola, *Oration on the Dignity of Man,* in E. Cassirer, P. O. Kristeller, and J. H. Randall Jr., eds., *The Renaissance Philosophy of Man* (Chicago, 1948), p. 225.
16. Ibid., pp. 247, 249.
17. Quoted in W. H. Woodward, *Vittorino da Feltre and Other Humanist Educators* (Cambridge, 1897), p. 102.
18. Quoted in Iris Origo, *The Light of the Past* (New York, 1959), p. 136.
19. Quoted in Elizabeth G. Holt, ed., *A Documentary History of Art* (Garden City, N.Y., 1957), vol.1, p. 286.
20. Quoted in Rosa M. Letts, *The Cambridge Introduction to Art: The Renaissance* (Cambridge, 1981), p. 86.
21. Quoted in Johan Huizinga, *The Waning of the Middle Ages* (Garden City, N.Y., 1956), p. 265.

## SUGGESTIONS FOR FURTHER READING

The classic study of the Italian Renaissance is **J. Burckhardt, *The Civilization of the Renaissance in Italy,* trans. S. G. C. Middlemore** (London, 1960), first published in 1860. General works on the Renaissance in Europe include **D. L. Jensen, *Renaissance Europe*** (Lexington, Mass., 1981); **P. Burke, *The European Renaissance: Centres and Peripheries*** (Oxford, 1998); **E. Breisach, *Renaissance Europe, 1300–1517*** (New York, 1973); **J. Hale, *The Civilization of Europe in the Renaissance*** (New York, 1994); and the classic work by **M. P. Gilmore, *The World of Humanism, 1453–1517*** (New York, 1962). Although many of its interpretations are outdated, **W. Ferguson's *Europe in Transition, 1300–1520*** (Boston, 1962), contains a wealth of information. The brief study by **P. Burke, *The Renaissance,* 2d ed.** (New York, 1997), is a good summary of recent literature on the Renaissance. For beautifully illustrated introductions to the Renaissance, see **G. Holmes, *Renaissance*** (New York, 1996), and **M. Aston, ed., *The Panorama of the Renaissance*** (New York, 1996).

Brief but basic works on Renaissance economic matters are **H. A. Miskimin, *The Economy of Early Renaissance Europe, 1300–1460*** (New York, 1975) and ***The Economy of Later Renaissance Europe, 1460–1600*** (New York, 1978). For a reinterpretation of economic matters, see **L. Jardine, *Worldly Goods*** (New York, 1996). On family and marriage, see **D. Herlihy, *The Family in Renaissance Italy*** (Saint Louis, Mo., 1974); **C. Klapisch-Zuber, *Women, Family, and Ritual in Renaissance Italy*** (Chicago, 1985); and the well-told story by **G. Brucker, *Giovanni and Lusanna: Love and Marriage in Renaissance Florence*** (Berkeley, Calif., 1986). On women, see **M. L. King, *Women of the Renaissance*** (Chicago, 1991), and **N. Z. Davis and A. Farge, eds., *A History of Women: Renaissance and Enlightenment Paradoxes*** (Cambridge, Mass., 1993).

The best overall study of the Italian city-states is **L. Martines, *Power and Imagination: City-States in Renaissance Italy*** (New York, 1979); **D. Hay and J. Law, *Italy in the Age of the Renaissance*** (London, 1989), is also a good survey. There is an enormous literature on Renaissance Florence. The best introduction is **G. Brucker, *Florence: The Golden Age, 1138–1737*** (Berkeley, Calif., 1988). On the *condottieri,* see **M. Mallett, *Mercenaries and Their Masters: Warfare in Renaissance Italy*** (Totowa, N.J., 1974). The work by **G. Mattingly, *Renaissance Diplomacy*** (Boston, 1955), remains the basic one on the subject. Machiavelli's life can be examined in **Q. Skinner, *Machiavelli*** (Oxford, 1981).

Brief introductions to Renaissance humanism can be found in **D. R. Kelley, *Renaissance Humanism*** (Boston, 1991); **C. G. Nauert Jr., *Humanism and the Culture of Renaissance Europe*** (Cambridge, 1995); and **F. B. Artz, *Renaissance Humanism, 1300–1550*** (Oberlin, Ohio, 1966). The fundamental work on fifteenth-century civic humanism is **H. Baron, *The Crisis of the Early Italian Renaissance,* 2d ed.** (Princeton, N.J., 1966). The impact of printing is exhaustively examined in **E. Eisenstein, *The Printing Press as an Agent of Change,*** 2 vols. (New York, 1978).

For brief introductions to Renaissance art, see **R. M. Letts, *The Cambridge Introduction to Art: The Renaissance*** (Cambridge, 1981), and **B. Cole and A. Gealt, *Art of the Western World*** (New York, 1989), ch. 6–8. Good surveys of Renaissance art include **F. Hartt, *History of Italian Renaissance Art,*** 4th ed. (Englewood Cliffs, N.J., 1994); **S. Elliott, *Italian Renaissance Painting,* 2d ed.** (London, 1993); **R. Turner, *Renaissance Florence: The Invention of a New Art*** (New York, 1997); **P. F. Brown, *Art and Life in Renaissance Venice*** (Upper Saddle River, N.J., 1997); and **L. Murray, *The High Renaissance*** (New York, 1967). For studies of individual artists, see **J. H. Beck, *Raphael*** (New York, 1994); **M. Kemp, *Leonardo da Vinci: The Marvellous Works of Nature and of Man*** (London, 1981); and **A. Hughes,**

*Michelangelo* (London, 1997). For a lively account of the painting of the Sistine Chapel ceiling, see **R. King, *Michelangelo and the Pope's Ceiling*** (New York, 2002).

For a general work on the political development of Europe in the Renaissance, see **J. H. Shennan, *The Origins of the Modern European State, 1450–1725*** (London, 1974). On France, see **R. J. Knecht, *The Rise and Fall of Renaissance France, 1483–1610,* 2d ed.** (Oxford, 2001). Early Renaissance England is examined in **J. R. Lander, *Crown and Nobility, 1450–1509*** (London, 1976). Good coverage of Renaissance Spain can be found in **J. N. Hillgarth, *The Spanish Kingdoms, 1250–1516,* vol. 2, *Castilian Hegemony, 1410–1516*** (New York, 1978). Two good works on eastern Europe include **P. W. Knoll, *The Rise of the Polish Monarchy*** (Chicago, 1972), and **C. A. Macartney, *Hungary: A Short History*** (Edinburgh, 1962). On the Ottomans and their expansion, see **H. Inalcik, *The Ottoman Empire: The Classical Age, 1300–1600*** (London, 1973), and the classic work by **S. Runciman, *The Fall of Constantinople, 1453*** (Cambridge, 1965).

On problems of heresy and reform, see **C. Crowder, *Unity, Heresy and Reform, 1378–1460*** (London, 1977). Aspects of the Renaissance papacy can be examined in **E. Lee, *Sixtus IV and Men of Letters*** (Rome, 1978), and **M. Mallett, *The Borgias*** (New York, 1969). On Rome, see especially **P. Partner, *Renaissance Rome, 1500–1559: A Portrait of a Society*** (Berkeley, Calif., 1976).

## History  Now™

Enter *HistoryNow* using the access card that is available for *Western Civilization. HistoryNow* will assist you in understanding the content in this chapter with lesson plans generated for your needs. In addition, you can read the following documents, and many more, online:

   Giovanni Villani, selections from Books 8 and 9 of *Chronicle*

   Two Tractates from Vittorino da Feltre and other Humanist Educators

   Giorgio Vasari, Excerpts from *Life of Michelangelo* and *Life of da Vinci*

## INFOTRAC SEARCH TERMS

 For additional reading, go to InfoTrac College Edition, your online research library at http://infotrac.thomsonlearning.com

| *Key Term Search* | *Subject Guide Search* |
| --- | --- |
| Leonardo da Vinci | Renaissance |
| Machiavelli | humanism |

## WESTERN CIVILIZATION RESOURCES

Visit the *Western Civilization* Companion Web site for resources specific to this book:

   http://history.wadsworth.com/spielvogel06/

For a variety of tools to help you succeed in this course, visit the Western Civilization Resource Center at

   http://history.wadsworth.com/western/

Included are quizzes; images; documents; interactive simulations; maps and timelines; movie explorations; and a wealth of other sources.

CHAPTER

# *13*

# REFORMATION AND RELIGIOUS WARFARE IN THE SIXTEENTH CENTURY

## CHAPTER OUTLINE AND FOCUS QUESTIONS

**Prelude to Reformation**

● What were the chief ideas of the Christian humanists?

**Martin Luther and the Reformation in Germany**

● What were Martin Luther's main disagreements with the Roman Catholic church?

**The Spread of the Protestant Reformation**

● What were the chief tenets of Zwinglianism, Anabaptism, Anglicanism, and Calvinism?

**The Social Impact of the Protestant Reformation**

● What was the social impact of the Protestant Reformation?

**The Catholic Reformation**

● What measures did the Roman Catholic church take to reform itself and to combat Protestantism in the sixteenth century?

**Politics and the Wars of Religion in the Sixteenth Century**

● What role did religion play in the European wars of the sixteenth century?

## CRITICAL THINKING

● What were the main tenets of the major Protestant groups, and how did they differ from each other and from Catholicism? What were the results of these differences?

*A sixteenth-century engraving of Martin Luther in front of Charles V at the Diet of Worms*

© Bibliotheque Nationale, Paris, France/Bridgeman Art Library

*O*N APRIL 18, 1520, a lowly monk stood before the emperor and princes of Germany in the city of Worms. He had been called before this august gathering to answer charges of heresy, charges that could threaten his very life. The monk was confronted with a pile of his books and asked if he wished to defend them all or reject a part. Courageously, Martin Luther defended them all and asked to be shown where any part was in error on the basis of "Scripture and plain reason." The emperor was outraged by Luther's response and made his own position clear the next day: "Not only I, but you of this noble German nation, would be forever disgraced if by our negligence not only heresy but the very suspicion of heresy were to survive. After having heard yesterday the obstinate defense of Luther, I regret that I have so long delayed in proceeding against him and his false teaching. I will have no more to do with him." Luther's appearance at Worms set the stage for a serious challenge to the authority of the Catholic church. This was by no means the first crisis in the church's fifteen-hundred-year history, but its consequences were more far-reaching than anyone at Worms in 1520 could have imagined.

Throughout the Middle Ages, the Catholic church continued to assert its primacy of position. It had overcome defiance of its temporal authority by emperors, and challenges to its doctrines had been crushed by the Inquisition and combated by new religious orders that carried its message of salvation to all the towns and villages of medieval Europe. The growth of the papacy had paralleled the growth of the church, but by the end of the Middle Ages, challenges to papal authority from the rising power of monarchical states had resulted in a loss of papal temporal authority. An even greater threat to papal authority and church unity arose in the sixteenth century when the unity of Christendom was shattered by the Reformation.

The movement begun by Martin Luther when he made his dramatic stand quickly spread across Europe, a clear indication of dissatisfaction with Catholic practices. Within a short time, new forms of religious practices, doctrines, and organizations, including Zwinglianism, Calvinism, Anabaptism, and Anglicanism, were attracting adherents all over Europe. Although seemingly helpless to stop the new Protestant churches, the Catholic church also underwent a religious renaissance and managed to revive its fortunes by the mid-sixteenth century. All too soon, the doctrinal divisions between Protestants and Catholics led to a series of religious wars that dominated the history of western Europe in the second half of the sixteenth century.

# Prelude to Reformation

Martin Luther's reform movement was by no means the first. During the second half of the fifteenth century, the new classical learning that was part of Italian Renaissance humanism spread to northern Europe and spawned a movement called **Christian** or **northern Renaissance humanism** whose major goal was the reform of Christianity.

## Christian or Northern Renaissance Humanism

Like their Italian counterparts, northern humanists cultivated a knowledge of the classics, the bond that united all humanists into a kind of international fellowship. In returning to the writings of antiquity, northern humanists (also called Christian humanists because of their profound preoccupation with religion) focused on the sources of early Christianity, the Holy Scriptures and the writings of such church fathers as Augustine, Ambrose, and Jerome. In these early Christian writings, they discovered a simple religion that they came to feel had been distorted by the complicated theological arguments of the Middle Ages.

The most important characteristic of northern humanism was its reform program. Convinced of the ability of human beings to reason and improve themselves, the northern humanists felt that through education in the sources of classical, and especially Christian, antiquity, they could instill a true inner piety or an inward religious feeling that would bring about a reform of the church and society. For this reason, Christian humanists supported schools, brought out new editions of the classics, and prepared new editions of the Bible and writings of the church fathers. In the preface to his edition of the Greek New Testament, the famous humanist Erasmus wrote:

> I disagree very much with those who are unwilling that Holy Scripture, translated into the vulgar tongue, be read by the uneducated, as if Christ taught such intricate doctrines that they could scarcely be understood by very few theologians, or as if the strength of the Christian religion consisted in men's ignorance of it. . . . I would that even the lowliest women read the Gospels and the Pauline Epistles. And I would that they were translated into all languages so that they could be read and understood not only by Scots and Irish but also by Turks and Saracens. . . . Would that, as a result, the farmer sing some portion of them at the plow, the weaver hum some parts of them to the movement of his shuttle, the traveler lighten the weariness of the journey with stories of this kind![1]

This belief in the power of education would remain an important characteristic of European civilization. Like later intellectuals, Christian humanists believed that to change society, they must first change the human beings who compose it. Although some critics have called the Christian humanists naive, they were in fact merely optimistic. The turmoil of the Reformation, however, shattered much of this intellectual optimism, as the lives and careers of two of the most prominent Christian humanists, Desiderius Erasmus and Thomas More, illustrate.

**Erasmus**   The most influential of all the Christian humanists was Desiderius Erasmus (1466–1536), who formulated and popularized the reform program of Christian humanism. Born in Holland, Erasmus was educated at one of the schools of the Brothers of the Common Life. He wandered to France, England, Italy, Germany, and Switzerland, conversing everywhere in the classical Latin that might be called his mother tongue. The *Handbook of the Christian Knight*, printed in 1503, reflected his preoccupation with religion. He called his conception of religion "the philosophy of Christ," by which he meant that Christianity should be a guiding philosophy for the direction of daily life rather than the system of dogmatic beliefs and practices that the medieval church seemed to stress. In other words, he emphasized inner piety and deemphasized the external forms of religion (such as the sacraments, pilgrimages, fasts, veneration of saints, and relics). To return to the simplicity of the early church, people needed to understand the original meaning of the Scriptures and early church fathers. Because Erasmus thought that the standard Latin edition of the Bible, known as the Vulgate, contained errors, he edited the Greek text of the New Testament from the earliest available manuscripts and published it, along with a new Latin translation, in 1516.

To Erasmus, the reform of the church meant spreading an understanding of the philosophy of Jesus, providing enlightened education in the sources of early Christianity, and making commonsense criticism of the abuses in

**Erasmus.** Desiderius Erasmus was the most influential of the northern Renaissance humanists. He sought to restore Christianity to the early simplicity found in the teachings of Jesus. This portrait of Erasmus was painted in 1523 by Hans Holbein the Younger, who had formed a friendship with the great humanist while they were both in Basel.

the church. This last is especially evident in *The Praise of Folly,* written in 1511, in which Erasmus was able to engage in a humorous yet effective criticism of the most corrupt practices of his own society. He was especially harsh on the abuses within the ranks of the clergy (see the box on p. 349).

Erasmus' program did not achieve the reform of the church that he so desired. His moderation and his emphasis on education were quickly overwhelmed by the passions of the Reformation. Undoubtedly, though, his work helped prepare the way for the Reformation; as contemporaries proclaimed, "Erasmus laid the egg that Luther hatched." Yet Erasmus eventually disapproved of Luther and the Protestant reformers. He had no intention of destroying the unity of the medieval Christian church; rather, his whole program was based on reform within the church.

**Thomas More** The son of a London lawyer, Thomas More (1478–1535) received the benefits of a good education. Although trained in the law, he took an avid interest in the new classical learning and became proficient in both Latin and Greek. Like the Italian humanists, who believed in putting their learning at the service of the state, More embarked on a public career that ultimately took him to the highest reaches of power as lord chancellor of England.

His career in government service, however, did not keep More from the intellectual and spiritual interests that were so dear to him. He was well acquainted with other English humanists and became an intimate friend of Erasmus. He made translations from Greek authors and wrote both prose and poetry in Latin. A devout man, he spent many hours in prayer and private devotions. Contemporaries praised his household as a shining model of Christian family life.

More's most famous work, and one of the most controversial of his age, was *Utopia,* written in 1516. This literary masterpiece is an account of the idealistic life and institutions of the community of Utopia (Greek for "nowhere"), an imaginary island in the vicinity of the recently discovered New World. It reflects More's own concerns with the economic, social, and political problems of his day. He presented a new social system in which cooperation and reason replaced power and fame as the proper motivating agents for human society. Utopian society, therefore, is based on communal ownership rather than private property. All persons work nine hours a day, regardless of occupation, and are rewarded according to their needs. Possessing abundant leisure time and relieved of competition and greed, Utopians were free to do wholesome and enriching things. More envisioned Utopia as an orderly world where social relations, recreation, and even travel were carefully controlled for the moral welfare of society and its members.

In serving King Henry VIII, More came face to face with the abuses and corruption he had criticized in *Utopia.* But he did not allow idealism to outweigh his own ultimate realism, and in *Utopia* itself he justified his service to the king:

> If you can't completely eradicate wrong ideas, or deal with inveterate vices as effectively as you could wish, that's no reason for turning your back on public life altogether. You wouldn't abandon ship in a storm just because you couldn't control the winds. On the other hand, it's no use attempting to put across entirely new ideas, which will obviously carry no weight with people who are prejudiced against them. You must go to work indirectly. You must handle everything as tactfully as you can, and what you can't put right you must try to make as little wrong as possible. For things will never be perfect, until human beings are perfect—which I don't expect them to be for quite a number of years.[2]

More's religious devotion and belief in the universal Catholic church proved even more important than his service to the king, however. Always the man of conscience, More willingly gave up his life opposing England's break with the Roman Catholic church over the divorce of King Henry VIII.

## Church and Religion on the Eve of the Reformation

Corruption in the Catholic church was another factor that spurred people to want reform. No doubt the failure of the Renaissance popes to provide spiritual leadership had affected the spiritual life of all Christendom. The papal

# ERASMUS: IN PRAISE OF FOLLY

*HE PRAISE OF FOLLY* is one of the most famous pieces of literature of the sixteenth century. Erasmus, who wrote it in a short period of time during a visit to the home of Thomas More, considered it a "little diversion" from his "serious work." Yet both contemporaries and later generations have appreciated "this laughing parody of every form and rank of human life." In this selection, Erasmus belittles one of his favorite objects of scorn, the monks.

## Erasmus, *The Praise of Folly*

Those who are the closest to these [the theologians] in happiness are generally called "the religious" or "monks," both of which are deceiving names, since for the most part they stay as far away from religion as possible and frequent every sort of place. I cannot, however, see how any life could be more gloomy than the life of these monks if I [Folly] did not assist them in many ways. Though most people detest these men so much that accidentally meeting one is considered to be bad luck, the monks themselves believe that they are magnificent creatures. One of their chief beliefs is that to be illiterate is to be of a high state of sanctity, and so they make sure that they are not able to read. Another is that when braying out their gospels in church they are making themselves very pleasing and satisfying to God, when in fact they are uttering these psalms as a matter of repetition rather than from their hearts. . . .

Moreover, it is amusing to find that they insist that everything be done in fastidious detail, as if employing the orderliness of mathematics, a small mistake in which would be a great crime. Just so many knots must be on each shoe and the shoelace may be of only one specified color; just so much lace is allowed on each habit; the girdle must be of just the right material and width; the hood of a certain shape and capacity; their hair of just so many fingers' length; and finally they can sleep only the specified number of hours per day. Can they not understand that, because of a variety of bodies and temperaments, all this equality of restrictions is in fact very unequal? Nevertheless, because of all this detail that they employ they think that they are superior to all other people. And what is more, amid all their pretense of Apostolic charity, the members of one order will denounce the members of another order clamorously because of the way in which the habit has been belted or the slightly darker color of it. . . .

Many of them work so hard at protocol and at traditional fastidiousness that they think one heaven hardly a suitable reward for their labors; never recalling, however, that the time will come when Christ will demand a reckoning of that which he had prescribed, namely charity, and that he will hold their deeds of little account. One monk will then exhibit his belly filled with every kind of fish; another will profess a knowledge of over a hundred hymns. Still another will reveal a countless number of fasts that he has made, and will account for his large belly by explaining that his fasts have always been broken by a single large meal. Another will show a list of church ceremonies over which he has officiated so large that it would fill seven ships.

---

court's preoccupation with finances had an especially strong impact on the clergy. So did the economic changes of the fourteenth and fifteenth centuries. The highest positions among the clergy were increasingly held by either nobles or the wealthy members of the bourgeoisie. Moreover, to increase their revenues, high church officials (bishops, archbishops, and cardinals) took over more than one church office. This so-called **pluralism** led in turn to absenteeism: church officeholders ignored their duties and hired underlings who were sometimes not appropriately qualified. Complaints about the ignorance and ineptness of parish priests became widespread in the fifteenth century.

While the leaders of the church were failing to meet their responsibilities, ordinary people were clamoring for meaningful religious expression and certainty of salvation. As a result, for some the salvation process became almost mechanical. As more and more people sought certainty of salvation through veneration of relics, collections of such objects grew. Frederick the Wise, elector of Saxony and Martin Luther's prince, had amassed over nineteen thousand relics to which were attached indulgences that could reduce one's time in purgatory by nearly two million years. (An in-

dulgence, you will recall, is a remission, after death, of all or part of the punishment for sin.) Other people sought certainty of salvation in the popular mystical movement known as the Modern Devotion, which downplayed religious dogma and stressed the need to follow the teachings of Jesus. Thomas à Kempis, author of *The Imitation of Christ*, wrote that "truly, at the day of judgment we shall not be examined by what we have read, but what we have done; not how well we have spoken, but how religiously we have lived."

What is striking about the revival of religious piety in the fifteenth century—whether expressed through such external forces as the veneration of relics and the buying of indulgences or the mystical path—was its adherence to the orthodox beliefs and practices of the Catholic church. The agitation for certainty of salvation and spiritual peace occurred within the framework of the "holy mother Church." But disillusionment grew as the devout experienced the clergy's inability to live up to their expectations. The deepening of religious life, especially in the second half of the fifteenth century, found little echo among the worldly-wise clergy, and this environment helps explain the tremendous and immediate impact of Luther's ideas.

# Martin Luther and the Reformation in Germany

The Protestant Reformation began with a typical medieval question: What must I do to be saved? Martin Luther, a deeply religious man, found an answer that did not fit within the traditional teachings of the late medieval church. Ultimately, he split with that church, destroying the religious unity of western Christendom. That other people were concerned with the same question is evident in the rapid spread of the Reformation. But religion was so entangled in the social, economic, and political forces of the period that the Protestant reformers' hope of transforming the church quickly proved illusory.

## The Early Luther

Martin Luther was born in Germany on November 10, 1483. His father wanted him to become a lawyer, so Luther enrolled at the University of Erfurt, where he received his bachelor's degree in 1502. Three years later, after becoming a master in the liberal arts, the young man began to study law. But Luther was not content, not in small part due to his long-standing religious inclinations. That summer, while returning to Erfurt after a brief visit home, he was caught in a ferocious thunderstorm and vowed that if he survived unscathed, he would become a monk. He then

**Martin Luther.** This painting by Lucas Cranach the Elder in 1533 shows Luther at the age of fifty. By this time, Luther's reforms had taken hold in many parts of Germany, and Luther himself was a happily married man with five children.

entered the monastic order of the Augustinian Hermits in Erfurt, much to his father's disgust. In the monastery, Luther focused on his major concern, the assurance of salvation. The traditional beliefs and practices of the church seemed unable to relieve his obsession with this question, especially evident in his struggle with the sacrament of penance or **confession.** The sacraments were a Catholic's chief means of receiving God's grace; confession offered the opportunity to have one's sins forgiven. Luther spent hours confessing his sins, but he was always doubtful. Had he remembered all of his sins? Even more, how could a hopeless sinner be acceptable to a totally just and all-powerful God? Luther threw himself into his monastic routine with a vengeance:

> I was indeed a good monk and kept my order so strictly that I could say that if ever a monk could get to heaven through monastic discipline, I was that monk. . . . And yet my conscience would not give me certainty, but I always doubted and said, "You didn't do that right. You weren't contrite enough. You left that out of your confession." The more I tried to remedy an uncertain, weak and troubled conscience with human traditions, the more I daily found it more uncertain, weaker and more troubled.[3]

Despite his herculean efforts, Luther achieved no certainty.

To help overcome his difficulties, his superiors recommended that the monk study theology. He received his doctorate in 1512 and then became a professor in the theological faculty at the University of Wittenberg, lecturing on the Bible. Sometime between 1513 and 1516, through his study of the Bible, he arrived at an answer to his problem.

Catholic doctrine had emphasized that both faith and good works were required of a Christian to achieve personal salvation. In Luther's eyes, human beings, weak and powerless in the sight of an almighty God, could never do enough good works to merit salvation. Through his study of the Bible, especially his work on Paul's Epistle to the Romans, Luther rediscovered another way of viewing this problem. To Luther, humans are saved not through their good works but through faith in the promises of God, made possible by the sacrifice of Jesus on the cross. The doctrine of salvation or justification by grace through faith alone became the primary doctrine of the Protestant Reformation (**justification** is the act by which a person is made deserving of salvation). Because Luther had arrived at this doctrine from his study of the Bible, the Bible became for Luther, as for all other Protestants, the chief guide to religious truth. Justification by faith and the Bible as the sole authority in religious affairs were the twin pillars of the Protestant Reformation.

**The Indulgence Controversy** Luther did not see himself as either an innovator or a heretic, but his involvement in the indulgence controversy propelled him into an open confrontation with church officials and forced him to see the theological implications of justification by faith alone. In 1517, Pope Leo X had issued a special jubilee indulgence to finance the ongoing construction of Saint Peter's Basilica in Rome. Johann Tetzel, a rambunctious Dominican,

© Scala/Art Resource, NY

# LUTHER AND THE NINETY-FIVE THESES

O MOST HISTORIANS, the publication of Luther's Ninety-Five Theses marks the beginning of the Reformation. To Luther, they were simply a response to what he considered Johann Tetzel's blatant abuses in selling indulgences. Although written in Latin, Luther's statements were soon translated into German and disseminated widely across Germany. They made an immense impression on Germans already dissatisfied with the ecclesiastical and financial policies of the papacy.

## Martin Luther, *Selections from the Ninety-Five Theses*

5. The Pope has neither the will nor the power to remit any penalties beyond those he has imposed either at his own discretion or by canon law.

20. Therefore the Pope, by his plenary remission of all penalties, does not mean "all" in the absolute sense, but only those imposed by himself.

21. Hence those preachers of Indulgences are wrong when they say that a man is absolved and saved from every penalty by the Pope's Indulgences.

27. It is mere human talk to preach that the soul flies out [of purgatory] immediately the money clinks in the collection-box.

28. It is certainly possible that when the money clinks in the collection-box greed and avarice can increase; but the intercession of the Church depends on the will of God alone.

50. Christians should be taught that, if the Pope knew the exactions of the preachers of Indulgences,

he would rather have the basilica of St. Peter reduced to ashes than built with the skin, flesh and bones of his sheep.

81. This wanton preaching of pardons makes it difficult even for learned men to redeem respect due to the Pope from the slanders or at least the shrewd questionings of the laity.

82. For example: "Why does not the Pope empty purgatory for the sake of most holy love and the supreme need of souls? This would be the most righteous of reasons, if he can redeem innumerable souls for sordid money with which to build a basilica, the most trivial of reasons."

86. Again: "Since the Pope's wealth is larger than that of the crassest Crassi of our time, why does he not build this one basilica of St. Peter with his own money, rather than with that of the faithful poor?"

90. To suppress these most conscientious questionings of the laity by authority only, instead of refuting them by reason, is to expose the Church and the Pope to the ridicule of their enemies, and to make Christian people unhappy.

94. Christians should be exhorted to seek earnestly to follow Christ, their Head, through penalties, deaths, and hells.

95. And let them thus be more confident of entering heaven through many tribulations rather than through a false assurance of peace.

---

hawked the indulgences in Germany with the slogan "As soon as the coin in the coffer rings, the soul from purgatory springs."

Luther was greatly distressed by the sale of indulgences, certain that people were simply guaranteeing their eternal damnation by relying on these pieces of paper to assure themselves of salvation. Angered, he issued his Ninety-Five Theses, although scholars are unsure whether he nailed them to a church door in Wittenberg, as is traditionally alleged, or mailed them to his ecclesiastical superior. In either case, his theses were a stunning indictment of the abuses in the sale of indulgences (see the box above). It is doubtful that Luther intended any break with the church over the issue of indulgences. If the pope had clarified the use of indulgences, as Luther wished, he would probably have been satisfied and the controversy would have ended. But Pope Leo X did not take the issue seriously and is even reported to have said that Luther was simply "some drunken German who will amend his ways when he sobers up." A German translation of the Ninety-Five Theses was quickly printed in thousands of copies and received sympathetically in a Germany that had a long tradition of dissatisfaction with papal policies and power.

**The Quickening Rebellion** The controversy reached an important turning point with the Leipzig Debate in July 1519. In Leipzig, Luther's opponent, the capable Catholic theologian Johann Eck, forced Luther to move beyond indulgences and deny the authority of popes and councils. In effect, Luther was compelled to see the consequences of his new theology. At the beginning of 1520, he proclaimed: "Farewell, unhappy, hopeless, blasphemous Rome! The Wrath of God has come upon you, as you deserve. We have cared for Babylon, and she is not healed: let us then, leave her, that she may be the habitation of dragons, spectres, and witches."[4] At the same time, Luther was convinced that he was doing God's work and had to proceed regardless of the consequences.

In three pamphlets published in 1520, Luther moved toward a more definite break with the Catholic church. The *Address to the Nobility of the German Nation* was a political tract written in German in which Luther called on the German princes to overthrow the papacy in Germany and establish a reformed German church. The *Babylonian Captivity of the Church*, written in Latin for theologians, attacked the sacramental system as the means by which the pope and church had held the real meaning of the Gospel

**Woodcut: Luther Versus the Pope.** In the 1520s, after Luther's return to Wittenberg, his teachings began to spread rapidly, ending ultimately in a reform movement supported by state authorities. Pamphlets containing picturesque woodcuts were important in the spread of Luther's ideas. In the woodcut shown here, the crucified Jesus attends Luther's service on the left, while on the right the pope is at a table selling indulgences.

© Staatliche Museen, Bildarchiv Preussischer Kulturbesitz, Berlin/Art Resource, NY

captive for a thousand years. He called for the reform of monasticism and for the clergy to marry. Though virginity is good, Luther argued, marriage is better, and freedom of choice is best. *On the Freedom of a Christian Man* was a short treatise on the doctrine of salvation. It is faith alone, not good works, that justifies, frees, and brings salvation through Jesus. Being saved and freed by his faith in Jesus, however, does not free the Christian from doing good works. Rather, he performs good works out of gratitude to God. "Good works do not make a good man, but a good man does good works."[5]

Unable to accept Luther's forcefully worded dissent from traditional Catholic teachings, the church excommunicated him in January 1521. He was also summoned to appear before the Reichstag, the imperial diet of the Holy Roman Empire, in Worms, convened by the newly elected Emperor Charles V (1519–1556). Expected to recant the heretical doctrines he had espoused, Luther refused and made the famous reply that became the battle cry of the Reformation:

> Since then Your Majesty and your lordships desire a simple reply, I will answer without horns and without teeth. Unless I am convicted by Scripture and plain reason—I do not accept the authority of popes and councils, for they have contradicted each other—my conscience is captive to the Word of God. I cannot and I will not recant anything, for to go against conscience is neither right nor safe. Here I stand, I cannot do otherwise. God help me. Amen.[6]

Emperor Charles was outraged at Luther's audacity and gave his opinion that "a single friar who goes counter to all Christianity for a thousand years must be wrong." By the Edict of Worms, Martin Luther was made an outlaw within the empire. His works were to be burned, and Luther himself was to be captured and delivered to the emperor.

## The Rise of Lutheranism

After a brief period of hiding, Luther returned to Wittenberg in Electoral Saxony at the beginning of 1522 and began to organize a reformed church. Lutheranism had wide appeal and spread rapidly. The preaching of evangelical sermons, based on a return to the original message of the Bible, found favor throughout Germany. In city after city, the arrival of preachers presenting Luther's teachings was soon followed by a public debate in which the new preachers proved victorious. A reform of the church was then instituted by state authorities. Also useful to the spread of the Reformation were pamphlets illustrated with vivid woodcuts portraying the pope as a hideous Antichrist and titled with catchy phrases such as "I Wonder Why There Is No Money in the Land" (which, of course, was an attack on papal greed). Luther also insisted on the use of music as a means to teach the Gospel, and his own composition, "A Mighty Fortress Is Our God," became the battle hymn of the Reformation:

> Standing alone are we undone, the Fiend would soon enslave us;
> but for us fights a mighty One whom God has sent to save us.
> Ask you who is this? Jesus Christ is He, Lord God of Hosts.
> There is no other God; He can and will uphold us.

**The Spread of Luther's Ideas**   Lutheranism spread to both princely and ecclesiastical states in northern and central Germany as well as to two-thirds of the free imperial cities, especially those of southern Germany, where prosperous burghers, for both religious and secular reasons, became committed to Luther's cause. Nuremberg, where an active city council led by the dynamic city secretary

Lazarus Spengler brought a conversion as early as 1525, was the first imperial city to convert to Lutheranism. At its outset, the Reformation in Germany was largely an urban phenomenon.

A series of crises in the mid-1520s made it apparent, however, that spreading the word of God was not as easy as Luther had originally envisioned—the usual plight of most reformers. Luther experienced dissent within his own ranks in Wittenberg from people such as Andreas Carlstadt, who wished to initiate a more radical reform by abolishing all relics, images, and the Mass. Luther had no sooner dealt with them when he faced defection from the Christian humanists. Many had initially supported Luther, believing that he shared their goal of reforming the abuses within the church. But when it became apparent that Luther's movement threatened the unity of Christendom, the older generation of Christian humanists, including Erasmus, broke with the reformer. A younger generation of Christian humanists, however, played a significant role in Lutheranism. When Philip Melanchthon (1497–1560) arrived in Wittenberg in 1518 at the age of twenty-one to teach Greek and Hebrew, he was immediately attracted to Luther's ideas and became a staunch supporter.

**The Peasants' War** Luther's greatest challenge in the mid-1520s, however, came from the Peasants' War. Peasant dissatisfaction in Germany stemmed from several sources. Many peasants had not been touched by the gradual economic improvement of the early sixteenth century. In some areas, especially southwestern Germany, influential local lords continued to abuse their peasants, and new demands for taxes and other services caused them to wish for a return to "the good old days." Social discontent soon became entangled with religious revolt as peasants looked to Martin Luther for support. It was not Luther, however, but one of his ex-followers, the radical Thomas Müntzer, who inflamed the peasants against their rulers with his fiery language: "Strike while the iron is hot!" Revolt first erupted in southwestern Germany in June 1524 and spread northward and eastward.

Luther reacted quickly and vehemently against the peasants. In his pamphlet *Against the Robbing and Murdering Hordes of Peasants,* he called on the German princes to "smite, slay and stab" the stupid and stubborn peasantry (see the box on p. 354). Luther, who knew how much his reformation of the church depended on the full support of the German princes and magistrates, supported the rulers. To Luther, the state and its rulers were ordained by God and given the authority to maintain the peace and order necessary for the spread of the Gospel. It was the duty of

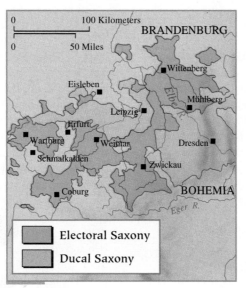

**Luther's Saxony**

princes to put down all revolts. By May 1525, the German princes had ruthlessly suppressed the peasant hordes. By this time, Luther found himself ever more dependent on state authorities for the growth and maintenance of his reformed church.

## Church and State

Justification by faith alone was the starting point for most of Protestantism's major doctrines. Since Luther downplayed the role of good works in salvation, the sacraments also had to be redefined. No longer were they merit-earning works; they were now divinely established signs signifying the promise of salvation.

Based on his interpretation of scriptural authority, Luther kept only two of the Catholic church's seven sacraments—baptism and the Lord's Supper. Baptism signified rebirth through grace. Regarding the Lord's Supper, Luther denied the Catholic doctrine of **transubstantiation,** which taught that the substance of the bread and wine consumed in the rite is miraculously transformed into the body and blood of Jesus. Yet he continued to insist on the real presence of Jesus' body and blood in the bread and wine given as a testament to God's forgiveness of sin.

Luther's emphasis on the importance of Scripture led him to reject the Catholic belief that the authority of Scripture must be supplemented by the traditions and decrees of the church. The word of God as revealed in the Bible was sufficient authority in religious affairs. A hierarchical priesthood was thus unnecessary since all Christians who followed the word of God were their own priests, constituting a "priesthood of all believers." Even though Luther thus considered the true church to be an invisible entity, the difficulties of actually establishing a reformed church led him to believe that a tangible, organized church was needed. Since the Catholic ecclesiastical hierarchy had been scrapped, Luther came to rely increasingly on the princes or state authorities to organize and guide the new Lutheran reformed churches. He had little choice. Secular authorities in Germany, as elsewhere, were soon playing an important role in church affairs. By 1530, in the German states that had converted to Lutheranism, both princes and city councils appointed officials who visited churches in their territories and regulated matters of worship. The Lutheran churches in Germany (and later in Scandinavia) quickly became territorial or state churches in which the state supervised and disciplined church members.

As part of the development of these state-dominated churches, Luther also instituted new religious services to replace the Mass. These featured a worship service consisting of a vernacular liturgy that focused on Bible reading,

# LUTHER AND THE "ROBBING AND MURDERING HORDES OF PEASANTS"

HE PEASANTS' WAR OF 1524–1525 encompassed a series of uprisings by German peasants who were suffering from economic changes they did not comprehend. Led by radical religious leaders, the revolts quickly became entangled with the religious revolt set in motion by Luther's defiance of the church. But it was soon clear that Luther himself did not believe in any way in social revolution. This excerpt is taken from Luther's pamphlet written in May 1525 at the height of the peasants' power but not published until after their defeat.

### Martin Luther, *Against the Robbing and Murdering Hordes of Peasants*

The peasants have taken on themselves the burden of three terrible sins against God and man, by which they have abundantly merited death in body and soul. In the first place they have sworn to be true and faithful, submissive and obedient, to their rulers, as Christ commands, when he says, "Render unto Caesar the things that are Caesar's," and in Romans XIII, "Let everyone be subject unto the higher powers." Because they are breaking this obedience, and are setting themselves against the higher powers, willfully and with violence, they have forfeited body and soul, as faithless, perjured, lying, disobedient knaves and scoundrels are wont to do. . . .

In the second place, they are starting a rebellion, and violently robbing and plundering monasteries and castles which are not theirs, by which they have a second time deserved death in body and soul, if only as highwaymen and murderers. . . . For rebellion is not simple murder, but is like a great fire, which attacks and lays waste a whole land. . . . Therefore, let everyone who can, smite, slay and stab, secretly or openly, remembering that nothing can be more poisonous, hurtful or devilish than a rebel. . . .

In the third place, they cloak this terrible and horrible sin with the Gospel, call themselves "Christian brothers," receive oaths and homage, and compel people to hold with them to these abominations. Thus they become the greatest of all blasphemers of God and slanderers of his holy Name, serving the devil, under the outward appearance of the Gospel, thus earning death in body and soul ten times over. . . . It does not help the peasants, when they pretend that, according to Genesis I and II, all things were created free and common, and that all of us alike have been baptized. . . . For baptism does not make men free in body and property, but in soul; and the Gospel does not make goods common. . . . Since the peasants, then, have brought both God and man down upon them and are already so many times guilty of death in body and soul, . . . I must instruct the worldly governors how they are to act in the matter with a clear conscience.

First, I will not oppose a ruler who, even though he does not tolerate the Gospel, will smite and punish these peasants without offering to submit the case to judgment. For he is within his rights, since the peasants are not contending any longer for the Gospel, but have become faithless, perjured, disobedient, rebellious murderers, robbers and blasphemers, whom even heathen rulers have the right and power to punish; nay, it is their duty to punish them, for it is just for this purpose that they bear the sword, and are "the ministers of God upon him that doeth evil."

---

preaching the word of God, and song. Following his own denunciation of clerical celibacy, Luther married a former nun, Katherina von Bora, in 1525. His union provided a model of married and family life for the new Protestant minister.

### Germany and the Reformation: Religion and Politics

From its very beginning, the fate of Luther's movement was closely tied to political affairs. In 1519, Charles I, king of Spain and grandson of Emperor Maximilian, was elected Holy Roman Emperor as Charles V (1519–1556). Charles V ruled over an immense empire, consisting of Spain and its overseas possessions, the traditional Austrian Habsburg lands, Bohemia, Hungary, the Low Countries, and the kingdom of Naples in southern Italy (see Map 13.1). The extent of his possessions was reflected in the languages he used: "I speak Spanish to God, Italian to women, French to men, and German to my horse." Politically, Charles wanted to maintain his dynasty's control over his enormous empire;

religiously, he hoped to preserve the unity of the Catholic faith throughout his empire. Despite his strengths, Charles spent a lifetime in futile pursuit of his goals. Four major problems—the French, the papacy, the Turks, and Germany's internal situation—cost him both his dream and his health. At the same time, the emperor's problems gave Luther's movement time to grow and organize before facing the concerted onslaught of the Catholic forces.

**The French, the Papacy, and the Turks**   Charles V's chief political concern was his rivalry with the Valois king of France, Francis I (1515–1547). Encircled by the possessions of the Habsburg empire, Francis became embroiled in conflict with Charles over disputed territories in southern France, the Netherlands, the Rhineland, northern Spain, and Italy. These conflicts, known as the Habsburg-Valois Wars, were fought intermittently for twenty-four years (1521–1544), preventing Charles from concentrating on the Lutheran problem in Germany.

Meanwhile, Charles faced two other enemies. The Habsburg emperor expected papal cooperation in deal-

CHART 13.1 **The Habsburgs as Holy Roman Emperors and Kings of Spain**

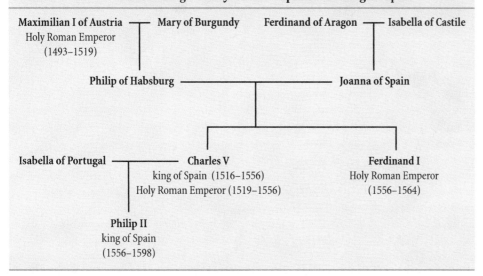

Maximilian I of Austria ——— Mary of Burgundy     Ferdinand of Aragon ——— Isabella of Castile
Holy Roman Emperor
(1493–1519)

Philip of Habsburg ————————————————— Joanna of Spain

Isabella of Portugal ——— Charles V                    Ferdinand I
                        king of Spain (1516–1556)        Holy Roman Emperor
                        Holy Roman Emperor (1519–1556)    (1556–1564)

Philip II
king of Spain
(1556–1598)

no desire to have a strong emperor.

Charles's attempt to settle the Lutheran problem at the Diet of Augsburg in 1530 proved completely inadequate, and the emperor wound up demanding that the Lutherans return to the Catholic church by April 15, 1531. In February 1531, fearful of Charles's intentions, eight princes and eleven imperial cities—all Lutheran—formed a defensive alliance known as the Schmalkaldic League. These Protestant German states vowed to assist each other "whenever any one of us is attacked on account of the Word of God and the doctrine of the Gospel." Religion was dividing the empire into two armed camps.

The renewed threat of the Turks against Vienna forced Charles once again to seek compromise instead of war with the Protestant authorities. From 1532 to 1535, Charles was forced to fight off a Turkish, Arab, and Barbary attack on the Mediterranean coasts of Italy and Spain. Two additional Habsburg-Valois Wars (1535–1538 and 1542–1544) soon

ing with the Lutheran heresy. Papal policy, however, was guided by political considerations, not religious ones. Fearful of Charles's power in Italy, Pope Clement VII (1523–1534) joined the side of Francis I in the second Habsburg-Valois War (1527–1529), with catastrophic results. In April 1527, the Spanish-imperial army of Charles V went berserk while attacking Rome and gave the capital of Catholicism a fearful and bloody sacking. Sobered by the experience, Clement came to terms with the emperor, and by 1530, Charles V stood supreme over much of Italy.

In the meantime, a new threat to the emperor's power had erupted in the eastern part of his empire. The Ottoman Turks, under Suleiman the Magnificent (1520–1566), had defeated and killed King Louis of Hungary, Charles's brother-in-law, at the Battle of Mohács in 1526. Subsequently, the Turks overran most of Hungary, moved into Austria, and advanced as far as Vienna, where they were finally repulsed in 1529.

**Politics in Germany**   By the end of 1529, Charles was ready to deal with Germany. The second Habsburg-Valois War had ended, the Turks had been defeated temporarily, and the pope had been subdued. The internal political situation in the Holy Roman Empire was not in his favor, however. Germany was a land of several hundred territorial states: princely states, ecclesiastical principalities, and free imperial cities. Though all owed loyalty to the emperor, Germany's medieval development had enabled these states to become quite independent of imperial authority. They had

**Charles V.** Charles V sought to create religious unity throughout his vast empire by keeping all his subjects within the bounds of the Catholic church. Due to his conflict with Francis I in addition to his difficulties with the Turks, the papacy, and the German princes, Charles was never able to check the spread of Lutheranism. This portrait of Charles V is by the Venetian painter Titian.

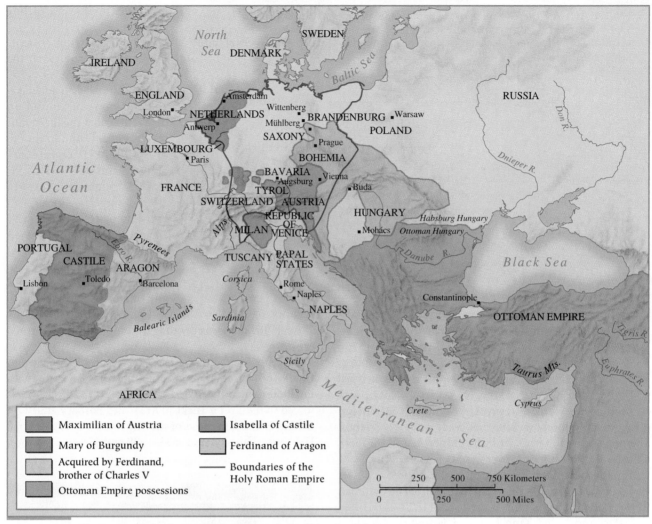

**MAP 13.1 The Empire of Charles V.** Charles V spent much of his reign fighting wars in Italy, against France and the Ottoman Empire, and within the borders of the Holy Roman Empire. He failed in his main goal to secure Europe for Catholicism: the 1555 Peace of Augsburg recognized the equality of Catholicism and Lutheranism and let each German prince choose his realm's religion. **?** Why would France feel threatened by the empire of Charles V? **View an animated version of this map or related maps at** http://history.wadsworth.com/spielvogel06/

followed and kept Charles preoccupied with military campaigns in southern France and the Low Countries. Finally, Charles made peace with Francis in 1544 and the Turks in 1545. Fifteen years after the Diet of Augsburg, Charles was finally free to resolve his problem in Germany.

By the time of Luther's death in February 1546, all hopes of a peaceful compromise had faded. Charles brought a sizable imperial army of German, Dutch, Italian, and Spanish troops to do battle with the Protestants. In the first phase of the Schmalkaldic Wars (1546–1547), the emperor's forces decisively defeated the Lutherans at the Battle of Mühlberg. Charles V was at the zenith of his power, and the Protestant cause seemed doomed.

Appearances proved misleading, however. The Schmalkaldic League was soon reestablished, and the German Protestant princes allied themselves with the new French king, Henry II (1547–1559)—a Catholic—to revive the war in 1552. This time Charles was less fortunate and was forced to negotiate a truce. Exhausted by his efforts to maintain religious orthodoxy and the unity of his empire, Charles abandoned German affairs to his brother Ferdinand, abdicated all of his titles in 1556, and retired to his country estate in Spain to spend the remaining two years of his life in solitude.

An end to religious warfare in Germany came in 1555 with the Peace of Augsburg, which marked an important turning point in the history of the Reformation. The division of Christianity was formally acknowledged, with Lutheranism granted equal legal standing with Catholicism. Moreover, the peace settlement accepted the right of each German ruler to determine the religion of his subjects (but not the right of the subjects to choose their religion). Charles's hope for a united empire had been completely dashed, and the ideal of medieval Christian unity was irretrievably lost. The rapid proliferation of new Protestant groups served to underscore that new reality.

| | |
|---|---|
| First Habsburg-Valois War | 1521–1525 |
| Battle of Mohács | 1526 |
| Second Habsburg-Valois War | 1527–1529 |
| Defeat of the Turks at Vienna | 1529 |
| Diet of Augsburg | 1530 |
| Formation of Schmalkaldic League | 1531 |
| Third Habsburg-Valois War | 1535–1538 |
| Fourth Habsburg-Valois War | 1542–1544 |
| Schmalkaldic Wars | 1546–1555 |
| Peace of Augsburg | 1555 |

# The Spread of the Protestant Reformation

For both Catholics and Protestant reformers, Luther's heresy raised the question of what constituted the correct interpretation of the Bible. The inability to agree on this issue led not only to theological confrontations but also to bloody warfare as each Christian group was unwilling to admit that it could be wrong.

## Lutheranism in Scandinavia

In 1397, the Union of Kalmar had brought about the unification of Denmark, Norway, and Sweden under the rule of one monarch, the king of Denmark. This union, however, failed to achieve any real social or political unification of the three states, particularly since the independent-minded landed nobles worked to frustrate any increase in monarchical centralization. By the beginning of the sixteenth century, the union was on the brink of disintegration. In 1520, Christian II (1513–1523) of Denmark, ruler of the three Scandinavian kingdoms, was overthrown by Swedish barons led by Gustavus Vasa. Three years later, Vasa became king of an independent Sweden (1523–1560) and took the lead in establishing a Lutheran Reformation in his country. By the 1530s, the Swedish Lutheran National Church had been created.

Meanwhile, Christian II had also been deposed as the king of Denmark by the Danish nobility; he was succeeded by his uncle, who became Frederick I (1523–1533). Frederick encouraged Lutheran preachers to spread their evangelical doctrines and to introduce a Lutheran liturgy into the Danish church service. In the 1530s, under Frederick's successor, Christian III (1534–1559), a Lutheran state church was installed with the king as the supreme authority in all ecclesiastical affairs. Christian was also instrumental in spreading Lutheranism to Norway. By the 1540s, Scandinavia had become a Lutheran stronghold. Like the German princes, the Scandinavian monarchs had been the dominant force in establishing state-run churches.

## The Zwinglian Reformation

In the sixteenth century, the Swiss Confederation was a loose association of thirteen self-governing states called cantons. Theoretically part of the Holy Roman Empire, they had become virtually independent in 1499. The six forest cantons were democratic republics; the seven urban cantons, which included Zürich, Bern, and Basel, were for the most part governed by city councils controlled by narrow oligarchies of wealthy citizens.

Ulrich Zwingli (1484–1531) was a product of the Swiss forest cantons. The precocious son of a relatively prosperous peasant, the young Zwingli eventually obtained both the bachelor of arts and master of arts degrees. During his university education at Vienna and Basel, Zwingli was strongly influenced by Christian humanism. Ordained a priest in 1506, he accepted a parish post in rural Switzerland until his appointment as a cathedral priest in the Great Minster of Zürich in 1518. Through his preaching there, Zwingli began the Reformation in Switzerland.

Zwingli's preaching of the Gospel caused such unrest that in 1523 the city council held a public disputation or debate in the town hall. The disputation became a standard method of spreading the Reformation to many cities. It gave an advantage to reformers, since they had the power of new ideas and Catholics were not used to defending their teachings. Zwingli's party was accorded the vic-tory, and the council declared that "Mayor, Council and Great Council of Zürich, in order to do away with disturbance and discord, have upon due deliberation and consultation decided and resolved that Master Zwingli should continue as heretofore to proclaim the Gospel and the pure sacred Scripture."[7]

**Reforms in Zürich** Over the next two years, evangelical reforms were promulgated in Zürich by a city council strongly influenced by Zwingli. Zwingli looked to the state to supervise the church. "A church without the magistrate is mutilated and incomplete," he declared. Relics and images were abolished; all paintings and decorations were removed from the churches and replaced by whitewashed walls. As Zwingli remarked, "The images are not to be endured; for all that God has forbidden, there can be no compromise."[8] The Mass was replaced by a new liturgy consisting of Scripture reading, prayer, and sermons. Music was eliminated from the service as a distraction from the pure word of God. Monasticism, pilgrim- ages, the veneration of saints, clerical celibacy, and the pope's authority were all abolished as remnants of papal Christianity. Zwingli's movement soon spread to other cities in Switzerland, including Bern in 1528 and Basel in 1529.

**A Futile Search for Unity** By 1528, Zwingli's reform movement faced a serious political problem as the forest cantons remained staunchly Catholic. Zürich feared an alliance between them and the Habsburgs. To counteract this danger, Zwingli attempted to build a league of evangelical cities by seeking an agreement with Luther and the German reformers. An alliance between them seemed possible, since the Reformation had spread to the southern German cities, especially Strasbourg, where a moderate reform movement containing characteristics of both Luther's and Zwingli's movements had been instituted by Martin Bucer (1491–1551). Both the German and the Swiss reformers realized the need for unity to defend against imperial and conservative opposition. Protestant political leaders, especially Landgrave Philip of Hesse, fearful of Charles V's ability to take advantage of the division between the reformers, attempted to promote an alliance of the Swiss and German reformed churches by persuading the leaders of both groups to attend a colloquy (conference) at Marburg to resolve their differences. Able to agree on virtually everything else, the gathering splintered over the interpretation of the Lord's Supper (see the box on p. 359). Zwingli believed that the scriptural words "This is my body" and "This is my blood" should be taken symbolically, not liter-

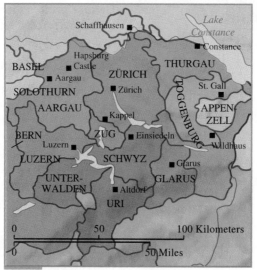

**Zwingli's Zürich**

ally. To Zwingli, the Lord's Supper was only a meal of remembrance, and he refused to accept Luther's insistence on the real presence of the body and blood of Jesus "in, with, and under the bread and wine." The Marburg Colloquy of 1529 produced no agreement and no evangelical alliance.

In October 1531, war erupted between the Swiss Protestant and Catholic cantons. Zürich's army was routed, and Zwingli was found wounded on the battlefield. His enemies killed him, cut up his body, burned the pieces, and scattered the ashes. This Swiss civil war of 1531 provided an early indication of what religious passions would lead to in the sixteenth century. Unable to find peaceful ways to agree on the meaning of the Gospel, the disciples of Christianity resorted to violence and decision by force. When he heard of Zwingli's death, Martin Luther, who had not forgotten the confrontation at Marburg, is supposed to have remarked that Zwingli "got what he deserved."

## The Radical Reformation: The Anabaptists

Although many reformers were ready to allow the state to play an important, if not dominant, role in church affairs, some people rejected this kind of magisterial reformation and favored a far more radical reform movement. Collectively called the Anabaptists, these radicals were actually members of a large variety of groups who shared some common characteristics. Anabaptism was especially attractive to the peasants, weavers, miners, and artisans who had been adversely affected by the economic changes of the age.

**The Ideas of the Anabaptists**   Anabaptists everywhere held certain ideas in common. All felt that the true Christian church was a voluntary association of believers who had undergone spiritual rebirth and had then been baptized into the church. Anabaptists advocated adult rather than infant baptism. No one, they believed, should be forced to accept the truth of the Bible. They also tried to return literally to the practices and spirit of early Christianity. Adhering to the accounts of early Christian communities in the New Testament, they followed a strict sort of democracy in which all believers were considered equal. Each church chose its own minister, who might be any mem-

**Zwingli.** Ulrich Zwingli began the Reformation in Switzerland through his preaching in Zürich. Zwingli's theology was accepted in Zürich and soon spread to other Swiss cities. This portrait of Zwingli was done by Hans Asper, probably in 1531.

# A Reformation Debate: The Marburg Colloquy

DEBATES PLAYED A CRUCIAL ROLE in the Reformation period. They were a primary instrument in introducing the Reformation into innumerable cities as well as a means of resolving differences among like-minded Protestant groups. This selection contains an excerpt from the vivacious and often brutal debate between Luther and Zwingli over the sacrament of the Lord's Supper at Marburg in 1529. The two protagonists failed to reach agreement.

## The Marburg Colloquy, 1529

**THE HESSIAN CHANCELLOR FEIGE:** My gracious prince and lord [Landgrave Philip of Hesse] has summoned you for the express and urgent purpose of settling the dispute over the sacrament of the Lord's Supper.... Let everyone on both sides present his arguments in a spirit of moderation, as becomes such matters.... Now then, Doctor Luther, you may proceed.

**LUTHER:** Noble prince, gracious lord! Undoubtedly the colloquy is well intentioned.... Although I have no intention of changing my mind, which is firmly made up, I will nevertheless present the grounds of my belief and show where the others are in error.... Your basic contentions are these: In the last analysis you wish to prove that a body cannot be in two places at once, and you produce arguments about the unlimited body which are based on natural reason. I do not question how Christ can be God and man and how the two natures can be joined. For God is more powerful than all our ideas, and we must submit to his word.

Prove that Christ's body is not there where the Scripture says, "This is my body!" Rational proofs I will not listen to.... God is beyond all mathematics and the words of God are to be revered and carried out in awe. It is God who commands, "Take, eat, this is my body." I request, therefore, valid scriptural proof to the contrary.

*Luther writes on the table in chalk, "This is my body," and covers the words with a velvet cloth.*

**OECOLAMPADIUS** [leader of the reform movement in Basel and a Zwinglian partisan]: The sixth chapter of John clarifies the other scriptural passages. Christ is not speaking there about a local presence. "The flesh is of no avail," he says. It is not my intention to employ rational, or geometrical, arguments—neither am I denying the power of God—but as long as I have the complete faith I will speak from that. For Christ is risen; he sits at the right hand of God; and so he cannot be present in the bread. Our view is neither new nor sacrilegious, but is based on faith and Scripture....

**ZWINGLI:** I insist that the words of the Lord's Supper must be figurative. This is ever apparent, and even required by the article of faith: "taken up into heaven, seated at the right hand of the Father." Otherwise, it would be absurd to look for him in the Lord's Supper at the same time that Christ is telling us that he is in heaven. One and the same body cannot possibly be in different places....

**LUTHER:** I call upon you as before: your basic contentions are shaky. Give way, and give glory to God!

**ZWINGLI:** And we call upon you to give glory to God and to quit begging the question! The issue at stake is this: Where is the proof of your position? I am willing to consider your words carefully—no harm meant! You're trying to outwit me. I stand by this passage in the sixth chapter of John, verse 63, and shall not be shaken from it. You'll have to sing another tune.

**LUTHER:** You're being obnoxious.

**ZWINGLI:** (*excitedly*) Don't you believe that Christ was attempting in John 6 to help those who did not understand?

**LUTHER:** You're trying to dominate things! You insist on passing judgment! Leave that to someone else! ... It is your point that must be proved, not mine. But let us stop this sort of thing. It serves no purpose.

**ZWINGLI:** It certainly does! It is for you to prove that the passage in John 6 speaks of a physical repast.

**LUTHER:** You express yourself poorly and make about as much progress as a cane standing in a corner. You're going nowhere.

**ZWINGLI:** No, no, no! This is the passage that will break your neck!

**LUTHER:** Don't be so sure of yourself. Necks don't break this way. You're in Hesse, not Switzerland.

---

ber of the community, since all Christians were considered priests (though women were often excluded). Those chosen as ministers had the duty to lead services, which were very simple and contained nothing not found in the early church. Like early Christians, Anabaptists, who called themselves "Christians" or "Saints," accepted that they would have to suffer for their faith. Anabaptists rejected theological speculation in favor of simple Christian living according to what they believed was the pure word of God. The Lord's Supper was interpreted as a remembrance, a meal of fellowship celebrated in the evening in private houses according to Jesus' example.

Unlike the Catholics and other Protestants, most Anabaptists believed in the complete separation of church and state. Not only was government to be excluded from the realm of religion, but it was not even supposed to exercise political jurisdiction over real Christians. Human law had no power over those whom God had saved. Anabaptists refused to hold political office or bear arms because many took the commandment "Thou shall not kill" literally, although some Anabaptist groups did become quite violent. Their political beliefs as much as their religious beliefs caused the Anabaptists to be regarded as dangerous radicals who threatened the very fabric of sixteenth-century society. Indeed, the chief thing Protestants and Catholics could agree on was the need to stamp out the Anabaptists.

**Varieties of Anabaptists** One early group of Anabaptists known as the Swiss Brethren arose in Zürich. Their ideas, especially adult baptism, frightened Zwingli, and they were soon expelled from the city. Because the first members of the Swiss Brethren who were baptized as adults had already been baptized as children (in the Catholic church), their opponents labeled them Anabaptists or Rebaptists. Under Roman law, such people were subject to the death penalty.

As the teachings of the Swiss Brethren spread through southern Germany, the Austrian Habsburg lands, and Switzerland, Anabaptists suffered ruthless persecution, especially after the Peasants' War of 1524–1525, when the upper classes resorted to repression. Virtually eradicated in Germany, Anabaptist survivors emerged in Moravia and Poland, and in the Netherlands, Anabaptism took on a strange form.

In the 1530s, the city of Münster, in Westphalia in northwestern Germany near the Dutch border, was the site of an Anabaptist uprising that determined the fate of Dutch Anabaptism. Seat of a powerful Catholic prince-bishop, Münster had experienced severe economic disasters, including crop failure and plague. Although converted to Lutheranism in 1532, Münster experienced a more radical mass religious hysteria that led to legal recognition for the Anabaptists. Soon Münster became a haven for Anabaptists from the surrounding neighborhood, especially the more wild-eyed variety known as Melchiorites, who adhered to a vivid **millenarianism.** They believed that the end of the world was at hand and that they would usher in the kingdom of God with Münster as the New Jerusalem. By the end of February 1534, these millenarian Anabaptists had taken control of the city, driven out everyone they considered godless or unbelievers, burned all books except the Bible, and proclaimed communal ownership of all property. Eventually, the leadership of this New Jerusalem fell into the hands of one man, John of Leiden, who proclaimed himself king of the New Jerusalem. As king, he would lead the elect from Münster out to cover the entire world and purify it of evil by the sword in preparation for Jesus' Second Coming and the creation of a New Age. In this new kingdom, John of Leiden believed, all goods would be held in common and the saints would live without suffering.

But it was not to be. As the Catholic prince-bishop of Münster gathered a large force and laid siege to the city, the new king repeatedly had to postpone the ushering forth from Münster. Finally, after many inhabitants had starved, a joint army of Catholics and Lutherans recaptured the city in June 1535 and executed the radical Anabaptist leaders in gruesome fashion. The New Jerusalem had ceased to exist.

Purged of its fantasies and its more extreme elements, Dutch Anabaptism reverted to its pacifist tendencies, especially evident in the work of Menno Simons (1496–1561), the man most responsible for rejuvenating Dutch Anabaptism. A popular leader, Menno dedicated his life to the spread of a peaceful, evangelical Anabaptism that stressed separation from the world in order to truly emulate the life of Jesus. Simons imposed strict discipline on his followers and banned those who refused to conform to the rules. The Mennonites, as his followers were called, spread from the Netherlands into northwestern Germany and eventually into Poland and Lithuania as well as the New World. Both the Mennonites and the Amish, who are also descended from the Anabaptists, maintain communities in the United States and Canada today.

## The Reformation in England

The English Reformation was initiated by King Henry VIII (1509–1547), who wanted to divorce his first wife, Catherine of Aragon, because she had failed to produce a male heir. Furthermore, Henry had fallen in love with Anne Boleyn, a lady-in-waiting to Queen Catherine. Anne's unwillingness to be only the king's mistress and the king's desire to have a legitimate male heir made their marriage imperative, but the king's first marriage stood in the way.

Henry relied on Cardinal Wolsey, the highest-ranking English church official and lord chancellor to the king, to obtain from Pope Clement VII an annulment of the king's marriage. Normally, the pope might have been willing to oblige, but the sack of Rome in 1527 had made the pope dependent on the Holy Roman Emperor Charles V, who happened to be the nephew of Queen Catherine. Discretion dictated delay in granting the English king's request. Impatient with the process, Henry dismissed Wolsey in 1529.

Two new advisers now became the king's agents in fulfilling his wishes. These were Thomas Cranmer (1489–1556), who became archbishop of Canterbury in 1532, and Thomas Cromwell (1485–1540), the king's principal secretary after the fall of Wolsey. They advised the king to obtain an annulment of his marriage in England's own ecclesiastical courts. The most important step toward this goal was the promulgation by Parliament of an act cutting off all appeals from English church courts to Rome, a piece of legislation that essentially abolished papal authority in England. Henry no longer needed the pope to obtain his annulment. He was now in a hurry because Anne Boleyn had become pregnant and he had secretly married her in January 1533 to legitimize the expected heir. In May, as archbishop of Canterbury and head of the highest ecclesiastical court in England, Thomas Cranmer ruled that the king's marriage to Catherine was "null and absolutely void" and then validated Henry's marriage to Anne. At the beginning of June, Anne was crowned queen. Three months later, a child was born. Much to the king's disappointment, the baby was a girl, whom they named Elizabeth.

In 1534, Parliament completed the break of the Church of England with Rome by passing the Act of Supremacy, which declared that the king was "taken, accepted, and reputed the only supreme head on earth of the Church of England." This meant that the English monarch now controlled the church in all matters of doctrine, clerical ap-

**Henry VIII and His Children.** The desire of Henry VIII for a male heir played a significant role in his break with the Catholic church. Pictured here in the central panel of this 1545 portrait by an unknown artist are Prince Edward, who became King Edward VI in 1547, Henry VIII, and Jane Seymour, his third wife. Although Jane Seymour died soon after giving birth to Edward, the artist chose to portray the mother with her grown son Edward in order to glorify the king and his family. On the far left is Princess Mary and on the far right is Princess Elizabeth.

pointments, and discipline. In addition, Parliament passed the Treason Act, making it punishable by death to deny that the king was the supreme head of the church.

Few challenged the new order. One who did was Thomas More, the humanist and former lord chancellor, who saw clearly to the heart of the issue: loyalty to the pope in Rome was now treason in England. More refused to support the new laws and was duly tried for treason. At his trial, he asked, rhetorically, what the effect of the actions of the king and Parliament would be: "Therefore am I not bound . . . to conform my conscience to the Council of one realm [England] against the general Council of Christendom?"[9] Because his conscience could not accept the victory of the national state over the church, nor would he, as a Christian, bow his head to a secular ruler in matters of faith, More was beheaded in London on July 6, 1535.

**The New Order** Thomas Cromwell worked out the details of the Tudor government's new role in church affairs based on the centralized power exercised by the king and Parliament. Cromwell also came to his extravagant king's financial rescue with a daring plan for the dissolution of the monasteries. About four hundred religious houses were closed in 1536, and their land and possessions were confiscated by the king. Many were sold to nobles, gentry, and some merchants. The king added enormously to his treasury and also to his ranks of supporters, who now had a stake in the new Tudor order.

Although Henry VIII had broken with the papacy, little change occurred in matters of doctrine, theology, and ceremony. Some of his supporters, such as Archbishop Thomas Cranmer, wished to have a religious reformation as well as an administrative one, but Henry was unyielding. Nevertheless, some clergymen ignored Henry on the matter of priestly celibacy and secretly married.

The final decade of Henry's reign was preoccupied with foreign affairs, factional intrigue, and a continued effort to find the perfect wife. Henry soon tired of Anne Boleyn and had her beheaded in 1536 on a charge of adultery. His third wife, Jane Seymour, produced the long-awaited male heir but died twelve days later. His fourth marriage, to Anne of Cleves, a German princess, was arranged for political reasons. Henry relied on a painted portrait of Anne when he made the arrangements, but he was disappointed at her physical appearance when he saw her in person and soon divorced her. His fifth wife, Catherine Howard, was more attractive but less moral. When she committed adultery, Henry had her beheaded. His last wife was Catherine Parr, who married the king in 1543 and outlived him. Henry was succeeded by the underage and sickly Edward VI (1547–1553), the son of his third wife.

Since the new king was only nine years old at the time of his accession to the throne, real control of England passed to a council of regency. During Edward's reign, Archbishop Cranmer and others inclined toward Protestant doctrines were able to move the Church of England in a more Protestant direction. New acts of Parliament instituted the right of the clergy to marry, the elimination of images, and the creation of a revised Protestant liturgy that was elaborated in a new prayer book and liturgical guide known as the Book of Common Prayer. These rapid changes in doctrine and liturgy aroused much opposition and prepared the way for the reaction that occurred when Mary, Henry's first daughter by Catherine of Aragon, came to the throne.

**Reaction under Mary** Mary (1553–1558) was a Catholic who fully intended to restore England to the Roman Catholic fold. But her restoration of Catholicism, achieved by joint action of the monarch and Parliament, aroused opposition. There was widespread antipathy to Mary's unfortunate marriage to Philip II, son of Charles V and the future king of Spain. Philip was strongly disliked in England, and Mary's foreign policy of alliance with Spain aroused further hostility, especially when her forces lost Calais, the last English possession from the Hundred Years' War. The burning of more than three hundred Protestant heretics aroused further ire against "bloody Mary." As a result of her policies, Mary managed to achieve the opposite of what she had intended: England was more Protestant by the end of her reign than it had been at the beginning. When she came to power, Protestantism had become identified with church destruction and religious anarchy. Now people identified it with English resistance to Spanish interference. Mary's death in 1558 ended the restoration of Catholicism in England.

## John Calvin and Calvinism

Of the second generation of Protestant reformers, one stands out as the systematic theologian and organizer of the Protestant movement—John Calvin (1509–1564). Calvin received a remarkably diverse education in humanistic studies and law in his native France. He was also influenced by Luther's writings, which were being circulated and read by French intellectuals as early as 1523. In 1533, Calvin

experienced a religious crisis that determined the rest of his life's work. He described it in these words:

> God, by a sudden conversion, subdued and brought my mind to a teachable frame, which was more hardened in such matters than might have been expected from one at my early period of life. Having thus received some taste and knowledge of true godliness, I was immediately inflamed with so intense a desire to make progress therein, although I did not leave off other studies, I yet pursued them with less ardor.[10]

Calvin's conversion was solemn and straightforward. He was so convinced of the inner guidance of God that he became the most determined of all the Protestant reformers.

After his conversion and newfound conviction, Calvin was no longer safe in Paris, since King Francis I periodically persecuted Protestants. Eventually, Calvin made his way to Basel, where in 1536 he published the first edition of the *Institutes of the Christian Religion,* a masterful synthesis of Protestant thought that immediately secured his reputation as one of the new leaders of Protestantism.

**Calvin's Ideas**   On most important doctrines, Calvin stood very close to Luther. He adhered to the doctrine of justification by faith alone to explain how humans achieved salvation. But Calvin also placed much emphasis on the absolute sovereignty of God or the "power, grace, and glory of God." Thus "God asserts his possession of omnipotence, and claims our acknowledgment of this attribute; not such as is imagined by sophists, vain, idle, and almost asleep, but vigilant, efficacious, operative and engaged in continual action."[11]

One of the ideas derived from his emphasis on the absolute sovereignty of God—**predestination**—gave a unique cast to Calvin's teachings. This "eternal decree," as Calvin called it, meant that God had predestined some people to be saved (the elect) and others to be damned (the reprobate). According to Calvin, "He has once for all determined, both whom he would admit to salvation, and whom he would condemn to destruction."[12] Calvin identified three tests that might indicate possible salvation: an open profession of faith, a "decent and godly life," and participation in the sacraments of baptism and communion. In no instance did Calvin ever suggest that worldly success or material wealth was a sign of election. Most important, although Calvin stressed that there could be no absolute certainty of salvation, some of his followers did not always make this distinction. The practical psychological effect of predestination was to give some later Calvinists an unshakable conviction that they were doing God's work on earth. Thus Calvinism became a dynamic and activist faith. It is no accident that Calvinism became the militant international form of Protestantism.

**John Calvin.** After a conversion experience, John Calvin abandoned his life as a humanist and became a reformer. In 1536, Calvin began working to reform the city of Geneva, where he remained until his death in 1564. This sixteenth-century portrait of Calvin pictures him near the end of his life.

# THE ROLE OF DISCIPLINE IN THE "MOST PERFECT SCHOOL OF CHRIST ON EARTH"

*J*OHN CALVIN HAD EMPHASIZED in his reform movement that the church should have the ability to enforce proper behavior. Consequently, the Ecclesiastical Ordinances of 1541, the constitution of the church in Geneva, provided for an order of elders whose function was to cooperate with the pastors in maintaining discipline, "to have oversight of the life of everyone," as Calvin expressed it. These selections from the official records of the Consistory show the nature of its work.

### Reports of the Genevan Consistory

Donna Jane Peterman is questioned concerning her faith and why she does not receive communion and attend worship. She confesses her faith and believes in one God and wants to come to God and the holy Church and has no other faith. She recited the Lord's Prayer in the vernacular. She said that she believes what the Church believes. Is questioned why she never participates in communion when it is celebrated in this town, but goes to other places. She answers that she goes where it seems good to her. Is placed outside the faith.

The sister of Sr. Curtet, Lucresse, to whom remonstrances have been made on account of her going with certain monies to have Masses said at Nessy by the monks of St. Claire. Questioned whether she has no scruples as to what she says. Replied that her father and mother have brought her up to obey a different law from the one now in force here. However, she does not desire the present law. Asked as to when was the festival of St. Felix, she replied that it was yesterday. Asked if she had not fasted, she replied that she fasted when it pleased her. Asked if she did not desire to pray to a single God; said that she did. Asked if she did not pray to St. Felix; said that she prayed to St. Felix and other saints who interceded for her. She is very obstinate. Decision that she be sent to some minister of her choice every sermon day and that the Lord's Supper be withheld from her.

At about this time, by resolution of the Consistory . . . the marriage contracted between the widow of Jean Archard, aged more than 70, and a servant of hers, aged about 27 or 28, was dissolved because of the too great inequality of age. The Consistory resolved further that Messieurs should be requested to make a ruling on this matter for the future.

---

To Calvin, the church was a divine institution responsible for preaching the word of God and administering the sacraments. Calvin kept the same two sacraments as other Protestant reformers, baptism and the Lord's Supper. Baptism was a sign of the remission of sins. Calvin believed in the real presence of Jesus in the sacrament of the Lord's Supper, but only in a spiritual sense. Jesus' body is at the right hand of God and thus cannot be in the sacrament, but to the believer, Jesus is spiritually present in the Lord's Supper.

**Calvin's Geneva**    Before 1536, John Calvin had essentially been a scholar. But in that year, he took up a ministry in Geneva that lasted until his death in 1564. Calvin achieved a major success in 1541 when the city council accepted his new church constitution, known as the Ecclesiastical Ordinances. This document created a church government that used both clergy and laymen in the service of the church. The Consistory, a special body for enforcing moral discipline, was set up as a court to oversee the moral life and doctrinal purity of Genevans (see the box above). As its power increased, the Consistory went from "fraternal corrections" to the use of public penance and excommunication. More serious cases could be turned over to the city council for punishments greater than excommunication. During Calvin's last years, stricter laws against blasphemy were enacted and enforced with banishment and public whippings.

Calvin's success in Geneva enabled the city to become a vibrant center of Protestantism. John Knox, the Calvinist reformer of Scotland, called it "the most perfect school of Christ on earth." Following Calvin's lead, missionaries trained in Geneva were sent to all parts of Europe. Calvinism became established in France, the Netherlands, Scotland, and central and eastern Europe. By the mid-sixteenth century, Calvinism had replaced Lutheranism as the international form of Protestantism, and Calvin's Geneva stood as the fortress of the Reformation.

## The Social Impact of the Protestant Reformation

Because Christianity was such an integral part of European life, it was inevitable that the Reformation would have an impact on the family, education, and popular religious practices.

Calvin's Geneva

## A PROTESTANT WOMAN

*I*N THE INITIAL ZEAL of the Protestant Reformation, women were frequently allowed to play unusual roles. Katherine Zell of Germany (c. 1497–1562) first preached beside her husband in 1527. After the death of her two children, she devoted the rest of her life to helping her husband and their Anabaptist faith. This selection is taken from one of her letters to a young Lutheran minister who had criticized her activities.

### Katherine Zell to Ludwig Rabus of Memmingen

I, Katherine Zell, wife of the late lamented Mathew Zell, who served in Strasbourg, where I was born and reared and still live, wish you peace and enhancement in God's grace. . . .

From my earliest years I turned to the Lord, who taught and guided me, and I have at all times, in accordance with my understanding and His grace, embraced the interests of His church and earnestly sought Jesus. Even in youth this brought me the regard and affection of clergymen and others much concerned with the church, which is why the pious Mathew Zell wanted me as a companion in marriage; and I, in turn, to serve the glory of Christ, gave devotion and help to my husband, both in his ministry and in keeping his house. . . . Ever since I was ten years old I have been a student and a sort of church mother, much given to attending sermons. I have loved and frequented the company of learned men, and I conversed much with them, not about dancing, masquerades, and worldly pleasures but about the kingdom of God. . . .

Consider the poor Anabaptists, who are so furiously and ferociously persecuted. Must the authorities everywhere be incited against them, as the hunter drives his dog against wild animals? Against those who acknowledge Christ the Lord in very much the same way we do and over which we broke with the papacy? Just because they cannot agree with us on lesser things, is this any reason to persecute them and in them Christ, in whom they fervently believe and have often professed in misery, in prison, and under the torments of fire and water?

Governments may punish criminals, but they should not force and govern belief, which is a matter for the heart and conscience not for temporal authorities. . . . When the authorities pursue one, they soon bring forth tears, and towns and villages are emptied.

## The Family

For centuries, Catholicism had praised the family and sanctified its existence by making marriage a sacrament. But the Catholic church's high regard for abstinence from sex as the surest way to holiness made the celibate state of the clergy preferable to marriage. Nevertheless, because not all men could remain chaste, marriage offered the best means to control sexual intercourse and give it a purpose, the procreation of children. To some extent, this attitude persisted among the Protestant reformers; Luther, for example, argued that sex in marriage allowed one to "make use of this sex in order to avoid sin," and Calvin advised that every man should "abstain from marriage only so long as he is fit to observe celibacy." If "his power to tame lust fails him," then he must marry.

But the Reformation did bring some change to the conception of the family. Both Catholic and Protestant clergy preached sermons advocating a more positive side to family relationships. The Protestants were especially important in developing this new view of the family. Because Protestantism had eliminated any idea of special holiness for celibacy, abolishing both monasticism and a celibate clergy, the family could be placed at the center of human life, and a new stress on "mutual love between man and wife" could be extolled. But were doctrine and reality the same? For more radical religious groups, at times they were (see the box above). One Anabaptist wrote to his wife before his execution, "My faithful helper, my loyal friend. I praise God that he gave you to me, you who have sustained me in all my trial."[13] But more often reality reflected the traditional roles of husband as the ruler and wife as the obedient servant whose chief duty was to please her husband. Luther stated it clearly:

> The rule remains with the husband, and the wife is compelled to obey him by God's command. He rules the home and the state, wages war, defends his possessions, tills the soil, builds, plants, etc. The woman on the other hand is like a nail driven into the wall . . . so the wife should stay at home and look after the affairs of the household, as one who has been deprived of the ability of administering those affairs that are outside and that concern the state. She does not go beyond her most personal duties.[14]

Obedience to her husband was not a wife's only role; her other important duty was to bear children. To Calvin and Luther, this function of women was part of the divine plan. God punishes women for the sins of Eve by the burdens of procreation and feeding and nurturing their children, but, said Luther, "it is a gladsome punishment if you consider the hope of eternal life and the honor of motherhood which had been left to her."[15] Although the Protestant reformers sanctified this role of woman as mother and wife, viewing it as a holy vocation, Protestantism also left few alternatives for women. Because monasticism had been destroyed, that career avenue was no longer available; for most Protestant women, family life was their only destiny. At the same time, by emphasizing the father as "ruler" and hence the center of household religion, Protestantism even removed the woman from her traditional role as controller of religion in the home.

Protestant reformers called on men and women to read the Bible and participate in religious services together.

In this way, the reformers provided a stimulus for the education of girls so they could read the Bible and other religious literature. The city council of Zwickau, for example, established a girls' school in 1525. But these schools were designed to encourage proper moral values rather than intellectual development and really did little to improve the position of women in society. Likewise, when women attempted to take more active roles in religious life, reformers—Lutheran and Calvinist alike—shrank back in horror. To them, the equality of the Gospel did not mean overthrowing the inequality of social classes or the sexes. Overall, the Protestant Reformation did not noticeably transform women's subordinate place in society.

## Education in the Reformation

The Reformation had an important effect on the development of education in Europe. Renaissance humanism had significantly altered the content of education, and Protestant educators were very successful in implementing and using humanist methods in Protestant secondary schools and universities. Unlike the humanist schools, however, which had been mostly for an elite, the sons and a few daughters of the nobility and wealthier bourgeoisie, Protestant schools were aimed at a much wider audience. Protestantism created an increased need for at least a semiliterate body of believers who could read the Bible for themselves.

While adopting the classical emphasis of humanist schools, Protestant reformers broadened the base of the people being educated. Convinced of the need to provide the church with good Christians and good pastors as well as the state with good administrators and citizens, Martin Luther advocated that all children should have the opportunity of an education provided by the state. To that end, he urged the cities and villages of Saxony to establish schools paid for by the public. Luther's ideas were shared by his Wittenberg coworker Philip Melanch-

thon, whose educational efforts earned him the title of *Praecepter Germaniae*, the Teacher of Germany. In his scheme for education in Saxony, Melanchthon divided students into three classes or divisions based on their age or capabilities.

Following Melanchthon's example, the Protestants in Germany were responsible for introducing the gymnasium, or secondary school, where the humanist emphasis on the liberal arts based on instruction in Greek and Latin was combined with religious instruction. Most famous was the school in Strasbourg founded by Johannes Sturm in 1538, which served as a model for other Protestant schools. John Calvin's Genevan Academy, founded in 1559, was organized in two distinct parts. The "private school" or gymnasium was divided into seven classes for young people who were taught Latin and Greek grammar and literature as well as logic. In the "public school," students were taught philosophy, Hebrew, Greek, and theology. The Genevan Academy, which eventually became a university, came to concentrate on preparing ministers to spread the Calvinist view of the Gospel.

## Religious Practices and Popular Culture

The attacks of Protestant reformers on the Catholic church led to radical changes in religious practices. The Protestant Reformation abolished or severely curtailed such customary practices as indulgences, the veneration of relics and saints, pilgrimages, monasticism, and clerical celibacy. The elimination of saints put an end to the numerous celebrations of religious holy days and changed a community's sense of time. Thus in Protestant communities, religious ceremonies and imagery, such as processions and statues, tended to be replaced with individual private prayer, family worship, and collective prayer and worship at the same time each week on Sunday.

In addition to abolishing saints' days and religious carnivals, some Protestant reformers even tried to eliminate

**A Sixteenth-Century Classroom.** Protestants in Germany developed secondary schools that combined instruction in the liberal arts with religious education. This scene from a painting by Ambrosius Holbein shows a schoolmaster instructing a pupil in the alphabet while his wife helps a little girl.

customary forms of entertainment. The Puritans (as English Calvinists were called), for example, attempted to ban drinking in taverns, dramatic performances, and dancing. Dutch Calvinists denounced the tradition of giving small presents to children on the feast of Saint Nicholas, in early December. Many of these Protestant attacks on popular culture were unsuccessful, however. The importance of taverns in English social life made it impossible to eradicate them, and celebrating at Christmastime persisted in the Dutch Netherlands.

## The Catholic Reformation

By the mid-sixteenth century, Lutheranism had become established in parts of Germany and Scandinavia, and Calvinism in parts of Switzerland, France, the Netherlands, and eastern Europe (see Map 13.2). In England, the split from Rome had resulted in the creation of a national church. The situation in Europe did not look favorable for Roman Catholicism. But constructive, positive forces for reform were at work within the Catholic church, and by the mid-sixteenth century, they came to be directed by a revived and reformed papacy, giving the church new strength. The revival of Roman Catholicism is often called the Catholic Reformation, although some historians prefer the term Counter-Reformation, especially for those elements of the Catholic Reformation that were directly aimed at stopping the spread of Protestantism.

### Revival of the Old

The Catholic Reformation was a mixture of old and new elements. The best features of medieval Catholicism were revived and then adjusted to meet new conditions, a situation most apparent in the revival of mysticism and monasticism. The emergence of a new mysticism, closely tied to the traditions of Catholic piety, was especially evident in the life of the Spanish mystic Saint Teresa of Avila (1515–1582). A nun of the Carmelite order, Teresa experienced a variety of mystical visions that she claimed resulted in the ecstatic union of her soul with God. But Teresa also believed that mystical experience should lead to an active life of service on behalf of her Catholic faith. Consequently, she founded a new order of barefoot Carmelite nuns and worked to foster their mystical experiences.

The regeneration of religious orders also proved valuable to the reform of Catholicism. Old orders, such as the Benedictines and Dominicans, were reformed and renewed. The Capuchins emerged when a group of Franciscans decided to return to the simplicity and poverty of Saint Francis of Assisi, the medieval founder of the Franciscan order. In addition to

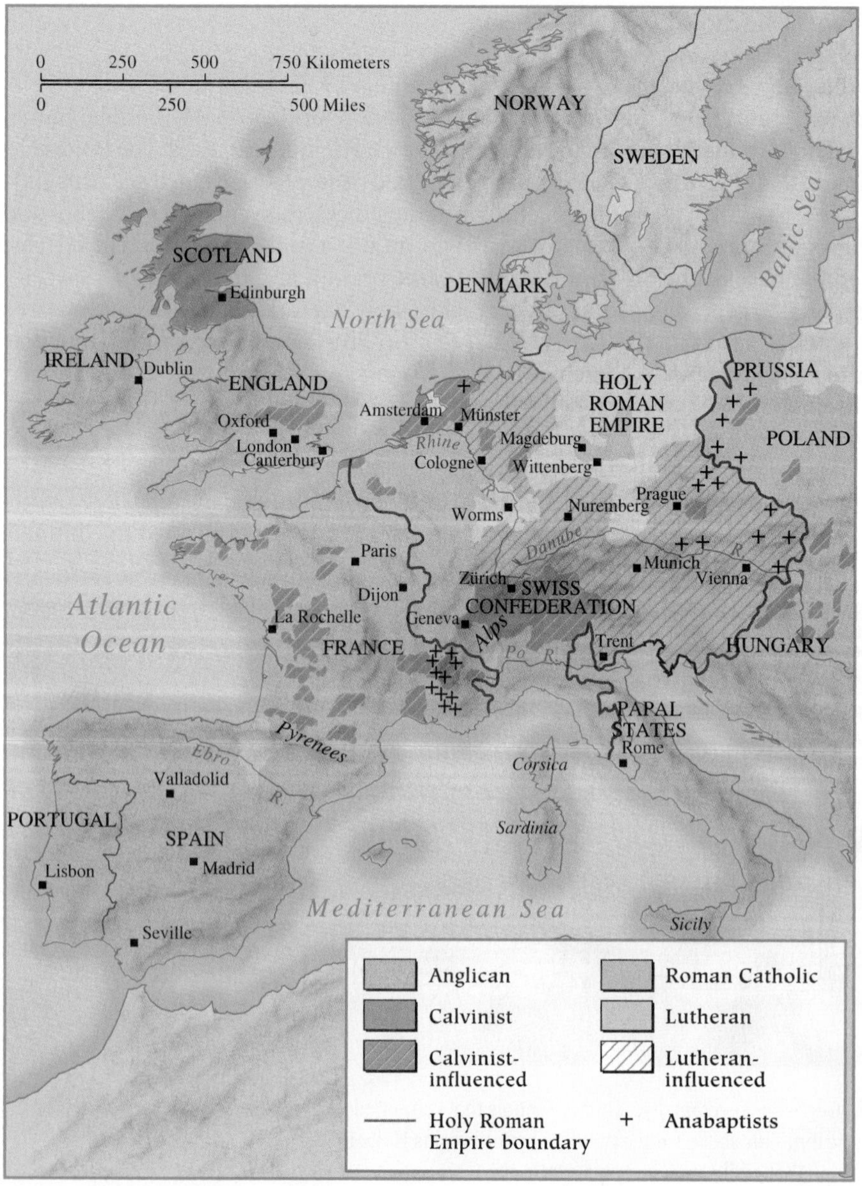

MAP 13.2 **Catholics and Protestants in Europe by 1560.** The Reformation continued to evolve beyond the basic split of the Lutherans from the Catholics. Several Protestant sects broke away from the teachings of Martin Luther, each with a separate creed and different ways of worship. In England, Henry VIII broke with the Catholic church for political and dynastic reasons. **?** Which areas of Europe were solidly Catholic, which were solidly Lutheran, and which were neither? View an animated version of this map or related maps at http://history.wadsworth.com/spielvogel06/

# LOYOLA AND OBEDIENCE TO "OUR HOLY MOTHER, THE HIERARCHICAL CHURCH"

*I*N HIS *SPIRITUAL EXERCISES,* Ignatius of Loyola developed a systematic program for "the conquest of self and the regulation of one's life" for service to the hierarchical Catholic church. Ignatius' supreme goal was the commitment of the Christian to active service under Jesus' banner in the Church of Christ (the Catholic church). In the final section of *The Spiritual Exercises,* Loyola explained the nature of that commitment in a series of "Rules for Thinking with the Church."

### Ignatius of Loyola, "Rules for Thinking with the Church"

The following rules should be observed to foster the true attitude of mind we ought to have in the Church militant.

1. We must put aside all judgment of our own, and keep the mind ever ready and prompt to obey in all things the true Spouse of Jesus Christ, our holy Mother, the hierarchical Church.
2. We should praise sacramental confession, the yearly reception of the Most Blessed Sacrament [the Lord's Supper], and praise more highly monthly reception, and still more weekly Communion. . . .
3. We ought to praise the frequent hearing of Mass, the singing of hymns, psalmody, and long prayers whether in the church or outside. . . .
4. We must praise highly religious life, virginity, and contingency; and matrimony ought not be praised as much as any of these.
5. We should praise vows of religion, obedience, poverty, chastity, and vows to perform other works of supererogation conducive to perfection. . . .
6. We should show our esteem for the relics of the saints by venerating them and praying to the saints.

We should praise visits to the Station Churches, pilgrimages, indulgences, jubilees, the lighting of candles in churches.

7. We must praise the regulations of the Church, with regard to fast and abstinence, for example, in Lent, on Ember Days, Vigils, Fridays, and Saturdays.
8. We ought to praise not only the building and adornment of churches, but also images and veneration of them according to the subject they represent.
9. Finally, we must praise all the commandments of the Church, and be on the alert to find reasons to defend them, and by no means in order to criticize them.
10. We should be more ready to approve and praise the orders, recommendations, and way of acting of our superiors than to find fault with them. Though some of the orders, etc., may not have been praiseworthy, yet to speak against them, either when preaching in public or in speaking before the people, would rather be the cause of murmuring and scandal than of profit. As a consequence, the people would become angry with their superiors, whether secular or spiritual. But while it does harm in the absence of our superiors to speak evil of them before the people, it may be profitable to discuss their bad conduct with those who can apply a remedy. . . .
13. If we wish to proceed securely in all things, we must hold fast to the following principle: What seems to me white, I will believe black if the hierarchical Church so defines. For I must be convinced that in Christ our Lord, the bridegroom, and in His spouse the Church, only one Spirit holds sway, which governs and rules for the salvation of souls.

caring for the sick and the poor, the Capuchins focused on preaching the Gospel directly to the people and emerged as an effective force against Protestantism.

New religious orders and brotherhoods were also created. The Theatines, founded in 1524, placed their emphasis on reforming the secular clergy and encouraging those clerics to fulfill their duties among the laity. The Theatines also founded orphanages and hospitals to care for the victims of war and plague. The Ursulines, a new order of nuns founded in Italy in 1535, focused their attention on establishing schools for the education of girls.

The Oratory of Divine Love, first organized in Italy in 1497, was not a new religious order but an informal group of clergy and laymen who worked to foster reform by emphasizing personal spiritual development and outward acts of charity. The "philosophy of Christ," advocated by the Christian humanist Erasmus, was especially appealing to many of them. The Oratory's members included a number of cardinals who favored the reform of the Catholic church.

###  The Society of Jesus

Of all the new religious orders, the most important was the Society of Jesus, known as the Jesuits, who became the chief instrument of the Catholic Reformation. The Society of Jesus was founded by a Spanish nobleman, Ignatius of Loyola (1491–1556), whose injuries in battle cut short his military career. Loyola experienced a spiritual torment similar to Luther's but, unlike Luther, resolved his problems not by a new doctrine but by a decision to submit his will to the will of the church. Unable to be a real soldier, he vowed to be a soldier of God. Over a period of twelve years, Loyola prepared for his lifework by prayer, pilgrimages, going to school, and working out a spiritual program in his brief but powerful book, *The Spiritual Exercises.* This was a training manual for spiritual development emphasizing exercises by which the human will could be strengthened and made to follow the will of God as manifested through his instrument, the Catholic church (see the box above).

**Ignatius of Loyola.** The Jesuits became the most important new religious order of the Catholic Reformation. Shown here in a sixteenth-century painting by an unknown artist is Ignatius of Loyola, founder of the Society of Jesus. Loyola is seen kneeling before Pope Paul III, who officially recognized the Jesuits in 1540.

© Scala/Art Resource, NY

Loyola gathered together a small group of individuals who were eventually recognized as a religious order, the Society of Jesus, by a papal bull in 1540. The new order was grounded on the principles of absolute obedience to the papacy, a strict hierarchical order for the society, the use of education to achieve its goals, and a dedication to engage in "conflict for God." The Jesuits' organization came to resemble the structure of a military command. A two-year novitiate weeded out all but the most dedicated adherents. Executive leadership was put in the hands of a general, who nominated all-important positions in the order and was to be revered as the absolute head of the order. Loyola served as the first general of the order until his death in 1556. A special vow of absolute obedience to the pope made the Jesuits an important instrument for papal policy.

**Activities of the Jesuits**   The Jesuits pursued three major activities. They established highly disciplined schools, borrowing freely from humanist schools for their educational methods. To the Jesuits, the thorough education of young people was crucial to combating the advance of Protestantism. In the course of the sixteenth century, the Jesuits took over the premier academic posts in Catholic universities, and by 1600, they were the most famous educators in Europe.

Another prominent Jesuit activity was the propagation of the Catholic faith among non-Christians. Francis Xavier (1506–1552), one of the original members of the Society of Jesus, carried the message of Catholic Christianity to the East. After converting tens of thousands in India, he traveled to Malacca and the Moluccas before reaching Japan in 1549. He spoke highly of the Japanese: "They are a people of excellent morals—good in general and not malicious."[16] Thousands of Japanese, especially in the southernmost islands, became Christians. In 1552, Xavier set out for China but died of a fever before he reached the mainland.

Although conversion efforts in Japan proved short-lived, Jesuit activity in China, especially that of the Italian Matteo Ricci (1552–1610), was more long-lasting. Recognizing the Chinese pride in their own culture, the Jesuits attempted to draw parallels between Christian and Confucian concepts and to show the similarities between Christian morality and Confucian ethics. For their part, the missionaries were impressed with many aspects of Chinese civilization, and reports of their experiences heightened European curiosity about this great society on the other side of the world.

The Jesuits were also determined to carry the Catholic banner and fight Protestantism. Jesuit missionaries succeeded in restoring Catholicism to parts of Germany and eastern Europe. Poland was largely won back for the Catholic church through Jesuit efforts.

## A Revived Papacy

The involvement of the Renaissance papacy in dubious finances and Italian political and military affairs had given rise to numerous sources of corruption. The meager steps taken to control corruption left the papacy still in need of serious reform, and it took the jolt of the Protestant Reformation to bring it about.

The pontificate of Pope Paul III (1534–1549) proved to be a turning point in the reform of the papacy. Raised in the lap of Renaissance luxury, Paul III continued Renaissance papal practices by appointing his nephews as cardinals, involving himself in politics, and patronizing arts and letters on a lavish scale. Nevertheless, he perceived the need for change and expressed it decisively. Advocates of reform, such as Gasparo Contarini and Gian Pietro Caraffa, were made cardinals. In 1535, Paul took the audacious step of appointing a reform commission to study the condition of the church. The commission's report in 1537 blamed the church's problems on the corrupt policies of popes and cardinals. Paul III also formally recognized the Jesuits and summoned the Council of Trent (see the next section).

A decisive turning point in the direction of the Catholic Reformation and the nature of papal reform came in the 1540s. In 1541, a colloquy had been held at Regensburg in a final attempt to settle the religious division peacefully. Here Catholic moderates, such as Cardinal Contarini, who favored concessions to Protestants in the hope of restoring Christian unity, reached a compromise with Protestant moderates on a number of doctrinal issues. When Contarini returned to Rome with these proposals, Cardinal Caraffa and other hard-liners, who regarded all compromise with Protestant innovations as heresy, accused him of selling out to the heretics. It soon became apparent that the conservative reformers were in the ascendancy when Caraffa was able to persuade Paul III to establish the Roman Inquisition or Holy Office in 1542 to ferret out doctrinal errors. There was to be no compromise with Protestantism.

When Cardinal Caraffa was chosen pope as Paul IV (1555–1559), he so increased the power of the Inquisition that even liberal cardinals were silenced. This "first true pope of the Catholic Counter-Reformation," as he has been called, also created the Index of Forbidden Books, a list of books that Catholics were not allowed to read. It included all the works of Protestant theologians as well as authors considered "unwholesome," a category general enough to include the works of Erasmus. Rome, the capital of Catholic Christianity, was rapidly becoming Fortress Rome; any hope of restoring Christian unity by compromise was fast fading. The activities of the Council of Trent made compromise virtually impossible.

### ⚜ The Council of Trent

In 1542, Pope Paul III took the decisive step of calling for a general council of Christendom to resolve the religious differences created by the Protestant revolt. It was not until March 1545, however, that a group of cardinals, archbishops, bishops, abbots, and theologians met in the city of Trent on the border between Germany and Italy and initiated the Council of Trent. But a variety of problems, including an outbreak of plague, war between France and Spain, and the changing of popes, prevented the council from holding regular annual meetings. Nevertheless, the council met intermittently in three major sessions between 1545 and 1563. Moderate Catholic reformers hoped that compromises would be made in formulating doctrinal definitions that would encourage Protestants to return to the church. Conservatives, however, favored an uncompromising restatement of Catholic doctrines in strict opposition to Protestant positions. After a struggle, the latter group won.

The final doctrinal decrees of the Council of Trent reaffirmed traditional Catholic teachings in opposition to Protestant beliefs. Scripture and tradition were affirmed as equal authorities in religious matters; only the church could interpret Scripture. Both faith and good works were declared necessary for salvation. The seven sacraments, the Catholic doctrine of transubstantiation, and clerical celibacy were all upheld. Belief in purgatory and in the efficacy of indulgences was affirmed, although the hawking of indulgences was prohibited. Of the reforming decrees that were passed, the most important established theological seminaries in every diocese for the training of priests.

After the Council of Trent, the Roman Catholic church possessed a clear body of doctrine and a unified church under the acknowledged supremacy of the popes, who had triumphed over bishops and councils. The Roman Catholic church had become one Christian denomination among many with an organizational framework and doctrinal pattern that would not be significantly altered for four hundred years. With a new spirit of confidence, the Catholic church entered a militant phase, as well prepared as the Calvinists to do battle for the Lord. An era of religious warfare was about to unfold.

# Politics and the Wars of Religion in the Sixteenth Century

By the middle of the sixteenth century, Calvinism and Catholicism had become militant religions dedicated to spreading the word of God as they interpreted it. Although this struggle for the minds and hearts of Europeans is at the heart of the religious wars of the sixteenth century, economic, social, and political forces also played an important role in these conflicts. Of the sixteenth-century religious wars, none were more momentous or shattering than the French civil wars known as the French Wars of Religion.

### ⚜ The French Wars of Religion (1562–1598)

Religion was the engine that drove the French civil wars of the sixteenth century. Concerned by the growth of Calvinism, the French kings tried to stop its spread by persecuting Calvinists but had little success. **Huguenots** (as the French Calvinists were called) came from all levels of society: artisans and shopkeepers hurt by rising prices and a rigid guild system; merchants and lawyers in provincial towns whose local privileges were tenuous; and members of the nobility. Possibly 40 to 50 percent of the French nobility became Huguenots, including the house of Bourbon, which stood next to the Valois in the royal line of succession and ruled the southern French kingdom of Navarre. The conversion of so many nobles made the Huguenots a potentially dangerous political threat to monarchical power. Though the Calvinists constituted only about 10 percent of the population, they were a strong-willed and well-organized minority.

The Catholic majority greatly outnumbered the Calvinist minority. The Valois monarchy was staunchly Catholic, and its control of the Catholic church gave it little incentive to look on Protestantism favorably. When King Henry II (1547–1559) was killed accidentally in a tournament, he was succeeded by a series of weak and neurotic sons, two of whom were dominated by their mother, Catherine de' Medici (1519–1589). As regent for her sons, the moderate Catholic Catherine looked to religious compromise as a way to defuse the political tensions but found to her consternation that both sides possessed their share of religious fanatics unwilling to make concessions. The extreme Catholic party—known as the ultra-Catholics—favored strict opposition to the Huguenots and was led by the Guise family. Possessing the loyalty of Paris and large sections of northern and northwestern France through their client-patronage system, the Guises could recruit and pay for large armies and received support abroad from the papacy and Jesuits who favored the family's uncompromising Catholic position.

But religion was not the only factor contributing to the French civil wars. Resentful of the growing power of monarchical centralization, towns and provinces were only too willing to join a revolt against the monarchy. This was also true of the nobility, and because so many of them were Calvinists, they formed an important base of opposition to the crown. The French Wars of Religion, then, presented a major constitutional crisis for France and temporarily halted the development of the French centralized territorial state. The claim of the state's ruling dynasty to a person's loyalties was temporarily superseded by loyalty to one's religious belief. For some people, the unity of France was less important than religious truth. But there also emerged in France a group of public figures who placed politics before religion and believed that no religious truth was worth the ravages of civil war. These *politiques* ultimately prevailed, but not until both sides were exhausted by bloodshed.

**Course of the Struggle**    The wars erupted in 1562 when the powerful duke of Guise massacred a peaceful congregation of Huguenots at Vassy. In the decade of the 1560s, the Huguenots held their own. Too small a group to conquer France, their armies were so good at defensive campaigns that they could not be defeated either, despite the infamous Saint Bartholomew's Day massacre.

This massacre of Huguenots in August 1572 occurred at a time when the Catholic and Calvinist parties had apparently been reconciled through the marriage of the sister of the reigning Valois king, Charles IX (1560–1574), and Henry of Navarre, the Bourbon ruler of Navarre. Henry was the son of Jeanne d'Albret, queen of Navarre, who had been responsible for introducing Calvinist ideas into her kingdom. Henry was also the acknowledged political leader of the Huguenots, and many Huguenots traveled to Paris for the wedding.

But the Guise family persuaded the king and his mother, Catherine de' Medici, that this gathering of Huguenots posed a threat to them. Charles and his advisers decided

François Dubois, La Saint Barthélemy, 1572/84. Huile sur bois, 94 × 154 cm, Musée cantonal des Beaux-Arts de Lausanne. Photo: J.-C. Ducret, Musée cantonal des Beaux-Arts de Lausanne

**The Saint Bartholomew's Day Massacre.**    Although the outbreak of religious war seemed unlikely in France, the collapse of the strong monarchy with the death of Henry II unleashed forces that led to a series of civil wars. Pictured here is the Saint Bartholomew's Day massacre of 1572. This contemporary painting by the Huguenot artist François Dubois vividly depicts a number of the incidents of that day when approximately three thousand Huguenots were murdered in Paris.

**CHRONOLOGY** The French Wars of Religion (1562–1598)

| | |
|---|---|
| Henry II | 1547–1559 |
| Charles IX | 1560–1574 |
| Duke of Guise massacres Huguenot congregation at Vassy | 1562 |
| Saint Bartholomew's Day massacre | 1572 |
| Henry III | 1574–1589 |
| Formation of the Holy League | 1576 |
| War of the Three Henries | 1588–1589 |
| Assassination of Henry III | 1589 |
| Coronation of Henry IV | 1594 |
| Edict of Nantes | 1598 |

to eliminate the Huguenot leaders with one swift blow. According to one French military leader, Charles and his advisers believed that civil war would soon break out anyway and that "it was better to win a battle in Paris, where all the leaders were, than to risk it in the field and fall into a dangerous and uncertain war."[17]

The massacre began early in the day on August 24 when the king's guards sought out and killed some prominent Huguenot leaders. These murders soon unleashed a wave of violence that gripped the city of Paris. For three days, frenzied Catholic mobs roamed the streets of Paris, killing Huguenots in an often cruel and bloodthirsty manner. According to one eyewitness account: "Then they took her [Françoise Lussault] and dragged her by the hair a long way through the streets, and spying the gold bracelets on her arms, without having the patience to unfasten them, cut off her wrists."[18] Three days of killing left three thousand Huguenots dead, although not Henry of Navarre, who saved his life by promising to turn Catholic. Thousands more were killed in provincial towns. The massacre boomeranged, however, because it discredited the Valois dynasty without ending the conflict.

The fighting continued. The Huguenots rebuilt their strength, and in 1576, the ultra-Catholics formed a "holy league," vowing to exterminate heresy and seat a true Catholic champion—Henry, duke of Guise—on the French throne in place of the ruling king, Henry III (1574–1589), who had succeeded his brother Charles IX. The turning point in the conflict came in the War of the Three Henries in 1588–1589. Henry, duke of Guise, in the pay of Philip II of Spain, seized Paris and forced King Henry III to make him chief minister. To rid himself of Guise influence, Henry III assassinated the duke of Guise and then joined with Henry of Navarre (who meanwhile had returned to Calvinism), who was next in line to the throne, to crush the Catholic Holy League and retake the city of Paris. Although successful, Henry III was assassinated in 1589 by a monk who was repelled by the spectacle of a Catholic king cooperating with a Protestant. Henry of Navarre now claimed the throne. Realizing, however, that

he would never be accepted by Catholic France, Henry took the logical way out and converted once again to Catholicism. With his coronation in 1594, the French Wars of Religion finally came to an end.

Nevertheless, the religious problem persisted until the Edict of Nantes was issued in 1598. The edict acknowledged Catholicism as the official religion of France but guaranteed the Huguenots the right to worship in selected places in every district and allowed them to retain a number of fortified towns for their protection. In addition, Huguenots were allowed to enjoy all political privileges, including the holding of public offices. Although the Edict of Nantes recognized the rights of the Protestant minority and ostensibly the principle of religious toleration, it did so only out of political necessity, not out of conviction.

## Philip II and Militant Catholicism

The greatest advocate of militant Catholicism in the second half of the sixteenth century was King Philip II of Spain (1556–1598), the son and heir of Charles V. Philip's reign ushered in an age of Spanish greatness, both politically and culturally.

The first major goal of Philip II was to consolidate and secure the lands he had inherited from his father. These included Spain, the Netherlands, and possessions in Italy (see Map 13.3) and the New World. For Philip, this meant strict conformity to Catholicism, enforced by aggressive use of the Spanish Inquisition, and the establishment of strong, monarchical authority. The latter was not an easy task because Philip had inherited a governmental structure in which each of the various states and territories of his empire stood in an individual relationship to the king. Philip did manage, however, to expand royal power in Spain by making the monarchy less dependent on the traditional landed aristocracy. Philip tried to be the center of the whole government and supervised the work of all departments, even down to the smallest details. Unwilling to delegate authority, he failed to distinguish between important and trivial matters and fell weeks behind on state correspondence, where he was inclined to make marginal notes and even correct spelling. One Spanish official said, "If God used the Escorial [the royal palace where Philip worked] to deliver my death sentence, I would be immortal."

One of Philip's aims was to make Spain a dominant power in Europe. To a great extent, Spain's preeminence depended on a prosperous economy fueled by its importation of gold and silver from its New World possessions, its agriculture, its commerce, and its industry, especially in textiles, silk, and leather goods. The importation of silver had detrimental effects as well, however, as it helped set off a spiraling inflation that disrupted the Spanish economy, eventually hurting both textile production and agriculture. Moreover, the expenses of war, especially after 1580, proved devastating to the Spanish economy. American gold and silver never constituted more than 20 percent of the royal revenue, leading the government to impose a crushing burden

**Philip of Spain.** This portrait by Titian depicts Philip II of Spain. The king's attempts to make Spain a great power led to large debts and crushing taxes, and his military actions in defense of Catholicism ended in failure and misfortune in both France and the Netherlands.

CHRONOLOGY    Philip II and Militant Catholicism

| | |
|---|---|
| Philip II | 1556–1598 |
| Outbreak of revolt in the Netherlands | 1566 |
| Battle of Lepanto | 1571 |
| Pacification of Ghent | 1576 |
| Union of Arras | 1579 |
| Spanish armada | 1588 |
| Twelve-year truce (Spain and Netherlands) | 1609 |
| Independence of the United Provinces | 1648 |

holy league against Turkish encroachments in the Mediterranean, especially the Muslim attack on the island of Cyprus, resulted in a stunning victory over the Turkish fleet in the Battle of Lepanto in 1571. Philip's greatest misfortunes came from his attempt to crush the revolt in the Netherlands and his tortured relations with Queen Elizabeth of England.

## Revolt of the Netherlands

As one of the richest parts of Philip's empire, the Spanish Netherlands was of great importance to the Most Catholic King. The Netherlands consisted of seventeen provinces (modern Netherlands, Belgium, and Luxembourg). The seven northern provinces were largely Germanic in culture and Dutch-speaking, while the French- and Flemish-speaking southern provinces were closely tied to France. Situated at the commercial crossroads of northwestern Europe, the Netherlands had become prosperous through commerce and a flourishing textile industry. Because of its location, the Netherlands was open to the religious influences of the age. Though some inhabitants had adopted Lutheranism or Anabaptism, by the time of Philip II, Calvinism was also making inroads. These provinces had no real political bond holding them together except their common ruler, and that ruler was Philip II, a foreigner who was out of touch with the local situation.

Philip II hoped to strengthen his control in the Netherlands, regardless of the traditional privileges of the separate provinces. This was strongly opposed by the nobles, towns, and provincial states, which stood to lose politically if their jealously guarded privileges and freedoms were weakened. Resentment against Philip was also aroused when the residents of the Netherlands realized that the taxes they paid were being used for Spanish interests. Finally, religion became a major catalyst for rebellion when Philip attempted to crush Calvinism. Violence erupted in 1566 when Calvinists—especially nobles—began to destroy statues and stained-glass windows in Catholic churches. Philip responded by sending the duke of Alva with ten thousand veteran Spanish and Italian troops to crush the rebellion.

The repressive policies of the duke proved counterproductive. The levying of a permanent sales tax alien-

of direct and indirect taxes. Even then the government was forced to borrow. Philip repudiated his debts seven times; still, two-thirds of state income went to pay interest on the debt by the end of his reign. The attempt to make Spain a great power led to its decline after Philip's reign.

Crucial to an understanding of Philip II is the importance of Catholicism to the Spanish people and their ruler. Driven by a heritage of crusading fervor, the Spanish had little difficulty seeing themselves as a nation of people divinely chosen to save Catholic Christianity from the Protestant heretics. Philip II, the "Most Catholic King," became the champion of Catholicism throughout Europe, a role that led to spectacular victories and equally spectacular defeats for the Spanish king. Spain's leadership of a

ated many merchants and commoners, who now joined the nobles and Calvinists in the struggle against Spanish rule. A special tribunal, known as the Council of Troubles (nicknamed by the Dutch the Council of Blood), inaugurated a reign of terror in which even powerful aristocrats were executed. As a result, the revolt now became organized, especially in the northern provinces, where William of Nassau, the prince of Orange, also known as William the Silent, and Dutch pirates known as the "Sea Beggars" mounted growing resistance. In 1573, Philip removed the duke of Alva and shifted to a more conciliatory policy to bring an end to the costly revolt.

William of Orange wished to unify all seventeen provinces, a goal seemingly realized in 1576 with the Pacification of Ghent. This agreement stipulated that all the provinces would stand together under William's leadership, respect religious differences, and demand that Spanish troops be withdrawn. But religious differences proved too strong for any lasting union. When the duke of Parma, the next Spanish leader, arrived in the Netherlands, he astutely played on the religious differences of the provinces and split their united front. The southern provinces formed a Catholic union—the Union of Arras—in 1579 and accepted Spanish control. To counter this, William of Orange organized the seven northern, Dutch-speaking states into a Protestant union—the Union of Utrecht—determined

to oppose Spanish rule. The Netherlands was now divided along religious, geographical, and political lines into two hostile camps. The struggle dragged on until 1609, when a twelve-year truce ended the war, virtually recognizing the independence of the northern provinces. These "United Provinces" soon emerged as the Dutch Republic, although the Spanish did not formally recognize them as independent until 1648. The ten southern provinces remained a Spanish possession (see Map 13.3).

## The England of Elizabeth

After the death of Queen Mary in 1558, her half-sister Elizabeth ascended the throne of England. During Elizabeth's reign, England rose to prominence as the relatively small island kingdom became the leader of the Protestant nations of Europe, laid the foundations for a world empire, and experienced a cultural renaissance.

The daughter of King Henry VIII and Anne Boleyn, Elizabeth had had a difficult early life. During Mary's reign, she had even been imprisoned for a while and had learned early to hide her true feelings from both private and public sight. Intelligent, cautious, and self-confident, she moved quickly to solve the difficult religious problem she had inherited from Mary, who had become extremely unpopular when she tried to return England to the Catholic fold.

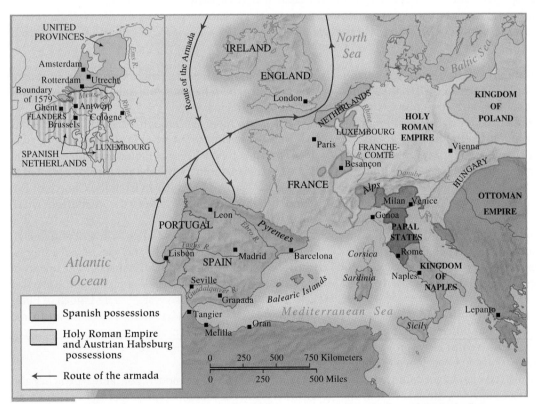

**MAP 13.3  The Height of Spanish Power under Phillip II.** Like his father, Charles V, Philip II, the "Most Catholic King," was a champion of the Catholic cause against Protestantism. He sought to maintain Habsburg control in the Netherlands by combating a Protestant revolt, a rebellion eventually supported by Queen Elizabeth of England. Spain's 1588 attempt to invade England ended in disaster. ❓ Why would England feel threatened by Spanish territory in the Netherlands? 🔊 **View an animated version of this map or related maps at** http://history.wadsworth.com/spielvogel06/

**Procession of Queen Elizabeth I.** Intelligent and learned, Elizabeth Tudor was familiar with Latin and Greek and spoke several European languages. Served by able administrators, Elizabeth ruled for nearly forty-five years and generally avoided open military action against any major power. This picture, painted near the end of her reign, shows the queen in a ceremonial procession.

**Religious Policy** Elizabeth's religious policy was based on moderation and compromise. As a ruler, she wished to prevent England from being torn apart over matters of religion. Parliament cooperated with the queen in initiating the Elizabethan religious settlement in 1559. The Catholic legislation of Mary's reign was repealed, and the new Act of Supremacy designated Elizabeth as "the only supreme governor of this realm, as well in all spiritual or ecclesiastical things or causes, as temporal." The Act of Uniformity restored the church service of the Book of Common Prayer from the reign of Edward VI with some revisions to make it more acceptable to Catholics. Elizabeth's religious settlement was basically Protestant, but it was a moderate Protestantism that avoided overly subtle distinctions and extremes.

The new religious settlement worked, at least to the extent that it smothered religious differences in England in the second half of the sixteenth century. Two groups, however, the Catholics and the Puritans, continued to oppose it. One of Elizabeth's greatest challenges came from her Catholic cousin, Mary, queen of Scots, who was next in line to the English throne. Mary was ousted from Scotland by rebellious Calvinist nobles in 1568 and fled for her life to England. There Elizabeth placed her under house arrest and for fourteen years tolerated her involvement in a number of ill-planned Catholic plots designed to kill Elizabeth and replace her on the throne with the Catholic Mary. Finally,

in 1587, after Mary became embroiled in a far more serious plot, Elizabeth had her cousin beheaded to end the threats to her regime.

Potentially more dangerous to Anglicanism in the long run were the **Puritans.** The word *Puritan* first appeared in 1564 when it was used to refer to Protestants within the Anglican church who, inspired by Calvinist theology, wanted to remove any trace of Catholicism from the Church of England. Elizabeth managed to keep the Puritans in check during her reign.

Elizabeth proved as adept in government and foreign policy as in religious affairs. She was well served administratively by the principal secretary of state. The talents of Sir William Cecil and Sir Francis Walsingham, who together held the office for thirty-two years, ensured much of Elizabeth's success in foreign and domestic affairs. Elizabeth also handled Parliament with much skill; it met only thirteen times during her entire reign (see the box on p. 375).

**Foreign Policy** Caution, moderation, and expediency also dictated Elizabeth's foreign policy. Fearful of other countries' motives, Elizabeth realized that war could be disastrous for her island kingdom and her own rule. Unofficially, however, she encouraged English seamen to raid Spanish ships and colonies. Francis Drake was especially adept at plundering Spanish fleets loaded with gold and silver from Spain's New World empire. While encouraging English

# Queen Elizabeth Addresses Parliament (1601)

UEEN ELIZABETH I ruled England from 1558 to 1603 with a consummate skill that contemporaries considered unusual in a woman. Though shrewd and paternalistic, Elizabeth, like other sixteenth-century monarchs, depended for her power on the favor of her people. This selection is taken from her speech to Parliament in 1601, when she had been forced to retreat on the issue of monopolies after vehement protest by members of Parliament. Although the speech was designed to make peace with Parliament, some historians also feel that it was a sincere expression of the rapport that existed between the queen and her subjects.

### Queen Elizabeth I, "The Golden Speech"

I do assure you there is no prince that loves his subjects better, or whose love can countervail our love. There is no jewel, be it of never so rich a price, which I set before this jewel: I mean your love. For I do esteem it more than any treasure of riches. . . . And, though God has raised me high, yet this I count the glory of my crown, that I have reigned with your loves. This makes me that I do not so much rejoice that God has made me to be a Queen, as to be a Queen over so thankful a people. . . .

Of myself I must say this: I never was any greedy, scraping grasper, nor a strait, fast-holding Prince, nor yet a waster. My heart was never set on any worldly goods, but only for my subjects' good. What you bestow on me, I will not hoard it up, but receive it to bestow on you again. Yea, mine own properties I account yours, to be expended for your good. . . .

I have ever used to set the Last-Judgement Day before mine eyes, and so to rule as I shall be judged to answer before a higher judge, to whose judgement seat I do appeal, that never thought was cherished in my heart that tended not unto my people's good. And now, if my kingly bounties have been abused, and my grants turned to the hurt of my people, contrary to my will and meaning, and if any in authority under me neglected or perverted what I have committed to them, I hope God will not lay their culps [crimes] and offenses to my charge; who, though there were danger in repealing our grants, yet what danger would I not rather incur for your good, than I would suffer them still to continue?

There will never Queen sit in my seat with more zeal to my country, care for my subjects, and that will sooner with willingness venture her life for your good and safety, than myself. For it is my desire to live nor reign no longer than my life and reign shall be for your good. And though you have had and may have many princes more mighty and wise sitting in this seat, yet you never had nor shall have any that will be more careful and loving.

---

piracy and providing clandestine aid to French Huguenots and Dutch Calvinists to weaken France and Spain, Elizabeth pretended complete aloofness and avoided alliances that would force her into war with any major power.

Gradually, however, Elizabeth was drawn into more active involvement in the Netherlands. This move accelerated the already mounting friction between Spain and England. After years of resisting the idea of invading England as impractical, Philip II of Spain was finally persuaded to do so by advisers who assured him that the people of England would rise against their queen when the Spaniards arrived. Moreover, Philip was easily convinced that the revolt in the Netherlands would never be crushed as long as England provided support for it. In any case, a successful invasion of England would mean the overthrow of heresy and the return of England to Catholicism, surely an act in accordance with the will of God. Accordingly, Philip ordered preparations for a fleet of warships that would rendezvous with the army of the duke of Parma in Flanders and escort his troops across the English Channel for the invasion.

**The Spanish Armada**   The armada proved to be a disaster. The Spanish fleet that finally set sail had neither the ships nor the troops that Philip had planned to send. A conversation between a papal emissary and an officer of the Spanish fleet before the armada departed reveals the fundamental flaw:

"And if you meet the English armada in the Channel, do you expect to win the battle?" "Of course," replied the Spaniard.

"How can you be sure?" [asked the emissary].

"It's very simple. It is well known that we fight in God's cause. So, when we meet the English, God will surely arrange matters so that we can grapple and board them, either by sending some strange freak of weather or, more likely, just by depriving the English of their wits. If we can come to close quarters, Spanish valor and Spanish steel (and the great masses of soldiers we shall have on board) will make our victory certain. But unless God helps us by a miracle the English, who have faster and handier ships than ours, and many more long-range guns, and who know their advantage just as well as we do, will never close with us at all, but stand aloof and knock us to pieces with their culverins [cannons], without our being able to do them any serious hurt. So," concluded the captain, and one fancies a grim smile, "we are sailing against England in the confident hope of a miracle."[19]

The hoped-for miracle never materialized. The Spanish fleet, battered by a number of encounters with the English, sailed back to Spain by a northward route around Scotland and Ireland, where it was further battered by storms. Although the English and Spanish would continue their war for another sixteen years, the defeat of the Spanish armada guaranteed for the time being that England would remain a Protestant country. Although Spain made up for its losses within a year and a half, the defeat was a psychological blow to the Spaniards.

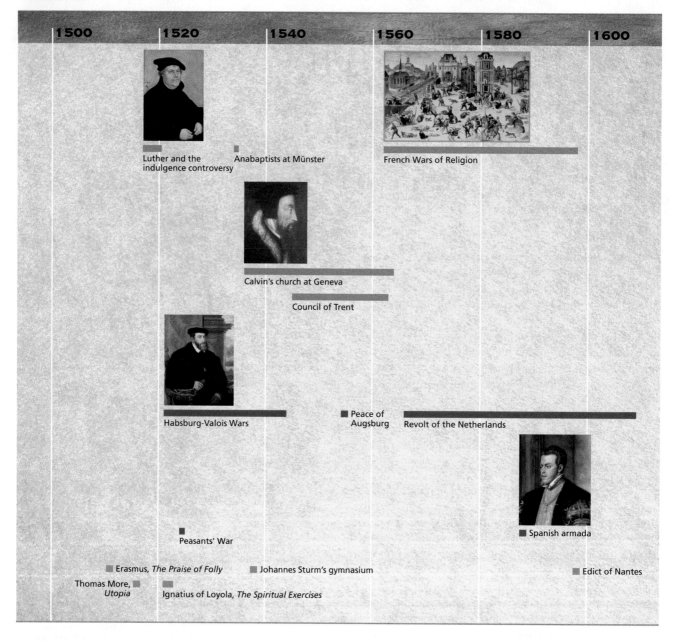

1500     1520     1540     1560     1580     1600

Luther and the indulgence controversy

Anabaptists at Münster

French Wars of Religion

Calvin's church at Geneva

Council of Trent

Habsburg-Valois Wars

Peace of Augsburg

Revolt of the Netherlands

Peasants' War

Spanish armada

Erasmus, *The Praise of Folly*

Johannes Sturm's gymnasium

Edict of Nantes

Thomas More, *Utopia*

Ignatius of Loyola, *The Spiritual Exercises*

## CONCLUSION

𝒲HEN THE AUGUSTINIAN MONK Martin Luther burst onto the scene with a series of theses on indulgences, few people suspected that his observations would eventually split all of Europe along religious lines. But the yearning for reform of the church and meaningful religious experience caused a seemingly simple dispute to escalate into a powerful movement.

Although Luther felt that his revival of Christianity based on his interpretation of the Bible should be acceptable to all, others soon appeared who also read the Bible but interpreted it in different ways. Protestantism fragmented into different sects, which, though united in their dislike of Catholicism, were themselves divided over the interpretation of the sacraments and religious practices. As reform ideas spread, religion and politics became ever more intertwined.

By 1555, Lutheranism had lost much of its momentum; its energy was largely replaced by the new Protestant form of Calvinism, which had a clarity of doctrine and a fervor that made it attractive to a whole new generation of Europeans. Although Calvinism's militancy enabled it to expand across Europe, Catholicism was also experiencing its own revival and emerged as a militant faith, prepared to do combat for the souls of the faithful. An age of religious passion was followed by an age of religious warfare.

That people who were disciples of the Apostle of Peace would kill each other—often in brutal and painful fashion—aroused skepticism about Christianity itself. As one German writer put it, "Lutheran, popish, and Calvinistic, we've got all these beliefs here; but there is some doubt about where Christianity has got."[20] It is surely no accident that the search for a stable, secular order of politics and for order in the universe through natural laws soon came to play important roles. Before we look at this search for order in the seventeenth century, however, we need first to look at the adventures that plunged Europe into its new role in the world.

## NOTES

1. Desiderius Erasmus, *The Paraclesis,* in John Olin, ed., *Christian Humanism and the Reformation: Selected Writings of Erasmus,* 3d ed. (New York, 1987), p. 101.

2. Thomas More, *Utopia,* trans. Paul Turner (Harmondsworth, England, 1965), p. 76.

3. Quoted in Alister E. McGrath, *Reformation Thought: An Introduction* (Oxford, 1988), p. 72.

4. Quoted in Gordon Rupp, *Luther's Progress to the Diet of Worms* (New York, 1964), p. 82.

5. Martin Luther, *On the Freedom of a Christian Man,* quoted in E. G. Rupp and Benjamin Drewery, eds., *Martin Luther* (New York, 1970), p. 50.

6. Quoted in Roland Bainton, *Here I Stand: A Life of Martin Luther* (New York, 1950), p. 144.

7. Quoted in De Lamar Jensen, *Reformation Europe* (Lexington, Mass., 1981), p. 83.

8. Quoted in Lee Palmer Wandel, *Voracious Idols and Violent Hands: Iconoclasm in Reformation Zurich, Strasbourg, and Basel* (New York, 1995), p. 81.

9. Quoted in A. G. Dickens and Dorothy Carr, eds., *The Reformation in England to the Accession of Elizabeth I* (New York, 1968), p. 72.

10. Quoted in Lewis W. Spitz, *The Renaissance and Reformation Movements* (Chicago, 1971), p. 414.

11. John Calvin, *Institutes of the Christian Religion,* trans. John Allen (Philadelphia, 1936), vol. 1, p. 220.

12. Ibid., vol. 1, p. 228; vol. 2, p. 181.

13. Quoted in Roland Bainton, *Women of the Reformation in Germany and Italy* (Minneapolis, 1971), p. 154.

14. Quoted in Bonnie S. Anderson and Judith P. Zinsser, *A History of Their Own: Women in Europe from Prehistory to the Present* (New York, 1988), vol. 1, p. 259.

15. Quoted in John A. Phillips, *Eve: The History of an Idea* (New York, 1984), p. 105.

16. Quoted in John O'Malley, *The First Jesuits* (Cambridge, Mass., 1993), p. 76.

17. Quoted in R. J. Knecht, *The French Wars of Religion, 1559–1598,* 2d ed. (New York, 1996), p. 47.

18. Quoted in Mack P. Holt, *The French Wars of Religion, 1562–1629* (Cambridge, 1995), p. 86.

19. Quoted in Garrett Mattingly, *The Armada* (Boston, 1959), pp. 216–217.

20. Quoted in Theodore Schieder, *Handbuch der Europäischen Geschichte* (Stuttgart, 1979), vol. 3, p. 579.

## SUGGESTIONS FOR FURTHER READING

Basic surveys of the Reformation period include **H. J. Grimm, *The Reformation Era, 1500–1650,*** 2d ed. (New York, 1973); **C. Lindberg, *The European Reformations*** (Cambridge, Mass., 1996); **D. L. Jensen, *Reformation Europe*** (Lexington, Mass., 1981); **G. R. Elton, *Reformation Europe, 1517–1559*** (Cleveland, Ohio, 1963); **J. D. Tracy, *Europe's Reformations, 1450–1650*** (Oxford, 1999); **D. MacCulloch, *The Reformation*** (New York, 2003); and **E. Cameron, *The European Reformation*** (New York, 1991). The significance of the Protestant Reformation is examined in **S. Ozment, *Protestants: The Birth of a Revolution*** (New York, 1992). A brief but very useful introduction to the theology of the Reformation can be found in **A. McGrath, *Reformation Thought: An Introduction,*** 3d rev. ed. (Oxford, 1999).

The development of humanism outside Italy is examined in **C. G. Nauert Jr., *Humanism and the Culture of Renaissance Europe*** (Cambridge, 1995). On Thomas More, see **R. Marius, *Thomas More: A Biography*** (New York, 1984). On Erasmus, see **J. McConica, *Erasmus*** (Oxford, 1991).

The classic account of Martin Luther's life is **R. Bainton, *Here I Stand: A Life of Martin Luther*** (New York, 1950). More recent works include **H. A. Oberman, *Luther*** (New York, 1992), and **J. M. Kittelson, *Luther the Reformer: The Story of the Man and His Career*** (Minneapolis, 1986). See also the brief biography by **M. Marty, *Martin Luther*** (New York, 2004). On the Peasants' War, see especially **P. Blickle, *The Revolution of 1525: The German Peasants' War from a New Perspective*** (Baltimore, 1981). The spread of Luther's ideas in Germany can be examined in **M. Hannemann, *The Diffusion of the Reformation in Southwestern Germany, 1518–1534*** (Chicago, 1975), and **B. Moeller, *Imperial Cities and the Reformation*** (Durham, N.C., 1982). On the role of Charles V, see **W. Maltby, *The Reign of Charles V*** (New York, 2002).

The best account of Ulrich Zwingli is **G. R. Potter, *Zwingli*** (Cambridge, 1976), although **W. P. Stephens's *Zwingli*** (Oxford, 1994) is an important study of the man's ideas. The most comprehensive account of the various groups and individuals who are called Anabaptists is **G. H. Williams, *The Radical Reformation,*** 2d ed. (Kirksville, Mo., 1992).

Two worthwhile surveys of the English Reformation are **A. G. Dickens, *The English Reformation,*** 2d ed. (New York, 1989), and **G. R. Elton, *Reform and Reformation: England, 1509–1558*** (Cambridge, Mass., 1977). On John Calvin, see **A. McGrath, *A Life of John Calvin: A Study in the Shaping of Western Culture*** (Cambridge, Mass., 1990), and **W. J. Bouwsma, *John Calvin*** (New York, 1988).

On the impact of the Reformation on the family, see **J. F. Harrington, *Reordering Marriage and Society in Reformation Germany*** (New York, 1995). **M. E. Wiesner's *Working Women in Renaissance Germany*** (New Brunswick, N.J., 1986) covers primarily the sixteenth century. There is also a good collection of essays in **S. Marshall, ed., *Women in Reformation and Counter-Reformation Europe: Public and Private Worlds*** (Bloomington, Ind., 1989). On education, see **G. Strauss, *Luther's House of Learning*** (Baltimore, 1978).

A good introduction to the Catholic Reformation can be found in the beautifully illustrated brief study by **A. G. Dickens, *The Counter-Reformation*** (New York, 1969). Also valuable are **M. R. O'Connell, *The Counter-Reformation, 1559–1610*** (New York, 1974), and **R. P. Hsia, *The World of Catholic Renewal, 1540–1770*** (Cambridge, 1998).

For new perspectives, see **R. Bireley,** *The Refashioning of Catholicism, 1450–1700* (Washington, D.C., 1999), and **John O'Malley,** *Trent and All That: Renaming Catholicism in the Early Modern Era* (Cambridge, Mass., 2002). On Loyola, see **P. Caravan,** *Ignatius Loyola: A Biography of the Founder of the Jesuits* (San Francisco, 1990). **J. O'Malley,** *The First Jesuits* (Cambridge, Mass., 1995), offers a clear discussion of the founding of the Jesuits.

For good introductions to the French Wars of Religion, see **M. P. Holt,** *The French Wars of Religion, 1562–1629* (Cambridge, 1995), and **R. J. Knecht,** *The French Wars of Religion, 1559–1598,* 2d ed. (New York, 1996). A good history of Spain in the sixteenth century is **J. Lynch,** *Spain, 1516–1598: From Nation-State to World Empire* (Cambridge, Mass., 1994). On Philip II, see **G. Parker,** *Philip II,* 3d ed. (Chicago, 1995). On the revolt of the Netherlands, see the classic work by **P. Geyl,** *The Revolt of the Netherlands, 1555–1609* (London, 1962), and **G. Parker,** *The Dutch Revolt* (London, 1977). Elizabeth's reign can be examined in two good biographies: **C. Haigh,** *Elizabeth I,* 2d ed. (New York, 1998), and **W. T. MacCaffrey,** *Elizabeth I* (London, 1993). The classic work on the Spanish armada is the beautifully written book *The Armada* by **G. Mattingly** (Boston, 1959).

# History ⌛ Now™

Enter *HistoryNow* using the access card that is available for *Western Civilization. HistoryNow* will assist you in understanding the content in this chapter with lesson plans generated for your needs. In addition, you can read the following documents, and many more, online:

Martin Luther, *Letter to the German Nobility, On Christian Liberty* and *Twelve Articles*

John Calvin, *Institutes of the Christian Religion*

Pope Paul III, Canons on Justification

King Henry IV, Edict of Nantes

## INFOTRAC SEARCH TERMS

 For additional reading, go to InfoTrac College Edition, your online research library at http://infotrac.thomsonlearning.com

*Subject Guide Search*            *Key Term Search*

Reformation                      Elizabeth I

Counter-Reformation

Martin and Luther not King

John Calvin

## WESTERN CIVILIZATION RESOURCES

 Visit the *Western Civilization* Companion Web site for resources specific to this book:

http://history.wadsworth.com/spielvogel06/

For a variety of tools to help you succeed in this course, visit the Western Civilization Resource Center at

http://history.wadsworth.com/western/

Included are quizzes; images; documents; interactive simulations; maps and timelines; movie explorations; and a wealth of other sources.

# Brief Contents

# PART 7

# CHRISTIANITY: THE NEW FAITH

Christianity arose from a combination of Greco-Roman and Jewish traditions, yet at the same time embodied a shift in ideology and customs. Although it originated as a small sect in the Jewish religion, Christianity quickly took hold of the populace of the entire Roman Empire, and as the Germanic tribes systematically destroyed the Roman state in the fifth century, it was the new faith that proved the most durable contribution to Western civilization. The transition from pagan Rome to a Christianized Europe was not a simple one, nor is the history of Christianity itself as a faith and a culture a straightforward one. There were many sects of the new faith and many interpretations of Christ's message, and even the fall of the Roman state did not necessarily represent a clear-cut triumph for the Christians. The transition actually lasted for several more centuries.

It is arguable that no one development had as much of an impact on the West as Christianity. Here are five sources that illustrate the origins of Christian beliefs, the attempt to stabilize Christian beliefs with the creation of a creed (statement of belief), and finally two sources that illustrate the complexity with which Christian and Roman cultures intersected.

# 7.1

## THE ANNUNCIATION TO MARY AND THE MAGNIFICAT, GOSPEL ACCORDING TO LUKE

*Jesus Christ was born c. 6 BC, during the reign of Augustus. The religion he founded had a profound impact on Western culture, and ultimately on the entire world. In the earliest days of the faith there were many oral traditions about Jesus circulating in the eastern provinces of the Roman Empire; some of these would be gathered up in the second century to form the Christian scriptures known as the New Testament. The four main sources for the life of Christ were the gospels of Matthew, Mark, Luke, and John, written some thirty to sixty years after the death of Christ. In the following excerpt from Luke, the most detailed of the gospels about Mary and the early life of Jesus, Mary learns that she is pregnant and delivers her longest speech of any of the gospel accounts, known as the Magnificat.*

---

### QUESTIONS

1. What is the significance of Elizabeth recognizing the holiness of Mary's pregnancy before Mary has told her anything about it?
2. Where are the men of this culture while this scene is taking place? Why are they not present?
3. How does Mary understand the role of God in history?

When his period of duty was completed Zechariah returned home. His wife Elizabeth conceived, and for five months she lived in seclusion, thinking, 'This is the Lord's doing; now at last he has shown me favour and taken away from me the disgrace of childlessness.

In the sixth month the angel Gabriel was sent by God to Nazareth, a town in Galilee, with a message for a girl betrothed to a man named Joseph; a descendant of David; the girl's name was Mary. The angel went in and said to her, 'Greetings, most favoured one! The Lord is with you.' But she was deeply troubled by what he said and wondered what this greeting could mean. Then the angel said to her, 'Do not be afraid, Mary, for God has been gracious to you; you will conceive and give birth to a son, and you are to give him the name Jesus. He will be great, and will be called Son of the Most High. The Lord God will give him the throne of his ancestor David, and he will be king over Israel for ever; his reign shall never end. 'How can this be?' said Mary. 'I am still a virgin.' The angel answered, 'The Holy Spirit will come upon you, and the power of the Most High will overshadow you; for that reason the holy child to be born will be called Son of God. Moreover your kinswoman Elizabeth has herself conceived a son in her old age; and she who is reputed barren is now in her sixth month, for God's promises can never fail. 'I am the Lord's servant,' said Mary; 'may it be as you have said.' Then the angel left her.

Soon afterwards Mary set out and hurried away to a town in the uplands of Judah. She went into Zechariah's house and greeted Elizabeth. And when Elizabeth heard Mary's greeting, the baby stirred in her womb. Then Elizabeth was filled with the Holy Spirit and exclaimed in a loud voice, 'God's blessing is on you above all women, and his blessing is on the fruit of your womb. Who am I, that the mother of my Lord should visit me? I tell you, when your greeting sounded in my ears, the baby in my womb leapt for joy. Happy is she who has had faith that the Lord's promise to her would be fulfilled!'

And Mary said:

'My soul tells out the greatness of the Lord,
my spirit has rejoiced in God my Savior;
for he has looked with favour on his servant,
lowly as she is.
From this day forward
all generations will count me blessed,
for the Mighty God has done great things for me.
His name is holy,
his mercy sure from generation to generation
toward those who fear him.
He has shown the might of his arm,
he has routed the proud and all their schemes;

he has brought down monarchs from their thrones,
and raised on high the lowly.
He has filled the hungry with good things,
and sent the rich away empty.
He has come to the help of Israel his servant,
as he promised to our forefathers;
he has not forgotten to show mercy
to Abraham and his children's children forever.'

Mary stayed with Elizabeth about three months and then returned home.

Source: *Gospel According to Luke, The Oxford Study Bible: Revised English Bible with the Apocrypha* (New York: Oxford University Press, 1992), 1:23-56.

# 7.2

❖

# THE SERMON ON THE MOUNT AND THE BEATITUDES, GOSPEL ACCORDING TO MATTHEW

*Matthew's gospel gives us this account of Jesus gathering followers and preaching, and serves as one of the most extensive illustrations of Jesus' message. It also contains one of the earliest Christian prayers, a series of statements beginning "Blessed are...," that make up the Beatitudes.*

❖

## QUESTIONS

1. From the references Jesus makes while preaching on the mount, how would you describe the social and economic background of his audience at this sermon?
2. What did this sermon tell the early Christians about the heaven that was being promised to them?
3. How does Jesus understand the concept of "law"? Is this a new understanding of law in the West?

From that day Jesus began to proclaim the message: 'Repent, for the kingdom of Heaven is upon you.'

Jesus was walking by the sea of Galilee when he saw two brothers, Simon called Peter and his brother Andrew, casting a net into the lake; for they were fishermen. Jesus said to them, 'Come with me, and I will make you fishers of men.' At once they left their nets and followed him.

Going on farther, he saw another pair of brothers, James son of Zebedee and his brother John; they were in a boat with their father Zebedee, mending their nets. He called them, and at once they left the boat and their father, and followed him.

He travelled throughout Galilee, teaching in the synagogues, proclaiming the good news of the kingdom, and healing every kind of illness and infirmity among the people. His fame spread throughout Syria; and they brought to him sufferers from various diseases, those racked with pain or possessed by demons, those who were epileptic or paralysed, and he healed them all. Large crowds followed him, from Galilee and the Decapolis, from Jerusalem and Judaea, and from Transjordan.

5 When he saw the crowds he went up a mountain. There he sat down, and when his disciples had gathered round him he began to address them. And this is the teaching he gave:

Blessed are the poor in spirit;
the kingdom of Heaven is theirs.
Blessed are the sorrowful;
they shall find consolation.
Blessed are the gentle;
they shall have the earth for their possession.
Blessed are those who show mercy;
mercy shall be shown to them.
Blessed are those whose hearts are pure;
they shall see God.
Blessed are the peacemakers;
they shall be called God's children.
Blessed are those who are persecuted in the cause of right;
the kingdom of Heaven is theirs.

Blessed are you, when you suffer insults and persecution and calumnies of every kind for my sake. Exult and be glad, for you have a rich reward in heaven; in the same way they persecuted the prophets before you.

You are the salt to the world. And if salt becomes tasteless, how is its saltness to be restored? It is good for nothing but to be thrown away and trodden underfoot.

You are light for all the world. A town that stands on a hill cannot be hidden. When a lamp is lit, it is not put under the meal-tub, but on the lampstand, where it gives light to everyone in the house. Like the lamp, you must shed light among your fellows, so that, when they see the good you do, they may give praise to your Father in heaven.

Do not suppose that I have come to abolish the law and the prophets; I did not come to abolish, but to complete. Truly I tell you: so long as heaven and earth endure, not a letter, not a dot, will diappear from the law until all that must happen has happened. anyone therefore who set aside even the least of the law's demands, and teaches others to do the same, will have the lowest place in the kingdom of Heaven, whereas anyone who keeps the law, and teaches others to do so, will rank high in the kingdom of Heaven. I tell you, unless you show yourselves far better than the scribes and Pharisees, you can never enter the kingdom of Heaven.

You have heard that our forefathers were told, "Do not commit murder; anyone who commits murder must be brought to justice." But what I tell you is this: Anyone who nurses anger against his brother must be brought to justice. Whoever calls his brother "good for nothing" deserves the sentence of the court; whoever calls him "fool" deserves hell-fire. So if you are presenting your gift at the altar and suddenly remember that your brother has a grievance against you, leave your gift where it is before the altar. First go and make your peace with your brother; then com back and offer your gift. If someone sues you, come to terms with him promptly while you are both on your way to court; otherwise he may hand you over to the judge, and the judge to the officer, and you will be thrown into jail. Truly I tell you: once you are there you will not be let out until you have paid the last penny.

You have heard that they were told, "Do not commit adultery." But what I tell you is this: If a man looks at a woman with a lustful eye, he has already committed adultery with her in his heart. If your right eye causes your downfall, tear it out and fling it away; it is better for you to lose one part of your body than for the whole of it to be thrown into hell. If your right hand causes your downfall, cut it off and fling it away; it is better for you to lose one part of your body than for the whole of it to go to hell.

Source: *Gospel According to Matthew, The Oxford Study Bible: Revised English Bible with the Apocrypha* (New York: Oxford University Press, 1992), 4: 17-25, 5: 1-30.

# 7.3

❖

# THE NICENE CREED

*In the first centuries of Christianity, in what might be called its formative years, there were numerous councils of church leaders, going back to the earliest meeting between Jesus and his disciples. (The Last Supper was one such meeting.) After the conversion of Constantine the Great in 312 AD, the Roman emperors also sent representatives to these councils. One function of the councils was to determine what constituted true Christian belief, about which there was often little consensus. Divergent interpretations of Jesus' preaching was common. One result was the creations of creeds, or statements of belief; there were several popular versions of these in the early church. One creed that has remained fundamental to most Christian sects today, although it exists in different forms, was created at the council of Nicea in 325. It was subsequently revised several times; the following form dates from approximately 374.*

❖

## QUESTIONS

1. What is the role of the believer in Christianity, as defined by the Creed?
2. How does the Nicene Creed present the concept of the Trinity? What are the three parts and how do they relate to one another?
3. What is the relationship of Jesus to God, as defined by this Creed?

We believe in one God the Father All-sovereign, maker of heaven and earth, and of all things visible and invisible;

And in one Lord Jesus Christ, the only-begotten Son of God, Begotten of the Father before all the ages, Light of Light, true God of True God, begotten not made, of one substance with the Father, through whom all things were made; who for us men and for our salvation came down from the heavens, and was made flesh of the Holy Spirit and the Virgin Mary, and became man, and was crucified for us under Pontius Pilate, and suffered and was buried, and rose again on the third day according to the Scriptures, and ascended into the heavens, and sitteth on the right hand of the Father, and cometh again with glory to judge living and dead, of whose kingdom there shall be no end:

And in the Holy Spirit, the Lord and the Life-giver, that proceedeth from the Father, who with Father and Son is worshipped together and glorified together, who spake through the prophets:

In one holy Catholic and Apostolic Church:

We acknowledge one baptism unto remission of sins. We look for a resurrection of the dead, and the life of the age to come.

Source: Henry Bettenson, ed., *Documents of the Christian Church*, (New York: Oxford University Press, 1963), p. 26.

# 7.4

✤

# DEFENSE OF CHRISTIANITY, ST. AUGUSTINE

*Augustine was Bishop of Hippo, in North Africa, from 396 to 430. He was one of the most prolific of the early Christian theologians, and although he himself claims to have destroyed some of his writings, many survive. In the* City of God, *Augustine set out to write a defense of Christians from the accusation that they were responsible for the sack of Rome in 410 by the Visigoths.*

✤

## QUESTIONS

1. In writing the *City of God*, what does Augustine reveal about the relationship between Christians and Pagans at the end of the Roman Empire?
2. Why does Augustine view the destruction of Rome as an act of Divine Providence?
3. What does Augustine mean by the phrase "City of God?"

CHAPTER 1

From this earthly city issue the enemies against whom the City of God must be defended. Some of them, it is true, abjure their worldly error and become worthy members in God's City. But many others, alas, break out in blazing hatred against it and are utterly ungrateful, notwithstanding its

Redeemer's signal gifts. For, they would no longer have a voice to raise against it, had not its sanctuaries given them asylum as they fled before the invaders' swords, and made it possible for them to save that life of which they are so proud.

Have not even those very Romans whom the barbarians spared for the sake of Christ assailed His Name? To this both the shrines of the martyrs and the basilicas of the Apostles bear witness: amid the city's devastation, these buildings gave refuge not only to the faithful but even to infidels. Up to the sacred threshold raged the murderous enemy, but the slayers' fury went no further. The merciful among the enemy conducted to the churches those whom they had spared even outside the holy precincts, to save them from others who lacked such mercy. Even these ruthless men, who in other places customarily indulged their ferocity against enemies, put a rein to their murderous fury and curbed their mania for taking captives, the moment they reached the holy places. Here, the law of sanctuary forbade what the law of war elsewhere permitted. Thus were saved many of those who now cry down Christian culture and who blame Christ for the calamities that befell the city. Indeed, that very mercy to which they owe their lives and which was exercised in Christ's Name they ascribe not to our Christ but to their Fate. Yet, if they only had sense, they would see that the hardships and cruelties they suffered from the enemy came from that Divine Providence who makes use of war to reform the corrupt lives of men. They ought to see that it is the way of Providence to test by such afflictions men of virtuous and exemplary life, and to call them, once tried, to a better world, or to keep them for a while on earth for the accomplishment of other purposes. As for the fact that the fierce barbarians, contrary to the usage of war, generally spared their lives for Christ's sake and, in particular, in places dedicated to Christ's Name — which by a merciful Providence were spacious enough to afford refuge to large numbers — this they should have credited to Christian culture. They should thank God and, if they would escape the pains of eternal fire, should turn to His Name with all sincerity — as many have, without sincerity, in order to escape the results of the present ruin.

For, many of those whom you see heaping impudent abuse on the servants of Christ would not have escaped the ruin and massacre had they not falsely paraded as servants of Christ. Now, with ungrateful pride, impious madness, and perversity of heart, they work against that Name. They who turned to that Name with a lying tongue, in order to enjoy this temporal light, deserve the penalty of eternal darkness....

## CHAPTER 3

Just think of the kind of gods to whose protection the Romans were content to entrust their city! No more pathetic illusion could be imagined. Yet, the pagans are angry with us because we speak so frankly of their divinities. However, they feel no anger against their own writers. They even pay them a fee to teach such nonsense, and think such teachers worthy of public salary and honors. Take Virgil. Children must read this greatest and best of all poets in order to impress their tender minds so deeply that he may never be easily forgotten, much as the well-known words of Horace suggest:

> The liquors that new vessel first contains
> Behind them leave a taste that long remains.

Now, in Virgil, Juno is pictured as the foe of the Trojans and as saying, while she goads Aeolus, King of the Winds, against them:

> The nation that I hate in peace sails by,
> With Troy and Troy's fallen gods to Italy.

Did they act wisely in placing Rome's immunity from defeat in the hands of such vanquished deities? Even assuming that Juno spoke these words in a fit of feminine anger, not knowing what she said, does not Aeneas himself, so often styled 'the pious,' relate how

> Panthus, a priest of Phoebus and the Tower,
> Rushed with his nephew and the conquered gods
> And, frantic, sought for shelter at my door.

Does he not admit that the very gods, whom he declares 'conquered' are entrusted to his protection rather than he to theirs when he is given the charge, 'To thee doth Troy commend her gods, her all'? If, then Virgil describes such gods as vanquished, and, because vanquished, needing a man's help even to escape, surely it is folly to believe that it was wise to entrust Rome to the safe-keeping of such divinities, and to believe that Rome could never be destroyed unless it lost its gods. In fact, to worship fallen gods as patrons and defenders is more like having poor odds than good gods. It is much more sensible to believe, not so much that Rome would have been saved from destruction had not the gods perished, but rather that the gods would have perished long ago had not Rome made every effort to save them.

For, who does not see, if only he stops to consider, how futile it is to presume that Rome could not be conquered when protected by conquered custodians, and that the reason it fell was that it lost its tutelary deities? Surely, the only possible reason why Rome should fall was that it wanted vincible protectors. Hence, when all these things were written and sung about the fallen gods, it was not because the poets took pleasure in lying, but because truth compelled intelligent men to avow them. However, this matter will be more fitly and more fully treated in subsequent chapters. Here I shall do my best to wind up in few words what I began to say about men's ingratitude.

These men, I say, hold Christ responsible for the evils which they deservedly suffer for their wicked lives. They have not the slightest appreciation of the fact, that, when they deserved to be punished, they were spared for Christ's sake. On the contrary, with impious perversity and bitterness, they attack His Name with those very tongues which falsely invoked that Name to save them. The very tongues which, like cowards, they held in check in the sacred places when safe, protected and unharmed by the enemy for Christ's sake, they now use to hurl malicious curses against Him....

## CHAPTER 7

All the destruction, slaughter, plundering, burning, and distress visited upon Rome in its latest calamity were but the normal aftermath of war. It was something entirely new that fierce barbarians, by an unprecedented turn of events, showed such clemency that vast basilicas were designated as places where refugees might assemble with assurance of immunity. There, no one was to be slain or raped; many destined for liberation were to be led there by the compassionate enemy; from there, none was to be dragged away to captivity by a cruel foe. That this was in honor of the Name of Christ and to the credit of Christian civilization is manifest to all. To see this and not acknowledge it with praise is ingratitude. To impugn those who give us credit is utterly unreasonable. Let no man with sense ascribe this to the savage ways of the barbarians. It was God who struck awe into ruthless and blood-thirsty hearts, who curbed and wondrously tamed them. God who long ago spoke these words by the mouth of the Prophet; 'I will visit their iniquities with a rod: and their sins with stripes. But My mercy I will not take away from them.

CHAPTER 8

But, someone will say: 'How, then, is it that this divine mercy was bestowed on impious and ungrateful man?' Surely, the answer is that mercy was shown by the One who, day by day, 'maketh His sun to rise upon the good and bad, and raineth upon the just and the unjust.' For, although some who reflect on these truths repent and are converted from their wickedness, others, according to the words of the Apostle, despise 'the riches of His goodness and long-suffering, in the hardness of their heart and the impenitence' and treasure up to themselves 'wrath against the day of wrath and revelation of the just judgment of God Who will render to every man according to his works.' Nevertheless, God's patience is an invitation to the wicked to do penance, just as God's scourge is a school of patience for the good. In the like manner, God's mercy embraces the good with love, just as His severity corrects the wicked with punishment. It has pleased Divine Providence to prepare for the just joys in the world to come in which the unjust will have no part; and for the impious, pains which will not afflict the virtuous. But, as for the paltry goods and evils of this transitory world, these He allotted alike to just and unjust, in order that men might not seek too eagerly after those goods which they see even the wicked to possess, or shrink too readily from those ills which commonly afflict the just....

Source: Augustine, *City of God*, trans. Gerald G. Walsh, Demetrius B. Zema, Grace Monahan, and Daniel J. Honan (New York: Doubleday, 1958), pp. 40-44.

# 7.5

# MARTYRDOM OF ST. PERPETUA

*Perpetua, born to a pagan Roman family, was martyred in Carthage in 203, in the persecutions of Emperor Septimus Severus. The following is her own account of arrest and imprisonment, and the account by Saturus (her teacher) of her subsequent death. At the time of her arrest Perpetua was a catechumen, preparing to be baptized as a Christian.*

## QUESTIONS

1. Why, according to Perpetua, is she being martyred? What was her crime according to the state of Rome?
2. Why were narratives such as the account of Perpetua's martyrdom so popular with early Christians?
3. Did the violent acts in the story add to or detract from its popularity?

If the ancient examples of faith, such as both testified to the grace of God, and wrought the edification of man, have for this cause been set out in writing that the reading of them may revive the past and so both God be glorified and man strengthened, why should not new examples be set out equally suitable to both those ends? For these in like manner will some day be old and needful for posterity, though in their own time because of the veneration secured to antiquity they are held in less esteem. But let them see to this who determine the one power of the one Spirit by times and seasons: since the more recent things should rather be deemed the greater, as being "later than the last." This follows from the pre-eminence of grace promised at the last lap of the world's race. For "In the last days, saith the Lord, I will pour forth of My Spirit upon all flesh, and their sons and their daughters shall prophesy: and on My servants and on My handmaidens will I pour forth of My Spirit: and their young men shall see visions, and their old men shall dream dreams." And so we who recognize and hold in honour not new prophecies only but new visions as alike promised, and count all the rest of the powers of the Holy Spirit as intended for the equipment of the Church, to which the same Spirit was sent bestowing all gifts upon all as the Lord dealt to each man, we cannot but set these out and make them famous by recital to the glory of God. So shall no weak or despairing faith suppose that supernatural grace, in excellency of martyrdoms or revelations, was found among the ancients only; for God ever works what He has promised, to unbelievers a witness, to believers a blessing. And so "what we have heard and handled declare we unto you also," brothers and little children, "that ye also" who were their eyewitnesses may be reminded of the glory of the Lord, and you who now learn by the ear "may have fellowship with" the holy martyrs, and through them with the Lord Jesus Christ, to whom belong splendour and honour for ever and ever. Amen.

Certain young catechumens were arrested, Revocatus and his fellow-slave Felicitas, Saturninus, and Secundulus. Among these also Vibia Perpetua, well-born, liberally educated, honourably married, having father and mother, and two brothers, one like herself a catechumen, and an infant son at the breast. She was about twenty-two years of age. The whole story of her martyrdom is from this point onwards told by herself as she left it written, hand and conception being alike her own.

"When I was still," she says, "with my companions, and my father in his affection for me was endeavouring to upset me by arguments and overthrow my resolution, 'Father,' I said, 'do you see this vessel, for instance, lying here, waterpot or whatever it may be?' 'I see it, 'he said. And I said to him 'Can it be called by any other name than what it is?' and he answered, 'No.' 'So also I cannot call myself anything else than what I am, a Christian.'

"Then my father, furious at the word 'Christian,' threw himself upon me as though to pluck out my eyes; but he was satisfied with annoying me; he was in fact vanquished, he and his Devil's arguments. Then I thanked the Lord for being parted for a few days from my father, and was refreshed by his absence. During those few days we were baptized, and the Holy Spirit bade me make no other petition after the holy water save for bodily endurance. A few days after we were lodged in prison; and I was in great fear, because I had never known such darkness. What a day of horror! Terrible heat, thanks to the crowds! Rough handling by the soldiers! To crown all I was tormented there by anxiety for my baby. Then Tertius and Pomponius, those blessed deacons who were ministering to us, paid for us to be removed for a few hours to a better part of the prison and refresh ourselves. Then all went out of the prison and were left to themselves. My baby was brought to me, and I suckled him, for he was already faint for want of food. I spoke anxiously to my mother on his behalf, and strengthened my brother, and commended my son to their charge. I was pining because I saw them pine on my account. Such anxieties I suffered for many days; and I obtained leave for my baby to remain in the prison with me; and I at once recovered my health, and was relieved of my trouble and anxiety for my baby; and my prison suddenly became a palace to me, and I would rather have been there than anywhere else...."

"After a few days a rumour ran that we were to be examined. Moreover, my father arrived from the city, worn with trouble, and came up the hill to see me, that he might overthrow my resolution, saying: 'Daughter, pity my white hairs! Pity your father, if I am worthy to be called father by you; if with these hands I have brought you up to this your prime of life, if I have preferred you to all your brothers! Give me not over to the reproach of men! Look upon your brothers, look upon your mother and your mother's sister, look upon your son who cannot live after you are gone! Lay aside your pride, do not ruin all of us, for none of us will ever speak freely again, if anything happen to you!' So spoke my father in his love for me, kissing my hands, and casting himself at my feet; and with tears called me by the name not of daughter but of lade. And I grieved for my father's sake, because he alone of all my kindred would not have joy in my suffering. And I comforted him, saying: 'It shall happen on that platform as God shall choose; for know well that we lie not in our own power but in the power of God.' and, full of sorrow, he left me.

"On another day when we were having our midday meal, we were suddenly hurried off to be examined; and we came to the market-place. Forthwith a rumour ran through the neighbouring parts of the market-place, and a vast crowd gathered. We went up onto the platform. The others, on being question, confessed their faith. So it came to my turn. And there was my father with my child, and he drew me down from the step, beseeching me: 'Have pity on your baby.' And the procurator Hilarian, who had then received the power of life and death in the room of the late pro-consul Minucius Timinianus, said to me: 'Spare your father's white hairs; spare the tender years of your child. Offer a sacrifice for the safety of the Emperors.' And I answered: 'No.' 'Are you a Christian?' said Hilarian. And I answered: 'I am.' And when my father persisted in trying to overthrow my resolution, he was ordered by Hilarian to be thrown down, and the judge struck him with his rod. And I was grieved for my father's plight, as if I had been struck myself, so did I grieve for the sorrow that had come on his old age. Then he passed sentence on the whole of us, and condemned us to the beasts; and in great joy we went down into the prison. Then because my baby was accustomed to take the breast from me, and stay with me in prison, I sent at once the deacon Pomponius to my father to ask for my baby. But my father refused to give him. And as God willed, neither had he any further wish for my breasts, nor did they become inflamed; that I might not be tortured by anxiety for the baby and pain in my breasts.

"After a few days, while we were all praying, suddenly in the middle of the prayer I spoke, and uttered the name of Dinocrates; and I was astonished that he had never come into mind till then; and I grieved, thinking of what had befallen him. And I saw at once that I was entitled, and ought, to make request for him. And I began to pray much for him, and make lamentation to the Lord. At once on this very night this was shown me. I saw Dinocrates coming forth from a dark place, where there were many other dark places, very hot and thirsty, his countenance pale and squalid; and the wound which he had when he died was in his face still. This Dinocrates had been my brother according to the flesh, seven years old, who had died miserably of a gangrene in the face, so that his death moved all to loathing. For him then I had prayed; and there was a great gulf between me and him, so that neither of us could approach the other. There was besides in the very place where Dinocrates was a font full of water, the rim of which was above the head of the child; and Dinocrates stood on tiptoe to drink. I grieved that the font should have water in it and that nevertheless he could not drink because of the height of the rim. And I woke and recognized that my brother was in trouble. But I trusted that I could relieve his trouble, and I prayed for him every day until we were transferred to the garrison prison, for we were to fight with the beasts at the garrison games on the Caesar Geta's birthday. And I prayed for him day and night with lamentations and tears that he might be given me.

"During the daytime, while we stayed in the stocks, this was shown me. I saw that same place which I had seen before, and Dinocrates clean in body, well clothed and refreshed; and where there had been a wound, I saw a scar; and the font which I had seen before had its rim lowered to the child's waist; and there poured water from it unceasingly; and on the rim a golden bowl full of water. And Dinocrates came forward and began to drink from it, and the bowl failed not. And when he had drunk enough of the water, he came forward, being glad to play as children will. And I awoke. Then I knew that he had been released from punishment.

"Then after a few days Pudens the adjutant, who was in charge of the prison, who began to show us honour, perceiving that there was some great power within us, began to admit many to see us, that both we and they might be refreshed by one another's company. Now when the day of the games approached, my father came in to me, worn with trouble, and began to pluck out his beard and cast it on the ground, and to throw himself on his face, and to curse his years, and to say such words as might have turned the world upside down. I sorrowed for the unhappiness of his old age....

As for Felicitas indeed, she also was visited by the grace of God in this wise. Being eight months gone with child (for she was pregnant at the time of her arrest), as the day for the spectacle drew near she was in great sorrow for fear lest because of her pregnancy her martyrdom should be delayed, since it is against the law for women with child to be exposed for punishment, and lest she should shed her sacred and innocent blood among others afterwards who were male-factors. Her fellow-martyrs too were deeply grieved at the thought of leaving so good a comrade and fellow-traveller behind alone on the way to the same hope. So in one flood of common lamentation they poured forth a prayer to the Lord two days before the games. Immediately after the prayer her pains came upon her. And since from the natural difficulty of an eight-months' labour she suffered much in child-birth, one of the warders said to her: "You who so suffer now, what will you do when you are flung to the beasts which, when you refused to sacrifice, you despised?" And she answered: "Now I suffer what I suffer: but then Another will be in me who will suffer for me, because I too am to suffer for Him." So she gave birth to a girl, whom one of the sisters brought up as her own daughter.

But He who had said: "Ask and ye shall receive" had granted to those who asked Him that death which each had craved. For, whenever they talked amongst themselves about their hopes of martyrdom, Saturninus declared that he wished to be cast to all the beasts; so indeed would he wear a more glorious crown. Accordingly at the outset of the show he was matched with the leopard and recalled from him; he was also (later) mauled on the platform by the bear. Saturus on the other hand had a peculiar dread of the bear, but counted beforehand on being dispatched by one bite of the leopard. And so when he was offered to the wild boar, the fighter with beasts, who had bound him to the boar, was gored from beneath by the same beast, and died after the days of the games were over, whereas Saturus was only dragged. And when he was tied up on the bridge before the bear, the bear refused to come out of his den. So Saturus for the second time was recalled unhurt.

For the young women the Devil made ready a mad heifer, an unusual animal selected for this reason, that he wished to match their sex with that of the beast. And so after being stripped and enclosed in nets they were brought into the arena. The people were horrified, beholding in the one a tender girl, in the other a woman fresh from childbirth, with milk dripping from her breasts. so theywere recalled and dressed in tunics without girdles. Perpetua was tossed first, and fell on her loins. Sitting down, she drew back her torn tunic from her side to cover her thighs, more mindful of her modesty than of her suffering. Then, having asked for a pin, she further fastened her disordered hair. For it was not seemly that a martyr should suffer with her hair dishevelled, lest she should seem to mourn in the hour of the glory. Then she rose, and seeing that Felicitas was bruised, approached, gave a hand to her, and lifted her up. And the two stood side by side, and the cruelty of the people being now appeased, they were recalled to the Gate of Life. There Perpetua was supported by a certain Rusticus, then a catechumen, who kept close to her; and being roused from what seemed like sleep, so completely had she been in the Spirit and in ecstasy, began to look about her, and said to the amazement of all: "When we are to be thrown to that heifer, I cannot tell." When she heard what had already taken place, she refused to believe it till she had observed certain marks of ill-usage on her body and dress. Then she summoned her brother and spoke to him and the catechumen, saying: "Stand ye all fast in the faith, and love one another; and be not offended by our sufferings."

Source: Anne Freemantle, ed., *A Treasury of Early Christianity*, (New York: Mentor Books, 1960), pp. 186-192, 195-197.

———— ✛ ————

## QUESTIONS FOR PART 7

1. Christianity is a religion that draws on the influences of many cultures. Using these documents, consider what connections Christianity has to Judaism, Greece, and Rome.
2. What was the role of women in early Christianity? Did that role differ in any way from how women functioned in the broader communities of the Jewish culture and Rome?
3. What was the relationship between early Christianity and the state? Christianity appears at the height of the Roman Empire, during the reign of Augustus, yet is often credited by historians with contributing to the fall of the Empire. Is early Christianity a divisive or unifying force in the late Roman world?

# PART 8

# THE EMERGING MEDIEVAL STATES

The medieval world was a synthesis of the Greco-Roman, Christian, and Germanic worlds. It was never an easy synthesis, and well into the modern period tensions between the three legacies remain, in such debates as the relationship between church and state, law and faith.

The collapse of the Roman political system in the West left a vacuum that was quickly filled by various Germanic tribes; in the East, the Roman state continued but transmuted into the theocratic, Greek state of the Byzantine Empire. Christianity, which had been splintered into diverse sects, had synthesized into a somewhat unified religion, only to begin to break apart again into very autonomous Latin and Greek churches. In the seventh century a new religion appeared in Arabia; Islam quickly overtook the Near East, northern Africa, and reached far into western Europe through the Iberian peninsula. There were, in fact, many medieval worlds.

The sources of this chapter illustrate some of those early medieval worlds, including the introduction of Christianity into the Germanic culture (the Conversion of Clovis), the Byzantine codification of Roman law in the *Corpus Juris Civilis*, the gradual development of papal authority over the Western church, and the earliest interaction between Islam and the West.

# 8.1

## CONVERSION OF CLOVIS

*Clovis became the first king of the Franks shortly before 500 AD. Until then, the Franks were ruled by a chieftain who answered to an assembly of warriors; it was a system of governance common to most Germanic tribes in the fifth and sixth centuries. At about the same time he also converted to Roman Christianity, as the following excerpt describes. It is not clear whether Clovis had pagan beliefs before this conversion, or whether he had converted to Arian Christianity, a sect viewed as heretical by the Roman church. Many of the Franks (and other Germans) had converted to Arianism by 500; gradually they would be converted to Roman Catholicism. The process of converting the Germans coincided with the conquests of several of the tribes by the Franks. Once he became king, Clovis was determined to build an empire to rule as well.*

---  ✦  ---

## QUESTIONS

1. If he had not yet converted to Catholicism, why does Clovis still punish the man who destroyed the vase from the church?
2. What role does Clotilda play in the conversion of Clovis?
3. Clovis' battlefield conversion mimics the conversion of Constantine the Great in 312, which also took place on a battlefield. Is it a coincidence that both men have the same conversion story?

**27** After these events Childeric died and Clovis his son reigned in his stead. In the fifth year of his reign Siagrius, king of the Romans, son of Egidius, had his seat in the city of Soissons which Egidius, who has been mentioned before, once held. And Clovis came against him with Ragnachar, his kinsman, because he used to possess the kingdom, and demanded that they make ready a battle-field. And Siagrius did not delay nor was he afraid to resist. And so they fought against each other and Siagrius, seeing this army crushed, turned his back and fled swiftly to king Alaric at Toulouse. And Clovis sent to Alaric to send him back, otherwise he was to know that Clovis would make war on him for his refusal. And Alaric was afraid that he would incur the anger of the Franks on account of Siagrius, seeing it is the fashion of the Goths to be terrified, and he surrendered him in chains to Clovis' envoys. And Clovis took him and gave orders to put him under guard, and when he had got his kingdom he directed that he be executed secretly. At that time many churches were despoiled by Clovis' army, since he was as yet involved in heathen error. Now the army had taken from a certain church a vase of wonderful size and beauty, along with the remainder of the utensils for the service of the church. And the bishop of the church sent messengers to the king asking that the vase at least be returned, if he could not get back any more of the sacred dishes. On hearing this the king said to the messenger: "Follow us as far as Soissons, because all that has been taken is to be divided there and when the lot assigns me that dish I will do what the father asks." Then when he came to Soissons and all the booty was set in their midst, the king said: "I ask of you, brave warriors, not to refuse to grant me in addition to my share, yonder dish," that is, he was speaking of the vase just mentioned. In answer to the speech of the king those of more sense replied: "Glorious king, all that we see is yours, and we ourselves are subject to your rule. Now do what seems well-pleasing to you; for no one is able to resist your power." When they said this, a foolish, envious and excitable fellow lifted his battle-ax and struck the vase, and cried in a loud voice: "You shall get nothing here except what the lot fairly bestows on you." At this all were stupefied, but the king endured the insult with the gentleness of patience, and taking the vase he handed it over to the messenger of the church, nursing the wound deep in his heart. And at the end of the year he ordered the whole army to come with their equipment of armor, to show the brightness of their arms on the field of March. And when he was reviewing them all carefully, he came to the man who struck the vase, and said to him: "No one has brought armor so carelessly kept as you; for neither your spear nor sword nor ax is in serviceable condition." And seizing his ax he cast it to the earth, and when the other had bent over somewhat to pick it up, the king raised his hands and drove his own ax into the man's head. "This," said he, "is what you did at Soissons to the vase." Upon the death of this man, he ordered the rest to depart, raising great dread of himself by this action. He made many wars and gained many victories. In the tenth year of his reign he made war on the Thuringi and brought them under his dominion.

28. Now the king of the Burgundians was Gundevech, of the family of king Athanaric the persecutor, whom we have mentioned before. He had four sons; Gundobad, Godegisel, Chilperic and Godomar. Gundobad killed his brother Chilperic with the sword, and sank his wife in water with a stone tied to her neck. His two daughters he condemned to exile; the older of these, who became a nun, was called Chrona, and the younger Clotilda. And as Clovis often sent embassies to Burgundy, the maiden Clotilda was found by his envoys. And when they saw that she was of good bearing and wise, and learned that she was of the family of the king, they reported this to King Clovis, and he sent an embassy to Gundobad without delay asking her in marriage. And Gundobad was afraid to refuse, and surrendered her to the men, and they took the girl and brought her swiftly to the king. The king was very glad when he saw her, and married her, having already by a concubine a son named Theodoric.

29. He had a first-born son by queen Clotilda, and as his wife wished to consecrate him in baptism, she tried unceasingly to persuade her husband, saying: "The gods you worship are nothing, and they will be unable to help themselves or any one else. For they are graven out of stone or wood or some metal. And the names you have given them are names of men and not of gods, as Saturn, who is declared to have fled in fear of being banished from his kingdom by his son; as Jove himself, the foul perpetrator of all shameful crimes, committing incest with men, mocking at his kinswomen, not able to refrain from intercourse with his own sister as she herself says: *Jovisque et soror et conjunx.* What could Mars or Mercury do? They are endowed rather with the magic arts than with the power of the divine name. But he ought rather to be worshipped who created by his word heaven and earth, the sea and all that in them is out of a state of nothingness, who made the sun shine, and adorned the heavens with stars, who filled the waters with creeping things, the earth with living things and the air with creatures that fly, at whose nod the earth is decked with creatures that fly, at whose nod the earth is decked with growing crops, the trees with fruit, the vines with grapes, but whose hand mankind was created, by whose generosity all that creation serves and helps man whom he created as his own." But though the queen said this the spirit of the king was by no means moved to belief, and he said: "It was at the command of our gods that all things were created and came forth, and it is plain that your God has not power and, what is more, he is proven not to belong to the family of the gods." Meantime the faithful queen made her son ready for baptism; she gave command to adorn the church with hangings and curtains, in order that he who could not be moved by persuasion might be urged to belief by this mystery. The boy, whom they named Ingomer, died after being baptized, still wearing the white garments in which he became regenerate. At this the king was violently angry, and reproached the queen harshly, saying: "If the boy had been dedicated in the name my gods he would certainly have lived; but as it is, since he was baptized in the name of your God, he could not live at all." To this the queen said: "I give thanks to the omnipotent God, creator of all, who has judged me not wholly unworthy, that he should deign to take to his kingdom one born from my womb. My soul is not stricken with grief for his sake, because I know that, summoned from this world as he was in his baptismal garments, he will be fed by the vision of God."

After this she bore another son, whom she named Chlodomer at baptism; and when he fell sick, the king said: "It is impossible that anything else should happen to him than happened to his brother, namely, that being baptized in the name of your Christ, he should die at once." But through the prayers of his mother, and the Lord's command, he became well.

30. The queen did not cease to urge him to recognize the true God and cease worshiping idols. But he could not be influenced in any way to this belief, until at last a war arose with the Alamanni, in which he was driven by necessity to confess what before he had of this free will denied. It came about that as the two armies were fighting fiercely, there was much slaughter, and Clovis's army began to be in danger of destruction. He saw it and raised his eyes to heaven, and with remorse in his heart he burst into tears

17

and cried: "Jesus Christ, whom Clotilda asserts to be the son of the living God, who art said to give aid to those in distress, and to bestow victory on those who hope in thee, I beseech the glory of thy aid, with the vow that if thou wilt grant me victory over these enemies, and I shall know that power which she says that people dedicated in thy name have had from thee, I will believe in thee and be baptized in thy name. For I have invoked my own gods, but, as I find, they have withdrawn from aiding me; and therefore I believe that they possess no power, since they do not help those who obey them. I now call upon thee, I desire to believe thee, only let me be rescued from my adversaries." And when he said this, the Alamanni turned their backs, and began to disperse in flight. And when they saw that their king was killed, they submitted to the dominion of Clovis, saying: "Let not the people perish further, we pray; we are yours now." And he stopped the fighting, and after encouraging his men, retired in peace and told the queen how he had had merit to win the victory by calling on the name of Christ. This happened in the fifteenth year of this reign.

31. Then the queen asked saint Remi, bishop of Rheims, to summon Clovis secretly, urging him to introduce the king to the word of salvation. And the bishop sent for him secretly and began to urge him to believe in the true God, maker of heaven and earth, and to cease worshiping idols, which could help neither themselves nor any one else. But the king said: "I gladly hear you, most holy father; but there remains one thing: the people who follow me cannot endure to abandon their gods; but I shall go and speak to them according to your words." He met with his followers, but before he could speak the power of God anticipated him, and all the people cried out together: "O pious king, we reject our mortal gods, and we are ready to follow the immortal God whom Remi preaches." This was reported to the bishop who was greatly rejoiced, and bade them get ready the baptismal font. The squares were shaded with tapestried canapies, the churches adorned with white curtains, the baptistery set in order, the aroma of incense spread, candles of fragrant odor burned brightly, and the whole shrine of the baptistery was filled with divine fragrance: and the Lord gave such grace to those who stood by that they thought they were placed amid the odors of paradise. And the king was the first to ask to be baptized by the bishop. Another Constantine advanced to the baptismal font, to terminate the disease of ancient leprosy and wash away with fresh water the foul spots that had long been borne. And when he entered to be baptized, the saint of God began with ready speech: "Gently bend your neck, Sigamber; worship what you burned; burn what you worshipped." The holy bishop Remi was a man of excellent wisdom and especially trained in rhetorical studies, and of such surpassing holiness that he equalled the miracles of Silvester. For there is extant a book of his life which tells that he raised a dead man. And so the king confessed all-powerful God in the Trinity, and was baptized in the name of the Father, Son and holy Spirit, and was anointed with the holy ointment with the sign of the cross of Christ. And of his army more than 3000 were baptized. His sister also, Albofled, was baptized, who not long after passed to the Lord. And when the king was in mourning for her, the holy Remi sent a letter of consolation which began in this way: "The reason of your mourning pains me, and pains me greatly, that Albofled your sister, of good memory, has passed away. But I can give you this comfort, that her departure from the world was such that she ought to be envied rather than mourned." Another sister also was converted, Lanthechild by name, who had fallen into the heresy of the Arians, and she confessed that the Son and the holy Spirit were equal to the Father, and was anointed....

Source: Gregory, Bishop of Tours, *History of the Franks*, trans. Ernest Brehaut (New York: W. W. Norton & Company, Inc., 1969), pp. 36-41.

# 8.2

## *CORPUS JURIS CIVILIS* OF JUSTINIAN

*The* Corpus Juris Civilis, *or Body of Civil Law, was both a compilation and a reworking of older Roman law codes. It is the single most important law code in the history of Western civilization. It was commissioned by the Byzantine Emperor Justinian in 529 and took four years to complete. In its finished form it was divided into four parts:* Code, Digests, *and* Institutes, *which were all written in Latin and based heavily on older Roman laws, and the* Novels, *which were new laws written in Greek. The very shape of the* Corpus — *Latin and Greek, old and new laws — exemplifies the Byzantine culture, itself a synthesis of old and new, West and East. Justinian was both a Roman emperor in the style of Augustus and Constantine, and an Eastern tyrant in the Greek tradition. The laws excerpted here are from the* Institutes.

### QUESTIONS

1. Does the *Corpus* define slavery as a natural state?
2. What rationale is used to determine whether a man and woman may marry or not? What determines impediment to marriage?
3. Who has more freedom under this law code, a slave in relation to a master, or a child in relation to a father?

## III. THE LAW OF PERSONS

All our law relates either to persons, or to things, or to actions. Let us first speak of persons; as it is of little purpose to know the law, if we do not know the persons for whose sake the law was made. The chief division in the rights of persons is this: men are all either free or slaves.

1. Freedom, from which men are said to be free, is the natural power of doing what we each please, unless prevented by force or by law.
2. Slavery is an institution of the law of nations, by which one man is made the property of another, contrary to natural right.
3. Slaves are denominated *servi*, because generals order their captives to be sold, and thus preserve them, and do not put them to death. Slaves are also called *mancipia*, because they are taken from the enemy by the strong hand.
4. Slaves either are born or become so. They are born so when their mother is a slave; they become so either by the law of nations, that is, by captivity, or by the civil law, as when a free person, above the age of twenty, suffers himself to be sold, that he may share the price given for him.
5. In the condition of slaves there is no distinction; but there are many distinctions among free persons; for they are either born free, or have been set free.

## IV. DE INGENIUS

A person is *ingenuus* who is free from the moment of his birth, by being born in matrimony, of parents who have been either both born free, or both made free, or one of whom has been born and the other made free; and when the mother is free, and the father a slave, the child nevertheless is born free; just as he is if his mother is free, and it is uncertain who is his father; for he had then no legal father. And it is sufficient if the mother is free at the time of the birth, although a slave when she conceived; and on the other hand, if she be free when she conceives, and is a slave when she gives birth to her child. If the child is held to be born free for the misfortune of the mother ought not to prejudice her unborn infant. The question hence arose, if a female slave with child is made free, but again becomes a slave before the child is born, whether the child is born free or a slave? Marcellus thinks it is born free, for it is sufficient for the unborn child, if the mother has been free, although only in the intermediate time; and this is true.

1. When a man has been born free he does not cease to be *ingenuus*, because he has been in the position of a slave, and has subsequently been enfranchised; for it has been often settled that enfranchisement does not prejudice the rights of birth.

## V. FREEDMEN...

1. Manumission is effected in various ways; either in the face of the Church, according to the imperial constitutions, or by *vindicta*, or in the presence of friends; or by letter, or by testament, or by any other expression of a man's last will. And a slave may also gain his freedom in many other ways, introduced by the constitutions of former emperors, and by our own.
2. Slaves may be manumitted by their masters at any time; even when the magistrate is only passing along, as when a praetor, or *praeses*, or proconsul is going to the baths, or the theater.

## IX. THE POWER OF PARENTS

Our children, begotten in lawful marriage, are in our power.

1. Marriage, or matrimony, is a binding together of a man and woman to live in an indivisible union.
2. The power which we have over our children is peculiar to the citizens of Rome; for no other people have a power over their children, such as we have over ours.
3. The child born to you and your wife is in your power. And so is the child born to your son of his wife, that is, your grandson or granddaughter; so are your great grandchildren, and all your other descendants. But a child born of your daughter is not in your power, but in the power of its own father.

## X. MARRIAGE

Roman citizens are bound together in lawful matrimony; when they are united according to law, the males having attained the age of puberty, and the females a marriageable age, whether they are fathers or sons of a family; but, of the latter, they must first obtain the consent of their parents, in whose power they are. For both natural reason and the law require this consent; so much so, indeed, that it ought to precede marriage. Hence the question has arisen, whether the daughter of a madman could be married, or his son marry? And as opinions were divided as to the son, we decided that as the daughter of a madman might, so may the son of a madman marry without the intervention of the father, according to the mode established by our constitution.

1. We may not marry every woman without distinction; for with some, marriage is forbidden. Marriage cannot be contracted between persons standing to each other in the relation of ascendant and descendant, as between a father and daughter, a grandfather and his granddaughter, a mother and her son, a grandmother and her grandson; and so on, *ad infinitum*. And, if such persons unite together, they only contract a criminal and incestuous marriage; so much so, that ascendants and descendants, who are only so by adoption, cannot intermarry; and even after the adoption is dissolved, the prohibition remains. You cannot, therefore, marry a woman who has been either your daughter or granddaughter by adoption, although you may have emancipated her.

2. There are also restrictions, though not so extensive, on marriage between collateral relations. A brother and sister are forbidden to marry, whether they are the children of the same father and mother, or of one of the two only. And, if a woman becomes your sister by adoption, you certainly cannot marry; but, if the adoption is destroyed by emancipation, you may marry her; as you may also, if you yourself are emancipated. Hence it follows, that if a man would adopt his son-in-law, he ought first to emancipate his daughter; and if he would adopt his daughter-in-law, he ought previously to emancipate his son.

3. A man may not marry the daughter of a brother, or a sister, nor the granddaughter, although she is in the fourth degree. For when we may not marry the daughter of any person, neither may we marry the granddaughter. But there does not appear to be any impediment to marrying the daughter of a woman whom your father has adopted; for she is no relation to you, either by natural or civil law.

4. The children of two brothers or two sisters, or of a brother and sister, may marry together.

5. So, too, a man may not marry his paternal aunt, even though she be so only by adoption; nor his maternal aunt; because they are regarded in the light of ascendants. For the same reason, no person may marry his great aunt, either paternal or maternal.

6. There are, too, other marriages from which we must abstain, from regard to the ties created by marriage; for example, a man may not marry his wife's daughter, or his son's wife, for they are both in the place of daughters to him; and this must be understood to mean those who have been our stepdaughters or daughters-in-law; for if a woman is still your daughter-in-law, that is, if she is still married to your son, you cannot marry her for another reason, as she cannot be the wife of two persons at once. And if your step-daughter, that is, if her mother is still married to you, you cannot marry her, because a person cannot have two wives at the same time.

7. Again, a man is forbidden to marry his wife's mother, and his father's wife, because they hold the place of mothers to him; a prohibition which can only operate when the affinity is dissolved; for if your step-mother is still your step-mother, that is, if she is still married to your father, she would be prohibited from marrying you by the common rule of law, which forbids a woman to have two husbands at the same time. So if your wife's mother is still your wife's mother, that is, if her daughter is still married to you, you cannot marry her, because you cannot have two wives at the same time.

8. The son of a husband by a former wife, and the daughter of a wife by a former husband, or the daughter of a husband by a former wife, and the son of a wife by a former husband, may lawfully contract marriage, even though they have a brother or sister born of the second marriage.

9. The daughter of a divorced wife by a second husband is not your step-daughter; and yet Julian says we ought to abstain from such a marriage. For the betrothed wife of a son is not your daughter-in-law; nor your betrothed wife your son's step-mother; and yet it is more decent and more in accordance with law to abstain from such marriage.

10. It is certain that the relationship of slaves is an impediment to marriage, even if the father and daughter or brother and sister, as the case may be, have been enfranchised.

Source: Oliver J. Thatcher, ed., *The Ideas that have Influenced Civilization in the Original Documents, Volume III* (Boston: Roberts-Manchester Publishing Co., 1901-1902), pp. 103-108

# 8.3

❖

# GREGORY I, LETTERS ON THE PAPACY

*Gregory I, pope from 590-604, is largely responsible for establishing Rome and the Papacy as the power center of the Western Church, and is thus known as Gregory the Great. The series of letters included here illustrate the vigorous approach he took to the many impediments faced by Rome in dominating the Western Church, including plague and the war between the Ostrogoths and the Byzantines for control of Italy, complicated by the invasion of the peninsula by the Lombards in 568. Gregory was also responsible for authorizing numerous missions that sent monks into the still pagan Germanic tribes of central and eastern Europe, as well as the British Isles. He also organized the music of the liturgy into the Gregorian Chants.*

❖

## QUESTIONS

1. How does Gregory interpret the calamities of the sixth century as an opportunity for Christians?
2. How does Gregory view his relationship to the temporal authorities?
3. Why does Gregory urge missionaries to incorporate local practices and the shrines of pagan idols into Christian worship?

## THE PRESENT AGE

*1. To the clergy of Milan*

Take note that all the things of this world, which we used to hear from sacred scripture were doomed to perish, we see now in ruins. Cities are overthrown, fortresses uprooted, churches destroyed, and no tiller of the soil inhabits our land any more. The sword of man incessantly rages in our midst — we, the very few who are left. Along with this, calamities smite us from above. Thus we see before our very eyes the evils that we long ago heard would descend upon the world, and the very regions of the earth have become like pages of books to us. As all things pass away, we should reflect how all that we have loved was nothing. Look with anxious heart, therefore, upon the approaching day of the Eternal Judge and, by repenting, anticipate its terrors. Wash away all the stains of your transgressions with your tears. Use lamentations that endure only for awhile to turn aside the wrath that hangs over you eternally. When our loving Creator comes to judge us, He will comfort us in direct proportion to what He now sees as the punishment that we inflict upon ourselves for our own transgressions.

## THE EMPEROR AND THE CHURCH OF CONSTANTINOPLE

### 2. To Emperor Maurice

Our most pious and God-appointed Lord, in addition to all the burdensome cares of empire, provides with true spiritual zeal for the preservation of Christian peace among the clergy. He righteously and correctly knows that no person can exercise proper rule on earth unless he knows how to deal with divine matters, and he also knows that the peace of the state depends on the peace of the universal Church. Indeed, Most Serene Lord, what human power, what strength of muscular arm, would dare raise a sacrilegious hand against the eminence of your most Christian empire, if all its priests strove with one mind, as they ought, to win the Redeemer's favor for you by prayer and the merit of their lives? What sword of a most savage people would advance with such cruelty to the slaughter of the faithful, were it not for the fact that the lives of us, who are called priests but who are not, are weighed down by perfidious deeds?...Our faults, which weigh down the forces of the state, sharpen the swords of the enemy. What shall we say for ourselves, who are unworthily set over God's people, when we oppress them with the burdens of our sins and destroy by example what we preach with our tongues?...Our bones are wasted by fasts, but we are bloated in our minds. Our body is covered with rags, but in the pride of our heart, we surpass the imperial purple. We lie in ashes but look down upon loftiness. Teachers of humility, we are masters of pride....God has inspired my most pious Lord to deter war against the empire by first establishing peace within the Church and by deigning to bring back the hearts of its priests to harmony. This, indeed, is what I desire, and for myself, I give glad obedience to your most serene commands.

Since, however, it is not my cause, but God's, since the holy laws, since the venerable councils, since the very commands of our Lord Jesus Christ are disturbed by the invention of a certain proud and haughty phrase, may you, My Most Pious Lord, cut out the sore and bind the resisting patient in the restraints of imperial authority. For in binding up these things tightly, you provide relief to the state, and when you cut off such things, you assure a longer reign for yourself.

To all who know the Gospel, it is clear that the Lord verbally committed to the holy apostle, Peter, the prince of all the apostles, care of the entire Church....For to Peter it was said: "You are Peter, and upon this rock I will build My Church, and the gates of hell shall not prevail against it. And I will give you the keys of the Kingdom of Heaven; whatever you bind on earth will be bound also in heaven, and whatever you loose on earth will be loosed also in heaven." Behold, Peter received the keys of the Kingdom of Heaven; the power to bind and loose is given him; the care of the entire Church is committed to him, and yet he is not called the *universal apostle*. Meanwhile, the most holy man, my fellow-priest John, attempts to be called universal bishop. I am compelled to cry out: "O tempora, O mores!"

Behold. all the regions of Europe are in the hands of barbarians, cities are overthrown, fortresses uprooted, provinces depopulated, no tiller of the soil inhabits the land, idol worshippers rage and daily dominate — all to the slaughter of the faithful — and still priests, who ought to lie weeping on the ground and in ashes, seek for themselves names of vanity, and they take pride in new and profane titles.

Do I, Most Pious Lord, defend my own cause? Am I resentful because of a wrong done me? No! It is the cause of Almighty God. It is the cause of the universal Church....In honor of Peter, prince of the apostles, [the title *universal*] was offered by the venerable synod of Chalcedon to the bishop of Rome. But not one bishop of Rome has ever consented to use this unique title, lest, by giving something special to one priest, priests in general would be deprived of the honor due them. How is it, then, that we do not seek the glory of this title, even when it is offered, but another presumes to seize it for himself, even though it has not been offered?...

Behold. We all suffer offense in this matter. Let the author of the offense be brought back to a proper way of life, and all priestly quarrels will end. For my part, I am the servant of all priests, as long as they live in a manner that befits priests. But whoever, through the swelling of vainglory, lifts up his neck against God Almighty and against the laws of the Church Fathers, I trust such a man will not bend my neck to himself, not even with a sword.

## PETRINE PRIMACY

### 3. To Eulogius, bishop of Alexandria

Your most sweet Holiness has spoken much in you letter to me about the chair of Saint Peter, prince of the apostles, saying that he himself now sits on it in the persons of his successors,...and, indeed, I gladly accepted all that was said, inasmuch as he has spoken to me about who occupies Peter's chair. Although special honor to me in no way delights me, I greatly rejoice because you, Most Holy One, have given to yourself what you have bestowed on me. For who can be unaware that the holy church has been made firm in the strength of the prince of the apostles, who derived his name from the firmness of his spirit, so that he was called *Petrus*, which comes from *petra*. And to him it is said by the voice of Truth: "I will give you the keys of the Kingdom of Heaven." And again it is said to him: "When you are converted, strengthen your brothers." And once more: "Simon, son of Jonah, do you love Me? Then feed My sheep." It follows from this that although there are many apostles, so far as primacy is concerned, the see of the prince of the apostles alone has grown strong in authority, which in three places is one see. For Peter himself exalted the see in which he deigned to reside and end his life on earth. Peter himself honored the see to which he sent his disciple as evangelist. Peter himself strengthened the see in which, although he would leave it, he sat for seven years. Because it is the see of one, and one see over which by Divine Authority three bishops now preside, whatever good I hear of you I impute to myself. If you believe anything good of me, impute this to your merits, because we are one in Him how says: "That they all may be one, as You, Father, are in Me and I in You, and that they may be one in Us.

## MISSIONARY POLICIES

### 4. To Augustine, bishop of the Angles

Augustine's third question.

Inasmuch as there is one faith, why do the practices of churches differ? The Roman Church has one type of mass; there is another in the churches of Gaul.

My brother, you are acquainted with the practices of the Roman Church, in which you have been nurtured. I wish, however, that if you have found any practices that might be more pleasing to God Almighty, be they the customs of the Church of Rome, or of Gaul, or of any Church whatsoever, you carefully select them out and diligently introduce to the Church of the Angles, which is still new to the faith, whatever you have been able to collect from these many Churches. We ought not love things for their location; rather, we should love locations for the good things that are attached to them. Therefore, choose from each particular Church those things that are holy, religious, and proper, and collecting them as it were into a bundle, plant them in the minds of the Angles for their use.

*5. To Mellitus, abbot traveling through Gaul*

Since the departure of our congregation that is with you, I have been most anxious because I have heard nothing about the success of your journey. When, however, Almighty God has brought you to our most reverend brother, Bishop Augustine, inform him that, after much deliberation, I have decided the following in regard to the issue of the Angles. The shrines of that people's idols should not be destroyed. Destroy only the idols that are in them. Take holy water and sprinkle it in these shrines. Build altars and deposit relics in them. For if the shrines are well built, it is necessary to transfer them from the worship of devils to the service of the True God. When the people see that their shrines are not destroyed, they will be able to banish error from their hearts and more comfortably come to places they are familiar with, now knowing and adoring the True God. Since they are also accustomed to kill many oxen as sacrifices to demons, they should also have some solemn festivity of this sort but in a changed form. On that day of dedication or on the feast days of the holy martyrs whose relics are deposited there, they may construct tents out of the branches of the trees that surround these shrines that have been transformed into churches, and they may celebrate that holy day with religious feasts. Do not let them sacrifice animals to the Devil any longer, but let them slay animals for their own eating in praise of God, and let them give thanks to the Giver of all for their full stomachs. In this way, while they retain some bodily pleasures they might more easily be able to incline their minds toward spiritual joys. Without a doubt, it is impossible to cut away everything all at once form hard hearts. One who strives to climb to the highest pinnacle must ascend by steps and paces, not be leaps.

Source: Alfred Andrea, ed., *The Medieval Record: Sources of Medieval History*, (Boston: Houghton Mifflin Company, 1997), pp. 116-118.

# 8.4

### ✤

# THE MUSLIM CONQUEST OF IBERIA

*In invading the Iberian Peninsula in 710, Islam continued its rapid expansion, as both a religion and a state. Founded in the early seventh century by Muhammad, by the eighth century the new civilization controlled most of the Middle East, including former Persian and Byzantine territories, and most of North Africa. It was now poised to conquer parts of western Europe. In 710 a Berber (a newly converted*

*North African people) named Tariq was sent by his king to invade Visigothic Iberia. Tariq founded a Muslim state that would last, at least partially, until the fall of Granada in 1492. Here is a Muslim chronicle account of Tariq's invasion.*

✤

## QUESTIONS

1. Why does Ilyan, a Visigoth, actually invite Tariq to invade Iberia?
2. Having accomplished the physical conquest of Iberia himself, why does Tariq hand it over to Musa Ibn Nosseyr?
3. How is this a holy war for the Muslims?

The encounter between Tariq and Ludhriq (Roderick) took place in the Wadi Lakka (Lago de la Janda) in Shudhuna (Sidonia). Allah put Roderick to flight. He was heavily encumbered with armour, and threw himself into the Wadi Lago; he was never seen again.

It is said that the Visigoth kings had a palace at Tulaitula (Toledo) in which was a sepulchre containing the Four Evangelists, on whom they swore their [coronation] oaths. The palace was greatly revered, and was never opened. When a king died, his name was inscribed there. When Roderick came to the throne, he put the crown on his head himself, which gave great offence to the Christians; then he opened the palace and the sepulchre, despite the attempts of the Christians to prevent him. Inside they found effigies of the Arabs, bows slung over their shoulders and turbans on their heads. At the bottom of the plinths it was written: "When this palace is opened and these images are brought out, a people in their likeness will come to al-Andalus and conquer it.

Tariq entered al-Andalus in Ramadan 92 (began 22 June 711). His reason for coming was as follows: One of the Spanish called Yulyan (Julian) used to come and go frequently between al-Andalus and the land of the Berbers (North Africa). Tanja (Tangiers) was [one of the places he regularly visited]. The people of Tangiers were Christian….He used to bring back from there fine horses and falcons for Roderick. The merchant's wife died, and he was left with his beautiful daughter. Roderick ordered him to proceed to al-'Udwa (North Africa), but Julian excused himself on the grounds that his wife had died and he had no-one with whom he could leave his daughter. He ordered her to be brought to the palace. When Roderick saw her, she pleased him greatly, and he took her. On his return, her father learned of this, and said to Roderick, "I have left behind horses and falcons such as you have never seen before." Roderick authorized him to go there and gave him money [to purchase them]. Julian went to Tariq b. Ziyad and excited his interest in al-Andalus, describing its fine points and the weakness of it inhabitants, and their lack of courage. Tariq b. Ziyad wrote to Musa b. Nusair with this information, and was ordered to invade al-Andalus. Tariq mustered the troops.

Once he was on board with this men, he couldn't keep his eyes open, and in his sleep he saw the Prophet (God bless him and grant him salvation), surrounded by the Muhajirun and the Ansar…girded with their swords and with their bows slung over their shoulders. The Prophet (on whom be peace) passed in front of Tariq and said to him, "Pursue your business!" Tariq saw the Prophet and his companions in his sleep until they entered al-Andalus. He took this as a good omen, and encouraged his men with the good news.

So Tariq crossed over the coast of al-Andalus and the first place he conquered was the town of Qartajanna (Carteya or Torre de Cartagena) in the district of al-Jazira (Algeciras). He ordered his men to chop up the captives whom they had killed, and boil their flesh in cauldrons. The remaining captives were set free. Those who were released told everyone they met, and God filled their hearts with fear. Then he advanced, and met Roderick, with the result already mentioned. He pushed on to Astija (Ecija) and Qurtuba (Cordova), then to Toledo and the pass known as the Pass of Tariq, through which he entered Jilliqiyya (Galicia). He overran Galicia, ending up in Usturqa (Astorga).

When Musa b. Nusair heard how successful he had been, he bacame envious of him, and set off with a large force... When he came to the coast of North Africa, he left the point from which Tariq b. Ziyad had entered and went [instead] to a place known as Marsa Musa (the anchorage of Musa; near Ceuta). He avoided the route followed by Tariq and took the Sidonia coast. He arrived one year after Tariq, and proceeded via Sidonia to Ishbiliyya (Seville), which he conquered. From there, he went to Laqant (Fuente de Cantos), to a place called Musa's Pass at the edge of Fuente de Cantos, [and from there] to Marida (Mérida). Some scholars say that the people of Mérida surrendered on terms and were not taken by storm. Musa advanced into Galicia through the pass named after him, and overran the territory he entered, and appeared before Tariq in Astorga.

When Tariq crossed over, the troops from Cordova went to meet him, and were scornful because they saw the small number of his followers. They fought a severe battle and were defeated; Tariq didn't cease slaughtering them until they reached Cordova. Roderick heard this and advanced from Toledo. They met at a place called Sidonia, on a river called today the Wadi Umm Hakim, and fought a hard battle. Almighty God killed Roderick and his men. Mughith al-Rumi, the slave of al-Walid b. 'Abd al-Malik [the Umayyad caliph, 705-15], was Tariq's cavalry commander and he marched on Cordova; Tariq went to Toledo. He entered it, and asked after the Table, which was the only thingt that concerned him. The People of the Book [the Jews or Christians] assert that it was the table of Solomon son of David [...]

[Tariq] conquered al-Andalus on behalf of Musa b. Nusair, and took from it the Table of Solomon son of David (on whom be peace!), and the crown. Tariq was told that the Table was in a fortress called Firas, two days' journey from Toledo, commanded by the son of Roderick's sister. Tariq sent him and his family a safe conduct; the prince cam down [from the castle] and Tariq carried out his promise towards him. Tariq said, "Hand over the Table to me," which he did; it had gold decoration and precious stones such as he had never seen. Tariq removed one of its legs together with its ornamentation of gold and jewels, and made a replacement leg for it. The Table was valued at 200,000 dinars because of its precious stones. Tariq took all the jewels, armour, gold, silver and plate he found there, and besides that acquired wealth such as had not been seen before. He collected it all up and went to Cordova, where he made his base. He then wrote to Musa b. Nusair informing him of the conquest of Spain and of the booty that he had acquired. [...]

It is also said that it was Musa, after his arrival in al-Andalus, who sent Tariq to Toledo, which is half way between Cordova and Arbuna (Narbonne). Narbonne marks the furthest extent of al-Andalus and the limit of where the writ of 'Umar b. 'Abd al-'Azia [Umayyad caliph, 717-720] was effective, before the polytheists overran it. It is still in their hands today. [It is also said that] it was only here that Tariq acquired the Table. Roderick was in possession of 2,000 miles of coast over and above that. [From these wide domains] the Muslims won great booty in gold and silver. "Abd al-Malik b. Maslama told me, on the authority of al-Laith b. Sa'd, "The carpets there were found [to be] woven with rods of gold, which formed a string of gold, pearls, rubies and emeralds. When the Berbers found one, and were unable to carry it away, they took an axe to it and cut it down the middle. Two of them took half each for themselves [and went off] together with a large crowd, while the troops were preoccupied with other things."

[The same authorities relate that] when al-Andalus was conquered, someone came to Musa b. Nusair and said to him, "Send someone with me and I will show you [buried] treasure." Musa sent people with him and the man said to them, "dig here." They did so, and emeralds and rubies such as they had never seen before poured out over them. When they saw it they were overawed, and said, "Musa b. Nusair will never believe us." They sent someone to get him and he saw it for himself. [The same sources] relate that when Musa b. Nusair conquered al-Andalus he wrote to [the caliph] 'Abd al-Malik: "It's not a conquest, so much as the Day of Judgement."

Source: Charles Melville and Ahmad Ubaydl, eds., *Christians and Moors in Spain, Vol. III, Arabic Sources (711-1501)*, (Warminster: Aris & Phillips, Ltd.., 1992), pp. 3-9.

⸺ ⚜ ⸺

## QUESTIONS FOR PART 8

1. Compare Tariq to Clovis. How are the two men similar in their approach to power? How are they different?
2. What role does the Roman Christian church play in the consolidation of Germanic and Byzantine power, respectively?
3. Which had more power in the emerging medieval world, the church or the state?

# PART 9

&

# THE EARLY MIDDLE AGES

The years between the fall of Rome, c. 500, to the Carolingian empire, c. 800, used to be known as the Dark Ages. In referring to them as such, historians were dismissing that period as lacking law and order, as a gap in civilization. We now know that civilization did not retreat entirely, and that the period was not nearly as dark as was once supposed. It is however, undeniable that the emergence of a new empire in the west in 800 represented a turning point in the Early Middle Ages. Charlemagne was crowned Emperor of the Romans by Pope Leo III on Christmas Day, 800; his empire would later be termed the Holy Roman Empire. Yet it was in not a recreation of the original Roman Empire. For one thing, in 800 there was still a "Roman Emperor," as that title had remained active with the Byzantines. For another thing, Charlemagne was crowned by the head of the Roman church, which leads to future power struggles between emperors and popes. Finally, Charlemagne's real power lay in his collection of various German titles, including king of the Franks and king of the Lombards, titles that remained separate from one another.

Simultaneously the Carolingian era resulted in increased power for the papacy and the Roman church. Bolstered by the support Charlemagne gave it and the frequency with which he relied on its help, the Catholic Church continued to expand its influence and its own attempts at centralized power. The following documents illustrate how Charlemagne consolidated and expanded his power, the expansion of Catholic faith, and the Carolingian culture that resulted from both. The final document gives us a glimpse of the impeding collapse of Carolingian power, which will be weakened by internal strife (dynastic wars) and external threats (Vikings, Magyars, and Muslims) in the ninth century.

# 9.1

✤

## CHARLEMAGNE'S WARS OF CONQUEST

*Charlemagne was the first emperor in the West since 476, when the last western Roman emperor had abdicated his title in face of a Barbarian sack of Rome. He established at his court at Aachen a center for learning and manuscript production that was unrivaled in western Europe for centuries. He sought to make government more efficient, replacing independent and land-wealthy nobles known as counts with subservient administrators, many of whom were drawn from the church. Charlemagne's efforts at centralizing power in a dynastic monarchy would not long survive after his death, but it set a precedent that would be copied by later medieval states.*

*Much of Charlemagne's power came from his incessant wars. He continued the tradition established by Clovis in 500 of conquering and converting the still pagan Germanic tribes of the East, spreading his idea of a revived Roman state far into central Europe and enabling the Catholic Church further access to the pagans.*

## QUESTIONS

1. What functions does the Catholic Church have in Charlemagne's wars of conquests?
2. How do we reconcile Charlemagne's faith with the fact that he spent most of his life at war?
3. Do the Franks recognize that they and the Saxons share a common Germanic heritage? Why or why not?

§7 Now that the war in Italy was over, the one against the Saxons, which had been interrupted for the time being, was taken up once more. No war ever undertaken by the Frankish people was more prolonged, more full of atrocities or more demanding of effort. The Saxons, like almost all the peoples living in Germany, are ferocious by nature. They are much given to devil worship and they are hostile to our religion. They think it no dishonour to violate and transgress the laws of God and man. Hardly a day passed without some incident or other which was well calculated to break the peace. Our borders and theirs were contiguous and nearly everywhere in flat, open country, except, indeed, for a few places where great forests or mountain ranges interposed to separate territories of the two peoples by a clear demarcation line. Murder, robbery and arson were of constant occurrence on both sides. In the end, the Franks were so irritated by these incidents that they decided that the time had come to abandon retaliatory measures and to undertake a full-scale war against these Saxons.

War was duly declared against them. It was waged for thirty three long years and with immense hatred on both sides, but the losses of the Saxons were greater than those of the Franks. This war could have been brought to a more rapid conclusion, had it not been for the faithlessness of the Saxons. It is hard to say just how many times they were beaten and surrendered as suppliants to Charlemagne, promising to do all that was exacted from them, giving the hostages who were demanded, and this without delay, and receiving the ambassadors who were sent to them. Sometimes they were so cowed and reduced that they even promised to abandon their devil worship and submit willingly to the Christian faith; but, however ready they might seem from time to time to do all this, they were always prepared to break the promises they had made. I cannot really judge which of these two courses can be said to have come the more easily to the Saxons, for, since the very beginning of the war against them, hardly a year passed in which they did not vacillate between surrender and defiance.

However, the King's mettlesome spirit and his imperturbability, which remained as constant in adversity as in prosperity, were not to be quelled by their ever-changing tactics, or, indeed, to be wearied by a task which he had once undertaken. Not once did he allow anyone who had offended in this way to go unpunished. He took vengeance on them for their perfidy and meted out suitable punishment, either by means of an army which he led himself or by dispatching a force against them under the command of his counts. In the end, when all those who had been offering resistance had been utterly defeated and subjected to his power, he transported some ten thousand men, taken from among those who lived both on this side of the Elbe and across the river, and dispersed them in small groups, with their wives and children, in various parts of Gaul and Germany. At long last this war, which had dragged on for so many years, came to an end on conditions imposed by the King and accepted by the Saxons. These last were to give up their devil worship and the malpractices inherited from their forefathers; and then, once they had adopted the sacraments of the Christian faith, and religion, they were to be united with the Franks and become one people with them....

§9. At a time when this war against the Saxons was being waged constantly and with hardly an intermission at all, Charlemagne left garrisons at strategic points along the frontier and went off himself with the largest force he could muster to invade Spain. He marched over a pass across the Pyrenees, received the surrender of every single town and castle which he attacked and then came back with his army safe and sound, except for the fact that for a brief moment on the return journey, while he was in the Pyrenean mountain range itself, he was given a taste of Basque treachery. Dense forests, which stretch in all directions, make this a spot most suitable for setting ambushes. At a moment when Charlemagne's army was stretched out in a long column of march, as the nature of the local defiles forced it to me, these Basques, who had set their ambush on the very top of one of the mountains, came rushing down on the last part of the baggage train and the troops who were marching in support of the rearguard and so protecting the army which had gone on ahead. The Basques forced them down into the valley beneath, joined battle with them and killed them to the last man. They then snatched up the baggage, and, protected as they were by the cover of darkness, which was just beginning to fall, scattered in all directions without losing a moment. In this feat the Basques were helped by the lightness of their arms and by the nature of the terrain in which the battle was fought. On the other hand, the heavy nature of their own equipment and the unevenness of the ground completely hampered the Franks in their resistance to the Basques. In this battle died Eggihard, who was in charge of the King's table, Anshelm, the Count of the Palace and Roland, Lord of the Breton Marches, along with a great number of others. What is more, this assault could not be avenged there and then, for, once it was over, the enemy dispersed in such a way that no one knew where or among which people they could be found....

§11. Next there suddenly broke out a war in Bavaria, but this was very soon over. It was occasioned by the pride and folly of Duke Tassilo. He was encouraged by his wife, who was the daughter of King Desiderius and thought that through her husband she could revenge her father's exile, to make an alliance with the Huns, the neighbours of the Bavarians to the East. Not only did Tassilo refuse to carry out Charlemagne's orders, but he did his utmost to provoke the king to war. Tassilo's arrogance was too much for the spirited King of the Franks to stomach. Charlemagne summoned his levies from all sides and himself marched against Bavaria with a huge army, coming to the River Lech, which divides the Bavarians from the Germans. He pitched his camp on the bank of this river. Before he invaded the province he determined to discover the intentions of the Duke by sending messengers to him. Tassilo realized that nothing could be gained for himself or his people by his remaining stubborn. He went in person to beg Charlemagne's forgiveness, handed over the hostages who had been demanded, his own son Theodo among them, and, what is more, swore an oath that he would never again listen to anyone who might try to persuade him to revolt against the King's authority. In this way a war which had all the appearance of becoming very serious was in the event brought to a swift conclusion. Tassilo was summoned to the King's presence and was not allowed to go back home afterwards. The government of the province over which he had ruled was entrusted from that moment onwards not to a single duke but to a group of counts.

§12. No sooner were these troubled over than Charlemagne declared war on the Slaves, whom we are accustomed to call Siltzes, but whose real name, in their own language, is the Welatabi. In this conflict the Saxons fought as allies alongside certain other nations who followed Charlemagne's standards, although their loyalty was feigned and far from sincere. The cause of the war was that the Welatabi refused to obey Charlemagne's orders and kept harassing with never-ending invasions the Abodrites, who earlier on had been allied to the Franks....

§13. The war Which cam next was the most important which Charlemagne ever fought, except the one against the Saxons: I mean the struggle with the Avars or Huns. He waged it with more vigour than any of the others and with much greater preparation. He himself led only one expedition into Pannonia, the province which the Huns occupied at that period. Everything else he entrusted to his son Pepin, to the governors of his provinces and to his counts and legates. The war was prosecuted with great vigour by these men and it came to an end in its eighth year.

Just how many battles were fought and how much blood was shed is shown by the fact that Pannonia is now completely uninhabited and that the site of the Khan's palace is now so deserted that no evidence remains that anyone ever lived there. All the Hun nobility died in this war, all their glory departed. All their wealth and their treasures assembled over so many years were dispersed. The memory of man cannot recall any war against the Franks by which they were so enriched and their material possessions so increased. These Franks, who until then had seemed almost paupers, now discovered so much gold and silver in the palace and captured so much precious booty in their battles, that it could rightly be maintained that they had in all justice taken from the Huns what these last had unjustly stolen from other nations....

§14. The last war which Charlemagne undertook was against those Northmen who are called Danes. They first came as pirates and then they ravaged the coasts of Gaul and Germany with a large fleet. Their King Godefrid was so puffed up with empty ambition that he planned to make himself master of the whole of Germany. He had come to look upon Frisia and Saxony as provinces belonging to him; and he had already reduced the Abodrites, who were his neighbours, to a state of subservience and made them pay him tribute. Now he boasted that he would soon come with a huge army to Aachen itself, where the King had his court. There was no lack of people to believe his boasting, however empty it really was. He was really considered to be on the point of trying some such manoeuvre, and was only prevented from doing so by the fact that he died suddenly. He was killed by one of his own followers, so that his own life and the war which he had started both came to a sudden end.

Source: Einhard, *Two Lives of Charlemagne*, trans. Lewis Thorpe (New York: Penguin Books, Ltd., 1969), pp. 61-68.

# 9.2

❖

# MISSIONS OF ST. BONIFACE

*Boniface is the Latin name for Winfrith, who died in 754. He was born in Wessex, one of several Anglo-Saxon kingdoms in England, and was renowned for his missionary activities both in England and in Europe. His missions among the Hessians, Frisians, and Saxons of the continent pre-date Charlemagne; they took place during the reign of Charlemagne's father Pepin, who was king of the Franks from 751-768. The peoples that Boniface was trying to convert to Christianity were the same tribes that Charlemagne spent most of his reign at war with. Later missionaries, who used the memory of Boniface's career and martyrdom for inspiration, would follow the progress of Charlemagne's army into Saxony and Frisia.*

--- ✦ ---

## QUESTIONS

1. The description of the pagan Germanic practices encountered by Boniface in 722 is nearly the same as descriptions from Roman writers of the first century. Why did these practices survive so long in the face of Christian missionary activity?
2. Boniface was not a Frank; do you think this gave him an advantage in his mission to the Frisians and Saxons, who were frequently at war with the Franks?
3. In the last scene, why do Boniface and his clergy refuse to fight back?

Many of the Hessians now were brought into the Catholic faith and received the sevenfold gift of the Holy Spirit and the laying on of hands. Others, however, whose spirit was still too feeble, refused to accept the unalloyed truths of the faith in their entirety. And there were also those who offered clandestine sacrifice to trees and springs, and even those who did it openly. There were occult, and even public, soothsayers who read the future in animals' entrails and in the flight of birds, and carried on all kinds of divining and spellbinding and sacrificial rites.

But there were also pagans with more sense who abhorred all this heathen impiety and would have nothing to do with it. With the advice of these latter he took a stand against all this by daring to cut down an immense oak tree which the pagans, in their own ancient language, called the Oak of Thunor [Donar], and which stood in a place called Geismar. While some of the brethren stood by, Boniface collected all his courage — for a great mob of pagans stood there, cursing bitterly in their hearts against this enemy of their gods — and cut into the tree. But though he had made only a small notch in the tree, suddenly its whole mighty mass, shaken by a divine blast from on high, which splintered its topmost branches, came crashing down and split asunder into four parts, as though by the avenging judgment of god. There for all to see were four giant sections of the trunk, all of equal length, though none of the brethren had laid a hand on it. At the sight of all this the pagans abruptly changed sides, left off their cursing of the moment before, and began to believe in the Lord and to bless Him. Afterwards the holy bishop talked the matter over with the brethren and decided to use the timber from this tree to build a wooden oratory which he dedicated in honor of St. Peter the Apostle.

...By some mysterious presentiment he was able to foretell the approaching day of this death to Bishop Lull and tell him even in what fashion death now at long last would come to him. He discussed with him detailed plans for the building of churches and the teaching of the people. And he said to him: "For I long to finish the journey which yet lies ahead of me. I am powerless to draw back from this pilgrimage of my heart. Even now the day of my departure is at hand and the hour of my death draws nearer. Shortly I shall escape from the prison of the body and return in freedom to claim my prize of immortality. Yours is the destiny, my dearest son, of completing the building of these churches in Thuringia which I have only begun. Yours is the most urgent task of leading this people out of the wasteland of their blind wandering. And I ask you to finish that church at Fulda which I started to build, and bring my old body there, worn out with its many years." After a pause he added: "And now, my son, prepare carefully all those things which must be packed up for our use on our journey. And do not forget to put a linen cloth in my chest of books to wrap my poor old body in." [...] But when the day grew light and the morning sunrise broke upon the world, it was a world turned upside down, for there advancing on them were not friends but enemies, not new Christian worshippers but new executioners. Brandishing spears and shields, a vast throng of the pagans burst into the camp. At once Boniface's escort rushed to arms on all sides and ran out against them. They stood poised to defend the saints — later martyrs — against this mindless mob of raging people, when the hero of God suddenly stepped out of his tent. At the first sound of the crowd's furious onslaught he had called the band of clergy to this side and had taken up the saints' relics which he always had with him. Now he immediately scolded his followers and forbade any fighting. "Do not fight them, lads. Lay down your weapons. What we are taught by the Gospel is true, and we must not give back evil for evil, but good for evil. This now is that very day we have long dreamed of. That moment of freedom we have yearned for is right here. So be heroic in the Lord and suffer this royal grace of his will gladly. Keep your trust in him and he will set your souls free."

Then he turned to the priests and deacons and other clerics standing beside him, God's sworn men all of them, and spoke to them like a father: "My hero brothers, be bold of heart. Have no terror of these slayers of the body, for they have no power to kill the soul, which lives forever. Take cheer in the Lord and fix the anchor of your hope in God, because in another instant he will give you your eternal reward and lead you to your rightful seat in the great hall of heaven among the fellowship of the angels noble beyond earthly measure. Do not surrender yourselves to the doomed love of this life. Snare not your heart with the base and hollow blandishments the heathen do. But submit courageously to this brief instant of death so that you may reign with Christ forever."

While he was lovingly urging his disciples on to the martyr's crown with these heartening words, suddenly the raging storm of pagans overwhelmed them with swords and every sort of weapon, and stained the bodies of the saints with the blood of a happy death.

Source: Clinton Albertson, S. J., *Anglo-Saxon Saints and Heroes* (New York: Fordham University Press, 1997), pp. 308-314.

# 9.3

✦

# A CAROLINGIAN WOMAN:
# GUIBERT OF NOGENT'S *MEMOIRS*

*Guibert was the abbot of Nogent from 1104-1121. His family were minor nobility (virtually a prerequisite for monastic promotion in the eleventh century) in France. His Memoirs recount not only his own story but also the story of his mother and her spiritual influence on him. The following account of his mother's conversion took place during the end of the Carolingian period.*

—————— ✦ ——————

## QUESTIONS

1. Although Guibert and his mother are Christians, why do they both believe that his mother was cursed on her wedding day?
2. Does Guibert resent his mother for abandoning him in order to join a monastery?
3. Why does Guibert not give his mother's name?

## CHAPTER 12

After these lengthy accounts I return to Thee, my God, to speak of the conversion of that good woman, my mother. When hardly of marriageable age, she was given to my father, a mere youth, by the provision of my grandfather, since she was of the nobility, had a very pretty face, and was naturally and most becomingly of sober mien. She had, however, conceived a fear of God's name at the very beginning of her childhood. she had learned to be terrified of sin, not from experience but from dread of some sort of blow from on high, and — as she often told me herself — this dread has so possessed her mind with the terror of sudden death that in later years she grieved because she no longer felt in maturity the same stings of righteous fear as she had in her unformed and ignorant youth.

Now, it so happened that at the very beginning of that lawful union conjugal intercourse was made ineffective through the bewitchments of certain persons. It was said that their marriage drew upon them the envy of a stepmother, who had some nieces of great beauty and nobility and who was plotting to slip one of them into my father's bed. Meeting with no success in her designs, she is said to have used magical arts to prevent entirely the consummation of the marriage. His wife's virginity thus remained intact for three years, during which he endured his great misfortune in silence; at last, driven to it by those close to him, my father was the first to reveal the facts. In all sorts of ways, his kinsmen endeavored to bring about a divorce, and by their constant pressure upon my father, who was then young and dull-witted, they tried to induce him to become a monk, although at that time there was little talk of this order. They did not do this for his soul's good, however, but with the purpose of getting possession of his property.

When their suggestion produced no effect, they began to hound the girl herself, far away as she was from her kinsfolk and harassed by the violence of strangers, into voluntary flight out of sheer exhaustion under their insults, and without waiting for divorce. She endured all this, bearing with calmness the abuse that was aimed at her, and if out of this rose any strife, she pretended ignorance of it. Besides this, certain rich men, perceiving that she was not in fact a wife, began to assail the heart of the young girl; but Thou, O Lord, the builder of inward chastity, didst inspire her with purity stronger than her nature or her youth. Thy grace it was that saved her from burning, though set in the midst of flames, Thy doing that her weak soul was not hurt by the poison of evil talk, and that when enticements from without were added to those impulses common to our human nature, like oil poured on the flames yet the young maiden's heart was always under her control and never won from her by any allurements. Are not such things solely Thy doing, O Lord? When she was in the heat of youth and continually engaged in wifely duties, yet for seven whole years Thou didst keep her is such contenence that, in the words of a certain wise man, even "rumour dare not speak lies about her."

O God, Thou knowest how hard, how almost impossible it would be for women of the present time to keep such chastity as this; whereas there was in those days such modesty that hardly ever was the good name of a married woman sullied by evil rumor. Ah! how wretchedly have modesty and honor in the state of virginity declined from that time to this our present age, and both the reality and the show of a married woman's protection fallen to ruin. Therefore coarse mirth is all that may be noted in their manners and naught but jesting heard, with sly winks and ceaseless chatter. Wantonness shows in their gait, only silliness in their behaviour. So much does the extravagance of their dress depart from the old simplicity that the enlargement of their sleeves, the tightness of their dresses, the distortion of their shoes of Cordovan leather with their curling toes, they seem to proclaim that everywhere modesty is a castaway. A lack of lovers to admire her is a woman's crown of woe, and on her crowds of thronging suitors rests her claim to nobility and courtly pride. There was a that time, I call God to witness, greater modesty in married men, who would have blushed to be seen in the company of such women, than there is now in brides. By such shameful conduct they turn men into greater braggarts and lovers of the market place and the public street.

What is the end of all this, Lord God, but that no one blushes for his own levity and licentiousness, because he knows that all are tarred with the same brush, and, seeing himself in the same case as all others, why the should he be ashamed of pursuits in which he knows all others engage? But why do I say "ashamed" when such men feel shame only if someone excels them as an example of lustfulness? A man's private boastfulness about the number of his loves or his choice of a beauty whom he has seduced is no reproach to him, nor is he scorned for vaunting his love affairs before Thee. Instead, his part in furthering the general corruption meets with the approval of all. Listen to the cheers when, with the inherent looseness of unbridled passions which deserve the doom of eternal silence, he shamelessly noises abroad what ought to have been hidden in shame, what should have burdened his soul with the guilt of ruined chastity and plunged him in the depths of despair. In this and similar ways, this modern age is corrupt and corrupting, distributing evil ideas to some, while the filth thereof, spreading to others, goes on increasing without end.

Holy God, scarcely any such thing was heard of in the time when Thy handmaid was behaving as she did; indeed, then shameful things were hidden under the cloak of sacred modesty and things of honor had their crown. In those seven years, O Lord, that virginity which Thou didst in wondrous fashion prolong in her was in agony under countless wrongs, as frequently they threatened to dissolve her marriage with my father and give her to another husband or to send her away to the remote houses of my distant relatives. Under such grievous treatment she suffered bitterly at times, but with Thy support, O God, she strove with wonderful self-control against the enticements of her own flesh and the inducements of others.

I do not say, gracious Lord, that she did this out of virtue, but that the virtue was Thine alone. For how could that be virtue that came of no conflict between body and spirit, no straining after God, but only from concern for outward honor and to avoid disgrace? No doubt a sense of shame has its use, if only to resist the approach of sin, but what is useful before a sin is committed is damnable afterward. What prostrates the self with the shame of propriety, holding it back from sinful deeds, is useful at the time, since the fear of God can bring aid, giving holy seasoning to shame's lack of savour, and can make that which was profitable at the time (that is, in the world) useful not for a moment but eternally. But after a sin is committed a sense of shame which leads to vanity is the more deadly the more it obstinately resists the healing of holy confession. The desire of my mother, Thy servant, O Lord God, was to do nothing to hurt her worldly honor, yet following Thy Gregory, whom, however, she had never read or heard read, she did not maintain that desire, for afterward she surrendered all her desires into Thy sole keeping, It was therefore good for her at that time to be attached to her worldly reputation.

Since the bewitchment by which the bond of natural and lawful intercourse was broken lasted seven years and more, it is all too easy to believe that, just as by prestidigitation the faculty of sight may be deceived so that conjurers seem to produce something out of nothing, so to speak, and to make certain things out of others, so reproductive power and effort may be inhibited by much less art; and indeed it is now a common practice, understood even by ignorant people. When that bewitchment was broken by a certain old woman, my mother submitted to the duties of a wife as faithfully as she had kept her virginity when she was assailed by so many attacks. In other ways she was truly fortunate, but she laid herself open not so much to endless misery as to mourning when she, whose goodness was ever growing, gave birth to an evil son who (in my own person) grew worse and worse. Yet Thou knowest, Almighty One, with what purity and holiness in obedience to Thee she raised me, how greatly she provided me with the care of nurses in infancy and of masters and teachers in boyhood, with no lack even of fine clothes for my little body, so that I seemed to equal the sons of kings and counts in indulgence....

While staying there, she resolved to retire to the monastery of Fly. After my master had a little house built for her there near the church, she then came forth from the place where she was staying. She knew that I should be utterly an orphan with no one at all on whom to depend, for great as was my wealth of kinsfolk and connections, yet there was no one to give me the loving care a little child needs at such an age; though I did not lack for the necessities of food and clothing. I often suffered from the loss of that careful provision for the helplessness of tender years that only a woman can provide. As I said, although she knew that I would be condemned to such neglect, yet Thy love and fear, O God, hardened her heart. Still, when on the way to that monastery she passed below the stronghold where I remained, the sight of the castle gave intolerable anguish to her lacerated heart, stung with the bitter remembrance of what she had left behind. No wonder indeed if her limbs seemed to be torn from her body, since she knew for certain that she was a cruel and unnatural mother. Indeed, she heard this said aloud, as she had in this way cut off her heart and left bereft of succor such a fine child, made worthy, it was asserted, by so much affection, since I was held in high regard not only by our own family but by outsiders. And Thou, good and gracious God, didst by Thy sweetness and love marvelously harden her heart, the tenderest in all the world, that it might not be tender to her own soul's harm. For tenderness would then have been her ruin, if she, neglecting her God, in her worldly care for me had put me before he own salvation. But "her love was strong as death," for the closer her love for Thee, the greater her composure in breaking from those she loved before.

Coming to the cloister, she found an old woman in the habit of a nun whom she compelled to live with her, declaring that she would submit to her discipline, as she gave the appearance of great piety. "Compelled," I say, because once she had tested the woman's character, she exerted all her powers of persuasion to get her companionship. And so she began gradually to copy the severity of the older woman, to imitate her meager diet, to choose the plainest food, to give up the soft mattress to which she had been accustomed, to sleep in contentment with only straw and a sheet. And since she still had much beauty and showed no sign of age, she purposely strove to assume the appearance of age with an old woman's wrinkles and bowed form. Her long flowing locks, which usually serve as a woman's crowning beauty, were frequently cut short with the scissors; her dress was black and unpleasant-looking, its unfashionable width adorned with countless patches; her cloak was undyed and her shoes were pierced with many a hole past mending, for there was within her One whom she tried to please with such mean apparel.

Since she had learned the beginning of good deeds from the confession of her old sins, she repeated her confessions almost daily. Consequently, her mind was forever occupied in searching out her past deeds, what she had thought or done or said as a maiden of tender years, or in her married life, or as a widow with a wider range of activities, continually examining the seat of reason and bringing what she found to the knowledge of a priest or rather to God through him. Then you might have seen the woman praying with such sharp sighs, pining away with such anguish of spirit that as she worshiped, there was scarcely ever a pause in the heart-rending sobs that went with her entreaties. She had learned the seven penitential psalms from the old woman I mentioned before, not by sight but by ear, and day and night she turned them over in her mind, chewing them with such savour, one might say, that the sighs and groans of those sweet angel songs never ceased to echo in Thy ears, O Lord. But whenever assemblies of people from outside disturbed her beloved solitude — for all who were acquainted with her, especially men and women of noble rank, took pleasure in conversing with her because of her wondrous wit and forbearance — on their departure, every untrue, idle, or thoughtless word she had uttered during their talk begat in her soul indescribable anguish until she reached the familiar waters of penitence or confession.

Source: Patrick Geary, ed., *Readings in Medieval History*, (Ontario: Broadview Press, 2003), pp. 369-371, 374-375.

# 9.4

## VIKING INVASIONS

*The invasions of the Vikings, or Northmen, in the ninth and tenth centuries represent the last wave of Germanic invasions, completing the process of the Germanization of Europe begun in the first century AD. These latest invaders (Danes, Swedes, and the Norse) were still pagan when they began migrating southward. Their invasions also came in many forms: violent military excursions, trade expeditions, and simple migrations of communities. By 1000 the invasions had ended, leaving Viking communities and states scattered across Europe. The most influential Viking settlements were in Greenland, Ireland, England, Francia, and Russia; an effort to establish a Viking colony in the Americas by Leif Erikson (an Icelander) in c. 1000 famously failed. Gradually, the Vikings settled into their new lands, converting to Christianity and adopting Carolingian and Anglo-Saxon titles and customs.*

*The following chronicle account is of the Viking invasions of Francia, the homeland of the Carolingians.*

## QUESTIONS

1. Compare the Viking invasions of the tenth century with the last war fought by Charlemagne against an earlier Viking invasion.
2. Why did the Vikings so frequently target Christian churches?
3. When the Vikings accept the offer of money in 885 to prevent the plunder of Paris, what does this say about the motives of these invaders?

## (b) THE SIEGE OF PARIS

885. The Northmen came to Paris with 700 sailing ships, not counting those of smaller size which are commonly called barques. At one stretch the Seine was lined with the vessels for more than two leagues, so that one might ask in astonishment in what cavern the river had been swallowed up, since it was not to be seen. The second day after the fleet of the Northmen arrived under the walls of the city, Siegfred, who was then king only in name but who was in command of the expedition, came to the dwelling of the illustrious bishop. He bowed his head and said: "Gauzelin, have compassion on yourself and on your flock. We beseech you to listen to us, in order that you may escape death. Allow us only the freedom of the city. We will do no harm and we will see to it that whatever belongs either to you or to Odo shall be strictly respected." Count Odo, who later became king, was then the defender of the city. The bishop replied to Siegfred, "Paris has been entrusted to us by the Emperor Charles, who, after God, king and lord of the powerful, rules over almost all the world. He has put it on our care, not at all that the kingdom may be ruined by our misconduct, but that he may keep it and be assured of its peace. If, like us, you had been given the duty of defending these walls, and if you should have done that which you ask us to do, what treatment do you think you would deserve?" Siegfred replied: "I should deserve that my head be cut off and thrown to the dogs. Nevertheless, if you do not listen to my demand, on the morrow our war machines will destroy you with poisoned arrows. You will be the prey of famine and of pestilence and these evils will renew themselves perpetually every year." So saying, he departed and gathered his comrades.

In the morning the Northmen, boarding their ships, approached the tower and attacked it. They shook it with their engines and stormed it with arrows. The city resounded with clamor, the people were aroused, the bridges trembled. All came together to defend the tower. There Odo, his brother Robert, and the Count Ragenar distinguished themselves for bravery; likewise the courageous Abbot Ebolus, the nephew of the bishop. A keen arrow wounded the prelate, while at his side the young warrior Frederick was struck by a sword. Frederick died, but the old man, thanks to God, survived. There perished many Franks; after receiving wounds they were lavish of life. At last the enemy withdrew, carrying off their dead. The evening came. The tower had been sorely tried, but its foundations were still solid, as were also the narrow *baies* which surmounted them. The people spent the night repairing it with boards. By the next day, on the old citadel had been erected a new tower of wood, a half higher than the former one. At sunrise the Danes caught their first glimpse of it. Once more the latter engaged with the Christians in violent combat. On every side arrows sped and blood flowed. With the arrows mingled the stones hurled by slings and war-machines; the air was filled with them. The tower which had been built during the night groaned under the strokes of the darts, the city shook with the struggle, the people ran hither and thither, the bells jangled. The warriors rushed together to defend the tottering tower and to repel the fierce assault. Among these warriors two, a count and an abbot [Ebolus], surpassed all the rest in courage. The former was the redoubtable Odo who never experienced defeat and who continually revived the spirits of the worn-out defenders. He ran along the ramparts and hurled back the enemy. On those who were secreting themselves so as to undermine the tower he poured oil, was, and pitch, which, being mixed and heated, burned the Danes and tore off their scalps. Some of them died; others threw themselves into the river to escape the awful substance....

Meanwhile Paris was suffering not only from the sword outside but also from a pestilence within which brought death to many noble men. Within the walls there was not ground in which to bury the dead....Odo, the future king, was sent to Charles, emperor of the Franks, to implore help for the stricken city.

One day Odo suddenly appeared in splendor in the midst of three bands of warriors. The sun made his armor glisten and greeted him before it illuminated the country around. The Parisians saw their beloved chief at a distance, but the enemy, hoping to prevent his gaining entrance to the tower, crossed the Seine and took up their position on the bank. Nevertheless Odo, his horse at a gallop, got past the Northmen and reached the tower, whose gates Ebolus opened to him. The enemy pursued fiercely the comrades of the count who were trying to keep up with him and get refuge in the tower. [The Danes were defeated in the attack.]

Now came the Emperor Charles, surrounded by soldiers of all nations, even as the sky is adorned with resplendent stars. A great throng, speaking many languages, accompanied him. He established his camp at the foot of the heights of Montmartre, near the tower. He allowed the Northmen to have the country of Sens to plunder; and in the spring he gave them 700 pounds of silver on condition that by the month of March they leave France for their own kingdom. Then Charles returned, destined to an early death.

## (c) THE BAPTISM OF ROLLO AND THE ESTABLISHMENT OF THE NORMANS IN FRANCE

The king had at first wished to give to Rollo the province of Flanders, but the Norman rejected it as being too marshy. Rollo refused to kiss the foot of Charles when he received from him the duchy of Normandy. "He who receives such a gift," said the bishops to him, "ought to kiss the foot of the king." "Never," replied he, "will I bend the knee to any one, or kiss anybody's foot." Nevertheless, impelled by the entreaties of the Franks, he ordered one of his warriors to perform the act in his stead. This man seized the foot of the king and lifted it to his lips, kissing it without bending and so causing the king to tumble over backwards. At that there was a loud burst of laughter and a great commotion in the crowd of onlookers. King Charles, Robert, Duke of the Franks, the counts and magnates, and the bishops and abbots, bound themselves by the oath of the Catholic faith to Rollo, swearing by their lives and their bodies and by the honor of all the kingdom, that he might hold the land and transmit it to his heirs from generation to generation throughout all time to come. When these things had been satisfactorily performed, the king returned in good spirits into his dominion, and Rollo with Duke Robert set out for Rouen.

In the year of our Lord 912 Rollo was baptized in holy water in the name of the sacred Trinity by Franco, archbishop of Rouen. Duke Robert, who was his godfather, gave to him his name. Rollo devotedly honored God and the Holy Church with his gifts....The pagans, seeing that their chieftain had become a Christian, abandoned their idols, received the name of Christ, and with one accord desire to be baptized. Meanwhile the Norman duke made ready for a splendid wedding and married the daughter of the king [Gisela] according to Christian rites.

Rollo gave assurance of security to all those who wished to swell in his country. The land he divided among his followers, and, as it had been a long time unused, he improved it by the construction of new buildings. It was peopled by the Norman warriors and by immigrants from outside regions. The duke established for his subjects certain inviolable rights and laws, confirmed and published by the will of the leading men, and he compelled all his people to live peaceably together. He rebuilt the churches, which had been entirely ruined; he restored the temples, which had been destroyed by the ravages of the pagans;

he repaired and added to the walls and fortifications of the cities; he subdued the Britons who rebelled against him; and with the provisions obtained from them he supplied all the country that had been granted to him.

Source: Frederic Austin Ogg, ed., *A Sourcebook of Mediaeval History* (New York: American Book Company, 1907), pp. 165-173.

✣

## QUESTIONS FOR PART 9

1. The sources in this chapter cover three and a half centuries. Why was there so much warfare during this period?
2. Compare the spiritual impulses of Boniface and Guibert's mother; why did people choose to be missionaries or nuns, when these choices bring danger or pain?
3. What role did women play in the Carolingian world?

# PART 10

❦

# THE HIGH MIDDLE AGES

The High Middle Ages, c. 1000-1300 AD, was a time of renewal and development in Western civilization. After several centuries in which cities and trade remained scarce, both re-emerged in the eleventh century, as the West stabilized. With the urbanization of Europe came new theories of spirituality, education, politics, and art. Much of what had begun in the early Middle Ages came to fruition, and even more than had been imagined. Catholicism had a complete hegemony on the West, and during this period the papacy (after a shaky start) reached the zenith of its power. New kingdoms and states were created, although dynastic feuds (both at the level of the aristocracy and of the monarchies) continued. These two developments will be explored in the next chapter.

In this chapter the religious and intellectual developments of the High Middle Ages are explored. At no other point in the Middle Ages could one say that Christian faith had such universal appeal as it did during these three centuries. The results of this communal commitment to Roman Catholicism resulted in the majesty of the Gothic cathedrals, the sublime beauty of polyphonic chant and liturgical music, the reform of established monastic houses and creation of new orders (such as the Franciscans and the Dominicans of the thirteenth century), and scholasticism, which attempted to explain faith and theology using classical philosophy as well as Christian faith and mysticism. The sources of this chapter highlight some of these cultural advancements.

# 10.1

✦

## *RULE* OF ST. FRANCIS OF ASSISI

*The first Christian monks were men and women of the third century who chose to live as solitary hermits in the deserts of Egypt and Syria. They followed the scriptural injunction of Christ, who said: "Go, sell everything you have, and give to the poor, and you will have treasure in heaven; then come and follow me" (Mark 10:21). Shortly thereafter monasteries were founded, in which men or women lived in groups, dedicating their lives to prayer. Each monastic house had its own* Rule, *or regulations to follow. The earliest monastic* Rule *in western Europe was that of St. Benedict in 529. Benedictine houses, which remained popular and powerful throughout the Middle Ages, emphasized isolation from the temporal world, daily prayer, farming or manuscript work, and meditation.*

*In 1210 a revolutionary approach to monasticism was created with the* Rule *of St. Francis. The Franciscans, or the Order of Friars Minor, were a mendicant order. They would not remove themselves from the world but instead wandered through the cities of western Europe preaching poverty and repentance.*

---- ✦ ----

## QUESTIONS

1. Under what circumstances could the Franciscan brothers have money?
2. What authority does the papacy have over individual Franciscans?
3. How is this a peculiarly urban *Rule*?

VIII.

THE RULE OF ST. FRANCIS OF ASSISI

("Bullarium Romanum, editio Taurinensis," vol. iii. p. 394)

1 This is the rule and way of living of the minorite brothers: namely to observe the holy Gospel of our Lord Jesus Christ, living in obedience, without personal possessions, and in chastity. Brother Francis promises obedience and reverence to our lord pope Honorius, and to his successors who canonically enter upon their office, and to the Roman Church. And the other brothers shall be bound to obey brother Francis and his successors.

2. If any persons shall wish to adopt this form of living, and shall come to our brothers, they shall send them to their provincial ministers; to whom alone, and to no others, permission is given to receive brothers. But the ministers shall diligently examine them in the matter of the catholic faith and the ecclesiastical sacraments. And if they believe all these, and are willing to faithfully confess them and observe them steadfastly to the end; and if they have no wives, or if they have them and the wives have already entered a monastery, or if they shall have given them permission to do so — they themselves having already taken a vow of continence by the authority of the bishop of the diocese, and their wives being such age that no suspicion can arise in connection with them: — the ministers shall say unto them the world of the holy Gospel, to the effect that they shall go and sell all that they have and strive to give it to the poor. But if they shall not be able to do this, their good will is enough. And the brothers and their ministers shall be on their guard and not concern themselves for their temporal goods; so that they may freely do with those goods exactly as God inspires them. But if advice is required, the ministers shall have permission to send them to some God-fearing men by whose counsel they shall dispense their goods to the poor. Afterwards there shall be granted to them the garments of probation: namely two gowns without cowls and a belt, and hose and a cape down to the belt; unless to these same ministers something else may at some time seem to be preferable in the sight of God. But, when the year of probation is over, they shall be received into obedience; promising always to observe that manner of living, and this Rule. And, according to the mandate of the lord pope, they shall never be allowed to break these bonds. For according to the holy Gospel, no one putting his hand to the plough and looking back is fit for the kingdom of God. And those who have now promised obedience shall have one gown with a cowl, and another, if they wish it, without a cowl. And those who are compelled by necessity, may wear shoes. And all the brothers shall wear humble garments, with the benediction of God. And I warn

and exhort them lest they despise or judge men whom they shall see clad in soft garments and in colours, using delicate food and drink; but each one shall the rather judge and despise himself.

3. The clerical brothers shall perform the divine service according to the order of the holy roman Church; excepting the psalter, of which they may have extracts. But the lay brothers shall say twenty four Paternosters at matins, five at the service of praise, seven each at the first, third, sixth and ninth hour, twelve at vespers, seven at the completorium; and they shall pray for the dead. And they shall fast from the feast of All Saints to the Nativity of the Lord; but as to the holy season of Lent, which begins from the Epiphany of the Lord and continues forty days, which the Lord consecrated with his holy fast — those who fast during it shall be blessed of the Lord, and those who do not wish to fast shall not be bound to do so; but otherwise they shall fast until the Resurrection of the Lord. But at other times the brothers shall not be bound to fast save on the sixth day (Friday); but in time of manifest necessity the brothers shall not be bound to fast with their bodies. But I advise, warn and exhort my brothers in the Lord Jesus Christ, that, when they go into the world, they shall not quarrel, nor contend with words, nor judge others. But they shall be gentle, peaceable and modest, merciful and humble, honestly speaking with all, as is becoming. And they ought not to ride unless they are compelled by manifest necessity or by infirmity. Into whatever house they enter they shall first say: peace be to this house. And according to the holy Gospel it is lawful for them to eat of all the dishes which are placed before them.

4. I firmly command all the brothers by no means to receive coin or money, of themselves or through an intervening person. But for the needs of the sick and for clothing the other brothers, the ministers alone and the guardians shall provide through spiritual friends, as it may seem to them that necessity demands, according to time, place and cold temperature. This one thing being always regarded, that, as has been said, they receive neither coin nor money.

5. Those brothers to whom God has given the ability to labour, shall labour faithfully and devoutly; in such way that idleness, the enemy of the soul, being excluded, they may not extinguish the spirit of holy prayer and devotion; to which other temporal things should be subservient. As a reward, moreover, for their labour, they may receive for themselves and their brothers the necessities of life, but not coin or money; and this humbly, as becomes the servants of God and the followers of most holy poverty.

6. The brothers shall appropriate nothing to themselves, neither a house, nor a place, nor anything; but as pilgrims and strangers in this world, in poverty and humility serving God, they shall confidently go seeking for alms. Nor need they be ashamed, for the Lord made Himself poor for us in this world. This is that height of most lofty poverty, which has constituted you my most beloved brothers heirs and kings of the kingdom of Heaven, has made you poor in possessions, has exalted you in virtues. This be your portion, which leads on to the land of the living. Adhering to it absolutely, most beloved brothers, you will wish to have for ever in Heaven nothing else than the name of our Lord Jesus Christ. And wherever the brothers are and shall meet, they shall show themselves as of one household; and the one shall safely manifest to the other his necessity. For if a mother loves and nourishes her son in the flesh, how much more zealously should one love and nourish one's spiritual brother? And if any of them fall into sickness, the other brothers ought to serve him, as they would wish themselves to be served.

7. But if any of the brothers at the instigation of the enemy shall mortally sin: for those sins concerning which it has been ordained among the brothers that recourse must be had to the provincial ministers, the aforesaid brothers shall be bound to have recourse to them, as quickly as they can, without delay. But those ministers, if they are priests, shall with mercy enjoin penance upon them. But if they are not priests, they shall cause it to be enjoined upon them through others, priests of the order; according as it seems to them to be most expedient in the sight of God. And they ought to be on their guard lest they

grow angry and be disturbed on account of the sin of any one; for wrath and indignation impede love in themselves and in others.

8. All the brothers shall be bound always to have one of the brothers of that order as general minister and servant of the whole fraternity, and shall be firmly bound to obey him. When he dies, the election of a successor shall be made by the provincial ministers and guardians, in the chapter held at Pentecost; in which the provincial ministers are bound always to come together in whatever place shall be designated by the general minister. And this, once in three years; or at another greater or lesser interval, according as shall be ordained by the aforesaid minister. And if, at any time, it shall be apparent to the whole body of the provincial ministers and guardians that the aforesaid minister does not suffice for the service and common utility of the brothers: the aforesaid brothers to whom the right of election has been given shall be bound, in the name of God, to elect another as their guardian. But after the chapter held at Pentecost the ministers and the guardians can, if they wish it and it seems expedient for them, in that same year call together, once, their brothers, in their districts, to a chapter.

9. The brothers may not preach in the bishopric of any bishop if they have been forbidden to by him. And no one of the brothers shall dare to preach at all to the people, unless he have been examined and approved by the general minister of this fraternity, and the office of preacher have been conceded to him. I also exhort those same brothers that, in the preaching which they do, their expressions shall be chaste and chosen, to the utility and edification of the people; announcing to them vices and virtues, punishment and glory, with briefness of discourse; for the words were brief which the Lord spoke upon earth.

10. The brothers who are the ministers and servants of the other brothers shall visit and admonish their brothers and humbly and lovingly correct them; not teaching them anything which is against their soul and against our Rule. But the brothers who are subjected to them shall remember that, before God, they have discarded their own wills. Wherefore I firmly command them that they obey their ministers in all things which they have promised God to observe, and which are not contrary to their souls and to our Rule. And wherever there are brothers who know and recognize that they can not spiritually observe the Rule, they may and should have recourse to their ministers. But the ministers shall receive them lovingly and kindly, and shall exercise such familiarity towards them, that they may speak and act towards them as masters to their servants; for so it ought to be, that the ministers should be the servants of all the brothers. I warn and exhort, moreover, in Christ Jesus the Lord, that the brothers be on their guard against all pride, vain-glory, envy, avarice, care and anxiety for this world, detraction and murmuring. And they shall not take trouble to teach those ignorant of letters, but shall pay heed to this that they desire to have the spirit of God and its holy workings; that they pray always to God with a pure heart; that they have humility, patience, in persecution and infirmity; and that they love those who persecute, revile and attack us. For the Lord saith: "Love your enemies and pray for those that persecute you and speak evil against you; blessed are they that suffer persecution for righteousness' sake, for of such is the kingdom of Heaven; He that is steadfast unto the end shall be saved."

11. I firmly command all the brothers not to have suspicious intercourse or to take counsel with women. And, with the exception of those whom special permission has been given by the Apostolic Chair, let them not enter nunneries. Neither may they become fellow god-parents with men or women, lest from this cause a scandal may arise among the brothers or concerning the brothers.

12. Whoever of the brothers by divine inspiration may with to go among the Saracens and other infidels, shall seek permission to do so from their provincial ministers. But to none shall the ministers give permission to go, save to those whom they shall see to be fit for the mission.

Furthermore, through their obedience I enjoin on the ministers that they demand from the lord pope one of the cardinals of the holy roman Church, who shall be the governor, corrector and protector of that fraternity, so that, always subjected and lying at the feet of that same holy Church, steadfast in the catholic faith, we may observe poverty and humility, and the only Gospel of our Lord Jesus Christ; as we have firmly promised.

Source: Ernest Henderson, ed. *Select Historical Documents of the Middle Ages* (New York: AMS Press, 1968), pp. 344-349.

# 10.2

# FOUNDATION OF THE UNIVERSITY OF HEIDELBERG, 1386

*The first university was created at Bologna in 1158. Emperor Frederick Barbarossa granted it a charter, primarily for the study of law. Its popularity was so immediate that other towns and other nobles wanted to charter their own universities. Most, such as the University of Paris, grew out of a pre-existing cathedral school. Each university also had its own focus: Bologna had law; Paris, Oxford and Cambridge had theology; and Salerno had medicine.*

*At all medieval universities, charters were signed between the students and the town or nobleman on whose land the school was to be run, such as this one between Heidelberg and a German prince, Rupert I.*

## QUESTIONS

1. What authority does the Bishop of Worms have over the students (or clerks)?
2. What do these regulations imply about the relationship between students and townspeople?
3. Why do you think Rupert used the University of Paris as a model?

1 We, Rupert the elder, by the grace of God count palatine of the Rhine, elector of the Holy Empire, and duke of Bavaria, — lest we seem to abuse the privilege conceded to us by the apostolic see of founding a place of study at Heidelberg similar to that at Paris, and lest, for this reason, being subjected to the divine judgement, we should deserve to be deprived of the privilege granted — do decree, with provident counsel (hich decree is to be observed unto all time), that the University of Heidelberg shall be ruled, disposed, and regulated according to the modes and manners accustomed to be observed in the University of Paris. Also that, as a handmaid of Paris — a worthy one let us hope — the latter's steps shall be imitated in every way possible; so that, namely, there shall be four faculties in it: the first, of sacred theology and divinity; the second, of canon and civil law, which, by reason of their similarity, we think best to comprise under one faculty; the third, of medicine; the fourth, of liberal arts — of the three-fold philosophy, namely, primal, natural, and moral, three mutually subservient daughters. We wish this institution to be divided and marked out into four nations, as it is at Paris; and that all these faculties shall

make one university, and that to it the individual students, in whatever of the said faculties they are, shall unitedly belong like lawful sons to one mother.

Likewise [we desire] that this university shall be governed by one rector, and that the various masters and teachers, before they are admitted to the common pursuits of our institution, shall swear to observe the statutes, laws, privileges, liberties, and franchises of the same, and not reveal its secrets, to whatever grade they may rise. Also that they will uphold the honor of the rector and the rectorship of our university, and will obey the rector in all things lawful and honest, whatever be the grade to which they may afterwards happen to be promoted. Moreover, that the various masters and bachelors shall read their lectures and exercise their scholastic functions and go about in caps and gowns of a uniform and similar nature, according as has been observed at Paris up to this time in the different faculties.

And we will that if any faculty, nation, or person shall oppose the aforesaid regulations, or stubbornly refuse to obey them, or any one of them — which God forbid — from that time forward that same faculty, nation, or person, if it do not desist upon being warned, shall be deprived of all connection with our aforesaid institution, and shall not have the benefit of our defense or protection. Moreover, we will and ordain that as the university as a whole may do for those assembled here and subject to it, so each faculty, nation, or province of it may enact lawful statutes, such as are suitable to its needs, provided that through them, or any one of them, no prejudice is done to the above regulations and to our institution, and that no kind of impediment arise from them. And we will that when the separate bodies shall have passed the statutes for their own observance, they may make them perpetually binding on those subject to them and on their successors. And as in the University of Paris the various servants of the institution have the benefit of the various privileges which its masters and scholars enjoy, so in starting our institution in Heidelberg, we grant, with even greater liberality, through these presents, that all the servants, i.e., its pedells, librarians, lower officials, preparers of parchment, scribes, illuminators, and others who serve it, may each and all, without fraud, enjoy in it the same privileges, franchises, immunities and liberties with which its masters or scholars are now or shall hereafter be endowed.

2. Lest in the new community of the city of Heidelberg, their misdeeds being unpunished, there be an incentive to the scholars of doing wrong, we ordain, with provident counsel, by these presents, that the bishop of Worms, as judge ordinary of the clerks of our institution, shall have and possess, now and hereafter while our institution shall last, prisons, and an office in our town of Heidelberg for the detention of criminal clerks. These things we have seen fit to grant to him and his successors, adding these conditions: that he shall permit no clerk to be arrested unless for a misdemeanor; that he shall restore any one detained for such fault, or for any light offense, to his master, or to the rector if the latter asks for him, a promise having been given that the culprit will appear in court and that the rector or master will answer for him if the injured parties should go to law about the matter. Furthermore, that, on being requested, he will restore a clerk arrested for a crime on slight evidence, upon receiving a sufficient pledge — sponsors if the prisoner can obtain them, otherwise an oath if he cannot obtain sponsors — to the effect that he will answer in court the charges against him; and in all these things there shall be no pecuniary exactions, except that the clerk shall give satisfaction, reasonably and according to the rule of the aforementioned town, for the expenses which he incurred while in prison. And we desire that he will detain honestly and without serious injury a criminal clerk thus arrested for a crime where the suspicion is grave and strong, until the truth can be found out concerning the deed of which he is suspected. And he shall not for any cause, moreover, take away any clerk from our aforesaid town, or permit him to be taken away, unless the proper observances have been followed, and he has been condemned by judicial sentence to perpetual imprisonment for a crime.

We command our advocate and bailiff and their servants in our aforesaid town, under pain of losing their offices and our favor, not to lay a detaining hand on any master or scholar of our said institution, nor to arrest him or allow him to be arrested, unless the deed be such that that master or scholar ought rightly to be detained. He shall be restored to his rector or master, if he is held for a slight cause, provided he will swear and promise to appear in court concerning the matter; and we decree that a slight fault is one for which a layman, if he had committed it, ought to have been condemned to a light pecuniary fine. Like-wise, if the master or scholar detained be found gravely or strongly suspected of the crime, we command that he be handed over by our officials to the bishop or to his representative in our said town, to be kept in custody.

3. By the tenor of these presents we grant to each and all the masters and scholars that, when they come to the said institution, while they remain there, and also when they return from it to their homes, they may freely carry with them, both coming and going, throughout all the lands subject to us, all things which they need while pursuing their studies, and all the goods necessary for their support, without any duty, levy, imposts, tolls, excises, or other exactions whatever. And we wish them and each one of them, to be free from the aforesaid imposts when purchasing corn, wines meat, fish, clothes and all things necessary for their living and for their rank. And we decree that the scholars from their stock in hand of provision, if there remain over on or two wagon loads of wine without their having practised deception, may after the feast of Easter of that year, sell it at wholesale without paying impost. We grant to them, moreover, that each day the scholars, of themselves or through their servants, may be allowed to buy in the town of Heidelberg, at the accustomed hour, freely and without impediment or hurtful delay, any eatables or other necessaries of life.

4. Lest the masters and scholars of our institution of Heidelberg may be oppressed by the citizens, moved by avarice, through extortionate prices of lodgings, we have seen fit to decree that henceforth each year, after Christmas, one expert from the university on the part of the scholars, and one prudent, pious, and circumspect citizen on the part of the citizens, shall be authorized to determine the price of the students' lodgings. Moreover, we will and decree that the various masters and scholars shall, through our bailiff, our judge and the officials subject to us, be defended and maintained in the quiet possession of the lodgings given to them free or of those for which they pay rent. Moreover, by the tenor of these presents, we grant to the rector and the university, or to those designated by them, entire jurisdiction concerning the payment of rents for the lodgings occupied by the students, concerning the making and buying of books, and the borrowing of money for other purposes by the scholars of our institution; also concerning the payment of assessments, together with everything that arises from, depends upon, and is connected with these.

In addition, we command our officials that, when the rector requires our and their aid and assistance for carrying out his sentences against scholars who try to rebel, they shall assist our clients and servants in this matter; first, however, obtaining lawful permission to proceed against clerks from the lord bishop of Worms, or from one deputed by him for this purpose.

---

Source: Frederic Austin Ogg, ed., *A Sourcebook of Medieval History* (New York: American Book Company, 1907), pp. 345-350.

# 10.3

## "ON THE ETERNALITY OF THE WORLD," ST. BONAVENTURA

*Scholasticism was the pre-eminent medieval intellectual system, which attempted to unite faith and reason into one coherent system. It is also a manifestation of the classical legacy; scholastic theologians endeavored to use classical philosophy to prove, logically, the existence and nature of God. The reintroduction of Aristotelian texts in the twelfth century became a primary motivation of scholastic explorations. Aristotle's ideas became so popular he was referred to simply as the Philosopher in most scholastic works.*

*Bonaventura (c. 1217-1274) was a Franciscan theologian at the University of Paris who argues here for rational proof that God, the Eternal, created the known world.*

### QUESTIONS

1. How did the creation of universities, such as the previous charter, promote scholasticism?
2. How does Bonaventura use "time" as evidence of creation?
3. Why did the scholastics feel it necessary to prove God using reason and logical philosophy?

ST. BONAVENTURA

(In *II Sent.* d.1, a.1, q.2)

The question is: Has the world been produced in time or from eternity. That it has not been produced in time is shown:

1. By the arguments based on motion, the first of which is demonstrative in the following way: *Before every motion and change, there is the motion of the first moveable thing (primum mobile)*; but everything which begins to be begins by way of motion or change; therefore that motion (viz., of the first moveable thing) is before all that which begins to be. But that motion could not have preceded itself or its movable thing (*mobile*); therefore it could not possibly have a beginning. The first proposition is a basic one and its proof is as follows: It is a basic principle in philosophy that "in every kind the complete is prior to the incomplete of that kind"; but movement toward place is the more perfect among all the kinds of motion inasmuch as it is the motion of a complete being, and circular motion is both the swifter and the more perfect among all the kinds of local motion; but the motion of the heaven is of this kind, therefore most perfect, therefore the first. Therefore it is evident that, etc.

2.   This is likewise shown by an absurdity consequent upon the alternative. *Everything which comes to be comes to be through motion or change*; consequently, if motion comes to be it comes to be through motion or change, and with regard to this latter motion the question is similarly raised. Therefore, either there is to be an infinite regress or a positing of some motion lacking a beginning; if the motion, then also the moveable thing and, consequently, also the world.

3.   Similarly, a demonstrative argument based on time as follows: *Everything which begins to be either begins to be in an instant or in time*. If, therefore, the world begins to be, it does so either in an instant or in time. But before every time there is time, and time is before every instant. Consequently there is time before all those things which have begun to be. But it could not have been before the world and motion; therefore the world has not had a beginning. The first proposition is *per se* known. The second, namely that before every time there is time, is evident from the fact that if it is flowing, it was of necessity flowing beforehand. Similarly, it is evident that there is time before every instant since time is a circular measure suited to the motion and the movable thing; but every point in a circle is a beginning even as it is an end; therefore every instant of time is a beginning of the future even as it is a terminus of the past. Accordingly, before every "now" there has been a past. It is evident, therefore, etc.

4.   Again, this is shown by the absurdity consequent upon the alternative. If time is produced, it is produced either in time or in an instant; therefore in time. But in every time there is a prior and a posterior, both a past and a future. Consequently, if time has been produced in time, there has been time before every time, and this is impossible. Therefore, etc.

   These are Aristotle's arguments based on the character of the world itself.

5.   Besides, these, there are other arguments based on the character of the producing cause. In general, there can be reduced to two, the first of which is demonstrative and the second based on the absurdity consequent upon the alternative. The first is as follows: *Given an adequate and actual cause, the effect is given*; but God from eternity has been the adequate and actual cause of this world; therefore, etc. The major premise is *per se* known. The minor, namely that God is the adequate cause, is evident. Since He needs nothing extrinsic for the creating of the world, but only the power, wisdom and goodness which have been most perfect in God from eternity, evidently He has, from eternity, been the adequate cause. That He has also been the actual cause is evident as follows:  God is pure act and is His own act of willing, as Aristotle says; and our philosophers (*Sancti*) say that He is His own acting. It follows, therefore, etc.

6.   Also, by the absurdity of the alternative. *Everything which begins to act or produce, when it was not producing beforehand, passes from rest into act*. If, therefore, God begins to produce the world, He passes from rest into act; but all such things are subject to rest and change or mutability. Therefore God is subject to rest and mutability. This, however, contradicts His absolute goodness and absolute simplicity, and, consequently, is impossible. It is to blaspheme God; and to say that the world has had a beginning amounts to the same thing.

   These are the arguments which the commentators and more recent men (*moderniores*) have added over and beyond the arguments of Aristotle; or, at least, they are reducible to these.

But there are arguments to the contrary, based on *per se* known propositions of reason and philosophy.

1.  The first of these is: It is impossible to add to the infinite. This is *per se* evident because everything which receives an addition becomes more; "but nothing is more infinite." If the world lacks a beginning, however, it has had an infinite duration, and consequently there can be no addition to its duration. But this is certainly false because every day a revolution is added to a revolution; therefore, etc. If you were to say that it is infinite in past time and yet is actually finite with respect to the present, which now is, and, accordingly, that it is in this respect, in which it is finite, that the "more" is to be found, it is pointed out to you that, to the contrary, it is in the past that the "more" is to be found. This is an infallible truth: If the world is eternal, then the revolutions of the sun in its orbit are infinite in number. Again, there have necessarily been twelve revolutions of the moon for every one of the sun. Therefore the moon has revolved more times than the sun, and the sun an infinite number of times. Accordingly, that which exceeds the infinite as infinite is discovered. But this is impossible; therefore, etc.

2.  The second proposition is: *It is impossible for the infinite in number to be ordered.* For every order flows from a principle toward a mean. Therefore, if there is no first, there is no order; but if the duration of the world or the revolutions of the heaven are infinite, they do not have a first; therefore they do not have an order, and one is not before another. But since this is false, it follows that they have a first. If you say that it is necessary to posit a limit (*statum*) to an ordered series only in the case of things ordered in a causal relation, because among causes there is necessarily a limit, I ask why not in other cases. Moreover, you do not escape in this way. For there has never been a revolution of the heaven without there being a generation of animal from animal. But an animal is certainly related causally to the animal from which it is generated. If, therefore, according to Aristotle and reason it is necessary to posit a limit among those things ordered in a causal relation, then in the generation of animals it is necessary to posit a first animal. And the world has not existed without animals; therefore, etc.

3.  The third proposition is: *It is impossible to traverse what is infinite.* But if the world had no beginning, there has been an infinite number of revolutions; therefore it was impossible fore it to have traversed them; therefore impossible for it to have come down to the present. If you say that they (i.e., numerically infinite revolutions) have not been traversed because there has been no first one, or that they well could be traversed in an infinite time, you do not escape in this way. For I shall ask you if any revolution has infinitely preceded today's revolution or none. If none, then all are finitely distant from this present one. Consequently, they are all together finite in number and so have a beginning. If some one is infinitely distant, then I ask whether the revolution immediately following it is infinitely distant. If not, then neither is the former (infinitely) distant since there is a finite distance between the two of them. But if it (i.e. the one immediately following) is infinitely distant, then I ask in a similar way about the third, the fourth, and so on to infinity. Therefore, one is not more distant than another from this present one, one is not before anothers, and so they are all simultaneous.

4.  The fourth proposition is: *It is impossible fore the infinite to be grasped by a finite power.* But if the world had no beginning, then the infinite is grasped by a finite power; therefore, etc. The proof

of the major is *per se* evident. The minor is shown as follows. I suppose that God alone is with a power actually infinite and that all other things have limitation. Also I suppose that there has never been a motion of the heaven without there being a created spiritual substance who would either cause or, at least, know it. Further, I also suppose that a spiritual substance forgets nothing. If, therefore, there has been no revolution of the heaven which he would not know and which would have been forgotten. Therefore, he is actually knowing all of them and they have been infinite in number. Accordingly, a spiritual substance with finite power is grasping simultaneously an infinite number of things. If you assert that this is not unsuitable because all the revolutions, being of the same species and in every way alike, are known by a single likeness, there is the objection that not only would he have known the rotations, but also their effects as well, and these various and diverse effects are infinite in number. It is clear, therefore, etc.

5. The fifth proposition is: *It is impossible that there be simultaneously an infinite number of things.* But if the world is eternal and without a beginning, then there has been an infinite number of men, since it would not be without there being men — for all things are in a certain way for the sake of man and a man lasts only for a limited length of time. But there have been as many rational souls as there have been men, and so an infinite number of souls. But, since they are incorruptible forms, there are as many souls as there have been; therefore an infinite number of souls exist. If this leads you to say that there has been a transmigration of souls or that there is but the one soul for all men, the first is an error in philosophy, because, as Aristotle holds, "appropriate act is in its own matter." Therefore, the soul, having been the perfection of one, cannot be the perfection of another, even according to Aristotle. The second position is even more erroneous, since much less is it true that there is but the one soul for all.

6. The last argument to this effect is: *It is impossible for that which has being after non-being to have eternal being,* because this implies a contradiction. But the world has being after nonbeing. Therefore it is impossible that it be eternal. That it has being after non-being is proven as follows: everything whose having of being is totally from another is produced by the latter out of nothing; but the world has its being totally from God; therefore the world is out of nothing. But not out of nothing as a matter (*materialiter*); therefore out of nothing as an origin (*originaliter*). It is evident that everything which is totally produced by something differing in essence has being out of nothing. For what is totally produced is produced in its matter and form. But matter does not have that out of which it would be produced because it is not out of God (*ex Deo*). Clearly, then, it is out of nothing. The minor, viz., that the world is totally produced by God, is evident from the discussion of another question.

## Conclusion

*Whether positing that all things have been produced out of nothing would imply saying that the world is eternal or has been produced eternally.*

I answer: It has to be said that to maintain that the world is eternal or eternally produced by claiming that all things have been produced by claiming that all things have been produced out of nothing is entirely against truth and reason, as the last of the above arguments proves; and it is so against reason that I do not believe that any philosopher, however slight his understanding, has maintained this.

For such a position involves an evident contradiction. But, with the eternity of matter presupposed, to maintain an eternal world seems reasonable and understandable, and this by way of two analogies which can be drawn. For the procession of earthly things from God is after the fashion of an imprint (*vestigium*). Accordingly, if a foot and the dust in which its print were formed were eternal, nothing would prevent our understanding that the footprint is co-eternal with the foot and, nevertheless, it still would be an imprint from the foot. If matter, or the potential principle, were in this fashion coeternal with the maker, what would keep that imprint from being eternal? Rather, on the contrary, it would seem quite fitting that it should be.

Again, another reasonable analogy offers itself. For, from God the creature proceeds as a shadow, the Son as brightness. But as soon as there is light, there is immediately brightness, and immediately shadow if there should be an opaque object in its way. If, therefore, matter, as opaque, is coeternal with the maker, just as it is reasonable to posit the Son, the brightness of the Father, to be coeternal, so it seems reasonable that creatures or the world, shadow in relation to the Highest Light, is eternal. Moreover, this view is more reasonable than its contrary, viz., that matter has been eternally incomplete, without form or the divine influence, as certain philosophers have maintained. In fact, it is more reasonable to such an extent that even that outstanding philosopher, Aristotle, has fallen into this error, according to the charges of our philosophers (*Sancti*), the exposition of the commentators, and the apparent meaning of his text.

On the other hand, modern scholars say that the Philosopher has never thought this nor did he intend to prove that the world had no beginning *in any way at all*, but rather that it did not begin *by way of natural motion.*

Which of these interpretations is the truer one I do not know. This one thing I do know, that if he held that the world has not begun *according to nature*, he maintained what is true, and his arguments based on motion and time are conclusive. But if he thought that it has *in no way begun*, he has clearly erred, as has been shown above by many arguments. Moreover, in order to avoid self-contradiction, he had to maintain either that the world has not been made, or that it has not been made out of nothing. In order to avoid an actual infinity, however, he had to hold for either the corruption of the rational soul, or its unicity, or its transmigration; thus, in any case, had had to destroy its beatitude. So it is that this error has both a bad beginning and the worst of endings.

Source: Patrick J. Geary, ed., *Readings in Medieval History* (Ontario: Broadview Press, 2003), pp. 493-497.

# 10.4

❖

## "ON GOD'S KNOWLEDGE," AVERROËS

*Not all of the scholastic philosophers of the High Middle Ages were Christian. In fact, Aristotelian philosophy had been lost to the Christian West from the sixth century onward, as the ability to read Greek was lost. Aristotle and other Greek texts had been preserved, largely through Arabic and Syrian translations, by Muslim scholars throughout the Islamic world. Ibn Rushd (1126-1198) was one of the most exceptional minds of the High Middle Ages. He excelled at medicine, pure philosophy, law, and of course theology, which in both Muslim and Christian worlds was considered to be the highest field of study. In the end, Muslim intellectual conservatism turned against philosophy and Ibn Rushd's works were lost, but they were translated into Latin and studied for centuries, in the West. Particularly important were his commentaries on Aristotle. The Latinized version of his name is Averroës.*

---------- ✤ ----------

## QUESTIONS

1. Compare the Averroës selection with the previous one by Bonaventura. Do their definitions of God differ substantially?
2. How is human knowledge different from God's knowledge?
3. Because of its association with the universities, Christian scholasticism was very much an urban philosophy; can we say the same of Averroës?

The difficulty is compelling, as follows. If all these things were in the Knowledge of God the Glorious before they existed, are they in their state of existence [the same] in His Knowledge as they were before their existence, or are they in their state of existence other in His Knowledge than they were before they existed? If we say that in their state of existence they are other in God's knowledge than they were before they existed, it follows that the eternal Knowledge is subject to change, and that when they pass from nonexistence to existence, there comes into existence additional Knowledge: but that is impossible for the eternal Knowledge. If on the other hand we say that the Knowledge of them in both states is one and the same it will be asked, 'Are they in themselves', i.e. the beings which come into existence, 'the same before they exist as when they exist?' The answer will have to be 'No, in themselves they are not the same before they exist as when they exist'; otherwise the existent and the non-existent would be one and the same. If the adversary admits this, he can be asked, 'Is not true Knowledge acquaintance with existence as it really is?' If he says 'Yes', it will be said, 'Consequently if the object varies in itself, the knowledge of it must vary; otherwise it will not be known as it really is'. Thus one of two alternatives is necessary: either the eternal Knowledge varies in Itself, or the things that come into existence are not know to It. But both alternatives are impossible for God the Glorius.

This difficulty is confirmed by what appears in the case of man: His knowledge of non-existent things depends on the supposition of existence, while his knowledge of them when they exist depends [on existence itself]. For it is self-evident that the two states of knowledge are different; otherwise he would be ignorant of things' existence at the time when they exist....

It is impossible to escape from this [difficulty] by the usual answer of the theologians about it, that God the Exalted knows things before their existence as they will be at the time of their existence, in respect of time, place and other attributes proper to each being. For it can be said to them: 'Then when they come to exist, does there occur any change or not?' — with reference to the passage of the thing from non-existence to existence. If they say "No change occurs', they are merely being supercilious. But if they say 'There does occur a change', it can be said to them: 'Then is the occurrence of this change known to the eternal Knowledge or not?' Thus the difficulty is compelling. In sum, it can hardly be conceived that the knowledge of a thing before it exists can be identical with the knowledge of it after it exists. Such, then, is the formulation of this problem in its strongest possible form, as we have explained it to you in conversation....

The way to resolve this difficulty, in our opinion, is to recognize that the position of the eternal Knowledge with respect to beings is different from the position of originated knowledge with respect to beings, in that the existence of beings is a cause and reason for our knowledge, while the eternal Knowledge is a cause and reason for beings. If, when beings come to exist after not having existed, there occurred an addition in the eternal Knowledge such as occurs in originated knowledge, it would follow that the eternal Knowledge would be an effect of beings, not their cause. Therefore there must not occur any change such as occurs in originated knowledge. The mistake in this matter has arisen simply from making an analogy between the eternal Knowledge and originated knowledge, i.e. between the suprasensible and the sensible; and the falsity of this analogy is well known. Just as no change occurs in an agent when his act comes into being, i.e. no change which has not already occurred, so no change occurs in the eternal Glorious Knowledge edge when the object of Its Knowledge results from It.

Thus the difficulty is resolved, and we do not have to admit that if there occurs no change, i.e. in the eternal Knowledge, He does not know beings at the time of their coming into existence just as they are; we only have to admit that He does not know them with originated knowledge but with eternal Knowledge. For the occurrence of change in knowledge when beings change is a condition only of knowledge which is caused by beings, i.e. originated knowledge....

Therefore eternal Knowledge is only connected with beings in a manner other than that in which originated knowledge is connected with them. This does not mean that It is not connected at all, as the philosophers have been accused of saying, in the context of this difficulty, that the Glorious One does not know particulars. Their position is not what has been imputed to them; rather they hold that He does not know particulars with originated knowledge, the occurrence of which is conditioned by their occurrence, since He is a cause of them, not caused by them as originated knowledge is. This is the furthest extent to which purification [of concepts] ought to be admitted.

For demonstration compels the conclusion that He knows things, because their issuing from Him is solely due to His knowing; it is not due to His being merely Existent or Existent with a certain attribute, but to His knowing, as the Exalted has said: 'Does He not know, He who created? He is the Penetrating, the Omniscient!' But demonstration also compels the conclusion that He does not know things with a knowledge of the same character as originated knowledge. Therefore there must be another knowledge of beings which is unqualified, the eternal Glorious Knowledge. And how is it conceivable that the Peripatetic philosophers could have held that the eternal Knowledge does not comprehend particulars, when they held that It is the cause of warning in dreams, of revelation, and of other kinds of inspiration?

### [Conclusion]

This is the way to resolve this difficulty, as it appears to us; and what has been said is incontestable and indubitable. It is God who helps us to follow the right course and directs us to the truth. Peace on you, with the mercy and blessing of God.

## SELECTION II

[Aristotle] means: Because of its not intellecting anything outside its own essence (since it is simple), its intellection of its own essence is something which can be subject to no mutation through all eternity; nor can there by any doubt regarding the fact that it is not subject therein to any weariness such as is the case in our intellection. The situation must be the same in the case of the rest of the separated intellects, save that the First is the simplest of them and for this reason is the One absolutely, since there is no multiplicity whatsoever in it, either through the intellect's being other than the intelligible or through the multiplicity of the intelligibles. For the multiplicity of intelligibles in one and the same intellect (as is the situation with our intellection) is something that is consequent on the otherness which exists in it, *acil.*, between the act of intellection and the intelligible. For when the intellect and the intelligible are united in a perfect union it follows that the many intelligibles which belong to that intellect and that intellect [itself] are united so as to become on thing, simple in all respects; but when the intelligibles that are actual in the single intellect remain many they are not united with its essence and its essence, then, is other than them.

This is what escaped Themistius where he holds that it is possible for the intellect to understand many intelligibles simultaneously. This contradicts our statement that it understands its own essence and understands nothing extrinsic to it and that the intellect and what it understands are one in all respects. He says that it understands all things by virtue of its understanding that it is a principle of theirs. All of this exemplifies the speech of one who does not grasp Aristotle's proofs here. Indeed, a disgraceful conclusion may follow, viz., that God is ignorant of what is here. Because of this, some people have said that he knows what is here through a universal knowledge, not through a particular knowledge. The truth is that since he knows his own essence alone he knows existent beings in that existence which is the cause of their [individual] existences. For example, one does not say of him who knows the heat of fire alone that he has no knowledge of the heat that is present in hot things but on the contrary it is he who knows the nature of heat *qua* heat. Thus it is the First (Be He Praised) who knows the nature of the existent *qua* existent absolutely which [existent] is his essence.

Source: John F. Wippel and Allan B. Wolter, ed., *Medieval Philosophy: From St. Augustine to Nicholas Cusa* (New York: The Free Press, 1969), pp. 235-240.

---

✦

---

## QUESTIONS FOR PART 10

1. Why did universities not appear before this part of the Middle Ages?
2. Scholastic Christians were reading writers such as Averroës at the same time as the crusades; how do we reconcile the contradiction two cultures sharing central theological ideas while they are also at war with one another?
3. Compare the *Rule* of St. Francis with the texts of Bonaventura and Averroës; is the Franciscan order anti-intellectual?

# PART 11

#### ❦

# EUROPEAN KINGDOMS OF THE MIDDLE AGES

The previous chapter explored the intellectual and spiritual developments of the High Middle Ages; this chapter explores the economic and political developments of the same period. One of the defining trends in these two fields was that of centralization; kings and popes alike were both seeking to consolidate their authority over land and subjects. Yet at the same time the newly emerging cities were also trying to protect their independence from the control of the new states. Individual elements within medieval society were more aware than ever of their personal liberties, and of the potential for states to infringe upon them. Furthermore, as kings and popes grew more powerful individually, they inevitably came into conflict with one another. Each after all was trying to rule over the same populaces. The documents of this section include regulations from the merchants of Southampton who wanted to protect their freedom of trade, two documents reflecting royal subjects trying to protect their rights against those of their kings, and finally, a series of documents illustrating the complex relationship between church and state.

# 11.1

#### ✤

## MERCHANT'S GUILD REGULATIONS

*Southampton was a town on the southeast coast of England, with heavy trade in raw wool for finished textiles and wine from the continent. Wool was the single most common trade good for England throughout most of the Middle Ages; controlling trade in that commodity was therefore of tremendous importance to the kings of England. Until 1199, Southampton was a royal demesne land, meaning it was directly under the control of the king. In that year, however, the merchants of Southampton formed an association known as a guild (or gild) and negotiated with King John for some autonomy. Over the next few centuries, the guild and various royal governments would add to the liberties of the guild. In turn, the guild effectively became the rulers of the town. In other cities, individual crafts would form their own guilds to negotiate with town and noble rulers, and to set standards for their own work and prices. The craft guilds were somewhat similar to the modern day labor unions, but played a much more central role in the day-to-day life of cities and citizens.*

———— ✤ ————

# QUESTIONS

1. Why do the merchants of Southampton ensure that guild members will be self-policing?
2. How does Regulation 20 ensure that the merchants' guild will be the most powerful organization in the town?
3. What advantage was there to the kings of England in agreeing to these concessions of power?

## THE MERCHANTS OF SOUTHAMPTON

### ORDANCES OF THE GILD MERCHANT OF SOUTHAMPTON

1 In the first place, there shall be elected from the gild merchant, and established, an alderman, a steward, a chaplain, four skevins, and an usher. And it is to be known that whosoever shall be alderman shall receive from each one entering into the gild fourpence, the steward, twopence; the chaplain, twopence; and the usher, one penny. And the gild shall meet twice a year: that is to say, on the Sunday next after St. John the Baptist's day, and on the Sunday next after St. Mary's day.

2. And when the gild shall be sitting, no one of the gild is to bring in any stranger, except when required by the alderman or steward. And the alderman shall have a sergeant to serve before him, the steward another sergeant, and the two skevins a sergeant, and the other two skevins a sergeant, and the chaplain shall have his clerk.

3. And when the gild shall sit, the alderman is to have, each night, so long as the gild sits, two gallons of wine and two candles, and the steward the same; and the four skevins and the chaplain, each of them one gallon of wine and one candle, and the usher one gallon of wine.

4. And when the gild shall sit, the lepers of La Madeleine shall have of the alms of the gild, two sesters of ale, and the sick of God's House and of St. Julian shall have two sesters of ale. And the Friars Minor shall have two sesters of ale and one sester of wine. And four sesters of ale shall be given to the poor whenever the gild shall meet.

5. And when the gild is sitting, no one who is of the gild shall go outside of the town for any business, without the permission of the steward. And if anyone does so, let him be fined two shillings, and pay them.

6. And when the gild sits, and any gildsman is outside of the city so that he does not know when it will happen, he shall have a gallon of wine, if his servants come to get it. And if a gildsman is ill and is in the city, wine shall be sent to him, two loaves of bread and a gallon of wine and a dish from the kitchen; and two approved men of the gild shall go to visit him and look after his condition.

7. And when a gildsman dies, all those who are of the gild and are in the city shall attend the service of the dead, and gildsmen shall bear the body and bring it to the place of burial. And whoever will not do this shall pay according to his oath, two pence, to be given to the poor. And those of the ward where the dead man shall be ought to find a man to watch over the body the night that the deal shall lie in his house. And so long as the service of the dead shall last, that is to say the vigil and the mass, there ought to burn four candles of the gild, each candle of two pounds weight or more, until the body is buried. And these four candles shall remain in the keeping of the steward of the gild.

8. The steward ought to keep the rolls and the treasure of the gild under the seal of the alderman of the gild.

9. And when a gildsman dies, his eldest son or his next heir shall have the seat of his father, or of his uncle, if his father was not a gildsman, and of no other one; and he shall give nothing for his seat. No husband can have a seat in the gild by right of his wife, nor demand a seat by right of his wife's ancestors.

10. And no one has the right or power to sell or give his seat in the gild to any man; and the son of a gildsman, other than his eldest son, shall enter into the gild on payment of ten shillings, and he shall take the oath of the gild.

11. And if a gildsman shall be imprisoned in England in time of peace, the alderman with the steward and with one of the skevins shall go, at the cost of the gild, to procure the deliverance of the one who is in prison.

12. And if any gildsman strikes another with his fist and is convicted thereof, he shall lost the gild until he shall have bought it back for ten shillings, and taken the oath of the gild again like a new member. And if a gildsman strikes another with a stick, or a knife, or any other weapon, whatever it may be, he shall lost the gild and the franchise, and shall be held as a stranger until he shall have been reconciled to the good men of the gild and has made recompense a fine to the gild of twenty shillings; and this shall not be remitted.

13. If any one does an injury, who is not of the gild, and is of the franchise or strikes a gildsman and is reasonably convicted, he shall lose his franchise and go to prison for a day and a night.

14. And if any stranger or any other who is not of the gild nor of the franchise strikes a gildsman, and is reasonable convicted thereof, let him be in prison two days and two nights, unless the injury is such that he should be more severely punished.

15. And if a gildsman reviles or slanders another gildsman, and a complaint of it comes to the alderman, and if he is reasonably convicted thereof, he shall pay two shillings fine to the gild, and if he is not able to pay he shall lose the gild.

16. And if anyone who is of the franchise speaks evil of a gildsman, and is convicted of this before the alderman, he shall pay five shillings for a fine or lose the franchise.

17. And no one shall come to the council of the gild if he is not a gildsman.

18. And if anyone of the gild forfeits the gild by any act or injury, and is excluded by the alderman and the steward and the skevins and the twelve sworn men of the city, and he wishes to have the gild again, he shall do all things anew just as one who has never been of the gild, and shall make amends for his injury according to the discretion of the alderman and the aforesaid approved men. And if anyone of the gild or of the franchise brings a suit against another outside of the city, by a writ or without a writ, he shall lose the gild and the franchise if he is convicted of it.

19. And no one of the city of Southampton shall buy anything to sell again in the same city, unless he is of the gild merchant or of the franchise. And if anyone shall do so and is convicted of it, all which he has so bought shall be forfeited to the king; and no one shall be quit of custom unless he proves that he is in the gild or in the franchise, and this from year to year.

20. And no one shall buy honey, fat, salf herrings, or any kind of oil, or millstones, or fresh hides, or any kind of fresh skins, unless he is a gildsman: nor keep a tavern for wine, nor sell cloth at retail, except in market or fair days, nor keep grain in his granary beyond five quarters, to sell at retail, if he is not a gildsman; and whoever shall do this and be convicted shall forfeit all to the king.

21. No one of the gild ought to be partner or joing dealer in any of the kinds of merchandise before mentioned with anyone who is not of the gild, by any manner of coverture, or art, or contrivance, or

collusion, or in any other manner. And whosoever shall do this and be convicted, the goods in such manner bought shall be forfeited to the king, and the gildsman shall lose the gild.

22. If any gildsman falls into poverty and has not the wherewithal to live, and is not able to work or to provide for himself, he shall have one mark from the gild to relieve his condition when the gild shall sit. No one of the gild nor of the franchise shall avow anothers goods for his by which the custom of the city shall be injured. And if any one does so and is convicted, he shall lose the gild and the franchise; and the merchandise so avowed shall be forfeited to the king.

23. And no private man nor stranger shall bargain for or buy any kind of merchandise coming into the city before a burgess of the gild merchant, so long as the gildsman is present and wishes to bargain for and buy this merchandise; and if anyone does so and is convicted, that which he buys shall be forfeited to the king.

24. And anyone who is of the gild merchant shall share in all merchandise which another gildsman shall buy or any other person, whosoever he is, if he comes and demands part and is there where the merchandise is bought, and also if he gives satisfaction to the seller and gives security for his part. But no one who is not a gildsman is able or ought to share with a gildsman, without the will of the gildsman.

25. And if any guildsman or other of the city refuse a part to the gildsman in the manner above said, he shall not buy or sell in that year in the town, except his victuals.

26. And if any merchant of the town buys wine or grain so that all the risk shall be on the buyer, he shall not pay custom for this merchandise. And if any risk is upon the seller, he shall pay.

27. It is provided that the chief alderman of the town, or the bailiffs and the twelve sworn men, shall give attention to the merchants as well strangers as private men, as often as it shall be required, to see that they have sufficient security for their debts, and recognizance from their debtors; and the day of this shall be enrolled before them, so that if the day is not kept, on proof by the creditor, the debtor should be then distrained according to the recognizance which he has made, in lands and chattels, to give satisfaction according to the usage of the town, without any manner of pleading, so that the men of the town should not have damage by the default of payment of the debtors aforesaid.

28. And if any guildsman for any debt which he may owe will not suffer himself to be distrained, or when he has been distrained, shall break through, or make removal or break the king's lock, and be convicted thereof, he shall lose his gildship until he has bought it again for twenty shillings, and this each time that he offends in such manner. And he shall be none the less distrained until he has made satisfaction for the debt he owes; and if he will not submit to justice as aforesaid and be thereof convicted, he shall go to prison for a day and a night like one who is against the peace; and if he will not submit to justice let the matter be laid before the king and his council in manner aforesaid....

32. Every year, on the morrow of St. Michael, shall be elected by the whole community of the town, assembled in a place provided, to consider the estate and treat of the common business of the town — then shall be elected by the whole community, twelve discreet men to execute the king's commands, together with the bailiffs, and to keep the peace and protect the franchise, and to do and keep justice to all persons, as well poor as rich, natives or strangers, all that year; and to this they shall be sworn in the form provided. And these twelve discreet men shall choose the same day two discreet men from among themselves and the other profitable and wise men to be bailiffs for the ensuing year, who shall take care that the customs shall be well paid; and they shall receive their jurisdiction the day after Michaelmas, as has been customary. And this shall be renewed every year, and the twelve aforesaid, if there is occasion. The same shall be done as to clear and sergeants of the city, in making and removing....

35. The common chest shall be in the house of the chief alderman or of the steward, and the three keys of it shall be lodged with three discreet men of the aforesaid twelve sworn men, or with three of the

skevins, who shall loyally take care of the common seal, and the charters and the treasure of the town, and the standards, and other muniments of the town, and no letter shall be sealed with the common seal, nor any charter taken out of the common-chest but in the presence of sex or twelve sworn men, and of the alderman or steward; and nobody shall sell by any kind of measure or weight that it is not sealed, under forfeiture of two shillings…..

63. No one shall go out to meet a ship bringing wine or other merchandise coming to the town, in order to buy anything, before the ship be arrived and come to anchor for unlading; and if any one does so and is convicted, the merchandise which he shall have bought shall be forfeited to the king.

Source: Andrea, Alfred, ed. *The Medieval Record: Sources of Medieval History.* Boston: Houghton Mifflin Company, 1997), pp. 249-252.

# 11.2

— ✣ —

## COMPLAINTS TO LOUIS IX FROM NORMAN SUBJECTS

*Louis IX, the king of France from 1226 to 1270, is remembered for reforming the civil administration and for twice leading Crusades. Before setting out for the Holy Land on his first crusade, Louis sent out royal judges known as* enquêteurs *to collect any grievances against royal administrators. He collected the grievances from Normandy, a dukedom that had been brought under French royal control in 1204 by King Philip II Augustus. The following excerpts from those complaints illustrate the centrality of revenue collection from royal lands.*

— ✣ —

### QUESTIONS

1. According to *Enquêt* 423, who is responsible for supplying the parish churches with money for the host?
2. Why are so many of the *Enquêts* petitions by women for restoration of land or revenue? What does this say about the power women had over their own lands?
3. What ultimately do the *Enquêts* say about the king's power over his subjects?

355. R…de Clerdoit, Richard Flori,…Herberti, Hugues Herberti, Buillaume, son of Hugh de Clerdoit, of Saint Jaques de…t, complain that both they and all others from the said parish for whom they similarly complain, were forced by the *baillis* and revenue farmers of the Lord King to pay a customs duty on all things they sell and purchase, wherever they sell or purchase them, just as they had been accustomed to do when there was a market at Montpinçon…on the Tuesday of each week, at the time when Raoul de Grandvilliers, knight and baron, held peaceful possession of his land before he want to England with King John; at which time he forfeited the land. And they say that they paid the said customs duty unjustly because, from the time when the land of the said baron came to the hand of King

Philip, there has been no market in the village of Montpinçon, as there had been at the aforesaid time; and nevertheless, they have paid the said customs duty from that time till the present and are still compelled to pay it....

359. Mabel, widow of Richard, son of Fulk, the knight, of Vieuxpont-en-Auge, complains that Girard de La Boiste acquired for the Lord King land lying in the parish of Castillon, of the diocese of Lisieux, and worth approximately 100s. annually, because the brother of the said woman, a lay person, after the death of his brother the priest, also died in England. It is the priest who had given the said land to Mabel, on the condition that he peacefully and with no interference hold the aforesaid land at farm from Mabel and her heirs throughout his lifetime for one pair of gloves worth 6d. The land was acquired by the Lord King last year on the previous Nativity of the Lord....

366. Emeline, daughter of Alain of Bretteville-sur-Dive complains that the revenue farmers of the Lord King acquired for the King 1-1/2 acres of land, which lie in the aforesaid parish. She was not able to recover them after the death of her father, who used to hold them from the said Lord King in fief for 3 capons, 3 hens, and 3 loaves to be paid annually; and the land was taken into the King's hand approximately 12 years ago. Nor in this matter was the Lord King injured....

374. Robert, called "the Blockhead" of Eraines, complains on behalf of his wife, since she is ill, saying that 20 years ago the Lord King retained in his possession the 3 quarts of barley that his wife used to collect in a certain land lying in the parish of Aubigny; for the *baillis* of the King did not wish to return the land to his wife's mother nor to her after the year and a day that it had been held in the hand of the King. [It was held] because of the outlawry of one of her men, who had been holding that land from [his wife's] mother; although it ought to have been returned after a year and a day....

385. Leceline, widow of G. Ferant, and Guillaume, her son, of the parish of Saint-Loup-Canivet, complain that they are not able to recover 4 acres of land, lying next to a certain field, which they hold from the Lord King, and which the Lord King gave 8 years ago to aforesaid Leceline to hold for herself and her heirs in return for 20s. to be paid annually for the said acres and the said field. And Girard de La Boiste was commanded to transfer the property to her, but he refused even though Jean de Vignes had commanded him to do it....

388. Giroth *de Treperel*, of the parish of Martigny, complains that Girard de La Boiste acquired for the Lord King 1 acre of land that Morel [de Falaise] the Jew had purchased in his fief during the life of his father [but] without the assent and permission of the said father. Giroth is not able to recover [the land] for the price that the Jew had given for the land....

395. Nicholas, rector of the church of Ussy, and Jean de Soulangy, priest, and Hugues, called "the Englishman," a clerk of the Lord King, complain for themselves and for all persons and vicars of the churches of the deanery of Aubigny, saying that the *prévôts* of Falaise exact a duty from them on those things, pertaining to [their] livelihood, which they buy for their own use — if they exceed the price of 5 pennies; briefly, on all the things that they purchase for their use and the use of their churches, just as from lay dues payers, so they say. The dean of Falaise and Thomas of Morteaux-Couliboeuf, a priest, make a similar complaint for all the priests of the aforesaid deanery....

411. Agnes *de Veilleio*, of Falaise, complains that King Philip, of illustrious memory, 2 years after the conquest of Normandy acquired possession of 2 plots, worth 48s. annually, and there fortified the castle of Falaise with moat-battlements and other structures; nor did he exchange [anything for them] with her although the said plots had been given to her as a marriage portion....

415. Acelin le Telier, of the parish of Aubigny, complains that 28 years ago, Pierre du Thillai took his son, W. Acelini into the King's hand, on account of land lying in the aforesaid parish and worth to the Lord King 5 bushels of barley at the Falaise measure to the Lord King. Pierre claimed that a certain

cousin of [Acelin's], whose land it had been, had gone into Poitou against the King, but [in fact] before he had left his province to set out for Poitou, the said cousin had sold the land to Acelin, so he says.

416. Raoul *de Cantepie* and Pierre, his brother, of Beaumais, complain that 40 years ago, Jean le Guerrier acquired for the King 20 acres of land and 1 fishpond, lying in the aforesaid parish and worth 40s. per year to the King, by asserting that their father owed one-third of 18l. to Morel [de Falaise] the Jew. However, King Philip, of illustrious memory, had quit him of that third part and had returned him that land which he had handed over to Morellus in pledge, so they say....

421. Robert Caffrei, of Olendon, complains that 6 years ago, Girard de La Boiste took in the Lord King's hand a certain *vavassoria* lying in the aforesaid parish and worth 10s. annually to [Robert], after the death of a certain man who was holding the said *vavassoriai* from him [Robert] — because the son of that man had acknowledged the lordship of the King after the death of [his] father; however, through an investigation [by jury] made about this it was discovered that the said *vavassoria* should have been held from the said Robert. And the said Girard had [collected] for the relief, 32s, for the aid of the host, 13s, and 10s from [Robert] for bailing himself out of jail — in which [Girard] had put him for claiming the said *vavassoria*....

423. Guillaume Martin, cleric, Buillaume de Villeray, Geoffroy *de Hamello*, Nicolas Chaperon, Roger Tustain, and Elnaud *de Fonte*, of Beaumais, complain that the revenue farmers of the Lord King refuse to help them pay the 36s. of aid for the host, which they were accustomed to pay for the demesne of the King. And they make the complaint for themselves and for their fellows. For the revenue farmers have not paid the said money for 3 years, although they [Guillaume Martin and company] have paid the aid for the host each year....

425. Nicolas *de Hamello*, of Cordey, Guillaume Fuchier, [and] Guillaume Eemelench complain on behalf of the entire parish, saying that they were accustomed to have a certain quittance, such that they did not pay the duty in Falaise on either wood or fields, for 1 penny, which each bordar of those [aforesaid] men used to pay to the *prévôt* of Falaise annually at the Circumcision of the Lord. Nevertheless, for the past 9 years the duty on forests and fields is demanded from them, although they are quit from the said rent.

Source: *"Enquêts* of King Louis," *Readings in Medieval History*, ed. Patrick J. Geary (Ontario: Broadview Press, 2003), pp. 705-714.

# 11.3

✤

# *MAGNA CARTA*

*In 1215 King John of England was confronted by his nobles, presented with a document called the* Great Charter (Magna Carta), *and told to sign it or risk being deposed. The* Charter *is famous for promoting individual freedoms, and protecting the common folk from royal abuses of power. In reality, the* Charter *only protects the noble class, and it includes few new protections that the nobles did not already have. The most important is the assurance by the king that he will respect the right of the nobles to approve taxes before he demanded them. It does, however, present a clear example of the feudal balance of power between kings and nobles.*

*The circumstances that precipitated the confrontation between John and his barons (as English nobles were collectively known) were a series of military and political failures by John. He had lost Normandy to the French in 1204 and another war to them in 1214. In both instances he turned to the barons and demanded extra taxes. He had lost a confrontation with Pope Innocent III over the archbishop of Canterbury. In 1213, Innocent legally deposed John, who had to sign a feudal oath of loyalty to the pope in order to get his title back. Collectively the barons felt manipulated, ignored, and bitter at John's repeated lack of success.*

---

## QUESTIONS

1. Is there anything innovative in the *Great Charter*?
2. Under what circumstances are women mentioned in the *Charter*?
3. At the end of the *Charter* John promises that the Church of England shall be free; from whom is he promising it freedom?

# MAGNA CARTA

...1. In the first place we have granted to God, and by this our present charter confirmed, for us and our hears forever, that the English church shall be free, and shall hold its rights entire and its liberties uninjured; and we will that it thus be observed; which is shown by this, that the freedom of elections, which is considered to be most important and especially necessary to the English church, we, of our pure and spontaneous will, granted, and by our charter confirmed, before the contest between us and our barons had arisen; and obtained a confirmation of it by the lord pope Innocent III; which we will observe and which we will shall be observed in good faith by our heirs forever.

We have granted moreover to all free men of our kingdom for us and our heirs forever all the liberties written below, to be had and held by themselves and their heirs from us and our heirs.

2. If any of our earls or barons, or others holding from us in chief by military service shall have died, and when he has died his heir shall be of full age and owe relief, he shall have his inheritance by the ancient relief; that is to say, the heir or heirs of an earl for the whole barony of an earl and hundred pounds; the heir or heirs of a baron for a whole barony a hundred pounds; the heir or heirs of a knight, for a whole knight's fee, a hundred shillings at most; and who owes less let him give less according to the ancient custom of fiefs.

3. If moreover the heir of any one of such shall be under age, and shall be in wardship, when he comes of age he shall have his inheritance without relief [that is, inheritance tax] and without a fine.

4. The custodian of the land of such a minor heir shall not take from the land of the heir any except reasonable products, reasonable customary payments, and reasonable services, and this without destruction or waste of men or of property; and if we shall have committed the custody of the land of any such a one to the sheriff or to any other who is to be responsible to us for its proceeds, and that man shall have caused destruction or waste from his custody we will recover damages from him, and the land shall be committed to two legal and discreet men of that fief, who shall be responsible for its proceeds to us or to him to whom we have assigned them; and if we shall have given or sold to anyone the custody, an it shall be handed over to two legal and discreet men of that fief who shall be in like manner responsible to us as is said above.

5. The custodian moreover, so long as he shall have the custody of the land, must keep up the houses, parks, warrens, fish ponds, mills, and other things pertaining to the land, from the proceeds of the land itself; and he must return to the heir, when he has come to full age, all his land, furnished with plows and implements of husbandry according as the time of cultivation requires and as the proceeds of the land are able reasonably to sustain.

6. Heirs shall be married without disparity, but so that before the marriage is contracted, it shall be announced to the heir's blood relatives.

7. A widow, after the death of her husband, shall have her marriage portion and her inheritance immediately and without obstruction, nor shall she give anything for her dowry or for her marriage portion, or for her inheritance which inheritance her husband and she held on the day of the death of her husband; and she may remain in the house of her husband for forty days after his death, within which time her dowry shall be assigned to her.

8. No widow shall be compelled to marry so long as she prefers to live without a husband, provided she gives security that she will not marry without our consent, if she holds from us, or without the consent of her lord from whom she holds, if she holds from another.

9. Neither we nor our bailiffs will seize any land or rent, for any debt, so long as the chattels of the debtor are sufficient for the payment of the debt; nor shall the pledges of a debtor be distrained so long as the principal debtor himself has enough for the payment of the debt; and if the principal debtor fails in the payment of the debt, not having the wherewithal to pay it, the pledges shall be responsible for the debt and if they wish, they shall have the lands and the rents of the debtor until they shall have been satisfied for the debt which they have before paid for him, unless the principal debtor shall have shown himself to be quit in that respect towards those pledges.

10. If anyone has taken anything from the Jews, by way of a loan, more or less, and ideas before that debt is paid, the debt shall not draw interest so long as the heir is under age, from whomsoever he holds; and if that debt falls into our hands, we will take nothing except the chattel contained in the agreement.

11. And if anyone dies leaving a debt owing to the Jews, his wife shall have her dower, and shall pay nothing of that debt; and if there remain minor children of the dead man, necessaries shall be provided for them corresponding to the holding of the dead man; and from the remainder shall be paid the debt, the service of the lords being retrained. In the same way debts are to be treated which are owed to others than the Jews.

12. No scutage or aid shall be imposed in our kingdom except by the common council of our kingdom, except for the ransoming of our body, for the making of our oldest son a knight, and for once marrying our oldest daughter, and for these purposes it shall be only a reasonable aid; in the same way it shall be done concerning the aids of the city of London.

13. And the city of London shall have all its ancient liberties and free customs, as well by land as by water. Moreover, we will and grant that all other cities and boroughs and villages and ports shall have all their liberties and free customs.

14. And for holding a common council of the kingdom concerning the assessment of an aid otherwise than in the three cases mentioned above, or concerning the assessment of a scutage [that is, payment by a vassal in lieu of military service], we shall cause to be summoned the archbishops, bishops, abbots, earls, and grater barons by our letters under seal; and besides we shall cause to be summoned generally, by our sheriffs and bailiffs, all those who hold from us in chief, for a certain day, that is at the end of forty days at least, and for a certain place; and in all the letters of that summons, we will express the cause of the summons, and when the summons has thus been given the business shall proceed on the

appointed day, on the advice of those who shall be present, even if not all of those who were summoned have come.

15. We will not grant to anyone, moreover, that he shall take an aid from his free men, except for ransoming his body, for making his oldest son a knight, and for once marrying his oldest daughter; and for these purposes only a reasonable aid shall be taken.

16. No one shall be compelled to perform any greater service for a knight's fee, or for any other free tenement, than is owed from it.

17. The common pleas shall not follow our court, but shall be held in some certain place.

18. The recognitions of *novel disseisin*, *mort d'ancestor*, and *darrein presentment* [that is, the common law procedures determining temporary possession of disputed land] shall be held only in their own counties and in this manner: we, or, if we are outside of the kingdom, our principal justiciar, will send two justiciars through each county four times a year, who with four knights of each county, elected by the county, shall hold in the county and one the day and in the place of the county court, the aforesaid assizes of the county.

19. And if the aforesaid assizes cannot be held within the day of the county court, a sufficient number of knights and free-holders shall remain from those who were present at the county court on that day to give the judgments, according as the business is more or less.

20. A free man shall not be fined for a small offense, except in proportion to the measure of the offense; and for a great offense he shall be fined in proportion to the magnitude of the offense, saving this freehold; and a merchant in the same way, saving his merchandise; and the villain shall be fined in the same way, saving his tools of civilization, if he shall be at our mercy; and none of the above fines shall be imposed except by the oaths of honest men of the neighborhood.

21. Earls and barons shall only be fined by their peers, and only in proportion to their offense.

22. A clergyman shall be fined, like those before mentioned, only in proportion to his lay holding, and not according to the extent of his ecclesiastical benefice.

23. No manor or man shall be compelled to make bridges over the rivers except those which ought to do it of old and rightfully.

24. No sheriff, constable, coroners, or other bailiffs of ours shall hold pleas of our crown.

25. All counties, hundreds, wapentakes, and tithings [that is, small traditional units of land] shall be at the ancient rents and without any increase, excepting our demesne manors.

26. If any person holding a lay fief from us shall die, and our sheriff or bailiff shall show our letters-patent of our summons concerning a debt which the deceased owed to us, it shall be lawful for our sheriff or bailiff to attach and levy on the chattels of the deceased found on his lay fief, to the value of that debt, in the view of legal men, but in such a way that nothing be removed thence until the clear debt to us shall be paid; and the remainder shall be left to the executors for the fulfillment of the will of the deceased, saving to his wife and children their reasonable shares.

27. If any free man dies intestate, his chattels shall be distributed by the hands of his near relatives and friends, under the oversight of the church, saving to each one the debts which the deceased owed to him.

28. No constable or other bailiff of ours shall take anyone's grain or other chattels, without immediately paying for them in money, unless he is able to obtain a postponement at the good-will of the seller.

29. No constable shall require any knight to give money in place of his ward of a castle if he is willing to furnish that ward in his own person or through another honest man, if he himself is not able to

do it for a reasonable cause; and if we shall lead or send him into the army he shall be free from ward in proportion to the amount of time by which he has been in the army for us.

30. No sheriff or bailiff of ours or anyone else shall take horses or wagons of any free man for carrying purposes except on the permission of that free man.

31. Neither we nor our bailiffs will take the wood of another man for castles, or for anything else which we are doing, except by the permission of him to whom the wood belongs.

32. We will not hold the lands of those convicted of a felony for more than a year and a day, after which the lands shall be returned to the lords of the fiefs.

33. All the fish-weirs in the Thames and the Medway, and throughout all England, shall be done away with, except those on the coast.

34. The writ which is called *praecipe* shall not be given for the future to anyone concerning any tenement by which a free man can lose his court.

35. There shall be one measure of wine our whole kingdom, and one measure of ale, and one measure of grain, that is the London quarter, and one width of died cloth and of russets and of halbergets, that is two ells within the selvages; of weights, moreover, it shall be as of measures.

36. Nothing shall henceforth be given or taken for a writ of inquisition concerning life or limbs, but it shall be given freely and not denied.

37. If anyone holds from us by fee farm or by non-military tenure or by urban tenure, and from another he holds land by military service, we will not have the guardianship of the heir of his land by military service, we will not have the guardianship of the heir of his land which is of the fief of another, on account of that fee farm, or soccage, or burgage; nor will we have the custody of that fee farm, or soccage, or burgage, unless that fee farm itself owes military service. We will not have the guardianship of the heir or of the land of anyone, which he holds from another by military service of paying to us knives or arrows, or things of that kind.

38. No bailiff for the future shall place anyone to his law on his simple affirmation, without credible witnesses brought for this purpose.

39. No free man shall be taken or imprisoned or dispossessed, or outlawed, or banished, or in any way destroyed, nor will we go upon him, nor send upon him, except by the legal judgment of his peers or by the law of the land.

40. To no one will we sell, to no one will we deny or delay, right or justice.

41. All merchants shall be safe and secure in going out from England and coming into England and in remaining and going through England, as well by land as by water, for buying and selling, free from all evil tolls, by the ancient and rightful customs, except in time of war; and if they are of a land at war with us, and if such are found in our land at the beginning of war, they shall be attached without injury to their bodies or goods, until it shall be known from us or from our principal justiciar in what way the merchants of our land are treated who shall be then found in the country which is at war with us; and if ours are safe there, the others shall be safe in our land.

42. It is allowed henceforth to anyone to go out from our kingdom, and to return, safely and securely, by land and by water, saving their fidelity to us, except in time or war for some short time, for the common good of the kingdom; excepting persons imprisoned and outlawed according to the law of the realm, and people of a land at war with us, and merchants, or whom it shall be done as is before said.

43. If anyone holds from any escheat [that is, a fief reverting to the lord in the absence of an heir], as from the honor of Wallingford, or Nottingham, or Boulogne, or Lancaster, or from other escheats which are in our hands and are baronies, and he dies, his heir shall not give any other relief, nor do to us

any other service than he would do to the baron, if that barony was in the hands of the baron; and we will hold it in the same way as the baron held it.

44. Men who dwell outside the forest shall not henceforth come before our justiciars of the forest, on common summons, unless they are in a plea of the forest, or are pledges for any person or persons who are arrested on account of the forest.

45. We will not make justiciars, constables, sheriffs or bailiffs except of such as know the law of the realm and are well inclined to observe it.

46. All barons who have founded abbeys for which they have charters of kings of England, or ancient tenure, shall have their custody when they have become vacant, as they ought to have.

47. All forests which have been afforested in our time shall be disafforested immediately; and so it shall be concerning river banks which in our time have been fenced in.

48. All the bad customs concerning forests and warrens and concerning foresters and warreners, sheriffs and their servants, river banks and their guardians shall be inquired into immediately in each county by twelve sworn knights of the same county, who shall be elected by the honest men of the same county, and within forty days after the inquisition has been made, they shall be entirely destroyed by them, never to be restored, provided that we be first informed of it, or our justiciar, if we are not in England.

49. We will give back immediately all hostages and charters which have been delivered to us by Englishmen as security for peace or for faithful service.

50. We will remove absolutely from their bailiwicks the relatives of Gerard de Athyes, so that for the future they shall have no bailiwick in England; Engelard de Cygony, Andrew, Peter and Gyon de Chancelles, Gyon de Cygony, Geoffrey de Martin and his brothers, Philip Mark and his brothers, and Geoffrey his nephew and their whole retinue.

51. And immediately after the re-establishment of peace we will remove from the kingdom all foreign-born soldiers, cross-bow men, servants, and mercenaries who have come with horses and arms for the injury of the realm.

52. If anyone shall have been dispossessed or removed by us without legal judgment of his peers, from his lands, castles, franchises, or his right we will restore them to him immediately; and if contention arises about this, then it shall be done according to the judgment of the twenty-five barons, of whom mention is made below concerning the security of the peace. Concerning all those things, however, from which anyone has been removed or of which he has been deprived without legal judgment of his peers by King Henry our father, or by King Richard our brother, which we have in our hand, or which others hold, and which is our duty to guarantee, we shall have respite till the usual term of crusaders; excepting those things about which the suit has been begun or the inquisition made by our writ before our assumption of the cross; when, however, we shall return from our journey, or if by chance we desist from the journey, we will immediately show full justice in regard to them.

53. We shall, moreover, have the same respite, in the same manner, about doing justice in regard to the forests which are to be disafforested or to remain forests, which Henry our father or Richard our brother made into forests; and concerning the custody of lands which are in the fief of another, custody of which we have until now had on account of a fief which anyone has held from us by military service; and concerning the abbeys which have been founded in fiefs of others than ourselves, in which the lord of the fee has asserted for himself a right; and when we return or if we should desist from our journey we will immediately show full justice to those complaining in regard to them.

54. No one shall be seized nor imprisoned on the appeal of a woman concerning the death of anyone except her husband.

55. All fines which have been imposed unjustly and against the law of the land, and all penalties imposed unjustly and against the law of the land are altogether excused, or will be on the judgment of the twenty-five barons of whom mention is made below in connection with the security of the peace, or on the judgment of the majority of them, along with the aforesaid Stephen, archbishop of Canterbury, if he is able to be present, and others whom he may wish to call for this purpose along with him. And if he should not be able to be present, nevertheless the business shall go on without him, provided that if any one or more of the aforesaid twenty-five barons are in a similar suit they should be removed as far as this particular judgment goes, and others who shall be chosen and put upon oath by the remainder of the twenty-five shall be substituted for them for this purpose along with him. And if he should not be able to be present, nevertheless the business shall go on without him, provided that if any one or more of the aforesaid twenty-five barons are in a similar suit they should be removed as far as this particular judgment goes, and others who shall be chosen and put upon oath by the remainder of the twenty-five shall be substituted for them for this purpose.

56. If we have dispossessed or removed any Welshmen from their lands, or franchises, or other things, without legal judgment of their peers, in England, or in Wales, they shall be immediately returned to them; and if a dispute shall have arisen over this, then it shall be settled in the borderland by judgment of their peers, concerning holdings of England according to the law of England, concerning holdings of Wales according to the law of Wales, and concerning holdings of the borderland according to the law of the borderland. The Welsh shall do the same to us and ours.

57. Concerning all those things, however, from which any one of the Welsh shall have been removed or dispossessed without legal judgment of his peers by King Henry our father, or King Richard our brother, which we hold in our hands, or which others hold, and we are bound to warrant to them, we shall have respite till the usual period of crusaders, except those about which suit was begun or inquisition made by our command before our assumption of the cross. When, however, we shall return or if by chance we shall desist from our journey, we will show full justice to them immediately, according to the laws of the Welsh and the aforesaid parts.

58. We will give back the son of Llewellyn immediately, and all the hostages from Wales and the charters which had been delivered to us as a security for peace.

59. We will act toward Alexander, king of the Scots, concerning the return of his sisters and his hostages, and concerning his franchises and his right, according to the manner in which we shall act toward our other barons of England, unless it ought to be otherwise by the charters which we hold from William his father, formerly king of the Scots, and this shall be by the judgment of his peers in our court.

60. Moreover, all those customs and franchises mentioned above which we have conceded in our kingdom, and which are to be fulfilled, as far as pertains to us, in respect to our men, all men of our kingdom shall observe as far as pertains to them, clergy as well as laymen, in respect to their men.

61. Since, moreover, for the sake of God, and for the improvement of our kingdom, and for the better quieting of the hostility sprung up lately between us and our barons, we have made all these concessions; wishing them to enjoy these in a complete and firm stability forever, we make and concede to them the security described below; that is to say, that they shall elect twenty-five barons of the kingdom, whom they will, who ought with all their power to observe, hold, and cause to be observed, the peace and liberties which we have conceded to them, and by this our present charter confirmed to them; in this manner, that if we or our justiciar, or our bailiffs, or any one of our servants shall have done wrong in any way toward anyone, or shall have transgressed any of the articles of peace or security; and the wrong shall have been shown to four barons of the aforesaid twenty-five barons, let those four barons come to us or to our justiciar, if we are out of the kingdom, laying before us the transgression, and let

them ask that we cause that transgression to be corrected without delay. And if we shall not have corrected the transgression, or if we shall be out of the kingdom, if our justiciar shall not have corrected it within a period of forty days, counting from the time in which it has been shown to us or to our justiciar, if we are out of the kingdom; the aforesaid four barons shall refer the matter to the remainder of the twenty-five barons, and let those twenty-five barons with the whole community of the country distress and injure us in every way they can; that is to say by the seizure of our castles, lands, possessions, and in such other ways as they can until it shall have been corrected according to their judgment, saving our person and that of our queen, and those of our children; and when the correction has been made, let them devote themselves to us as they did before. And let whoever in the country wishes take an oath that in all the above-mentioned measures he will obey the orders of the aforesaid twenty-five barons, and that he will injure us as far as he is able with them, and we give permission to swear publicly and freely to each one who wishes to swear, and no one will we ever forbid to swear. All those, moreover, in the country who of themselves and their own will are unwilling to take an oath to the twenty-five barons as to distressing and injuring us along with them, we will compel to take the oath by our mandate, as before said. And if any one of the twenty-five barons shall have died or departed from the land or shall in any other way be prevented from taking the above-mentioned action, let the remainder of the aforesaid twenty-five barons choose another in his place, according to their judgment, who shall take an oath in the same way as the others. In all those things, moreover, which are committed to those five and twenty barons to carry out, if perhaps the twenty-five are present, and some disagreement arises among them about something, or if any of them when they have been summoned are not willing or are not able to be present, let that be considered valid and firm which the greater part of those who are present arrange or command, just as if the whole twenty-five had agreed in this; and let the aforesaid twenty-five swear that they will observe faithfully all the things which are said above, and with all their ability cause them to be observed. And we will obtain nothing from anyone, either by ourselves or by another by which any of these concessions and liberties shall be revoked or diminished; and if any such thing shall have been obtained, let it be invalid and void, and we will never use it by ourselves or by another.

62. And all ill-will, grudges, and anger sprung up between us and our men, clergy and laymen, from the time of the dispute, we have fully renounced and pardoned all. Moreover, all transgressions committed on account of this dispute, from Easter in the sixteenth year of our reign till the restoration of peace, we have fully remitted to all, clergy and laymen, and as far as pertains to us, fully pardoned. And moreover we have caused to be made for them testimonial letters-patent of lord Stephen, archbishop of Canterbury, lord Henry, archbishop of Dublin, and of the aforesaid bishops and of master Pandulf, in respect to that security and the concession named above.

63. Wherefore we will and firmly command that the church of England shall be free, and that the men of our kingdom shall have and hold all the aforesaid liberties, rights and concessions, well and peacefully, freely and quietly, fully and completely, for themselves and their heirs, from us and our heirs, in all things and places, forever, as before said. It has been sworn, moreover, as well on our part as on the part of the barons, that all these things spoken of above shall be observed in good faith and without any evil intent. Witness the above names and many others. Given by our hand in the meadow which is called Runnymede, between Windsor and Staines, on the fifteenth day of June, in the seventeenth year of our reign.

Source: Emilie Amt, ed., *Medieval England, 1000-1500: A Reader* (Ontario: Broadview Press, Ltd., 2001), pp. 214-223.

# 11.4

## INVESTITURE CONTROVERSY DOCUMENTS

*The* Magna Carta *came about, in part, because of a struggle for power between a king and a pope. Such struggles were common throughout the High and Late Middle Ages. No such struggle had as substantial an effect as the Investiture Controversy between the Holy Roman Emperor Henry IV and Pope Gregory VII. The controversy began in 1075, when the pope issued a list of papal claims to authority and power,* Dictatus Papae *("Proclamations of the Pope"). In 1076 Henry IV responded by calling for a synod, or council, to reform abuses within the church, clearly ignoring the pope's authority to call such councils; in fact, the "abuses" Henry intended to clear up included Gregory's claims to power. In Henry IV then decided to test papal claims to jurisdiction over internal church appointments in the Holy Roman Empire by appointing, or investing, his own choices for bishops, without the pope's approval, leading to his deposition and excommunication by Gregory. Henry would get his title back, and his excommunication lifted, but only after public penance. Gregory would re-depose and re-excommunicate Henry again in 1080; finally Henry would have Gregory himself deposed and exiled in 1084. The feud does not officially end until the Concordat of Worms in 1122, between Calixtus II (pope from 1119-1124) and Emperor Henry V (r. 1106-1125).*

*It must be noted that there are antecedents to this struggle which go back to centuries of conflicting theories about imperial and papal power, and that even the oath taken by Henry V at Worms in 1122 did not really resolve this underlying power struggle. It merely settled the specific fight over investiture.*

## QUESTIONS

1. Who ultimately do you think wins the Investiture Controversy, the pope or the king?
2. What authorities does Gregory VII base the claims of *Dictatus Papae* on?
3. What do these documents tell us about how emperors viewed the function of the earthly church?

## DICTATUS PAPAE

1. That the Roman church was established by God alone.
2. That the Roman pontiff alone is rightly called universal.
3. That he alone has the power to depose and reinstate bishops.
4. That his legate, even if he be of lower ecclesiastical rank, presides over bishops in council, and has the power to give sentence of deposition against them.
5. That the pope has the power to depose those who are absent.
6. That, among other things, we ought not to remain in the same house with those whom he has excommunicated.

7. That he alone has the right, according to the necessity of the occasion, to make new laws, to create new bishoprics....
8. That he alone may use the imperial insignia.
9. That all princes shall kiss the foot of the pope alone.
10. That his name alone is to be recited in the churches.
11. That the name applied to him belongs to him alone.
12. That he has the power to depose emperors.
13. That he has the right to transfer bishops from one see to another when it becomes necessary.
14. That he has the right to ordain as a cleric anyone from any part of the church whatsoever.
15. That anyone ordained by him may rule [as bishop] over another church....
16. That no general synod may be called without his order.
17. That no action of a synod and no book shall be regarded as canonical without his authority.
18. That his decree can be annulled by no one, and that he can annul the decrees of anyone.
19. That he can be judged by no one.
20. That no one shall dare to condemn a person who has appealed to the Apostolic See.
21. That the important cases of any church whatsoever shall be referred to the Roman Church.
22. That the Roman Church has never erred and will never err to all eternity, according to the testimony of the holy scriptures.
23. That the Roman pontiff who has been canonically ordained is made holy by the merits of St. Peter....
24. That by his command or permission subjects may accuse their rulers.
25. That he can depose and reinstate bishops without the calling of a synod.
26. That no one can be regarded as catholic who does not agree with the Roman Church.
27. That he has the power to absolve subjects from their oath of fidelity to wicked rulers.

✢ ✢ ✢

## THE LETTER OF HENRY IV TO GREGORY VII, JANUARY 24, 1076

Henry, king not by usurpation, but by the holy ordination of God, to Hildebrand, not pope, but false monk.

This is the salutation which you deserve, for you have never held any office in the Church without making it a source of confusion and a curse to Christian men instead of an honor and a blessing. To mention only the most obvious cases out of many, you have not only dared to touch the Lord's anointed, the archbishops, bishops, and priests, but you have scorned them and abused them, as if they were ignorant servants not fit to know what their master was doing. This you have done to gain favor with the vulgar crowd. You have declared that the bishops know nothing and that you know everything; but if you have such great wisdom you have used it not to build but to destroy. Therefore we believe that St. Gregory, whose name you have presumed to take, had you in mind when he said: "The heart of the prelate is puffed up by the abundance of subjects, and he thinks himself more powerful than all others." All this we have endured because of our respect for the papal office, but you have mistaken our humility for fear, and have dared to make an attack upon the royal and imperial authority which we received from God. You have even threatened to take it away, as if we had received it from you, and as if the empire and kingdom were in your disposal and not in the disposal of God. Our Lord Jesus Christ has called us to the government of the empire, but he never called you to the rule of the Church. This is the way you have gained advancement in the Church: through craft you have obtained wealth; through wealth you have obtained favor; through favor, the power of the sword; and through the power of the sword, the papal seat, which is the seat of peace; and then from the seat of peace you have expelled peace. For you have incited subjects to rebel against their prelates by teaching them to despise the bishops, their rightful rulers. You have given to laymen the authority over priests, whereby they condemn and depose those whom the bishops have put over them to teach them. You have attacked me, who, unworthy as I am, have yet been anointed to rule among the anointed of God, and who, according to the teaching of the fathers, can be judged by no one save God alone, and can be deposed for no crime except infidelity. For the holy fathers in the time of the apostate Julian did not presume to pronounce sentence of deposition against him, but left him to be judged and condemned by God. St. Peter himself said: "Fear God, honor the king" [1 Pet. 2:17]. But you, who fear not God, have dishonored me, whom He has established. St. Paul, who said that even an angel from heaven should be accursed who taught any other than the true doctrine, did not make an exception in your favor, to permit you to teach false doctrines. For he says: "But though we, or an angel from heaven, preach any other gospel unto you than that which we have preached unto you, let him be accursed" [Gal. 1:8]. Come down, then, from that apostolic seat which you have obtained by violence; for you have been declared accursed by St. Paul for your false doctrines and have been condemned by us and our bishops for your evil rule. Let another ascend the throne of St. Peter, one who will not use religion as a cloak of violence, but will teach the life-giving doctrine of that prince of the apostles. I, Henry, king by the grace of God, with all my bishops, say unto you: "Come down, come down, and be accursed through all the ages."

✤ ✤ ✤

# GREGORY VII'S FIRST EXCOMMUNICATION AND DEPOSITION OF HENRY IV

St Peter, prince of the apostles, incline your ear to me, I beseech you, and hear me, your servant, whom you have nourished from my infancy and have delivered from my enemies who hate me for my fidelity to you. You are my witness, as are also my mistress, the mother of God, and St. Paul your brother, and all the other saints, that your holy Roman church called me to its government against my own will, and that I did not gain your throne by violence; that I would rather have ended my days in exile than have obtained your place by fraud or for worldly ambition. It is not by my efforts, but by your grace, that I am set to rule over the Christian world which was specially entrusted to you by Christ. It is by your grace and as your representative that God has given to me the power to bind and to loose in heaven and in earth. Confident of my integrity and authority, I now declare in the name of omnipotent God, the Father, Son, and Holy Spirit, that Henry, son of the emperor Henry, is deprived of his kingdom of Germany and Italy; I do this by your authority and in defense of the honor of your church, because he has rebelled against it. He who attempts to destroy the honor of the Church should be deprived of such honor as he may have held. He has refused to obey as a Christian should, he has not returned to God from whom he had wandered, he has had dealings with excommunicated persons, he has done many iniquities, he has despised the warnings which, as you are witness, I sent to him for his salvation, he has cut himself off from your Church, and has attempted to rend it asunder; therefore, by your authority, I place him under a curse. It is in your name that I curse him, that all people may know that you are Peter, and upon your rock the Son of the living God has built his Church, and the gates of hell shall not prevail against it.

✤ ✤ ✤

# THE CONCORDAT OF WORMS

*The Oath of Calixtus II*

Calixtus, bishop, servant of the servants of God, to his beloved son, Henry, by the grace of God emperor of the Romans, Augustus.

We hereby grant that in Germany the elections of the bishops and abbots who hold directly from the crown shall be held in you presence, such elections to be conducted canonically and without simony or other illegality. In the case of disputed elections you shall have the right to decide between the parties, after consulting with the archbishop of the province and his fellow-bishops. You shall confer the regalia of the office upon the bishop or abbot elect by the scepter, and this shall be done freely without exacting any payment from him; the bishop or abbot elect on his part shall perform all the duties that go with the holding of the regalia.

In other parts of the empire the bishops shall receive the regalia from you in the same manner within six months of their consecration, and shall in like manner perform all the duties that go with them. The undoubted rights of the Roman Church, however, are not to be regarded as prejudiced by this concession. If at any time you shall have occasion to complain of the carrying out of these provisions, I will undertake to satisfy your grievances as far as shall be consistent with my office. Finally, I hereby make a true and lasting peace with you and with all of your followers, including those who supported you in the recent controversy.

*The Oath of Henry V*

In the name of the holy and undivided Trinity.

For the love of God and his holy church and of Pope Calixtus, and for the salvation of my soul, I, Henry, by the grace of God, emperor of the Romans, Augustus, hereby surrender to God and his apostles, Sts. Peter and Paul, and to the holy Catholic Church, all investiture by ring and staff. I agree that elections and consecrations shall be conducted canonically and shall be free from all interference. I surrender also the possessions and regalia of St. Pater which have been seized by me during this quarrel, or by my father in his lifetime, and which are now in my possession, and I promise to aid the Church to recover such as are held by any other persons. I restore also the possessions of all other churches and princes, clerical or secular, which have been taken away during the course of this quarrel, which I have, and promise to aid them to recover such as are held by any other persons.

Finally, I make true the lasting peace with Pope Calixtus and with the holy Roman Church and with all who are or have ever been of his party. I will aid the Roman Church whenever my help is asked, and will do justice in all matters in regard to which the Church may have occasion to make compliant.

Source: Andrea, Alfred, ed. *The Medieval Record: Sources of Medieval History*. Boston: Houghton Mifflin Company, 1997), pp. 314-317.

❖

## QUESTIONS FOR PART 11

1.  By the end of the High Middle Ages, which has more power over individual Europeans, the church or the state?
2.  What options did royal subjects have to express their dissatisfaction with their kings? Were those options class based?
3.  Compare these documents with those of the previous section; what common themes can you identify from this three hundred year period of Western history?

# PART 12

❧

# INTERSECTION OF MEDIEVAL CULTURES: THE CRUSADES

From Spain to Jerusalem, the most common interaction between western Europeans and other cultures in the High and Late Middle Ages was one of warfare. In addition to warfare, there were other modes of contact between Europe and other cultures, primarily trade and missionary activity, although it usually overlapped with military activity. In Spain, Christian kingdoms had been fighting to regain control of the peninsula since the Muslim invasion of the eighth century. The *Reconquista* would finally end in 1492, when Ferdinand of Aragon defeated the last Muslim stronghold of Granada and the last Spanish Jews were either exiled or converted to Christianity. Other Jewish communities in Europe were also targets of Christian violence. From 1096 onward Jews were massacred, marginalized by the Catholic Church at the Fourth Lateran Council of 1215, and exiled by England and France.

In 1095, Western Christians turned their military attention outside the continent, launching a series of Crusades that would last until the thirteenth century. The First Crusade turned out to be only one of many, and the end result was not just warfare between Christian and Muslim, but ultimately between Christian and Christian. In 1204 Venice led a Crusade against the city of Constantinople itself, and in 1226 a Crusade was called against Christian heretics in France, known as the Albigensian Crusade.

# 12.1

⚜

## URBAN II'S CALL FOR THE FIRST CRUSADE

*The First Crusade began in 1095 when Pope Urban II sent out a call for all "servants of God" to take up arms and rescue the Byzantine Empire from Muslim expansion. Urban also wanted to recapture the Holy Land, restoring Christian control to Jerusalem. The Call came in response to a plea from Byzantine Emperor Alexius II Comnenus, who had written a letter to Urban requesting soldiers to augment his forces. Instead, Christians of all social classes answered the Call; the first Crusader "army" to reach Constantinople was made up of ordinary pilgrims, men and women, most of who lacked any military training. Successive waves of actual soldiers, divided by feudal allegiance and nationality into fiercely competitive armies, succeeded in capturing the Holy Land in 1099, and established several Christian kingdoms.*

162

————— ✦ —————

## QUESTIONS

1. How does Urban use the Call for a Crusade to bolster his own power as pope?
2. What benefit does Urban promise those who die in battle or on the way to the Crusade? What else might motivate someone to go on Crusade?
3. Of the four accounts, Guibert of Nogent was probably not present when Urban gave the actual speech. How does his account differ from the other three?

*Fulcher of Chartres*

Most beloved brethren: Urged by necessity, I Urban, by the permission of God chief bishop and prelate over the whole world, have come into these parts as an ambassador with a divine admonition to you, the servants of God....

"Although, O sons of God, you have promised more firmly than ever to keep the peace among yourselves and to preserve the rights of the church, there remains still an important work for you to do. Freshly quickened by the divine correction, you must apply the strength of your righteousness to another matter which concerns you as well as God. For your brethren who live in the east are in urgent need of your help, and you must hasten to give them the aid which has often been promised them. For, as most of you have heard, the Turks and Arabs have attacked them and have conquered the territory of Romania [that is, the Greek empire] as far west as the shore of the Mediterranean and the Hellespont, which is called the Arm of St. George. They have occupied more and more of the lands of those Christians, and have overcome them in seven battles. They have killed and captured many, and have destroyed the churches and devastated the empire. If you permit them to continue thus for a while with impunity, the faithful of God will be much more widely attacked by them. On this account I, or rather the Lord, beseech you as Christ's heralds to publish this everywhere and to persuade all people of whatever rank, footsoldiers and knights, poor and rich, to carry aid promptly to those Christians and to destroy that vile race from the lands of our friends. I say this to those who are present, but it is meant also for those who are absent. Moreover, Christ commands it.

"All who die by the way, whether by land or by sea, or in battle against the pagans, shall have immediate remission of sins. This I grant them through the power of God with which I am invested. O what a disgrace, if such a despised and base race, which worships demons, should conquer a people which has the faith of omnipotent God and is made glorious with the name of Christ! With what reproaches will the Lord overwhelm us if you do not aid those who, with us, profess the Christian religion! Let those who have been accustomed to wage unjust private warfare against the faithful now go against the infidels and end with victory this war which should have been begun long ago. Let those who for a long time have been robbers now become knights. Let those who have been fighting against their brothers and relatives now fight in a proper way against the barbarians. Let those who have been serving as mercenaries for small pay now obtain the eternal reward. Let those who have been wearing themselves out in both body and should now work for a double honor. Behold! on this side will be the sorrowful and poor, on that, the rich; on this side, the enemies of the Lord, on that, his friends. Let those who go not put off the journey, but rent their lands and collect money for their expenses; and as soon as winter is over and spring comes, let them eagerly set out on the way with God as their guide."

*Robert the Monk*

In 1095 a great council was held at Auvergne, in the city of Clermont. Pope Urban II, accompanied by cardinals and bishops, presided over it. It was made famous by the presence of many bishops and princes from France and Germany. After the council had attended to ecclesiastical matters, the pope went out into a public square, because no house was able to hold the people, and addressed them in a very persuasive speech, as follows:

"O race of Franks, O people who live beyond the mountains [that is, from Rome], O people loved and chosen by God, as is clear from your many deeds, distinguished over all other nations by the situation of your land, your catholic faith, and your regard for the holy church, we have a special message and exhortation for you. For we wish you to know what a grave matter has brought us to your country. The sad news has come from Jerusalem and Constantinople that the people of Persia, an accursed and foreign race, enemies of God, 'a generation that set not their heart aright, and whose spirit was not steadfast with God' [Ps. 78-8], have invaded the lands of those Christians and devastated them with the sword, rapine, and fire. Some of the Christians they have carried away as slaves; others they have put to death. The churches they have either destroyed or turned into mosques. They desecrate and overthrow the altars. They circumcise the Christians and pour the blood from the circumcision on the altars or in the baptismal fonts. Some they kill in a horrible way by cutting open the abdomen, taking out a part of the entrails and tying them to a stake; they then beat them and compel them to walk until all their entrails are drawn out and they fall to the ground. Some they use as targets for their arrows. They compel some to stretch out their necks, and then they try to see whether they can cut off their heads with one stroke of the sword. It is better to say nothing of their horrible treatment of the women. They have taken from the Greek empire a tract of land so large that it takes more than two months to walk through it. Whose duty is it to avenge this and recover that land, if not yours? For to you more than to other nations the Lord has given military spirit, courage, agile bodies, and the bravery to strike down those who resist you. Let your minds be stirred to bravery by the deeds of your forefathers, and by the efficiency and greatness of Charles the Great, and of Louis his son, and of the other kings who have destroyed Turkish kingdoms and established Christianity in their lands. You should be moved especially by the holy grave of our Lord and Savior which is now held by unclean peoples, and by the holy places which are treated with dishonor and irreverently befouled with their uncleanness.

"O bravest knights, descendants of unconquered ancestors, do not be weaker than they, but remember their courage. If you are kept back by your love for your children, relatives, and wives, remember what the Lord says in the Gospel: 'He that loveth father or mother more than me is not worthy of me' [Matt. 10:37]; 'and everyone that hath forsaken houses, or brothers, or sisters, or father, or mother, or wife, or children, or land for my name's sake shall receive a hundredfold and shall inherit everlasting life' [Matt. 19:29]. Let no possessions keep you back, no solicitude for your property. Your land is shut in on all sides by the sea and mountains and is too thickly populated. There is not much wealth here and the soil scarcely yields enough to support you. On this account you kill and devour each other, and carry on war and mutually destroy each other. Let your hatred and quarrels cease, your civil wars come to an end and all your dissensions stop. Set out on the road to the holy sepulcher, take the land from that wicked people and make it your own. That land which, as the scriptures says, if lowing with milk and honey, God gave to the children of Israel. Jerusalem is the best of all lands, more fruitful than all others, as it were a second paradise of delights. This land our Savior made illustrious by his birth, beautiful with his life, and sacred with his suffering; he redeemed it with his death and glorified it with his tomb. This royal city is now held captive by her enemies, made pagan by those who know not God.

She asks and longs to liberated and does not cease to beg you to come to her aid. She asks aid especially from you because, as I have said, God has given more of the military spirit to you than to other nations. Set out on this journey and you will obtain the remission of your sins and be sure of the incorruptible glory of the kingdom of heaven."

When Pope Urban had said this and much more of the same sort, all who were present were moved to cry out with one accord, "It is the will of God, it is the will of God." When the pope heard this he raised his eyes to heaven and gave thanks to God, and commanding silence with a gesture of his hand, he said: "My dear brethren, today there is fulfilled in you that which the Load says in the Gospel, 'Where two or three are gathered together in my name, there I am in the midst' [Matt. 18:20]. For unless the Lord God had been in your minds you would not all have said the same thing. For although you spoke with many voices, nevertheless, it was one and the same thing that made you speak. So I say unto you, God, who put those words into your hearts, has caused you to utter them. Therefore let these words be your battle cry because God caused you to speak them. Whenever you meet the enemy in battle, you shall all cry out, 'It is the will of God, it is the will of God.' And we do not command the old or weak to go, or those who cannot bear arms. No women shall go without their husbands, or brothers, or proper companions, for such would be a hindrance rather than a help, a burden rather than an advantage. Let the rich aid the poor and equip them for fighting and take them with them. Clergymen shall not go without the consent of their bishop, for otherwise the journey would be of no value to them. Nor will this pilgrimage be of any benefit to a layman if he goes without the blessing of his priest. Whoever therefore shall determine to make this journey and shall make a vow to God and shall offer himself as a living sacrifice, holy, acceptable to God [Rom. 12:1], shall wear a cross on his brow or on his breast. And when he returns after having fulfilled his vow he shall wear the cross on his back. I this way he will obey the command of the Lord, 'Whosoever doth not bear this cross and come after me is not worthy of me'" [Luke 1:27].

When these things had been done, while all prostrated themselves on the earth and beat their breasts, one of the cardinals, named Gregory, made confession for them, and they were given absolution for all their sins. After the absolution, they received the benediction and permission to go home.

*Baldric of Dol*

"We have heard, most beloved brethren, and you have heard what we cannot recount without deep sorrow — how, with great hurt and dire sufferings, our Christian brothers, members in Christ, are scourged, oppressed, and injured in Jerusalem, in Antioch, and the other cities of the East. Your own blood-brothers, your companions, your associates (for you are sons of the same Christ and the same church) are either subjected in their inherited homes to other masters, or are driven from them, or they come as beggars among us; or, which is far worse, they are flogged and exiled as slaves for sale in their own land. Christian blood, redeemed by the blood of Christ, has been shed, and Christian flesh, akin to the flesh of Christ, has been subjected to unspeakable degradation and servitude. Everywhere in those cities there is sorrow, everywhere misery, everywhere groaning (I say it with a sigh). The churches in which divine mysteries were celebrated in olden times are now, to our sorrow, used as stables for the animals of these people! Holy men do not possess those cities; nay, base and bastard Turks hold sway over our brothers. The blessed Peter first presided as bishop at Antioch; behold, in his own church the gentiles [that is, the non-Christians] have established their superstitions, and the Christian religion, which they ought rather to cherish, they have basely shut out from the hall dedicated to God! The estates given for the support of the saints and the patrimony of nobles set aside for the sustenance of the poor are subject to pagan tyranny, while cruel masters abuse for their own purposes the returns from these lands. The priesthood of God has been ground down into the dust. The sanctuary of God (unspeakable shame!) is everywhere profaned. Whatever Christians still remain in hiding there are sought out with unheard of tortures.

"Of holy Jerusalem, brethren, we dare not speak, for we are exceedingly afraid and ashamed to speak of it. This very city, in which, as you all know; Christ himself suffered for us, because our sins demanded it, has been reduced to the pollution of paganism and, I say it to our disgrace, withdrawn from the service of God. Such is the heap of reproach upon us who have so much deserved it! Who now serves the church of the blessed Mary in the valley of Josaphat, in which church she herself was buried in body? But why do we pass over the Temple of Solomon, nay of the Lord, in which the barbarous nations placed their idols contrary to law, human and divine? Of the Lord's Sepulcher we have refrained from speaking, since some of you with your own eyes have seen to what abominations it has been given over. The Turks violently took from it the offerings which you brought there for alms in such vast amounts, and in addition, they scoffed much and often at your religion. And yet in that place (I say only what you already know) rested the Lord; there he died for us; there he was buried. How precious would be the longed-for, incomparable place of the Lord's burial, even if God failed there to perform the yearly miracle! For in the days of his passion all the lights in the Sepulcher and round about in the church, which have been extinguished, are re-lighted by divine command. Whose heart is so stony, brethren, that it is not touched by so great a miracle? Believe me, that man is bestial and senseless whose heart such divinely manifest grace does not move to faith! And yet the gentiles see this in common with the Christians and are not turned from their ways! They are, indeed, afraid, but they are not converted to the faith; nor is it to be wondered at, for a blindness of mind rules over them. With what afflictions they wronged you who have returned and are now present, you yourselves know too well, you who there sacrificed your substance and your blood for God....

"What are we saying? Listen and learn! You, girt about with the badge of knighthood, are arrogant with great pride; you rage against your brothers and cut each other in pieces. This is not the [true] soldiery of Christ which rends asunder the sheep-fold of the Redeemer. The holy church has reserved a soldiery for herself to help her people, but you debase her wickedly to her hurt. Let us confess the truth, whose heralds we ought to be; truly, you are not holding to the way which leads to life. You, the oppressors of children, plunderers of widows; you, guilty of homicide, of sacrilege, robbers of another's rights, you who await the pay of thieves for the shedding of Christian blood — as vultures smell fetid corpses, so do you sense battles from afar and rush to them eagerly. Verily, this is the worst way, for it is utterly removed from God! If, forsooth, you wish to be mindful of your souls, either lay down the girdle of such knighthood, or advance boldly, as knights of Christ, and rush as quickly as you can to the defense of the eastern church. For she it is from whom the joys of your whole salvation have come forth, who poured into your mouths the milk of divine wisdom, who set before you the holy teachings of the Gospels. We say this, brethren, that you may restrain your murderous hands from the destruction of your brothers, and in behalf of your relatives in the faith oppose yourselves to the gentiles. Under Jesus Christ, our leader, may you struggle for your Jerusalem, in Christian battle-line, most invincible line, even more successfully than did the sons of Jacob of old — struggle, that you may assail and drive out the Turks, more execrable than the Jebusites, who are in this land, and may you deem it a beautiful thing to die for Christ in that city in which he died for us. But if it befall you to die this side of it, be sure that to have died on the way is of equal value, if Christ shall find you in his army. God pays with the same shilling, whether at the first or eleventh hour. You should shudder, brethren, you should shudder at raising a violent hand against Christians; it is less wicked to brandish your sword against Saracens. It is the only warfare that is righteous, for it is charity to risk your life for your brothers. That you may not be troubled about the concerns of tomorrow, know that those who fear God want nothing, nor those who cherish him in truth. The possessions of the enemy, too, will be yours, since you will make spoil of their treasures and return victorious to your own; or empurpled with our own blood, you will have gained everlasting glory. For such a commander you ought to fight, for one who lacks neither might nor wealth with which to reward you. Short is the way, little the labor, which, nevertheless, will repay you with the crown that fades not away. Accordingly, we speak with the authority of the prophet: 'Gird they sword upon thy thigh, O mighty one.' Gird yourselves, everyone of you, I say, and be valiant sons; for it is better for you to die in battle than to behold the sorrows of your race and of your holy places. Let neither property nor the alluring charms of your wives entice you from going; nor let the trials that are to be borned so deter you that you remain here."

And turning to the bishops, he said, "You brothers and fellow bishops; you, fellow priests and sharers with us in Christ, make this same announcement through the churches committed to you, and with your whole soul vigorously preach the journey to Jerusalem. When they have confessed the disgrace of their sins, do you, secure in Christ, make this same announcement through the churches committed to you, and with your whole soul vigorously preach the journey to Jerusalem. When they have confessed the disgrace of their sins, do you, secure in Christ, grant them speedy pardon. Moreover, you who are to go shall have us praying for you; we shall have you fighting for God's people. It is our duty to pray, yours to fight against the Amalekites [that is, biblical enemies of the Hebrews]. With Moses, we shall extend unwearied hands in prayer to heaven, while you go forth and brandish the sword, like dauntless warriors, against Amalek."

As those present were thus clearly informed by these and other words of this kind from the apostolic lord, the eyes of some were bathed in tears; some trembled, and yet others discussed the matter. However, in the presence of all at that same council, and as we looked on, the bishop of Puy, a man of great renown and of highest ability, went to the pope with joyful countenance and on bended knee sought and entreated blessing and permission to go. Over and above this, he won from the pope the command that all should obey him, and that he should hold sway over al the army in behalf of the pope, since all knew him to be a prelate of unusual energy and industry.

Source: S. J. Allen and Emilie Amt, eds., *The Crusades: A Reader* (Ontario: Broadview Press, 2003), pp 39-46.

# 12.2

## MASSACRE OF JEWS

*On their way to Constantinople to join with other Crusading armies, the first pilgrims who responded to Urban's Call (source 12.1) for the First Crusade launched a series of attacks on Jewish communities in Germany. These Crusaders decided that Jewish "infidels" were just as worthy a target as Muslims. This source is a Jewish description of the massacre of Jews in Mayence (Mainz) in 1096.*

---
&#10013;
---

## QUESTIONS

1. Why do the Jews view their own destruction as a sentence from God?
2. Why do some of the Jews choose suicide, or to kill their own families, when threatened by the Christians?
3. Besides the religious differences between Christians and Jews, what other motivation might the Crusaders have had for killing Jews?

. . . The hand of the Lord was heavy against His people. All the Gentiles were gathered together against the Jews in the courtyard to blot out their name, and the strength of our people weakened when they saw the wicked Edomites overpowering them. [The Edomites were the traditional foes of the Jews; here, Christians are meant.] The bishop's men, who had promised to help them, were the very first to flee, thus delivering the Jews into the hands of the enemy. They were indeed a poor support; even the bishop himself fled from his church for it was thought to kill him also because he had spoken good things of the Jews....[Archbishop Ruthard had been paid to remain and defend the Jews. He was later accused of having received some of the plunder taken from them.]

When the children of the holy covenant saw that the heavenly decree of death had been issued and that the enemy had conquered them and had entered the courtyard, then all of them — old men and young, virgins and children, servants and maids — cried out together to their Father in heaven and, weeping for themselves and for their lives, accepted as just the sentence of God. One to another they said: "Let us be strong and let us bear the yoke of the holy religion, for only in this world can the enemy kill us — and the easiest of the four deaths is by the sword. But we, our souls in paradise, shall continue to live eternally, in the great shining reflection [of divine glory]." [In Jewish law the four death penalties were: stoning, burning, beheading, strangulation.]

With a whole heart and with a willing soul they then spoke: "After all it is not right to criticize the acts of God — blessed by He and blessed by His name — who has given to us His Torah and a command to put ourselves to death, to kill ourselves for the unity of His holy name. Happy are we if we do His will. Happy is anyone who is killed or slaughtered, who dies for the unity of His name, so that he is ready to enter the World to Come, to dwell in the heavenly camp with the righteous — with Rabbi Akiba and his companions, the pillars of the universe, who were killed for His name's sake. [The Romans martyred Akiba during the Bar Kikba revolt, about 135 C.E.] Not only this; but he exchanges the world of darkness for the world of light, the world of trouble for the world of joy, and the world that passes away for the world that lasts for all eternity." Then all of them, to a man, cried out with a loud voice: "Now we must delay no longer for the enemy are already upon us. Let us hasten and offer ourselves as a sacrifice to the Lord. Let him who has a knife examine it that it not be nicked, and let him come and slaughter us for the sanctification of the Only One, the Everlasting, and then let him cut his own throat or plunge the knife into his own body." [A nick in the slaughterer's knife would make it ritually unfit.]

As soon as the enemy came into the courtyard they found some of the very pious there with our brilliant master, Isaac ben Moses. He stretched out his neck, and his head they cut off first. The others, wrapped in their fringed praying-shawls, sat by themselves in the courtyard, eager to do the will of their Creator. They did not care to flee into the chamber to save themselves for this temporal life, but out of love they received upon themselves the sentence of God. The enemy showered stones and arrows upon them, but they did not care to flee; and [Esther 9:5] "with the stroke of the sword, and with slaughter, and destruction" the foe killed all of those whom they found there. When those in the chambers saw the deed of these righteous ones, how the enemy and already come upon them, they then cried out, all of them: "There is nothing better than for us to offer our lives as a sacrifice." [The outnumbered Jews had no chance to win: Emico is reported to have had about 12,000 men.]

The women there girded their loins with strength and slew their sons and their daughters and then themselves. Many men, too, plucked up courage and killed their wives, their sones, their infants. The tender and delicate mother slaughtered the babe she had played with; all of them, men and women arose and slaughtered one another. The maidens and the young brides and grooms looked out of the windows and in a loud voice cried: "Look and see, O our God, what we do for the sanctification of Thy great name in order not to exchange you for a hanged and crucified one...."

Thus were the precious children of Zion, the Jews of Mayence, tried with ten trials like Abraham, our father, and like Hananiah, Mishael, and Azariah [who were thrown into a fiery furnace, Daniel 3:21]. They tied their sons as Abraham tied Isaac his son, they received upon themselves with a willing soul the yoke of the fear of god, the King of the Kings of Kings, the Holy One, blessed be He, rather than deny and exchange the religion of our King for [Isaiah 14:19] "an abhorred offshoot [Jesus]...." [Christians and Jews of those days often spoke contemptuously of each other's religion.] They stretched out their necks to the slaughter and they delivered their pure souls to their Father in heaven. Righteous and pious women bared their throats to each other, offering to be sacrificed for the unity of the Name. A father turning to his son or brother, a brother to his sister, a woman to her son or daughter, a neighbor to a neighbor or a friend, a groom to a bride, a fiancée to a fiancée, would kill and would be killed, and blood touched blood. The blood of the men mingled with their wives', the blood of the fathers with their children's, the blood of the brothers with their sisters', the blood of the teachers with their disciples', the blood of the grooms with their brides', the blood of the leaders with their cantors', the blood of the judges with their scribes', and the blood of infants and sucklings with their mothers'. For the unity of the honored and awe-inspiring Name were they killed and slaughtered.

The ears of him who hears these things will tingle, for who has ever heard anything like this? Inquire now and look about, was there ever such an abundant sacrifice as this since the days of the primeval Adam? Were there ever eleven hundred offerings on one day, each one of them like the sacrifice of Isaac, the son of Abraham?

For the sake of Isaac who was ready to be sacrificed on Mount Moriah, the world shook, as it is said [Isaiah 33:7]: "Behold their valiant ones cry without; [the angels of peace weep bitterly]" and [Jeremiah 4:28] "the heavens grow dark." Yet see what these martyrs did! Why did the heavens not grow dark and the stars not withdraw their brightness? Why did not the moon and the sun grow dark in their heavens when on one day, on the third of Siwan, on a Tuesday, eleven hundred souls were killed and slaughtered, among them so many infants and sucklings who had not transgressed nor sinned, so many poor, innocent souls?

Wilt Thou, despite this, still restrain Thyself, O Lord? For Thy sake it was that these numberless souls were killed. Avenge quickly the blood of Thy servants which was spilt in our days and in our sight. Amen.

## II. Rachel and Her Children

Now I shall recount an tell of the most unusual deeds that were done on that day [May 27, 1096] by these righteous ones....Who has ever seen anything like this? Who has ever heard of a deed like that which was performed by this righteous and pious woman, the young Rachel, the daughter of Rabbi Isaac ben Asher, the wife of Rabbi Judah? For she said to her friends: "I have four children. Do not spare even them, lest the Christians come, take them alive, and bring them up in their false religion. Through them, too, sanctify the name of the Holy God."

So one of her companions came and picked up a knife to slaughter her son. But when the mother of the children saw the knife, she let out a loud and bitter lament and she beat her face and breast, crying: "Where are Thy mercies, O God?" In the bitterness of her soul she said to her friend: "Do not slay Isaac in the presence of his brother Aaron lest Aaron see his brother's death and run away." The woman then took the lad Isaac, who was small and very pretty, and she slaughtered him while the mother spread out her sleeves to receive the blood, catching it in her garment instead of a basin. When the child Aaron saw that his brother Isaac was slain, he screamed again and again: "Mother, mother, do not butcher me," and ran and hid under a chest.

She had two daughters also who still lived at home, Bella and Matrona, beautiful young girls, the children of her husband Rabbi Judah. The girls took the knife and sharpened it themselves that it should not be nicked. Then the woman bared their necks and sacrificed them to the Lord God of Hosts who has commanded us not to change His pure religion but to be perfect with Him, as it is written [Deuteronomy 18:13]: "Perfect shall you be with the Lord your God."

When this righteous woman had made an end of sacrificing her three children to their Creator, she then raised her voice and called out to her son Aaron: "Aaron, where are you? You also I will not spare nor will I have any mercy." Then she dragged him out by his foot from under the chest where he had hidden himself, and she sacrificed him before God, the high and exalted. She put her children next to her body, two on each side, covering them with her two sleeves, and there they lay struggling in the agony of death. When the enemy seized the room they found her witting and wailing over them. "Show us the money that is under your sleeves," they said to her. But when it was the slaughtered children they saw, they struck her and killed her, upon her children, and her spirit flew away and her soul found peace at last. To her applied the Biblical verse [Hosea 10:14]: "The mother was dashed in pieces with her children."...

When the father saw the death of his four beautiful, lovely children, he cried aloud, weeping and wailing, and threw himself upon the sword in his hand so that his bowels came out, and he wallowed in blood on the road together with the dying who were convulsed, rolling in their life's blood. The enemy killed all those who were left in the room and then stripped them naked; [Lamentations 1:11] "See, O Lord, and behold, how abject I am become." Then the crusaders began to give thanks in the name of "the hanged one" because they had done what they wanted with all those in the room of the bishop so that not a soul escaped. [The crusaders now held a thanksgiving service in the archbishop's palace where the massacre took place.]

Source: Jacob R. Marcus, *The Jew in the Medieval World: A Sourcebook: 315-1791* (New York: Harper & Row Publishers, 1938), pp. 115-120.

# 12.3

## RICHARD I AND SALADIN: THE THIRD CRUSADE

*After nine decades of Christian control, Muslims re-conquered Jerusalem in 1187. Inevitably this led to a renewed call for crusading. Unlike previous crusades, this time the Europeans faced well-organized Muslim forces, which were unified under a Sunni Kurd named Saladin. Saladin proved a formidable enemy but also earned the respect of the Crusaders. Three European kings set sail for the Third Crusade: Richard I (d. 1199) of England, Philip II (d. 1223) of France, and Holy Roman Emperor Frederick Barbarossa (d. 1190). Only Richard I, the Lionhearted, would achieve any success, although he would fail to take Jerusalem.*

*Richard had to settle for capturing Acre in 1187. It is one of the most controversial moments in the history of the Crusades. In the capture of Jerusalem Saladin had promised not to harm Christian civilians; Richard made no such promises and slaughtered thousands of Muslim prisoners at Acre. Saladin responded by ending his ban on killing Christian prisoners. In the end, however, Richard and Saladin negotiated access for Christian pilgrims to Jerusalem.*

*The following descriptions provide a chance to compare Saladin and Richard. The first is from Baha ad-Din, an Arab biographer of Saladin, and the second is from the* Deeds of Richard.

+

## QUESTIONS

1. Baha ad-Din states that Saladin showed respect for infidels by suggesting they convert to Islam. How is this respectful?
2. What are the political and military advantages for Saladin in not slaughtering Christian prisoners?
3. What are the political and military advantages for Richard in slaughtering the Muslim prisoners?

*1. What I have observed of Saladin's attachment to the principles of religion, and his respect for every part of the holy law*

In our collection of authentic traditions stands the following saying of the holy Prophet [that is, Mohammed]: "Islam is built upon five columns: confession of the unity of God, the regular performance of prayer, payment of the tenth in charity, the fast of the month Ramadon, and pilgrimage to the holy house of God [in Mecca]. Saladin — may God be merciful to him! — truly believed in the doctrines of the faith, and often recited prayers in praise of God. He had accepted the dogmas of religion upon demonstrable proofs, the result of his conversations with the most learned doctors and the most eminent jurisconsults. In these arguments he acquired knowledge that enabled him to speak to the purpose when a discussion took place in his presence, although he did not employ the technical language of the lawyers. These conversations confirmed him in a true faith, which remained undisturbed by any doubt, and, in his case, prevented the arrow of speculation from overshooting the mark, and striking at last on doubt and infidelity.

The learned doctor Kotb ed-Uin en-Nisaburi had composed an exposition of Islam for the benefit of this prince, containing all that was necessary for him to know. As [Saladin] was much pleased with this treatise, he made his younger sons learn it by heart, so that good doctrine might be established in their souls from their tenderest years. I have myself seen him take this book and read it aloud to his children, after they had committed its contents to memory.

As to prayer, he was always regular in his attendance at the public service [on Fridays], and he said one day that for several years he had never failed in this duty. When he was ill, he used to send for the imam [that is, teacher] alone, and forcing himself to keep on his feet, would recite the Friday prayers. He recited the usual prayers regularly, and, if he woke during the night, said a prayer. If he did not wake, he used to pray before the morning prayer. As long as consciousness lasted, he never failed to say his prayers. I saw him perform this duty regularly during his last illness, and he discontinued it only during the three days in which his mind was wandering. When he was traveling, he used to get down from his horse at the appointed hours to pray.

Let us speak of his tenth in charity. The sum of money he left at his death was not large enough to be submitted to this tax; his private charities had absorbed everything. He who had possessed such abundant wealth left in his treasury, when he died, only forty-seven Nasri dirhems [equivalent to Greek drachmas], and a single Tyrian gold piece [that is, a gold coin minted at Tyre]. He left neither goods, nor house, nor real estate, neither garden, nor village, nor cultivated land, nor any other species of property....

## 5. Of his zeal in fighting in God's cause

God almighty said (Quran 29:69): "Those who fight strenuously for us we will surely guide in our way, for, verily, God is with those who do well." There are numerous texts in the Quran exhorting us to fight for the faith. And, of a truth, the sultan entertained an ardent passion for the holy war; his mind was always filled with it. Therefore one might swear, in absolute security and without risk of perjury, that from the time when he first issued forth to fight the infidel, he spent not a single piece of gold or silver except for the carrying on of the holy war or for distribution among his troops. With him to wage war in God's name was a veritable passion; his whole heart was filled with it, and he gave body and soul to the cause. He spoke of nothing else; all his thoughts were of instruments of war; his soldiers monopolized every idea. He showed all deference to those who talked of the holy war and who encouraged the people to take part in it. His desire to fight in God's cause forced him to leave his family, his children, his native land, the place of his abode, and all else in his land. Leaving all these earthly enjoyments, he contented himself with dwelling beneath the shadow of a tent, shaken to the right hand and to the left by the breath of every wind....

## 8. His care to be polite:

The holy Prophet said: "I have been sent to make manifest in all their beauty the noble qualities of the soul." When any man gave his hand to the Prophet he clasped it until the other withdrew it. And so, too, our sultan was very noble of heart; his face expressed kindliness, his modesty was great, and his politeness perfect. No visitor ever came to him without being given to eat, and receiving what he desired. He greeted everyone, even infidels, politely. For instance, after the conclusion of peace in the month of

Shawâl, in the year 588 [that is, Oct. to Nov. 1192], he left Jerusalem to journey to Damascus, and whilst he was on his way he saw the [Frankish] prince of Antioch, who had come up unexpectedly, and was standing at the entrance of his tent. This prince had come to ask something from him, and the sultan gave him back el 'Amk, which territory he had acquired in the year 584 [that is, 1188-1189), at the time of the conquest of the coastal lands. So, too, I was present at Nazareth when the sultan received the visit of the [Frankish] lord of Sidon; he showed him every mark of respect, treated him with honor, and admitted him to his own table. He even proposed to him that he should embrace Islam, set before him some of the beauties of our religion, and urged him to adopt it....

I was present one day when a Frankish prisoner was brought before him. This man was in such a state of excitement that his terror was visible in every feature. The interpreter asked him the cause of his fear, and God put the following answer in the mouth of the unfortunate fellow: "Before I saw his face I was greatly afraid, but now that I am in the presence [of Saladin] and can see him, I am certain that he will do me no harm." The sultan, moved by these words, gave him his life, and sent him away free.

I was attending the prince on one of the expeditions he used to make on the flanks of the enemy, when one of the scouts brought up a woman, rending her garments, weeping and beating her breast without ceasing. "This woman," the soldier said, "came out from among the Franks, and asked to be taken to the sultan; so I brought her here." The sultan asked her, through his interpreter, what was the matter, and she replied: "Some Muslim thieves got into my tent last night and carried off my child, a little girl. All night long I have never ceased begging for help, and our princes advised me to appeal to the king of the Muslims. 'He is very merciful,' they said. 'We will allow you to go out to seek him and ask for your daughter.' Therefore they permitted me to pass through the lines, and in you lies my only hope of finding my child." The sultan was moved by her distress; tears came into his eyes, and, acting from the generosity of his heart, he sent a messenger to the market-place of the camp, to seek her little one and bring her away, after repaying her purchaser the price he had given. It was early morning when her case was heard, and in less than an hour the horseman returned, bearing the little girl on his shoulder. As soon as the mother caught sight of her, she threw herself on the ground, rolling her face in the dust, and weeping so violently that it drew tears from all who saw her. She raised her eyes to heaven, and uttered words which we did not understand. We gave her back her daughter, and she was mounted to return to the enemy's army.

The sultan was very averse to the infliction of corporal punishment on his servants, even when they cheated him beyond endurance. On one occasion two purses filled with Egyptian gold pieces had been lodged in the treasury; these were stolen, and two purses full of copper coins left in their place. All he did was to dismiss the people employed in that department of his service.

In the year 583 [that is, 1187], at the battle of Hattin — a famous day's fight of which, please God, we shall speak in its proper place — Prince Arnat [that is, Reynald of Châtillon], lord of el-Kerak, and the king of the Franks of the seacoast [that is, Guy of Lusignan], were both taken prisoner, and the sultan commanded them to be brought before him. This accursed Arnat was a great infidel, and a very strong man. On one occasion, when there was a truce between the Muslims and the Franks, he had treacherously attacked and carried off a caravan that passed through his territory, coming from Egypt. He seized these people, put them to torture, and put some of them in grain-pits, and imprisoned some in narrow cells. When they objected that there was a truce between the two peoples, he replied: "Ask your Mohammed to deliver you." The sultan, to whom these words were reported, took an oath to slay the infidel with his own hand, if God should ever place him in his power. The day of the battle of Hattin God delivered this man into the hands of the sultan, and he resolved at once to slay him, that he might fulfill his oath. He commanded him to be brought before him, together with the king. The latter complained of thirst, and the sultan ordered a cup of sherbet to be given him. The king, having drunk some of if, handed the cup to Arnat, whereupon the sultan said to the interpreter: "Say to the king, 'It is you who give him drink, but I give him neither to drink nor to eat.'" By these words he wished it to be understood that honor forbade him to harm any man who had tasted his hospitality. He then struck him on the neck with his own hand, to fulfill the vow he had made. After this, when he had taken Acre, he delivered all the prisoners, to the number of about four thousand, from their wretched durance, and sent them back to their own country and their homes, giving each of them a sum of money for the expenses of his journey. This is what I have been told by many persons, for I was not present myself when it took place....

King Richard...turned his attention to packing up the petraries and mangonels for transportation. For when the time had expired which had been fixed by the Turks for the restoration of the cross and the ransom of the hostages, after waiting three weeks, according to the conditions, to see if Saladin would keep his word and covenant, the king regarded him as a transgressor, as Saladin appeared not to care about it at all; and perhaps this happened by the dispensation of God, so that something more advantageous might be obtained. But the Saracens asked further time to fulfill their promise and make search for the cross....

When it became clearly evident to King Richard that a longer period had elapsed than had been agreed, and that Saladin was obdurate and would not bother to ransom the hostages, he called together a council of the chiefs of the people, by whom it was resolved that the hostages should all be hanged, except a few nobles of the higher class, who might ransom themselves or be exchanged for some Christian captives. King Richard, aspiring to destroy the Turks root and branch, and to punish their wanton arrogance, as well as to abolish the law of Mohammed, and to vindicate the Christian religion, on the Friday before the Assumption of the blessed virgin Mary, ordered 2,700 of the Turkish hostages to be led forth from the city and hanged; his soldiers marched forward with delight to fulfill his commands and to retaliate, with the assent of divine grace, by taking revenge upon those who had destroyed so many of the Christians with missiles from bows and crossbows.... [The crusaders then moved toward Jerusalem, arriving in it vicinity in mid-1192, after much fighting and many delays.]

✦ ✦ ✦

*Itinerary of the Pilgrims and Deeds of Richard*

The [German] army now entered the Armenian territories: all rejoiced at having left a hostile kingdom, and at their arrival in the country of the faithful. But, alas! a more fatal land awaited them, which was to extinguish the light and joy of all.... On the boarders of Armenia there was a place, surrounded on one side by steep mountains, on the other side by the river Selesius. While the packhorses and baggage were passing this river, the victorious emperor [Frederick Barbarossa] halted... [and] in consequence of the packhorses crossing the river, became at last impatient of the delay; and wishing to accelerate the march, he prepared to cross the nearest part of the stream, so as to get front of the packhorses and be at liberty to proceed. O sea! O earth! O heaven! the ruler of the [Holy] Roman Empire, ever august, in whom the glory of ancient Rome again flourished,...was overwhelmed in the waters and perished! And though those who were near him hastened to his assistance, yet his aged spark of life was extinguished by a sudden through not premature death....

When his funeral rites had been performed, they left the fatal spot as soon as possible, bearing with them the body of the emperor adorned with royal magnificence, that it might be carried to Antioch. There the flesh, being boiled from the bones, reposes in the church of the apostolic see, and the bones were conveyed by sea to Tyre, to be transported from there to Jerusalem.... The [emperor's army], arriving at Antioch after many and long fastings, gave way too plentifully to their appetites, and [many] died of sudden repletion, and so...the greater part of the great army perished, and most of the survivors returned to their own countries. A small body of them, ashamed to return, served under the emperor's son....

After Easter [1191] there arrived [at Acre] Philip, king of France, and not long after him, Richard, king of England.... Around [Acre] the besiegers lay in countless multitudes, chosen from every nation throughout Christendom and under the face of heaven, and well fitted for the labors and fatigues of war; for the city had now been besieged a long time, and had been afflicted by constant toil and tribulation, but the pressure of famine, and every kind of adversity, as we have before described. Moreover, beyond the besiegers was seen the Turkish army, not in a compact body, but covering the mountains and valleys, hills and plains, with tents, the colors of whose various forms were reflected by the sun.... King Richard beheld and counted all their army, and when he arrived in port, the king of France and a whole army of natives, and the princes, chiefs, an nobles, came forth to meet him and welcome him, with joy and exultation, for they had eagerly long for his arrival....

The city of Acre, from its strong position, and its being defended by the choicest men of the Turks, appeared difficult to take by assault. The French had hitherto spent their labor in vain in constructing machines and engines for breaking down the walls, with the greatest care; for whatever they erected, at a great expense, the Turks destroyed with Greek fire or some devouring conflagration....

Source: S. J. Allen and Emilie Amt, eds., *The Crusades: A Reader* (Ontario: Broadview Press, 2003), pp. 148-153, 170-172.

# 12.4

⚜

# TEUTONIC KNIGHTS IN POLAND

*Crusading orders — knights who took religious vows yet remained primarily soldiers — became popular after the success of the First Crusade. The Knights Templar, the Knights of St. John (the Hospitallers) and the Teutonic Knights are just three of these warrior monastic orders. Even when there were no more crusades to the Holy Land these orders remained active; the Templars became bankers until their dissolution in 1312, the Knights of St. John controlled Rhodes and established hospitals, and the Teutonic Knights turned their attention to eastern Europe and the conquest of the Prussians of Poland, and the conversion of the Slavs.*

⚜

## QUESTIONS

1. Do these German chronicles present anything to admire about the Prussians?
2. Compare these documents to the following source on the Mongols (Source 12.5); do the European observers view each of these groups the same?
3. Which temporal lord had final authority over the Teutonic Knights?

*Concerning Brother Herman von Salza, fourth master of the German house*

This powerful hero received God's blessing in many manifestations of grace. In all his actions he was eloquent, wise, far-seeing, just, honorable, and kind. When he saw the order, as master of which the brothers had elected him, in such a miserable condition, he said with a sigh: "Oh, heavenly God, I would gladly lose an eye if only the order, in my time, would increase enough so that it could equip ten knightly brothers." Thus he prayed fervently. And you, most gentle Christ, who are always willing to fulfill the wishes of the just who beseech you, what did you do? Did you let his prayer go unheard? No, your sweet kindness gave him all he prayed for: while he was master, the order increased in wealth and power so greatly that after his death it numbered two thousand brothers of German origin and of excellent manly strength....

Master Hermann also acquired for his order the most useful and best papal and imperial privileges. Also the order was given many a territory in Apulia, Greece, Cilicia, and Germany, Transylvania, Livonia, and Prussia....

God loved Master Hermann because he obeyed his orders, and he therefore helped him to rise high. All people loved him; pope and emperor, kings, dukes, famous princes, and other courageous lords were drawn to Master Hermann to such an extent that all his wishes were fulfilled to the benefit, honor, and advantage of the order.

*How the Prussians devastated the land of Duke Conrad of Masovia and Kujavia*

The Prussians often did much harm to these lands. They burned, destroyed, murdered men and drove women and children into eternal slavery. And if a pregnant woman could not keep up with their army, they killed her, together with the unborn child. They tore children from their mothers' arms and impaled them on fence poles where the little ones died in great misery, kicking and screaming. They devastated the duke's lands to such an extent that, of all the weaker and stronger fortresses of his territory, only Plock on the Vistula was left to him.

The heathen also destroyed about two hundred and fifty parish houses and many beautiful monasteries in which monks, nuns, and the secular clergy had served God. The heathen stormed about everywhere like madmen. They killed the priests before their altars while the body and blood of our Lord Jesus Christ were devoutly being consecrated. The heathen threw God upon the ground to the outrage and infamy of the sacred object, and stamped upon the sacred body of Christ and his blood in their fury. One could further see the unclean heathen stealing in their hate chalices, lamps, and all sorts of sacred vessels. It was pitiful to see how they treated not only the worldly virgins but also those devoted to God. The devilish crowd dragged them out of the cloisters by force and, to their great distress of heart, used them for their disgusting lust.

*The Brothers of the Sword*

When Duke Conrad saw his land so miserable destroyed, and he was not able to protect it, he conferred with Bishop Christian of Prussia and the great nobles of his court about what would help him and them most. He thus created for the protection of his country the Brotherhood of the Knights of Christ. They wore white tunics with red swords and stars on them. (The duke gave the order the castle of Dobrin on the Vistula.)

*How the lands of Prussia and Kulm were given to the brothers of the order of the German house*

The fame of the heroic deeds of the Teutonic order spread so far that Conrad of Masovia heard of it. Then the idea came to him — and the spirit of God moved him so that he did not relinquish it again — to invite these brothers for the protection of his country; to ask them whether they could not, with their force, free the Christians from their heathen oppressors since the Brothers of the Sword were unable to do so.

*Imperial confirmation of the gift of land of Kulm to the Teutonic order (1226)*

In the name of the holy and undivided Trinity, Amen. Frederick II, by the grace of God, emperor of the Romans, Augustus, king of Jerusalem and Sicily. God has raised our emperorship over all kings of the earth, and expanded the sphere of our power over different zones that his name may be magnified in this world and the faith be spread among the heathen peoples. Just as he created the Holy Roman Empire for the preaching of the Gospel, so likewise we must turn our care and attention to the conquest and conversion of the heathen....

For this reason we make known to and inform with this proclamation all living and future members of our empire: Brother Hermann, the worthy master of the Holy German Hospital of St. Mary at Jerusalem and our trustworthy servant, has informed us in all submissiveness that our dear Conrad, duke of Masovia and Kujavia, intends to make provision for him and his brothers in the land of Kuhn and the land between his march and the territories of the Prussians. Therefore the brothers shall take upon themselves the trouble and, on a suitable occasion, to the honor and glory of the true God, enter into the Prussian land and occupy it. Hermann postponed the acceptance of this offer and approached our majesty first with his submissive application; if we should deign to agree, he would begin the great task, trusting in our authorization. Our majesty should then confirm to him and his house all the land which the duke gave him, as well as all the land they would gain in Prussia through their efforts; also we should grant his house through a charter all rights and liberties for this area. Then he would accept the gift of said duke and use the goods and men of his house for the invasion and conquest of the county in tireless, unremitting effort.

Considering the attitude of active Christianity of this master, and how he eagerly desires to acquire these lands for his house in the name of God, and since this land belongs to our empire; trusting also in the wisdom of this master, a man mighty in word and deed, who will take up the matter forcefully with his brothers and carry through the conquest manfully, not abandoning it as many did before him, who wasted so much energy in this undertaking for nothing, we give this master the authority to invade the land of Prussia with the forces of his house, and with all means at his disposal.

We also permit and confirm to this master, his successors and his house for all time that they shall hold the said land which they will get from Duke Conrad according to his promise, any other lands which he may give them in the future, finally, all they conquer in Prussia with the grace of God, with rights to the mountains, the flat country, rivers, forests, and lakes as if it were an ancient imperial right, freely and unencumbered by any services or taxes, without any ordinary burdens, and no one shall have to give account for this, their land. They also shall be allowed in the land they conquer now or in the future, for the benefit of their house to erect road and other toll stations, hold fairs and markets, coin money, collect taxes and other tributes, set up traffic laws for their rivers and the sea as it seems good to them; they also shall always have the right of mining gold, silver, and other metals, and salt if such are at present found in their territories, or should be found there in the future. We also give them the right to set up judges and administrators, thus to govern and lead justly the people subject to them, both those who have been converted to the true faith as well as those who live in their delusion; to punish crimes of evil-doers wisely, to examine civil and criminal matters and to make decisions according to the dictates of reason. To this we add, out of our especial grace, that this master and his successors shall have and exercise sovereign rights in all their lands in the same manner as they are enjoyed by princes of the empire exercising the fullest rights in their lands, so that they may introduce good customs and promulgate regulations through which the faith of the Christians may be strengthened and their subjects enjoy peace and quiet.

Through this charter we prohibit any prince, duke, margrave, count, court official, magistrate, bailiff, every person of high or low estate, whether temporal or spiritual, to infringe on these privileges and authorizations. Should anyone dare to do so, let him know that he will have to pay a fine of one thousand pounds of gold, one half to our treasury, the other to the ones that were injured....

*Of the images, disbeliefs, and customs of the Prussians*

[The Prussians knew neither writing nor books.] and they were very much surprised at first when they saw the letters of the knights. And thus God was unknown to them; and thence came their error that they, in their foolishness, worshipped any creature as god: thunder, sun, moon, stars, birds, animals, and even toads. They also had fields, woods, and waters which were holy to them, so that they neither plowed nor fished nor cut wood in them....

The Prussians also believed in a resurrection, but not correctly. They believed that as he is on earth, noble or common, poor or rich, powerful or not, just so would he be after the resurrection. Therefore it was customary after the death of a noble to burn with him his weapons and horse, servants and maids, beautiful clothes, hunting dogs, falcons, and whatever else belongs to the equipment of a noble. Also with the common people everything they owned was burned, because they believed it all would rise with them and continue to serve them.

Also there was a devilish fraud connected with such a death, for the relatives of the dead came to the priest and asked if he had seen somebody go or drive by his house at such and such a time of the day or night. The priest then generally described to them exactly the figure of the dead man, his gestures, his weapons and dress, servants and horses. And to make them believe him more readily, he often showed them some mark which the dead man cut or scratched into his door while driving by.

After a victory, the heathen, for their salvation, usually sacrificed to their idols one-third of their booty which they gave to the priest, who burned it for the gods. [They also sacrificed horses and cast lots.]...

Wealth and good-looking clothes they value very slightly; as they take off their furs today, they put them on tomorrow. They are ignorant of soft beds and fine food. They drink, since ancient times, only three things: water, mead, and mares' milk....

[Their greatest virtue is hospitality.] They freely and willingly share food and drink. They think they have not treated their guests politely and well if they are not so full of drink that they vomit. Usually they urge each other mutually to take an innumerable number of drinks of equal measure. When they sit down to drink, every member of the household brings a measure to his host, drinks to him out of it, and the host then gladly finishes the drink. Thus they drink to each other, and let the cup go round without rest, and it runs to and fro, now full, now empty. They do this until man and woman, host and friends, big and small, all are drunk; that is pastime to them and a great honor — to me that does not seem honorable at all.

According to an old custom, they buy their women with money. The husband keeps his wife like a maid; she is not allowed to eat at his table, and daily has to wash the feet of the members of the household and the guests.

Nobody has to beg, because the poor man can go from house to house and eat wherever he likes.

If there is a murder, there is no reconciliation until the friends of the dead have killed the guilty person or one of his close relatives. If a Prussian is met suddenly by a great calamity, he usually kills himself in his distress....

Some Prussians, in honor of their gods, bathe daily; others never. Man and woman spin thread; some wool, the others linen, whichever they think the gods like most. Some never mount a black horse; some never a white one, or one of some other color.

Source: S. J. Allen and Emilie Amt, eds., *The Crusades: A Reader* (Ontario: Broadview Press, 2003), pp. 280-284.

# 12.5

## ENCOUNTERING THE MONGOLS, WILLIAM OF RUBRUCK

*The Mongols were a nomadic, tribal people from the Asiatic steppes who were virtually unknown to the West until c. 1167. In that year, a warrior named Temuchin unified the tribes under his control and conquered the Far East, Central Asia, and the Russian kingdoms, reaching as far west as Poland and Hungary. Temuchin was granted the title of Genghis Khan, or "universal ruler." When he died in 1227, his vast empire was divided amongst his four grandsons. The European part of his empire, known as the Golden Horde, lasted only a few more decades before being gradually pushed back into the east or converted to Christianity and absorbed into the emerging Russian state.*

*In 1253 a Franciscan monk named William of Rubruck was sent by Louis IX of France into the Golden Horde to convert the Mongols (or Tartars) to Christianity. He wrote the following account of the Mongol culture for the king.*

### QUESTIONS

1. What does William hope the Crusaders of Europe will learn from his description of the Mongols?
2. How do the Mongols treat their dead?
3. Do you feel that William's mission to the Mongols was successful?

WILLIAM OF RUBRUCK ON THE MONGOLS

*William of Rubruck, and Franciscan friar, traveled into Mongol territories in 1253 as part of the ongoing Christian missionary effort to convert the Mongols to Christianity. He was probably in the* service of the French king Louis IX, to whom his account of his journey, excerpted below, is addressed. William's writings are important for their detailed (albeit western) view of Mongol life.

Source: trans. W.W. Rockhill, *The Journey of William Rubruck to the Eastern Parts of the World, 1253-55...* (London: The Hakluyt Society, 1900), second series, vol. 4, pp. 52-55, 75-84, 95-96, 1-3-105, 107, 116, 281-82; revised.

After having left Sodaia we came on the third day across the Tartars, and when I found myself among them it truly seemed to me that I had been transported into another century. I will describe to you as well as I can their mode of living and manners.

Nowhere do they have fixed dwelling-places, nor do they know where their next will be. They have divided Scythia among themselves, which extends from the Danube to the rising of the sun; and every captain, depending on the number of men under him, knows the limits of his pasture lands and where to graze in winter and in summer, spring and autumn. For in winter they go down to warmer regions in the south: in summer they go up to cooler regions towards the north. The pasture lands without water they graze over in winter when there is snow there, for the snow serves them as water.

They set up the dwelling in which they sleep on a circular frame of interlaced sticks converging into a little round hoop on the top, from which projects above a collar as a chimney, and this framework they cover over with white felt.... and they make these houses so large that they are sometimes 30 feet in width. I myself once measured the width between the wheel-tracks of a cart 20 feet, and when the house was on the cart it projected beyond the wheels on either side five feet at least....

It is the duty of the women to drive the carts, get the dwellings on and off them, milk the cows, make butter and sour curds, and dress and sew skins, which they do with a thread made of tendons. They divide the tendons into fine shreds, and then twist them into one long thread. They also sew boots, the socks and the clothing. They never wash clothes, for they say that God would be angered at this, and that it would thunder if they hung them up to dry. They will even beat those they find washing them.... Furthermore, they never wash their bowls, but when the meat is cooked they rinse out the dish in which they are about to put it with some of the boiling broth from the kettle, which they pour back into it. The women also make the felt and cover the houses.

The men make bows and arrows, manufacture stirrups and bits, make saddles, do the carpentering on [the framework] of their dwellings and the carts; they take care of the horses, milk the mares, churn the *cosmos* or mare's milk, make the skins in which it is put; they also look after the camels and load them. Both sexes look after the sheep and goats, sometimes the men, other times the women milking them....

As to their marriages, you must know that no one among them has a wife unless he buys her; so it sometimes happens that girls are well past marriageable age before they marry, for their parents always keep them until they sell them. They observe the first and second degrees of consanguinity, but no degree of affinity; thus one [man] will have at the same time or successively two sisters [as his wives]. Among them no widow marries, for the following reason: they believe that all who serve them in this life shall serve them in the next, so they believe that a widow will always return to her first husband after death. Hence this shameful custom prevails among them: that sometimes a son marries all his father's wives, except his own mother; for the dwellings of the father and mother always belong to the youngest son, so it is he who must provide for all his father's wives who come to him with the paternal household, and if he wishes it he uses them as wives, for he does not think himself injured if they return to his father after death. So when anyone has made a bargain with a man to marry his daughter, the father of the girl gives a feast, and the girl flees to her relatives and hides there. Then the father says: "Here, my daughter is yours: take her wherever you find her." Then [the bridegroom] searches for her with his friends till he finds her, and must take her by force and carry her off with a semblance of violence to his house....

When anyone dies, they lament with loud wailing, and then they are free, for they pay no taxes for the year. And if anyone is present at the death of an adult, he may not enter the dwelling even of Mangu Khan [the emperor] for the year. If it is a child who dies, the person who was present may not enter it for a month. Beside the tomb of the dead they always leave a tent if he is one of the nobles, that is, of the family of Genghis Khan, who was their first father and lord. Of him who is dead, the burying place is not known. And around these palaces where they bury their nobles there is always a camp with men watching the tombs. I did not understand that they bury treasures with their dead....

When therefore we found ourselves among these barbarians, it seemed to me, as I said before, that I had been transported into another world. They surrounded us on their horses, after having made us wait for a long while seated in the shade under our carts. The first question [they asked] was whether we had ever been among them before.... Then they asked where we came from and where we wanted to go. I told them...that we had heard that Sartach was a Christian, and that I wanted to go to him, for I had your letters to deliver to him....

There were five of us [Europeans], and the three [Mongols] who were conducting us, two driving the carts and one going with us to Sartach. The meat they had given us was insufficient, and we could find nothing to buy with money. To add to this, when we were seated in the shade under our carts, [the people of the neighborhood] pushed in most importunately among us, to the point of crushing us, in their eagerness to see all our things.... Above all this, however, I was distressed because I could do no preaching to them; the interpreter would say to me, "You cannot make me preach, I do not know the proper words to use." And he spoke the truth; for after a while, when I had learned something of the language, I saw that when I said one thing, he said a totally different one, according to what came uppermost in his mind. So, seeing the danger of speaking through him, I made up my mind to keep silence....

And so we came to Sartach's dwelling, and they raised the felt which hung before the entry, so that he could see us. Then they made the clerk and the interpreter bow [to him]; of us they did not demand it. Then they enjoined us earnestly to be most careful in going in and coming out not to touch the threshold of the dwelling, and also to chant some blessing for him. So we went in chanting, "*Salve, regina!*"...Then Coiac [A Nestorian priest who served Sartach] handed [Sartach] the censer with the incense, and he examined it, holding it in his hand most carefully. After that he handed the psalter [we had brought], at which he took a good look, as did the wife who was seated beside him. Then he handed him the Bible, and he asked if the Gospels were in it. I said that it contained all the sacred writings. He also took in his hand the cross, and asked if the image on it were that of Christ. I replied that it was. Those Nestorians and Hermenian [Christians] never make the figure of Christ on their crosses; they would thus appear to entertain some doubt of the Passion, or to be ashamed of it. Then I presented to him your letter, with translations in Arabic and Syiac, for I had had them both translated and written in these languages at Acon....

Before we left Sartach, the above-mentioned Coiac and a number of scribes of the court said to us, "You must not say that our lord is a Christian. He is not a Christian, but a Moal" [or Mongol]. For the name of Christian seems to them that of a nation. They have risen so much in their pride, that though they may believe somewhat in Christ, yet they do not wish to be called Christians, wishing to exalt their own name of Moal above all others, nor do they wish to be called Tartars. The Tartars were another people....

Of Sartach I know not whether he believes in Christ or not. This I do know, that he will not be called a Christian, and it even seemed to me that he mocked the Christians. For he is on the road of the [local] Christians,...all of whom pass by him when going to his father's household carrying presents to him, so he shows himself most attentive to them. Should, however, Saracens come along carrying more presents than they, they are sent along more expeditiously. He has Nestorian priests around him who [conduct their worship services]....

...[I]f the army of the church were to come to the Holy Land, it would be very easy to conquer or to pass through [the lands on the way]. The king of Hungary has at most 30,000 soldiers. From Cologne to Constantinople it is not more than forty days in a cart. From Constantinople it is not so far as that to the country of the king of Hermenia. In times past valiant men passed through these countries, and succeeded, though they had most powerful adversaries, whom God has since removed from the earth. Nor should we [if we followed the road] be exposed to the dangers of the sea or to the mercies of the sailor men, and the price which would have to be given for a fleet would be enough for the expenses of the land journey. I state it with confidence, that if you peasants — to say nothing of the princes and noblemen — would only travel like the Tartar princes, and be content with similar provisions, they would conquer the world.

It seems to me inexpedient to send another friar to the Tartars as I went, or as the preaching friars go; but if the lord pope, who is head of all Christians, wishes to send with proper state a bishop, and reply to the foolishness [the Mongols] have already written three times to the Franks (once to Innocent IV of blessed memory [from Guyuk Khan], and twice to you...), he would be able to tell them whatever he pleased, and also make them reply in writing. They listen to whatever an ambassador [as opposed to a lower-level envoy like a friar] has to say, and always ask if he has more to say; but he must have a good interpreter — nay, several interpreters — abundant travelling funds, and so on.

Source: S. J. Allen and Emilie Amt, eds., *The Crusades: A Reader*, ed. S. J. Allen and Emilie Amt (Ontario: Broadview Press, 2003), pp 393-396.

———— ✠ ————

## QUESTIONS FOR PART 12

1. In what ways did all the warfare of the High Middle Ages benefit Europe economically and culturally?
2. Were the Crusades an indication of how powerful the Christian faith had become in Europe, or a sign of weakness within the faith?
3. What role did monarchs play in crusading? How did the Crusades help them politically?

# PART 13

## ❧

# CRISES OF THE LATER MIDDLE AGES

The fourteenth and fifteenth centuries were two of the most catastrophic throughout the Middle Ages. Western Europe faced a series of disasters in this period: the first appearance of the Black Death in 1347, dramatic social upheavals exemplified by peasant rebellions and renewed persecutions of Jews, disintegration of the Catholic Church through the Avignon exile and the Great Schism, over a century of warfare between England and France, and finally the eruption of civil war in England. The results of these calamities were diverse, although in general the mood of Europe was one of doom and gloom for most of the period.

In spite of the dark mood, it was also a period of tremendous advancement and development. New technologies were discovered, admittedly most of them military. The decrease in population from the plague eased the burden on Europe's over-extended food supplies. Overall, cities grew more prosperous in spite of populations fleeing disease and warfare for the countryside. Although people's faith was weakened by the crises of Avignon and Schism, the Church emerged stronger. External and internal warfare only revealed the resilience of England and France. Finally, during (and often in direct response to) all of this, Europe rediscovered its classical past and the artistic and cultural movement known as the Renaissance began.

# 13.1

## ✦

# BONIFACE VIII'S BULL "UNAM SANCTUM"

*Boniface VIII was only pope for nine years, between 1294 and 1303, yet his impact on the Catholic Church was felt for the next century and a half. In 1296, Philip IV, the Fair, levied a tax on French clergy. Boniface saw this as an infringement of ecclesiastical privilege and ordered the clergy to ignore the tax. The feud between king and pope escalated, resulting in the bull "Unam Sanctum" in 1302, the broadest claim of papal power yet issued. In retaliation, royal troops seized Boniface, who was freed by Italians but quickly died (perhaps of shock from the attack). Upon the death of Boniface, Philip forced the College of Cardinals to elect a French pope, Clement V, who was encouraged to move the papal court from Rome to Avignon, where Philip promised the protection of French troops. This began the Babylonian Captivity of the Papacy, which lasted from 1305-1377.*

---- ✤ ----

## QUESTIONS

1. According to Boniface, who has the authority to judge the pope?
2. What is the two-sword theory of power?
3. Do you feel that Boniface has any justification for his claims of authority?

*(From the latest revision of the text in "Revue des Questions historiques," July, 1889, p. 255.)*

We are compelled, our faith urging us, to believe and to hold — and we do firmly believe and simply confess — that there is one holy catholic and apostolic church, outside of which there is neither salvation nor remission of sins; her Spouse proclaiming it in the canticles: "My dove, my undefiled is but one, she is the choice one of her that bare her;" which represents one mystic body, of which body the head is Christ; but of Christ, God. In this church there is one Lord, one faith and one baptism. There was one ark of Noah, indeed, at the time of the flood, symbolizing one church; and this being finished in one cubit had, namely, one Noah as helmsman and commander. And, with the exception of this ark, all things existing upon the earth were, as we read, destroyed. This church, moreover, we venerate as the only one, the Lord saying through His prophet: "Deliver my soul from the sword, my darling from the power of the dog." He prayed at the same time for His soul — that is, for Himself the Head — and for His body, — which body, namely, he called the one and only church on account of the unity of the faith promised, of the sacraments, and of the love of the church. She is that seamless garment of the Lord which was not cut but which fell by lot. Therefore of this one and only church there is one body and one head — not two heads as if it were a monster: — Christ, namely, and the vicar of Christ, St. Peter, and the successor of Peter. For the Lord Himself said to Peter, Feed my sheep. My sheep, He said, using a general term, and not designating these or those particular sheep; from which it is plain that He committed to Him *all* His sheep. If, then, the Greeks or others say that they were not committed to the care of Peter and his successors, they necessarily confess that they are not of the sheep of Christ; for the Lord says, in John, that there is one fold, one shepherd and one only. We are told by the word of the gospel that in this His fold there are two swords, — a spiritual, namely, and a temporal. For when the apostles said "Behold here are two swords" — when, namely, the apostles were speaking in the church — the Lord did not reply that this was too much, but enough. Surely he who denies that the temporal sword is in the power of Peter wrongly interprets the world of the Lord when He says: "Put up thy sword in its scabbard." Both swords, the spiritual and the material, therefore, are in the power of the church; the one, indeed, to be wielded for the church, the other by the church; the one by the knights, but at the will and sufferance of a priest. One word, moreover, ought to be under the other, and the temporal authority to be subjected to the spiritual. For when the apostle says "there is no power but of God, and the powers that are of God are ordained," they would not be ordained unless sword were under sword and the lesser one, as it were, were led by the other to great deeds. For according to St. Dionysius the law of divinity is to lead the lowest through the intermediate to the highest things. Not therefore, according to the law of the universe, are all things reduced to order equally and immediately; but the lowest through the intermediate to the highest things. Not therefore, according to the law of the universe, are all things reduced to order equally and immediately; but the lowest through the intermediate, the intermediate through the higher. But that the spiritual exceeds any earthly power in dignity and nobility we ought the more openly to confess the more spiritual things excel temporal ones. This also is made plain to our eyes from the giving of tithes, and the benediction and the sanctification; from the acceptation of this same power, from the control over those same things. For, the truth bearing witness, the spiritual power has to establish the earthly power, and to judge it if it be not good. Thus concerning the church and the ecclesiastical power is verified the prophecy of Jeremiah: "See, I have this day set thee over the nations and over the kingdoms," and the other things which follow. Therefore if the earthly power err it shall be judged by the spiritual power; but if the lesser spiritual power err, by the greater. But if the greatest, it can be judged by God alone, not by man, the apostle bearing witness. A spiritual man judges all things, but he himself is judged by no one. This authority, moreover, even though it is given to man and exercised through man, is not human but rather divine, being given by divine lips to Peter and founded on a rock for him and his successors through Christ himself whom he has confessed; the Lord himself saying to Peter: "Whatsoever thou shalt bind," etc. Whoever, therefore, resists this power thus ordained by God, resists the ordination of God, unless he makes believe, like the Manichean, that there are two beginnings. This we consider false and heretical, since by the testimony of Moses, not "in the beginnings," but "in the beginning" God created the Heavens and the earth. Indeed we declare, announce and define, that it is altogether necessary to salvation for every human creature to be subject to the Roman pontiff.

The Lateran, Nov. 14, in our 8th year. As a perpetual memorial of this matter.

Source: Ernest Henderson, ed. *Select Historical Documents of the Middle Ages* (New York: AMS Press, 1968), pp. 435-37.

# 13.2

## PEASANT REBELLION OF 1381

*There were several peasant rebellions in the fourteenth century. In 1320, French peasants rebelled, and again in the 1358 Jacquerie ("Jack Goodman," which was a colloquial term for peasant). In 1381 English peasants revolted against Richard II, and there were also rebellions that year in Flanders and in the Italian city-states. There were many reasons why individual rebellions occurred, but one common theme was the frustration by the peasants with taxes and feudal dues.*

*Jean Froissart's* Chronicle *recorded many significant events of the century, including the English Peasant Rebellion, as excerpted here.*

## QUESTIONS

1. What role does the Catholic Church play in causing this rebellion?
2. As they marched toward London, why do the rebels claim that they stand "for the King"?
3. If this is a rebellion about feudal dues and taxes, why to the rebels attack Lombards (i.e., foreigners) in London?

In these machinations they had been greatly encouraged originally by a crack-brained priest of Kent called John Ball, who had been imprisoned several times for his reckless words by the Archbishop of Canterbury. This John Ball had the habit on Sundays after mass, when everyone was coming out of church, of going to the cloisters or the graveyard, assembling the people round him and preaching thus:

'Good people, things cannot go right in England and never will, until goods are held in common and there are no more villains and gentlefolk, but we are all one and the same. In what way are those whom we call lords greater masters than ourselves? How have they deserved it? Why do they hold us in bondage? If we all spring from a single father and mother, Adam and Eve, how can they claim or prove that they are lords more than us, except by making us produce and grow the wealth which they spend? They are clad in velvet and camlet lined with squirrel and ermine, while we go dressed in coarse cloth. They have the wines, the spices and the good bread; we have the rye, the husks and the straw, and we drink water. They have shelter and ease in their fine manors, and we have hardship and toil, the wind and the rain in the fields. And from us must come, from our labour, the things which keep them in luxury. We are called serfs and beaten if we are slow in our service to them, yet we have no sovereign lord we can complain to, none to hear us and do us justice. Let us go to the King — he is young — and show him how we are oppressed, and tell him that we want things to be changed, or else we will change them ourselves. If we go in good earnest and all together, very many people who are called serfs and are held in subjection will follow us to get their freedom. And when the King sees and hears us, he will remedy the evil, either willingly or otherwise.'

These were the kind of things which John Ball usually preached in the villages on Sundays when the congregations came out from mass, and many of the common people agreed with him. Some, who were up to no good, said: 'He's right!' and out in the fields, or walking together from one village to another, or in their homes, they whispered and repeated among themselves: 'That's what John Ball says, and he's right.'...

These promises incited the people of Kent, Essex, Sussex, Bedford and the neighbouring districts and they set off and went towards London. They were a full sixty thousand and their chief captain was one Wat Tyler. With him as his companions were Jack Straw and John Ball. These three were the leaders and Wat Tyler was the greatest of them. He was a tiler of roofs, and a wicked and nasty fellow he was....

When those people saw that they would obtain nothing more, they were aflame with fury. They went back to the hill where the main body was and reported what had been said to them and that the King had gone back to the Tower. The whole mass of them began shouting together: 'To London! Straight to London!' They started off and swept down towards the city, ransacking and destroying the houses of abbots, lawyers and court officials, and came to the immediate outskirts, which are fine and extensive. They levelled several fine buildings and, in particular, the King's prisons, which are called Marshalseas, setting free all the prisoners inside. They committed many outrages in the suburbs and, when they reached the bridge, they began to threaten the Londoners because they had closed its gates. They said they would set fire to all the suburbs and then take London by storm, burning and destroying it. The common people of London, many of whom were on their side, assembled together and said: 'Why not let these good people come into the town? They are our own people and they are doing all this to help us.' So the gates had to be opened and all those famished men entered the town and rushed into the houses which had stocks of provisions. Nothing was refused them and everyone made haste to welcome them in and set out food and drink to appease them. After that, their leaders John Ball, Jack Straw and Wat Tyler, with more than thirty thousand men, went straight through London to the Palace of the Savoy, a very fine building on the Thames as you go towards the King's Palace of Westminster, and belonging to the Duke of Lancaster. They quickly got inside and killed the guards, and then sent it up in flames. Having committed this outrage they went on to the palace of the Hospitallers of Rhodes, known as St. John of Clerkenwell, and burnt it down, house, church, hospital and everything. Besides this, they went from street to street, killing all the Flemings they found in churches, chapels, and houses. None was spared. They broke into many houses belonging to Lombards and robbed them openly, no one daring to resist them. In the town they killed a wealthy man called Richard Lyon, whose servant Wat Tyler had once been during the wars in France. On one occasion Richard Lyon had beaten his servant and Wat Tyler remembered it. He led his men to him, had his head cut off in front of him, and then had it stuck on a lance and carried through the streets. So those wicked men went raging about in wild frenzy, committing many excesses on that Thursday throughout London....

They were all agreeing to this plan when suddenly the King appeared, accompanied by perhaps sixty horsemen. He had not been thinking about them, but had been intending to go on and leave London behind. When he reached the Abbey of St. Bartholomew which stands there, he stopped and looked at the great crowd and said that he would not go on without hearing what they wanted. If they were discontented, he would placate them. The nobles who were with him stopped when he did, as they must. When Wat Tyler saw this, he said to his men: 'Here's the King, I'm going to talk to him. Don't budge from here unless I give you the signal, but if I make this sign (he showed them one), move forward and kill the lot. Except the King, don't touch the King. He's young, we will make him do as we want, we can take him with us anywhere in England and we shall be the lords of the realm. No doubt of that.' There was a tailor there called John Tickle, who had delivered sixty doublets for some of those scoundrels to wear and Tyler was wearing one himself. Tickle said to him: 'Hi, sir, who's going to pay for my doublets? I want at least thirty marks.' 'Be easy now,' said Tyler. 'You'll be paid in full by tomorrow. Trust me, I'm a good enough guarantee.'

With that, he stuck his spurs into a horse he had mounted, left his companions and went straight up to the King, going so near that his horse's tail was brushing the head of the King's horse. The first words he said to the King were: 'Well, King, you see all those men over there?' 'Yes,' said the King. 'Why do you ask?' 'Because they are all under my command. They've sworn their sacred oath to do anything I tell them.' 'Good,' said the King, 'I see nothing wrong in that.' 'So,' said Tyler, who only wanted a quarrel, 'do you think, King, that these men here, and as many again in London, all under my command, are going to leave you without getting their letters? No, we're going to take them with us.'...

Just then the Lord Mayor of London arrived on horseback with a dozen others, all fully armed beneath their robes, and broke through the crowd. He saw how Tyler was behaving and said to him in the sort of language he understood: 'Fellow, how dare you say such things in the King's presence? You're getting above yourself.' The King lost his temper and said to the Mayor: 'Lay hands on him, Mayor.' Meanwhile Tyler was answering: "I can say and do what I like. What's it to do with you?' 'So, you stinking boor,' said the Mayor, who had once been a King's Advocate, 'you talk like that in the presence of the King, my natural lord? I'll be hanged if you don't pay for it.'

With that he drew a great sword he was wearing and struck. He gave Tyler such a blow on the head that he laid him flat under his horse's feet. No sooner was he down than he was entirely surrounded, so as to hide him from the crowds who were there, who called themselves his men. One of the King's squires called John Standish dismounted and thrust his sword into Tyler's belly so that he died.

Those crowds of evil men soon realized that their leader was dead. They began to mutter: 'They've killed our captain. Come on, we'll slay the lot!" They drew themselves up in the square in a kind of battle-order, each holding before him the bow which he carried. Then the King did an extraordinarily rash thing, but it ended well. As soon as Tyler was dispatched, he left his men, saying: 'Stay here, no one is to follow me,' and went alone towards those half-crazed people, to whom he said: 'Sirs, what more do you want? You have no other captain but me, I am your king, behave peaceably.' On hearing this, the majority of them were ashamed and began to break up. They were the peace-loving ones. But the bad ones did not disband; instead they formed up for battle and showed that they meant business. The King rode back to his men and asked what should be done next. He was advised to go on towards the country, since it was no use trying to run away. The Mayor said: 'That is the best thing for us to do, for I imagine the loyal men on our side who are waiting armed in their houses with their friends.'...

So those crazy men departed and split up, some going one way, some another. The King, with the nobles and their companies, went back in good order into London, to be received with joy. The first thing the King did was to visit his lady mother the Princess, who was still in the Tower Royal. When she saw her son, she was overjoyed and said: 'Ah, my son, how anxious I have been today on your account!' 'Yes, my lady,' the King answered, 'I know you have. But now take comfort and praise God, for it is a time to praise him. Today I have recovered my inheritance, the realm of England which I had lost.'

The King remained with his mother for the whole day and the lords and nobles went back peaceably to their houses. A royal proclamation was drawn up and cried from street to street, ordering all persons who were not natives of London or had lived there for less than a year to leave at once. If they were still found three at sunrise on the Sunday, they would be counted as traitors to the King and would lose their heads. When this order became known, none dared to disobey it. Everyone left in haste on that same Saturday and started back for their own districts. John Ball and Jack Straw were found hiding in an old ruined building, where they had hoped to escape the search. But they did not; their own people gave them away. The King and the nobles were delighted by their capture, for then their heads were cut off, and Tyler's too, although he was dead already, and posted up on London Bridge in place of those of the worthy men whom they had beheaded on the Thursday. News of this quickly spread around London. All the people from the distant counties who had flocked there at the summons of those wicked men set off hurriedly for their own places, and never dared to come back again.

Source: Jean Froissart, *Chronicles*, trans. Geoffrey Brereton (New York: Penguin Books, Ltd., 1968, 1978), pp. 211-230.

# 13.3

---

## THE TWELVE CONCLUSIONS OF THE LOLLARDS

*In late fourteenth century England the first heresy native to England appeared. John Wyclif (c. 1328-1384) was an Oxford theologian who questioned and ultimately rejected papal claims of authority as well as many traditional Catholic beliefs and practices. His objections were based on his close reading of scripture, which he claimed did not support the traditional power of the papacy. Wyclif's ideas were officially declared heretical by the Church, but continued to find support across England and on the continent. His English followers were known as Lollards. In 1394 they offered the following list of twelve "conclusions" on the corruption of the Church.*

--- ⚜ ---

## QUESTIONS

1. How do the Conclusions of the Lollards represent a type of crisis for the later Middle Ages?
2. Who do the Lollards blame most for what they see as the corruption of the fourteenth-century Church: the papacy, the priests, or the laity? Why?
3. Are the Lollards hopeful about humanity's potential to be saved?

1 That when the Church of England began to go mad after temporalities, like its great step-mother the Roman Church, and churches were authorized by appropriation in divers places, faith, hope, and charity began to flee from our Church, because pride, with its doleful progeny of moral sins, claimed this under title of truth. This conclusion is general, and proved by experience, custom, and manner or fashion, as you shall afterwards hear.

2. That our usual priesthood which began in Rome, pretended to be of power more lofty than the angels, is not that priesthood which Christ ordained for His apostles. This conclusion is proved because the Roman priesthood is bestowed with signs, rites, and pontifical blessing, of small virtue, nowhere exemplified in Holy Scripture, because the bishop's ordinal and the New Testament scarcely agree, and we cannot see that the Holy Spirit, by reason of any such signs, confers the gift, for He and all His excellent gifts cannot consist in any one with mortal sin. A corollary to this is that it is a grievous play for wise men to see bishops trifle with the Holy Spirit in the bestowal for orders, because they give the tonsure in outward appearance in the place of white hearts; and this is the unrestrained introduction of antichrist into the Church to give colour to idleness.

3. That the law of continence enjoined on priests, which was first ordained to the prejudice of women, brings sodomy into all the Holy Church, but we excuse ourselves by the Bible because the decree says that we should not mention it, though suspected. Reason and experience prove this conclusion: reason, because the good living of ecclesiastics must have a natural outlet or worse; experience, because the secret proof of such men is that they find delight in women, and when thou hast proved such a man mark him well, because he is one of them. A corollary to this is that private religions and the originators or beginning of this sin would be specially worthy of being checked, but God of His power with regard to secret sin sends open vengeance in His Church.

4. That the pretended miracle of the sacrament of bread drives all men, but a few, to idolatry, because they think that the Body of Christ which is never away from heaven could by power of the priest's word be enclosed essentially in a little bread which they show the people; but God grant that they might be willing to believe what the evangelical doctor says in his Trialogus (iv 7), that the bread of the altar is habitually the Body of Christ, for we take it that in this way any faithful man and woman can by God's law perform the sacrament of that bread without any such miracle. A final corollary is that although the Body of Christ, for we take it that in this way any faithful man and woman can by God's law perform the sacrament of that bread without any such miracle. A final corollary is that although the Body of Christ has been granted eternal joy, the service of Corpus Christi, instituted by Brother Thomas [Aquinas], is not true but is fictitious and full of false miracles. It is no wonder; because Brother Thomas, at that time holding with the pope, would have been willing to perform a miracle with a hen's egg; and we know well that any falsehood openly preached turns to the disgrace of Him who is always true and without any defect.

5.   That exorcisms and blessings performed over wine, bread, water and oil, salt, wax, and incense, the stones of the altar, and church walls, over clothing, mitre, cross, and pilgrims' staves, are the genuine performance of necromancy rather than of sacred theology. This conclusion is proved as follows, because by such exorcisms creatures are honoured as being of higher virtue than they are in their own nature, and we do not see any change in any creature which is so exorcized, save by false faith which is the principal characteristic of the Devil's art. A corollary: that if the book of exorcizing holy water, read in church, were entirely trustworthy we think truly that the holy water used in church would be the best medicine for all kinds of illnesses—sores, for instance; whereas we experience the contrary day by day.

6.   That king and bishop in one person, prelate and judge in temporal causes, curate and officer in secular office, puts any kingdom beyond good rule. This conclusion is clearly proved because the temporal and spiritual are two halves of the entire Holy Church. And so he who has applied himself to one should not meddle with the other, for no one can serve two masters. It seems that hermaphrodite or ambidexter would be good names for such men of double estate. A corollary is that we, the procurators of God in this behalf, do petition before Parliament that all curates, as well superior as inferior, be fully excused and should occupy themselves with their own charge and no other.

7.   That special prayers for the souls of the dead offered in our Church, preferring one before another in name, are a false foundation of alms, and for that reason all houses of alms in England have been wrongly founded. This conclusion is proved by two reasons: the one is that meritorious prayer, and of any effect, ought to be a work proceeding from deep charity, and perfect charity leaves out no one, for 'Thou shalt love thy neighbour as thyself.' And so it is clear to us that the gift of temporal good bestowed on the priesthood and houses of alms is a special incentive to private prayer which is not far from simony. For another reason is that special prayer made for men condemned is very displeasing to God. And although it be doubtful, it is probable to faithful Christian people that founders of a house of alms have for their poisonous endowment passed over for the most part to the broad road. The corollary is: effectual prayer springing from perfect love would in general embrace all whom God would have saved, and would do away with that well-worn way or merchandise in special prayers made for the possessionary mendicants and other hired priests, who are a people of great burden to the whole realm, kept in idleness: for it has been proved in one book, which the king had, that a hundred houses of alms would suffice in all the realm, and from this would rather accrue possible profit to the temporal estate.

8.   That pilgrimages, prayers, and offerings made to blind crosses or roods, and to deaf images of wood or stone, are pretty well akin to idolatry and far from alms, and although these be forbidden and imaginary, a book of error to the lay folk, still the customary image of the Trinity is specially abominable. This conclusion God clearly proves, bidding alms to be done to the needy man because they are the image of God, and more like than wood or stone; or God did not say, 'let us make wood or stone in our likeness and image,' but man; because the supreme honour which clerks call *latria* appertains to the Godhead only; and the lower honour which clerks call *dulia* appertains to man and angel and to no inferior creature. A corollary is that the service of the cross, performed twice in any year in our church, is full of idolatry, for if that should, so might the nails and lance be so highly honoured; then would the lips of Judas be relics indeed if any were able to possess them. But we ask you, pilgrim, to tell us when you offer to the bones of saints placed in a shrine in any spot, whether you relieve the saint who is in joy, or that almshouse which is so well endowed and for when men have been canonized. God knows how. And to speak more plainly, a faithful Christian supposes that the wounds of that noble man, whom men call St. Thomas, were not a case of martyrdom.

9.    That auricular confession which is said to be so necessary to the salvation of a man, with its pretended power of absolution, exalts the arrogance of priests and gives them opportunity of other secret colloquies which we will not speak of; for both lords and ladies attest that, for fear of their confessors, they dare not speak the truth. And at the time of confession there is a ready occasion for assignation, that is for 'wooing,' and other secret understandings leading to mortal sins. They themselves say that they are God's representatives to judge of every sin, to pardon and cleanse whomsoever they please. They say that they have the keys of heaven and of hell, and can excommunicate and bless, bind and loose, at their will, so much so that for a drink, or twelve pence, they will sell the blessing of heaven with charter and close warrant sealed with the common seal. This conclusion is so notorious that it needs not any proof. It is a corollary that the pope of Rome, who has given himself out as treasurer of the whole Church, having in charge that worthy jewel of Christ's passion together with the merits of all saints in heaven, whereby he grants pretended indulgence from penalty and guilt, is a treasurer almost devoid of charity, in that he can set free all that are prisoners in hell at his will, and cause that they should never come to that place. But in this any Christian can well see there is much secret falsehood hidden away in our Church.

10.    That manslaughter in war, or by pretended law of justice for a temporal cause, without spiritual revelation, is expressly contrary to the New Testament, which indeed is the law of grace and full of mercies. This conclusion is openly proved by the examples of Christ's preaching here on earth, for he specially taught a man to love his enemies, and to show them pity, and not to slay them. The reason is this, that for the most part, when men fight, after the first blow, charity is broken. And whoever dies without charity goes the straight road to hell. And beyond this we know well that no clergyman can by Scripture or lawful reason remit the punishment of death for one mortal sin and not for another; but the law of mercy, which is the New Testament, prohibits all manner of manslaughter, for in the Gospel: 'It was said unto them of old time, Thou shalt not kill.' The corollary is that it is indeed robbery of poor folk when lords get indulgences from punishment and guilt for those who aid their army to kill a Christian people in distant lands for temporal gain, just as we too have seen soldiers who run into heathendom to get them a name for the slaughter of men; much more do they deserve ill thanks from the King of Peace, for by our humility and patience was the faith multiplied, and Christ Jesus hates and threatens men who fight and kill, when He says: 'He who smites with the sword shall perish by the sword.'

11.    That the vow of continence made in our Church by women who are frail and imperfect in nature, is the cause of bringing in the gravest horrible sins possible to human nature, because, although the killing of abortive children before they are baptized and the destruction of nature by drugs are vile sins, yet connexion with themselves or brute beasts of any creature not having life surpasses them in foulness to such an extent as that they should be punished with the pains of hell. The corollary is that, widows and such as take the veil and the ring, being delicately fed, we could wish that they were given in marriage, because we cannot excuse them from secret sins.

12.    That the abundance of unnecessary arts practised in our realm nourishes much sin in waste, profusion, and disguise. This, experience and reason prove in some measure, because nature is sufficient for a man's necessity with few arts. The corollary is that since St. Paul says: 'having food and raiment, et us be therewith content,' it seems to us that goldsmiths and armourers and all kinds of arts not necessary for a man, according to the apostle, should be destroyed for the increase of virtue; because although these two said arts were exceedingly necessary in the old law, the New Testament abolishes them and many others.

This is our embassy, which Christ has bidden us fulfil, very necessary for this time for several reasons. And although these matters are briefly noted here they are however set forth at large in another book, and many others besides, at length in our own language, and we wish that these were accessible to all Christian people. We ask God then of His supreme goodness to reform our Church, as being entirely out of joint, to the perfectness of its first beginning.

Source: Henry Bettenson, ed., *Documents of the Christian Church*, (New York: Oxford University Press, 1963), pp. 175-179.

# 13.4

## SONG OF JOAN OF ARC, CHRISTINE DE PISAN

*Few medieval figures still attract as much debate as Joan of Arc. An illiterate peasant born in 1412, she claimed to have visions that led her to fight against the English on behalf of the Dauphin Charles, heir to the French throne. After Joan defeated the English at Orleans in 1429, the Dauphin was crowned Charles VII and the tide of the Hundred Years' War turned in favor of the French. In 1430 Joan was captured by the Burgundians, who although French were allies of the English. Joan was tried by French clergy, under English control, and executed for witchcraft and heresy in 1431. She was nineteen years old. Rallying around the memory of Joan, Charles and his French forces gradually reconquered his kingdom and by 1453 English territory in France was reduced to one town, Calais. In 1920 the Catholic Church declared Joan a saint.*

*The controversies surrounding Joan then and now center on the questions of whether her visions were "true," and what role she actually played in the battle. In 1429, immediately after the capture of Orleans, a French writer named Christine de Pisan wrote a poem (or* ditiè, *a song) applauding Joan's success and her holiness. It is the first poem dedicated to Joan.*

### QUESTIONS

1. What significance is there in the fact that the author of the poem is a woman?
2. How does Christine use Biblical examples to explain the success of Joan?
3. Why does Christine think God has chosen to use a young girl for this "miraculous" victory over the English?

*I*      I, Christine, who have wept for eleven years in a walled abbey where I have lived ever since Charles (how strange this is!) the king's son — dare I say it? — fled in hast from Paris, I who have lived enclosed there on account of the treachery, now, for the first time, begin to laugh…

*III*     In 1429 the sun began to shine again. It brings back the good, new season which had not really been seen for a long time — and because of that many people had lived out their lives in sorrow; I myself am one of them. But I no longer grieve over anything, now that I can see what I desire.

*V*      The reason is that the rejected child of the rightful king of France, who has long suffered many a great misfortune and who now approaches, rose up as if towards prime, coming as a crowned king in might and majesty, wearing spurs of gold.

*VI*      Now let us greet our king! Welcome to him on his return! Overjoyed at the sight of his noble array, let us all, both great and small, step forward to greet him joyously — and let no one hold back — praising God, who has kept him safe, and shouting "Noël!" in a loud voice...

*X*      Did anyone, then, see anything quite so extraordinary come to pass (something that is well worth noting and remembering in every region), namely, that France (about whom it was said she had been cast down) should see her fortunes change, by divine command, from evil to such great good,

*XI*      as the result, indeed, of such a miracle that, if the matter were not so well-known and crystal-clear in every aspect, nobody would ever believe it? It is a fact well worth remembering that God should nevertheless have wished (and this is the truth!) to bestow such great blessings on France, through a young virgin.

*XII*      And what honor for the French crown, this proof of divine intervention! For all the blessings which God bestows upon it demonstrate how much He favors it and that He finds more faith in the Royal House than anywhere else; as far as it is concerned, I read (and there is nothing new in this) that the Lilies of France never erred in matters of faith.

*XIII*      And you Charles, king of France, seventh of that noble name, who have been involved in such a great war before things turned out at all well for you, now, thanks be to God, see your honor exalted by the Maid who has laid low your enemies beneath your standard (and this *is* new!)

*XIV*      in a short time; for it was believed quite impossible that you should ever recover your country which you were on the point of losing. Now it is manifestly yours for, no matter who may have done you harm, you have recovered it! And all this has been brought about by the intelligence of the Maid who, God be thanked, has played her part in this matter!

*XV*      And I firmly believe that God would never have bestowed such grace upon you if it were not ordained by Him that you should, in the course of time, accomplish and bring to completion some great and solemn task; I believe too that He has destined you to be the author of very great deeds.

*XVI*      For there will be a king of France called Charles, son of Charles, who will be supreme ruler over all kings. Prophecies have given him the name of "The Flying Stag," and many a deed will be accomplished by this conqueror (God has called him to this task) and in the end he will be emperor....

*XIX*      And how will you ever be able to thank God enough, serve and fear Him in all your deeds (for He has led you from such great adversity to peace and raised up the whole of France from such ruin) when His most holy providence made you worthy of such signal honor?...

*XXI*   And you, blessed Maid, are you to be forgotten, given that God honored you so much that you untied the rope which held France so tightly bound? Could one ever praise you enough for having bestowed peace on this land humiliated by war?

*XXII*   Blessed be He who created you, Joan, who were born at a propitious hour! Maiden sent from God, into whom the Holy Spirit poured His great grace, in whom [i.e. the Holy Spirit] there was and is an abundance of noble gifts, never did Providence refuse you any request. Who can ever begin to repay you?

*XXIII*   and what more can be said of any other person or of the great deeds of the past? Moses, upon whom God in His bounty bestowed many a blessing and virtue, miraculously and indefatigably led God's people out of Egypt. In the same way, blessed Maid, you have led us out of evil!

*XXIV*   When we take your person into account, you who are a young maiden, to whom God gives the strength and power to be the champion who casts the rebels down and feeds France with the sweet, nourishing milk of peace, here indeed is something quite extraordinary!

*XXV*   For if God performed such a great number of miracles through Joshua who conquered many a place and cast down many an enemy, he, Joshua, was a strong and powerful *man*. But, after all, a *woman* — a simple shepherdess — braver than any man ever was in Rome! As far as God is concerned, this was easily accomplished.

*XXVI*   But as for us, we never heard tell of such an extraordinary marvel, for the prowess of all the great men of the past cannot be compared to this woman's whose concern it is to cast out our enemies. This is God's doing: it is He who guides her and who has given her a heart greater than that of any man.

*XXVII*   Much is made of Gideon, who was a simple workman, and it was God, so the story tells, who made him fight; nobody could stand firm before him and he conquered everything. But whatever guidance God gave [him], it is clear that He never performed so striking a miracle as He does for this woman.

*XXVIII*   I have heard of Esther, Judith and Deborah, who were women of great worth, through whom God delivered His people from oppression, and I have heard of many other worthy women as well, champions every one, through them He performed many miracles, but He has accomplished more through this Maid.

*XXIX*   She was miraculously sent by divine command and conducted by the angel of the Lord to the king, in order to help him. Her achievement is no illusion for she was carefully put to the test in council (in short, a thing is proved by its effect)

*XXX*  and well examined, before people were prepared to believe her; before it became common knowledge that God had sent her to the king, she was brought before clerks and wise men so that they could find out if she was telling the truth. But it was found in history-records that she was destined to accomplish her mission....

*XXXIII*  Oh, how clear this was at the siege of Orléans where her power was first made manifest! It is my belief that no miracle was ever more evident, for God so came to the help of His people that our enemies were unable to help each other any more than would dead dogs. It was there that they were captured and put to death.

*XXXIV*  Oh! What honor for the female sex! It is perfectly obvious that God has special regard for it when all these wretched people who destroyed the whole kingdom — now recovered and made safe by a woman, something that 5000 *men* could not have done — and the traitors [have been] exterminated. Before the event they would scarcely have believed this possible.

*XXXV*  A little girl of sixteen (isn't this something quite supernatural?) who does not even notice the weight of the arms she bears — indeed her whole upbringing seems to have prepared her for this, so strong and resolute is she! And her enemies go fleeing before her, not one of them can stand up to her. She does all this in full view of everyone,

*XXXVI*  and drives her enemies out of France recapturing castles and towns. Never did anyone see greater strength, even in hundreds or thousands of men! And she is the supreme captain of our brave and able men. Neither Hector nor Achilles had such strength! This is God's doing: it is He who leads her.

*XXXVII*  And you trusty men-at-arms who carry out the task and prove yourselves to be good and loyal, one must certainly make mention of you (you will be praised in every nation!) and not fail to speak of you and your valor in preference to everything else,

*XXXVIII*  you who, in pain and suffering, expose life and limb in defence of what is right and dare to risk confronting every danger. Be constant, for this, I promise, will win you glory and praise in Heaven. For whoever fights for justice wins a place in Paradise — this I do venture to say.

*XL*  You thought you had already conquered France and that she must remain yours. Things have turned out otherwise, you treacherous lot! Go and beat your drums elsewhere, unless you want to taste death, like your companions, whom wolves may well devour, for their bodies lie dead amidst the furrows!

*XLI*  And know that she will cast down the English for good, for this is God's will: He hears the prayer of the good whom they wanted to harm! The blood of those who are dead and have no hope of being brought back to life again cries out against them. God will tolerate this no longer — He has decided, rather, to condemn them as evil.

*XLII*    She will restore harmony in Christendom and the Church. She will destroy the unbelievers people talk about, and the heretics and their vile ways, for this is the substance of a prophecy that has been made. Nor will she have mercy on any place which treats faith in God with disrespect.

*XLIII*    She will destroy the Saracens, by conquering the Holy Land. She will lead Charles there, whom God preserve! Before he dies he will make such a journey. He is the one who is to conquer it. It is there that she is to end her days and that both of them are to win glory. It is there that the whole enterprise will be brought to completion.

*XLIV*    Therefore, in preference to all the brave men of times past, this woman must wear the crown, for her deeds show clearly enough already that God bestows more courage upon her than upon all those men about whom people speak. And she has not yet accomplished her whole mission! I believe that God bestows her here below so that peace may be brought about through her deeds.

*XLV*    And yet destroying the English race is not her main concern for her aspirations lie more elsewhere: it is her concern to ensure the survival of the Faith. As for the English, whether it be a matter for joy or sorrow, they are done for. In days to come scorn will be heaped on them. They have been cast down!

*XLVI*    And all you base rebels who have joined them, you can see now that it would have been better for you to have gone forwards rather than backwards as you did, thereby becoming the serfs of the English. Beware that more does not befall you (for you have been tolerated long enough!), and remember what the outcome will be!

*XLVII*    Oh, all you blind people, can't you detect God's hand in this? If you can't, you are truly stupid for how else could the Maid who strikes you all down have been sent to us? — And you don't have sufficient strength! Do you want to fight against God?

Source: Alfred J. Andrea, ed., *The Medieval Record: Sources of Medieval History* (Boston: Houghton Mifflin Company, 1997), pp. 437-440.

## QUESTIONS FOR PART 13

1. In what ways do all four of these documents reflect a new awareness of the individual?
2. Although the crises of the fourteenth and fifteenth centuries were traumatic, how do these documents also present positive opportunities?
3. Had the status of women changed since the Early Middle Ages?

# PART 14

❧

# ITALIAN RENAISSANCE

Between 1350-1550, a new artistic, cultural, and political movement began in Italy and moved gradually northward across the continent. The movement was later called the "Renaissance," a French word meaning "rebirth." Most prominent was the rediscovery of classical ideas, techniques, and philosophy. The very languages of the classical world were revived; throughout the Middle Ages, Latin was the language of the Church and Greek was virtually unknown in western Europe. In the fourteenth and fifteenth centuries, classical Latin was studied again, and Greek was re-introduced into Europe by Byzantine scholars fleeing the conquest of Constantinople in 1453 by Ottoman Turks.

It was also a period of rebirth of trade and cities, particularly after the 1450's, when the Hundred Years' War had ended and more wealth increased the interest in luxury goods. Warfare was certainly not over; if anything it increased between the Italian city-states, and between the Italians and the French. But new theories about states and war changed how both were organized and conducted. Faith also underwent a revolution; the Protestant Reformation was a manifestation of the Renaissance, although in a more subtle way.

The single most important Renaissance philosophy was humanism, which was a part of every endeavor of European culture during this period. Humanist ideals emphasized the potential of humanity and praised human endeavors and led to the celebration of humanity in a characteristically classical manner. Humanism also sought to counter the rigidity to which scholasticism had been reduced by the thirteenth century. The sources in this chapter show the poetic, artistic, and political sides of the Renaissance.

# 14.1

⚜

## *SONNETS*, DANTE ALIGHIERI

*Dante Alighieri (1265-1321) was both a Medieval and a Renaissance writer, thus perfectly indicative of the gradual shift in literary styles and tastes that took place in the fourteenth century. Although his masterpiece epic,* The Divine Comedy, *is a classic example of medieval piety and world-view, his sonnets (three of which are included here) show the humanist influences of the early Renaissance. The sonnets are dedicated to Beatrice, with whom Dante first fell in love when they were both children and continued to love and idealize long after her death.*

*It is worth noting that Dante was from Florence, as with many of the most influential Renaissance artists (in many media) and thinkers. The Florence of Dante's day was wracked with internal strife and blood feuds (Dante was himself exiled from Florence because of one such feud), and torn between imperial and papal politics. None of this would change over the course of the Renaissance, but within a century of Dante's death Florence would also be the most powerful and wealthy city in Italy.*

## QUESTIONS

1. Can you pick out examples of classical influence from these sonnets?
2. Is Beatrice a real woman for Dante?
3. Are these Christian poems?

To every captive soul and gentle lover
   Into whose sight this present rhyme may chance,
That, writing back, each may expound its sense,
Greetings in Love, who is their Lord, I offer.
   Already of those hours a third was over
Wherein all stars display their radiance,
When lo! Love stood before me in my trance:
Recalling what he was fills me with horror.
Joyful Love seemed to me and in his keeping
   He held my heart; and in his arms there lay
My lady in a mantle wrapped, and sleeping.
   Then he awoke her and, her fear not heeding,
My burning heart fed to her reverently.
   Then he departed from my vision, weeping

These eyes of mine beheld the tenderness
   Which marked your features when you turned your gaze
Upon my doleful bearing and the ways
I many times assume in my distress.
   I understood then that you fain would guess
The nature of the dolour of my days;
And so straightway I grew afraid to raise
My eyes lest they reveal my abjectness.
And as I from your vision then withdrew
   The tears within my heart began to well,
Where all was stirred to tumult by your sight;
   And to my soul I murmured in my plight:
'With her indeed that self-same Love must dwell
Who makes you go thus weeping as you do.'...

✠ ✠ ✠

No woman's countenance has ever worn
  In such miraculous degree the hue
    Of love and pity's look, from yielding to
    The sight of gentle eyes or folk who mourn,
    As does your own when I approach forlorn
    And with my grieving face for mercy sue.
    Such thoughts then come to mind because of you
    My heart with fear and suffering is torn.
My wasted eyes I find I cannot keep
    From gazing at you ever and again,
    For by a tearful longing they are led.
    Beholding you then so augments their pain
    They are consumed by their desire to weep,
    Yet in your presence tears they cannot shed.

Sources:  Dante Alighieri, *La Vita Nuova [Poems of Youth]*, trans. Barbara Reynolds (New York: Penguin Books, Ltd., 1969), pp. 33, 90-91.

# 14.2

✠

# THE LIFE OF LEONARDO DA VINCI

*The term "renaissance man" might have been invented just to describe Leonardo da Vinci (1452-1519). Da Vinci was a painter, sculptor, and poet; his notebooks are filled with writings and drawings in mathematics, optics, anatomy, mechanics, chemistry, and philosophical speculation. Although not the most successful artist in his day (that title belongs to Michelangelo), to many people da Vinci was the epitome of everything that made up the Renaissance fusion of classical and Christian humanism. Two of the most famous pieces of art ever created by Western civilization are paintings by him: Mona Lisa and The Last Supper.*

*The following passages are from a biography of da Vinci by a contemporary painter, Vasari, who wrote biographies of several of his fellow artists.*

✠

## QUESTIONS

1. How is the very idea of writing a biography of an artist a "Renaissance" concept?
2. Why, according to Vasari, does da Vinci leave so many of his works unfinished?
3. What is humanist about da Vinci's approach to art?

Leonardo's disposition was so lovable that he commanded everyone's affection. He owned, one might say, nothing and he worked very little, yet he always kept servants as well as horses. These gave him great pleasure as indeed did all the animal creation which he treated with wonderful love and patience. For example, often when he was walking past the places where birds were sold he would pay the price asked, take them from their cages, and let them fly off into the air, giving them back their lost freedom. In return he was so favoured by nature that to whatever he turned his mind or thoughts the results were always inspired and perfect; and his lively and delightful works were incomparably graceful and realistic.

Clearly, it was because of his profound knowledge of painting that Leonardo started so many things without finishing them; for he was convinced that his hands, for all their skill, could never perfectly express the subtle and wonderful ideas of his imagination. Among his many interests was included the study of nature; he investigated the properties of plants and then observed the motion of the heavens, the path of the moon, and the course of the sun.

I mentioned earlier that when he was still young Leonardo entered the workshop of Andrea del Verrocchio. Now at that time Verrocchio was working on a panel picture showing the baptism of Christ by St. John, for which Leonardo painted an angel who was holding some garments; and despite his youth, he executed it is such a manner that his angel was far better than the figures painted by Andrea. This was the reason why Andrea would never touch colours again, he was so ashamed that a boy understood their use better than he did. Leonardo was then commissioned to make a cartoon (for a tapestry to be woven of gold and silk in Flanders an sent to the king of Portugal) showing the sin of Adam and Eve in the Garden of Paradise. For this he drew with the brush in chiaroscuro, with the lights in lead-white, a luxuriant meadow full of different kinds of animals; and it can truthfully be said that for diligence and faithfulness to nature nothing could be more inspired or perfect. There is a fig tree, for example, with its leaves foreshortened and its branches drawn from various aspects, depicted with such loving care that the brain reels at the thought that a man could have such patience. And there is a palm tree, the radiating crown of which is drawn with such marvellous skill that no one without Leonardo's understanding and patience could have done it. The work was not carried any farther and so today the cartoon is still in Florence, in the blessed house of the Magnificent Ottaviano de' Medici to whom it was presented not long ago by Leonardo's uncle....

Leonardo also executed in Milan, for the Dominicans of Santa Maria delle Grazie, a marvellous and beautiful painting of the Last Supper. Having depicted the heads of the apostles full of splendour and majesty, he deliberately left the head of Christ unfinished, convinced he would fail to give it the divine spirituality it demands. This all but finished work has ever since been held in the greatest veneration by the Milanese and others. In it Leonardo brilliantly succeeded in envisaging and reproducing the tormented anxiety of the apostles to know who had betrayed their master; so in their faces one can read the emotions of love, dismay, and anger, or rather sorrow, at their failure to grasp the meaning of Christ. And this excites no less admiration than the contrasted spectacle of the obstinacy, hatred, and treachery in the face of Judas or, indeed, than the incredible diligence with which every detail of the work was executed. The texture of the very cloth on the table is counterfeited so cunningly that the linen itself could not look more realistic.

It is said that the prior used to keep pressing Leonardo, in the most importunate way, to hurry up and finish his work, because he was puzzled by Leonardo's habit of sometimes spending half a day at a time contemplating what he had done so far; if the prior had had his way, Leonardo would have toiled like one of the labourers hoeing in the garden and never put his brush down for a moment. Not satisfied with this, the prior then complained to the duke, making such a fuss that the duke was constrained to send for

Leonardo and, very tactfully, question him about the painting, although he showed perfectly well that he was only doing so because of the prior's insistence. Leonardo, knowing he was dealing with a prince of acute and discerning intelligence, was willing (as he never had been with the prior) to explain his mind at length; and so he talked to the duke for a long time about the art of painting. He explained that men of genius sometimes accomplish most when they work the least; for, he added, they are thinking out inventions and forming in their minds the perfect ideas which they subsequently express and reproduce with their hands. Leonardo then said that he still had two heads to paint: the head of Christ was one, and for this he was unwilling to look for any human model, nor did he dare suppose that his imagination could conceive the beauty and divine grace that properly belonged to the incarnate Deity. Then, he said, he had yet to do the head of Judas, and this troubled him since he did not think he could imagine the features that would form the countenance of a man who, despite all the blessing he had been given, could so cruelly steel his will to betray his own master and the creator of the world. However, added Leonardo, he would try to find a model for Judas, and if he did not succeed in doing so, why then he was not without the head of that tactless and importunate prior. The duke roared with laughter at this and said that Leonardo had every reason in the world for saying so. The unfortunate prior retired in confusion to worry the labourers working in his garden, and he left off worrying Leonardo, who skilfully finished the head of Judas and made it seem the very embodiment of treachery and inhumanity. The head of Christ remained, as was said, unfinished.

This noble painting was so finely composed and executed that the King of France subsequently wanted to remove it to his kingdom. He tried all he could to find architects to make cross-stays of wood and iron with which the painting could be protected and brought safely to France, without any regard for expense, so great was his desire to have it. But as the painting was done on a wall his majesty failed to have his way and it remained in the possession of the Milanese. While he was working on the Last Supper, in the same refectory where there is a painting of the Passion done in the old manner, on the end wall, Leonardo portrayed Ludovico himself with his eldest son, Massimiliano; and on the other side, with the Duchess Beatrice, his other son Francesco, both of whom later became dukes of Milan; and all these figures are beautifully painted....

For Francesco del Giocondo Leonardo undertook to execute the portrait of his wife, Mona Lisa. He worked on this painting for four years, and then left it still unfinished; and today it is in the possession of King Francis of France, at Fontainebleau. If one wanted to see how faithfully art can imitate nature, one could readily perceive it from this head; for here Leonardo subtly reproduced every living detail. The eyes had their natural lustre and moistness, and around them were the lashes and all those rosy and pearly tints that demand the greatest delicacy of execution. The eyebrows were completely natural, growing thickly in one place and lightly in another and following the pores of the skin. The nose was finely painted, with rosy and delicate nostrils as in life. The mouth, joined to the flesh-tints of the face by the red of the lips, appeared to be living flesh rather than paint. On looking closely at the pit of her throat one could swear that the pulses were beating. Altogether this picture was painted in a manner to make the most confident artist — no matter who — despair and lose heart. Leonardo also made use of this device: while he was painting Mona Lisa, who was a very beautiful woman, he employed singers and musicians or jesters to keep her full of merriment and so chase away the melancholy that painters usually give to portraits. As a result, in this painting of Leonardo's there was a smile so pleasing that it seemed divine rather than human; and those who saw it were amazed to find that it was as alive as the original....

Leonardo went to Rome with Duke Giuliano de' Medici on the election of Pope Leo who was a great student of natural philosophy, and especially of alchemy. And in Rome he experimented with a paste made out of a certain kind of wax and made some light and billowy figures in the form of animals which he inflated with his mouth as he walked along and which flew above the ground until all the air escaped. To the back of a very odd-looking lizard that was found by the gardener of the Belvedere he attached with a mixture of quicksilver some wings, made from the scales stripped from other lizards, which quivered as it walked along. Then, after he had given it eyes, horns, and a beard he tamed the creature, and keeping it in a box he used to show it to this friends and frighten the life out of them. Again, Leonardo used to get the intestines of a bullock scraped completely free of their fat, cleaned and made so fine that they could be compressed into the palm of one hand; then he would fix one end of them to a pair of bellows lying in another room, and when they were inflated they filled the room in which they were and forced anyone standing there into a corner. Thus he could expand this translucent and airy stuff to fill a large space after occupying only a little, and he compared it to genius. He perpetrated hundreds of follies of this kind, and he also experimented with mirrors and made the most outlandish experiments to discover oils for painting and varnish for preserving the finished works....

Sources: Georgio Vasari, *The Lives of the Artists*, trans. George Bull (Baltimore: Penguin Books, Ltd., 1965), pp. 255-271.

# 14.3

## *THE PRINCE*, MACHIAVELLI

*The Renaissance was much more than an artistic change. It also included new approaches to politics and new definitions of power. Nothing epitomizes this new idea of power better than Niccolo Machiavelli's political treatise* The Prince. *Written in 1513,* The Prince *was a radically different approach to statecraft; according to Machiavelli (d. 1527), rulers were justified in taking whatever actions that are necessary to protect their own power, whether that action is morally acceptable or not, or if it benefits the ruler's subjects or not. He used as his model contemporary rulers from Italy (Machiavelli was himself from Florence) as well as his knowledge of Roman political history. Perhaps the most important innovation of Machiavelli's political theory was his secularism.*

## QUESTIONS

1. *The Prince* has been described as either a cynical or realistic view of politics. Which do you think it is?
2. According to Machiavelli, why should a ruler avoid a reputation for generosity?
3. Is there a place for faith in Machiavelli's theory of statehood?

## CHAPTER XVII — CONCERNING CRUELTY: WHETHER IT IS BETTER TO BE LOVED THAT TO BE FEARED, OR THE REVERSE

Turning to some other of the afrementioned qualities, I say that ever prince ought to wish to be considered kind rather than cruel. Nevertheless, he must take care to avoid misusing his kindness. Cesare Brogia was considered cruel; yet his cruelty restored Romagna, uniting it in peace and loyalty. If this result is considered good, then he must be judged much kinder than the florentines who, to avoid being called cruel, allowed Pistoia to be destroyed. A prince, therefore, must be indifferent to the charge of cruelty if he is to keep his subjects loyal and united. Having set an example once or twice, he may thereafter act far more mercifully than the princes who, through excessive kindness, allow disorders to arise from which murder and rapine ensue. Disorders harm the entire citizenry, while the executions ordered by a prince harm only a few individuals. Indeed, of all princes, the newly-established one can least of all escape the charge of cruelty, for new states are encumbered with dangers. As Virgil has Dido say,

> *Res dura, et regni novitas me talia cogunt*
> *Moliri, et late fines custode tueri.*

Nevertheless, he ought to be slow to believe what he hears and slow to act. Nor should he fear imaginary dangers, but proceed with moderation, prudence, and humanity, avoiding carelessness born of overconfidence and unbearable harshness born of excessive distrust.

Here a question arises: whether it is better to be loved than feared, or the reverse. The answer is, of course, that it would be best to both loved and feared. But since the two rarely come together, anyone compelled to choose will find greater security in being feared than in being loved. For this can be said about the generality of men: that they are ungrateful, fickle, dissembling, anxious to flee danger, and covetous of gain. So long as you promote their advantage, they are all yours, as I said before, and will offer you their blood, their goods, their lives, and their children when the need for these is remote. When the need arises, however, they will turn against you. The prince who bases his security upon their word, lacking other provision, is doomed; for friendships that are gained by money, not by greatness and nobility of spirit, may well be earned, but cannot be kept; and in time of need, they will have fled your purse. Men are less concerned about offending someone they have cause to love than someone they have cause to fear. Love endures by a bond which men, being scoundrels, may break whenever it serves their advantage to do so; but fear is supported by the dread of pain, which is ever present.

Still a prince should make himself feared in such a way that, though he does not gain love, he escapes hatred; for being feared but not hated go readily together. Such a condition he may always attain if he will not touch the property of his citizens and subjects, nor their women. And if he finds it necessary to take someone's life, he should do so when there is suitable justification and manifest cause; but above all, he should refrain from the property of others, for men are quicker to forget the death of a father than the loss of a patrimony. Furthermore, excuses for seizing property are never lacking and, indeed, anyone who begins to live by plunder will always find pretexts for taking over what belongs to someone else. On the other hand, pretexts for taking someone's life arise more rarely and last a shorter time.

But when a prince is at the head of his armies and must command multitudes of soldiers, then more than ever must he be indifferent to a reputation for cruelty, for without such a reputation no army was ever held together, nor was it every fit for combat. Among the marvelous deeds of Hannibal is numbered this one: that though he had an enormous army composed of a great variety of races fighting in a foreign land, no dissension ever arose among the troops or between the troops and their leader, either in good times or in bad. This could have had no other source but his inhuman cruelty which, together with his extraordinary qualities of leadership, made him an object of constant reverence and terror to his soldiers. To produce such an effect without this cruelty, his other qualities would have been insufficient. Writers of scant judgment in this matter have, on the one hand, admired his accomplishments and, on the other, condemned their chief source.

The proof that his other qualities would have been insufficient may be seen in the case of Scipio — a most exceptional man not only in his own times but in all remembered history — whose soldiers mutinied in Spain for no reason other than his excessive leniency, which allowed them more freedom than was consonant with military discipline. Fabius Maximus reproved him for it in the Senate and called him the corrupter of Roman arms. When one of his lieutenants ravaged the Locrians, Scipio neither avenged them nor took action to correct his lieutenant's insolence. This too grew out of his mild nature, so much so, in fact, that someone seeking to excuse Scipio's conduct before the Senate observed that many men have more skill in avoiding errors than in correcting them. This propensity would in time have damaged Scipio's fame and glory if he had persevered in it, but since he was ruled by the Senate, its potential harmfulness remained hidden, and it redounded to his glory.

Returning to the question, then, of being loved or feared, I conclude that since men love as they themselves determine but fear as their ruler determines, a wise prince must rely upon what he and not others can control. He need only strive to avoid being hated, as I said....

## CHAPTER XXIII — HOW TO AVOID FLATTERERS

One important point I do not want to overlook concerns a failing against which princes cannot easily protect themselves unless they are especially prudent or have good advisers. I refer to the flatterers with whom the courts of princes are crowded. Because men are so easily pleased with their own qualities and are so readily deceived in them, they have difficulty in guarding against these pests, and in attempting to guard against them, they run the risk of being scorned. For there is no way of avoiding flattery except by letting men know that they will not offend by telling the truth; yet if every man is free to tell you the truth, you will not receive due respect.

Therefore, a prudent prince will pursue a third course, choosing the wise men of his state and granting only to them the freedom to tell him the truth, but only concerning those matters about which he asks, and no others. Yet he should question them about all maters, listen to their opinions, and then decide for himself as he wishes. He should treat these councils and the individual advisers in such a way as to make it clear that their words will be the more welcome the more freely they are spoken. Except for these men, he should listen to no one, but rather pursue the course agreed upon and do so resolutely. Anyone who does otherwise will fall victim to flatterers or, as a result of the various opinions he hears, will often change his mind and thereby lose reputation.

Regarding this, I should like to cite a recent example. Pre' Luca, the ambassador of Maximilian, the present emperor, used to say that His Majesty never sought counsel from anyone, yet never did anything as he wished to do it. This grows out of his acting contrary to what has just been suggested. Being a very secretive man, the Emperor never consults anyone and never reveals his intentions. But as soon as he begins to put them into effect, they are discovered. Then they are opposed by the men he has about him, and, lacking resolution, he is easily dissuaded from them. The result in that what he does on one day he destroys on the next, and it is never possible to know what he is seeking or planning, or to have any confidence in his decisions.

A prince, therefore, should always seek advice, but only when he, not someone else, chooses. Indeed, he should discourage everyone from giving advice unless he has asked for it. In fact, if he should observe that someone is withholding the truth for some reason, he should show annoyance. Since many people believe that some princes are reputed wise, thanks rather to their wise counselors than to their own natural gifts, they ought to be told that they deceive themselves. For this is a general rule that never fails: a prince who is not wise himself cannot be wisely counseled, unless by chance he should have a sole counselor by whom he is ruled in all matters. There could be such a situation, but it would not last long, for the counselor would soon deprive the prince of his state. An unwise prince, having to consider the advice of several counselors, would never receive concordant opinions, and he would not be able to reconcile them on his own. His counselors would pursue their own interests and he would know neither how to rule them nor how to understand them. They could not do otherwise, for men will always prove bad unless necessity compels them to be good. Therefore I conclude that good advice, no matter where it comes from, ultimately derives from the prudence of the prince, and the prudence of the prince does not derive from good advice.

Source: Niccolo Machiavelli, *The Prince*, trans. Daniel Donno (New York: Bantam Books1966, 1981), pp. 56-64, 81-82

# 14.4

## ❧

## *BOOK OF THE COURTIER*, CASTIGLIONE

*Machiavelli was not the only political theorist of the Renaissance. Indeed, the field of political philosophy seemed to explode in the fifteenth and sixteenth centuries, and would forever remain one of the most popular fields of Western intellectual endeavor. Baldesar Castiglione (1478-1529) wrote the definitive handbook for the aristocratic class of Italy. Unlike Machiavelli, who focused on the skills necessary to be a good ruler, Castiglione's* Book of the Courtier *was aimed at all aristocrats and thus presented a broader picture of what education, skills, morals, and even fashion sense an ambitious nobleman needed to have. It drew very heavily on classical learning as well as current Italian history.*

## ❧

## QUESTIONS

1. Compare Castiglione's discussion of flattery with Machiavelli's in the previous source.
2. What kind of education should a courtier have? Why?
3. In what way does Castiglione use classical references? Which ones does he choose, and why?

'I should like our courtier to be a more than average scholar, at least in those studies which we call the humanities; and he should have a knowledge of Greek as well as Latin, because of the many different things that are so beautifully written in that language. He should be very well acquainted with the poets, and no less with the orators and historians, and also skilled at writing both verse and prose, especially in our own language; for in addition to the satisfaction this will give him personally, it will enable him to provide constant entertainment for the ladies, who are usually very fond of such things. But if because of his other activities or through lack of study he fails to achieve a commendable standard in his writing, then he should take pains to suppress his work, to avoid ridicule, and he should show it only to a friend he can trust. And the exercise of writing will be profitable for him at least to the extent that it will teach him how to judge the work of others. For it is very unusual for someone who is not a practised writer, however erudite he may be, to understand completely the demanding work done by writers, or appreciate their stylistic accomplishments and triumphs and those subtle details characteristic of the writers of the ancient world. Moreover, these studies will make our courtier well informed and eloquent and (as Aristippus said to the tyrant) self-confident and assured no matter whom he is talking to. However, I should like our courtier to keep one precept firmly in mind: namely, that in what I have just discussed and in everything else he should always be diffident and reserved rather than forward, and he should be on his guard against assuming that he knows what he does not know. For we are instinctively all too greedy for praise, and there is no sound or song that comes sweeter to our ears; praise, like Sirens' voices, is the king of music that causes shipwreck to the man who does not stop his ears to its deceptive harmony. Recognizing this danger, some of the philosophers of the ancient world wrote books giving advice on how a man can tell the difference between a true friend and a flatterer. Even so, we may well ask what use is this, seeing that there are so many who realize perfectly well that they are listening to flattery, and yet love the flatterer and detest the one who tells them the truth. Indeed, very often, deciding that the one who praises them is not being fulsome enough, they lend him a hand themselves and say such things that even the most outrageous flatterer feels ashamed. Let us leave these blind fools to their errors and decide that our courtier should possess such good judgement that he will not be told that black is white or presume anything of himself unless he is certain that it is true, and especially in regard to those flaws which, if you remember, when he was suggesting his game for the evening Cesare recalled we had often used to demonstrate the particular folly of this person or another. To make no mistake at all, the courtier should, on the contrary, when he knows the praises he receives are deserved, not assent to them too openly nor let them pass without some protest. Rather he should tend to disclaim them modestly, always giving the impression that arms are, as indeed they should be, his chief profession, and that all his other fine accomplishments serve merely as adornments; and this should especially be his attitude when he is in the company of soldiers, lest he behave like those who in the world of scholarship want to be taken for warriors and among warriors want to seem men of letters. In this way, as we have said, he will avoid affectation, and even his modest achievements will appear great.'

At this point, Pietro Bembo interrupted: 'I cannot see, my dear Count, why you wish this courtier, who is so literate and so well endowed with other worthy qualities, to regard everything as serving to adorn the profession of arms, and not arms and the rest as serving to adorn the profession of letter, which, taken by themselves, are as superior in dignity to arms as is the soul to the body, since letters are a function of the soul, just as arms are of the body.'

    Then the Count answered: 'On the contrary, the profession of arms pertains both to the soul and to the body. But I should not want you to be the judge of this, Pietro, because by one of the parties concerned it would be assumed that you were prejudiced. And as this is a controversy that the wisest men have already thrashed out, there is no call to re-open it. As it is, I consider that it has been settled in favour of arms; and since I may form our courtier as I wish, I want him to be of the same opinion. If you think the contrary, wait until you hear of a contest in which the man who defends the cause of arms is allowed to use the, just as those who defend the cause of letters make use of letters in their defence; for if each one uses his own weapons, you will see that the men of letters will lose.'

'Ah,' said Pietro Bembo, 'you were only too ready earlier on to damn the French for their scant appreciation of letters, and you mentioned the glory that they bring to men and the way they make a man immortal. And now you seem to have changed your mind. Do you not remember that:

> Giunto Alessandro alla famosa tomba
> del fero Achille, sospirando disse:
> O fortunato, che sì chiara tromba
> trovasti, e chi di te sì alto scrisse!

And if Alexander was envious of Achilles not because of what he had done himself but because of the way he was blessed by fortune in having his deeds celebrated by Homer, we must conclude that he put a higher value on the writings of Homer than on the arms of Achilles. What other judge do you want, or what other verdict on the relative worth of arms and letters than the one delivered by one of the greatest commanders that has ever lived?

The Count replied: 'I blame the French for believing that letters are harmful to the profession of arms, and I maintain myself that it is more fitting, joined together in our courtier. I do not think that this means I have changed my opinion. But, as I said, I do not wish to argue which of them is more praiseworthy. Let it be enough that men of letters hardly ever choose to praise other than great men and glorious deeds, which deserve praise both on their own account and because, in addition, they provide writers with a truly noble theme. And this subject-matter embellishes what is written and, no doubt, is the reason why such writings endure, for otherwise, if they dealt not with noble deeds but with vain and trivial subjects, they would surely be read and appreciated less. And if Alexander was envious of Achilles because he was praised by Homer, it still does not necessarily follow that he thought more of letters than of arms; and if he had thought that he was as inferior to Achilles as a soldier as he believed that all those who would write about him were inferior to Homer as writers, he would, I am sure, have far preferred brave exploits on his own part to brave talk from others. Therefore I believe that when he said what he did, Alexander was tacitly praising himself, and expressing a desire for what he thought he lacked, namely supreme ability as a writer, rather than for what he took for granted he already had, namely prowess as a warrior, in which he was far from acknowledging Achilles as his superior. So when he called Achilles fortunate he meant that if so far his own fame did not rival that of Achilles (which had been made bright and illustrious through so inspired a poem) this was not because his valour and merits were less notable or less deserving of the highest praise but because of the way fortune had granted Achilles a born genius to be his herald and to trumpet his deeds to the world. Moreover, perhaps Alexander wanted to encourage some gifted person to write about him, showing that his pleasure in this would be as great as his love and respect for the sacred monuments of literature. And now we have said enough about this subject.'...

...the Count continued as follows:

'Gentlemen, I must tell you that I am not satisfied with our courtier unless he is also a musician and unless as well as understanding and being able to read music he can play several instruments. For, when we think of it, during our leisure time we can find nothing more worthy or commendable to help our bodies relax and our spirits recuperate, especially at Court where, besides the way in which music helps everyone to forget his troubles, many things are done to please the ladies, whose tender and gentle souls are very susceptible to harmony and sweetness. So it is no wonder that both in ancient times and today they have always been extremely fond of musicians and have welcomed music as true refreshment for the spirit.'

Sources: Baldesar Castiglione, *The Book of the Courtier*, trans. George Bull (New York: Penguin Books, Ltd., 1967, 1986), pp. 90-96, 98-102.

## QUESTIONS FOR PART 14

1. The term "renaissance" literally means rebirth. What was reborn and how?
2. How was the Renaissance also a time of continuity of medieval culture?
3. Why did the Renaissance begin first in the Italian city-states?

# PART 15

# REFORMATION AND THE WARS OF RELIGION

There were many Reformations in the sixteenth century. Some of the movement's leaders began as reformers and became protesters, while others remained reformers. Furthermore, these Reformations did not appear without precedent or cause; humanism and renaissance ideas also contributed to the Reformations. Martin Luther's objections to particular Catholic practices in 1517 was certainly one starting point of one Reformation, but it had inherited fifteenth-century humanism and movements that emphasized personal piety. John Calvin and Ulrich Zwingli introduced their own Reformations in the decade after Luther's, and while they both agreed with Luther (and each other) on some doctrines and beliefs, they disagreed with Luther (and each other) on many more. All three, as well as other reformers were influenced by emerging national awareness. It seemed as if every European country had its own version of a Reformation. The Catholic Church had its own as well, although it did so without changing any doctrine; instead it underwent an internal renewal and rid itself of abuses.

All Reformations, whether Protestant or Catholic, ended up the period embroiled in violence. Religious wars swept across Europe in the mid-sixteenth century and would continue into the seventeenth. One particularly horrific manifestation of the religious violence was the witch hunts, which admittedly began in the Late Middle Ages, but which increased in both scope and degree of violence as the Reformation progressed. Reformation and religious violence were both aided by the new technology of printing, which made ideas more readily available to a wider audience than ever before.

# 15.1

# *NINETY-FIVE THESES*, MARTIN LUTHER

*The most important document of the Protestant Reformation was the* Ninety-Five Theses *of Martin Luther. Luther (1483-1546) was an intensely devout monk with legal training and humanist interests who was obsessed with salvation. In 1517 Luther was teaching at the university in Wittenberg when the Dominican Tetzel arrived to preach a special indulgence. Indulgences were papal dispensations (releases) from either penance or time in purgatory in exchange for an act of faith. The Crusades are an example of how indulgences had been used by the Church; Crusaders had been promised full remission of their sins in exchange for fighting. Tetzel promised salvation if people donated money for the construction of St. Peter's in Rome. Luther was confused by the theology of the indulgence and offended by the apparent "sale" of salvation preached by Tetzel. Luther posited ninety-five points on penance, indulgences, and salvation; he proposed this topic for discussion in the traditional university manner by posting his theses on the church door.*

## QUESTIONS

1. How does Luther's legal background reveal itself in how he thinks about indulgences?
2. Find an example of how Luther uses scripture to argue against the theory of indulgence.
3. How is Luther using this opportunity to criticize papal abuses?

# NINETY-FIVE THESES
*or*
## DISPUTATION ON THE POWER AND EFFICACY OF INDULGENCES

1. When our Lord and Mater Jesus Christ said, "Repent" [Matt. 4:17], he willed the entire life of believers to be one of repentance.
2. This word cannot be understood as referring to the sacrament of penance, that is, confession and satisfaction, as administered by the clergy.
3. Yet it does not mean solely inner repentance; such inner repentance is worthless unless it produces various outward mortifications of the flesh.
4. The penalty of sin remains as long as the hatred of self, that is, true inner repentance, until our entrance into the kingdom of heaven.
5. The pope neither desires nor is able to remit any penalties except those imposed by his own authority or that of the canons.
6. The pope cannot remit any guilt, except by declaring and showing that it has been remitted by God; or, to be sure, by remitting guilt in cases reserved to his judgment. If his right to grant remission in these cases were disregarded, the guilt would certainly remain unforgiven.
7. God remits guilt to no one unless at the same time he humbles him in all things and makes him submissive to his vicar the priest.
8. The penitential canons are imposed only on the living, and, according to the canons themselves, nothing should be imposed on the dying.
9. Therefore the Holy Spirit through the pope is kind to us insofar as the pope in his decrees always makes exception of the article of death and of necessity.
10. Those priests act ignorantly and wickedly who, in the case of the dying, reserve canonical penalties for purgatory.
11. Those tares of changing the canonical penalty to the penalty of purgatory were evidently sown while the bishops slept [Matt. 13:25].
12. In former times canonical penalties were imposed, not after, but before absolution, as tests of true contrition.
13. The dying are freed by death from all penalties, are already dead as far as the canon laws are concerned, and have a right to be released from them.

14. Imperfect piety or love on the part of the dying person necessarily brings with it great fear; and the smaller the love, the greater the fear.
15. This fear or horror is sufficient in itself, to say nothing of other things, to constitute the penalty of purgatory, since it is very near the horror of despair.
16. Hell, purgatory, and heaven seem to differ the same as despair, fear, and assurance of salvation.
17. It seems as though for the souls in purgatory fear should necessarily decrease and love increase.
18. Furthermore, it does not seem proved, either by reason or Scripture, that souls in purgatory are outside the state of merit, that is, unable to grow in love.
19. Nor does it seem proved that should in purgatory, at least not all f them, are certain an assured of their own salvation, even if we ourselves may be entirely certain of it.
20. Therefore the pope, when he uses the words "plenary remission of all penalties," does not actually mean "all penalties," but only those imposed by himself.
21. Thus those indulgence preachers are in error who say that a man is absolved from every penalty and saved by papal indulgences.
22. As a matter of fact, the pope remits to souls in purgatory no penalty which, according to canon law, they should have paid in this life.
23. If remission of all penalties whatsoever could be granted to anyone at all, certainly it would be granted only to the most perfect, that is, to very few.
24. For this reason most people are necessarily deceived by that indiscriminate and high-sounding promise of release from penalty.
25. That power which the pope has in general over purgatory corresponds to the power which any bishop or curate has in a particular way in his own diocese and parish.
26. The pope does very well when he grants remission to souls in purgatory, not by the power of the keys, which he does not have, but by way of intercession for them.
27. They preach only human doctrines who say that as soon as the money clinks into the money chest, the soul flies out of purgatory.
28. It is certain that when money clinks in the money chest, greed and avarice can be increased; but when the church intercedes, the result is in the hands of God alone.
29. Who knows whether all souls in purgatory wish to be redeemed, since we have exceptions in St. Severinus and St. Paschal, as related in a legend.
30. No one is sure of the integrity of his own contrition, much less of having received plenary remission.
31. The man who actually buys indulgences is as rare as he who is really penitent; indeed, he is exceedingly rare.
32. Those who believe that they can be certain of their salvation because they have indulgence letters will be eternally damned, together with their teachers.
33. Men must especially be on guard against those who say that the pope's pardons are that inestimable gift of God by which man is reconciled to him.
34. For the graces of indulgences are concerned only with the penalties of sacramental satisfaction established by man.
35. They who teach that contrition is not necessary on the part of those who intend to buy souls out of purgatory or to buy confessional privileges preach unchristian doctrine.
36. Any truly repentant Christian has a right to full remission of penalty and guilt, even without indulgence letters.
37. Any true Christian, whether living or dead, participates in all the blessings of Christ and the church; and this is granted him by God, even without indulgence letters.

38. Nevertheless, papal remission and blessing are by no means to be disregarded, for they are, as I have said (Thesis 6), the proclamation of the divine remission.

39. It is very difficult, even for the most learned theologians, at one and the same time to commend to the people the bounty of indulgences and the need of true contrition.

40. A Christian who is truly contrite seeks and loves to pay penalties for his sins; the bounty of indulgences, however, relaxes penalties and causes men to hate them -- at least it furnishes occasion for hating them.

41. Papal indulgences must be preached with caution, lest people erroneously think that they are preferable to other good works of love.

42. Christians are to be taught that the pope does not intend that the buying of indulgences should in any way be compared with works of mercy.

43. Christians are to be taught that he who gives to the poor or lends to the needy does a better deed than he who buys indulgences.

44. Because love grows by works of love, man thereby becomes better. Man does not, however, become better by means of indulgences but is merely freed from penalties.

45. Christians are to be taught that he who sees a needy man and passes him by, yet gives his money for indulgences, does not buy papal indulgences but God's wrath.

46. Christians are to be taught that, unless they have more than they need, they must reserve enough for their family needs and by no means squander it on indulgences.

47. Christians are to be taught that they buying of indulgences is a matter of free choice, not commanded.

48 Christians are to be taught that the pope, in granting indulgences, needs and thus desires their devout prayer more than their money.

49. Christians are to be taught that papal indulgences are useful only if they do not put their trust in them, but very harmful if they lose their fear of God because of them.

50. Christians are to be taught that if the pope knew the exactions of the indulgence preachers, he would rather that the basilica of St. Peter were burned to ashes than built up with the skin, flesh, and bones of his sheep.

51. Christians are to be taught that the pope would and should wish to give of his own money, even though he had to sell the basilica of St. Peter, to many of those from whom certain hawkers of indulgences cajole money.

52. It is vain to trust in salvation by indulgence letters, even though the indulgence commissary, or even the pope, were to offer his soul as security.

53. They are the enemies of Christ and the pope who forbid altogether the preaching of the Word of God in some churches in order that indulgences may be preached in others.

54. Injury is done to the Word of God when, in the same sermon, an equal or larger amount of time is devoted to indulgences than to the Word.

55. It is certainly the pope's sentiment that if indulgences, which are a very insignificant thing, are celebrated with one bell, one procession, and one ceremony, then the gospel, which is the very greatest thing, should be preached with a hundred bells, a hundred processions, a hundred ceremonies.

56. The true treasures of the church, out of which the pope distributes indulgences, are not sufficiently discussed or known among the people of Christ.

57. That indulgences are not temporal treasures is certainly clear, for many indulgence sellers do not distribute them freely but only gather them.

58. Nor are they the merits of Christ and the saints, for, even without the pope, the latter always work grace for the inner man, and the cross, death, and hell for the outer man.

59. St. Lawrence said that the poor of the church were the treasures of the church, but he spoke according to the usage of the word in his own time.

60. Without want of consideration we say that the keys of the church, given by the merits of Christ, are that treasure.

61. For it is clear that the pope's power is of itself sufficient for the remission of penalties and cases reserved by himself.

62. The true treasure of the church is the most holy gospel of the glory and grace of God.

63. But this treasure is naturally most odious, for it makes the first to be last (Mt. 20:16).

64. On the other hand, the treasure of indulgences is naturally most acceptable, for it makes the last to be first.

65. Therefore the treasures of the gospel are nets with which one formerly fished for men of wealth.

66. The treasures of indulgences are nets with which one now fishes for the wealth of men.

67. The indulgences which the demagogues acclaim as the greatest graces are actually understood to be such only insofar as they promote gain.

68. They are nevertheless in truth the most insignificant graces when compared with the grace of God and the piety of the cross.

69. Bishops and curates are bound to admit the commissaries of papal indulgences with all reverence.

70. But they are much more bound to strain their eyes and ears lest these men preach their own dreams instead of what the pope has commissioned.

71. Let him who speaks against the truth concerning papal indulgences be anathema and accursed.

72. But let him who guards against the lust and license of the indulgence preachers be blessed.

73. Just as the pope justly thunders against those who by any means whatever contrive harm to the sale of indulgences.

74. Much more does he intend to thunder against those who use indulgences as a pretext to contrive harm to holy love and truth.

75. To consider papal indulgences so great that they could absolve a man even if he had done the impossible and had violated the mother of God is madness.

76. We say on the contrary that papal indulgences cannot remove the very least of venial sins as far as guilt is concerned.

77. To say that even St. Peter if he were now pope, could not grant greater graces is blasphemy against St. Peter and the pope.

78. We say on the contrary that even the present pope, or any pope whatsoever, has greater graces at his disposal, that is, the gospel, spiritual powers, gifts of healing, etc., as it is written, 1 Co 12[:28].

79. To say that the cross emblazoned with the papal coat of arms, and set up by the indulgence preachers is equal in worth to the cross of Christ is blasphemy.

80. The bishops, curates, and theologians who permit such talk to be spread among the people will have to answer for this.

81. This unbridled preaching of indulgences makes it difficult even for learned men to rescue the reverence which is due the pope from slander or from the shrewd questions of the laity.

82. Such as: "Why does not the pope empty purgatory for the sake of holy love and the dire need of the souls that are there if he redeems an infinite number of souls for the sake of miserable money with which to build a church?" The former reason would be most just; the latter is most trivial.

83. Again, "Why are funeral and anniversary masses for the dead continued and why does he not return or permit the withdrawal of the endowments founded for them, since it is wrong to pray for the redeemed?"

84. Again, "What is this new piety of God and the pope that for a consideration of money they permit a man who is impious and their enemy to buy out of purgatory the pious soul of a friend of God and do not rather, because of the need of that pious and beloved soul, free it for pure love's sake?"

85. Again, "Why are the penitential canons, long since abrogated and dead in actual fact and through disuse, now satisfied by the granting of indulgences as though they were still alive and in force?"

86. Again, "Why does not the pope, whose wealth is today greater than the wealth of the richest Crassus, build this one basilica of St. Peter with his own money rather than with the money of poor believers?"

87. Again, "What does the pope remit or grant to those who by perfect contrition already have a right to full remission and blessings?"

88. Again, "What greater blessing could come to the church than if the pope were to bestow these remissions and blessings on every believer a hundred times a day, as he now does but once?"

89. "Since the pope seeks the salvation of souls rather than money by his indulgences, why does he suspend the indulgences and pardons previously granted when they have equal efficacy?"

90. To repress these very sharp arguments of the laity by force alone, and not to resolve them by giving reasons, is to expose the church and the pope to the ridicule of their enemies and to make Christians unhappy.

91. If, therefore, indulgences were preached according to the spirit and intention of the pope, all these doubts would be readily resolved. Indeed, they would not exist.

92. Away, then, with all those prophets who say to the people of Christ, "Peace, peace," and there is no peace! (Jer 6:14)

93. Blessed be all those prophets who say to the people of Christ, "Cross, cross," and there is no cross!

94. Christians should be exhorted to be diligent in following Christ, their Head, through penalties, death and hell.

95. And thus be confident of entering into heaven through many tribulations rather than through the false security of peace (Acts 14:22).

Source: *Luther's Works, Volume 31, Career of the Reformer: I*, ed. Harold J. Grimm (Philadelphia: Muhlenberg Press, 1957), pp. 25-33.

# 15.2

---- ✥ ----

## SIXTY-SEVEN ARTICLES, ULRICH ZWINGLI

*With the Ninety-Five Theses of Luther, the Protestant Reformation had begun. Luther had probably not intended to break away from the church when he first questioned the practice of indulgences, but that was the end result. Particularly appealing to many Christians across Europe was Luther's insistence that scripture alone should be the source of Christian doctrine. Ulrich Zwingli (1484-1531) began preaching on the centrality of scripture in 1523 and was immediately controversial; a town council was called after much debate proclaimed Zwingli to be the spiritual leader of the city and encouraged him to continue his preaching. The Reformation begun by Luther in Germany had spread to Switzerland.*

*Although he was influenced by Luther, Zwingli was no Lutheran. The two theologians differed greatly on certain doctrines, particularly their interpretation of the nature of the sacraments and the relationship between church and state. Zwingli envisioned Zurich as a "Christian" city, and theorized that the civil authority came from God.*

*The following source lists Zwingli's plan for Zurich.*

---- ✦ ----

## QUESTIONS

1. What is Zwingli's view of the papacy?
2. According to Zwingli, what is the relationship between the individual and God?
3. How does Zwingli define the priesthood?

The articles and opinions below, I, Ulrich Zwingli, confess to have preached in the worthy city of Zurich as based upon the Scriptures which are called inspired by God, and I offer to protect and conquer with the said articles, and where I have not now correctly understood said Scriptures I shall allow myself to be taught better, but only from said Scriptures.

I. All who say that the Gospel is invalid without the confirmation of the Church err and slander God.

II. The sum and substance of the Gospel is that our Lord Jesus Christ, the true Son of God, has made known to us the will of his heavenly Father, and has with his innocence released us from death and reconciled God.

III. Hence Christ is the only way to salvation for all who ever were, are and shall be.

IV. Who seeks or points out another door errs, yea, he is a murderer of souls and a thief.

V. Hence all who consider other teachings equal to or higher than the Gospel err, and do not know what the Gospel is.

VI. For Jesus Christ is the guide and leader, promised by God to all human beings, which promise was fulfilled.

VII. That he is an eternal salvation and head of all believers, who are his body, but which is dead and can do nothing without him.

VIII. From this follows first that all who dwell in the head are members and children of God, and that is the church or communion of the saints, the bride of Christ, *Ecclesia catholica.*

IX. Furthermore, that as the members of the body can do nothing without the control of the head, so no one in the body of Christ can do the least without his head, Christ.

X. As that man is mad whose limbs (try to) do something without his head, tearing, wounding, injuring himself; thus when the members of Christ undertake something without their head,

Christ, they are mad, and injure and burden themselves with unwise ordinances.

XI. Hence we see in the clerical (so-called) ordinances, concerning their splendor, riches, classes, titles, laws, a cause of all foolishness, for they do not also agree with the head.

XII. Thus they still rage, not on account of the head (for that one is eager to bring forth in these times from the grace of God,) but because one will not let them rage, but tries to compel them to listen to the head.

XIII. Where this (the head) is hearkened to one learns clearly and plainly the will of God, and man is attracted by his spirit to him and changed into him.

XIV. Therefore all Christian people shall use their best diligence that the Gospel of Christ be preached alike everywhere.

XV. For in the faith rests our salvation, and in unbelief our damnation; for all truth is clear in him.

XVI. In the Gospel one learns that human doctrines and decrees do not aid in salvation.

## ABOUT THE POPE

XVII. That Christ is the only eternal high priest, wherefrom it follows that those who have called themselves high priests have opposed the honor and power of Christ, yea, cast it out.

## ABOUT THE MASS

XVIII. That Christ, having sacrificed himself once, is to eternity a certain and valid sacrifice for the sins of all faithful, wherefrom it follows that the mass is not a sacrifice, but is a remembrance of the sacrifice and assurance of the salvation which Christ has given us.

XIX. That Christ is the only mediator between God and us.

XX. That God desires to give us all things in his name, whence it follows that outside of this life we need no mediator except himself.

XXI. That when we pray for each other on earth, we do so in such fashion that we believe that all things are given to us through Christ alone.

## ABOUT GOOD WORKS

XXII. That Christ is our justice, from which follows that our works in so far as they are good, so far they are of Christ, but in so far as they are ours, they are neither right nor good.

## CONCERNING CLERICAL PROPERTY

XXIII. That Christ scorns the property and pomp of this world, whence from it follows that those who attract wealth to themselves in his name slander him terribly when they make him a pretext for their avarice and wilfullness.

## CONCERNING THE FORBIDDING OF FOOD

XXIV. That no Christian is bound to do those things which God has not decreed, therefore one may eat at all times all food, wherefrom one learns that the decree about cheese and butter is a Roman swindle.

## ABOUT HOLIDAY AND PILGRIMAGE

XXV. That time and place is under the jurisdiction of Christian people, and man with them, wherefrom is learnt that those who fix time and place deprive the Christians of their liberty.

## ABOUT HOODS, DRESS, INSIGNIA

XXVI. That God is displeased with nothing so much as with hypocrisy; whence is learnt that all is gross hypocrisy and profligacy which is mere show before men. Under this condemnation fall hoods, insignia, plates, etc.

## ABOUT ORDER AND SECTS

XXVII. That all Christian men are brethren of Christ and brethren of one another, and shall create no father (for themselves) on earth. Under this condemnation fall orders, sects, brotherhoods, etc.

## ABOUT THE MARRIAGE OF ECCLESIASTS

XXVIII. That all which God has allowed or not forbidden is righteous, hence marriage is permitted to all human beings.

XXIX. That all who are called clericals sin when they do not protect themselves by marriage after they have become conscious that God has not enabled them to remain chaste.

## ABOUT THE VOW OF CHASTITY

XXX. That those who promise chastity [outside of matrimony] take foolishly or childishly too much upon themselves, whence is learnt that those who make such vows do wrong to the pious being.

## ABOUT THE BAN

XXXI. That no special person can impose the ban upon any one, but the Church, that is the congregation of those among whom the one to be banned dwells, together with their watch man, *i.e.,* the pastor.

XXXII. That one may ban only him who gives public offence.

## ABOUT ILLEGAL PROPERTY

XXXIII. That property unrighteously acquired shall not be given to temples, monasteries, cathedrals, clergy or nuns, but to the needy, if it cannot be returned to the legal owner.

## ABOUT MAGISTRY

XXXIV. The spiritual (so-called) power has no justification for its pomp in the teaching of Christ.

XXXV. But the lay has power and confirmation from the deed and doctrine of Christ.

XXXVI. All that the spiritual so-called state claims to have of power and protection belongs to the lay, if they wish to be Christians.

XXXVII. To them, furthermore, all Christians owe obedience without exception.

XXXVIII. In so far as they do not command that which is contrary to God.

XXXIX. Therefore all their laws shall be in harmony with the divine will, so that they protect the oppressed, even if he does not complain.

XL. They alone may put to death justly, also, only those who give public offence (if God is not offended let another thing be commanded).

XLI. If they give good advice and help to those for whom they must account to God, then these owe to them bodily assistance.

XLII. But if they are unfaithful and transgress the laws of Christ they may be deposed in the name of God.

XLIII. In short, the realm of him is best and most stable who rules in the name of God alone, and his is worst and most unstable who rules in accordance with his own will.

## ABOUT PRAYER

XLIV. Real petitioners call to God in spirit and truly, without great ado before men.

XLV. Hypocrites do their work so that they may be seen by men, also receive their reward in this life.

XLVI. Hence it must always follow that church-song and outcry without devoutness, and only for reward, is seeking either fame before the men or gain.

## ABOUT OFFENCE

XLVII. Bodily death a man should suffer before he offend or scandalize a Christian.

XLVIII. Who through stupidness or ignorance is offended without cause, he should not be left sick or weak, but he should be made strong, that he may not consider as a sin which is not a sin.

XLIX. Greater offence I know not than that one does not allow priests to have wives, but permits them to hire prostitutes. Out upon the shame!

## ABOUT REMITTANCE OF SIN

L. God alone remits sin through Jesus Christ, his Son, and alone our Lord.

LI. Who assigns this to creatures detracts from the honor of God and gives it to him who is not God; this is real idolatry.

LII. Hence the confession which is made to the priest or neighbor shall not be declared to be a remittance of sin, but only a seeking for advice.

LIII. Works of penance coming from the counsel of human beings (except the ban) do not cancel sin; they are imposed as a menace to others.

LIV. Christ has borne all our pains and labor. Hence whoever assigns to works of penance what belongs to Christ errs and slanders God.

LV. Whoever pretends to remit to a penitent being any sin would not be a vicar of God or St. Peter, but of the devil.

LVI. Whoever remits any sin only for the sake of money is the companion of Simon and Balaam, and the real messenger of the devil personified.

## ABOUT PURGATORY

LVII. The true divine Scriptures know naught about purgatory after this life.

LVIII. The sentence of the dead is known to God only.

LVIX. And the less God has let us know concerning it, the less we should undertake to know about it.

LX. That man earnestly calls to God to show mercy to the dead I do not condemn, but to determine a period of time therefor (seven years for a mortal sin), and to lie for the sake of gain, is not human, but devilish.

## ABOUT THE PRIESTHOOD.

LXI. About the consecration which the priests have received in late times the Scriptures know nothing.

LXII. Furthermore, they know no priests except those who proclaim the word of God.

LXIII. They command honor should be shown, i.e., to furnish them with food for the body.

## ABOUT THE CESSATION OF MISUSAGES

LXIV. All those who recognize their errors shall not be allowed to suffer, but to die in peace, and thereafter arrange in a Christian manner their bequests to the Church.

LXV. Those who do not wish to confess, God will probably take care of. Hence no force shall be used against their body, unless it be that they behave so criminally that one cannot do without that.

LXVI. All the clerical superiors shall at once settle down, and with unanimity set up the cross of Christ, not the money-chests, or they will perish, for I tell thee the ax is raised against the tree.

LXVII. If any one wishes conversation with me concerning interest, tithes, unbaptized children or confirmation, I am willing to answer.

Let no one undertake here to argue with sophistry or human foolishness, but come to the Scriptures to accept them as the judge (foras cares! the Scriptures breathe the Spirit of God), so that the truth either may be found, or if found, as I hope, retained.

Amen.

Thus may God rule.

The basis and commentary of these articles will soon appear in print.

Sources: *Ulrich Zwingli (1484-1531): Selected Works*, ed. Samuel Macauley Jackson (Philadelphia: University of Philadelphia Press, 1901, 1972), pp. 111-117.

# 15.3

---  ✣  ---

## "RAPTURE OF THE SOUL," TERESA OF AVILA

*The Catholic Church was not unresponsive to the charges of reformers such as Luther and Zwingli. There were two stages to the Counter-Reformation that took place within the Catholic Church. One was the official response by both pope and emperor, which were to condemn Luther and the Protestants, and to summon a church council at Trent in 1545-1563, which confirmed all Catholic doctrines and practices. The second response was a movement of spiritual renewal, which promoted a more personal relationship between humanity and God. New religious orders such as the Society of Jesus (the Jesuits) and the Capuchins (a reformed Franciscan order) emerged. Missionary activity also increased, helped by the discovery of the Americas and new access to Asia. Mysticism had a resurgence in popularity, which incorporated personal piety and traditional Catholic faith. Teresa of Avila (1515-1582) was a Carmelite nun who had intense visions of God. In the following excerpt from her mystical text, the Interior Castle, she discusses the soul's rapturous union with God.*

---  ✣  ---

### QUESTIONS

1. How is Teresa's understanding of rapture related to her gender?
2. Compare this with Luther's Ninety-Five Theses. How do the two differ in their description of how the soul knows God?
3. Who do you think was the intended audience of this mystical text?

• • • I want to put down here some kinds of rapture that I've come to understand because I've discussed them with so many spiritual persons. But I don't know whether I shall succeed as I did when I wrote elsewhere about them and other things that occur in this dwelling place. On account of certain reasons it seems worthwhile to speak of these kinds of rapture again — if for no other reason, so that everything related to these dwelling places will be put down here together.

3. One kind of rapture is that in which the soul even though not in prayer is touched by some word it remembers or hears about God. It seems that His Majesty from the interior of the soul makes the spark we mentioned increase, for He is moved with compassion in seeing the soul suffer so long a time from its desire. All burnt up, the soul is renewed like the phoenix, and one can devoutly believe that its faults are pardoned. Now that it is so pure, the Lord joins it with Himself, without anyone understanding what is happening except these two; nor does the soul itself understand in a way that can afterward be explained. Yet, it does have interior understanding, for this experience is not like that of fainting or convulsion; in these latter nothing is understood inwardly or outwardly.

4. What I know in this case is that the soul was never so awake to the things of God nor did it have such deep enlightenment and knowledge of His Majesty. This will seem impossible, for if the faculties are so absorbed that we can say they are dead, and likewise the senses, how can a soul know that it

understands this secret? I don't know, nor perhaps does any creature but only the Creator. And this goes for many other things that take place in this state — I mean in these two dwelling places, for there is no closed door between the one and the other. Because there are things in the last that are not revealed to those who have not yet reached it, I thought I should divide them.

5. When the soul is in this suspension, the Lord likes to show it some secrets, things about heaven, and imaginative visions. It is able to tell of them afterward, for these remain so impressed on the memory that they are never forgotten. But when the visions are intellectual, the soul doesn't know how to speak of them. For there must be some visions during these moments that are so sublime that it's not fitting for those who live on this earth to have the further understanding necessary to explain them. However, since the soul is in possession of its senses, it can say many things about these intellectual visions.

It could be that some of you do not know what a vision is, especially an intellectual one. I shall explain at the proper time, for one who has the authority ordered me to do so. And although the explanation may not seem pertinent, it will perhaps benefit some souls.

6. Well now you will ask me: If afterward there is to be no remembrance of these sublime favors granted by the Lord to the soul in this state, what benefit do they have? O daughters, they are so great one cannot exaggerate! For even though they are unexplainable, they are well inscribed in the very interior part of the soul and are never forgotten.

But, you will insist, if there is no image and the faculties do not understand, how can the visions be remembered? I don't understand this either; but I do understand that some truths about the grandeur of God remain so fixed in this soul that even if faith were not to tell it who God is and of its obligation to believe that He is God, from that very moment it would adore Him as God, as did Jacob when he saw the ladder. By means of the ladder Jacob must have understood other secrets that he didn't know how to explain, for by seeing just a ladder on which angels descended and ascended he would not have understood such great mysteries if there had not been deeper interior enlightenment. I don't know if I'm guessing right in what I say, for although I have heard this story about Jacob, I don't know if I'm remembering it correctly.

7. Nor did Moses know how to describe all that he saw in the bush, but only what God wished Him to describe. But if God had not shown secrets to his soul along with a certitude that made him recognize and believe that they were from God, Moses could not have entered into so many severe trials. But he must have understood such deep things among the thorns of that bush that the vision gave him the courage to do what he did for the people of Israel. So, sisters, we don't have to look for reasons to understand the hidden things of God. Since we believe He is powerful, clearly we must believe that a worm with as limited a power as ours will not understand His grandeurs. Let us praise Him, for He is pleased that we come to know some of them.

8. I have been wanting to find some comparison by which to explain what I'm speaking about, and I don't think there is any that fits. But let's use this one: You enter into the room of a king or great lord, or I believe they call it the treasure chamber, where there are countless kinds of glass and earthen vessels and other things so arranged that almost all of these objects are seen upon entering. Once I was brought to a room like this in the house of the Duchess of Alba where, while I was on a journey, obedience ordered me to stay because of this lady's insistence with my superiors. I was amazed on entering and wondered what gain could be gotten from that conglomeration of things, and I saw that one could praise the Lord at seeing so many different kinds of objects, and now I laugh to myself on realizing how the experience has helped me here in my explanation. Although I was in that room for a while, there was so much there to see that I soon forgot it all; none of those pieces has remained in my memory any more than if I had never seen them, nor would I know how to explain the workmanship of any of them. I can

only say in general that I remember seeing everything. Likewise with this favor, the soul, while it is made one with God, is placed in this empyreal room that we must have interiorly. For, clearly, the soul has some of these dwelling places since God abides within it. And although the Lord must not want the soul to see these secrets every time it is in this ecstasy, for it can be so absorbed in enjoying Him that a sublime good like that is sufficient for it, sometimes He is pleased that the absorption decrease and the soul see at once what is in that room. After it returns to itself, the soul is left with that representation of the grandeurs it saw; but it cannot describe any of them, nor do its natural powers grasp any more than what God wished that it see supernaturally.

9. You, therefore, might object that I admit that the soul sees and that the vision is an imaginative one. But I'm not saying that, for I'm not dealing with an imaginative vision but with an intellectual one. Since I have no learning, I don't know how in my dullness to explain anything. If what I have said up to now about this prayer is worthwhile, I know clearly that I'm not the one who has said it.

I hold that if at times in its raptures the soul doesn't understand these secrets, its raptures are not given by God but are caused by some natural weakness. It can happen to persons with a weak constitution, as is so with women, that any spiritual force will overcome the natural powers, and the soul will be absorbed as I believe I mentioned in reference to the prayer of quiet. These experiences have nothing to do with rapture. In a rapture, believe me, God carries off for Himself the entire soul, and, as to someone who is His own and His spouse, He begins showing it some little part of the kingdom that it has gained by being espoused to Him. However small that part of His kingdom may be, everything that there is in this great God is magnificent. And He doesn't want any hindrance from anyone, neither from the faculties nor from the senses, but He immediately commands the doors of all these dwelling places to be closed; and only that door to His room remains open so that we can enter. Blessed be so much mercy; they will be rightly cursed who have not wanted to benefit by it and who have lost this Lord.

10. O my sisters, what nothingness it is, that which we leave! Nor is what we do anything, nor all that we could do for a God who thus wishes to communicate Himself to a worm! And if we hope to enjoy this blessing even in this present life, what are we doing? What is causing us to delay? What is enough to make us, even momentarily, stop looking for this Lord as did the bride in the streets and in the squares? Oh, what a mockery everything in the world is if it doesn't lead us and help us toward this blessing even if its delights and riches and joys, as much of them as imaginable, were to last forever! It is all loathsome dung compared to these treasures that will be enjoyed without end. Nor are these anything in comparison with having as our own the Lord of all the treasures of heaven and earth.

11. O human blindness! How long, how long before this dust will be removed from our eyes! Even though among ourselves the dust doesn't seem to be capable of blinding us completely, I see some specks, some tiny pebbles that if we allow them to increase will be enough to do us great harm. On the contrary, for the love of God, Sisters, let us benefit by these faults so as to know our misery, and they will give us clearer vision as did the mud to the blind man cured by our Spouse. Thus, seeing ourselves so imperfect, let us increase our supplications that His Majesty may draw good out of our miseries so that we might be pleasing to Him.

12. I have digressed a great deal without realizing it. Pardon me, Sisters, and believe me that having reached these grandeurs of God (I mean, reached the place where I must speak of them), I cannot help but feel very sorry to see what we lose through our own fault. Even though it is true that these are blessing the Lord gives to whomever He wills, His Majesty would give them all to us if we loved Him as He loves us. He doesn't desire anything else than to have those to whom to give. His riches do not lessen because He gives them away.

13. Well now, to get back to what I was saying, the Spouse commands that the doors of the dwelling places be closed and even those of the castle and the outer wall. For in desiring to carry off this soul, He takes away the breath so that, even though the other senses sometimes last a little longer, a person cannot speak at all; although at other times everything is taken away at once, and the hands and the body grow cold so that the person doesn't seem to have any life; nor sometimes is it known whether he is breathing. This situation lasts but a short while, I mean in its intensity; for when this extreme suspension lets up a little, it seems that the body returns to itself somewhat and is nourished so as to die again and give more life to the soul. Nevertheless, so extreme an ecstasy doesn't last long.

Source: Teresa of Avila, *Interior Castle*, trans. Kieran Kavanaugh and Otilio Rodriquez (New York: Paulist Press, 1979), pp. 126-133.

# 15.4

---✣---

# THE EDICT OF NANTES

*The Wars of Religion began in 1524 with a peasant rebellion in Germany. In France, the religious divisions turned into a civil war between noble families. John Calvin (1509-1564) began preaching in Paris in 1533, although he fled in 1536 to avoid persecution. Many people (including nobles) were still drawn to Calvinism (known in France as Huguenots) for spiritual reasons; others saw this as a chance to demand social and political reforms. In 1559 the monarchy faced another crisis: a series of weak kings, whose state was run by their mother Catherine de' Medici and the fanatically anti-Protestant Guise family. By 1562 the powerful Bourbons, relatives of the king and rivals of the Guise, were Huguenots. War broke out in 1562 when the Duc of Guise massacred Huguenots. In 1572 a larger massacre of Huguenots occurred on St. Bartholomew's Day, ordered by the king, Catherine, and Guise family. Huguenots had been invited to Paris to celebrate the marriage of Henry of Navarre (a Huguenot himself) to the king's sister.*

*But Henry did marry Margaret, the king's sister. When her two remaining brothers died, Henry became the next king of France (1594). He agreed to convert to Catholicism, but remained sympathetic to the Huguenots. In 1598 he issued this Edict.*

---✣---

## QUESTIONS

1. Does the Edict offer full toleration to the Huguenots? Explain why or why not.
2. How does Henry think the state should best deal with the recent violence?
3. How much freedom is actually promised to the Huguenots?

*Henry, by the grace of God king of France and of Navarre, to all to whom these presents come, greeting:*

Among the infinite benefits which it has pleased God to heap upon us, the most signal and precious is his granting us the strength and ability to withstand the fearful disorders and troubles which prevailed on our advent in this kingdom. The realm was so torn by innumerable factions and sects that the most legitimate of all the parties was fewest in numbers. God has given us strength to stand out against this storm; we have finally surmounted the waves and made our port of safety, — peace for our state. For which his be the glory all in all, and ours a free recognition of his grace in making use of our instrumentality in the good work.... We implore and await from the Divine Goodness the same protection and favor which he has ever granted to this kingdom from the beginning....

We have, by this perpetual and irrevocable edict established and proclaimed and do establish and proclaim:

I. First, that the recollection of everything done be one party or the other between March, 1585, and our accession to the crown, and during all the preceding period of troubles, remain obliterated and forgotten, as if no such things had ever happened.

III. We ordain that the Catholic Apostolic and Roman religion shall be restored and reestablished in all places and localities of this our kingdom and countries subject to our sway, where the exercise of the same has been interrupted, in order that it may be peaceably and freely exercised, without any trouble or hindrance: forbidding very expressly all persons, of whatsoever estate, quality, or condition, from troubling, molesting, or disturbing ecclesiastics in the celebration of divine service, in the enjoyment or collection of tithes, fruits, or revenues of their benefices, and all other rights and dues belonging to them: and that all those who during the troubles have taken possession of churches. Houses, goods or revenues, belonging to the said ecclesiastics, shall surrender to them entire possession and peaceable enjoyment of such rights, liberties, and sureties as they had before they were deprived of them.

VI. And in order to leave no occasion for troubles or differences between our subjects, we have permitted, and herewith permit, those of the said religion called Reformed to live and abide in all the cities and places of this our kingdom and countries of our sway, without being annoyed, molested, or compelled to do anything in the matter of religion contrary to their consciences, . . . upon condition that they comport themselves in other respects according to that which is contained in this our present edict.

VII. It is permitted to all lords, gentlemen, and other persons making profession of the said religion called Reformed, holding the right of high justice [or a certain feudal tenure], to exercise the said religion in their houses.

IX. We also permit those of the said religion to make and continue the exercise of the same in all villages and places of our dominion where it was established by them and publicly enjoyed several and divers times in the year 1597, up to the end of the month of August, notwithstanding all decrees and judgments to the contrary.

XIII. We very expressly forbid to all those of the said religion its exercise, either in respect to ministry, regulation, discipline, or the public instruction of children, or otherwise, in this our kingdom and lands of our dominion, otherwise than in the places permitted and granted by the present edict.

XIV. It is forbidden as well to perform any function of the said religion in our court or retinue, or in our lands and territories beyond the mountains, or in our city of Paris. or within five leagues of the said city.

XVIII. We also forbid all our subjects, of whatever quality and condition, from carrying off be force or persuasion, against the will of their parents, the children of the said religion, in order to cause them to be baptized or confirmed in the Catholic Apostolic and Roman Church; and the same is forbidden to those of the said religion called Reformed, upon penalty of being punished with especial severity.

XXI. Books concerning the said religion called Reformed may not be printed and publicly sold, except in cities and places where the public exercise of the said religion is permitted.

XXII. We ordain that there shall be no difference or distinction made in respect to the said religion, in receiving pupils to be instructed in universities, colleges, and schools; nor in receiving the sick and poor into hospitals, retreats and public charities.

XXIII. Those of the said religion called Reformed shall be obliged to respect the laws of the Catholic Apostolic and Roman Church, recognized in this our kingdom, for the consummation of marriages contracted, or to be contracted, as regards the degrees of consanguinity and kinship.

Source: James Harvey Robinson, ed., *Readings in European History*, Vol. II, (Boston: Ginn and Company, 1904, 1934), pp. 183-85.

# 15.5

## *MALLEUS MALEFICARUM*

*Another manifestation of the Wars of Religion was the witch hunts. There had been restrictions against witchcraft within the medieval Catholic Church, but active persecution of people suspected of witchcraft began in 1484 with a papal bull, which specifically allowed the inquisition to use torture on suspected witches. The witch trials begin in earnest in the mid-sixteenth century, and continue until about mid-seventeenth century. "Witches" were yet another target of religious violence: both Catholics and Protestants persecuted men and women suspected of witchcraft.*

*The following source is from 1486. It is an excerpt from the* Malleus Maleficarum, *the "Hammer of Witches" written by two Dominican friars. It was intended to be handbook for the identification, capture, torturing, and execution of suspected witches. The* Malleus *was popular with both Catholics and Protestants. The following excerpt identifies a group that was deemed particularly susceptible to interest in witchcraft: women.*

### QUESTIONS

1. How exactly is "witch craft" being defined in this period?
2. Why were women supposed to be so susceptible?
3. This text was written by a Catholic, yet the basic principles of it were also used by Protestant witch hunters. What "authority" does this text have for Protestants?

*Why Superstition is chiefly found in Women.*

As for the first question, why a greater number of witches is found in the fragile feminine sex than among men; it is indeed a fact that it were idle to contradict, since it is accredited by actual experience, apart from the verbal testimony of credibly witnesses. And without in any way detracting from a sex in which God has always taken great glory that His might should be spread abroad, let us say that various men have assigned various reasons for this fact, which nevertheless agree in principle. Wherefore it is good, for the admonition of women, to speak of this matter; and it has often been proved by experience that they are eager to hear of it, so long as it is set forth with discretion.

For some learned men propound this reason; that there are three things in nature, the Tongue, an Ecclesiastic, and a Woman, which know no moderation in goodness or vice; and when they exceed the bounds of their condition they reach the greatest heights and the lowest depths of goodness and vice. When they are governed by a good spirit, they are most excellent in virtue; but when they are governed by an evil spirit, they indulge the worst possible vices....

Now the wickedness of women is spoken of in *Ecclesiasticus* xxv: There is no head above the head of a serpent: and there is no wrath above the wrath of a woman. I had rather dwell with a lion and a dragon than to keep house with a wicked woman. And among much which in that place precedes and follows about a wicked woman, he concludes: All wickedness is but little to the wickedness of a woman. Wherefore S. John Chrysostom says on the text, It is not good to marry (*S. Matthew* xix): What else is woman but a foe to friendship, an unescapable punishment, a necessary evil, a natural temptation, a desirable calamity, a domestic danger, a delectable detriment, an evil of nature, painted with fair colours! Therefore if it be a sin to divorce her when she ought to be kept, it is indeed a necessary torture; for either we commit adultery by divorcing her, or we must endure daily strife. Cicero in his second book of *The Rhetorics* says: The many lusts of men lead them into one sin, but the lust of women leads them into all sins; for the root of all women's vices is avarice. And Seneca says in his *Tragedies:* A woman either loves or hates; there is no third grade. And the tears of woman are a deception, for they may spring from true grief, or they may be a snare. When a woman thinks alone, she thinks evil....

And all this is made clear also in the New Testament concerning women and virgins and other holy women who have by faith led nations and kingdoms away from the worship of idols to the Christian religion. Anyone who looks at Vincent of Beauvais (*in Spe. Histo.*, XXVI. 9) will find marvellous things of the conversion of Hungary by the most Christian Gilia, and of the Franks by Clotilda, the wife of Clovis. Wherefore in many vituperations that we read against women, the word woman is used to mean the lust of the flesh. As it is said: I have found a woman more bitter than death, and good woman subject to carnal lust.

Other again have propounded other reasons why there are more superstitious women found than men. And the first is, that they are more credulous; and since the chief aim of the devil is to corrupt faith, therefore he rather attacks them. See *Ecclesiasticus* xix: He that is quick to believe is light-minded, and shall be diminished. The second reason is, that women are naturally more impressionable, and more ready to receive the influence of a disembodied spirit; and that when they use this quality well they are very good, but when they use it ill they are very evil.

The third reason is that they have slippery tongues, and are unable to conceal from the fellow-women those things which by evil arts they know; and, since they are weak, they find an easy and secret manner of vindicating themselves by witchcraft. See *Ecclesiasticus* as quoted above: I had rather dwell with a lion and a dragon than to keep house with a wicked woman. All wickedness is but little to the wickedness of a woman. And to this may be added that, as they are very impressionable, they act accordingly.

There are also others who bring forward yet other reasons, of which preachers should be very careful how they make use. For it is true that in the Old Testament the Scriptures have much that is evil to say about women, and this because of the first temptress, Eve, and her imitators; yet afterwards in the New Testament we find a change of name, as from Eva to Ave (as S. Jerome says), and the whole sin of Eve taken away by the benediction of Mary. Therefore preachers should always say as much praise of them as possible.

But because in these times this perfidy is more often found in women than in men, as we learn by actual experience, if anyone is curious as to the reason, we may add to what has already been said the following: that since they are feebler both in mind and body, it is not surprising that they should come more under the spell of witchcraft.

For as regards intellect, or the understanding of spiritual things, they seem to be of a different nature from men; a fact which is vouched for by the logic of the authorities, backed by various examples from the Scriptures. Terence says: Women are intellectually like children. And Lactantius (*Institutiones*, III): No woman understood philosophy except Temeste. And *Proverbs* xi, as it were describing a woman, says: As a jewel of gold in a swine's snout, so is a fair woman which is without discretion.

But the natural reason is that she is more carnal than a man, as is clear from her many carnal abominations. And it should be noted that there was a defect in the formation of the first woman, since she was formed from a bent rib, that is, a rib of the breast, which is bent as it were in a contrary direction to a man. And since through this defect she is an imperfect animal, she always deceives. For Cato says: When a woman weeps she weaves snares. And again: When a woman weeps, she labours to deceive a man. And this is shown by Samson's wife, who coaxed him to tell her the riddle he had propounded to the Philistines, and told them the answer, and so deceived him. And it is clear in the case of the first woman that she had little faith; for when the serpent asked why they did not eat of every tree in Paradise, she answered: Of every tree, etc. - lest perchance we die. Thereby she showed that she doubted, and had little in the word of God. And all this is indicated by the etymology of the word; for *Femina* comes from *Fe* and *Minus*, since she is ever weaker to hold and preserve the faith. And this as regards faith is of her very nature; although both by grace and nature faith never failed in the Blessed Virgin, even at the time of Christ's Passion, when it failed in all men.

Therefore a wicked woman is by her nature quicker to waver in her faith, and consequently quicker to abjure the faith, which is the root of witchcraft.

And as to her other mental quality, that is, her natural will; when she hates someone whom she formerly loved, then she seethes with anger and impatience in her whole soul, just as the tides of the sea are always heaving and boiling. Many authorities allude to this cause. *Ecclesiasticus* xxv: There is no wrath above the wrath of a woman. And Seneca (*Tragedies*, VIII): No might of the flames or the swollen winds, no deadly weapon, is so much to be feared as the lust and hatred of a woman who has been divorced from the marriage bed....

And indeed, just as through the first defect in their intelligence they are more prone to abjure the faith; so through their second defect of inordinate affections and passions they search for, brood over, and inflict various vengeances, either by witchcraft, or by some other means. Wherefore it is no wonder that so great a number of witches exist in this sex.

Women also have weak memories; and it is a natural vice in them not to be disciplined, but to follow their own impulses without any sense of what is due; this is her whole study, and all that she keeps in her memory. So Theophrastus says: If you hand over the whole management of the house to her, but reserve some minute detail to your own judgement, she will think that you are displaying a great want of faith in her, and will stir up strife; and unless you quickly take counsel, she will prepare poison for you, and consult seers and soothsayers; and will become a witch....

If we inquire, we find that nearly all the kingdoms of the world have been overthrown by women. Troy, which was a prosperous kingdom, was, for the rape of one woman, Helen, destroyed, and many thousands of Greeks slain. The kingdom of the Jews suffered much misfortune and destruction through the accursed Jezebel, and her daughter Athaliah, queen of Judah, who caused her son's sons to be killed, that on their death she might reign herself; yet each of them was slain. The kingdom of the Romans endured much evil through Cleopatra, Queen of Egypt, that worst of women. And so with others. Therefore it is no wonder if the world now suffers through the malice of women.

And now let us examine the carnal desires of the body itself, whence has arisen unconscionable harm to human life. Justly may we say with Cato of Utica: If the world could be rid of women, we should not be without God in our intercourse. For truly, without the wickedness of women, to say nothing of witchcraft, the world would still remain proof against innumerable dangers. Hear what Valerius said to Rufinus: You do not know that women is the Chimaera, but it is good that you should know it; for that monster was of three forms; its face was that of a radiant and noble lion, it had the filthy belly of a goat, and it was armed with the virulent tail of a viper. And he means that a woman is beautiful to look upon, contaminating to the touch, and deadly to keep.

Let us consider another property of hers, the voice. For as she is a liar by nature, so in her speech she stings while she delights us. Wherefore her voice is like the song of the Sirens, who with their sweet melody entice the passers-by and kill them. For they kill them by emptying their purses, consuming their strength, and causing them to forsake God. Again Valerius says to Rufinus: When she speaks it is a delight which flavours the sin; the flower of love is a rose, because under its blossom there are hidden many thorns. See *Proverbs* v, 3-4: Her mouth is smoother than oil; that is, her speech is afterwards as bitter as absinthium. [Her throat is smoother than oil. But her end is as bitter as wormwood.]

Let us consider also her gait, posture, and habit, in which is vanity of vanities. There is no man in the world who studies so hard to please the good God as even an ordinary woman studies by her vanities to please men. An example of this is to be found in the life of Pelagia, a worldly woman who was wont to go about Antioch, tired and adorned most extravagantly. A holy father, name Nonnus, saw her and began to weep, saying to his companions, that never in all his life had he used such diligence to please God; and much more he added to this effect, which is preserved in his orations.

It is this which is lamented in *Ecclesiastes* vii, and which the Church even now laments on account of the great magnitude of witches. And I have found a woman more bitter than death, who is the hunter's snare, and her heart is a net, and her hands are bands. He that pleaseth God shall escape from her; but he that is a sinner shall be caught by her. More bitter than death, that is, than the devil: *Apocalypse* vi, 8, His name was Death. For though the devil tempted Eve to sin, yet Eve seduced Adam. And as the sin of Eve would not have brought death to our soul and body unless the sin had afterwards passed on to Adam, to which he was tempted by Eve, not by the devil, therefore she is more bitter than death....

To conclude. All witchcraft comes from carnal lust, which is in women insatiable. See *Proverbs* xxx: There are three things that are never satisfied, yea, a forth thing which says not, It is enough; that is, the mouth of the womb. Wherefore for the sake of fulfilling their lusts they consort even with devils.

Source: Heinrich Kramer and James Sprenger, *The Malleus Maleficarum,* trans. Montague Summers (New York: Dover Publications, Inc., 1971), pp. 41-47. Reprinted with permission.

# QUESTIONS FOR PART 15

1. Did Luther and Zwingli see their Reformation as making Christianity easier for believers?
2. Was the Reformation (Protestant or Catholic) good for women?
3. How did the Reformation exacerbate the witch-hunts?

# Brief Contents

# Part Two: Late Antiquity and the Middle Ages

The Roman political system dissolved in the western provinces and was replaced by smaller kingdoms, empires, and principates. In the east, however, Roman government remained stable and despite invasions and migrations was able to forge a long lasting Late Roman or "Byzantine" state. The Middle Ages, therefore, developed very differently in the east and west. The western regions were transformed by the influences of German, Celtic, Slavic, and other traditions. The East, while not untouched by new ideas, maintained ancient Greek and Roman traditions, even in the face of strong Arab and Islamic pressure.

## Competing Empires: Byzantines and Carolingians

The Frankish (Merovingian) kingdom controlled the old Roman province of Gaul for several centuries. This was a united Christian kingdom. By the seventh century, however, the kingdom was divided and beginning to weaken. As a result, Charles Martel, the mayor of the palace of Austrasia, gained power and, most importantly, defeated the Muslims at Poitiers. But it was his son, Pepin, who, with the help of the Catholic Church, would depose the Merovingians and create a new Frankish kingdom—that of the Carolingians. The Pepin's son, Charlemagne (or Charles the Great) was the most renowned and powerful of the Carolingian leaders.

In the eastern half of the old Roman Empire the government remained stable and powerful. This Eastern Roman Empire has become known as the Byzantine Empire, although the people continued to consider themselves "Roman." The emperors of the east treated the Germans in the west as regents of Roman power. In the sixth century, however, a real attempt was made to reunite the old empire into a territorial and institutional whole. The Emperor Justinian was the mastermind behind this plan, and he was partially and temporarily successful. Friction, not unnaturally, resulted from conflicting ideas about the nature and ownership of power in the west.

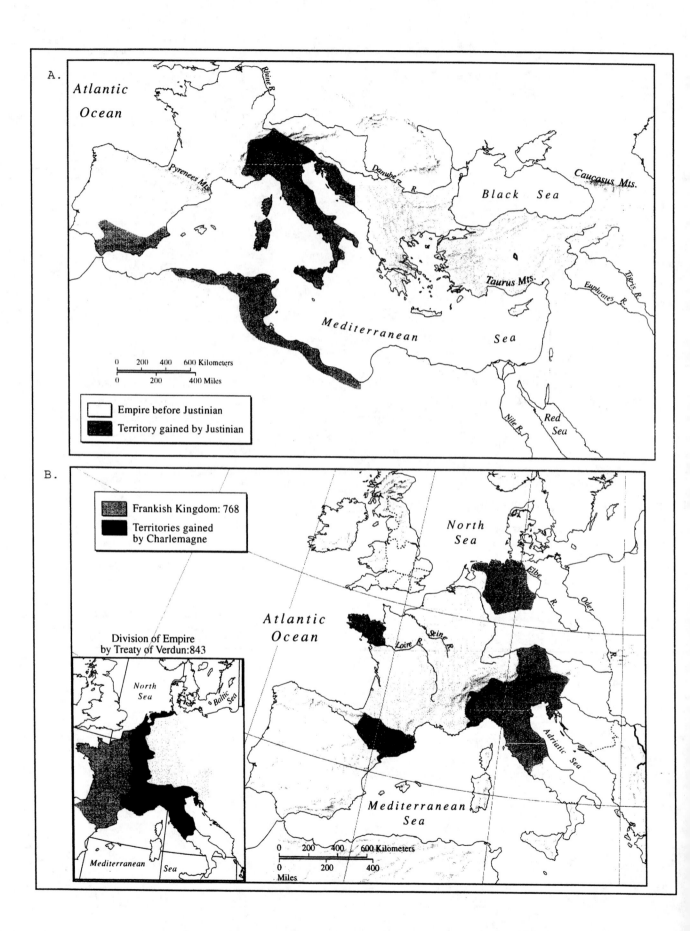

A.

Atlantic
Ocean

Pyrenees Mts.

Rhine R.

Danube R.

Black Sea

Caucasus Mts.

Taurus Mts.

Euphrates R.

Tigris R.

Mediterranean Sea

Nile R.

Red Sea

0  200  400  600 Kilometers
0  200  400 Miles

☐ Empire before Justinian
■ Territory gained by Justinian

B.

▨ Frankish Kingdom: 768
■ Territories gained by Charlemagne

North Sea

Atlantic Ocean

Elbe R.

Oder R.

Seine R.

Loire R.

Adriatic Sea

Mediterranean Sea

Division of Empire by Treaty of Verdun: 843

North Sea

Baltic Sea

Mediterranean Sea

0  200  400  600 Kilometers
0  200  400 Miles

# Locations

On the appropriate inset on Map 4, using different colors for each group, shade in the boundaries and number the territories of the new western kingdoms listed below. Also number and place on the map cities and geographical features listed below.

**Kingdoms and Regions**
1. Alemanni
2. Arabia
3. Austrasia
4. Bulgars
5. Burgundy
6. Celts
7. Franks
8. Kingdom of Sicily
9. Lombards
10. Mercia
11. Neustria
12. Ostrogoths
13. Picts
14. Vandals
15. Visigoths

**Cities**
16. Aachen
17. Belgrade
18. Bordeaux
19. Constantinople
20. Cracow
21. Danzig
22. Leipzig
23. Nuremberg
24. Paris
25. Verdun

**Byzantine Neighbors**
26. Alemanni
27. Arabia
28. Bulgars
29. Burgundians
30. Ostrogoths
31. Persian Empire
32. Syria

**Geographical Features**
33. Baltic Sea
34. Danube River
35. Rhine River

# Environment

1.    What were the material and environmental advantages of the territories held by Justinian?

_____
_____
_____
_____
_____
_____
_____

2.    Describe the major trade routes in the Byzantine Empire.

_____

_____

_____

_____

_____

_____

3.    What, and from where, were the major goods being imported? Exported?

_____

_____

_____

_____

_____

4.    What affect did the location of Constantinople have on trade in the Byzantine Empire?

_____

_____

_____

_____

_____

5.    Describe the environmental difficulties encountered by the agricultural populations in the era of the Carolingians.

_____

_____

_____

_____

_____

6.    Describe the major trade routes of the Carolingians.

_____

_____

_____

_____

_____

# Human Society and Civilizations

7.    What were the main socio-political characteristics of the Byzantine Empire in the eighth century? And how do they relate to the geographical context of the Byzantine world?

_____

_____

_____

_____

_____

8.    In the west, what were the long-term political and economic results of the Treaty of Verdun?

_____

_____

_____

_____

9.    Describe the linguistic and cultural differences that were emerging in the divided territories of the Carolingian Empire.

_____

_____

_____

_____

_____

10.    What nations would emerge from the Carolingian territories?

_____

_____

_____

_____

11.    List at least five of the major regions of the Holy Roman Empire. Try to explain these divisions of the Holy Roman Empire. Did they help or hinder stability in the empire? Explain.

_____

_____

_____

_____

_____

_____

_____

# Life in the Byzantine and Carolingian Worlds

12.  Imagine that you are a merchant from Constantinople and that you are traveling to the Carolingian court. Write an essay describing what sorts of goods might you be trading and your impressions of daily life in Early Medieval Europe. Note especially the things that differ most dramatically from your own experiences in the east.

# New People: Goths, Germans, and Slavs

As we have seen, the Roman political system was weakened in the western provinces; in Eastern Europe, it eventually was replaced by numerous small Germanic and Slavic kingdoms. A few of these kingdoms like the Carolingians would prove to be fairly long lived. The Christian Church also benefited from the withdrawal of Roman power from the west. Some form of Christianity was accepted by most of the German people who gained the old Roman territories. Around the territories on each side of the Oder River, there was considerable intermixing of German with Slavs (which, incidentally, resulted in instability in Polish borders which characterized Poland well into the twentieth century).

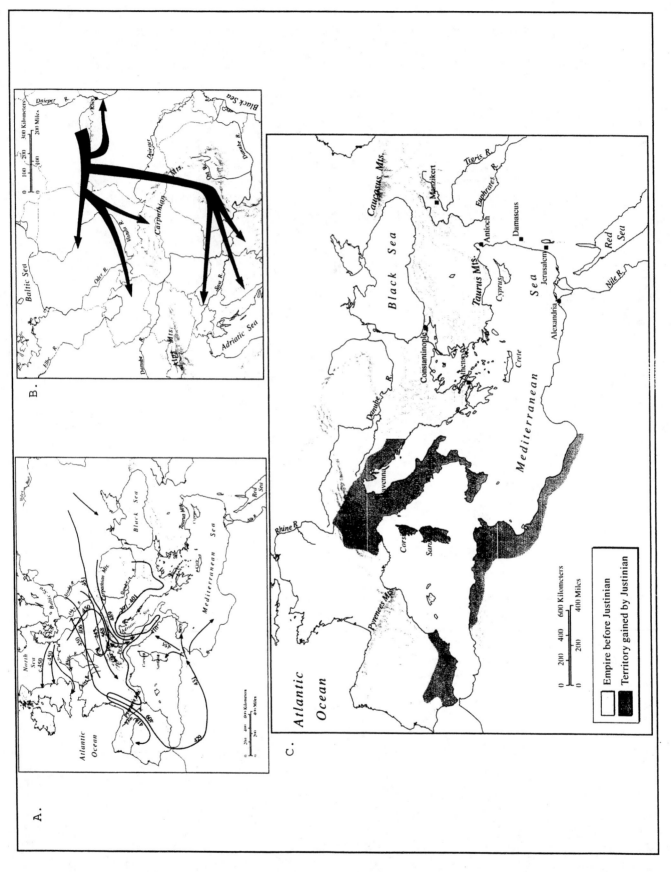

A.

B.

C.

Atlantic
Ocean

Rhine R.

Pyrenees Mts.

Ravenna

Corsica

Sardinia

Danube R.

Constantinople

Athens

Crete

Caucasus Mts.

Black Sea

Taurus Mts.

Cyprus

Mediterranean Sea

Mandzikert

Tigris R.

Euphrates R.

Antioch

Damascus

Jerusalem

Alexandria

Red Sea

Nile R.

0    200    400    600 Kilometers

0         200         400 Miles

☐ Empire before Justinian

■ Territory gained by Justinian

MAP 05

8

# Locations

Migrating and invading people took over the territories of the former Roman Empire in the west. On the appropriate inset on Map 5, using different colors for each group, lightly shade in the territories of and number the following successor groups. On the other maps, label the migrations of the Slavs, and the "Barbarian" migration and invasion routes:

**Kingdoms**

1. Alemanni
2. Celts
3. Franks
4. Lombards
5. Merovingians
6. Picts
7. Saxons
8. Scots
9. Vandals

**Germanic Peoples**

11. Franks
12. Huns
13. Ostrogoths
14. Vandals
15. Visigoths

# Environment

1. How did the environment and geography of Europe contribute to the migrations and invasions of the Germanic, Gothic, and Slavic peoples?

_____

_____

_____

_____

_____

_____

_____

_____

_____

_____

_____

_____

_____

_____

_____

2.    What cultural characteristics of the Germans can you identify as having an environmental explanation?

_____
_____
_____
_____
_____
_____

3.    What cultural characteristics of the Slavs can you identify as having an environmental explanation?

_____
_____
_____
_____
_____
_____

## Human Society And Civilizations

4.    What were the main causes of friction between the ancient Italian peoples and their German rulers?

_____
_____
_____
_____
_____
_____

5.    How did German law and society differ from that of the ancient Romans? In what ways was the natural world a contributor to these differences?

_____
_____
_____
_____
_____
_____

6.    What long term impact did the German and Slavic people have on the development of political systems and territorial boundaries in the west?

_____

_____

_____

_____

_____

_____

_____

7.    What long term cultural impact did the German and Slavic people have on the west?

_____

_____

_____

_____

_____

_____

_____

8.    Briefly summarize the family structure of the ancient Franks.

_____

_____

_____

_____

_____

_____

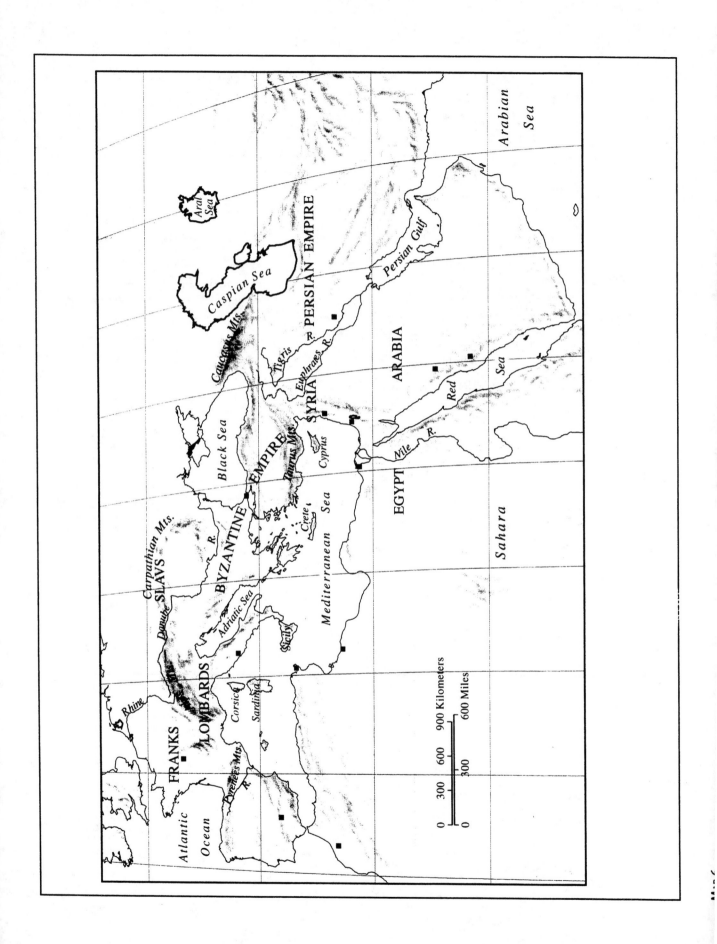

Aral Sea

Caspian Sea

PERSIAN EMPIRE

Arabian Sea

Persian Gulf

Caucasus Mts.

Tigris R.

Euphrates R.

ARABIA

Red Sea

SYRIA

Black Sea

Cyprus

Taurus Mts.

BYZANTINE EMPIRE

Nile R.

EGYPT

Crete

Mediterranean Sea

Sahara

Carpathian Mts.

SLAVS

Danube R.

Adriatic Sea

Sicily

LOMBARDS

Corsica

Sardinia

Rhine

FRANKS

Pyrenees Mts.

Atlantic Ocean

0    300    600    900 Kilometers

0    300    600 Miles

12

# New Ideas: Christianity and Islam

The Roman political system in the western provinces was eventually replaced by numerous small Germanic kingdoms, and the Christian Church benefited from the withdrawal of Roman power. Some form of Christianity was accepted by most of the German people who gained the old Roman territories. This exercise locates the German successor states and identifies important Christian centers.

In the seventh century, Arab tribes began to accept a new religion, Islam, and to expand their influence in both the eastern and western Mediterranean world. The acceptance of Islam by the Arabs was rapid and complete. The reasons for such a rapid and successful religious revolution are still not clear. Upon unifying politically as well as religiously, the Arabs began to expand their territory.

## Locations

On Map 6, shade in and label the territories gained by Islamic peoples by about 632. In another color, shade in and label the territories held by 661. Finally, in a third color, shade in and label the territories held through Islamic expansion by 750 CE. Also, place the number or name of the following cities on your map:

| | | | |
|---|---|---|---|
| 1. | Alexandria | 6. | Mecca |
| 2. | Antioch | 7. | Medina |
| 3. | Baghdad | 8. | Poitiers |
| 4. | Cordoba | 9. | Tripoli |
| 5. | Jerusalem | 10. | Tunis |

## Environment

1.   What impact did geography have on the spread of Christianity in Europe? Be specific.

_____

_____

_____

_____

_____

2.    What impact did geography have on the spread of Islam in the Middle East, Africa, and Europe? Be specific.

_____
_____
_____
_____
_____
_____
_____
_____
_____
_____

## Human Society And Civilizations

3.    Name at least five major centers of Christian diffusion in the western territories. Describe the locations of these centers and explain their importance.

_____
_____
_____
_____
_____
_____
_____
_____
_____
_____

4.    Name at least five major centers of Christian diffusion in the eastern territories. Describe the locations of these centers and explain their importance.

_____
_____
_____
_____
_____
_____
_____
_____
_____
_____

5.    Briefly, describe the routes and processes of the Christianization of Britain.

_____

_____

_____

_____

_____

_____

6.    In the sixth and seventh centuries, the Latin Christian church gained considerable power and prestige. Name at least two reasons why this was so.

_____

_____

_____

_____

_____

_____

7.    What factors enabled the territorial expansion of Islam on such a large scale?

_____

_____

_____

_____

_____

_____

8.    What factors or events stopped the territorial expansion of Islam into Christian Europe?

_____

_____

_____

_____

_____

_____

9.    What impact did the Islamic conquests have on Christian Europe?

_____

_____

_____

_____

_____

_____

## Life in the Islamic World

10.     Using your texts and other sources, write an essay describing how the advent of Islam changed the roles of women in Arabic society. Be sure to clarify the status of women before the birth of Muhammed (ca. 570 CE). At the end of your essay, please properly cite any sources that you used.

_____

_____

_____

_____

_____

_____

_____

_____

_____

_____

_____

_____

_____

_____

_____

_____

_____

_____

_____

_____

_____

_____

_____

_____

_____

_____

_____

_____

_____

_____

_____

_____

_____

_____

_____

# Late Antiquity and the Middle Ages: Test Your Knowledge

Next to each of the following regions and cities, write in its associated religion and the approximate date of conversion to that religion. When the region underwent more that one conversion, e.g., from pagan to Christian to Muslim, you will need to list all major conversions and their dates.

1.  Aachen _____

2.  Alexandria _____

3.  Antioch _____

4.  Canterbury _____

5.  Cologne _____

6.  Cordoba _____

7.  Ephesus _____

8.  Fez _____

9.  Marseilles _____

10. Mecca _____

11. Medina _____

12. Milan _____

13. Nicaea _____

14. Paris _____

15. Tours _____

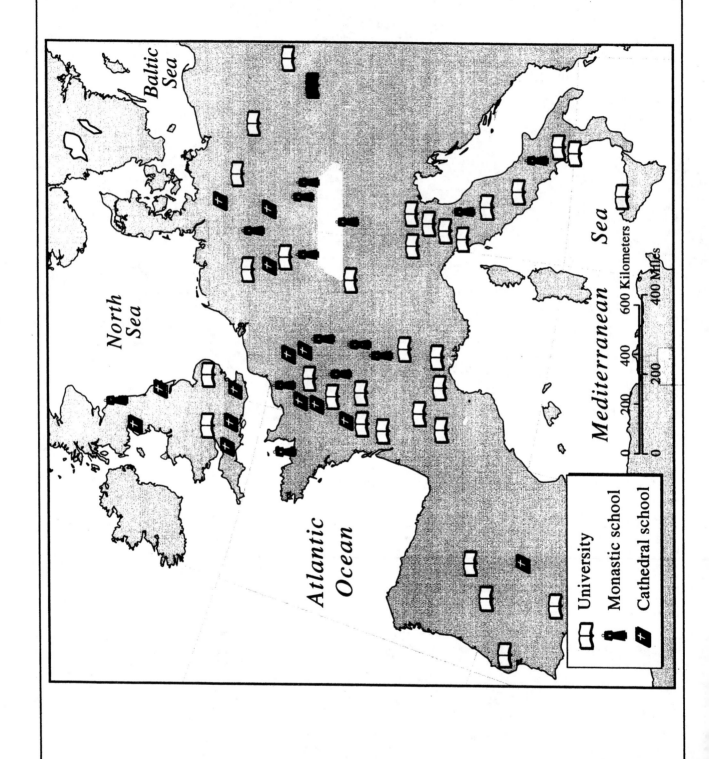

North Sea

Baltic Sea

Mediterranean Sea

Atlantic Ocean

University

Monastic school

Cathedral school

600 Kilometers

400 Miles

0    200    400

0    200    400

# Part Three: Late Middle Ages to the Reformation

The 12th through the 16th centuries saw a myriad of rapid, and profoundly influential, developments. Technological transformations, the creation of universities, population fluctuations and the infusion of dramatically new ideas led to the foundations of modern religious divisions and systems of government. There were a variety of reasons for these changes, including but not limited to, new ways of thinking imported from the east though peaceful trade and the violence of the Crusades, dislocations caused by the Black Death, (which was a disaster of enormous magnitude), and conflicts within and surrounding the Catholic church.

## The Spread of New Ideas: Education

Intellectual life in the later Middle Ages reflected a period of exceptional vitality and change. The clergy, hitherto the main educators in the European world, began to lose some of their dominance and influences in education began to be felt from the work of secular officials, warriors, courtiers, philosophers and aristocrats. The university, in its modern form, developed during this era in order to train both an educated clergy and educated secular citizenry.

### Locations

On Map 7, place the appropriate city center next to its university, monastic school, or cathedral school icon.

| | | | | | |
|---|---|---|---|---|---|
| 1. | Bologna | 6. | Naples | 11. | Reims |
| 2. | Cambridge | 7. | Notre Dame | 12. | Rome |
| 3. | Chartres | 8. | Oxford | 13. | Seville |
| 4. | Durham | 9. | Paris | 14. | Toledo |
| 5. | Mainz | 10. | Prague | 15. | Vienna |

# Society and Civilization

1.    Briefly, list five of the earliest major Universities with the date of their foundation.

_____

_____

_____

_____

_____

_____

2.    What were the origins of these schools? Why did schools arise in the locations that they did?

_____

_____

_____

_____

_____

_____

3.    What physical and educational characteristics did these early universities share?

_____

_____

_____

_____

_____

4.    Can you explain why there were fewer universities in Spain than in France?

_____

_____

_____

_____

_____

5.    What effect did the humanist movement have on education and the locations of schools?

_____

_____

_____

_____

_____

# Life In A Medieval University

6.    Imagine that you are a student in Bologna. Write a letter to your father describing your location and experiences.

_____

_____

_____

_____

_____

_____

_____

_____

_____

_____

_____

_____

_____

_____

_____

_____

_____

_____

_____

_____

_____

_____

_____

_____

_____

_____

_____

_____

_____

_____

_____

_____

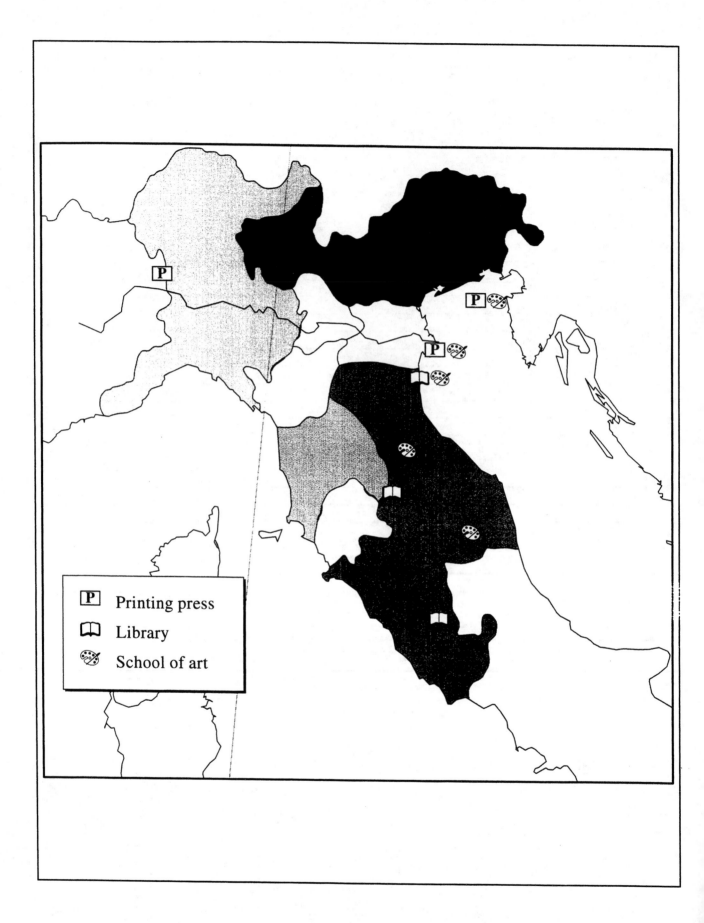

MAP 8

# Culture and Politics: Italy and the Renaissance

State systems varied by region and era. For example, though in the fourteenth century Italy had a well-established system of city-state governments, often in conflict with one another, by the fifteenth century there were only a few, very powerful states left. They vied with one another for a variety of reasons, often calling on the Papacy or the Holy Roman Empire of the Germans to support their claims. Frequent warfare was the result, and unification of nations such as Italy was a long way away. Europe had entered a period of turmoil and rebirth exemplified by political rivalries as well as intellectual and artistic achievements of the Renaissance and Reformation.

## Locations

On Map 8, next to the symbols for presses, libraries, and schools of art, write the name of the associated city. In the proper area, also write in the following regions:

Duchy of Ferarra          Papal States

Duchy of Milan            Republic of Florence

Duchy of Modena           Republic of Lucca

Duchy of Savoy            Republic of Siena

Kingdom of Naples         Republic of Venice

## Culture And Society

1.    How did the five major 15th-century powers in Italy come to dominance?

_____

_____

_____

_____

_____

_____

_____

_____

_____

_____

2.  What role did geography play in the development of these regional powers?

_____
_____
_____
_____
_____
_____
_____
_____

3.  Compare and contrast the Renaissance of Italy and the Northern Renaissance. In what ways were these "rebirths" most similar and in what ways were they most different?

_____
_____
_____
_____
_____
_____
_____
_____
_____

4.  How did geography and location affect regional developments? Be specific.

_____
_____
_____
_____
_____
_____
_____
_____

5.  Using Renaissance recipes and menus as guides, discuss how trade in Renaissance Italy affected the daily lives of the elite.

_____
_____
_____
_____
_____
_____
_____

# Politics and Religion: The Reformation

In contrast to Italy, Spain was home to several independent Christian nations that had managed, militarily, to take the peninsula from those practicing Islam and Judaism. The Spanish enforced strict orthodoxy. Unlike the leaders and states of Italy, Isabella of Castile and Ferdinand of Aragon made major progress toward early unification of the Iberian Peninsula. Their combined power and wealth, plus the support of the Catholic Church would make them a real threat to countries near and far. Yet, at the same time the Christian church in the sixteenth century was suffering from the consequences of abuses by Catholics (in particular the papacy) and was reaching a crisis point. Many reform movements grew out of the frustration of the times; some made surprisingly influential by the dissemination of these new ideas through the written word, now easily spread because of the printing press. The Reformation in Germany led by Martin Luther was to be one of the most influential. It was not long before the populations of Europe had chosen sides: Protestant (e.g., Lutheran, Calvinist, Anglican) or Catholic.

1.    Compare and contrast the Reformation in England and Germany. How did local conditions affect the different approaches to reformation?

_____
_____
_____
_____
_____
_____
_____
_____
_____

2.    What impact did the Reformation generally have on the economy of Europe? Give several examples.

_____
_____
_____
_____
_____
_____
_____
_____

3. What impact did the Reformation have on the political life and territorial boundaries of Europe? And, on the other hand, what impact did existing territorial divisions have on the progress of the Reformation?

_____
_____
_____
_____
_____
_____
_____
_____
_____
_____

4. What impact did the Reformation have on the society of Europe? Give several examples.

_____
_____
_____
_____
_____
_____
_____
_____
_____

5. Next to the following cities, list the appropriate religious affiliation (Anglican, Calvinist, Calvinist influenced, Roman Catholic, Lutheran, Lutheran influenced).

A. Amsterdam _____

B. Cologne _____

C. Dijon _____

D. Edinburgh _____

E. Geneva _____

F. London _____

G. Madrid _____

H.  Oxford  _____

I.  Paris  _____

J.  Rome  _____

K.  Seville  _____

L.  Trent  _____

M.  Vienna  _____

N.  Wittenberg  _____

O.  Worms  _____

## Life and Death in the Middle Ages

The Black Death killed from 25 to 50% of the population of Europe. In some cases, entire villages were wiped out. Some cities saw their populations reduced by more than half. The disaster had cultural, economic and religious results.

6.    Briefly describe the nature of the Black Death and outline its progress through Europe.

_____
_____
_____
_____
_____
_____
_____
_____
_____

7.    How did the environment of Europe influence the progress of the Black Death?

_____
_____
_____
_____
_____
_____
_____

8.  Discuss European responses to the Black Death. What were some of the psychological and religious responses experienced by the inhabitants of Europe? Give specific examples.

_____
_____
_____
_____
_____
_____
_____
_____
_____
_____
_____

9.  What economic ramifications did the Black Death have? Be detailed.

_____
_____
_____
_____
_____
_____
_____
_____
_____

10. In what ways did the Black Death have long term political effects?

_____
_____
_____
_____
_____
_____
_____
_____
_____

# Late Middle Ages to the Reformation: Test Your Knowledge

Next to the name listed below, list the individual's date, major achievements or characteristics, and main location of activity:

1.  Botticelli, Sandro

_____
_____
_____
_____

2.  Charles V (Holy Roman Emperor)

_____
_____
_____
_____
_____
_____

3.  da Vinci, Leonardo

_____
_____
_____
_____
_____

4.  della Mirandola, Pico

_____
_____
_____
_____

5.  di Donatello, Donato

_____
_____
_____
_____
_____

6. Dufay, Guillaume

_____

_____

_____

_____

_____

_____

7. Erasmus, Desiderius

_____

_____

_____

_____

_____

8. Gutenberg, Johannes

_____

_____

_____

_____

_____

9. Henry VIII

_____

_____

_____

_____

_____

10. Hus, John

_____

_____

_____

_____

_____

11. Isabella of Castile

_____
_____
_____
_____
_____
_____

12. King Louis XI of France

_____
_____
_____
_____
_____
_____

13. Loyola, Ignatius

_____
_____
_____
_____
_____
_____

14. Luther, Martin

_____
_____
_____
_____
_____
_____

15. Michelangelo

_____
_____
_____
_____
_____
_____

16.  More, Thomas

_____
_____
_____
_____
_____
_____

17.  Pope Paul III

_____
_____
_____
_____
_____
_____

18.  Prince Ivan III

_____
_____
_____
_____
_____
_____

19.  Raphael

_____
_____
_____
_____
_____

20.  Zwingli, Ulrich

_____
_____
_____
_____
_____
_____